JAMES AGEE

JAMES AGEE

FILM WRITING AND SELECTED JOURNALISM

Agee on Film: Reviews and Comments
Uncollected Film Writing
The Night of the Hunter
Journalism and Book Reviews

THE LIBRARY OF AMERICA

—

First Printing
The Library of America—160

MICHAEL SRAGOW
SELECTED THE CONTENTS AND WROTE THE NOTES
FOR THIS VOLUME

Contents

AGEE ON FILM

Reviews and Comments

A LETTER TO THE EDITORS OF "THE NATION"

Dear Sirs: In the good old days before pseudo-science and feminism ruined her, it was considered rude to congratulate one's hostess on her meals, since praise would imply that they could have been bad, and by the same rule of courtesy it should be unnecessary to write grateful letters to editors.

Astonishing excellence, however, is the exception, and James Agee's film column seems to this reader, and to many others he has spoken with, just that.

I do not care for movies very much and I rarely see them; further, I am suspicious of criticism as the literary genre which, more than any other, recruits epigones, pedants without insight, intellectuals without love. I am all the more surprised, therefore, to find myself not only reading Mr. Agee before I read anyone else in *The Nation* but also consciously looking forward all week to reading him again.

In my opinion, his column is the most remarkable regular event in American journalism today. What he says is of such profound interest, expressed with such extraordinary wit and felicity, and so transcends its ostensible—to me, rather unimportant—subject, that his articles belong in that very select class—the music critiques of Berlioz and Shaw are the only other members I know—of newspaper work which has permanent literary value.

One foresees the sad day, indeed, when Agee on Films will be the subject of a Ph.D. thesis.

W. H. AUDEN

Swarthmore, Pa., October 16, 1944.

A NOTE ON THIS BOOK

James Agee was considered by many people—both in and out of Hollywood—as the most brilliant and perceptive movie critic of his time. The body of his comment on film was large, original and varied. From late 1941 to the middle of 1948, he was movie reviewer for *Time*, and from the fall of 1942 to 1948, he also wrote the movie column for *The Nation*. In addition, he was responsible for the famous article on silent comedy, which was the cover story for *Life* on September 3, 1949, as well as various other pieces on films or directors, including the one on John Huston, which also came out in *Life*.

For years, lovers of movies and film technique urged a collection of these unique contributions to film criticism, and when Agee's posthumous novel, *A Death in the Family*, appeared, dozens of reviewers demanded *Agee on Film*. The plans for this book were already under way when *A Death in the Family* won the Pulitzer Prize for the most distinguished work of fiction published in 1957.

Agee had a very clear sense of what he looked for in a movie, and he felt strongly that the movie (essentially an industry for entertainment) had within it the obvious potential of a virile modern art form, yet one only occasionally fulfilled. He was frequently impatient with those who were responsible for so many lost opportunities. As he stated in his article on John Huston, "Most movies are made in the evident assumption that the audience is passive and wants to remain passive; every effort is made to do all the work—the seeing, the explaining, the understanding, even the feeling. . . . Huston's pictures are not acts of seduction or of benign enslavement but of liberation, and they require, of anyone who enjoys them, the responsibilities of liberty. They continually open the eye and require it to work vigorously; and through the eye they awaken curiosity and intelligence. That, by any virile standard, is the essential to good entertainment. It is unquestionably essential to good art."

The second part of this passage defines the central tenet of Agee's film philosophy.

CONTENTS

ILLUSTRATIONS

Comedy's Greatest Era

*The appearance of "Comedy's Greatest Era" in Life maga-
zine, September 3, 1949, received one of the greatest responses
in the magazine's history. The surprising element was the
reaction from people who could have seen few, if any, of the
silent comedies, simply because they were too young. The
article makes it possible for everyone to be nostalgic for
something that perhaps they have never known.*

In the language of screen comedians four of the main
grades of laugh are the titter, the yowl, the bellylaugh and the
boffo. The titter is just a titter. The yowl is a runaway titter.
Anyone who has ever had the pleasure knows all about a bellylaugh. The boffo is the laugh that kills. An ideally good gag,
perfectly constructed and played, would bring the victim up
this ladder of laughs by cruelly controlled degrees to the top
rung, and would then proceed to wobble, shake, wave and
brandish the ladder until he groaned for mercy. Then, after the
shortest possible time out for recuperation, he would feel the
first wicked tickling of the comedian's whip once more and
start up a new ladder.

The reader can get a fair enough idea of the current state of
screen comedy by asking himself how long it has been since he
has had that treatment. The best of comedies these days hand
out plenty of titters and once in a while it is possible to achieve
a yowl without overstraining. Even those who have never seen
anything better must occasionally have the feeling, as they
watch the current run or, rather, trickle of screen comedy, that
they are having to make a little cause for laughter go an awfully
long way. And anyone who has watched screen comedy over
the past ten or fifteen years is bound to realize that it has
quietly but steadily deteriorated. As for those happy atavists
who remember silent comedy in its heyday and the bellylaughs
and boffos that went with it, they have something close to an
absolute standard by which to measure the deterioration.

When a modern comedian gets hit on the head, for example, the most he is apt to do is look sleepy. When a silent
comedian got hit on the head he seldom let it go so flatly. He

9

realized a broad license, and a ruthless discipline within that license. It was his business to be as funny as possible physically, without the help or hindrance of words. So he gave us a figure of speech, or rather of vision, for loss of consciousness. In other words he gave us a poem, a kind of poem, moreover, that everybody understands. The least he might do was to straighten up stiff as a plank and fall over backward with such skill that his whole length seemed to slap the floor at the same instant. Or he might make a cadenza of it—look vague, smile like an angel, roll up his eyes, lace his fingers, thrust his hands palms downward as far as they would go, hunch his shoulders, rise on tiptoe, prance ecstatically in narrowing circles until, with tallow knees, he sank down the vortex of his dizziness to the floor, and there signified nirvana by kicking his heels twice, like a swimming frog.

Startled by a cop, this same comedian might grab his hat-brim with both hands and yank it down over his ears, jump high in the air, come to earth in a split violent enough to tele-scope his spine, spring thence into a coattail-flattening sprint and dwindle at rocket speed to the size of a gnat along the grand, forlorn perspective of some lazy back boulevard.

Those are fine clichés from the language of silent comedy in its infancy. The man who could handle them properly com-bined several of the more difficult accomplishments of the acrobat, the dancer, the clown and the mime. Some very gifted comedians, unforgettably Ben Turpin, had an immense vo-cabulary of these clichés and were in part so lovable because they were deep conservative classicists and never tried to break away from them. The still more gifted men, of course, simpli-fied and invented, finding out new and much deeper uses for the idiom. They learned to show emotion through it, and comic psychology, more eloquently than most language has ever managed to, and they discovered beauties of comic mo-tion which are hopelessly beyond reach of words.

It is hard to find a theater these days where a comedy is playing; in the days of the silents it was equally hard to find a theater which was not showing one. The laughs today are piti-fully few, far between, shallow, quiet and short. They almost never build, as they used to, into something combining the jabbering frequency of a machine gun with the delirious mo-

mentum of a roller coaster. Saddest of all, there are few comedians now below middle age and there are none who seem to
learn much from picture to picture, or to try anything new.

To put it unkindly, the only thing wrong with screen comedy today is that it takes place on a screen which talks. Because
it talks, the only comedians who ever mastered the screen cannot work, for they cannot combine their comic style with talk.
Because there is a screen, talking comedians are trapped into a
continual exhibition of their inadequacy as screen comedians
on a surface as big as the side of a barn.

At the moment, as for many years past, the chances to see
silent comedy are rare. There is a smattering of it on television
—too often treated as something quaintly archaic, to be
laughed at, not with. Some two hundred comedies—long and
short—can be rented for home projection. And a lucky minority has access to the comedies in the collection of New York's
Museum of Modern Art, which is still incomplete but which is
probably the best in the world. In the near future, however,
something of this lost art will return to regular theaters. A
thick straw in the wind is the big business now being done by
a series of revivals of W. C. Fields's memorable movies, a kind
of comedy more akin to the old silent variety than anything
which is being made today. Mack Sennett now is preparing a
sort of pot-pourri variety show called *Down Memory Lane*
made up out of his old movies, featuring people like Fields and
Bing Crosby when they were movie beginners, but including
also interludes from silents. Harold Lloyd has re-released *Movie
Crazy*, a talkie, and plans to revive four of his best silent comedies (*Grandma's Boy, Safety Last, Speedy* and *The Freshman*).
Buster Keaton hopes to remake at feature length, with a minimum of dialogue, two of the funniest short comedies ever
made, one about a porous homemade boat and one about a
prefabricated house.

Awaiting these happy events we will discuss here what has
gone wrong with screen comedy and what, if anything, can be
done about it. But mainly we will try to suggest what it was
like in its glory in the years from 1912 to 1930, as practiced by
the employees of Mack Sennett, the father of American screen
comedy, and by the four most eminent masters: Charlie Chaplin, Harold Lloyd, the late Harry Langdon and Buster Keaton.

The father of silent comedy, Mack
Sennett, and Kipling, son of Numa
the studio lioness.

Mack Sennett made two kinds of comedy: parody laced with
slapstick, and plain slapstick. The parodies were the unceremo-
nious burial of a century of hamming, including the new hamming in serious movies, and nobody who has missed Ben
Turpin in *A Small Town Idol*, or kidding Erich von Stroheim in
Three Foolish Weeks or as *The Shriek of Araby*, can imagine how
rough parody can get and still remain subtle and roaringly
funny. The plain slapstick, at its best, was even better: a profu-
sion of hearty young women in disconcerting bathing suits,
frisking around with a gaggle of insanely incompetent policemen and of equally certifiable male civilians sporting museum-
piece mustaches. All these people zipped and caromed about
the pristine world of the screen as jazzily as a convention of
water bugs. Words can hardly suggest how energetically they
collided and bounced apart, meeting in full gallop around the
corner of a house; how hard and how often they fell on their
backsides; or with what fantastically adroit clumsiness they got
themselves fouled up in folding ladders, garden hoses, tethered
animals and each other's headlong cross-purposes. The ges-

tures were ferociously emphatic; not a line or motion of the body was wasted or inarticulate. The reader may remember how splendidly upright wandlike old Ben Turpin could stand for a Renunciation Scene, with his lampshade mustache twittering and his sparrowy chest stuck out and his head flung back like Paderewski assaulting a climax and the long babyish back hair trying to look lionlike, while his Adam's apple, an orange in a Christmas stocking, pumped with noble emotion. Or huge Mack Swain, who looked like a hairy mushroom, rolling his eyes in a manner patented by French Romantics and gasping in some dubious ecstasy. Or Louise Fazenda, the perennial farmer's daughter and the perfect low-comedy housemaid, primping her spit curl; and how her hair tightened a good-looking face into the incarnation of rampant gullibility. Or snouty James Finlayson, gleefully foreclosing a mortgage, with his look of eternally tasting a spoiled pickle. Or Chester Conklin, a myopic and inebriated little walrus stumbling around in outsize pants. Or Fatty Arbuckle, with his cold eye and his loose, serene smile, his silky manipulation of his bulk and his satanic marksmanship with pies (he was ambidextrous and could simultaneously blind two people in opposite directions).

The intimate tastes and secret hopes of these poor ineligible dunces were ruthlessly exposed whenever a hot stove, an electric fan or a bulldog took a dislike to their outer garments: agonizingly elaborate drawers, worked up on some lonely evening out of some Godforsaken lace curtain; or men's underpants with big round black spots on them. The Sennett sets—delirious wallpaper, megalomaniacally scrolled iron beds, Grand Rapids *in extremis*—outdid even the underwear. It was their business, after all, to kid the squalid braggadocio which infested the domestic interiors of the period, and that was almost beyond parody. These comedies told their stories to the unaided eye, and by every means possible they screamed to it. That is one reason for the India-ink silhouettes of the cops, and for convicts and prison bars and their shadows in hard sunlight, and for barefooted husbands, in tigerish pajamas, reacting like dervishes to stepped-on tacks.

The early silent comedians never strove for or consciously thought of anything which could be called artistic "form," but they achieved it. For Sennett's rival, Hal Roach, Leo McCarey once devoted almost the whole of a Laurel and Hardy two-reeler to pie-throwing. The first pies were thrown thoughtfully, almost philosophically. Then innocent bystanders began to get caught into the vortex. At full pitch it was Armageddon. But everything was calculated so nicely that until late in the picture, when havoc took over, every pie made its special kind of point and piled on its special kind of laugh.

Sennett's comedies were just a shade faster and fizzier than life. According to legend (and according to Sennett) he discovered the sped tempo proper to screen comedy when a green cameraman, trying to save money, cranked too slow.* Realizing the tremendous drumlike power of mere motion to exhilarate, he gave inanimate objects a mischievous life of their own, broke every law of nature the tricked camera would serve him for and made the screen dance like a witches' Sabbath. The thing one is surest of all to remember is how toward the end of nearly every Sennett comedy, a chase (usually called the "rally") built up such a majestic trajectory of pure anarchic motion that bathing girls, cops, comics, dogs, cats, babies, automobiles, locomotives, innocent bystanders, sometimes what seemed like a whole city, an entire civilization, were hauled along head over heels in the wake of that energy like dry leaves following an express train.

"Nice" people, who shunned all movies in the early days, condemned the Sennett comedies as vulgar and naive. But millions of less pretentious people loved their sincerity and sweetness, their wild-animal innocence and glorious vitality. They could not put these feelings into words, but they flocked to the silents. The reader who gets back deep enough into that world will probably even remember the theater: the barefaced honky-tonk and the waltzes by Waldteufel, slammed out on a mechanical piano; the searing redolence of peanuts and demi-rep perfumery, tobacco and feet and sweat; the laughter of unrespectable people having a hell of a fine time, laughter as violent and steady and deafening as standing under a waterfall.

---

*Silent comedy was shot at 12 to 16 frames per second and was speeded up by being shown at 16 frames per second, the usual rate of theater projectors at that time. Theater projectors today run at 24, which makes modern film taken at the same speed seem smooth and natural. But it makes silent movies fast and jerky.

Sennett wheedled his first financing out of a couple of ex-bookies to whom he was already in debt. He took his comics out of music halls, burlesque, vaudeville, circuses and limbo, and through them he tapped in on that great pipeline of horsing and miming which runs back unbroken through the fairs of the Middle Ages at least to ancient Greece. He added all that he himself had learned about the large and spurious gesture, the late decadence of the Grand Manner, as a stage-struck boy in East Berlin, Connecticut, and as a frustrated opera singer and actor. The only thing he claims to have invented is the pie in the face, and he insists, "Anyone who tells you he has discovered something new is a fool or a liar or both."

The silent-comedy studio was about the best training school the movies have ever known, and the Sennett studio was about as free and easy and as fecund of talent as they came. All the major comedians we will mention worked there, at least briefly. So did some of the major stars of the twenties and since —notably Gloria Swanson, Phyllis Haver, Wallace Beery, Marie

The Sennett Girls were born when Sennett saw that "a nice-looking Jane" made the front page, but President Wilson was buried on page three.

Dressler and Carole Lombard. Directors Frank Capra, Leo McCarey and George Stevens also got their start in silent comedy; much that remains most flexible, spontaneous and visually alive in sound movies can be traced, through them and others, to this silent apprenticeship. Everybody did pretty much as he pleased on the Sennett lot, and everybody's ideas were welcome. Sennett posted no rules, and the only thing he strictly forbade was liquor. A Sennett story conference was a most informal affair. During the early years, at least, only the most important scenario might be jotted on the back of an envelope. Mainly Sennett's men thrashed out a few primary ideas and carried them in their heads, sure the better stuff would turn up while they were shooting, in the heat of physical action. This put quite a load on the prop man; he had to have the most improbable apparatus on hand—bombs, trick telephones, what not—to implement whatever idea might suddenly turn up. All kinds of things did—and were recklessly used. Once a low-comedy auto got out of control and killed the cameraman, but he was not visible in the shot, which was thrilling and undamaged; the audience never knew the difference.

Sennett used to hire a "wild man" to sit in on his gag conferences, whose whole job was to think up "wildies." Usually he was an all but brainless, speechless man, scarcely able to communicate his idea; but he had a totally uninhibited imagination. He might say nothing for an hour; then he'd mutter "You take . . ." and all the relatively rational others would shut up and wait. "You take this cloud . . ." he would get out, sketching vague shapes in the air. Often he could get no further; but thanks to some kind of thought-transference, saner men would take this cloud and make something of it. The wild man seems in fact to have functioned as the group's subconscious mind, the source of all creative energy. His ideas were so weird and amorphous that Sennett can no longer remember a one of them, or even how it turned out after rational processing. But a fair equivalent might be one of the best comic sequences in a Laurel and Hardy picture. It is simple enough —simple and real, in fact, as a nightmare. Laurel and Hardy are trying to move a piano across a narrow suspension bridge. The bridge is slung over a sickening chasm, between a couple of Alps. Midway they meet a gorilla.

Had he done nothing else, Sennett would be remembered for giving a start to three of the four comedians who now began to apply their sharp individual talents to this newborn language. The one whom he did not train (he was on the lot briefly but Sennett barely remembers seeing him around) wore glasses, smiled a great deal and looked like the sort of eager young man who might have quit divinity school to hustle brushes. That was Harold Lloyd. The others were grotesque and poetic in their screen characters in degrees which appear to be impossible when the magic of silence is broken. One, who never smiled, carried a face as still and sad as a daguerreotype through some of the most preposterously ingenious and visually satisfying physical comedy ever invented. That was Buster Keaton. One looked like an elderly baby and, at times, a baby dope fiend; he could do more with less than any other comedian. That was Harry Langdon. One looked like Charlie Chaplin, and he was the first man to give the silent language a soul.

When Charlie Chaplin started to work for Sennett he had chiefly to reckon with Ford Sterling, the reigning comedian. Their first picture together amounted to a duel before the assembled professionals. Sterling, by no means untalented, was a big man with a florid Teutonic style which, under this special pressure, he turned on full blast. Chaplin defeated him within a few minutes with a wink of the mustache, a hitch of the trousers, a quirk of the little finger.

With *Tillie's Punctured Romance*, in 1914, he became a major star. Soon after, he left Sennett when Sennett refused to start a landslide among the other comedians by meeting the raise Chaplin demanded. Sennett is understandably wry about it in retrospect, but he still says, "I was right at the time." Of Chaplin he says simply, "Oh well, he's just the greatest artist that ever lived." None of Chaplin's former rivals rate him much lower than that; they speak of him no more jealously than they might of God. We will try here only to suggest the essence of his supremacy. Of all comedians he worked most deeply and most shrewdly within a realization of what a human being is, and is up against. The Tramp is as centrally representative of humanity, as many-sided and as mysterious, as Hamlet, and it seems unlikely that any dancer or actor can ever have excelled him in eloquence, variety or poignancy of motion. As for pure motion, even if he had never gone on to make his magnificent feature-length comedies, Chaplin would have made his period in movies a great one singlehanded even if he had made nothing except *The Cure*, or *One A.M.* In the latter, barring one immobile taxi driver, Chaplin plays alone, as a drunk trying to get upstairs and into bed. It is a sort of inspired elaboration on a soft-shoe dance, involving an angry stuffed wildcat, small rugs on slippery floors, a Lazy Susan table, exquisite footwork on a flight of stairs, a contretemps with a huge, ferocious pendulum and the funniest and most perverse Murphy bed in movie history—and, always made physically lucid, the delicately weird mental processes of a man ethereally sozzled.

Before Chaplin came to pictures people were content with a couple of gags per comedy; he got some kind of laugh every second. The minute he began to work he set standards—and continually forced them higher. Anyone who saw Chaplin eating a boiled shoe like brook trout in *The Gold Rush*, or embarrassed by a swallowed whistle in *City Lights*, has seen perfection. Most of the time, however, Chaplin got his laughter less from the gags, or from milking them in any ordinary sense, than through his genius for what may be called *inflection*—the perfect, changeful shading of his physical and emotional attitudes toward the gag. Funny as his bout with the Murphy bed is, the glances of awe, expostulation and helpless, almost whimpering desire for vengeance which he darts at this infernal machine are even better.

A painful and frequent error among tyros is breaking the comic line with a too-big laugh, then a letdown; or with a laugh which is out of key or irrelevant. The masters could ornament the main line beautifully; they never addled it. In *A Night Out* Chaplin, passed out, is hauled along the sidewalk by the scruff of his coat by staggering Ben Turpin. His toes trail; he is as supine as a sled. Turpin himself is so drunk he can hardly drag him. Chaplin comes quietly to, realizes how well he is being served by his struggling pal, and with a royally delicate gesture plucks and savors a flower.

The finest pantomime, the deepest emotion, the richest and most poignant poetry were in Chaplin's work. He could prob-

Charlie Chaplin and Jackie Coogan are wary of The Law in Chaplin's first real masterpiece, "The Kid" (1920).

ably pantomime Bryce's *The American Commonwealth* without ever blurring a syllable and make it paralyzingly funny into the bargain. At the end of *City Lights* the blind girl who has regained her sight, thanks to the Tramp, sees him for the first time. She has imagined and anticipated him as princely, to say the least; and it has never seriously occurred to him that he is inadequate. She recognizes who he must be by his shy, confident, shining joy as he comes silently toward her. And he recognizes himself, for the first time, through the terrible changes in her face. The camera just exchanges a few quiet close-ups of the emotions which shift and intensify in each face. It is enough to shrivel the heart to see, and it is the greatest piece of acting and the highest moment in movies.

Harold Lloyd worked only a little while with Sennett. During most of his career he acted for another major comedy producer, Hal Roach. He tried at first to offset Chaplin's influence and establish his own individuality by playing Chaplin's exact opposite, a character named Lonesome Luke who wore clothes much too small for him and whose gestures were like-wise as unChaplinesque as possible. But he soon realized that an opposite in itself was a kind of slavishness. He discovered his own comic identity when he saw a movie about a fighting parson: a hero who wore glasses. He began to think about those glasses day and night. He decided on horn rims because they were youthful, ultravisible on the screen and on the verge of becoming fashionable (he was to make them so). Around these large lensless horn rims he began to develop a new char-acter, nothing grotesque or eccentric, but a fresh, believable young man who could fit into a wide variety of stories.

Lloyd depended more on story and situation than any of the other major comedians (he kept the best stable of gagmen in Hollywood, at one time hiring six); but unlike most "story" comedians he was also a very funny man from inside. He had, as he has written, "an unusually large comic vocabulary." More particularly he had an expertly expressive body and even more expressive teeth, and out of his thesaurus of smiles he could at a moment's notice blend prissiness, breeziness and asininity, and still remain tremendously likable. His movies were more extroverted and closer to ordinary life than any others of the best comedies: the vicissitudes of a New York taxi driver; the unaccepted college boy who, by desperate courage and in-spired ineptitude, wins the Big Game. He was especially good at putting a very timid, spoiled or brassy young fellow through devastating embarrassments. He went through one of his most uproarious Gethsemanes as a shy country youth courting the nicest girl in town in *Grandma's Boy.* He arrived dressed "strictly up to date for the Spring of 1862," as a subtitle ob-served, and found that the ancient colored butler wore a simi-lar flowered waistcoat and moldering cutaway. He got one wandering, nervous forefinger dreadfully stuck in a fancy little vase. The girl began cheerfully to try to identify that queer smell which dilated from him; Grandpa's best suit was rife with mothballs. A tenacious litter of kittens feasted off the goose grease on his home-shined shoes.

Lloyd was even better at the comedy of thrills. In *Safety Last,* as a rank amateur, he is forced to substitute for a human fly and to climb a medium-sized skyscraper. Dozens of awful things happen to him. He gets fouled up in a tennis net. Popcorn falls on him from a window above, and the local pigeons treat him like a cross between a lunch wagon and St. Francis of Assisi. A mouse runs up his britches-leg, and the crowd below salutes his desperate dance on the window ledge with wild applause of the daredevil. A good deal of this full-length picture hangs thus by its eyelashes along the face of a building. Each new floor is like a new stanza in a poem; and the higher and more horrifying it gets, the funnier it gets.

In this movie Lloyd demonstrates beautifully his ability to do more than merely milk a gag, but to top it. (In an old, simple example of topping, an incredible number of tall men get, one by one, out of a small closed auto. After as many have clambered out as the joke will bear, one more steps out: a midget. That tops the gag. Then the auto collapses. That tops the topper.) In *Safety Last* Lloyd is driven out to the dirty end of a flagpole by a furious dog; the pole breaks and he falls, just managing to grab the minute hand of a huge clock. His weight promptly pulls the hand down from IX to VI. That would be more than enough for any ordinary comedian, but there is further logic in the situation. Now, hideously, the whole clockface pulls loose and slants from its trembling springs above the street. Getting out of difficulty with the clock, he makes still further use of the instrument by getting one foot caught in one of these obstinate springs.

A proper delaying of the ultrapredictable can of course be just as funny as a properly timed explosion of the unexpected. As Lloyd approaches the end of his horrible hegira up the side of the building in *Safety Last*, it becomes clear to the audience, but not to him, that if he raises his head another couple of inches he is going to get murderously conked by one of the four arms of a revolving wind gauge. He delays the evil moment almost interminably, with one distraction and another, and every delay is a suspense-tightening laugh; he also gets his foot nicely entangled in a rope, so that when he does get hit, the payoff of one gag sends him careening head downward through the abyss into another. Lloyd was outstanding even among the master craftsmen at setting up a gag clearly, culminating and getting out of it deftly, and linking it smoothly to the next. Harsh experience also taught him a deep and fundamental rule: never try to get "above" the audience.

Lloyd tried it in *The Freshman*. He was to wear an unfinished, basted-together tuxedo to a college party, and it would gradually fall apart as he danced. Lloyd decided to skip the pants, a low-comedy cliché, and lose just the coat. His gagmen warned him. A preview proved how right they were. Lloyd had to reshoot the whole expensive sequence, build it around defective pants and climax it with the inevitable. It was one of the funniest things he ever did.

When Lloyd was still a very young man he lost about half his right hand (and nearly lost his sight) when a comedy bomb exploded prematurely. But in spite of his artificially built-out hand he continued to do his own dirty work, like all of the best comedians. The side of the building he climbed in *Safety Last* did not overhang the street, as it appears to. But the nearest landing place was a roof three floors below him, as he approached the top, and he did everything, of course, the hard way, that is, the comic way, keeping his bottom stuck well

Harold Lloyd as the campus fool who became a campus idol in "The Freshman" (1925).

out, his shoulders hunched, his hands and feet skidding over perdition.

If great comedy must involve something beyond laughter, Lloyd was not a great comedian. If plain laughter is any criterion—and it is a healthy counterbalance to the other—few people have equaled him, and nobody has ever beaten him.

Chaplin and Keaton and Lloyd were all more like each other, in one important way, than Harry Langdon was like any of them. Whatever else the others might be doing, they all used more or less elaborate physical comedy; Langdon showed how little of that one might use and still be a great silent-screen comedian. In his screen character he symbolized something as deeply and centrally human, though by no means as rangily so, as the Tramp. There was, of course, an immense difference in inventiveness and range of virtuosity. It seemed as if Chaplin could do literally anything, on any instrument in the orchestra. Langdon had one queerly toned, unique little reed. But out of it he could get incredible melodies.

Like Chaplin, Langdon wore a coat which buttoned on his wishbone and swung out wide below, but the effect was very different: he seemed like an outsized baby who had begun to outgrow his clothes. The crown of his hat was rounded and the brim was turned up all around, like a little boy's hat, and he looked as if he wore diapers under his pants. His walk was that of a child which has just gotten sure on its feet, and his body and hands fitted that age. His face was kept pale to show off, with the simplicity of a nursery-school drawing, the bright, ignorant, gentle eyes and the little twirling mouth. He had big moon cheeks, with dimples, and a Napoleonic forelock of mousy hair; the round, docile head seemed large in ratio to the cream-puff body. Twitchings of his face were signals of tiny discomforts too slowly registered by a tinier brain; quick, squirty little smiles showed his almost prehuman pleasures, his incurably premature trustfulness. He was a virtuoso of hesitations and of delicately indecisive motions, and he was particularly fine in a high wind, rounding a corner with a kind of skittering toddle, both hands nursing his hatbrim.

He was as remarkable a master as Chaplin of subtle emotional and mental process and operated much more at leisure. He once got a good three hundred feet of continuously bigger laughs out of rubbing his chest, in a crowded vehicle, with Limburger cheese, under the misapprehension that it was a cold salve. In another long scene, watching a brazen showgirl change her clothes, he sat motionless, back to the camera, and registered the whole lexicon of lost innocence, shock, disapproval and disgust, with the back of his neck. His scenes with women were nearly always something special. Once a lady spy did everything in her power (under the Hays Office) to seduce him. Harry was polite, willing, even flirtatious in his little way. The only trouble was that he couldn't imagine what in the world she was leering and pawing at him for, and that he was terribly ticklish. The Mata Hari wound up foaming at the mouth.

There was also a sinister flicker of depravity about the Langdon character, all the more disturbing because babies are pre-moral. He had an instinct for bringing his actual adulthood and figurative babyishness into frictions as crawley as a fingernail on a slate blackboard, and he wandered into areas of strangeness which were beyond the other comedians. In a nightmare in one movie he was forced to fight a large, muscular young man; the girl Harry loved was the prize. The young man was a good boxer; Harry could scarcely lift his gloves. The contest took place in a fiercely lighted prize ring, in a prodigious pitch-dark arena. The only spectator was the girl, and she was rooting against Harry. As the fight went on, her eyes glittered ever more brightly with blood lust and, with glittering teeth, she tore her big straw hat to shreds.

Langdon came to Sennett from a vaudeville act in which he had fought a losing battle with a recalcitrant automobile. The minute Frank Capra saw him he begged Sennett to let him work with him. Langdon was almost as childlike as the character he played. He had only a vague idea of his story or even of each scene as he played it; each time he went before the camera Capra would brief him on the general situation and then, as this finest of intuitive improvisers once tried to explain his work, "I'd go into my routine." The whole tragedy of the coming of dialogue, as far as these comedians were concerned —and one reason for the increasing rigidity of comedy every since—can be epitomized in the mere thought of Harry Langdon confronted with a script.

The simple pleasures were a specialty of the simple-minded character created by Harry Langdon. Most of his troubles were equally simple.

Langdon's magic was in his innocence, and Capra took beautiful care not to meddle with it. The key to the proper use of Langdon, Capra always knew, was "the principle of the brick." "If there was a rule for writing Langdon material," he explains, "it was this: his only ally was God. Langdon might be saved by the brick falling on the cop, but it was *verboten* that he in any way motivate the brick's fall." Langdon became quickly and fantastically popular with three pictures, *Tramp, Tramp, Tramp, The Strong Man* and *Long Pants,* from then on he went downhill even faster. "The trouble was," Capra says, "that high-brow critics came around to explain his art to him. Also he developed an interest in dames. It was a pretty high life for such a little fellow." Langdon made two more pictures with high-brow writers, one of which (*Three's A Crowd*) had some wonderful passages in it, including the prize-ring nightmare;

then First National canceled his contract. He was reduced to mediocre roles and two-reelers which were more rehashes of his old gags; this time around they no longer seemed funny. "He never did really understand what hit him," says Capra. "He died broke [in 1944]. And he died of a broken heart. He was the most tragic figure I ever came across in show business."

Buster Keaton started work at the age of three and one-half with his parents in one of the roughest acts in vaudeville ("The Three Keatons"); Harry Houdini gave the child the name Buster in admiration for a fall he took down a flight of stairs. In his first movies Keaton teamed with Fatty Arbuckle under Sennett. He went on to become one of Metro's biggest stars and earners; a Keaton feature cost about $200,000 to make and reliably grossed $2,000,000. Very early in his movie career friends asked him why he never smiled on the screen. He didn't realize he didn't. He had got the dead-pan habit in variety; on the screen he had merely been so hard at work it had never occurred to him there was anything to smile about. Now he tried it just once and never again. He was by his whole style and nature so much the most deeply "silent" of the silent comedians that even a smile was as deafeningly out of key as a yell. In a way his pictures are like a transcendent juggling act in which it seems that the whole universe is in exquisite flying motion and the one point of repose is the juggler's effortless, uninterested face.

Keaton's face ranked almost with Lincoln's as an early American archetype; it was haunting, handsome, almost beautiful, yet it was irreducibly funny; he improved matters by topping it off with a deadly horizontal hat, as flat and thin as a phonograph record. One can never forget Keaton wearing it, standing erect at the prow as his little boat is being launched. The boat goes grandly down the skids and, just as grandly, straight on to the bottom. Keaton never budges. The last you see of him, the water lifts the hat off the stoic head and it floats away.

No other comedian could do as much with the dead pan. He used this great, sad, motionless face to suggest various related things: a one-track mind near the track's end of pure insanity; mulish imperturbability under the wildest of circumstances; how dead a human being can get and still be alive; an awe-inspiring sort of patience and power to endure, proper to granite but uncanny in flesh and blood. Everything that he was and did bore out this rigid face and played laughs against it. When he moved his eyes, it was like seeing them move in a statue. His short-legged body was all sudden, machinelike angles, governed by a daft aplomb. When he swept a semaphore-like arm to point, you could almost hear the electrical impulse in the signal block. When he ran from a cop his transitions from accelerating walk to easy jogtrot to brisk canter to headlong gallop to flogged-piston sprint—always floating, above this frenzy, the untroubled, untouchable face—were as distinct and as soberly in order as an automatic gearshift.

Keaton was a wonderfully resourceful inventor of mechanistic gags (he still spends much of his time fooling with Erector sets); as he ran afoul of locomotives, steamships, prefabricated and over-electrified houses, he put himself through some of the hardest and cleverest punishment ever designed for laughs. In *Sherlock Jr.*, boiling along on the handlebars of a motorcycle quite unaware that he has lost his driver, Keaton whips through city traffic, breaks up a tug-of-war, gets a shovelful of dirt in the face from each of a long line of Rockette-timed ditch-diggers, approaches a log at high speed which is hinged open by dynamite precisely soon enough to let him through and, hitting an obstruction, leaves the handlebars like an arrow leaving a bow, whams through the window of a shack in which the heroine is about to be violated, and hits the heavy feet-first, knocking him through the opposite wall. The whole sequence is as clean in motion as the trajectory of a bullet.

Much of the charm and edge of Keaton's comedy, however, lay in the subtle leverages of expression he could work against his nominal dead pan. Trapped in the side-wheel of a ferryboat, saving himself from drowning only by walking, then desperately running, inside the accelerating wheel like a squirrel in a cage, his only real concern was, obviously, to keep his hat on. Confronted by Love, he was not as dead-pan as he was cracked up to be, either; there was an odd, abrupt motion of his head which suggested a horse nipping after a sugar lump.

Keaton worked strictly for laughs, but his work came from so far inside a curious and original spirit that he achieved a great deal besides, especially in his feature-length comedies. (For

plain hard laughter his nineteen short comedies—the negatives
of which have been lost—were even better.) He was the only
major comedian who kept sentiment almost entirely out of his
work, and he brought pure physical comedy to its greatest
heights. Beneath his lack of emotion he was also uninsistently
sardonic; deep below that, giving a disturbing tension and
grandeur to the foolishness, for those who sensed it, there was
in his comedy a freezing whisper not of pathos but of melan-
cholia. With the humor, the craftsmanship and the action
there was often, besides, a fine, still and sometimes dreamlike
beauty. Much of his Civil War picture *The General* is within
hailing distance of Mathew Brady. And there is a ghostly, unforgettable moment in *The Navigator* when, on a deserted,
softly rolling ship, all the pale doors along a deck swing open

Buster Keaton, whose face was always a stoic mask,
puts character and comedy into a simple exercise in
equilibrium.

as one behind Keaton and, as one, slam shut, in a hair-raising illusion of noise.

Perhaps because "dry" comedy is so much more rare and odd than "dry" wit, there are people who never much cared for Keaton. Those who do cannot care mildly.

As soon as the screen began to talk, silent comedy was pretty well finished. The hardy and prolific Mack Sennett made the transfer; he was the first man to put Bing Crosby and W. C. Fields on the screen. But he was essentially a silent-picture man, and by the time the Academy awarded him a special Oscar for his "lasting contribution to the comedy technique of the screen" (in 1938), he was no longer active. As for the comedians we have spoken of in particular, they were as badly off as fine dancers suddenly required to appear in plays.

Harold Lloyd, whose work was most nearly realistic, naturally coped least unhappily with the added realism of speech; he made several talking comedies. But good as the best were, they were not so good as his silent work, and by the late thirties he quit acting. A few years ago he returned to play the lead (and play it beautifully) in Preston Sturges's *The Sin of Harold Diddlebock*, but this exceptional picture—which opened, brilliantly, with the closing reel of Lloyd's *The Freshman*—has not yet been generally released.

Like Chaplin, Lloyd was careful of his money; he is still rich and active. Last June, in the presence of President Truman, he became Imperial Potentate of the A.A.O.N.M.S. (Shriners). Harry Langdon, as we have said, was a broken man when sound came in.

Up to the middle thirties Buster Keaton made several feature-length pictures (with such players as Jimmy Durante, Wallace Beery and Robert Montgomery); he also made a couple of dozen talking shorts. Now and again he managed to get loose into motion, without having to talk, and for a moment or so the screen would start singing again. But his dark, dead voice, though it was in keeping with the visual character, tore his intensely silent style to bits and destroyed the illusion within which he worked. He gallantly and correctly refuses to regard himself as "retired." Besides occasional bits, spots and minor roles in Hollywood pictures, he has worked on summer stages, made talking comedies in France and Mexico and clowned in a French circus. This summer he has played the straw hats in *Three Men on a Horse*. He is planning a television program. He also has a working agreement with Metro. One of his jobs there is to construct comedy sequences for Red Skelton.

The only man who really survived the flood was Chaplin, the only one who was rich, proud and popular enough to afford to stay silent. He brought out two of his greatest nontalking comedies, *City Lights* and *Modern Times*, in the middle of an avalanche of talk, spoke gibberish and, in the closing moments, plain English in *The Great Dictator*, and at last made an all-talking picture, *Monsieur Verdoux*, creating for that purpose an entirely new character who might properly talk a blue streak. *Verdoux* is the greatest of talking comedies though so cold and savage that it had to find its public in grimly experienced Europe.

Good comedy, and some that was better than good, outlived silence, but there has been less and less of it. The talkies brought one great comedian, the late, majestically lethargic W. C. Fields, who could not possibly have worked as well in silence; he was the toughest and the most warmly human of all screen comedians, and *It's A Gift* and *The Bank Dick*, fiendishly funny and incisive white-collar comedies, rank high among the best comedies (and best movies) ever made. Laurel and Hardy, the only comedians who managed to preserve much of the large, low style of silence and who began to explore the comedy of sound, have made nothing since 1945. Walt Disney, at his best an inspired comic inventor and teller of fairy stories, lost his stride during the war and has since regained it only at moments. Preston Sturges has made brilliant, satirical comedies, but his pictures are smart, nervous comedy-dramas merely italicized with slapstick. The Marx Brothers were sidesplitters but they made their best comedies years ago. Jimmy Durante is mainly a nightclub genius; Abbott and Costello are semi-skilled laborers, at best; Bob Hope is a good radio comedian with a pleasing presence, but not much more, on the screen.

There is no hope that screen comedy will get much better than it is without new, gifted young comedians who really belong in movies, and without freedom for their experiments. For everyone who may appear we have one last, invidious comparison to offer as a guidepost.

One of the most popular recent comedies is Bob Hope's *The Paleface*. We take no pleasure in blackening *The Paleface*; we single it out, rather, because it is as good as we've got. Anything that is said of it here could be said, with interest, of other comedies of our time. Most of the laughs in *The Paleface* are verbal. Bob Hope is very adroit with his lines and now and then, when the words don't get in the way, he makes a good beginning as a visual comedian. But only the beginning, never the middle or the end. He is funny, for instance, reacting to a shot of violent whisky. But he does not know how to get still

Ben Turpin was a high-grade low parodist. Here he appears as The Man You Love to Hate (Erich von Stroheim).

funnier (*i.e.*, how to build and milk) or how to be funniest last (*i.e.*, how to top or cap his gag). The camera has to fade out on the same old face he started with.

One sequence is promisingly set up for visual comedy. In it, Hope and a lethal local boy stalk each other all over a cow town through streets which have been emptied in fear of their duel. The gag here is that through accident and stupidity they keep just failing to find each other. Some of it is quite funny. But the fun slackens between laughs like a weak clothesline, and by all the logic of humor (which is ruthlessly logical) the biggest laugh should come at the moment, and through the way, they finally spot each other. The sequence is so weakly thought out that at that crucial moment the camera can't afford to watch them; it switches to Jane Russell.

Now we turn to a masterpiece. In *The Navigator* Buster Keaton works with practically the same gag as Hope's duel. Adrift on a ship which he believes is otherwise empty, he drops a lighted cigarette. A girl finds it. She calls out and he hears her; each then tries to find the other. First each walks purposefully down the long, vacant starboard deck, the girl, then Keaton, turning the corner just in time not to see each other. Next time around each of them is trotting briskly, very much in earnest; going at the same pace, they miss each other just the same. Next time around each of them is going like a bat out of hell. Again they miss. Then the camera withdraws to a point of vantage at the stern, leans its chin in its hand and just watches the whole intricate super structure of the ship as the protagonists stroll, steal and scuttle from level to level, up, down and sidewise, always managing to miss each other by hair's-breadths, in an enchantingly neat and elaborate piece of timing. There are no subsidiary gags to get laughs in this sequence and there is little loud laughter; merely a quiet and steadily increasing kind of delight. When Keaton has got all he can out of this fine modification of the movie chase he invents a fine device to bring the two together: the girl, thoroughly winded, sits down for a breather, indoors, on a plank which workmen have left across sawhorses. Keaton pauses on an upper deck, equally winded and puzzled. What follows happens in a couple of seconds at most: air suction whips his silk topper backward down a ventilator; grabbing frantically for it, he backs against the lip of the ventilator, jacknifes and falls in backward. Instantly the camera cuts back to the girl. A topper falls through the ceiling and lands tidily, right side up, on the plank beside her. Before she can look more than startled, its owner follows, head between his knees, crushes the topper, breaks the plank with the point of his spine and proceeds to the floor. The breaking of the plank smacks Boy and Girl together.

It is only fair to remember that the silent comedians would have as hard a time playing a talking scene as Hope has playing his visual ones, and that writing and directing are as account-able for the failure as Hope himself. But not even the humblest journeymen of the silent years would have let themselves off so easily. Like the masters, they knew, and sweated to obey, the laws of their craft.

The Nation
1942–1948

In the fall of 1942, James Agee was asked to do a movie column for The Nation. *Margaret Marshall, then Literary Editor, gave him free rein to cover what he wanted and to write as he pleased. As a result of her understanding attitude, the reviews became the highly personalized expression of an extremely gifted and sensitive American artist.*

December 26, 1942

I WOULD like so to use this column about moving pictures as to honor and discriminate the subject through interesting and serving you who are reading it. Whether I am qualified to do this is an open question to which I can give none of the answers. But I can begin by describing my condition as a would-be critic.

I suspect that I am, far more than not, in your own situation: deeply interested in moving pictures, considerably experienced from childhood on in watching them and thinking and talking about them, and totally, or almost totally, without experience or even much second-hand knowledge of how they are made. If I am broadly right in this assumption, we start on the same ground, and under the same handicaps, and I qualify to be here, if at all, only by two means. It is my business to conduct one end of a conversation, as an amateur critic among amateur critics. And I will be of use and of interest only in so far as my amateur judgment is sound, stimulating, or illuminating.

That my own judgment, and yours, is that of an amateur, is only in part a handicap. It is also a definition. It can even be an advantage, of a sort, in so far as a professional's preoccupation with technique, with the box-office, with bad traditions, or simply with work, can blur, or alter the angle of, his own judgment. I would talk to even so good a director as John Ford, for instance, with deep respect for him as a technician and as a serious man, but I might at the same time regret ninety-nine feet in every hundred of *The Grapes of Wrath*, and be able to specify my regret; and it would be a question entirely of the maturity of my judgment, and not in the least of my professional or amateur standing, whether I were right or wrong. If I were a professional, on the other hand, my realization of the complexity of making any film would be so much clarified that I would be much warier than most critics can be in assigning either credit or blame. Indeed, if you could follow out all the causes of that sort of high-serious failure, you would be involved as much in the analysis of an industry, a form of government, and the temper of a civilization, as in the analysis of a film.

As an amateur, then, I must as well as I can simultaneously recognize my own ignorance and feel no apology for what my eyes tell me as I watch any given screen, where the proof is caught irrelevant to excuse, and available in proportion to the eye which sees it, and the mind which uses it.

If only I had seen enough of the candidates I would like, now, to make some of the customary seasonal comments on the ten best films of the year. Not having seen even *Mrs. Miniver*, I have nothing to say, beyond mentioning that one look at the *Miniver* stills was enough to keep me away.

The best picture I saw this year was *The Gold Rush*. Next to that were various non-fiction shots of war. Next to them was *In Which We Serve*, which sets its limits so discreetly and fills them so nearly perfectly, and thus so likably, that my qualifying remarks must seem ungrateful.

They are that a blend, no matter how successful, of high-mediocre cinematic realism with Noel Coward's unexcelled particular kind of theatrical skill and tact cannot achieve anything first-rate but only one of the few next-best things, and that good as it is, it is a hollow filled with persuasive shadows and echoes where full excellence is solid, if transfigured, flesh and blood. I think the chief lack and the outstanding talent of such a man as Coward have the same root: a peculiarly sentimental kind of sensitiveness which is common to many witty, sad, able, and fastidious men. Their feeling for phenomena, whether human or inanimate, is at the same time sensuously sharp, shy, and critical, without either great energy or vulgarity or depth; so that when they are confronted with simple people, toward whom they feel remote and tender, or with a powerful and simple subject, they are at an essential loss, against which, on a secondary level, they have excellently equipped themselves.

In that sense of loss they retreat to two forts: that of "kitsch," used gently and with the severe withdrawal of irony of which ironists are best capable; and that of the taste, the devices, the exquisite sense of detail, the regard for form, by which they rectify and perfect the kitsch, refine their essential sentimentality, and set up defenses against any attack on it. This reverent and just evaluation of kitsch takes the place of that depth of heart and mind from which a first-rate artist works; and taste, tricks, detail, a dancer's delight in form, are the deft and of themselves respectable substitutes for a first-rate artist's perfecting of his perception. The result is that it is almost too elegantly geared for almost too many "effects." It has been so subtly used by the fingertips, rather than born out of the whole of the body, that discriminating watchers, in turn, are liable to find it merely touching, and pleasing to touch, whereas the undiscriminating watcher, taking this delicate imitation of power for power itself, is subtly hornswoggled.

I rather regret having used this space so generally, and would like at least to say that Coward himself is exceedingly good in the film, that Bernard Miles, whose chief petty officer looks like a Gothic angel, is even better, and that Coward's farewell to his crew is a really remarkable and moving tour de force. I would like also to recommend *Random Harvest* to those who can stay interested in Ronald Colman's amnesia for two hours and who could with pleasure eat a bowl of Yardley's shaving soap for breakfast, and *Life Begins at 8:30* to those who can still be tickled by Monty Wooley's beard and Nunnally Johnson's lines (both good things in moderation), at the end of what seems hours. I also urge that *Ravaged Earth*, which is made up of Japanese atrocities, be withdrawn until, if ever, careful enough minds, if any, shall have determined whether or not there is any morally responsible means of turning it loose on the public.

January 23, 1943

Wᴵᴸᴸᴵᴬᴹ Dᴵᴱᴛᴱᴿᴸᴱ is to be respected as a man who obviously wants to make fine moving pictures, and to use them for serious teaching. It would be a pleasure to say better of him, but that is at best a pleasure deferred. *Tennessee Johnson* is another of those screen biographies for which thousands of cultivated people will lay aside *Jalna* for an evening because they like to feel benevolent toward a really good movie. It is as sincere as Henry Wallace, whom it is perhaps prenominating, and now and then, helped usually by Van Heflin, the sincerity breaks loose from its male nurses and becomes vigorous and warming for a minute or two. Lionel Barrymore, too, is sometimes better than you could think possible after all these years of grunting to stay awake under the boredom of his assignments. The rest is Dieterle's customary high-minded, high-polished mélange of heavy "touches" and "intelligent" performances. Within the limits of its nearsighted traditions it does its very best; but anyone who wants a measure for the inadequacy of that should watch Morris Ankrum, as Jefferson Davis, announcing the secession of Mississippi.

It is unimportant whether Ankrum is perfect, or anywhere near it. The important thing is that he works in a world apart from the rest of the company; a world where good historical films have a chance to exist. He looks like a daguerreotype, not an impersonation. He bears himself like a man of 1860, not like a studious actor in a costume picture. He talks like a half-crazy devil. He supplies, in fact, the two primal requirements of the camera, in whose neglect or dilution you might better not use a camera at all: living—rather than imitative—visual, aural, and psychological authenticity, and the paralyzing electric energy of the present tense as against the rest of the show's glossy, comfortably researched reenactment at eighty years' remove.

Perhaps it is unkind to knock a picture for its neglect of problems which never occurred to its makers, and which are habitually neglected throughout an industry; but I cannot feel it is irrelevant. Here by some accident is this actor, dead right in every essential, showing up the bumbling of the rest. If all that he means had been realized, and studied, the following suggestions would be unnecessary.

Since Americans of the nineteenth and twentieth centuries differ in face, bearing, speech, and spirit as deeply as the men of different races, scour the country for the atavisms and actors who can at least suggest the difference, and preserve us from any more of these affable masquerades.

The historical events or inventions must look like newsreels made under ideal conditions, or poor ones if that edges the illusion of veracity.

The "private-life" scenes must attempt a related kind of realism which so far has only been dabbled at, stagily, in Lubitsch's earliest films, and innocently, through transcendent chromos, in *The Birth of a Nation*.

If you can give this realism poetic clarity without blurring its naturalistic clarity, you will have the beginnings, at least, of a good historical film, instead of a Drinkwater play.

All this detail will be as dead weight as its neglect is unless it is given present-tense immediacy rather than the customary optative pluperfect. The use of orthochromatic film will at least help toward this; whereas the seed-pearl shine which is so rarely appropriate to romance, irony, and special atmosphere, and which possesses even newsreels today, will drown in fatuousness every other care you take.

In this film, instead, where the common people are intended to mean so much, the one faintly convincing rural face is Heflin's when he briefly recalls Barthelmess in the first production of *Tol'able David*. Much more nearly typical is a bit by a supposed country boy who has a city face and body and a new straw hat which is scissored into a calendar reminiscence of a Whittier poem.

Those who think that I am quibbling over detail instead of deploring an ignorance of basic obligations should logically think the same if I objected to a performance of a Mozart quartet on a bass ocharina, a kazoo, and a team of Hickman whistles, or pointed out inadequacies in a production of *Coriolanus* which was staged by a particularly art-minded group of fox terriers.

I have given perhaps exorbitant space to *Tennessee Johnson* because it furnishes, for many, the illusion that Hollywood is "coming of age," and because a lifetime subscription to the *Atlantic Monthly* does not seem to me synonymous with "coming of age." In the little space left, a few regrets and recommendations.

Hitchcock's *Shadow of a Doubt* is a much better and more interesting picture, with some real attention to what places and people really look like, in Santa Rosa and in New Jersey, some very good (and some fussy) photography by Joseph Valentine, and some clever observation of rabbity white-collar life which, in spite of a specious sweetness, is the best since W. C. Fields's *It's a Gift*.

The Commandos Strike at Dawn will remind you why John Farrow won the Critics' Award for direction with *Wake Island*. It is "mature," for Paul Muni begins as a meteorologist widower and ends as a corpse. It glorifies the common man, for Muni says, "We Norwegians are a sturdy folk." Its climax is a commando raid in which no point is made of the likelihood that every trick of fighting has its countertrick and that the enemy, having boned up on them, may not be entirely cooperative. The raid is done in what currently passes for montage, so freely used in *Wake Island*. It has about the relation to Eisenstein's montage that a whickering prose, punctuated entirely by dashes, has to good poetry. Lillian Gish, formal and archaic though she is, shows how far pictures have degenerated since her time.

Journey for Margaret contains a few poignant flashes on children and parental emotion, some writing ("I'm mad at 1940," etc., etc.) as awful as the people who talk like that, and a well-meant performance by Fay Bainter which suggests that if Anna Freud—whom she is supposed to echo—really treats children like that, they were far better left shocked in the bomb-rubble than deshocked in her clinic. Those who want to see evil, cruelty, and some archetypical national diseases should see *The Powers Girl* and two out of three other musicals; few other films manage, even inadvertently, to get down so much. The subject here is American bitchery, with a demon photographer and his insurance-ad Mom and Pop thrown in, and some overloaded music from Benny Goodman, who should have refused to take off his glasses.

The best recent war short is *Conquer by the Clock*. It develops some questionable emotion over a munitions girl who, through sneaking time for a cigarette in the ladies' room, sends a dead cartridge to a soldier and the soldier to his death. It fails to suggest that the same thing might have happened if her visit to the toilet had been sincere; but like *Private Smith of the U.S.A.* it shows that when Slavko Vorkapich can keep his hands off a fancy transition (he still cannot) he is one of the straightest and most sharp-eyed men in Hollywood.

February 20, 1943

Not counting the films I have had to miss, it has been a dull month. Certainly the most interesting show I have seen is *The Hard Way*, in which, evidently, several frustrated talents have done their best to eat their cake and have it. The story—the pathetic, cheated woman who wrecks lives right and left in the effort to realize herself through a younger sister—is liable to go ham even aside from Bette Davis's virtual patent on it. The neatly sneaked-in sexual-economic explanations help, here, only a little; the show-business setting is an unlucky concession to glamor. This theme is either cruelly relevant on a grand native scale or better let alone; and a good deal even of the best of this treatment of it is coarse-grained, stagy, and sentimental.

Even so, there is a good deal in it to excite and to please. Much of the dialogue of Daniel Fuchs and Peter Viertel is a dozen times more loaded and acute than the average, and Fuchs's genius for writing quarrels (as in *Homage to Blenholt*) would alone make the picture worth seeing. Vincent Sherman directed it; he holds a large cast to a pitch of diversified accuracy which is seldom even attempted, and the vaudeville and theatrical sequences are the first in years to convince me (who knows little about either). A good deal of credit—how much, it is impossible to guess—must go to Jerry Wald, who wrote the original story and was the producer. I particularly liked Jack Carson as the more amorphous of two hoofers, and I thought Dennis Morgan made a good deal of his cold, complicated partner. Ida Lupino I feel sorry about. She has fine moments, especially one of Zazu Pitts in *Greed*, but I felt too often that her favorite expression of strained intensity would be less quickly relieved by a merciful death than by Ex-Lax. It is good to learn that in spite of her casting as Emily Brontë,

Miss Lupino still wants to play comedy, at which she is excellent. James Wong Howe's first few minutes with the camera, in a Pennsylvania mill town, all but floored me with gratitude. He goes on the list with Hitchcock as one of the few men of whom it can be hoped that, given the chance (and in Hitchcock's case travel, and still sharper advice from natives), they may yet take advantage of the $5,000 ceiling on sets to use this country as it ought to be used in films, and as it has scarcely been touched.

The well-paid shamming of forms of violence and death which millions a day are meeting in fact seems of an order more dubious than the shamming of all other forms of human activity; so I cannot be sure how I feel about *Air Force*. It is loud, loose, sincere, violently masculine, and at times quite exciting. Its disasters are well arranged and, in the Coral Sea sequence, nicely cut. There is some gladdening effort to get away from movie faces and to give the men diverse and authentic speech; the success is only occasional. Bits of the music are imaginative; all of it vitiates what it is intended to enhance. The sound, if plain realism is enough, is unusually good. I think it unfortunate, since the crew of this bomber is supposed to be going night after night without sleep, that the cast was not required to. The camera work varies between competence in the air and the gummiest sort of "Rembrandt" sentimentalities on the ground. A few all but annihilating cut-ins of actual combat adequately measure the best of the fiction, and my own uneasiness about it.

Barring a few infallible bits of slap-stick and one or two kitschy ingenuities with color, *Saludos Amigos* depresses me. Self-interested, belated ingratiation embarrasses me, and Disney's famous cuteness, however richly it may mirror national infantilism, is hard on my stomach. (I have not yet seen Donald Duck's income-tax film, but from what I hear, it will be worth as vicious invective as the Führer's Face.) *Journey into Fear* is disappointing, too. It is good to see so likable an entertainer as Welles making an unpretentious pleasure-picture; but to make a good one you need to be something of an artist, and Welles has little if any artistry. Since costume pictures leave me cold and oblique editorials—especially when I disagree with them—leave me colder, *Young Mr. Pitt* held nothing for me

but Morley's suaveness, my lingering liking for Donat, and respect for some smooth dialogue and for Carol Reed's intelligent walk across the intrinsically hopeless flypaper of his first
super-production.

Apparently *Casablanca*, which I must say I liked, is working
up a rather serious reputation as a fine melodrama. Why? It is
obviously an improvement on one of the world's worst plays;
but it is not such an improvement that that is not obvious.
Any doubters should review the lines of Claude Rains. Rains,
Bogart, Henried, Veidt, Lorre, Sakall, and a colored pianist
whose name I forget were a lot of fun, and Ingrid Bergman
was more than that; but even so, Michael Curtiz still has a
twenties director's correct feeling that everything, including
the camera, should move; but the camera should move for purposes other than those of a nautch-dancer, and Mr. Curtiz's
bit players and atmospheric scenes are not even alien corn.
Thanks to a friend, moreover, I can now quote two lines which
I snickered at and then, I blush to say, forgot. One, Miss
Bergman's plea to her husband, takes the season's prize for exposition: "Oh, Victor, please don't go to the underground
meeting tonight." The other, more tender, is Miss Bergman's
too, just after she collapses on to a sofa with Humphrey
Bogart: "From now on you'll have to do the thinking for both
of us, dear."

Social psychiatrists might, I think, regard the following as
sinister wartime symptoms. In two current films there are
heroines named Charlie; in a third there is a heroine named
Chris. In the only two films I have seen in which young men
got notices from their government informing them whether
they were, or were not, acceptable for armed service, the
young men first trembled in agonies of suspense, next, after
glancing at the notice, showed their very tonsils for joy, and
next made quite sure that the audience would share in their
pleasure by cavorting in a manner to fit Mickey Rooney for
wheel-chair roles. In the long run it became clear, in both
cases, that they got the job.

March 20, 1943

The Human Comedy is an effort to create, through a series of lyrically casual, almost plotless scenes, the image of a good family in a good town in wartime. Most of my friends detest it. A good many millions of other people, I suspect, will like it, as they liked the Andy Hardy films and Rupert Hughes's *The Old Nest*, whose traditions it returns to rather more than improves on. I do not agree with either side. I think my friends are too frightened of tearjerkers to grant that they can be not only valid but great, and that the audience at large is too friendly, too gullible, too eager to be seduced. The picture is mainly a mess, but as a mixture of typical with atypical failure, and in its rare successes, it interests me more than any other film I have seen for a good while.

Many of its faults, and most of its virtues, are those of its author. What angers me is that Saroyan's original story, cut perhaps twenty per cent and sternly dry-cleaned, might have been the basis for a film which, though I might not wholly have liked or agreed with it, would have had a great deal of beauty and importance. That, of course, would have had to depend on every detail of its screen treatment; and in nearly every respect the treatment it gets wobbles between that stultifying kind of slick-paper competence which is worse than no competence at all and unforgivable errors of taste and judgment. The best one can say of it, with few exceptions, is that it tries on the whole to be "faithful" to Saroyan; not invariably a good idea. The worst, in my opinion, lies less in its active failures of taste or of plain sense than in its easygoing, self-pleased, Mortimer Snerdish neglect of some magnificent opportunities.

There are, as I say, exceptions. Most of them involve the one sound piece of casting and performance, that of Jack Jenkins as the four-year-old Ulysses, who, I fervently hope, will not be used again; otherwise he will become just another actor. When Ulysses is trying to learn "My Old Kentucky Home" from his brother, or is asking his mother what the man meant when he sang weep-no-more—adding another weep-no-more with exquisite quickness and quiet—or when, watching an also well-played store-window robot, he first learns the meaning of terror, something perfectly limpid, true, warm, and powerful comes alive which gives Saroyan and this film, for all their lapses, a rare and honorable right to existence. There are other very good bits: the gentle leavetaking of three soldiers who have picked up two nice girls; the sound, filled with death and enigma, as they recede along a rainy night sidewalk; the beautifully timed, very moving sound, late in the film, of the first two horseshoes as they hit the dirt in the dusk. I am sorry Mickey Rooney was cast in the leading role, but I was touched to see how sensitive and earnest an actor this usually unfortunate young man can be. I thought he did almost as well with the part as an "actor" could.

It would be hard, I grant, to find anyone beyond childhood who might be capable of purity and directness of performance, which are hopelessly unavailable to most actors; but I wish it had occurred to everyone to try. The Hollywood traditions of acting, to say nothing of those of the stage, are incapable even at best of convincing one, except in the frankest kind of myth. I like some of the myths very well and some of the actors in them, but when there is any pretense whatever of portraying "real" people—as in *The Grapes of Wrath* and in this film— such actors are painfully out of place. Acting, even in the films I would like to see made, must inevitably develop a tradition, a style, which must as inevitably, in the long run, stultify and destroy itself. All I am urging here is that the present tradition be recognized for worse than dead, except within its limited and also half-dead bounds, and that new sources be drawn on, new styles—drastically new ones—developed. Some time I hope to make some suggestions on this matter, at length. Here, there is time to say only that nearly every performance in this film, from the skilfully well-intended but traditional (Frank Morgan's) to the hopelessly unfortunate but also traditional (Fay Bainter's, Van Johnson's, Ray Collins's), strangles at birth every hope of a truly vivid reality. And surely there are enough Mexican mothers in California to make unnecessary the use, for a Mexican mother, of a sexy young actress with flour all over her hair who can't even make the accent convincing.

Saroyan's brand of Christian anarchy I find about equally genuine, sympathetic, professional, and muddled. I think his all but glandular inability to take evil seriously not only limits his world but leads him sometimes into foolishness and unintentional deceit; but I do not question, as some of my friends do, his right to make a story which is not "class conscious," nor do I disapprove of the film for its failure to rectify this presumed lack. I do notice, however, that MGM has used exactly as much of Saroyan's feelings (or ideas) as it pleases, and no more; which is only too liable to be the fate of men of good-will who are capable of good-will alone.

What annoyed me much more was the neglect of opportunities which, one would think, would be only too obvious to film makers with a grain of cinematic sense. Take three salient examples.

A premental child hears a freight train coming, runs up close to it, waves, is answered by a singing Negro. Made, with any imagination, from the point of view of the child—and of plain fact—this could have been a roaring and miraculous half-minute. Not one thing in it is taken advantage of. To make the shame complete, the Negro himself has the fruity vibrato of a "well-trained" singer.

On another train, deep in the night—here referred to as "an American night"—crowded troops, on their way to war, get tired of talking and of dirty songs and by gradual stages take to singing a Moody-and-Sankey-style hymn. I think it is perfectly conceivable, or properly inventable, that they would. But if they did, it would take some doing, and if we got it, it could be unforgettable. Here, all we get is a few mushy salon shots of a night train; the well-groomed, well-rested faces of about nine in the evening; an obnoxiously emphasized Chinese and Filipino (?) to prove that, despite the absence of Negroes, this is the century of the common man; one excellent face, that of a big-eared prep-school type of child; aside from this, about a three-point-two amount of sensitiveness to faces; the song starting, unreally, much too soon; the soldiers getting into it with the overswift, disgraceful "informality" of a musical-comedy chorus, and sounding like one; a total absence of the complexity, the weariness, the power, the pity, the great beauty which it seems incomprehensible not to have imagined, and which one night's ride in a contemporary day coach could so richly have taught those who made, and were presumably content with, this scene. Or could it have taught them? Are

Hollywood "professionals" so engulfed in their "profession" that they are incapable of seeing beyond the ends of their cameras? I rather suspect that most of them are.

I suspect it all the more in their general and specific failure to realize that here they might for once have used a real town in all its intricacy, individuality, and beauty. In the closing sequence a young man, an orphan, arrives who has never seen the town before but has heard much of it. He wants to look at it, tenderly and at leisure. He might have been the vehicle for as fine a summation as an American town could ever get. What does the camera do instead? Close-ups of his face, while his stream of consciousness murmurs that there is the library, and the Presbyterian Church, and so on.

Why did they bother to make the film at all? Why, for that matter, do they bother to make any? Surely, not twice in any hundred thousand feet can they flatter themselves that they qualify to.

May 1, 1943

Desert Victory is the first completely admirable combat film, and if only film makers and their bosses can learn the simple lessons it so vigorously teaches, its service to the immediate future and to history will be incalculably great. The most heartening thing about it is that its lessons are learnable. It takes something approaching great talent to learn from great talent, but the men who made this film are not men of great talent. They are simply men of intelligence, courage, and aesthetic honor who have been given a chance to use their abilities in the recording of a worthy theme. That they were given the apparently unhindered chance is as important as the fact that they knew how to use it; on both counts, the makers of American films have virtually everything to learn.

It is so good, and so simply good, that it is hard to do more than urge that you see it. In the camera work, the cutting, the music and sound, the commentary, it is a clean, simple demonstration that creative imagination is the only possible substitute for the plainest sort of good sense—and is, after all, merely an intensification of good sense to the point of incandescence.

There is hardly one moment in the collaboration of cameras that implies a truly creative eye, that makes a subject be itself with the intensity of a diamond; but on the other hand there is hardly a shot which by any sort of dramatizing, prearrangement, or sentimentalization gets in the way of the high honest average chance for magnificence which any face or machine or light or terrain possesses, left to its own devices. The captured German film hits a similar level.

The cutting—here I include the broad scenario—is a shade or two more perceptive, though again it gets along, proudly and well, with plain sense and sensitiveness instead of brilliance. It is distinguished from most cutting simply in being the work of men who have thought, felt, and cared a great deal about the power and honesty of given film images, in themselves simply, in juxtaposition and careful series, in rhythm, and in a rhythmic and spatial whole. The results of this sort of thought and feeling, carved out without compromise, are inevitable. Whereas the average nonfiction film, even if the material is well photographed—which it seldom is—moves in great blotches of ill-punctuated gabble, filled with uh's, ah's, and as-I-was-sayings, this moves at worst in clean, resonant sentences, which construct irreducible paragraphs, and develops, at discreet intervals, the small fine poems of which honesty without inspiration is capable. Very notable, I think, is the fact that here, for the first time in a strictly record film, record has been used without abuse to create an organized whole rather than a gifted, spotty sprawl. (The camera work in *June 13th*, for instance, is more sophisticated, but over-all, *June 13th* is diffuse and a little posterish, without anything like the solidity and internal rhyming of the British film.)

Sound and music commentary follow, here, the same pattern: that is, they are used when and as they should be. The music goes a little vulgar at the end, but there are two movements—the industrial build-up and the build-up of the barrage—which almost for the first time are made in intelligent relations to natural sound, and which spike rather than water the screen's images. The commentary is especially worth American study. The normal native commentary, well measuring our loss of cinematic instinct, heckles and humiliates the screen image, and pounds it, like the nagging of a shrew, a

salesman, a preacher, a demagogue, a pimp, or all five combined; we use films to illustrate the rotten words we worship.
Here, for once, the words really illuminate when they are used
at all; and here, for once, the voice is right which speaks them.
The natural sound rises, in one scene, to a solid attempt to annihilate the audience which a friend of mine has properly compared with Beethoven. The second time I heard it, it was
muted into a defeat of this intention. I urge that by every means
possible you require that it be given full blast. It is the first serious attempt to make an audience participate in the war. No
audience should be spared it.

These men have taken painful care with every foot of this
film. The attitude of the average American film maker—and
his boss—will, of course, be conditioned by the fact that
neither knows much about moving pictures, about care and
honesty, or about the great potential sensitiveness of the general audience, toward which they have been acting like house-
broken Nazis for the past twenty years. But that even they
must suspect that the general audience is capable of receiving
better than they know how to give is suggested by the mere
rumor that Darryl Zanuck has refused to see this film, and that
its release was delayed in favor of his own shorn lamb.

Desert Victory is a stunning textbook on how to make a nonfiction war film. *Hangmen Also Die*, *This Land Is Mine*, and
The Moon Is Down open the question whether serious fiction
films on the subject had better be made at all. I would believe
that plain melodramas, through their innate artificiality and
unpretentiousness, have a good right to exist and may even,
within their special formalism, give a remote but decent echo
of the truth. I can even respectfully conceive of the attempt at
a head-on embodiment of the truth. But that would be a
much more difficult and serious job than the makers of these
three films realize. It would require a sensitiveness which they
totally lack to the speed with which the noblest reported actions and principles can become the most vulgar sentiment, especially as served to civilians at a comfortable remove. It would
require an ingenuity which they seem never to have conceived
of in finding and developing kinds of acting, setting, and
lighting which might render an audience incapable of feeling,
first, that all they are seeing is, after all, only a picture, and

second—and still worse—that the occupied nations are filled, not with the terrific human and historical chemistry which is in fact at work in them, but with a pack of posturing Donlevys and Laughtons and Traverses spouting inhuman lines like "You cannot keel de speerit off a free pipples." Seriously, I think such shows can create a dullness of heart, a schizophrenia, from which we might never recover. Whether I am right or wrong about that, I find this sort of stodgy heroism, about such subjects, incredulously indecent.

Of the three films, Lang and Bert Brecht's *Hangmen* is the most interesting. They have chosen to use brutality, American gangster idiom, and Middle High German cinematic style to get it across, and it is rich with clever melodrama, over-*maestoso* directional touches, and the sort of *Querschnitt* sophistication for detail which Lang always has. It is most interesting as a memory album. There's a heroine straight out of the Berlin of the middle twenties, and the Nazis are also archaic, nicely presented types: the swaggering homosexual, the cannonball-headed plainclothesman, the tittering, torturing androgyne who, one can imagine, is a revenge on some boyhood misery of Lang's in a Teutonic school. They are all conceivable, as Nazis; but they are all old-fashioned. The New Order has produced men of a new kind, and it would be more to the point to show some of them.

This Land Is Mine eschews physical terror in favor of mental, and tries to give an exposition of the obligations of free men under those circumstances. That is a courageous but foredoomed idea. I doubt, first, whether physical and mental terror and obligation can in this context be separated. You cannot afford to dislocate or internationalize your occupied country; or to try to sell it to Americans by making your citizens as well-fed, well-dressed, and comfortably idiomatic as Americans; or to treat the show to the corrupted virtuosities of studio lighting and heavy-ballet composition. This film, like Lang's, is filled with bitter, anachronistic, interesting talent under pressures, but it is a question where the pressure begins and the self-deception ends.

The Moon Is Down is a stale quarrel by now which I see no point in reheating. I respect Steinbeck's insistence that both the Nazis and their enemies are human beings, but too many things get in the way of any proof of the fact. Colonel Lanser, as written and played, is very intelligent, but poorly representative. The sort of Nazi Steinbeck must have intended is post-humanistic and unprecedented, as Walter Slezak brilliantly suggests, with far less to use, in *This Land Is Mine*. Irony, I am told, comes from *eironikos*, which could be translated as false naivete. Steinbeck's "little people" use it so much that they become false and naive out of all conscious proportions. So the irony itself becomes unpalatable, and the people become dehumanized victims of a well-intended, unconscious patronage. Worse still, they become stagy—in the worst recent (Group Theater) tradition—with their bursts of song during executions and their scornful smiles, which so falsely dismay Nazi soldiers. To state frankly your deep fear of torture or death ought to be an advance over the traditional false-heroics. Instead, it becomes its own kind of vulgar boast and takes its place in that growing, already over-ripe vocabulary of democratic claptrap which all but destroys our realization that modest heroism is possible, constant, and implicit in this war.

I have inadequate room left to regret an ill-directed nastiness, in my review of *The Human Comedy*, which should have been more accurately directed. I think of Clarence Brown, who directed it, in the most praiseworthy and respectful terms, as the man who piloted Garbo's best films and who, before that, made the excellent and bold films *Smoldering Fires* and *The Signal Tower*. I have still to insist that he has become a dope, and to offer the negligencies in *The Human Comedy* as proof. But he is a sympathetic and likable casualty rather than the sort of born star-spangled Judas I directed that review against.

May 22, 1943

As CINEMA and as warfare, *Mission to Moscow* is an important piece. Not entirely without skill, it inaugurates for a great general audience a kind of pamphleteering and of at least nominal nonfiction whose responsibilities, whose powers for good or evil, enlightenment or deceit, are appalling; and of which we are likely to get a great deal from now on. (Walter Huston

touring Mr. Willkie's One World seems like a foregone conclusion.) This first film is likely to hasten and intensify our cooperation with the Soviet Union. It may even help frustrate those
who—if my naive impression is correct—plan to win this
particular peace by destroying the Soviet Union, dominating
Europe with the help of Bryn Mawr graduates and domesticated democrats, and reducing China to an Anglo-American–
owned, Japanese-policed laundry. To whatever degree the film
may help frustrate such intentions, and enrich our alliance, I
feel considerable passion in its favor. It will be the first time
that moving pictures have even flexed their muscles in a human
crisis. Aside from these purely practical issues, however, the
picture fascinates me chiefly as a phenomenon. So does the
question how it came to be made in the first place.

There are other questions. Did the government urge the
film on Warner Brothers? Is it federally subsidized or lend-
lease? Are the sacred treatment of the President and the adroit
suggestion that all isolationists were Republicans parts of a
deal or mere good-will? We can only suspect, through rumor
and internal inference, that the Stalinists here stole or were
handed such a march that the film is almost describable as the
first Soviet production to come from a major American studio.
Almost, but not quite. For it is indeed, as Manny Farber has
well said, a mishmash: of Stalinism with New Dealism with
Hollywoodism with journalism with opportunism with shaky
experimentalism with mesmerism with onanism, all mosaicked
into a remarkable portrait of what the makers of the film think
that the American public should think the Soviet Union is
like—a great glad two-million-dollar bowl of canned borscht,
eminently approvable by the Institute of Good Housekeeping.

As such, it is as rich a subject for diagnosis as any other
dream.

Up to a point—not far short of first base—it is serviceable.
It is good to see the conservatives of this country, Great
Britain, France, and Poland named even for a fraction of their
responsibility for this war. It is good to see the Soviet Union
shown as the one nation during the past decade which not
only understood fascism but desired to destroy it, and which
not only desired peace but had some ideas how it might be

preserved and how it would otherwise inevitably be lost. It is good for that matter to hear even an oblique line spoken in favor of Basic English—a line by the way which underlines the rumor that Madame Litvinov played a strong hand behind-screen.

But that is about as much good as I can find, barring some sincere performances and some rather inchoate directorial nervous energy. The rest is shameful rot. Not that *Mission to Moscow* is either remarkably more true or more false than the characteristic reflexes of Hollywood, the press, the schools, the politicians, or civilization in general: simply, it indulges the all but universal custom of using only so much of the truth as may be convenient and of regarding aesthetic integrity, human verisimilitude, and psychological credibility as scullions, dismissible without notice if employable at all. This sort of irresponsibility is insulting and inimical to its producers, appraisers, and consumers alike, and those who accept or excuse it insult and endanger themselves still again, from within. The immediate incidental pragmatic effect may be good. But the deeper effect is shame, grief, anaesthesia, the ruin of faith and conscience and the roots of intelligence; and the real end, as should be reasonably clear just now, is disaster.

Letting that be for the moment, what are some examples?

Mr. Davies himself is one in his prologue, indorsing the gospel truth of this production—a figure as much of dream as of reality. As a big business man, the figure which has replaced Lincoln as the American archetype, he is a creature whose wisdom, disinterest, reliability are final and above question.

The man whom Ambassador Huston faithfully calls "Boss" is another. Boss is here accorded almost the divine invisibility of "good taste" which Jesus Christ rated in Fred Niblo's *Ben Hur*, where a Mazda bulb stood in for the Nazarene; and his voice, even in intimate conversation with Joe, sounds as if he were telling a hundred and thirty million of his friends that we planned it that way.

Ambassador Huston is still another, as he carries his honest Tarkingtonian charm around brightest Russia, Seeing for Himself with an Open Mind. He sees little of the colossal country and the astonishing people Warner Brothers might at least have half tried to let him see. But Davies himself didn't see either, actually. He saw what ambassadors, officials see; and the film shows him doing just that, no more. This is one of the most faithful notes in the film, really. What little Mr. Huston does see, however, will be mighty illuminating to those fifty million-odd moviegoers who have never had his advantages. For there is no essential difference, it turns out, between the Soviet Union and the good old U.S.A., except that in Russia everybody affects a Weber and Fields accent and women run locomotives and you get tailed by a pair of harmless comics who claim to be GPU men. The Ambassador learns this sort of good news in a series of dialogues on that "educational" radio level in which a mere scientist asks a Pasteur, "Just what *is* this H_2O, Doctor Coffee-Nerves?" and gets a wrong answer. Mrs. Davies and Madame Molotov, meanwhile, put on a woman's-page skit with a serving maid which makes Elinor Ames's *The Correct Thing* look like the correct thing. Later, at a "history"-making reception, two 'cello-voiced Soviet officials stroll past the camera with the most endearing Daisy Ashfordism in years. Commissar Cox opines, "We are entering a new era, don't you think so?" Commissar Box retaliates, feelingly, "*I* think we have done *remarkably* well!"

About the trials I am not qualified to speak. On surface falsifications of fact and atmosphere I might, but on the one crucial question, whether Trotsky and Trotskyists were or were not involved with Germany and Japan in a plot to overthrow the government and to partition the country, I am capable of no sensible opinion. I neither believe it nor disbelieve it. I neither believe nor disbelieve evidence to the contrary. I am unable to trust the politicians of either camp or of any other to supply me, the world in general, or even their closest associates, with the truth. I am unable to be sure, even, that men of such intelligence, courage, and integrity as Professor Dewey are undeceivable in such matters, deeply as I respect them; so I am unable, in turn, to be convinced by their findings and opinions. It may be that this painful impotence is an impotence merely of my own spirit; it may be that I am immobilized, rather, by my conviction that a primary capacity for telling or discovering the truth is possible, today, to few human beings in few types of occupation or allegiance. In any case I can attempt to learn the truth, and can defend, or attack, only in

areas where I can rely in some small degree on the hope of
emergent truthfulness in the material and in those who are
handling it.

June 12, 1943

Prelude to War is the first of the army orientation films put
out by Lieutenant Colonel Frank Capra's Special Services
Unit. It is the sort of thing one can expect when capable film
makers work for a great and many-leveled audience—the best,
I suspect, which this country has ever had—under no obligation to baby or cajole, and for a serious purpose.

The intention of the film is to tell the history of fascism from
the Mukden incident through the invasion of Ethiopia. Interested experts will object that it does not tell that history *whole*;
I think it more important that here for the first time an American film tries to give the general dimensions of a theory and
practice which has customarily been treated, in government
and Hollywood films alike, as if it were the hate that dare not
speak its name.

The method is more verbose than I wish it were or am sure
it need be; but if the American addiction to word-dominated
films is crystallizing into an American form, this is a useful
model. The profuse text has been vigilantly researched and on
the whole is respectably written. More shrewdness has been
used here to make screen images point, edge, impregnate, or
explode the spoken text than I have seen used before; at times
the border line is crossed into full cinematic possibility, and
words serve the screen instead or even do it the greatest service, of withdrawal. For a film made up chiefly of old newsreels
and confiscated enemy footage, a surprising amount is new,
and a surprising amount of the new is excellent. There is an
eye for the unprecedented powers which can reside in simple
record photographs—the ferocious inadvertent caricature, the
moment when a street becomes tragic rather than a mere
street, the intricate human and political evidence in unknown
faces—which is here equaled only by the quiet, dry-touched
forcefulness with which such images are cut in. A newsreel poll
of American war sentiment in 1939 is brilliantly used. There is a

long, pouring, speechless sequence, intelligently sustained by rudimentary drumbeats, of marching children, youths, and men which is a virtuoso job of selection and cutting, and the grimmest image of fascism I have seen on a screen.

There are also faults. Over-all, the film is so crowded and so ramified that it has no ultimate musical coherence. Things like the drummed march, which had every right to be cinematically overwhelming, are merely impressive. I found repeated references to a Mr. John Q. Public embarrassing, for I felt they betrayed an underestimation of the audience of which the picture as a whole is hearteningly free. A few production shots, like the salon bit showing the withered, rosaried hands of an old woman (which may, heaven forbid, be a stock shot after all; the salon manner has infected so much), are unnecessarily dissonant. In the effort to relieve the monotony of one commentator's voice, too many voices are used, and too many of these voices suggest the cheerful drawers peddlers and the flunked divinity students who are the normal cantors for our nonfiction films. I also noticed with regret that many of the shots devoted to demonstrating that John Q. Public's country is a horse of another color were indeed of another color, glossy and insipid; but I blame this less on the country than on the fact that few of us, conspicuously excepting Walker Evans, have yet learned how to make a camera show what a country it is. It was extremely disconcerting at the end to see a "two worlds" image of Vice-President Wallace's overdrawn to a point at which an image of the Western Hemisphere, described as "free," totally eclipses the "slave" hemisphere. The film as a whole indicates that this unfortunate piece of misorientation could not have been deliberate, but it should be rectified.

Suffocating to meet nose to nose (it is over two hours of Virginia Dare wine, women, and song), *Stage Door Canteen* is beautiful as a preview of a period piece. Any film is, but this one carries a saturation of the mannerisms of fourth-decade entertainment, patriotism, and sub-idealized lovemaking which could supply almost any twenty others. The best of the patriotism is implicit rather than overt. The lovemaking is strictly church-supper. The entertainment is best. Lack of space, libel laws, and a fondness for entertainers, all prevent any detail on the subject; but we can safely remember that every piece of entertainment, like every political speech or swatch of advertising copy, has nightmarish accuracy as a triple-distilled image of a collective dream, habit, or desire. My favorite few minutes was Gracie Fields's rendition of the Lord's Prayer as set, it sounded, by Stainer or more so. In the music itself, in every gesture used to sell it and every inflection, in the reverent, faintly embarrassed audience, this is the most touching and complex bit of religious history which has ever reached the screen; the whole footage of *The King of Kings* is just a Ford hour by comparison. *Stage Door Canteen* is achingly long; a lot of the dialogue is dragged in by heels who should never have been hired even to drag it out; and Frank Borzage should have used a spare cameraman with first-rate eyes to work the Canteen floor for its wonderful possibilities. Yet this is a nice harmless picture for the whole family; and it is a gold mine for those who are willing to go to it in the wrong spirit.

George Stevens's last film as a civilian (*The More the Merrier*) is partly nice and partly disappointing. The chiseling, cringing sex and claustrophobia of war-torn Washington might have delivered a really original, really native comedy, and the types set up to carry this comedy are not bad in conception; they are spoiled in the execution. Stevens has a free, pretty feeling for business (like Jean Arthur's awkwardness after the love scene on the steps), for special colorations of talk (there is some good adlibbing), and for gratuitous satire (a poke at the G-men and a snort at the surplus of women in Washington). Yet the film as a whole is a tired soufflé, for unfortunately Stevens doesn't know where to stop. Farce, like melodrama, offers very special chances for accurate observation, but here accuracy is avoided ten times to one in favor of the easy burlesque or the easier idealization which drops the bottom out of farce. Every good moment frazzles or drowns. The most flagrant example is Jean Arthur, whose mugging and whinnying seemed to me as redundant and, at length, as uningratiating, as if a particularly cute monkey, instead of merely holding out his hat for a penny which I might gladly have made a quarter, insisted that he was working his way through Harvard.

I recommend a look at *Wings Up*, the best OWI short I have seen, and at Paramount's *African Report* because it seems to try, even though it fails, to learn some much-needed lessons from *Desert Victory*. I wanted to write here of fifteen fragments of avant-garde films which were recently shown by Hans Richter at the Museum of Modern Art, but there is only room to say that though I respected their intentions, and believed great things can still or always come of small-audience films proudly made on shoestrings, there is no substitute for the born cinematic talent which René Clair's *Entr'Acte* so delightfully showed and which nearly all the rest so depressingly lacked. Finally, I regret having missed *The Ox-Bow Incident* and for the moment can only pass on the word of trustworthy people that it is worth seeing, as I would expect a William Wellman film to be.

July 3, 1943

I ONLY hope Major de Seversky and Walt Disney know what they are talking about, for I suspect an awful lot of people who see *Victory Through Air Power* are going to think they do. Certainly I am not equipped to argue with them. I have the feeling I was sold something under pretty high pressure, which I don't enjoy, and I am staggered by the ease with which such self-confidence, on matters of such importance, can be blared all over a nation, without cross-questioning. Beyond that, I can only talk of it as a certain kind of moving picture.

When Disney is attending strictly to mechanics and to business, it is good poetry and, barring its overpersuasiveness, good teaching. When, instead, he is being poetic, or cute, or in this case funny, it is neither. Such images as that of the Nazi wheel are vivid and instructive. Such images as that of the bird which nests in a Maginot gunmouth are the defective side of this notably split talent or composite of talents. The human animations, like all of Disney's, are so bad they become interesting as misanthropic footnotes. The real poetic energy in Disney's films has always come of the children and grandchildren of his basic metaphors—the sounds and images of impingement, for instance, as the Nazi wheel is assaulted—and usually these are finely detailed and polished. Here they are not much more than roughed-in. The nonmusical sound is good without his occasional brilliance; the music is a loss. The color undersea (as in Disney's forest glades, etc.—there is something fishy about either him or me) is subdued and quite pretty; the extroverted color is so much loud candy, if candy were to develop aesthetic pretensions. The patronizing comic cuteness with which early aviation is treated and the gay dreams of holocaust at the end seem to me as ill-advised as the finely mechanized expository stuff between them is new and correct.

I noticed, uneasily, that there were no suffering and dying enemy civilians under all those proud promises of bombs; no civilians at all, in fact. Elsewhere, the death-reducing virtues of De Seversky's scheme—if he is right—are mentioned; but that does not solve the problem. It was necessary here either (1) to show bombed civilians in such a manner as to enhance the argument, (2) to omit them entirely, or (3) to show them honestly, which might have complicated an otherwise happy sales talk. I am glad method 1 was not used, and of method 3 I realize that animated cartoons, so weak—at least as Disney uses them—in the whole human world, would be particularly inadequate to human terror, suffering, and death. Even so, I cannot contentedly accept the antiseptic white lies of method 2. The sexless sexiness of Disney's creations has always seemed to me queasy, perhaps in an all-American sense; in strict descent from it is this victory-in-a-vacuum which is so morally simple a matter—and so salubrious for the postwar if only it were true—of machine-eat-machine.

At last I saw *The Ox-Bow Incident*. I also saw *Bataan*. Between the two of them there is a great deal one might talk about on the difficult question of the proper and the incestuous relationship, in any work of art or entertainment, between nature and artifice. After a good deal of effort to get it on to paper and into feasible space, I'm afraid it is wiser to give up, saying only as follows. *Ox-Bow* is one of the best and most interesting pictures I have seen for a long time, and it disappointed me. *Bataan* is incomparably less of a picture, and I liked it very much. It seems to me that in *Ox-Bow* artifice and nature got jammed in such a way as to give a sort of double focus, like off-printing in a comic strip. Here was a remarkably controlled and intelligent film; and in steady nimbus, on every detail, was the stiff over-consciousness of those who made it of the excellence of each effect, to such a degree that the whole thing seemed a mosaic of over-appreciated effects which continually robbed nature of its own warmth and energy, and the makers of the ambitious claims which they had made on nature. This complicatedness of attitude, as I infer it, accounts for occasional flagrant mistakes, like the phonily gnarled lynching tree or the angelic soprani which are used as motif for the Negro preacher; and accounts also for unluckier, more intrinsic flaws than those—for the literariness and theatricality, the essential patronage and indirect self-pity, which braid and infuse the best of the show. Henry Fonda is a good median example. His performance is the most sympathetic of his career; and beneath it his personal fondness for "the part" and his awareness how to temper his mannerisms to an unshorn wind show like several inches of slip. If I seem to be going out of my way to find faults to explain what was chiefly a troubling of intuition—and I'm afraid I may be—let me at least pay my respects to this film by adding that I find the same arteriosclerotic fault-of-attitude harming still better things—nearly all the good writing of this century, the films of Pudovkin and Pabst, and some of the music of Brahms.

But not in Mozart, and not, far down the scale, in *Bataan*. Its claims on nature are modest enough to be almost shamefully safe, being only those which a certain kind of melodrama can dare to claim; and from there on what still might have been very bad becomes instead a small triumph of pure artifice. And that becomes possible, I think, thanks again to creative attitude. The people who made this film, I judge, were lucky enough to believe in it so warmly and innocently that the small area they staked out in nature remained at the fertile center of their affection, and their cinematic intelligence and skill—with none left over for self-congratulation from the sidelines—were released entirely to the proper business of embodiment. What they had to embody was as formal and naive as a pulp story. Thirteen men defend a bridgehead against hopeless odds. Like their number, their types and their troubles and their deaths are conclusions so forgone that to try to freshen them by tampering and basic invention would have been a deep aesthetic mistake (again, as with Disney, the power of the secondary and tertiary metaphor). The mistake was not made. The story was simply put into patient and fecund detail, excellently written, acted, photographed, paced, above all directed (by Tay Garnett) into something as perfectly artificial, and as strongly rooted also in nature, as good ballet or, in another aspect, Italian opera, which like the pulp story has a large believing, yet critical audience. It seems to me irrelevant to criticism on any other grounds so long as it ventures on to no other grounds. I have heard *Bataan* criticized for presuming so shallowly to portray war. But I think it much less shallow than most of the more ambitious war pictures, which are indeed insults both to the men who make real war and to the men who made the images. We may not yet recognize the tradition, but it is essentially, I think, not a drama but a certain kind of native ritual dance. As such its image of war is not only naive, coarse-grained, primitive; it is also honest, accomplished in terms of its aesthetic, and true.

Eric Ambler's stories are not yet getting very good breaks on the screen. Orson Welles's *Journey into Fear* had sophistication without much journeying, in the kinesthetic sense of the word, still less fear. *Background to Danger* has plenty of danger, in lively motion at that, without a background keenly drawn enough to make it really dangerous. Short of the really "creative" men, Raoul Walsh is one of my favorite directors; but—besides thoroughly enjoying it—you could use this film for one kind of measurement of the unconquerable difference between a good job by Hitchcock and a good job of the Hitchcock type.

There is still doubt—and should be none—about the American release of two English "documentaries," both of which deserve better than that rubber truncheon of a categorizer. *World of Plenty*, about past, present, and future food, was energetically and well written by the late Eric Knight and surprisingly (to me) well edited by Paul Rotha, with some adroit pedagogical help from the Isotype Institute and a general boldness of ideology which I would like to see cutting grease in as many American theaters as possible. *The Silent Village* is a reenactment by Welsh miners of the story of the mining village of Lidice. The unobstreperous sensitiveness of those who made it and the fistlike authenticity, dignity, and seriousness of those who performed in it make this an expiation for every odious advantage which has been taken of that village. It is a question, probably a sad one, whether any group of miners in this country would have been capable of it.

July 24, 1943

Horses may send their children to *For Whom the Bell Tolls* without fear. That offensive word "stallion" (not to be confused with *Joseph* Stallion) which appeared in Mr. Hemingway's novel and even in Dudley Nichols's original script has been changed, in the finished production, to read "blazed face."

Human beings should proceed more cautiously; else they are liable to be misinformed. When f-sc-sts are actually mentioned, the one time they are, the context makes it clear that they are just Italians who, in company with German Nazis and those dirty Russian Communists, are bullyragging each other and poor little Spain, which wants only peace and quiet. In the same speech, if you are not careful, you may easily get the impression that Gary Cooper is simply fighting for the Republican Party in a place where the New Deal has got particularly out of hand. The next speech, which suggests that not all Americans have Mr. Cooper's disinterested historical foresight, appears in the Nichols script but not on the screen. There is, on the other hand, General Golz's joke about how full of accents Spain is these days, which I suppose can be regarded as a small triumph by screen workers defeated enough to seek their victories through microscopes. There is a faint hint that Gary Cooper (strictly in character) favors Russian cigarettes; I suppose if it were any more specific the run on Novotnys would be excelled only by the Norway-rat stampede of the millions to fling themselves at Earl Browder's feet. Miss Bergman is allowed to use the International Brigade's *Salud* once when Mr. Cooper says g'by, but when Mr. Cooper is saving a comrade from capture by shooting him through the head, neither of them can bear to say more than *adios*, though the script read differently. A line of Mr. Nichols's invention, "I come from Stalin," as it is excitingly delivered by Konstantin Shayne in the best use of a bit in years, may cheer some excitable sectors; I thought it highly ambiguous and, except as a piece of acting, unimportant. Mr. Nichols's original script is fairly riddled with the word fascist. The release script and the production prefer the word nationalist. I thought I once caught the word phalangist, but it may have been fuh land sakes.

Paramount, in other words, has crashed through. It has covered itself, too, against any pink nigglers who might bring the accusation of dodging political issues. The speech in which Mr. Cooper mentions fascists and the grand old party so misleadingly does at least—and with abominably clumsy hindsight—go on to say that Spain, as the old phrase went, is a proving-ground, a dress rehearsal for a greater war. But even this has no more organic connection with the film as a whole than a Gideon Bible has with a hotel bedroom.

There is, on the other hand, Ingrid Bergman. Miss Bergman not only bears a startling resemblance to an imaginable human being; she really knows how to act, in a blend of poetic grace with quiet realism which almost never appears in American pictures. Hemingway's conception of Maria is partly adolescent I think, and for a while her understanding of the role seems still more so. She seems never to have dreamed that a young girl who has seen death and suffered gang rape cannot in all reason bounce into her role looking like a Palmolive ad. But in many moments of the early love stuff—in flashes of shy candor and in the pleasures of playing *femme esclave*—she does very pretty things, and later on she does some very powerful ones. Her confession of the rape is an exquisitely managed tearjerker. Her final scene of farewell is shattering to watch. Not that it's perfect. But its sources and intention are so right, and so astonishingly out of key with the rest of the production. She seems really to have studied what a young woman might feel and look like in such a situation (not a moving picture)—half-nauseated and nine-tenths insane with grief, forced haste, and utter panic. Semi-achieved though it is, it is devastating and wonderful to see.

A lot of other actors ought to be mentioned if there were space. Katina Paxinou's Pilar is sometimes stagy, but she does have style and grandeur. Akim Tamiroff's Pablo would have been a great performance, I believe, if only it had had the chance. The best of Vladimir Sokoloff's Anselmo has real sweetness, as against the stock-company naive cuteness to which the production reduces his conscience over killing. Frank Puglia's Captain Gomez and Fortunio Bonanova's Fernando are solid and very likable, and a young Cuban named Lilo Yarson gives a gentle, fine performance as Joaquin. Gary Cooper is self-effacing and generally a little faint, like the character he plays, but the faintness has its moments of paying off, and his general support of Miss Bergman is nearly as good as the law will allow.

That is more than can be said of the coarse-grained general tone of the show. Mikhail Rasumny, who might have made a good nature symbol of the amoral gipsy, is reduced to a D. W. Griffith comic with overtones of a fine-arts survey course. Joseph Calleia's El Sordo, by no likely fault of his, is just a blend of Wallace Beery and Tully Marshall; and the famous stand on the hill, which needs mathematical cold-processing, is nearly illegible. Hemingway perhaps crowded in more grand-scale characters than he could handle, but at least they had the benefit of the whole of his great talent and intention; here, though they talk forever, they are just a mush with mica flashing on it, half-developed, nervously tossed aside, incoherent. One single shot of the desperate love and hopeful intuition which prompts Agostino to strike his leader could have given that scene intact terror, even greatness, as a tragic image of appeasement; as it is, it is like a fine dog running on three legs. The suspensive intercutting of the long last night, sedulous as it is in its derivation from *Intolerance*, where that was invented, only increases my reverence for the old picture; the new has all the suspense of a clothesline swaybacked with wet-wash. The suspense at the bridge as dynamite is laid is boldly protracted to the point of ridicule. I sympathized with the boldness and was had by the suspense but could not help realizing that, properly conceived and cut, it could have been ten times as exciting in half the footage. The rhythm of this film, in fact, is the most defective I have ever seen in a super-production.

The Technicolor is even unluckier. It is as good as the best experts, at this stage, can make it: which still means the rankest kind of magazine-illustration and postcard art. Color is very nice for costume pieces and musical comedies, and has a great aesthetic future in films, but it still gets fatally in the way of any serious imitation of reality.

Of all the rumbling rumors and denials of political interference on the part of the Franco government, the Catholic church, and the State Department, it has been possible chiefly to find only the clogged-drain smell which the picture bears out. Franco's ambassador tried to get the State Department to suppress it and was refused. The San Francisco consul, Francisco Amat, saw the script and objected to everything you might expect him to, and was reputedly disregarded. Adolph Zukor says, "It is a great picture, without political significance. We are not for or against anybody." Other Paramount executives have delivered lines almost as distinguished. On the question whether the opening was delayed from March to July because Robert Jordan—pardon me, Murphy—had work to do in Spain, the State Department declines comment. There are people in Washington, however, who are not eager to tie their names to it, who say that the whole affair is "too hot to talk about." Why, is any man's guess. And how this production could possibly have offended anyone politically, except a few million powerless characters who retain some vestige of moral nerve, is beyond any guessing.

Mr. Hemingway's sleeping bag, by the way, is so discreetly used that you can never at any moment be sure who is in or out nuendo.

September 4, 1943

Seeing Ernst Lubitsch's *Heaven Can Wait* was a little like hearing Louis Armstrong play at his present best. It brought back a time when people really made good movies: it was so good I half believed Lubitsch could still do as well as the best he ever did, if he had half a chance.

Heaven Can Wait is not up to his best; nothing has been, for nearly twenty years. Its real matrix, for that matter, is the sort of smirking, "civilized," Central European puff paste with which the Theater Guild used to claim to bring vitality to the American stage. But it looks like a jewel against the wood-silk and cellophane which passes for a moving picture now that Hollywood has come of age. It has few of the jaw-breaking Lubitsch touches which at last I got tired of years ago and a lot of the gentler ones which, ham or not, I shall always like, and it has a good deal of the dry sparkle, the shrewd business, and the exquisite timing which made pictures like *Forbidden Paradise* and *Three Women* some of the best nonmajor jobs ever done. The sets, costumes, and props are something for history. I have to speak of it with less authority than intuition, but I thought the period work, in these respects—as in Lubitsch's modulations in styles of posture and movement—was about the prettiest and the most quietly witty I had ever seen. The color was just as good; it was used with sensitiveness and wit, I thought, for the first time. The script was hardly less accomplished, a beautifully set mosaic of kidded clichés. I saw nothing but good, anywhere, in the doll-like selection, manipulation, and performance of the large cast. That does not surprise me in people like Charles Coburn and Louis Calhern and Laird Cregar, but when you find it also in Don Ameche and Gene Tierney, amazed tribute is due somebody. It is certainly due Lubitsch; and (another superlative is unavoidable) it is due the most resourceful make-up job I have ever seen; and finally (I can still hardly believe it) it is due Mr. Ameche and Miss Tierney.

Good sets and props have done a lot for still another picture this month; excellent lighting, good camera work, and unusually good bit-casting have added so much edge and vitality that *The Fallen Sparrow* passes among many people for the almost-Hitchcock spy melodrama it certainly is not. Otherwise, the show is no harm and no special good; about the speed of second-best Pocket Book mysteries. Someone should tell Maureen O'Hara that if she is pretending to be a granddaughter of a French prince, she should leave off aiding China long enough to avoid calling him "France Wah." I have heard mild pleasure expressed over the fact that in this film the hero comes right out and says he fought the fascists in Spain. That seems to me to be now the strict equivalent of coming right out and saying that you were with Lee in Virginia. I should add that Mr. Garfield is required to explain that he has come of melodramatic age only since the outbreak of the World War (which set in, I understand, in 1939), and went to Spain merely as an eye-dillist, doing what any kid would do.

Diana Trilling, writing about *Claudia* in book form, has

said everything about her that so badly needed saying. Of the film version I can add only that it is very much worth seeing if you have a healthy mind and a sound stomach. What you see is a rather shrewdly lighted demonstration, on the part of a baby wife, an anthropophagous mother, and a gosh-all-friday husband, of their fetal, and nationally archetypical, incompetence to live; so presented that the audience, in a grand passion of self-recognition, cackles with delight. I cannot believe that this is good for the audience. A comic catharsis is as possible as a tragic and is, I suspect, more beneficent as well as more true (I still wait for an adequate comic treatment of *Hamlet* or *Lear*). But those aspects of *Claudia* which make it funny (to some) and the powder-puff gags which point it up, to say nothing of the processes of self-dethronement which must be shanghaied into service if one is to laugh at it, or pass it off, are not possible of catharsis, which is possible only to the pure in heart, the fearless; the whole business is, rather, auto-intoxication of the most sinister and endemic sort. There could be, and usually are, more thunderous diagnostic epitaphs upon dead civilizations, but when this one gets its turn, one that will do as well as any other ("Honesty is the best policy," "A boy's best friend is his mother," "I've got my living to make," "I got my orders," "Do you love me?" "How do you feel?" and "The price of liberty is eternal vigilance" are other apt candidates) is "Grin and bear it."

As Robert Stebbins wrote several years ago, Fred Astaire has a lot, besides his Mozartian abilities as a tap-dancer, which is as great, in its own way, as the best of Chaplin. It is in the walk, the stance, the face, the voice, the cool, bright, yet shadowless temper, and it would require the invention of a new character, the crystallization of a new manner, probably the development of a new cinematic form, to be adequately realized. It is present in *The Sky's the Limit*, and gives the first half hour such charm and flow I half expected another *Top Hat*. I didn't get it. I liked the idea of a short, quiet musical about three people who, for once, play a triangle which is not an Iscariot marathon; but it would have required first-rate style and polishing in every department to come off, and had it in none. Astaire's new partner Joan Leslie has something, too, of a primitive sort.

The not very eloquent but mailable way of saying it is that she is sometimes very uncomplicatedly pretty.

September 25, 1943

It is hard to have clear judgment about war pictures, especially nonfiction war pictures, and the current excitement over the record of the defense of Stalingrad—the full, painfully pleonastic title is *The City That Stopped Hitler—Heroic Stalingrad* —is a good example of how hard it is. The very name of the city is such a sounding-board in most minds, such a bid to emotions and sympathies which addle the power of judgment, that the water is muddied from the start. Added to that, *Stalingrad*, like most other record films or newsreels of war, contains images of war so grand or so touching, so much more worth seeing than nearly anything else we ever see on the screen, that we are liable on their account to feel that we are seeing a great picture or, for that matter, that any critical assessment of the picture is vulgar, small, and irrelevant. But that is like being moved by words like love, death, blood, sweat, tears, regardless of how well or ill they are used. It may be harder to use honest cinematic images dishonestly—the truth insists on pushing through—than to use words dishonestly; but nearly every war film proves how actually easy it is, and suggests how hard it would be to use those images honestly, to say nothing of adequately. *Stalingrad* is sensibly and often sensitively edited. But there is hardly a moment in it where the editing—rather than the single shot—even begins to lift a series of images above prose coherence and toward the plain-featured, heroic poetry which might possibly be deserving of the subject. The commentary, meanwhile, almost constantly reduces, or lily-gilds, or angles the power of the images; never does better; occasionally does worse, as in its strange suggestion that it is better for Russians to use flamethrowers on living Germans than for Germans to use them on dead Russians; or in its managing, several times, to make the audience laugh and applaud at the sight of dead, dying, suffering, or humiliated Germans.

Actually, I suppose such films are better assembled and set to words than might be hoped for, so hot after the event; but that does not reduce the fact that they are nearly always inadequate to, and often a dishonoring of, the event, the people recorded, and the people who did the recording. The war cameramen themselves, of course, are subject to critical assessment. Varying degrees of judgment, courage, taste, and luck are continuously implied in what they record, and you can see sharp national differences in their styles of eyesight, with the Russians and British generally leading, and the Germans and Americans generally trailing. There is much room for analysis of their work, and for improvement; but I suspect that their several styles are more nearly appropriate to what they are doing than more detached developed judgment could make them. In any case the cameramen on both sides of every front are making a record which in proper editorial hands, sooner or later, could be made to yield some of the greatest works of art—or whatever term might have to be substituted—ever known.

It surprises me to find *So Proudly We Hail* confusing many people almost as much. I realize that a good deal of sincerity, emotion, and desire to honor went into it, and I have no desire to laugh at that; but it is impossible to accept the result, except in a kind of fascination. This is probably the most deadly-accurate picture that will ever be made of what war looks like through the lenses of a housewives'-magazine romance. In those terms it is to be recommended. Some reviewers who grant that the story itself is painful feel that the picture is redeemed by the deep sincerity of the players and by the powerful realism of the war scenes. But it seemed to me the most sincere thing Paramount's young women did was to alter their make-up to favor exhaustion (and not too much of it) over prettiness (and not too little of that); and that the bombings of hospitals and the strafings of wounded accurately met their level in the honest matron behind me who kept saying tst-tst-tst. Sonny Tufts, as Miss Goddard's marine, I rather like; but he is making a hit walking rope between mild credibility and the shucks-jeeze brand of ladies'-darlingism, and that rope has just one side to fall on.

The Adventures of Tartu disguises British Agent Robert

Donat as an oleaginous Rumanian whose business it is to destroy a Nazi poison-gas plant and escape the consequences
with Valerie Hobson. It is so easy to enjoy that it is easy to overrate: that is, it gave me nearly as much simple fun as thrillers a
dozen times better; but not quite. You are seeing all it has, and
bald spots as well, the first time around, whereas with a good
Hitchcock or even a good Carol Reed, even the pleasures visible at a first seeing stand up, or intensify, under a third and a
fifth; new ones turn up with each seeing, and it is a long time
before the whole work wears thin or takes on the staleness of a
classic indulged too often.

Very belatedly I want to say that *The Watch on the Rhine*
seemed much better on the screen than it did, almost identi-
cally, on the stage—though I still wished Henry James might
have written it; and that I join with anyone whose opinion of
Paul Lukas's performance is superlative. Also that a simple-
hearted friendliness generated between audience and screen at
This Is the Army made that film happy to see even when it was
otherwise boring; though I am among an apparent minority
which feels that Warner Brothers' cuddly-reverential treatment
of President Roosevelt—in *Mission to Moscow*, *This Is the Army*,
and the forthcoming *Princess O'Rourke*—is subject to charges
certainly of indecent exposure and, quite possibly, of alienation
of affections.

October 8, 1943

Sahara. Humphrey Bogart and several less high-salaried but
no less talented soldiers, stranded at an oasis, hold off and then
capture a full Nazi battalion. Anyone who can make that believable, even for so long as you watch it, knows how to make
a good war melodrama. *Sahara* is the best one since *Bataan*.
Cinematically it is better. It borrows, chiefly from the English,
a sort of light-alloy modification of realism which makes the
traditional Hollywood idiom seem as obsolete as a minuet.

A Lady Takes a Chance is not the new kind of realistic sex
comedy it might have been, but once in a while it's on the
edge. Too often both ends of Jean Arthur are played against
the middle; but John Wayne suggests how sensational he might

be in a sufficiently evil story about a Reno gigolo. Besides the unusually frank erotic undertones there are some good harsh street and rodeo shots, a fine small hotel, and a saloon scene which gets down the crowded, deafening glamor which unforeseen daylight drunkenness can have, better than I have ever seen it filmed before.

Hostages, made from Stefan Heym's novel, lacks the cinematic edge, detail, and inventiveness which the story could have afforded, but at worst it is competent, politically focused, and fairly exciting. William Bendix, though he mugs, is a valuable surprise. He evidently understands—as nobody else in Hollywood seems to—the almost beyond-death detachment which is at the center of everything a deeply political man does.

Corvette K-225 is an unusually decent and unpretentious—but not very interesting—semi-documentary about Corvette K-225. Some of it, made in Canada and on the North Atlantic, is fresh and pretty to see; even genuinely moving. The more violent stuff, though well-contrived, is strictly studio, and suffers by comparison.

True to Life is a rather crass and moderately amusing comedy about two soap-opera laureates (Dick Powell and Franchot Tone) who deceive and exploit a (far from true-to-life) Queensboro family, for "material." There is some fair radio-ribbing, and I liked Victor Moore and some daft gadgets derived from old Buster Keaton comedies. Mary Martin, I notice with some alarm, is playing Jean Arthur—a tendency which even Miss Arthur must learn to curb.

Lassie Come Home is a dog story which I had hardly expected to enjoy, and cannot be sure who will and who won't. I did, though. Those who made it seem to have had a pretty fair sense of the square naivete which most good stories for children have, or affect; they also manipulate some surprisingly acute emotions out of the head dog. Whether from private remembrance or from the show, I got several reverberations of that strangely pure, half-magical tone which certain books, regardless of their other qualities, have for many children.

Thousands Cheer is a thoroughly routine musical distinguished only by Gene Kelly with nothing to use his talents on, a terrible piece of trash by Shostakovich, and the unpleasant

sight of José Iturbi proving he is a real guy by playing the sort
of boogie-woogie anyone ought to be able to learn through a
correspondence course.

Sweet Rosie O'Grady has some fairly pretty color and sets
(1880), a few glimpses of Betty Grable's façade, and the power
to remind you that the right director and author could make
wonderful use of her.

Wintertime, Sonja Henie's ten-thousandth baked alaska,
proves that skating musicals do not have to be half as boring as
they usually are; also that that fact is of no great importance.

Thank Your Lucky Stars is the loudest and most vulgar of the
current musicals. It is also the most fun, if you are amused
when show people kid their own idiom, and if you find a cruel-
compassionate sort of interest in watching amateurs like Bette
Davis do what they can with a song.

October 30, 1943

SO PROUDLY WE FAIL

WE SUFFER—we vaguely realize—a unique and constantly
intensifying schizophrenia which threatens no other nation involved in this war. Geography is the core of the disease. Those
Americans who are doing the fighting are doing it in parts of
the world which seem irrelevant to them; those who are not,
remain untouched, virginal, prenatal, while every other considerable population on earth comes of age. In every bit of
information you can gather about breakdowns of American
troops in combat, overseas, even in the camps, a sense of un-
utterable dislocation, dereliction, absence of contact, trust,
wholeness, and reference, in a kind and force which no other
soldiers have to suffer, clearly works at the root of the disaster.
Moreover, while this chasm widens and deepens daily between
our fighting and civilian populations and within each mind,
another—much deeper and wider than any which geography
alone could impose—forms and increases between this nation
and the other key nations of the world. Their experience of
war is unprecedented in immediacy and unanimity. Ours, even
in the fraction which has the experience at all, is essentially
specialized, lonely, bitter, and sterile; our great majority will

emerge from the war almost as if it had never taken place; and not all the lip-service in the world about internationalism will make that different. This, and more and worse, is all so obvious, so horrifying, and so apparently unalterable that, being a peculiarly neurotic people, we are the more liable to nod and pay it the least possible attention. That is unfortunate. Our predicament is bad enough as it stands; the civil and international prospect is unimaginably sinister.

Since it is beyond our power to involve ourselves as deeply in experience as the people of Russia, England, China, Germany, Japan, we have to make up the difference as well as we can at second hand. Granting that knowledge at second hand, taken at a comfortable distance is of itself choked with new and terrible liabilities, I believe nevertheless that much could be done to combat and reduce those liabilities, and that second-hand knowledge is at least less dangerous than no knowledge at all. And I think it is obvious that in imparting it, moving pictures could be matchlessly useful. How we might use them, and how gruesomely we have failed to, I lack room to say; but a good bit is suggested by a few films I want to speak of now.

Even the Army Orientation films, through no fault intrinsic to them, carry their load of poison, of failure. You can hear from every sort of soldier from the simplest to the most intricate what a valuable job they are doing. But because they are doing it only for service men they serve inadvertently to widen the abyss between fighters and the civilians who need just as urgently to see them. Civilians, however, get very little chance to learn anything from moving pictures. We are not presumed to be brave enough. And the tragic thing is that after a couple of decades of Hollywood and radio, we are used to accepting such deprivations and insults quite docilely; often, indeed, we resent anyone who has the daring to try to treat us as if we were human beings.

Just now it is a fought question whether numbers four and five of the Orientation Series, *The Battle of Britain* and *The Battle of Russia*, will get public distribution. Whether they do depends on what is laughingly called the Office of War Information and on what is uproariously called the War Activities Committee. The OWI's poor little pictures, blue-born with timidity from the start, have finally been sabotaged out of existence; and judging by the performance to date of the WAC, it is not very likely that we shall see these films. And if we do see them, it is more than likely that we shall see them with roast albatrosses like *The Keeper of the Flame* hung around their necks.

I can only urge you to write your Congressman, if he can read. For these films are responsible, irreplaceable pieces of teaching. *Britain*, one hour's calculated hammering of the eye and ear, can tell you more about that battle than you are ever likely otherwise to suspect, short of having been there. *Russia*, though it is a lucid piece of exposition, is cut neither for fact nor for political needlepoint but purely, resourcefully, and with immensely powerful effect, for emotion. It is by no means an ultimate handling of its material, but it is better than the Russian records from which it was drawn, and next to the tearful magnificence of *The Birth of a Nation* is, I believe, the best and most important war film ever assembled in this country.

Beside it Samuel Goldwyn's *The North Star* is something to be seen more in sorrow than in anger and more in the attitude of the diagnostician than in any emotion at all. It represents to perfection some crucially symptomatic characteristics of Hollywood and of the American people in so far as Hollywood reflects, or is accepted by, the people. Hollywood's noble, exciting, all but unprecedented intention here is to show the conduct of the inhabitants of a Russian border village during the first days of their war; to show real people, involved in realities, encumbered by a minimum of star-spotlighting or story. The carrying out of that intention implies in every detail the hopeless mistrust in which Hollywood holds its public. To call this "commercial" and to talk about lack of intelligence and taste is, I think, wide of the main mark. The attitude is more nearly that of the fatally misguided parent toward the already all but fatally spoiled child. The result is one long orgy of meeching, sugaring, propitiation, which, as a matter of fact, enlists, develops, and infallibly corrupts a good deal of intelligence, taste, courage, and disinterestedness. I am sorry not to talk at length and in detail about this film. I can only urge you to watch what happens in it: how every attempt to use a reality brings the romantic juice and the annihilation of any possible reality pouring from every gland. In its basic design Lillian

Hellman's script could have become a fine picture: but the characters are stock, their lines are tinny-literary, their appearance and that of their village is scrubbed behind the ears and "beautified"; the camera work is nearly all glossy and overcomposed; the proudly complicated action sequences are stale from overtraining; even the best of Aaron Copland's score has no business ornamenting a film drowned in ornament: every resourcefulness appropriate to some kinds of screen romance, in short, is used to make palatable what is by no remote stretch of the mind romantic. I think the picture represents the utmost Hollywood can do, within its present decaying tradition, with a major theme. I am afraid the general public will swallow it whole. I insist, however, that that public must and can be trusted and reached with a kind of honesty difficult, in so mental-hospital a situation, to contrive; impossible, perhaps, among the complicated pressures and self-defensive virtuosities of the great studios.

The thing that so impresses me about the nonfiction films which keep coming over from England is the abounding evidence of just such a universal adulthood, intelligence, and trust as we lack. I lack space to mention them in detail (the new titles are *I Was a Fireman*, *Before the Raid*, and, even better, *ABCA* and the bleak, beautiful, and heartrending *Psychiatry in Action*), but I urge you to see every one that comes your way. They are free, as not even our Orientation films are entirely, of salesmanship; they are utterly innocent of our rampant disease of masked contempt and propitiation. It comes about simply enough: everyone, on and off screen and in the audience, clearly trusts and respects himself and others.

There is a lot of talk here about the need for "escape" pictures. To those who want to spend a few minutes in a decently ventilated and healthful world, where, if only for the duration, human beings are worthy of themselves and of each other, I recommend these British films almost with reverence as the finest "escapes" available.

November 6, 1943

V ERY LATE—but the film is ready for national release, I am glad to say—I hacked through the thicket of "delightfuls" and "enchantings" which had kept me at a distance, to see *Jeannie*, a gently characterized British-made comedy about a Scottish peasant woman who discovers, in the course of a trip to prewar Vienna, that she doesn't have to feel like an old maid after all. A more acute pointing of the roles of an English business man (Michael Redgrave) and an almost traditional sponging count, more accuracy with the Viennese bourgeoisie (the hotel personnel seems very good), and sets much more evocative in details could have made it an entirely beautiful film. But Barbara Mullen alone (as Jeannie), in her prim, sharp-tuned delicateness, would make it one of the easiest, sweetest of light comedies; and I must apologize for my slowness in agreeing with everyone else who has seen it.

The Cagney brothers' first independent piece, *Johnny Come Lately*, seems to persuade many people that the Cagneys (and others) should stay dependent. I do not agree. The film does show a fatal commercial uneasiness and, I half suspect, radical loss or atrophy of cinematic judgment. But *Johnny*, before it breaks down into a panic of melodramatic and comic propitiation, does give a gentle and leisured if not very memorable first hour whose tone and pace would never have survived a big studio; there is a very appealing performance by Grace George; and there is a general ambience of hope and pleasure about the production, which, regrettably, loses its glow. The hazards of independence are great unless you have daring, brains, ability, and a basic unconfused carelessness about whether you go bankrupt or not; but with very few exceptions I believe that anything good in films which comes out of this country, at all soon, is bound to come from the independents.

Something I have learned only by hearsay is, I think, worth passing on as plausible. A former Hollywood man, now with the Signal Corps, went along with the raid on Kiska. On the way he did a fair amount of shooting of the colossal paraphernalia, the slow inflation of the controlling personalities, and (I hope) the generalized tension between life, memory, future, and death, which are bound so laboriously to converge upon

any such action. Once there he also photographed, enthusias-
tically, the two dogs, the scrupulously impudent inscriptions,
and the general letdown which were all the Japanese left. He exposed, in all, a good many thousand feet. They may have been
the record of what some people feel to have been the turning-
point of the war—the moment at which the Japanese went
somewhere else in preference to heaven, as we have learned to
expect of them. Or they may have been the matrix of one of
the funniest and most mitigating pictures about war which
could ever conceivably be made. I suspect they may have been
both at once, and I suggest that the title *Desert Victory* was
used too soon. In any case, if I have heard right, my conjec-
tures are as irrelevant as my hearsay must be counted unreli-
able. The complete negative, unless my informant has been
misinformed, was destroyed in Washington.

November 13, 1943

Guadalcanal Diary, an adaptation of the Richard Tregaskis
book, is unusually serious, simple, and honest, as far as it goes;
but it would be a shame and worse if those who made or will
see it got the idea that it is a remotely adequate image of the
first months on that island. The picture is worth talking about
at some length, and I hope to do that when there is space.
Meanwhile I think it is to be rather respected, and recommended, but with very qualified enthusiasm.

We Will Come Back, a furious and very entertaining Russian
melodrama about guerrillas and a Nazi spy, is as phony in its
way as *The North Star*. But it can tell you even more about the
Russians than *The North Star* can tell you about Americans,
with about a hundredth the tedium and chagrin. It can tell you
a good deal, for that matter, which the Russian war record
films cannot: for as a piece of popular entertainment it is as
intensely and internally Russian as a small, florid, vociferous
opera company might be Italian. What you see inferred in it is
violent, hysterical, innocent, reckless, and realistic almost beyond our comprehension. (Watch especially the guerrilla leader,
the girl, and the two leading Nazis.) I was particularly interested to see the almost slapstick scorn with which a dying Ger-

man is treated (good, I infer, for howls of laughter), and the attitude toward religion. God is repeatedly scratched behind the ears as He passes and slapped affectionately on the rump to make it stick; and toward the end, in a clear bid for applause, an old priest grabs a Nazi soldier and bashes his skull in with a rock. It looks as if Cherkassov in *The Calling of Dan Matthews* were only a question of a very short time.

Old Acquaintance is a typical woman's duet on the standard musical saws favored by any housewives' magazine (the tune is "Love Is the Sweetest Thing but We Have No Bananas Today"). What perplexes me is that I could sit through it with some interest. The two chief characters seem to represent, between them, all that a suburban housewife at her worst likes to think she is and thanks God she is not (honorable, realistic, and self-denying, like Bette Davis), and all that she thanks God she is not, but is (Miriam Hopkins as a frenzied tea-cosy sheltering the opposite characteristics). Miss Davis loses two lovers for the sake of Miss Hopkins and her daughter; Miss Hopkins loses everything except Miss Davis. Miss Davis is noble enough and Miss Hopkins ignoble enough to make it unnecessary for any housewife to take the morality play personally, beyond comfortably checking on what she knew already, that virtue's peculiar rewards are hardly worth the candle. The odd thing is that the two ladies and Vincent Sherman, directing, make the whole business look fairly intelligent, detailed, and plausible; and that on the screen such trash can seem, even, mature and adventurous.

November 20, 1943

Princess O'Rourke, I had thought, might be treated like other social errors of its sort: an unobtrusive raising of the window, and the less said the better. But since it is being acclaimed, by everyone in sight so far as my eyes carry, as one of the best comedies of the year, I am forced to reconsider. Reconsidering, I accept it as a jaw-breaking rebuke to anyone, like myself, who likes to think that Hollywood underestimates its audience. This noisome show is about a Princess who, with the help of her jolly old chum President Roosevelt, married an

American air pilot. The two basic lines of comedy are snobbery of the sorriest native kind: the common man's worship of the titled one, and the common man's even more abandoned, even less understandable adoration of himself. Along the inside of this vicious-cycle track, neck and neck, scamper the ideas that all titled European males are sterile and that all untitled works-in-progress from God's little acre, are guaranteed capable of bringing on any number of sons just like them. This ugly rubbish is packaged in the kind of prime government-inspected whimsy which you might expect if the *New Yorker*'s humorists were picking up egg money from *Railway Age*: Princess-meets-banana-split, and so on. There is also a grisly saucer of musical chop suey called *Honorable Moon*. Jack Carson I like and Jane Wyatt I am eager to forgive, in spite of everything; and I am vulnerable to Olivia de Havilland in every part of my being except the ulnar nerve. But if ever a standing indication were needed that as a people we do not deserve to mouth such words as "democracy," let alone "common sense" or "minimum human decency," this is it.

The Iron Major is a respectful, rather dull picture about the football coach Frank Cavanaugh. Such able, unintellectual, cagy teachers are very much worth talking about, but all the talk here is in words of less than one syllable. All you get is Pat O'Brien's nicely controlled performance and a few pretty period-shots of Worcester, Mass.

Deerslayer, on the other hand, can be recommended to any-one who would not feel that an eight-year-old boy who gallops up howling "Wah-wah, I'm an Indian" needs to consult a psychiatrist. I don't feel that most bad pictures are "bad enough to be funny"; they are just bad enough to be fascinating, not to say depressing as hell. But this defenseless and disarming show is the purest dumb delight I have seen in a long time.

December 4, 1943

The Cross of Lorraine is a melodrama about French soldiers in a German military prison. Tay Garnett, who made *Bataan*, directed it, and did an even better job. Half a football team worked on the story, yet except for a foolish coda it is one of the most edged, well-characterized, and naturally cinematic scripts of the year. There are no performances below pretty good in the whole of a large cast; I especially like Hume Cronyn as a born appeaser, Gene Kelly as his opposite, Jean Pierre Aumont as a man in the middle, Sir Cedric Hardwicke as a priest, Joseph Calleia as a leftist, and Tonio Selwart as a Nazi. There is some second-rate theatrical, literary, and merely political mannerism, but a surprising amount of it comes to life. There is also a good deal of shock and brutality, for which Mr. Garnett seems to have a special talent. Some of the camera work is very good.

Cry Havoc is a sincere fourth-rate picture made from a sincere fifth-rate play about nurses on Bataan. By fourth-rate I mean it is incomparably less offensive than *So Proudly We Hail*. In fact, in spite of many very bad things in it and its intrinsic staginess, I was often touched by it, simply because the members of the cast (Margaret Sullavan, Ann Sothern, Joan Blondell, Ella Raines, and several others) seemed to care a great deal about the thing they were reenacting.

Government Girl, a comedy about wartime Washington, is Dudley Nichols's first shot at directing. Some of it is awful, especially some of the things gentle little Miss De Havilland has to do for the laughs of the canaille. But some more of it has a crude energy and lack of timidity and polish which are a pleasure even when nothing much else is doing. And here and there—especially with the surprising Sonny Tufts and other men—Nichols gets down some sharp, nasty, funny comment on business men and politicians.

December 18, 1943

Happy Land tells how the ghost of a man who fought in the Civil War comes to comfort his middle-aged grandson, whose own son has just been killed in the present war. The old man leads him through the small town and through his own remembrance and his remembrance of the life of the son. Some of this is idyllic and pretty, which is fair enough. But you get no impression that the son had any troubles that a glass of Pepsi-Cola wouldn't cure; so that you wonder whether such a life could have been lived and whether it was worth the bother. The idea advanced here is, quite to the contrary, that the son's life, being American, was worth dying for. This idea seems to me arguable, at least as it is served up here; far too much of it is the sort of boiled-and-buttered native corn, fresh from the can, for which MacKinlay Kantor is beloved by some.

However, the thing is quietly and sincerely played, especially by Don Ameche and Henry Morgan, and as quietly and sincerely directed by Irving Pichel. Also, it was shot in a real town (the more Iowan-looking parts of Santa Rosa and Healdsburg, California; Santa Rosa was first used for Hitchcock's *Shadow of a Doubt*); so a real town's irreducible beauty and validity keep forcing the softly handled theme toward its proper dignity. All of Joseph La Shelle's photography is good; some of it is so cool, flexible, and sensitive that—along with the work of Alfred Valentine in *Shadow of a Doubt*—it takes up the Magna Charta for American films from the cellar corner where it was tossed along with the lost thirty-two reels of *Greed*. Also I am glad to see even an attempt to show what a war death means to a family. Therefore, though I think *Happy Land* is tainted with dextrose and with that nasty-nationalistic self-pitying self-congratulation for which we plain Amurrican folks—in more ways than one like ostriches—are developing an ever more sinister and indiscriminate appetite, I also think it is worth seeing.

What a Woman! (what a title!) is about Rosalind Russell, a high-paid genius peddler who harpoons a college professor (Willard Parker) to play the romantic lead in a filmed best-selling piece of trash his fantasy life had spilled on to paper. As a profilist for the *Knickerbocker Magazine*, Brian Aherne looks on, and tells her that she is using only ten per cent of her womanliness—a generous estimate—in the sort of life she leads. The professor goes gaga. I suppose it is amusing if, like me, you are at all likely to laugh at a kind of smartness on the screen which you—or I, anyhow—would yawn at on Broadway. Either sophistication is highly relative to context or I am, I suspect, and had better worry about, the latter. Anyhow, some of the interiors are nice pieces of kidding.

Girl Crazy has nothing in it I can recommend unless you are curious to see what makes one of the biggest box-office successes of the year; unless, like me, you find Mickey Rooney much more bearable since he quit putting his soul into his comedy—he seems now just a detached and very competent vaudeville actor; and unless, like me, you like Judy Garland. Miss Garland is a good strident vaudeville actor too; and has an apparent straightness and sweetness with which I sympathize. Judging by her infrequent "emotional" moments I would like very much to see her in straight dramatic roles.

The Gang's All Here highlights Alice Faye singing "No Love, No Nothing," as torturing a piece of torching as the war has evolved, but is mainly made up of Busby Berkeley's paroxysmic production numbers, which amuse me a good deal. There is one routine with giant papier-mâché bananas, cutting to thighs, then feet, then rows of toes, which deserves to survive in every case-book of blatant film surreption for the next century. But then, for anthropological reasons, so does "No Love, No Nothing," as here filmed.

The Heat's On is a stale-ale musical in which a lot of good people apathetically support the almost equally apathetic Mae West. There is one wonderful shot, epitomizing a flop legshow trying to be dirty, in which a lot of peeled girls writhe rather wearily on a flight of steps. Victor Moore is good except for his big seduction scene with Mae, at which both of them merely sniff as if it were a saucer of black-market dog food. Mae West is mainly as good as ever, which is still plenty good enough for me; but evidently she and her colleagues feel that too few people agree with me.

Madame Curie is a smooth, rather horrible romanticization of a subject I am sorry to see romanticized. More about that later.

December 25, 1943

PRIZE DAY

A YEAR is ending. It ends our second at war, the fiftieth—or twentieth, as you prefer—in the history of the great recording, communicative, educational, and artistic medium of our time. In another fifty years—or ten, I am willing to bet—moving pictures will no longer be the central medium. Radio will have taken their place; television, very likely, will have taken the place of both.

Let us try to assess what has and has not been done in moving pictures, particularly those made in this country, during the year.

Our only really good films have been our straight record films. Of these, the best have been of war, whose special intensity requires a minimum of intelligence to do fairly well with. Of these, we can still have no idea how much is kept from us or for what good or insufficient reason. Of the material we have seen it is clear that nearly always, when there has been a chance to prepare for the shot through the mind and the mind's eye rather than the eye purely of courage and of the camera, the mind has been painfully inferior to the possibility offered. The presentation invariably has been worse. The prevailing quality has been that of American commercial romanticism, as taught, for example, by the *Life* school.

In Russia, in occasional shots, great records of war have been made. But much is still staged and falsified and rhetorical in the shooting itself, and the editing, still more, has been posterish, opportunistic, and anti-human. In neither camera work nor editing have I seen anything which was not derived, and degraded, from Dziga-Vertov or Eisenstein.

In England warmly casual, humane, mature, cinematically firm films have been made; the most essentially good and perceptive which I have seen from anywhere this year—good enough, and strange enough to us, so that I am not surprised by what amounts to a conspiracy in this country against showing them at all widely. But there is no use thinking too well of these films. *Desert Victory* is unquestionably the best film of the year; but it is the result of a great subject handled rather with thorough cinematic common sense than with cinematic creative energy. Humphrey Jennings's *Listen to Britain* so uses the one first-rate creative idea of the year that after making a few clear—and several fuddled—statements the idea apologizes and limps out quietly by the back way.

In this country the spectators are treated as fools, more often than not by other fools. Or call them misled. The proof is in every commentator's voice, his phrasing, his abject mawkishness and political childishness, and in the puff-paste, onanistic, heartless quality of most of the camera work, whose nearest equivalent is the tradition Leni Riefenstahl froze in Germany. In Russian films people are photographed and appealed to essentially as animals and are treated as human individuals only to force-feed inhuman, anti-individualistic points. In England they are regarded as human individuals, and the jumbled leftish-democratic line accordingly holds more hope; but here too, when creativity is not absent, it is tempered to shorn lambs or is abdicated for equally sorry reasons.

Here, the only films I can feel any well-grounded excitement over are the army orientation films. Of these only two out of the six completed have reached the civilian public. Of these the first, *Prelude to War*, was treated like a poor relation by most exhibitors, and the second, *The Battle of Russia*, was gelded of its already sterile political equipment. *Battle of Russia*, next to *Desert Victory*, is the best film of the year. But like the other orientation films it is saturated with words and only begins to use the possibilities of the screen, as such, to show and teach. And like all the others it can make you sick to the very soul with its political timidity.

Nearly all of the most talented people in moving pictures work in fiction, and most of the greatest possibilities lie within fiction. The record in fiction is not a happy one.

In disagreement with most qualified people I think more well than ill of *Shadow of a Doubt*; but I must admit that its skill is soft and that it is distinctly below the standard set by Hitchcock's best English work. *The Hard Way* is one of the few films of the year worth seeing again; but seeing it again, group-theatricality, Bette-Davism, and compromise impair even its justly famous first half hour. *The Ox-Bow Incident* I underpraised; it stands in memory very firm, respectable, and sympathetic. But I still think it suffers from *rigor artis*. *The Watch on the Rhine* was a carefully screened play about which, cinematically, I feel little beyond respect for Paul Lukas's beautiful performance. *Casablanca* is still reverently spoken of as (1) fun, (2) a "real movie." I still think it is the year's clearest measure of how willingly, *faute de mieux*, people will deceive themselves. Even *Jeannie*, hardly a movie at all, was better fun; or even that affable imitation-of-an-imitation, *Tartu*.

As for those pictures in which Hollywood "grew up," or began to pull its weight, I won't waste space even naming them. The solemn, expensive anti-fascist and war dramas like *The Moon Is Down* are just as depressing; even *This Land Is Mine* is just sincerely polished bone. The sterterous underground melodrama *Hangmen Also Die* stands up better than most of them. *The Human Comedy* and *Happy Land* put up the so-called home front in syrup but deserve at least a polite bow each, the first for a few moments of genuine sweetness, the second because, along with *Shadow of a Doubt*, *The Hard Way*, and some of the RKO shorts, it is photographically the only hopeful work of the year.

The semi-documentaries—such as *Air Force*—learned absolutely nothing of value. All alike they tried to combine hopelessly ill-appreciated primer smatterings of technical realism and studio combat with romanticized men and talk which chemically guaranteed the defeat of all possible reality. The easier, more traditional task of making war melodramas brought *Bataan*, *Sahara*, and *The Cross of Lorraine*. However essentially formularistic they were, and however rectally fed their cinematic, psychological, and political intelligence, they were among the few cinematically alert and pleasing jobs of the year.

In the line of plain "entertainment" there was no indication that anybody realizes that entertainment and artistry are inseparable and virtually synonymous. The musicals I saw gave perhaps twenty seconds of genuine pleasure with each two hours of annihilation. *The More the Merrier* was fair fun until the whole cast began dancing the joke into my ribs. *A Lady Takes a Chance* was amusing when you could see past Jean Arthur's *moues* and the thick snow of Captain Billy's *Whiz-Bang*. I can recommend *Lassie Come Home* to any dog who will check his interest in films in the theater lobby. But if you want simple pleasure you may as well go to another Maisie picture or a Laurel and Hardy or an Abbott and Costello; and even there you have to work for it. I regret my failure, still, to see *Holy Matrimony*, which I hear is really good. I wish it well; but I wonder whether Aristophanes himself could alter the balance of this year.

The whole business has been dying here, ten years or more. Last year, it seems to me, was the all-time low—so far.

And a very good New Year to you, too.

Madame Curie enlists an unusual amount of competence, patience, and commercialized sincerity in the production, which rather saddens than angers or pleases me, of the screen equivalent to Harpers' Prize "literature": safe, smooth, respectable, an epitome of all that the bourgeois likes what he calls his art to be. One could use it as a model of all that is most to be regretted in Hollywood at this stage, and I had thought I might. I suggest, instead, that you look up, in a recent issue of *Life*, two photographs: one of Pierre Curie and his brother and their parents, the other of Walter Pidgeon and three colleagues, representing them. Between them, those two pictures will tell you more than enough.

Higher and Higher, which introduces Frank Sinatra to the screen, is one for the museums; nor is that just a crack. Sinatra adds to his more famous advantages that of being, obviously, a decent enough sort; he also has weird fleeting resemblances to Lincoln, which I think may help out in the audience subconscious. (Heaven help us all if Booth had missed and Lincoln had a larynx!) Through most of the film Sinatra is just a sort of male Mary Pickford, a mock-shy, poised young man huskily husking Occidental and very mortal corn. At the end, thanks to a stroke of simple genius on the part of the director, Tim Whelan, he stands without visible support among clouds, in an effect which could be described only in the unmailable terms of an erotic dream, and swells from a pinpoint to a giant. Higher and higher indeed. The Messiah Himself will have to sweat to work out a better return engagement.

Destination Tokyo combines a good deal of fairly exciting submarine warfare with at least as much human interest, which I found neither very human nor at all interesting. Warner does a lot of this sort of thing and of "socially conscious" work and is, I believe, more to be respected than any other American studio so far as maturity of intention is concerned. But even in that respect there is all the sky from knee-high left to grow in. And the cinematic achievement, as a rule, is just about what you get from any other studio.

January 8, 1944

A Guy Named Joe is just a title. The story is about a ghost named Pete (Spencer Tracy) who, solid and cheerful as ever—except that the living cast cannot see or hear him—gets busy like the other dead aces, showing neophytes how to fly, fight, and make love. His star pupil (Van Johnson) becomes interested in Pete's former sweetheart (Irene Dunne), who is still inconsolable, and Pete's hardest job is to divorce her from the remembrance of the easygoing, slick-paper love scenes she played with Spencer Tracy. It is, as you can see, a story about wartime love and death, a theme lacking neither in dignity nor in appositeness. Like *Happy Land* it neatly obtunds death's sting as ordinary people suffer it by not only assuming but photographing a good, busy, hearty hereafter. I am of course in no position to offer contrary proof, and can indeed imagine the general idea not only as believable but as dramatically amenable to very good use. But I don't care to see it so blandly used, as unqualified aspirin, before an audience of which the majority, I fear, believes everything it sees on a screen, nor can I respect the dramatic uses to which the idea has been put here. Miss Dunne feels nothing like real love or anxiety over Pete while he is alive, and only a nominal, ornamental, plot-extending grief after he dies. Pete and the audience are also spared what might have happened if she had really got either frozen or tender with Mr. Johnson, while Pete looked on. So, when she matures in her bereavement, every genuine bereavement and maturing which the film by implication claims to reflect and preach to is cruelly exploited and insulted for the sake of what is, at best, an otherwise harmless and medium-silly romance. If you are so generous as to overlook these minor faults, however, the picture will serve as well as two hours spent over the *Woman's Home Companion*. Spencer Tracy is better than the show deserves, and Victor Fleming's direction is of itself, as usual, likable enough.

Riding High is a musical show featuring Western landscapes in Technicolor, Victor Moore as a swindler, a blood-curdling sucker-delighter named Cass Daly, some loud, cheerful, uninteresting tunes, and Dorothy Lamour. Miss Lamour wears one costume which must be seen to be believed, and which hopefully suggests to me that the gentlemen or ladies of the Hays office either refused to believe their eyes, did not see at all, or modestly take care never, when a lightly-dressed woman appears, to look below the wishbone.

Erratum: The title of *Destination Tokyo*, reviewed last week, was incorrectly given as *Destiny, Tokyo*.

January 15, 1944

Lost Angel undertakes one of the few dramatic subjects worth a second thought: the bringing-up of a child. The child, who is, with occasional skids, very poignantly played by Margaret O'Brien, is a foundling whom a set of psychologists adopt, name Alpha, and do their worst with. By the time she is six she is an air-conditioned genius. Then a newspaper reporter flicks a wild card into her deck. For the first time she hears of, and experiences, the possibilities of the irrational, the irregular, the inexplicable, the magical. For the first time she becomes aware of love, and suffers it. Moral: Never trust your own, or anybody's, intelligence about a child; love is all that really matters.

There are grimly misleading and mismanaged things about this picture. Much as I mistrust the run of child-psychologists and progressive educators I don't like to see it implied, even in myth, that they are unaware of the indispensable importance, to a child, of parental love or the best available substitute. They are likely to militate against any fruitful love far more frighteningly through the antiseptic, utilitarian, neo-pietistic quality of their recognition than through ignorance. It is unlikely, too, that a child under their seal would see the city, or meet another child, for the first time, only after running away from them. Rather, the child would be so hermetically "well adjusted," so thoroughly anaesthetized, to both that a naked realization of either would be one of its gravest difficulties. I like hardly better seeing the loose sentimentalities of a narcissistic reporter (James Craig) set up as a working model for the cure-all. And I don't like at all such needless complications as the gunman who is tossed in for *New Yorkerish* laughs, or the general unimaginativeness through which "magic" is shown the child by means of the remarkable things of a city street at night—sandwichmen with neon shirtfronts, etc.—rather than the unremarkable. Almost anything, in such contexts of childhood, can seem miraculous; and through the child's eyes and mind the wonder of a city, which is intrinsic in a well-used camera anyhow, could have been shown many people, instead of the easily glamorous mist, a pipe-smoking dog, some Chinese, a night club, and similar easy outs; and could have become one of the most beautiful sequences I can imagine. But barring a brief examination of a popcorn machine, that chance is forfeited.

Nevertheless, I was often moved, impressed, and excited by this film. It does get down something of the detachment and paradoxical defenselessness-inviolability of a young child, and —for all its softening and cheating—some broad warnings against attitudes one should fear. And toward the end it had, for me, a good deal of the beauty and power of Mann's *Early Sorrow*, all the more because I would hardly have expected it on the screen. I can only hope it will be more useful than deceitful; either way, I think it is important.

January 22, 1944

CROCODILE tears over the alleged decline of Alfred Hitchcock have for years been a favorite cocktail among those who take moving pictures seriously. That has always seemed to me an impatient and cheap attitude to take toward any kind of change, or disturbance, in the work of a good artist. It still does. Nevertheless, because my space is limited, I am going to use it almost exclusively to specify things which strike me as limiting, or disappointing, about *Lifeboat*.

The initial idea—a derelict boat and its passengers as

microcosm—is itself so artificial that, like the problems set by keeping a story moving for two hours within a gunwale frame, it sets the whole pride and brain too sharply to work on a tour de force for its own sake.

These two handicaps, adequately undertaken, could have become leverages upon great advantages, working like, say, the formal stringencies of a sonnet.

It seems to me that the only way to counteract the basic artificiality and to bring it through to absolute success—the more so when you count in the necessary stripping away of the sort of detail of streets, machines, garments which Hitchcock has a genius for putting to work—would have been through (1) an implacable physical and psychological realism, which was not attempted, (2) squeezing the poetic and symbolic power out of the final intensities of this realism—the essence of most good cinema—rather than tempering the realism to the allegory.

As allegory, the film is nicely knit, extensively shaded and detailed, and often fascinating. But the allegory itself is always too carefully slide-ruled. None of it gives off the crazy, more than ambiguous, nascent-oxygen quality of first-rate allegories like those of Shakespeare or Kafka or Joyce. And little of it effloresces into pure human or even pure theatrical emotion; it is too thought-out, too superficial, and too much in thrall to its somewhat sentimental intelligence. Though every performance has, within the limits which seem so arduously and coldly set, fine spirit and propriety, only William Bendix occasionally transcends those limits and becomes an immediate human being.

The handling of the cinematic problems is extremely astute, in spite of a smell of studio about most of it. But since too little was ventured of what followed as a logical obligation out of the root of the idea, it remains an interesting, disappointing demonstration of possibilities at a second or third remove. What disturbs me is the question whether Hitchcock recognizes this, as I would certainly be inclined to assume; or whether, like too many good but less gifted film artists, he has at last become so engrossed in the solution of pure problems of technique that he has lost some of his sensitiveness toward the purely human aspects of what he is doing. A friend of mine justly remarks that *Lifeboat* is more a Steinbeck picture than a

Hitchcock. In *Shadow of a Doubt*, too, I felt that Hitchcock was dominated by his writers. In his finest films he has always shown, always cinematically, qualities of judgment and perception which to my mind bring him abreast of all but the few best writers of his time, and which set him far beyond the need, conscious or otherwise, of going to school to anyone. But too many people rock *Lifeboat*; and they lull what had every right and need, if it were undertaken at all, to be a great and terrifying film.

January 29, 1944

SINCE nothing is more repugnant to me than the pseudo-religious, I went to *The Song of Bernadette* gritting my teeth against my advance loathing. But since, also, many of the deepest resonances of my childhood are Catholic; and since I intensely suspect and fear the implacable pieties of those who deny the rationally inexplicable even when they are being beaten over the head with it; and since, accordingly, I feel a triumphant pride in the work or mere existence of true artists and of the truly experienced in religion, I was unexpectedly and greatly moved by a great many things in the film. I owe this somewhat indecently subjective preface because I doubt that the film can be strongly recommended to anyone whose mind and emotions lack some similar shape. I can add only that the picture is unusually well made—within limits.

The limits are those of middle-class twentieth-century genteelism, a fungus which by now all but chokes the life out of any hope from Hollywood and which threatens any vivid appetite in Hollywood's audience. In proportion to the excellence any given film achieves within these limits—which can be considerable—I suppose it is the more pernicious. If that is so, *Bernadette* is a champion enemy. For within those genteel limits I have seldom seen so tender and exact an attention to mood, to over-all tone, to cutting, to the edging of an emotion, and to giving vitality, sometimes radiance, in terms of the image and the sound more than of the character, the story, the line, the music. Jennifer Jones especially, as Bernadette, whether through Henry King's direction or her own ability, impossibly combines the waxen circumspections of a convent school with abrupt salients of emotion of which Dostoevski himself need not have been ashamed.

But Bernadette Soubirous and the cruel, ridiculous, and unfathomable concentrics which spread from her naive ecstasy composed one of the most appalling and instructive events of our time; to the reproduction of which only an almost unimaginably brilliant film could have been adequate. What you have here, instead, is a tamed and pretty image, highly varnished, sensitively lighted, and exhibited behind immaculate glass, the window at once of a shrine and of a box-office.

February 5, 1944

The Miracle of Morgan's Creek, the new Preston Sturges film, seems to me funnier, more adventurous, more abundant, more intelligent, and more encouraging than anything that has been made in Hollywood for years. Yet the more I think of it, the less I esteem it. I have, then, both to praise and defend it, and to attack it.

The essential story is hardly what you would expect to see on an American screen: a volcanically burgeoning small-town girl (Betty Hutton) gets drunk and is impregnated by one of several soldiers, she can't remember which; her father (William Demarest), her younger sister (Diana Lynn), and her devoted 4-F lover (Eddie Bracken) do all they can to help her out; the result is a shambles, from which they are delivered by a "miracle" which entails its own cynical comments on the sanctity of law, order, parenthood, and the American home—to say nothing of a number of cherished pseudo-folk beliefs about bright-lipped youth, childhood sweethearts, Mister Right, and the glamor of war. Sturges tells this story according to a sound principle which has been neglected in Hollywood—except by him—for a long time: in proportion to the inanity and repressiveness of the age you live in, play the age as comedy if you want to get away with murder. The girl's name, Trudy Kockenlocker, of itself relegates her to a comic-strip world in which nothing need be regarded as real; the characters themselves are extremely stylized—a skipping little heifer, a choleric father, an updated Florence Atwater, a classical all-American dope; and the wildly factitious story makes comic virtues of every censor-dodging necessity. Thanks to these devices the Hays office has been either hypnotized into a liberality for which it should be thanked, or has been raped in its sleep.

Having set up these formalized characters, each in a different comic key, and this thin-ice version of the story he is really telling, Sturges has just begun. He also doubles the characters on their own trails, into sharp pathos, into slapstick (some of which falls flat), into farce as daftly unsettling as being licked to death by a lioness, to the edge of tragi-comedy, and into moments of comedy which could emerge only from their full quality as human beings. He plays every twist of his story for sharp realism as well as laughs; his small-town doctor, banker, lawyer, and, most notably, Porter Hall as a justice of the peace are bits of comic realism finely graded against the chameleon-like principals. Above all, Sturges carries farther than he has ever done before his bold blends and clashes of comic and realistic angles of attack. In a typically fine scene on Christmas Eve, when Trudy's pregnancy has developed the comic-emotional portentousness of a delayed-action bomb, he manages to sustain an atmosphere of really tender pathos and, at the same time, (1) to cue in "Silent Night," (2) to show irate Constable Kockenlocker hammering the hell out of a recalcitrant Christmas star, (3) to let him comfort his restive daughter with the noble reminder (deleted the second time I saw the film) "You may be waiting for the President of the United States," and (4) to cap that, for Bethlemayhem, by having young Emily inquire, gently, what that cow is doing in the kitchen.

Besides resonating many traditions of comedy against a firm basic realism, the film rests on an apparently complex emotional and philosophic base which seems to me not really complex but simply mature, being—on its smaller scale—at once as nihilistic as Céline, at least as deeply humane as Dickens, and at all times inviolably, genuinely, and intelligently gay. Excepting a few moments when Sturges forces everything too far, the film is also beautifully played, especially by William Demarest, whose performance stands with Paul Lukas's in *The Watch on the Rhine* among the finest I have seen.

But you may, I have to realize, disagree with me. I have incredulously heard some people dismiss the show as "comedy"; they should stick to something really vital and serious like *Zola*. Others feel it is too frantic and too rough; it has enough mental, creative, and merely brutal energy for a hundred average pictures. Others object to various errors of taste, mainly connected with making laughs out of pregnancy. Here again I partly agree; but I would rather see pregnancy remain a subject for questionable laughter than see it become taboo against any laughter at all. Still others dislike the film for its multiple attack, its shiftiness of style; but if you accept that principle in Joyce or in Picasso, you will examine with interest how brilliantly it can be applied in moving pictures and how equally promising, as against the lovely euphonies René Clair achieved according to the same principle, astute cacophony can be. For barring Chaplin's this seems to me the largest American attempt, on the level of full consciousness, to stir up from the bottom the whole history and possibility of moving pictures into one broth; to draw, like Clair, on the blackloam, instinctive genius of the Mack Sennett comedies; and to amuse and excite the simplest at once with the most complex customers. In fact, in the degree that this film is disliked by those who see it, whether consciously or passively, I see a measure less of its inadequacies than of the progress of that terrible softening, solemnity, and idealization which, increasing over several years, has all but put an end to the output and intake of good moving pictures in this country.

Yet the more I think about the film, the less I like it. There are too many things that Sturges, once he had won all the victories and set all the things moving which he managed to here, should have achieved unhindered, purely as a good artist; and he has not even attempted them. He is a great broken-field runner; once the field is clear he sits down and laughs. The whole tone of the dialogue, funny and bright as it often is, rests too safely within the pseudo-cute, pseudo-authentic, patronizing diction perfected by Booth Tarkington. And in the stylization of action as well as language it seems to me clear that Sturges holds his characters, and the people they comically represent, and their predicament, and his audience, and the best potentialities of his own work, essentially in contempt.

His emotions, his intelligence, his aesthetic ability never fully commit themselves; all the playfulness becomes rather an avoidance of commitment than an extension of means for it. Cynicism, which gives the film much of its virtue, also has it by the throat; the nihilism, the humaneness, even the gaiety become, in that light, mere postures and tones of voices; and whereas nearly all the mischief is successful, nearly every central and final responsibility is shirked. Of course there is always the danger, in trying to meet those ultimate human and aesthetic responsibilities, of losing your gaiety; but that never happened to Mozart—or to René Clair at his best.

I mention Clair again because Sturges has so many similar abilities so richly—and because there is such a difference between the two. Whether or not he ever makes another film under favorable circumstances, and up to his best, Clair is one of the few great artists of this century. Sturges, in his middle forties, is still just the most gifted American working in films, vividly successful in the kind of artful-dodging which frustrates Clair; hollow and evasive at those centers in which Clair is so firm. I suspect that Sturges feels that conscience and comedy are incompatible. It would be hard for a man of talent to make a more self-destructive mistake.

February 12, 1944

I HAVE never read *Jane Eyre*, but I think there may be some use in comparing the screen version with a not very good version which Luther Adler and Sylvia Sidney brought to the Boston stage several months ago. Judging by the play, the novel must have a good deal of inter-class, feminist, ethical, and erotic tension, and Rochester, besides having a good deal of disintegrating romantic splendor, must in some degree symbolize the predicament and decay of the best of England in his time. Judging by the film, the novel must also have the kind of darkly transparent, hypnotic tone and pace which seem never, any more, to be achieved or even attempted in writing. There is almost no symbolic resonance and almost no really taking or revealing tension in the film; there is very little, in fact, after the first twenty minutes or so that makes it at all seriously worth seeing. Those first twenty minutes, however, which are devoted to Jane's schooling and her first meeting with Rochester, are a lush, beetlebrowed, unusually compelling piece of highly romantic screen rhetoric. I suspect Orson Welles had a hand in this stretch—for good and for bad; it has a good deal of his black-chenille-and-rhinestones manner. After that, all you get is a careful and tame production, a sadly vanilla-flavored Joan Fontaine, and Welles treating himself to road-operatic sculpturings of body, cloak, and diction, his eyes glinting in the Rembrandt gloom, at every chance, like side-orders of jelly. It is possible to enjoy his performance as dead-pan period parody; I imagine he did. I might have more if I hadn't wanted, instead, to see a good performance.

It is also possible, I gather from many people, to be as excited and scared by *The Lodger*, the adaptation of Mrs. Belloc Lowndes's story about Jack the Ripper, as the adaptors intended. I wish I could have been, for it is years since a horror picture has given me my money's worth, and I feel that today only Val Lewton, who makes such B pictures as *The Seventh Victim*, has occasional promising ideas how to go about it. For me the main troubles with *The Lodger* were that everyone was trying for gentlemanly, intelligent horror, sustained only by tricks of secondary suspense (you know from the start who the Ripper is), in too gentlemanly and too little incisively intelligent a manner. As a result the beautiful interiors, the sometimes beautiful streets, and the too beautiful lighting and photography drew too much attention to their own sumptuous but very passive vitality, and the good performances of Laird Cregar, Sir Cedric Hardwicke, Sara Allgood, and Merle Oberon also remained a purely visual pleasure. Doris Lloyd, however, does project a moment of solid, old-fashioned fright.

February 26, 1944

Phantom Lady is the first picture produced by Joan Harrison, who worked with Hitchcock as secretary, idea woman, and script writer from 1934 to 1941. Much of it is good. It is also a pleasure to see because Miss Harrison got to make it, apparently, through a combination of the strong arm, luck, and the sensible willingness of Universal's executives to take a chance on a B thriller; because within limits she clearly knows what she is doing; and because the critical and popular success of the film may possibly encourage other film executives to take chances on other dark horses and may also encourage other horses, dark or white-haired, to take chances with their best rather than their merely safe ideas and abilities.

Even so, I feel the film is being talked about a little too excitedly. Miss Harrison is doing nothing that Hitchcock has not done a great deal better, and little, for that matter, which was not a commonplace ten to fifteen years ago in American city melodramas. She is simply an intelligent, entertaining worker in an idiom which badly needs not only restoring but developing. She gets from Hitchcock none of his fine-grained business and eye for detail, only some of the broad and show-wise aspects of his style. She knows, for instance, when and how to use silence, and she has a better than average sense of place, mood, timing, cutting, and sound. She has a nicely unconventional sense of casting which brings one fine bit by a hatmaker who looks like a maltreated Renaissance angel, and which uses Franchot Tone as a cultivated paranoiac; but Tone's performance cannot get above his mediocre lines and her fancy lighting of his obsessed hands. Miss Harrison seems, in fact, to know much less about people, and how they think, feel, talk, and move, than about effects. Some of the dialogue ("You should see how they've twisted him, hurt him . . . and his mind was so full of beautiful plans for model cities") is like a nail on a slate; and the producer also permits a good deal of amateurish reading. Even the effects are not all they might be. There is a suspense scene on a late-night Elevated platform which is excellent up to the ten seconds which should tighten and pay it off; there it shifts into second gear, and not even the frightening jolt of the turnstile which relieves it can rescue it. There is another scene, a jam session used as a metaphor for orgasm and death—which in turn become metaphors for the jam session—which is good but would gain, I think, if it were less intensely romanticized; the chief mistake there, it seems to me, is a narrow table crowded to all its edges with liquor bottles. That, too, is good, physically vivid metaphor; but it is juvenile-delinquent jazz. The late reels of the picture slacken, and the ending, upon which Universal insisted, is half-heartedly done. But this is written as a would-be corrective of too much indiscriminate praise. There is plenty in *Phantom Lady* to enjoy, and to be glad of.

March 4, 1944

THE ISSUES and fragments of the army's *Screen Magazine* which were recently given a civilian airing at the Museum of Modern Art are at once heartening, disappointing, and disturbing. It is disturbing to any anti-authoritarian to have to realize that we work more honestly and more effectively as semi-totalitarians than as semi-democrats; these films are miles ahead of any rough American equivalent—mainly newsreels—made for civilians. Even so, high-mediocre is the general ceiling. The commentators' voices are not, thank God, trying to strangle the buyer and embalm his corpse in the same inflection; but they do tend to be smoothly, unpleasantly folksy. There is an obligatory hell-and-damn or so to each issue, a rather frequent use of naked soldiers bathing, a good bit of backside comedy. Barring a slightly uneasy sort of chumminess, however, the tone and pace are generally relaxed and sensible, wonderfully pleasing to experience after waltzing across the little bits of broken mirror which make the average newsreel, or suffering the riveting-hammer, maniacal yammer of a March of Time. There is frequent intelligent use of an excellent device which ought to be recognized as basic to decent film grammar: the shot introduced and given its own pure power, for a few seconds—it ought often to be minutes—without sound, music, explanation, or comment. Private Snafu, a cartooned cluck full of instinctive bad habits, would be fun to see, I imagine, on any front; but I wonder why there is no animated version of *Yank*'s Private Sadsack. The Magazine seems a little short on fun, and lamentably short on pretty women. As teaching and as morale tonic I presume it would be very valuable even if it were much less good than it is; but on both counts it seems tame and unimaginative compared with what it might be. I have to speak, with the sense of a very limited right to, of my objection to hearing the Japanese referred to as "cockroaches," "rats," and so forth. With combat experience, I must realize, this might strike me differently; I only hope not. I also hope that I would under no circumstances accept the Magazine's muted sneer at a Japanese shrine. There are some tenderly crude and on the whole nice pieces of sentimentality about soldiers' parents who cannot write their sons in English, army dogs, and sailors' children at Christmas time. There are some fine, terrible shots of Tarawa. A few minutes of Kiska under quiet steady rain make about as beautiful an image of desolation as I have ever seen.

March 11, 1944

THIS WEEK I want briefly to mention several films which should have been reviewed sooner.

The Army Orientation film *The Negro Soldier* is straight and decent as far as it goes, and means a good deal, I gather, to most of the Negro soldiers who have seen it. It is also pitifully, painfully mild; but neither the film nor those who actually made it should be criticized for that. The mildness is, rather, a cruel measure of the utmost that the War Department dares or is willing to have said on the subject. The same mildness makes the film amenable to very broad public distribution, without wholly obviating its almost certain good effect upon a massive white audience which needs to be reached and influenced, however tamely. Whether tougher treatments ever get to the screen depends, in part, on how many people see this one. And that may largely depend on the efforts of the Negroes and whites whom this particular film is surest to disappoint. For I suspect that most exhibitors are going to need encouragement from the audience, in one form or another, to ask for the film at all—to say nothing of advertising it. And I believe that to many people the screen presentation of the Negro as something other than a clown, a burnt-cork Job, or a plain imbecile, will be more startling and more instructive than we are likely to imagine.

The Purple Heart is Darryl Zanuck beating his Hollywood rivals to the draw with a Japanese atrocity picture. It is a fictional account, much more controlled than it might have been, of the trial and torture of eight American fliers who were captured after the Doolittle raid. Under Lewis Milestone's direction, his best in years, it is unusually edged, well-organized, and solidly acted. But I feel extremely queasy watching fiction —especially persuasive fiction—which pretends to clarify facts that are not clear, and may never become so. Conditioned by such amphibious and ambiguous semi-information, we are still more likely than otherwise to do things to defeated enemies which, both morally and materially, will finally damage us more deeply even than them.

I feel an even sharper objection to the moment, in *Passage to Marseille*, when Humphrey Bogart, on a ship representing France, slaughters the surviving helpless crew of a wrecked plane which represents conquered Germany. Victor Francen is shocked, to be sure; but Bogart is the star, from whom the majority will accordingly accept advice on what to do with Germany. Aside from this scene the picture is regulation Nordhoff and Hall, Warner Brothers, Michael Curtiz fustian about Devil's Island, French fascists, and French patriots—fair-to-dull melodramatic entertainment, needled with political consciousness.

In *The Fighting Seabees* American bulldozers engage in direct combat with Japanese tanks, but this opportunity for a few minutes of wonderful film is almost completely muffed. The Japanese are represented, both verbally and by mannerism, as subhuman. One is caught up screaming in the jaws of a steamshovel; he is shot and dropped. The dramatic intention is apparently one of grim humor but I wonder whom the laugh is on.

The Sullivans sketches the life story of the five brothers who were killed at once in the South Pacific. The streets, backyards, porch-life, and interiors are quite good. The treatment of the human being is limpid, simple, and nearly always unimaginative. The emotional impact, for me, was almost nil, in part because nobody really came to life, in part because the effort to reenact and to exploit these real and vanished lives seemed to me somehow scarcely sane; I wish I knew why.

No Greater Love, a Russian film about a woman guerrilla leader, has a kind ferocity and ugliness which none of these American films approach; but I feel less uneasy about it than about them. I think the thing which gives this film a full existence and a full right to it is an earned immediacy and passion which the American films entirely lack. The acting is furious and hyperbolic yet proper to the over-all key of frenzy. The photography would be discarded by any Hollywood studio: it is harsh, often crude, always sensitive to time, place, weather, substance, atmosphere, and the presence of life. I would have preferred superimposed printed dialogue to the dramatic-school and Theatre Union sorts of voices which were dubbed in; even if they had been excellent I suspect that their safe, hermetic, reenacted quality would have been inescapable, and would have created a strange and disturbing lesion of one's time sense in seeing and hearing the film. On the screen you see it happening; at the same moment the voices are saying, this happened, and this is roughly how. But dubbing is likely to lift this and future Russian films clear of their pitifully narrow American circuit of a few dozen little "art" theaters, and that is all to the good. People may now get a chance to learn what they, and Hollywood, are cheating each other out of. Ideally, *No Greater Love* should be double-billed, all over the country, with *The North Star.*

The Uninvited, through an adroit counterpointing, syncopating, and cumulation of the natural and the supernatural, turns a mediocre story and a lot of shabby clichés into an unusually good scare-picture. It seems to me harder to get a fright than a laugh, and I experienced thirty-five first-class jolts, not to mention a well-calculated texture of minor frissons.

Standing Room Only does pretty well with stale material too —Toryish tropes like the Washington room shortage, feminized husbands, female soldiers, imbecilic bureaucrats, pitiless servants. The lines are utterly insincere and slickly witty, the directing is fairly flip and observant, and some of the performances are fine, especially that of Roland Young, who is able to make anything he appears in seem much more intelligent, human, and amusing than it has any intrinsic right to.

Lady in the Dark is something I'm not sure I can talk about fairly, for the whole idea of mixing psychoanalysis and production numbers leaves me irrecoverably cold. Sketching my ideal MGM production of *The Brothers Karamazov* years ago, I cast Fred Astaire as Alyosha (against a more logical MGM choice of Hardie Albright) to make possible a great dancing sequence called Alyosha's Dream, in which Grushenka (Marlene Dietrich) would appear variously as herself, the Virgin, Mary Magdalene, and Father Zossima. Those who would like to see such a sequence done sincerely, the only proper way, may find a good deal to enjoy in *Lady in the Dark*. But I like my dreams the hard way.

Up In Arms, which puts Danny Kaye through a Sam Goldwyn war, ought logically to leave me just as cold, but I enjoyed it. The war is nothing like that fought on land, sea, or even in *The North Star*. The Goldwyn Girls look like real live women instead of the customary radio-cap sculptures. There are some pleasant, silly gags by Don Martman of the Crosby-Hope-Lamour Roads-to-everywhere. All that aside, Danny Kaye is the whole show, and everything depends on whether or not you like him. I do.

March 18, 1944

Although it lasts just nineteen minutes, *With the Marines at Tarawa* gave me, in that time, a sharper realization of combat than any other film I have seen. I also respected its craftsmanship and its taste, barring an ill-timed utterance of the line "their lives mean nothing to them" while the camera is examining Japanese corpses. It interests me that color, so harmless to musical fantasies and so generally fatal to films which deal, even nominally, with peacetime realism, adds a lot to the power and immediacy of these war scenes. A man who was at Tarawa tells me that it is impossible to duplicate the sounds of such an operation, and that with such material as was photographed, the editors have pulled no punches, as I suspected they might have; the cameras simply failed to get down some of the things we read of in the newspapers. This eyewitness— he was a correspondent there—thought the picture a good job but was, I could see, a little amused that it had moved and excited me so intensely. I don't wonder he was. But I think it can be highly recommended to anyone who, like myself, needs to diminish so far as he can the astronomical abyss which exists between the experienced and the inexperienced in war. The

faces of individual marines, at the end, are even more hum-
bling and more instructive than the worst of the records of
combat.

See Here, Private Hargrove suffers a proper disadvantage,
compared with *Tarawa*. It is callow, puppyish, whimsically
amusing—to those who can easily swallow that contradiction
—and uninterested in telling the truth even about training.
Taken within its own modest comic intentions it is harmless
enough, I suppose, and reasonably entertaining—it may perhaps genuinely amuse men in training camps—and there are
good performances by Bill Phillips and Keenan Wynn. But
there is something unpleasantly cuddly about it—a sort of
cross between *Stalky* and the pansy-truck-driver sort of *New
Yorker* humor.

Voice in the Wind, a heartfelt shoestring quickie shot in thirteen days, is a pretty awful moving picture, I realize, but I was
touched by its sincerity and by a number of things in it, and
was sympathetically interested in a good deal more. It is being
advertised as "a strange new kind of moving picture," and that
makes me realize, as the excitement over the "originality" of
Citizen Kane used to, that already I belong to a grizzling generation. The picture is like a middle-thirties French melodrama
drenched in the Rembrandt-and-molasses manner of German
"art" films of the early to middle twenties. Even within those
terms it is much less good than it might be, solemn, unimaginative, thinly detailed; but it is also richly nostalgic if you have
any affection for bad period art. (I have an idea that the less
discriminating among the German refugees will go crazy over
it.) Also I enjoyed hearing a piece of Chopin played without
interruption and with appropriate oversensitivity, while the
tragedy came to a standstill, sniffling and wiping its eyes. It
takes a lot of anti-commercial courage to do that in a film; and
however wrong most of it goes, *Voice in the Wind* has a great
deal of that sort of courage.

The Impostor is a piece of anxious manufacture about Jean
Gabin as a fugitive killer, masquerading as a Free French hero,
in Equatorial Africa. Gabin himself, artificiality and all, is
good. The rest of the show sadly proves just how nearly impossible it is to make a French film in Hollywood, or anywhere
else except France.

March 25, 1944

Tunisian Victory is bound to be compared with *Desert Victory*. That it suffers by comparison is by no means entirely the fault of the Englishmen and Americans who made it. *Desert Victory* started with great advantages, and took highly intelligent further advantage of each of them. History imposed upon the film a grand and simple form; it was possible to personify anonymous forces in two, rather than two dozen, opposing leaders who had the further advantage of being psychologically provocative figures; and the film was made under a single, focused control and for a single purpose. *Tunisian Victory* had to tell of a campaign much more complex, in political as well as military respects; it was apparently necessary to highlight, and bow and scrape to, every half-sized military wig in sight; the film suffered the liabilities of "full collaboration"; it evidently suffered too at the hands of people whose concern was purely political and propagandistic; and its makers were trying not only to give a short screen history of a vast and intricate action but at the same time to play international Gaston and Alphonse. The questionable political overtones of the invasion never so much as smudge the sound track—though one good look at the people involved is perhaps enough; the military story, on the other hand, is told so doggedly, with such textbookish wordiness, that the film never escapes for more than a few seconds at a time into the sort of pure tragic excitement which *Desert Victory* proved a war film can be. There are shots, and clusters of shots, as fine as any in the British film, but they never get a chance to gather cinematic momentum; the words, the verbalized facts, forever nag them to heel, and their competently edited heeling is no acceptable substitute. It was a mistake too, I think, to try to "humanize" American and English soldiers, whose screen faces hardly need that service, by means of two disembodied voices, one Cockney, one Kansas City, for they give the film the pseudo-democratic, demagogic coloration of most vernacular literature. *Tunisian Victory* is, in fact, at its worst whenever it tries to be "human" for humanity's sake; I, at least, felt that the people on the screen and in front of it were being unconsciously patronized, which is one cut worse than consciously; and judging by the run of British

and American films I have seen, I feel pretty sure whose national disease that is. For the privilege of producing a Lincoln
we have been paying through our tinhorn nose, in counterfeit
kind, ever since we brought him down with a Roman phrase.

Beyond provoking friendly mention of ripe Ann Sheridan,
decent Dennis Morgan, and shrewd S. Z. Sakall, *Shine On,
Harvest Moon* offers nothing worth talking about. *Tender
Comrade*—"wife," that means—is very much worth talking
about, and I hope that adequate strength and space will coin-
cide in a week or two. Meanwhile I can say only that it is one
of the god-damnedest things ever seen.

April 1, 1944

TARDILY, I arch my back and purr deep-throated approval of
The Curse of the Cat People, which I caught by pure chance,
one evening, on a reviewer's holiday. Masquerading as a routine case of Grade B horrors—and it does very well at that job
—the picture is in fact a brave, sensitive, and admirable little
psychological melodrama about a lonely six-year-old girl, her
inadequate parents, a pair of recluses in a neighboring house,
and the child's dead, insane mother, who becomes the friend
and playmate of her imagination. Since you have probably
heard about it already from other reviewers, and since it is the
sort of picture anyhow which deserves to give one the pleasure
of personal discovery, I will not do more than say that dozens
of the details are as excellent as the whole intention. Certain
confusions in the plot—especially one scene in which the imaginary playmate, by pinning a gift to her gown, momentarily
seems to categorize herself as a mere studio wraith—suggests
that the people who made the film worked out two versions,
one with conventional supernatural trimmings, the other, the
far from conventional story they got away with. I was rather
pleased than not, incidentally, by the trick, or accident, or both,
which kept me and the audience uncertain, clear to the end,
whether the ghost was a "real" ghost or the far more real fantasy of the child. In the same way I liked the ambiguous melodrama about the daft old actress and her tortured daughter, in
the sinister house; though here I would have liked even better

the much purer, quieter realism which they would have achieved if they had taken their key from the wonderfully chosen house itself. I wish that the makers of the film, and RKO, might be given some special award for the whole conception and performance of the family servant, who is one of the most unpretentiously sympathetic, intelligent, anti-traditional, and individualized Negro characters I have ever seen presented on the screen. And I hope that the producer, Val Lewton, and the rest of his crew may be left more and more to their own devices; they have a lot of taste and talent, and they are carrying films a long way out of Hollywood.

Even so, they have things to learn. This had every right to be a really first-rate movie; but good as it is, it is full of dead streaks —notably the writing, directing, and playing of the parts of the parents and the kindergarten teacher—and there are quite a few failures of imagination and of taste. The people with whom I saw the film—a regular Times Square horror audience —were sharply on to its faults and virtues. When the Ideal Playmate (Simone Simone) first appeared to the imagination of the infant in a dress and a lascivious lighting which made her façade look like a relief map from What Every Young Husband Should Know, they laughed their heads off. They laughed again, with tender and perceptive spontaneity, when, confronted by snobbery, the little girl caught her shoulders into a bewildered, instinctively pure shrug of distaste. And when the picture ended and it was clear beyond further suspense that anyone who had come to see a story about curses and were-cats should have stayed away, they clearly did not feel sold out; for an hour they had been captivated by the poetry and danger of childhood, and they showed it in their thorough applause.

That is, I grant, a specialized audience, unobstreperous, poor, metropolitan, and deeply experienced. The West Times Square audience is probably, for that matter, the finest movie audience in the country (certainly, over and over, it has proved its infinite superiority to the run of the "art theater" devotees —not to mention, on paper which must brave the mails, the quality and conduct of Museum of Modern Art film audiences). As long as such an audience exists, no one in Hollywood has a right to use the stupidity of the public for an alibi; and I suspect that a few more films as decent and human as this

one would indicate that there is a very large and widely distributed audience indeed for good films.

THERE is no reason, after all, why a movie musical should
not be as good as any other sort of movie. *Cover Girl* is the
first since *Top Hat* which even suggests the possibilities. There
is nothing in it that approaches the dance in the jigsawed pavil-
ion in the rain in the old Astaire-Rogers film. Much of *Cover
Girl*, for that matter, is not as fresh as it may seem; but its
second-handedness and its occasional failures cannot obliterate
the pleasure of seeing the work of a production company which
obviously knows, cares about, and enjoys what it is doing.

The story, of itself, is conventional enough: a Brooklyn
nightclub dancer (Rita Hayworth) leaves her boss (Gene Kelly),
who loves her, for Broadway and for smoother, richer men
(Otto Kruger, Lee Bowman), and ultimately thinks better of
it; in period flashbacks her grandmother (Miss Hayworth
again) describes a similar trajectory. But scene by scene—with
some skids—this story is written with intelligence as well as wit
and is acted sincerely and with a deft evocation of background,
trade, character, and various true-to-life implications which are
not verbally permissible in a Hollywood script. As a result, most
of the Kelly-Hayworth-Bowman triangulations carry an interest and an emotional weight which are rare enough in straight
dramatic films, to say nothing of musicals. In general, the
songs and dances, besides being quite good as numbers, intensify the characterizations: Kelly, in fact, does his best acting in
the course of singing two versions of "Put Me to the Test"; his
nightclub and the observant charm of the best of the show are
put exactly in their idealized-realistic key by the eight-girl chorus which—with a finely exhilarating bang—starts the picture.
Most of the costumes are the most shrewdly pretty I have seen
for a long time; many of the sets and colors are as good as
those in *Heaven Can Wait*. The color still goes manic occasionally—one moment the flesh of the chorus-girls is almost as
happy-looking as if Renoir had been technical adviser, the next
it looks as if the girls had just skipped out of a blood-bath. But

there are some appreciative shades of brick, pavement, and blind glass in the night streets which for the first time, so far as I know, begin to colonize the proper potential universe of color in films.

In a show so surprisingly full of achievement the failures set one's teeth all the more on edge. The period flashbacks slacken the picture and, within themselves, clash two periods forty years apart. The one big production number is just about like any average thing of its kind. Some of the Brooklyn sets are too cute and air-conditioned to support the relatively genuine characterizations or to help achieve the moods which are tried for. Some of the tunes and incidental music are pseudonacreous, routine Jerome Kern; some of the lyrics are Roget's-Thesauric, routine Ira Gershwin. Several of the dances, after establishing uncommonly good emotion, plan, and focus, lose everything in a mere dashing around. Even Kelly's most ambitious dance—a double-exposed duet with his conscience, down a late-night street—in spite of some hair-raising moments, wavers between convincing and pumped-up despair. It is further vitiated by lush orchestration, after a very exciting start on bare-boned piano to which, I suggest, only the driest sort of drumming should have been added.

There are plenty of other letdowns. Yet *Cover Girl* would be worth seeing if only for Rita Hayworth at her prettiest (at certain other moments she looks as if she were daring you to stick your head in her mouth) or, still more important, Gene Kelly. Kelly is limited and is capable of failure, as he occasionally proves here. But I can think of no one in Hollywood, just now, who is more satisfying or more hopeful to watch for singing, dancing or straight acting.

April 15, 1944

Memphis Belle is the story of one bomber's twenty-fifth mission over Germany. You realize, as you watch it, that if the crew survives, it will be retired from combat service. What this means to the men of the crew, to those whose survival will not mean retirement, and to those who are not flying that day is so unobstreperously clear in the faces of all of them that I could not guess which shots were reenacted and which were straight records. This same vigorous and pitiful sense of the presence, danger, skill, and hope of several human beings so pervades the flying, flak, bombing, and fighting scenes that not even one of the dozen or so superhuman shots allows you to feel that either it or you are there for the view. Everything is seen, done, and experienced as if from inside one or another of the men in the plane. Color and the sudden amazements of the air help to create this immediacy, but so do the very experienced, vigilant photography, the even better cutting, and a general good taste which knows better than to use any rhetoric of image, word, or sound in dealing with such facts. *With the Marines at Tarawa* shudders like a new wound, and is as terrible to see. *Memphis Belle* does not have that kind of power or sensitiveness. But of its very different kind of war process, at once more aloof and more intimate, it seems as good a record. Taken together, the films are documentaries with which for the first time we can look the English in the eye.

The man in over-all charge of making this good film was William Wyler, whose talent I respected in *Wuthering Heights* and even in *Mrs. Miniver*, without caring for the pictures. Postwar planners should work out a better fate for him than going back to Hollywood.

May 6, 1944

DEATH TAKES A POWDER

DEATH, lately, and bereavement have been getting a good deal of friendly attention from Hollywood. God has been let in out of the rain, too (though I must save discussion of that for another time). Adversity makes strange bedfellows; and there are always people on hand to go through their pants' pockets while they sleep, just on the chance. The real wonder is not that Hollywood is so eager to exploit the grief, anguish, fear, premonition, and troubled spiritual apprehension of everyone on earth it can reach, but that it has been so slow in recognizing the magnificence of its opportunity to do so. It is more than possible, too, that a good deal of this extremely lucrative exploitation is "sincere." Certainly it would seem a natural, even inevitable function of a popular art which was half worthy of its reach, its responsibilities, and its potentialities—which was, in other words, even half healthy, even a fraction alive—to undertake these immense experiences and preoccupations and to bring to them some measure, however meek, of understanding, order, and illumination.

But nothing of that sort occurs in the films I am thinking of; indeed, every effort is made to keep anything of that sort from occurring.

Happy Land set up a pretty, prettily photographed American town without an ounce of meanness or ugliness or even complicatedness in it, set up an American boy to match, took him off to war, killed him, and assured his grieving father that that special boyhood, in that special town, was unarguably worth dying for. This questionable thesis was demonstrated by Harry Carey, a ghostly grandfather who made it clear that just as there is nothing much to worry about above ground in our native land, the American Hereafter is a pleasant Old Soldiers' Home.

A Guy Named Joe told of an ace who was killed and who promptly got steady employment from his heavenly boss, Lionel Barrymore, teaching a neophyte how to become an ace too. This ghost has also to watch his young pupil court his former sweetheart, and to cure her of her grief over himself. In bare outline and idea this story offers a good workable metaphor for tradition in an art of skill, and wonderful possibilities for drama. The jealousy of a living lover for a dead man made one of Joyce's finest stories; the emotions a ghost might feel who watched a living man woo and cajole his former mistress seem just as promising to me; the paralysis and slow healing of a bereaved woman is not a bad subject, of itself. But to make such a film—above all at such a time as this—would require extraordinary taste, honesty, and courage. The makers of *A Guy Named Joe* had courage, if a moral idiot has it; I doubt whether taste and honesty enter into it at all. I can hardly conceive of a picture more stonily impious. Joe's affability in the afterlife is enough to discredit the very idea that death in combat amounts to anything more than getting a freshly pressed uniform; and he is so unconcerned as he watches Van Johnson palpitate after Irene Dunne that he hardly bothers to take his gum out of his mouth. The people who have the best right to picket God on this matter, or at least Metro-Goldwyn-Mayer, are the dead whom the film is supposed to honor; failing that, widows, and the surviving pupils and lovers, can hardly make adequate protest.

The astonishing *Tender Comrade* is one in the eye for widows, with plenty for mere war wives too, and nothing I can imagine for anyone else except the hardiest misogynists, for whom it should prove the biggest treat and the most satisfying textbook in years. *Tender Comrade* gets along without dry ice and well-fed ghosts; its comfortable realism suggests an infinitely degraded and slickened *Little Women*. The highest-salaried tender comrade is Ginger Rogers, hilt-deep in her specialty as a sort of female Henry Fonda. She is a girl named Jo. In flashbacks you are given her courtship, marriage tiffs, etc., with *her* tender comrade, who is now away at war. They have the curious accuracy of those advertising dialogues in which Mr. and Mrs. Patchogue eliminate their erotic blockages by wrangling their way through to a good laxative. Jo is waiting out the war in a rented house with four other female comrades, of whom three are working in an aircraft plant. The fourth shows how any decent refugee can meet the servant shortage by refusing any pay for house-keeping; the others prove their Americanism by splitting their wages with her—whether she pays for their food out of her cut is not indicated. The only one who shows any signs of disliking all the cooperative, sorority-house democracy, which all but suffocated me, and of having enough sex in her to suggest that many women may be inconvenienced or even tempted, at present, is branded also as a sucker for Axis propaganda and as especially undiscriminating about men. Miss Rogers consistently addresses these companions as "kids," her baby as "little guy" or "Chris Boy." At the climax, getting news of her husband's death, she subjects this defenseless baby to a speech which lasts twenty-four hours and five minutes by my watch and which, in its justifications of the death, the obligations it clamps on the child, and its fantastic promises of a better world to come, is one of the most nauseating things I have ever sat through. It is terribly pitiful—to choose the mildest word—to think how much of America this scene and the picture as a whole are likely to move, console, corroborate, and give eloquence to. For in every word, inflection, gesture, motive, and act, the thing seems as fiercely, ultimately exact as Gertie MacDowell. A mass of women, frightening to conceive of, and the women's magazines, and the movies must have created each other mutually to belong so wholly to each other; and when you see such a film as this you have seen the end. What God hath joined together, let no man put asunder.

Compared with such sugartit treatments of death and its consequences *Between Two Worlds* seems very decent indeed. But really it isn't, very; it is just *Outward Bound* brought up to date, sad to think of as the best we can do. Most of the newly dead on this ocean liner bound for eternity are killed by a very up-to-date bomb, but the bomb also helps destroy the highly theatrical but quite chilly suspense which was the best thing in the play; you know they are all dead from the start, instead of discovering the fact as gradually as they do. Also there are no soldiers aboard—to say nothing of an enemy; and for ferry service from a world so saturated with death, the ship seems strangely empty—a fact that was not obtrusive in a day when death was not obtrusive. The characters, though they are sincerely played, are convincing neither as individuals nor as generalizations. They are drawn with the coarseness peculiar to genteelism, and their dramatic gyrations, even at best, are operatic-Piccadilly, as of twenty years ago. Their inventor does have the nerve—which we seem to have lost—to conceive that such characters face judgment and that it is a judgment worth fearing; and the judgment seems, within its liberal-agnostic limits, compassionate and gently—too gently—intelligent. That people ever took this for a distinguished play is a measure of something stultified and sadly hungry, in that time, about the general sense of life and death; today, the play speaks through moral and theatrical traditions which are receding so rapidly that the whole business is like a politely murmured withdrawal from a drawing-room which turned out to be a slaughterhouse. Whether we like it or not we are beyond things like *Between Two Worlds*, however decent and sober their intention. And whether we know it or not—and I believe most soldiers and many civilians know it—we are beyond and above the cruel, fetid, criminal little myths about death which are the best, so far, that Hollywood has furnished out of its own immediate day. They are as evil as cosmetics on a cadaver.

May 13, 1944

SOME of the following films are worth more detailed comment and may get it in the course of time. Meanwhile here is a check-list.

Going My Way, a rather saccharine story about priests, has a gentle, engaging performance by Bing Crosby, a very full and fine one by Barry Fitzgerald, and a general leisure and appreciation of character which I think highly of. It would have a little more stature as a "religious" film if it dared suggest that evil is anything worse than a bad cold and that lack of self-knowledge can be not merely cute and inconvenient but also dangerous to oneself and to others. *It Happened Tomorrow* is the deftest, prettiest film René Clair has made here, and a few moments in it—notably a box-office holdup—are beautiful. But its basic idea seems a limp one, the story is over-ingenious, and there are only glimmers of the pure joy which was so abundant in Clair's great films; I doubt that anyone could achieve such joy, or its equivalent, in contemporary Hollywood. *The Adventures of Mark Twain* gets long and soggy but has frequent good intentions and occasional near-successes, especially when it forgets to be a biography and stretches its points for the fun of it. The jumping-frog contest is really funny.

The Hitler Gang fascinates me as all waxworks do; otherwise it worries me because of its solemn effort to stick to the "facts" before an audience which is liable, on that account, to swallow it whole. Hitler strikes me as something other than a pitiful, vicious psychotic incapable of an idea, and I don't enjoy the picture's apparent suggestion—through the respectful portrayal of Gregor Strasser—that there would be nothing wrong with National Socialism if only the vicious ringleaders were eliminated. *Address Unknown* is rather vapid anti-fascism, too: full of sincere and, in their uninteresting way, skilful shadows by William Cameron Menzies. But neither Paul Lukas nor anyone else can give it much bite. Lukas can do nothing for the Errol Flynn vehicle *Uncertain Glory*, either, beyond increasing one's respect for an actor who refuses to sink to the level of his material. In *Buffalo Bill* William Wellman has constructed a Technicolored Indian battle, derived perhaps from the battle in *Alexander Nevsky*, which is fun to watch, and in general he makes good use of the plains and the movement of people on them. But most of the picture is boring. *Up in Mabel's Room* is as horrible, and wonderful, as watching a Gopher Prairie dramatic club play a mail-order farce (6m., 6f.). *The Yellow Canary* is mediocre British spy stuff, relieved only by British film cliché, which is several times as realistic and intelligent as ours. *The Lady and the Monster* is a mad-scientist movie featuring Erich von Stroheim and a Czech ex-skating champion named Vera Hruba Ralston, who does not skate in this one and whom I thought unusually attractive. The picture is two-thirds mildly amusing cliché and one-third mildly successful sharpening or avoidance of cliché.

My regret at having somewhat overrated *Cover Girl* is more than counterbalanced by even a glancing remembrance of other current musicals. If I really sat down to think of them, I'm afraid I'd rate it even higher. I serve warning, in no special order of disgrace, against seeing the following—mentioning any good thing I can, about each: *Follow the Boys* shows you the sort of entertainment American soldiers and sailors are subjected to at home and abroad, and shows you also how very proud Hollywood is of its role in the war. Purple Hearts should be handed out after every projection. *Broadway Rhythm* contains perhaps three minutes of good acrobatic dancing and lasts nearly two hours. In *Show Business* there are a few bits of archaic vaudeville which give off a moderately pleasant smell of peanuts and cigar smoke. During the making of *Pin-Up Girl* Betty Grable was in the early stage of pregnancy; everyone else was evidently in a late stage of paresis. *Knickerbocker Holiday* uses the smirking mannerisms and attitudes of Gilbert and Sullivan as one might use Sanka dregs the fifth time. In *Seven Days Ashore* I thought Alan Carney pleasant and promising; Margaret Dumont very funny. I also liked glints of cynicism in the script and of flexibility in the camera work. But in the aggregate these good things cannot amount to better than five per cent of the picture. If music be the breakfast food of love, kindly do not disturb until lunch time.

May 27, 1944

Watching *The White Cliffs of Dover* is like drinking cup after cup of tepid orange pekoe at a rained-out garden party staged by some deep-provincial local of the English-speaking Union. Like the Alice Duer Miller "poem" from which it derives, it is a natural for our better Bovaries and their male equivalents. As the whalebone-collar *Tender Comrade*, and a lot besides, it may also be unequivocally urged upon anyone who has a sufficient appetite for suffering, hatred, and a study of the devout exposition of unqualified snob dream-life. One of the movie trade papers has observed that some well-known Englishman—who apparently did not dare to give his name—thought the film unfortunate, even as an effort to foster Anglo-American amity, but that Lord Halifax liked it very much. This seems adequate check on a story Curt Riess once printed: that on the night before the Anschluss, Halifax kept an Austrian diplomat (I forget the name) who was trying to beg him to avert it waiting for hours on the ground that he was detained with a friend. The diplomat heard their gay laughter, and never saw Halifax. The friend, according to Mr. Riess's story, was von Ribbentrop.

And the Angels Sing is a Paramount shy at comedy, involving four small-town sisters (Dorothy Lamour, Betty Hutton, Diana Lynn, and Mimi Chandler) who pursue a dishonest jazz-band leader (Fred MacMurray) to Brooklyn. A lot of it—cruel, soggily professional, over-elaborate, and inclined toward snobbish whimsy—makes me tired, and I am especially sorry to watch the exciting potentialities of Diana Lynn turning, more and more, into mere narcissistic chilly cuteness. But Betty Hutton is almost beyond good and evil, so far as I am concerned, and I like a good many bits about the jazz musicians—the vulpine performance of Eddie Foy, Jr. (until he horses it); the jammed, harsh-lighted, pitiful Brooklyn dance hall; the faces of the musicians as they background silly songs; the moment when the band leader leaves the gasping jitterbugs to the mercy of a Hawaiian "prince" "and his Schultz Island Serenaders"; and the show's funniest, most authentic line, a warning yapped into the middle of a mass attack on the leader-trumpeter, the band's meal-ticket: "Don't hit him on the lip!"

IF AN automatic movie camera could have been set up in the Roman Forum on no matter what day two thousand years ago, every foot of it would have for us a special quality of wonder. I feel that sort of wonder in watching the March of Time's *Underground Report.* Made up mainly of captured film, it gives the fullest image of occupied Europe I have seen, and gives us, above all, an image of a world, a phase, which we shall never see by any other means, since it will be wholly altered by the mere presence of our fighters, cameramen, and observers, once they get there. One might discuss the film in detail and at length, for the moral and psychological charge of many of these shots is complex, and a surprising number of the single shots are magnificent. But I will merely recommend *Underground Report*, very highly, to anyone who would like to be walking in the cities of Europe, invisibly, today.

I didn't see *The Eve of St. Mark* on the stage. As a film, though it is smooth, careful, and full of decent intentions, it depresses me. It has a good deal of that flavor of corn syrup which becomes continually more official in honest, homely celebrations of our local way of living; what bothers me quite as much is its equally characteristic passion for eating its cake and having it. The sufferings of wartime love and the difficulties of celibacy are conveyed in gentle glimmers by the drafted hero (William Eythe) and his sweetheart (Anne Baxter), but never frankly or painfully enough to trouble the audience. In the same way, later, a choice between honorable withdrawal from a hopeless military predicament and a still more honorable, useful death is "faced" and as promptly about-faced. There is no mention of other soldiers whose lives the deaths of these soldiers may save; the men do discuss, rather bitterly, whether their country and its future, judging by past and present performance, are worth dying for. When one of them insists that the purpose of this war is to guarantee an end of poverty everywhere, they all choose to stay and die—only to have that necessity removed by the demolition of their gun. This sort of half-honesty, which so comfortably spikes every possible charge of dishonesty, can be very deceitful; I'm not sure but what it is worse than none at all.

I never read *Mr. Skeffington*, by "Elizabeth," either. Judging by the film, I can't have missed much. It is another of those pictures in which Bette Davis demonstrates the horrors of egocentricity on a marathonic scale; it takes her just short of thirty years' living and two and a half hours' playing time to learn, from her patient husband (Claude Rains), that "a woman is beautiful only when she is loved" and to prove this to an audience which, I fear, will be made up mainly of unloved and not easily lovable women. Miss Davis, Director Vincent Sherman, and several others put a great deal of hard work and some that is good into this show, and there are some expert bits of middle-teens and 1920s New York atmosphere. But essentially *Mr. Skeffington* is just a super soap opera, or an endless woman's-page meditation on What to Do When Beauty Fades. The implied advice is dismaying: hang on to your husband, who alone will stand by you then, and count yourself blessed if, like Mr. Rains in his old age, he is blinded.

June 10, 1944

Dr. Corydon M. Wassell, an unspectacular man, too compassionate and brave to mesh smoothly, in crisis, with authoritarians, was ordered, when Java was about to fall, to abandon several helplessly wounded sailors who were in his charge. He refused, stayed with them, kept them alive, and with great difficulty got all but one of them out of Java to Australia. I do not feel I need to have been there to know that his story is one of the great ones of this war; also, that it could be much better told through moving pictures than by any other means; also that on both counts Cecil de Mille's screen version of it is to be regretted beyond qualification. It whips the story, in every foot, into a nacreous foam of lies whose speciousness is only the more painful because Mr. de Mille is so obviously free from any desire to alter the truth except for what he considers to be its own advantage. All the more touching, and terrifying, is the fact that Dr. Wassell himself thinks that the picture, with a few trifling exceptions, is true and good.

Well, he has a right to be generous, or deceived, which none of us can dispute with him, far less claim for ourselves. One measure of the truth and goodness of the film is the difference between the elderly, simple face of the doctor and the simple yet far from simple face of the high-priced male beauty who enacts him. I like Gary Cooper; but God himself, assisted by all nine Muses, could not have made an appropriate film of *Dr. Wassell* once that piece of casting was settled on. For another measure, I choose one minor detail. When the ship out of Java is strafed and a young woman is wounded, and her ankle is being bandaged, the occasion is used to slip in a discreet bit of leg art. That, I can promise you, is typical of every shot in the movie. If you'd like another sample—I could go on forever—I offer the cinegenic idiocy of a moment when Dr. Wassell, wheeling out of a shelled road, drives his lorry through every roadside fowl-pen which, in his urgent predicament, he can get within range. Here are three brief respective counter-suggestions: (1) If you must use an actor in this sort of film, where no actors belong, get an inexperienced, unknown man who looks right and is right inside and who lacks mytholo-gizing power, and train him only so much as need be. Failing that, use an obscure, realistically competent, somewhere nearly appropriate professional like Edward Ellis. (2) If a woman is wounded, her flesh may very possibly be exposed, but for heaven's sake photograph it in such a way that nobody in your audience can possibly gobble it up—or vomit it out—as crimi-nally misplaced cheese cake. (3) Dr. Wassell was a country man, and a gentle one. I would assume that his country-bred re-flexes might cause him to try his best to avoid juggernauting livestock; and I know that this frightening conflict of reflexes could have made a wonderful moment in the film.

This viciously bad picture and a fine one called *Attack!—The Invasion of New Britain* furnish between them an oppor-tunity—almost an obligation—to discuss our war movies to date. I hope I can do so soon, and do some justice also to *Attack!* Meanwhile I urge you to see both pictures if they are available; one as a sumptuous demonstration of our confused sense of reality—a confusion which amounts almost to insan-ity; the other as an antidote, a cleanser of the eyesight, and a restorer of hope and respect for what we can do when we honor and understand our subject and our craft.

June 17, 1944

WHEN Roger Touhy and his six colleagues broke out of Stateville Penitentiary they managed it, so far as I can make out by the old papers, without outside help. The greenness, fewness, and carelessness of the guards—their personnel changed and diminished by the war—seem to have been responsible. In *Roger Touhy, Gangster* the mob does get outside help, and it is not indicated that the guards were green, few, or careless. Again, in fact the fugitives knocked over an armored car for $20,000 for a hideout nest egg. In the film no such holdup occurs, and I kept wondering what they were living on. In fact they got draft cards, through a series of holdups, which roughly fitted their descriptions. In the film they get draft cards by holdups, but nothing is done about the effort of the men, which must have been awful, comic, and cinematically promising, to single out victims who bore them a reasonable resemblance. In fact they comforted themselves abundantly with women and liquor. In the film there are no women around their hideouts and most of them stay sober as judges. In fact they lived in such excruciating claustrophobia, plus agoraphobia, plus mutual mistrust, plus general terror and anxiety, that as time wore on they became all but incapable of swallowing solid food; they seem to have lived largely on whiskey and coffee. In the film you get only the mildest idea of this physical and psychic misery. Ten to fifteen years ago the makers of such a film would have had a natural, vigorous feeling for the value of such detail. They would never have allowed it to be by-passed —or, if this or that in it seemed libelous or censorable, they would have invented some tougher equivalent which was not. *Touhy* has some fairly exciting and intelligent things in it, and anyone who loves the best of the old gangster films will get some nostalgic pleasure out of it; but it is a long way short even of the ordinary ones in immediacy, drive, tension, and imagination.

Seeing the screen version of *The Hairy Ape* I wonder whether it was really such a very good play in the first place. In any case it is hardly worth seeing as it stands here. The obsessed stoker is sincerely played by William Bendix, but Bendix is not a man to inspire the sort of fear or the sort of pity that is needed; and the character, robbed of all biological-political meaning and of the best of his talk, and glossed over with sub-comedy, could inspire neither emotion even if Bendix could. Susan Hayward, as the loathsome girl who makes him trouble, is more interesting. She is of the wrong social wave length to carry this particular role; but there are roles, not yet invented so far as I know, in which she could do a paralyzingly good job on one important kind of vicious American woman. Who would be left in the audience is harder to imagine.

June 24, 1944

IF AS a civilian, you feel the importance of experiencing what little you can about the war, you had better avoid practically every foot of fiction film which we have made about it, and you had of course better see all the newsreels and war-record films you can. At their weakest they have things to show which no nonrecord war films, not even the greatest that might be made, could ever hope to show. The latest and best of these films are *Attack!—the Invasion of New Britain*, the first invasion newsreels, and, I am reliably told, the newsreels about the fall of Cassino. The great things in such films are nearly always single shots. The good things, which sometimes approach and could attain greatness, are the cutting, the sound, the quality of the text and voice of the commentary. But even the weakest shots, and even some of the prepared or posed ones, seem to me to have great power and wonder. In *Attack!* there are morning shots, getting men and matériel ashore in the not quite misty, sober light, which overwhelmed me with their doubleness of beauty, almost sublimity, and their almost fragrant immediacy, which made me doubt my right to be aware of the beauty at all; and these were very intelligently, restrainedly enhanced by the rather quiet sounds of metal and motors—sounds which seemed as if stopped-down by the foliage and by the quality of the light and air.

The same petrifying immediacy turns up in the newsreel of a landing barge under fire off the Normandy coast, crowded with the crouched soldiers—their almost smiling officer standing—who soon leave its protection, the housetops of the French shore standing insanely near and distinct above the end of the barge, and abruptly disclosed full-length as by the rise (or fall) of a theater curtain, as the barge opens and the men begin their hip-deep wade ashore. But fully as moving and as worthy of watching, over and over, were the shots of men receiving medical pellets and their last Communion before battle, in *Attack!*; or those of Eisenhower on the first day of invasion, grinning as uncontrollably and sympathetically as an eight-year-old; or of a disconsolate young German prisoner getting his wrist bandaged.

Such material could be used still more powerfully, I think, if we dared—and knew how—to make the central intention that of communicating war to civilians and did not stop with recording it. Stop-shots, slow-motion repetitions, and blow-ups of especially significant faces or images or bits of action, with or without comment or sound, would be one device; un-rehearsed interviews would be another; a still more intrusive use of the camera in places where cameras are most unwel-come might, I uneasily believe, be a third; since the reaction of those who resent the prying would react in turn upon the con-sciousness and conscience of the audience. I regret tinges of slightly complacent "American" stuff in the *Attack!* commen-tary; this far from complacent film is well above the need for any such help. The newsreel commentary is more straightforward and less morally and psychologically appalling than it used to be but, as ought not to have to be expected, is still rather a mixture of parochial orotundity and sports-announcing. I re-gret still more the failure, in the invasion newsreels, to use at least one good long stretch of the extraordinary shots which were made from strafing planes; these were chopped down barely short of their most catastrophically effective few sec-onds. The principle is as misguided in films as it would be in music. I wish I might see a newsreel or longer film which first presented its images in the most powerful order and weaving possible, without a word of explanation; then got down, with diagrams and with recapitulated shots, to explanation. I am in-terested in explanations, but a thousand times more interested that an image have its full power. On the whole, however, the invasion films are well organized, well cut, and free of the affectations into which the use of more adventurous cutting might dangerously lead.

We could be getting still better record films of war if, like the British, our men were supplied with Cunningham Combat cameras instead of Eyemoes (the standard—and disliked—equipment); if, like the Germans and Russians, we had a much larger supply of telephoto lenses and more men trained to use them; and if we and the British used, per day, more than an average of 500 feet of film and assigned, per division, more than two movie cameramen, plus two still cameramen and two drivers. The invasion of Europe is being covered more thoroughly, we are told, than any other military operation in history; I am glad of that. But after all, the inadequate coverage of the Second Punic War hardly justifies any present complacency. It would be hard to conceive how many good cameramen, with how many good cameras and how much film, would begin to be enough. As for the recording of sound and speech, both calibrated with moving images and for its own sake, that seems still to be in the mere novelty stage.

July 1, 1944

ONLY one of the following movies seems to me worth more than a note, though three or four of them can be seen without more than a pint or so of anaesthetic.

The only one I really enjoyed was *They Met in Moscow*, which, without seeming to take any trouble to do so, makes monkeys out of us in the field of musical comedy. It tells of the meeting, separation, longing, and reunion of a southern shepherd and a northern girl who herds swine. The songs they sing are excessive, vivid, pretty, uncommercial, and solidly rooted in alphabetic emotions. They are handled and photographed as if real faces and real fresh-air landscapes could not but be more pleasing than death masks peopling a vacuum-sealed magniloquence of scarlet linoleum and dry-ice mist. I wish I thought such a film could be made in this country; but our idea of "freshness" is pretty aptly embalmed, I'm afraid, in an inadvertent horror show about youth hostels called *Song of the*

Open Road, which made something so loathsome of youth that even *Home in Indiana* seemed comparatively harmless.

Home in Indiana is about adolescent love and harness racing. There are some half-appreciative Technicolor landscapes; there is about as little pleasure in horses as I have ever seen achieved in a horse movie. One of the female adolescents looks attractive in dungarees; another wears a couple of rather extreme bathing suits. None of them act their age or any other.

Bathing Beauty swarms with bathing suits and their contents; most often and most carnally in focus is Esther Williams, lolloping in a friendly way before underwater cameras. Above water level Harry James and Xavier Cugat play, and Red Skelton, for my leathery taste, is occasionally rather funny. I could not resist the wish that Metro-Goldwyn-Mayer had topped its aquatic climax—a huge pool full of girls, fountains, and spouts of flame—by suddenly draining the tank and ending the show with the entire company writhing like goldfish on a rug. But MGM resisted it.

Why *Two Girls and a Sailor* is the hit it seems to be must be explained by those who mistake the all-American bitchiness of the heroines for all-American cuteness, Van Johnson for homely charm, and what seemed hours of suffocating boredom for air-conditioned summer entertainment. But Gracie Allen does a funny number in it, and I would recommend it to anyone who cares remotely as much for Jimmy Durante as I do. He ought to have a great deal more to do. But even as a stage corpse he would make me grateful.

Christmas Holiday is fair enough while Deanna Durbin sings a quiet arrangement of "Always"; aside from that it is pseudo-tragic mush, about a New Orleans cabaret singer, her weak husband (Gene Kelly, wasting his time), and an insipid officer on furlough.

In *They Met in Moscow* the Russians show us how to make a musical comedy; in *Days of Glory*—the Russian *White Cliffs of Dover*—we show them how not to make a Russian war movie. I have an unhappy feeling that Casey Robinson, who wrote and produced it, wanted to do something artistically first-rate about the guerrillas; but the film interests only as a possibly accurate image of the Russia which may exist in the minds of the more fatuous contributors to Russian War Relief. Aside from

Robinson's sincere intentions, I can speak courteously only of Tamara Toumanova's anachronistic beauty, which, I imagine, might have wrung dithyrambs out of Lord Byron.

July 8, 1944

To *The People's Avengers* eighteen Soviet cameramen contribute their records of guerrilla life and warfare, and Norman Corwin contributes his commentary and his voice. Mr. Corwin, in spite of being a radio man, lets gratifyingly long stretches of film run by without saying a word; when he does speak, the words are generally continent. The voice itself has, it seems to me, a slightly officious resonance, and I don't think he should be forgiven the remark "One down" when a German sentry falls dead, or the remark "Reluctant superman" as partisans drag a frantically abject German soldier from his hiding place in a haystack. (Just before this shot ends or is cut, by the way, there is a sudden clenching of people round the prostrate soldier, ambiguous but horribly suggestive, which makes the crack still more off color, and tempts me to wonder how global the anthology of post-war atrocity films might be, if every nation has the historical conscience to preserve its stock.)

The harvest of the cameras is fascinating even when it is tacky—some intensely rhetorical filter shots; or suspect—some silhouettes, before a dawn attack, which could easily have been discarded from *The North Star* but which may easily, and disconcertingly, be straight records. Some of the shots imply first-rate poetic foresight and imagination—most impressively, those of a German train, visible above rich deep-country foliage only in its soft walking tower of smoke as it moves slowly toward ambushed dynamite. Even shots which are heavily posed or reenacted—a newly decorated hero with the prettiest available girl—break the boundaries of faking; they betray, between subject and photographer, an unaffected quality of comradeship which is also seen sometimes in English films, almost never in ours. To me some of the most interesting moments showed the guerrillas at rest rather than at work—deep in the woods with their women, their stew kettles and pecking hens, and their death-experienced little boys—the faces all deep-rural, bottomlessly and naturally resolute, and incomparably secure. They reminded me, sharply, of people in parts of the back country, and of tag-ends of frontier, here. I felt reasonably sure that under similar circumstances such American civilians would react as well, and wondered how many of that kind are left.

Marine Raiders is a formula war movie (Pat O'Brien versus Robert Ryan and Ruth Hussey, all versus the Japanese) which mildly transcends its formula through bits of truer-than-average dialogue, studio combat, acting, and direction, and an occasional flexibility of insight or camera work which seems to distinguish RKO pictures as political decency distinguishes those made by Warner Brothers. (There are some moments in San Diego—notably in a crowded, forlorn record-your-voice joint—which I thought very good even though they misfired.) Robert Ryan, if he is allowed to forget about Gary Cooper, may become one of the few good leading men. *Secret Command* is about shipyards, saboteurs, and saboteur hounds. It contains two pieces of melodrama which set records for wilful denial of suspense (more frequent cutting-in of a loosening bolt in one, a dial-and-needle in the other, would have fixed everything); aside from that, and another of Pat O'Brien's experienced soft-shoe performances, the film is in no way memorable.

Two weeks ago in this column I wrote telescopic lens for telephoto. Three weeks ago vivacious roles were recommended for Susan Hayward. The word should have been vicious.

July 15, 1944

IN Humphrey Jennings's *The Silent Village* Welsh miners movingly pretended that Germans had made a Lidice of their town. In Cavalcanti's *48 Hours* (from a story by Graham Greene) some very good professional and unprofessional actors pretend that disguised German parachutists try to capture a Gloucestershire village. The thing never seems really to have happened, as *The Silent Village* almost did; nor is the film the fanged masterpiece Hitchcock alone might have made it; but it falls on a very solid stool between. The village types are the sort of entomologically observed, remarkably lifelike, charming dolls which not only Greene but Coward and Waugh so often create instead of characters—a dear-old-boy rector, his passionate, constricted daughter, the merry, warm old woman who handles the switchboard and the mail, the robinlike lady of the manor, the marked-down Heathcliff who helps the Germans, etc., etc. Well written and directed and beautifully played, these characters are not to be scorned, even though they are the soberer, still self-satirizing and self-congratulatory grandnieces and nephews of Gilbert and Sullivan; we have never yet managed to set up in films as good a portrait of an American small town, and there is poetic force in this puppetry though it lacks complexity and depth.

When men kill in this film they do it much more abruptly and simply than in ours; the reactions of women who kill or cause death—most of them have to use guile to get within striking distance—are seriously studied, and good and terrible to see. I only wish this cleavage by sex had not been as oversimple as knocking shale apart. I think the best of *48 Hours* is neither in its people nor, mainly, in their exciting, melodramatically plausible actions—aside from one gentle, marvelous, awful shot in which four cycling Home Guards oscillate and spill under machine-gun fire—but in its relating of the people and their actions to their homes, their town, their tender, lucid countryside. As the audience watches from a hill, with the eyes at once of a helpless outsider, a masked invader, and a still innocent defender, a mere crossroads imparts qualities of pity and terror which, to be sure, it always has, but which it seldom shows us except under tilted circumstances. And at moments, when the invaders prowlingly approach through the placid gardens of the barricaded manor in the neat morning light, the film has the sinister, freezing beauty of an Auden prophecy come true.

July 22, 1944

I HAVE not read Chekhov's story *The Shooting Party* from which Douglas Sirk derives *Summer Storm*, but it looks as if Mr. Sirk had wanted to be faithful to something plotty, melodramatic, and second-grade, with psychological possibilities in it which he, or his actors, failed to make much of. As a provincial judge going to the dogs under the influence of Linda Darnell, a ruthless peasant beauty, George Sanders gets across no impression of moral disintegration, struggle, helplessness, or compensatory pleasures; even when he allows her innocent husband to be punished for her murder it seems like little more than His Most Embarrassing Moment. Edward Everett Horton, as a twiddling, infatuated provincial count, has lighter baggage to carry and carries it amusingly, within rather amateurish, highly theatrical limits; in a stagy, but never in a human sense, you realize that the man he is playing and the class he is representing are loose as ashes. Linda Darnell, flashing her eyes and teeth and flexing her glands at both men, is probably the weakest of the three so far as performance goes; but since, in general appearance, she is a kind of person I can imagine going on all fours for, especially if I were a provincial judge, I thought her not entirely ill cast. There are bits of acting and photography in *Summer Storm* which put it as far outside the run of American movies as it laudably tries to be. But most of it had, for me, the sporty speciousness of an illustrated drugstore classic. "'Speaking of women,' murmured the Baron, toying with his aperient . . ."

It would be nice to see some screen "fantasy" if it were done by anyone with half a heart, mind, and hand for it. But when the studios try to make it, duck and stay hid until the mood has passed. The story of a dancing caterpillar which became an international personality, a political and religious symbol, and a baby Armageddon for science, commercialism, and what is popularly thought of as innocence and idealism might, with great skill, imagination, and avoidance of whimsy, become wonderful. But *Once Upon a Time* is not wonderful. It is just less witty and more gently intentioned than the overrated radio hit—the Corwin *My Client Curley*—from which it was developed; and both, to be plain about it, fancy gossamer as building material and then try to manufacture it out of two-by-fours. *The Cantervile Ghost*, played in mock-pansy, mock-Shakespearian style by Charles Laughton, is a quondam coward who can only go to his rest when a descendant, Robert Young, proves himself brave in warfare. The possibilities here seem thin at best, but a sufficient understanding of cowardice might still have made them amount to something. Margaret O'Brien is involved in this, too, and gives the film what little charm it has; but more still makes it an unhappy experience. She is an uncannily talented child, and it is infuriating to see her handled, and gradually being ruined, by oafs.

Candlelight in Algeria is a smooth routine British melodrama centered on a camera which contains film showing where General Clark and others will meet to plot the invasion of North Africa. There is no harm in it, and no special interest either, except in Walter Rilla's performance and in watching the English try, pretty successfully, to make American types. But one gets tired of saying that the British do this sort of melodrama well. They do; but too often, well is not so awfully well as all that. Educated Englishmen by the gross who have nothing to say and don't even realize it can write well, if by well one means plumply cadenced classical prose, fairly accurate about nothing worth accuracy, without one spark of urgency, insight, or wilfulness in it. I feel that by now they can do the movie equivalent in their sleep, and should not be too highly credited for it, even though our own somnambulistic utterance draws rather on Oley Speaks and S. Parkes Cadman than on Cicero and Burke.

July 29, 1944

DAVID O. SELZNICK'S *Since You Went Away* is a movie about an American home in wartime. It is clear that Mr. Selznick thinks of it as *the* American home and that the Hiltons, who live in it, are supposed to be *the* Amercan family. I even suspect that Selznick, who is nothing if not ambitious, hoped to make a contemporary native equivalent to the home-front sections of *War and Peace*. What he has managed, instead, is an immense improvement on a *Ladies' Home Journal* story so sticky I couldn't get through it, which has, as he finishes it, something of the charm of an updated and cellophaned *Little Women*. *Since You Went Away* is not a good film, by any standards I care for, and I would not dare to recommend it to anyone who cares exclusively for good films. But I enjoyed it a good deal, even when I was most dissatisfied with it, and I was very much interested by it.

I always enjoy and am interested in Mr. Selznick's particular blend of serious talent with smart, safe showmanship; I am the more interested—if not more joyful—now that I suspect that his style will dominate Hollywood for the next ten years or so. What I might best do here is discuss this lively but aesthetically self-defeating, peculiar yet imitable style, which gives all but identical tone and character to such disparate films as *King Kong*, *David Copperfield*, *Gone with the Wind*, and this new, relatively realistic film. But I am still more interested in its perfect if often fortuitous appropriateness to the subject of *Since You Went Away*.

Somebody, some day, must do a *Tobacco Road* about the Hiltons, their habits and their home; they need it perhaps more than any other Americans. But until that or a still better day comes, I shall have as much respect as disrespect for Mr. Selznick's conception of them. He is not what I would call perceptive, for he is obviously, and I think disarmingly, in love with his subject. Since his subject is also in love with itself, this creative attitude has its points. So far as conscious intention and perception last, it means a fidelity to detail—of properties, costumes, voices, gestures—which the most detached of artists could not hope to improve on. When consciousness blurs into love, it means a fidelity to dream, easy enough to scorn unless you realize that the Hiltons and their kind live as much in a dream of themselves as in anything one would venture to call "reality."

Without irony, then, I accept as creatures partaking of the inevitability and superior realism of a dream Neil Hamilton as the all-American husband, Claudette Colbert as his all-American wife, Jennifer Jones as the all-American seventeen-year-old, "the new Shirley Temple"—strapped in like a child prodigy with broken ribs—as her thirteen-year-old sister, Hattie McDaniel as the ultimate colored cook, and so forth and so on, taking care not to omit the best piece of casting of all: Joseph Cotten as the forever rejected bachelor suitor who, clouding the screen with discreetly alarming threats of adulterous desire, forever comes back to Miss Colbert for more. It is thus too, in their wonderful blend of acute authenticity with authentic self-delusion, that I accept most of the things the Hiltons and their friends do, not to mention Mr. Selznick's masterpiece, the Hilton home—one of those pitiful suburban brick things which is indeed *the* American home if you agree with me that seven out of ten Americans would sell their souls for it.

It is hard to separate the conscious Hiltoniana from the semi-conscious and the unconscious. The handwritings of Mr. and Mrs. Hilton—as candid, efficient, soulless, and definitely proper to their class and country as the very best watercrests —seem a typical and laudable piece of Selznick vigilance. The Hilton furniture, quite as properly, looks as little used and unlovable as it is, presumably, much used and loved, for such homes are incurably virginal; but I wonder whether Mr. Selznick intended this. Now and then, in the effort fully to cover the home front, Selznick does the sort of pelvis-cracking split you can only get away with in a dream—or in life so actual you can hardly make fiction of it. The Hilton cook, satisfying all that anyone could possibly desire of a Negro in these restive times, not only keeps strict union hours on the job she takes when Mrs. Hilton can no longer afford her; when she is done she hustles back to the Hiltons to get in her day's measure of malapropisms, comic relief, mother wit, and free labor. I also wonder how many Mrs. Hiltons really become welders.

Mr. Selznick's attitude toward the Hiltons deprives him— like them—of any very clear psychological understanding, beyond fairly rudimentary and gracefully glossed-over stuff; yet now and then this innocence achieves remarkable things on its own. Mrs. Hilton's "Don't ever grow up," a request tenderly made of the bachelor who has spent his best years enslaved to her, is worthy of *Sentimental Education*; but I have no feeling that it was recognized as piercing and sinister, or that any irony or pity was intended when, with equal authenticity, Nazimova identified Miss Colbert with the America which she, an old, poor, working-class immigrant, had always dreamed of. I thought it just as brilliantly correct, and as clear of conscious malice, that both Hilton children were girls.

Since it seems possible that wives and children in England, and in Russia, and in China, and even, conceivably, in Germany and in Japan, are missing their men and cherishing their homes very much as we are, I don't like to see these phenomena presented as the peculiar glory of one particular country and its one true cause and justification and aim of war. But that, like much of *Since You Went Away*, is a law of dream life for which, I am afraid, neither Mr. Selznick nor anyone else can be blamed, and is so broad and deep that one's sense of reality can, at best, only hope to stay afloat in it.

August 5, 1944

L ATE as it seems, and little use as it is likely to be, and bad as in most respects it is, I am glad to see a moving picture which may help to remind a few millions of us of the people who—along with their attackers—have been involved in this war longest, most exhaustingly, and with the least help from their nominal allies. There are other things about *Dragon Seed* which I am more than glad to see in a movie. It is good to hear a man have the simplicity to tell his war-eroded wife, when she asks him whether he would have married her if she had been as she now is during their courtship, that he probably wouldn't have. It is good to hear it explained of a collaborationist that he was motivated entirely by devotion to his family. It is good to be shown, even sketchily, the mutually enriching sources of the reverence and contentment and fortitude of an old and upright man—his land, his wife, his sons, his grandchild. It is good to see this natural piety of his, and his sense of the sovereignty of the family, yield so slowly and with such pain to the imperious force of mere generalized community; and to see for the first time in a film even a little of the enormity and anguish it is for a family to destroy and to abandon its home and its farm.

It is good, too, to watch a man who feels that killing, under no matter what circumstances, is a fearful act, as thorough in its consequences in the killer as in the killed. Or to hear a young man—an ally and a patriot—who has developed a vengeful obsession for cruel killing, spoken of by his father as "the sort of man I hate and fear most." Or to see a man wonder—and doubt—whether a people which has spent years at war can ever hope, as he says, to "get back to ourselves," except possibly through the memories of peace which the old transmit to those who are too young to have endured the guilt.

Such matters aside, however, *Dragon Seed* is an almost unimaginably bad movie. Mrs. Buck persists in a questionable habit of making her Chinese peasants talk like a Bible revised by Butcher-Leaf-Lang-and-Myers. This Metro-Goldwyn-Mayer film is a limp-leather-bound, goosefleshy Golden Treasury of such talk—"the wind has brought the rain" instead of "it's raining" or just watching it fall; "you place the book where my hand cannot reach it" instead of "put that back, damn it." I wouldn't like it any better, I must grant, if the same characters talked like vaudeville laundrymen, or internationalized themselves with phrases like "by heck" or "tarnation strike me"; in fact I think that finding a diction proper to so-called simple folk is one of the most embarrassing, not to say hopeless, literary problems we have set ourselves.

MGM was up against still other problems. The California countryside they chose for location shots, Mrs. Buck is reported to have said, was a dead-ringer for parts of China before they got busy terracing it, reterracing it, and finally painting the terraces to make sure they would show. The film's backgrounds are full of the evidence of this immense, earnest, rather pathetic labor: they look about as real and as habitable as a miniature golf course, and very likely cost as much as it would have to transfer the whole company to China.

Against these unearthly, sepia-tinted landscapes, speaking their inhuman language, move such distinguished Chinese as Katharine Hepburn and Walter Huston and Aline MacMahon and Akim Tamiroff and Henry Travers and Agnes Moorehead and Turhan Bey; indeed, I've never seen another picture so full of wrong slants. Since there are plenty of genuine and good Chinese actors around Hollywood, some of whom appear as the Japanese in this film, it was entirely unnecessary for these principals to undertake their hopeless assignments, and I shan't even try to say how awful and silly they looked—Miss Hepburn especially, in her shrewdly tailored, Peck-&-Peckish pajamas— with the occasional exception of Miss MacMahon and the rather frequent exception of Mr. Huston. Both of them obviously realized that it was much more important to convey the emotions of human beings than the charade mannerisms of Little Theater Chinese. In fact I cannot think of any other non-Chinese actor simple and sincere enough to manage so finely, under such difficult circumstances, as Walter Huston has done. To mention only two more of the main things wrong with this picture, "quaint" pseudo-Chinese background-music was never more insultingly out of place. And I have never so intensely deplored the more and more stylish device of transitional narration, which here cosily, rather patronizingly, as if it were prodding those whom it talks of with its pipestem, comments upon the courage and endurance of a people—in the wheel-chair voice, if I'm not mistaken, of Dr. Gillespie.

August 19, 1944

Wilson is by no means the first film in which one might watch Hollywood hopping around on one foot, trying to put on long pants. Nor are the immense responsibilities and potentialties of moving pictures so nearly Mr. Darryl Zanuck's personal discovery, patent applied for, as he apparently feels them to be (*Intolerance*, after all, is nearly thirty years old). Yet Mr. Zanuck may be better than excused for regarding his new film as an important one, a test case. Very likely it is, not only for him but for Hollywood in general, for a long time to come. For as a hymn to internationalism, performed with all the stops pulled out, at just this time, *Wilson* becomes an extremely powerful campaigner for the Fourth Term, whether or not Mr. Zanuck so intended it. It thus undertakes more crucial and specific political responsibilities, more boldly, than any other American film to date. Still more important, from Hollywood's point of view, it represents the steepest investment, so far, in a would-be serious picture. When you count in a million dollars' exploitation costs, *Wilson* set Mr. Zanuck and the other little Foxes back about $5,200,000. No other film has ever cost so much.

If *Wilson* fails, Darryl Zanuck has promised never again to make a picture without Betty Grable. If *Wilson* fails, worse things than that may happen. It seems very possible that even any attempt at making "serious" or "idea" films of this sort might be postponed in this country for years to come. If *Wilson* succeeds, on the other hand, it is likely that we will get a lot of other pictures like it, not only because a new box-office formula will have been established but also because, I feel sure, Hollywood is as full as any other place of men of fairly good will who would gladly devote some of it to the public weal so long as no risk is involved.

If this conception of maturing and seriousness becomes generally accepted, I will be more sorry than glad. Pictures like *Wilson* have little if anything to do with mature serious cinema as such, and those who think of *Wilson* as a mature film are not in the least concerned with its liveliness or deadness as a work of art; they are excited because serious ideas are being used on the screen. Something well worth excitement, I'll grant; but how much? None of the ideas used in *Wilson* is expressed in any better than primer fashion. Anyone who cares to can still get twice as much out of a newspaper and a dozen times as much out of even a mediocre book, so far as ideas are concerned. Perhaps this is a moment to be generous, as if toward a child who stumbles over unexpectedly big words; but that kind of contempt is peculiar to those who hate movies and think they like them, and is unavailable to those who love movies and are thought to loathe them. Furthermore, I believe that political ideas at their most mature and serious are still childish and frivolous as compared with those ideas or conceptions which attempt to work in, to perceive, and to illuminate, the bottoms of the souls of human beings. If political issues and a reverence for fact on the journalistic (or even the historical) level become a popular criterion for seriousness and maturity in films, the proper study of mankind is likely to be deferred even longer than by the present prospects. On the other hand, if great audiences, and those who fearfully try to give them what they want, get used to the idea that thinking and entertainment are by no means autonomous, this postponement-period may serve both ends, valuably, as a period of transition and training.

The whole business makes me a little tired when I reflect that it is 99 per cent waste motion—that a dozen really good, really mature films, each made on a B-budget or less, would be more likely to do overnight what in this way won't happen with any firmness in twenty years. But the distinguishing faculty of the realist in his preference for the longest distance between two points—a preference which becomes virtually beatitude if the second point is never reached. As a realist, then, I hope that *Wilson* grosses ten million dollars and that no matter how disastrously misleading the whole process may be, the studios will spend the next few years tearing each other's throats out over political and social issues. Seriousness and courage on a political level are infinitely preferable, heaven knows, to no seriousness and courage at all.

I have left myself very little space in which to talk about *Wilson* in detail; but perhaps that is just as well. It is essentially a very sincere and even a brave picture, and I am bound to salute even an attempt to help prevent a third world war, and to wish it well. One might at great length talk about its virtues —for on its own level, and in so far as its tight intersection of anxious showmanship, conventional talent, and journalistic conscience allows it, it has a great many more virtues than faults, and is a big, splendid, competent, resourceful show. One might at even greater length, and still with no lack of basic sympathy, analyze its extremely characteristic fits and starts down to the least evidence of the effort to give it all that money can buy and that honest research can edge it with: for in every grand effect and little mannerism it is both fascinating and instructive. They copied the cracks in the paint in the original portraits of Presidents in the White House; but they were unable to learn anything whatever of primary value from their study of 160,000 feet of relevant newsreel.

But here again, I am just as glad to shirk my duty. No matter how friendly I feel toward *Wilson* and the people who made it, any such review would amount chiefly to a specification of occupational psychosis. With the best intentions in the world, Hollywood took a character and a theme of almost Shakespearian complexity and grandeur, and reduced the character to an astutely played liberal assistant professor of economics; the theme to a few generalizations which every schoolboy has half-forgotten; the millennial, piteous surge of hope and faith which bore Wilson to Paris, to nothing at all; the colossal struggles between Wilson and Clemenceau and Senator Lodge, to one firmly written tizzy and one softly written one; Wilson's terrifying, possessed trip around the United States, to a set of pretty Thomas-Wolfean train-montages, culminating in the unprepared breakdown of a good insurance risk; the American people, to a passive murmurous backdrop; and an extraordinarily grandiose prospect of powerful and original cinema, to a high-grade sort of magazine illustration. Every major problem, opportunity, and responsibility which the picture set its makers was, in other words, flunked—now through timidity, again through habitual half-blindness, and most of all perhaps through the desire to sell and ingratiate and essentially to render a two-and-a-half-hour apology for one sustained impulse of daring and disinterestedness.

If *Wilson* fails, I believe it will be because Mr. Zanuck and his associates were not up to their subject. For I am quite sure that the tremendous audiences which may or may not accept it as it stands would have been found more than ready for the same story, maturely told.

September 9, 1944

Nunnally Johnson has turned the old Floyd Dell–Thomas Mitchell farce *Little Accident* into *Casanova Brown*, a large slice of brisket for Gary Cooper. Mr. Cooper's role breaks into four parts for which he is peculiarly well qualified —or perhaps typed is the word. For the first few reels, very much worried, he talks to Frank Morgan as he might if the Hays office would allow him to pretend to be a young man who, a few hours before his wedding, is informed that he is the father of an illegitimate child. Then in flashback, very much embarrassed, he calls on his parents-in-law with his bride, Teresa Wright, and, by accident, burns their house down. Next, he is so farcically manhandled in a lying-in hospital that he all but loses certainty which sex he is. Last, extremely Cooperish, he kidnaps his baby (and Miss Wright's) and earnestly, laboriously takes care of it. How these tableaux of masculinity at bay fit together and are motivated is not important enough to go into; neither, perhaps, is the film itself. But like most of Johnson's screen plays it is reasonably and at times more than reasonably amusing. It is also the first production of International

Pictures, a new "independent" corporation for which both Cooper and Johnson will produce from now on. I put independent in quotes without vindictiveness or deep sorrow, merely to indicate that, judging by *Casanova Brown*, nothing independent in any very interesting sense is likely to come from the new studio. It's just Hollywood with its stays a little loosened; but even that is better than nothing, and far better than the bad serious stuff which independent producers sometimes attempt.

That is more than one can say for *The Seventh Cross*; Metro-Goldwyn-Mayer has used it, with every good intention I am sure, to crucify the possibilities of a very fine movie. Spencer Tracy is a sincere actor and in many respects a good one, but he is hopelessly ill-qualified to suggest a German anti-fascist who has escaped from a concentration camp; very little else in the film helps out, either. In almost every respect, in fact, the picture is an ultra-typical MGM "major" production; it is perhaps unnecessary to add that that style is fatal to any sort of film except the purest low-ceilinged romance. Hume Cronyn, Steve Geray, and Agnes Moorehead do manage to cut a few glints of living acid through all the glossy lard, and one street shot of coarse legs in black cotton stockings, walking with casual peculiarity, has a suddenness, sadness, and individuality which should have taught those who made this film how to create and photograph a city. One has to wonder, instead, how on earth it got into so conventional a show.

The Impatient Years made me very impatient indeed. The difficulties of a discharged soldier and the wife whom he had known, before he went off to war, for only four days, could have become a first-rate film. So long as the script allows them to stay within hailing distance of that idea, Jean Arthur and Lee Bowman and Charles Coburn make a semi-bearable third-rate comedy of it.

Hail the Conquering Hero, of course, is pretty nearly the only film of the year worth talking about. I hope to try, next week.

September 23, 1944

Hail the Conquering Hero is the story of a pitiful discard from the Marines (Eddie Bracken) who, helped and forced by a group of marines just back from Guadalcanal, returns as a false hero to his mother and his girl and his home town just before a local election, is put up for mayor against his guilty will, endures a day of comic-satiric hell which includes three extraordinary civic speeches, and at length, in an awful public confession, makes a genuine hero of himself. It is a bewilderingly skilful picture, and the skill is used no more brilliantly to tell the story than to cover up the story's weaknesses and those of its author, Preston Sturges.

If the story is to tell itself at all, and keep going to feature length, everything depends on the marines who befriend and bully Mr. Bracken into it. But Sturges never lets you know why they are forcing their victim through the show. What Sturges does instead, though, is both interesting and highly characteristic of him. Getting Bracken home in the first place forces him to invent one of his most arresting characters, a psychopathic marine, embodied by the ex-boxer Freddie Steele with a legendary, almost supernatural quality of serene, unfathomable, frightening energy. This marine happens to feel a maniacal reverence toward mothers, and shocked into fury by the hero's neglect of his own mother, he sets everything moving. Once they are all in the small town and the young man is desperately eager to clear up the misunderstanding, Sturges shifts the weight to a marine sergeant played by William Demarest, whose great skill in registering a kind of daft innocence and brutal sentimentality, helped by Sturges, can make you believe anything.

Here, however, you hardly know what to believe, for Sturges takes care never to give Demarest time for more than a hint and a laugh. Unless we are to believe that the sergeant is simply so maddened by all the homely excitement that he refuses to let either himself or Bracken jump off the merry-go-round, his motives would have to be of Dostoevskian cruelty and mysteriousness to hold water at all; but of this possibility the hints are so vague that I suspect myself of supplying them. The long and the short of it is that the more you think of the evidence supplied you the less you understand why the marines are

there, and why you ever believed it at all. The trick here, a favorite one with Sturges, is to keep everything so jotted, so
shrewdly and ambiguously shaded, so rapid, and so briskly full
of irrelevant pleasures, that you neither think nor care to, at
all. Flickers of motive, most of them faked or questionable,
succeed each other so restively that like the successive frames
of a strip of film they create an illusory flowing image of
motive which one is liable to swallow whole at the time. But in
thoroughly good pieces of work there is an aesthetic and moral
discipline which, however richly it indulges in certain kinds of
illusion, strictly forbids itself others. It never fakes or dodges a
motive, a character, an emotion, or an idea. And it never uses
its power to entertain as an ace-in-the-hole against one's objection to that sort of faking.

I'd like not to be so owlish about a picture which gave me so
much more delight than displeasure, but now that Sturges is
being compared, I am told, with people like Voltaire—there
are semi-defensible reasons to compare him with Shakespeare,
for that matter—I think there is some point in putting on the
brakes. Most certainly Sturges has fine comic and satiric gifts,
and knows how to tell more truth than that when he thinks it
expedient; but he seldom does. This film has enough themes
for half a dozen first-rate American satires—the crippling myth
of the dead heroic father, the gentle tyranny of the widowed
mother, the predicament of the only child, the questionable
nature of most heroism, the political function of returning soldiers, these are just a few; I suppose in a sense the whole story
is a sort of *Coriolanus* on all fours. But not one of these themes
is honored by more attention than you get from an inconti-
nent barber in a railway terminal, and the main theme, which I
take to be a study of honor, is dishonored by every nightingale
in Sturges's belfry. When Bracken makes his strongly written,
beautifully spoken confession, his fellow-townsmen, persuaded
by the sergeant and their own best citizen, promptly make him
mayor. This is doubtless supposed to pass as irony, since the
townspeople and by implication the general audience, not to
say the American voting public, are represented as incurable
jackasses. But jackasses or not, people in small towns don't
reward virtue in any such way; so I'm sorry to see them rewarding Mr. Sturges.

The small-town types themselves, by the way, smartly cast and dressed and detailed and edited as they are, are very little nearer genuine small-town than Broadway is. The Mayor is so well played by Raymond Walburn that it is impossible to take him simply as a meaningful figure of satire. The hero's girl (Ella Raines), after some well and cruelly drawn phases of mixed motive, comes through solid gold when he is at his nadir. The two bits which best survive all of Sturges's deviousness are a paralyzingly high-charged, many-sided moment in which Bracken hits the psychopath, and Franklin Pangborn's unemphasized, terribly sad, and revealing shifts of face as he reflects Bracken's confession in the depths of the character he plays. Sturges is by far the smartest man for casting in Hollywood; this use of Pangborn, an extremely fine actor, is the one thing that improves on his role in *The Bank Dick*.

Any adequate review of this remarkable movie would devote at least as much space to its unqualified praise as I have to qualifying the praise; it would have to spend more space than that, I think, getting at even a tentative explanation of why Sturges functions as he does. "Hollywood" is no explanation, surely; "Hollywood" was made for Sturges and he in turn is its apotheosis; but why? It seems to me that Sturges had reason, through his mother, to develop, as they caromed around high-Bohemian Europe during his childhood, from opera to opera and gallery to gallery, not only his singular mercurialism and resourcefulness, which come especially natural to some miserably unhappy children, but also a retching, permanently incurable loathing for everything that stank of "culture," of "art." I gather further that through his stepfather, a stable and charming Chicago sportsman and business man, he developed an all but desperate respect and hunger for success, enhanced by a sickening string of failures as a business man and inventor up to the age of about thirty; and that this again assumed the dimensions of a complex. I believe that in his curious career as a never-quite-artist of not-quite-genius he has managed to release and guide the energies of these influences in the only way open to him.

I hesitate to write this sort of thing, drawn only from such superficialities as have appeared in print and from some remarkable photographs of Sturges as a child and young man which appeared in the *Saturday Evening Post*; but I risk the worse than questionable taste because I see no other way to understand what Sturges's films are about. They are wonderful as comedies and they are wonderfully complex and ingenious; they seem to me also wonderfully, uncontrollably, almost proudly corrupt, vengeful, fearful of intactness and self-commitment; most essentially, they are paradoxical marvels of self-perpetuation and self-destruction; their mastering object, aside from success, seems to be to sail as steep into the wind as possible without for an instant incurring the disaster of becoming seriously, wholly acceptable as art. They seem to me, indeed, in much of their twisting, the elaborately counterpointed image of a neurosis. It is an especially interesting neurosis, not only because Sturges is a man of such talent and not only because it expresses itself in such fecund and in themselves suggestive images, but also because, in relation to art, it seems the definitive expression of this country at present—the stranglehold wedlock of the American female tradition of "culture," the male tradition of "success."

For East is East, and West is West, and Maggie and I are out.

September 30, 1944

It is a tremendous pleasure to see something done in American movies which you can be proud of—however foolish and suspect that sort of pride may be. I feel pride in and respect for everyone, from start to finish, who was involved in the shooting, cutting, writing, and speaking of the Marine Corps' and Warner Brothers' *The Battle for the Marianas*; I feel all the better because, coming after *Tarawa*, *Memphis Belle*, and *Attack*, the picture so clearly proves that fine honest work can become a habit, and is not necessarily a result of the bitter attempt and the frustrated desire of scattered individuals. Key individuals, unquestionably, are in the long run responsible for the excellence of these films, and some of the most important of them, very likely, are not movie men at all but simply executives whose taste and decency and good sense make it possible. Such men are of course quite as indispensable as good craftsmen and good artists; I wish one might know their names and might thank them, both publicly and privately. *The Marianas* does not seem to me to have quite the clarity of force of *Tarawa*; and by now, inevitably, even a civilian watching combat films from a theater chair begins to feel some pinhead fraction of the fatigue which transforms soldiers. But I would recommend this picture highly if that were all I could say for it; and I could say a great deal more if there were room.

It is quite as great a pleasure, and a much more startling one, to see such a film as *Youth Runs Wild* coming out of a Hollywood studio—a far better piece of news than films like the much more resourceful, polished, and entertaining *Hail the Conquering Hero*. Not even its faults are the Hollywood kind: it is gawky, diffuse, rather boyscoutish in its social attitudes (but it does have attitudes); often as not its characters go wooden (but they never turn into ivory-soap sculpture); too often the photography goes velvety (but always in earnestly striving for a real, not a false, atmosphere, and never striving for a sumptuous look). When the picture is good—and its over-all inadequacy flashes with good all through—you are seeing pretty nearly the only writing and acting and directing and photography in Hollywood which is at all concerned with what happens inside real and particular people among real and particular objects—not with how a generalized face can suggest a generalized emotion in a generalized light. As pleasing to watch as what these people do, both in front of and behind the camera, is the clearly very simple, earnest, and honorable attitude which they have toward their work. To watch most of them, you would hardly think they had ever heard of Hollywood, much less wanted to go there. For a fuller and more specific appraisal of *Youth Runs Wild* and its producer, Val Lewton, I can only recommend that you read Manny Farber's review in a recent issue of the *New Republic*; it would be senseless for me merely to repeat, in other words, what I so thoroughly agree with. Mr. Lewton may well run into hard times with his work if he develops much of a reputation, either popular or critical. So it is with mixed feelings that I realize, and write, that all over the country he must already have the respect and the hopeful wishes of everyone who cares two cents for what a moving picture is.

October 14, 1944

IF YOU laid *Double Indemnity* and *Frenchman's Creek* end to end you might still prefer to spend the evening with *Madame Bovary*; yet you might find a few things mildly worth examining in these two so different, so similar reflections of current attitudes toward bourgeois adultery. The James Cain story, under Billy Wilder's control, is to a fair extent soaked in and shot through with money and the coolly intricate amorality of money; you can even supply the idea, without being contradicted by the film, that among these somewhat representative Americans money and sex and a readiness to murder are as inseparably interdependent as the Holy Trinity. Wilder also has a real feeling, on a not-quite-real, smart level, for the streets and suffocating marriage hutches and calm-lighted Piggly Wigglies and heartlessly resonant offices of his city, and I agree that his casting of Fred MacMurray and Barbara Stanwyck and Edward G. Robinson is perceptive. But not that it is wholly successful.

Indeed, the picture never fully takes hold of its opportunities, such as they are, perhaps because those opportunities are appreciated chiefly as surfaces and atmospheres and as very tellable trash. It is proper enough, for instance, that Barbara Stanwyck should suggest a greatly coarsened *Esquire* drawing and that her affair with MacMurray should essentially be as sexless as it is loveless. Her icy hair and teeth and dresses are well worked out toward communicating this idea. But in Wilder's apparent desire to make it clear that nympholepts are cold he has neglected to bring to life the sort of freezing rage of excitations which such a woman presumably inspires in such a fixer as Walter Neff; this sort of genre love-scene ought to smell like the inside of an overwrought Electrolux. Wilder has not made much, either, of the tensions of the separateness of the lovers after the murder, or of the coldly nauseated despair and nostalgia which the murderer would feel.

In many ways *Double Indemnity* is really quite a gratifying and even a good movie, essentially cheap I will grant, but smart and crisp and cruel like a whole type of American film which developed softening of the brain after the early thirties. But if at the same time you are watching for all that could have been got out of it, you cannot help being disappointed as well as pleased.

The Cain story is trash at best; at its worst it is highly respectable, set beside Daphne du Maurier's little bathroom classic, *Frenchman's Creek*. I have always thought—not very originally, I imagine—that the essence of Madame Bovary and her millions of great-granddaughters is masturbation, literal as often as figurative. This film, like the "novel" it improves on, is masturbation-fantasy triple-distilled, infallible as any real-life dream and as viciously fascinating as reading such a dream over the terrible dreamer's shoulder.

The shoulder of the actual dreamer, here, and of the audience, is unmistakably that of a suburban fat-mama. But on the screen there is magically no such thing: she is an English noblewoman of the Restoration, and lovely to look at, at that. Her husband is no sacksuited dollar-chaser but a London fop. Her country refuge is not some little place in Connecticut; it is a whackingly beautiful mansion on the Cornish coast. Her lover, a local pirate who loves life and lives it as he likes, is more of a composite. With his accent, his gently insolent bearing, and his knowledgeable eyes, he is that sort of European who panics sensitive young matrons by observing that your "Amarican men, sharming and antoozieyestic as they are, know noddinx oof lahv"—or, as usefully, by sad-eyed muting of reference to his experience in concentration camps he never saw; at the same time he is easily recognizable as the sort of tousleheaded, briar-sucking commercial artist who fancies himself as a second Gauguin on Sundays, who has gone hermit at $20,000 a year, and who threatens every smug harbor on both shores of Long Island Sound with his trim little launch. None of the unusually resourceful Technicolor, wax-fruit dialogue, or munificence of costume and social degree conceals the fact that this is really just an archetypally sordid, contemporary middle-bracket flirtation, told without perception, warmth, honor, or irony from the center of a soul like a powder-parlor—but told, in those terms, with the gloves off, and every cowardly emotion and creepy desire and sniveling motive caught red-handed.

As the life of this party Joan Fontaine has a prettiness and vivacity which I had not suspected of her. She also develops, in place of any believable semblance of erotic or emotional passion, a sort of excitement which I find appropriate to the story, and revealing of its audience beyond cavil. As she conducts her discreet little coastal cruise along the coves and peninsulas of adultery, she never once suggests a woman in love or even in confusion; but she does constantly suggest a Vassar girl on a picket line.

November 4, 1944

To ANYONE who has noticed, except with relief, the recent absence of this column, I want to apologize. I am sorry, too, that it will take me a couple of weeks to catch up. There ought to be some special tense for this warmed-over sort of re-viewing; I can think, instead, only of a rough emotional equiva-lent: how much I wish I could have made a screen biography of Thomas E. Dewey, with Raymond Walburn in the title role.

Well, let me, like the Young Pretender, seize opportunity by the crupper. Of the movies I have seen lately the one I like best was *To Have and Have Not.* It has so little to do with Ernest Hemingway's novel that I see no point in discussing its "faith-fulness"; it is, rather, a sort of call-house version of *Going My Way.* It is not, I scuttle to explain, an upstairs story about priests. But like the better film it gets along on a mere thin ex-cuse for a story, takes its time without trying to brag about its budget or to reel up footage for footage's sake, is an unusually happy exhibition of teamwork, and concentrates on character and atmosphere rather than plot. The best of the picture has no plot at all, but is a leisurely series of mating duels between Humphrey Bogart at his most proficient and the very enter-taining, nervy, adolescent new blonde, Lauren Bacall. Whether or not you like the film will depend I believe almost entirely on whether you like Miss Bacall. I am no judge. I can hardly look at her, much less listen to her—she has a voice like a chorus by Kid Ory—without getting caught in a dilemma between a low whistle and a bellylaugh. It has been years since I have seen such amusing pseudo-toughness on the screen. About all that Howard Hawkes and his writers (William Faulkner and Jules Furthman) and Bogart try to do is to set this arrogant neophyte off to the best possible advantage, to cover up her weaknesses —or turn them into assets—and to toss campstools under her whenever she wobbles. This in itself is a pleasure to watch; so is the way she rewards them; still more, I enjoyed watching something that obviously involved relaxed, improvising fun for those who worked on it, instead of the customary tight-lipped and hammer-hearted professional anxiety. I also enjoyed Hoagy Carmichael and his tunes, and the picture's general romantic, kidding appreciation of honky-tonk. The best of it had for me at least a little of the nostalgia of highballs that taste like rotten mahogany, defective mechanical pianos at implacable fortissimo, or gents-rooms strangled with the fragrance of mentholated raspberries. This sort of slumgullion is, I must grant, fully as specious as stuff like *The White Cliffs of Dover* and perhaps even more reprehensible, since—I flatter myself—it seduces a better class of people. I still have a weakness for it, and cannot recommend *To Have and Have Not* to anyone who hasn't.

For *Thunder Rock*, a much more high-minded movie, I can't say as much. It is well produced and on the whole very well acted, especially by Barbara Mullen; there were moments when it really moved me; and it is not only on the side of the angels but sometimes takes their side with passion and some eloquence. But angels bore me at least as much as anyone else when they arrange themselves so little theatrically: in a lighthouse, from dusk to dawn, the ghosts of some defeated nineteenth-century prometheans reenact their struggles before an embittered young man of our time, and persuade him that the world is worth fighting to save whether it likes it or not. I was glad of some outspoken virulence against some of the people —those, next to the Nazis, most often blamed—who did most to get the world into this war, until I reflected that even when it was written, around 1940, it came late enough to be safe. To find oneself, and others, approving this sort of intrepid *esprit d'escalier* is not only shaming but frightening. Such self-congratulatory, horribly late approval anaesthetizes us against an awareness of matters which, ten years from now, will become the material for bold, bitter, instructive pieces of surefire hindsight like *Thunder Rock*.

San Diego I Love You is a coarse-weft, easygoing little farce about an inventor (Edward Everett Horton), his daughter (Louise Albritton), a girl-shy financier (Jon Hall), and some pleasant comics (notably Buster Keaton). I can't exactly recommend it, but if you see it by accident it will cause no particular pain. *Bride by Mistake* is more nearly a comedy of manners, I suppose (the heiress who wants to be sure she is loved for herself alone, etc.); its lines and characters are often almost human, and I thought that Laraine Day, whom I have not seen play comedy before, was attractive both in person and performance. I would like to see what Ernst Lubitsch could do for her. I rather liked *1812*, a Russian film, when I saw it. Thinking it over, it reduces to a few flamboyant military shots, a lot of Moscow-Arty close-ups, and a good deal too much smell of studio. *Tall in the Saddle* is a medium-silly Western, done, however, as if those who made it knew that, and were getting and giving what mild pleasure they could out of the knowledge. *Dangerous Journey*, an Armand Denis travel film, offers a script so inexpressibly smug and jeering that even a caption writer for the *National Geographic* would choke over it; one terrifying sequence in which a Burmese priestess and a king cobra carry on a dancelike dialogue about fertility; a scattering of other interesting shots, some of them lifted from *Dark Rapture* and most of them lamely put together; and a very gratifying one in which some sixty savage canoeists, paddling like mad, founder themselves, their craft, and Mr. Denis.

November 18, 1944

THE NEW Russian film, *The Rainbow*, is a ferocious anthology of the atrocities perpetrated by German soldiers upon the women and children and babies and old men of an occupied Ukrainian village. It is fiction, derived from a prize-winning novel which I would infer to be monstrously trashy and teacher's-petty, and it is done on the whole with a good deal less than the customary Russian ability to make screen fiction look at least as true as fact. Yet its maniacal quality—not to mention the bulk of its subject matter—is of itself bullyingly persuasive; still more so is one's realization that crimes at least as terrible have been a commonplace in the war in Russia and elsewhere. I have endured none of these things, but it is easy for me to realize that others who have and still others who haven't may be strongly moved by them, in the way the makers of the picture intended to move them. I, however, am still more strongly moved by other considerations.

I wonder whether one has any business making or accepting a film about war or cruelty or brutality unless some sort of attempt is made, in the film, to understand them. I wonder whether certain dreadful events, of the sort this picture is full of, are not so incalculably rich in the possibilities of moral and aesthetic blackmail that they can never be represented maturely or even undeceitfully, and so had better not be represented at all. I wonder, too, at the reception of the film here. The reactions of the audience at the Stanley were as cheerfully bestial as they might be if that audience had, through similar experience, earned some semblance of right to them; and so far as I have seen or heard, only one reviewer, Manny Farber, has stood up against the perniciousness of the movie. It is the utter simplicity of feeling, among those who approve *The Rainbow*, which is particularly disturbing. The picture presents data which, backed by one's knowledge of fact, make it hard to keep one eye open; but if there are so few people who can even try to, who can so much as doubt the full validity of their approval of the film, in a relatively untouched country where it is popularly supposed to be easiest on earth to keep and cultivate and utter the freedom of one's mind and conscience, that suggests to me a deeper disaster than all other disasters of war and peace combined.

I am curious, for that matter, why this picture was made in Russia, and for Russians (it seems understandable enough as a foreign editorial). It seems possible that with the shift toward certain victory, after terrible danger and loss and ferocity and suffering, a general reaction may have set in among the Russian people in thousands of liberated towns which has tended to make them sick of hatred and vengeance and incapable of it; and that this film is to be understood less as a spontaneous outburst of rage and loathing than as a carefully deliberated effort to combat war weariness and the restoration of any semblance of moral tenderness and skepticism. Whatever the motives or sentiments of those who made the film, it seems to me as unadulterated and violent a piece of agit-prop as I have ever seen, and whether you approve or deplore it depends chiefly, I think, on how you feel about agit-prop.

I have no doubt about my own feelings; it is my idea of anathema. I do believe, to be sure, that a kind of propaganda is possible whose constant effort is to clarify rather than merely simplify, not to say falsify or exploit, issues and motives and causes and needs; to forge, in Joyce's words, the uncreated conscience of the race. But I am afraid the believers in agit-prop will dismiss that sort of propaganda, scornfully, as mere art; and I am afraid they are right. In any case there is not one ounce of such effort in *The Rainbow*. Indeed, few films ever made have so vigorously seized the spectator by the throat and so implacably insisted, with one unprincipled bang over the head after another, that he turn himself into the wildest animal possible, and mistrust and hate with all his might any lingering question which troubles him about his obligation to do so. It is more than understandable that such a film should come out of the sort of war that has been fought in Russia; but that does not mean that the film is fit for human consumption. For all its studio artificiality and its still more essential falseness it seems, rather, almost of a piece with war itself. Like war it is bursting with energy, with passion, and with skill of itself both good and bad, but hardly a foot of it so much as suspects the most elementary, most indispensable obligation of the true artist, or of anyone, for that matter, who seriously desires to walk on his hind feet: to try, under whatever confusion of pressures, to understand and illuminate and conduct oneself in accordance with the truth, in so far as one experiences it.

All of the passion and resource of this film are used systematically, according to the most blunt and amoral means available, to demolish one's moral and aesthetic judgment by splitting both and by turning the split forces of both against each other. When, for just one instant, a woman, rather than betray her comrades and her country, suffers her newborn baby to be shot before her eyes, she has committed a tremendous act, and it is one which of itself all but annihilates one's feeling of the right, not to say the invincible, obligation to keep one's senses. But the fact remains that whatever she did or did not do in that predicament, she would have presented, not solved, a terrible moral problem. But everything is solved in this film; every most important thing may be incalculably hard to do right by, but the right itself is easy.

When you can make such a picture, or watch it with untroubled approval, some crucially important moral nerve has, I believe, gone dead in you. Temporarily, perhaps incurably, you have been rendered helpless in the most disastrous way I can conceive of. There are frightening, flagrant symptoms of such a death in this film, as in its general American reception. In the film God—in Whom I very much doubt that the makers of the film believe—is represented as available only to Russian patriots, not to cowards or traitors and not to Germans. It is explained of the enemy that "they are Germans and that is why they kill." The idea of postwar justice is summed up in a woman's speech about German prisoners: after they have watched their armies starved and beaten, their cities destroyed, their wives and children recoil from them, and after they "answer for their crimes before a People's Court—then, a quick death." When you are capable of regarding God as a party member in good standing; of agreeing with the National Socialists that various tendencies or actions are explicable in terms of race or nation and that all members in that race or nation are infected with those tendencies and are liable to those actions; of stating, in the same breath, that the enemy should stand trial and then should and shall be annihilated; it seems merely inevitable that you will have lost, as well, even the simplest sort of eye for faces. The woman who delivers this closing oration about justice is presented virtually as the embodiment of her people, and strikes me as one of the most coldly and irremediably horrifying human beings I have ever laid eyes on. It is a complex face, and I will not attempt an analysis of it or of my reactions, but I can give a rough idea of the latter by suggesting that the substitution of King Kong would have left me with a far better opinion of the judgment of the makers of the film, and a far happier hope for the future, if the innocent and whole-hearted approval of such a work is any kind of measure of the present. But then Kong, I must grant, is one of the few reasonably human movie heroes I can remember.

O<small>F THE</small> new films, *None but the Lonely Heart* most respectably bids for appreciation, general courtesy, and even enthusiasm; but on the whole I preferred *Meet Me in St Louis*. Most of its rather pretty new and old tunes are sung in an up-to-date chromium-and-glucose style which bitterly imposes on one's ability to believe that the year is 1903; and most of its sets and costumes and colors and characters are too perfectly waxen to belong to that or any other year. Indeed, this habit of sumptuous idealization seriously reduces the value even of the few scenes on which I chiefly base my liking for the picture; but at the same time, and for that matter nearly all the time, it gives you, for once, something most unusually pretty to watch. I can't remember ever having seen studio-sealed Technicolor better used, and would like particularly to mention three shots: one in which a mother and four daughters, all in festal, cake-frosting white, stroll across their lawn in spring sunlight, so properly photographed that the dresses all but become halations; one of a fine black horse and buggy in a brisk and resonant autumn night—an atmosphere you can all but get the temperature and cider fragrance and staidly sporty erotic tension of; and one of Halloween, which I will speak of later.

I liked the general intention of the movie: to let its tunes and other musical-comedy aspects come as they may, and to concentrate rather on making the well-heeled middle-class life of some adolescent and little girls in St. Louis seem so beautiful that you can share their anguish when they are doomed to move to New York. I must confess I could have liked it much better still. For by a process of elementary reasoning on which I hold no patent and which, indeed, I would be only too happy to see appropriated by people in a better position to make use of it, I am persuaded that this very good because very real idea might have been adequately served only in proportion as the girls, and the visual and emotional climate they move in and are supposed to love, themselves approached and honored rather than flouted and improved on reality. The one member of the cast who proved my childishly blunt point by turning it, over and over again, into a heart-piercing sword was the incredibly vivid and eloquent Margaret O'Brien; many

of her possibilities and glints of her achievement hypnotize me
as thoroughly as anything since Garbo.

What she is playing here is still, as usual, safely glossed and
thinned and sweetened; but someone has surrounded her with
an air of generosity and ease and perception in which she does
some of her most satisfying work so far. (I imagine it may be
the director, Vincente Minelli, especially if he is also responsible for a kind of graciousness and sense of joy in many of the
shots, and sometimes in their succession, which seem to me
Italian.) Her merely cute acts, like her song and her cakewalk,
or her pleasure when she sits high beside a carriage driver,
manage to mix stock cuteness with enchantment and with accurate psychology; the scene in which she is lugged in with her
lip cut, screaming half-lies and gibberish, is about the most impressive and complex job of crying I have ever seen put on. I
can hardly wait for her to be old enough to take on Hedwig's
fearful jag in *The Wild Duck*—and can less than bear to realize
what miraculous things she will almost certainly never get the
chance to do between now and then.

Her annihilation of the snowmen she can't take to New
York would have been terrifying if only she had had adequate
support from the snowmen and if only the camera could have
had the right to dare to move in close. Being only the well-
meant best that adult professionals could design out of corn-
flakes or pulverized mothballs or heroin or whatever they are
making snow out of just now, these statues were embarrassingly handicapped from their birth, and couldn't even reach
you deeply by falling apart. Her walk on Halloween, away from
the bonfire into the deepening dark of the street, her fear and
excitement intensifying as she approaches her destination (the
insulting of the most frightening man in the neighborhood)
and follows the camera (which withdraws a few feet ahead of
her in a long soft curve) are a piece of acting, of lovely, simple
camera movement, and of color control which combined,
while they lasted, to make my hair stand on end. If the rest of
the picture's autumn section, which is by far its best, had lived
up to the best things about that shot, and if the rest of the
show, for all its prettiness, had been scrapped, *Meet Me in
St. Louis* would have been, of all things on earth it can never
have intended to be, a great moving picture—the first to be

made in this country, so far as I can remember, since *Modern Times.*

Of Clifford Odets's first job of directing, *None but the Lonely Heart,* I have left myself room to say only that it is worth seeing. So is *Mademoiselle Fifi,* a Val Lewton production. I hope to review both films next week.

December 2, 1944

*N*one but the Lonely Heart, a story about the education of a young man in London's prewar slums, is an unusually sincere, almost-good film and was made under unusually unexpected auspices. Its star, Cary Grant, asked that it be made, and plays its far from Cary Grantish hero so attentively and sympathetically that I all but overlooked the fact that he is not well constituted for the role. Its most notable player, Ethel Barrymore, seemed miscast too, but I was so soft as to be far more than satisfied by her beauty and authority. Its director, Clifford Odets, who also turned Richard Llewellyn's novel into the screen play, is still liable to write—or preserve from the book—excessive lines like "dreaming the better man"; he suggests his stage background as well as his talent by packaging his bits too neatly; and his feeling for light, shade, sound, perspective, and business is too luscious for my taste. But I believe that even if he doesn't get rid of such faults he will become a good director. I base my confidence in him chiefly on the genuine things about his faith in and love for people, which are as urgent and evident here as his sentimentalities; on two very pretty moments in the film, one of two drunken men playing with their echoes under an arch, the other of two little girls all but suffocated by their shy adoration of the hero; and on the curiously rich, pitiful, fascinating person, blended of Cockney and the Bronx, whom he makes of a London girl, with the sensitive help of June Duprez. I suppose I should be equally impressed by the fact that the picture all but comes right out and says that it is a bad world which can permit poor people to be poor; but I was impressed rather because Odets was more interested in filling his people with life and grace than in explaining them, arguing over them, or using them as boxing-gloves.

While big-timers with big money were creditably risking it on *None but the Lonely Heart*, small-timers with small money, in the same studio, were squeezing it into *Mademoiselle Fifi*, which is quite skilfully combined with *Boule de Suif*. I could not wish Producer Val Lewton and Director Robert Wise and their associates much more money to work with, because it seems to me that a small budget has on the whole sharpened their resourcefulness and the general quality of all the films Lewton supervises. But I certainly could wish them more money in terms of more time to get things done as they want them.

Too much of *Fifi* is clearly just the best that could be half-translated from a well-edged script in a pathetic race against schedule; and now and then its poverty results in makeshift of a rather stagy, or even musty, sort rather than in bringing out the bones in its face. It seems possible, too, that some of the picture's inadequacies are inadequacies of depth and keenness of talent rather than of time and money; none of its characters, from the script on out, ever fully identify themselves as characters on a screen rather than in print or on a stage. Yet it has many good and near-good moments, as pure movie; and I don't know of any American film which has tried to say as much, as pointedly, about the performance of the middle class in war. There is a gallant, fervent quality about the whole picture, faults and all, which gives it a peculiar kind of life and likeableness, and which signifies that there is one group of men working in Hollywood who have neither lost nor taken care to conceal the purity of their hope and intention.

30 Seconds over Tokyo is in some respects the pleasantest of current surprises: a big-studio, big-scale film, free of artistic pretension, it is transformed by its not very imaginative but very dogged sincerity into something forceful, simple, and thoroughly sympathetic in spite of all its big-studio, big-scale habits. Its characters are hardest to take when they are most intimately in character, though even then they are played with a straightforwardness you don't normally expect of marquee names. The flying sequences, especially one long fluid stretch of low flight from the carrier's deck to Tokyo, backgrounded as in Dovzhenko's great *Frontier* only by the calmly sublime roar of engines, are really well made, powerful, and exciting.

The Chinese, nearly all of them amateur, are the best thing in the picture and the best Chinese in any American picture: I can only hope they make a great many people in Hollywood aware of the tremendous advantages of using non-actors in films, which are quite as great as those of "getting outdoors," even for interiors, as against the careful reconstruction of all outdoors inside a studio. There are also some shots facing, even emphasizing, the ugliness, humiliation, and pity of losing a leg, which are precisely the honest sort one had learned never to expect in American war films.

December 9, 1944

The Very Thought of You, a story about the wives of absent soldiers, entangles some sincerity and even insight, and some pretty good family quarrels, and some straight acting in so much wincing embarrassment of over-stylized talk and of rubbing the audience's nose in emotions that it is hardly if at all worth seeing. *Dark Waters* is a thriller about a young woman, convalescent from shock, who suffers among cryptic surroundings and ambiguous people on a swampy Louisiana sugar plantation. It has many—perhaps too many is one trouble—of the elements of a good fright-picture, but most of the time they either get in each other's way or suggest their possibilities without achieving them. *Together Again* is a comedy about a small-town female mayor, too much on her dignity to be interested in love, and a big-town sculptor who changes her mind. There are flashes of wit in it, verbal, even psychological, and even visual, but nearly all of them, like the story itself, are suicidally professional and forced. *And Now Tomorrow* is about a deaf upper-class girl and an ex-proletarian doctor who, after some machine-turned comedy of sex antagonism, restores her hearing and, presumably, dissolves her snobbery. As John McManus of *PM* points out, it is rather cruel to quite a number of people in the audience to show a cure for the kind of deafness that results from meningitis without letting you know whether there is in fact any such cure.

Lost in a Harem is a flat Abbott and Costello comedy with a rather amusing use of a ham actor, his hallucinations, which remain invisible to the audience, the sound track which records them, and some pantomime which, scarcely developed as it is, is still as tantalizing and refreshing, against all the screen-paralyzing contemporary blabber, as a teaspoonful of water in the middle of a desert. Two current cartoon shorts, whose titles and author for some reason slip my mind, alternate heavy but sometimes funny facetiousness with bits of active imagination. Both star Warner Brothers' anarchic rabbit; one burlesques a South Sea travelogue, the other a Western. *V-1*, an English short about robot bombs, is well edited, better written than average—it is wordy but at least some of the words count for something—and honestly narrated in an unaffected voice. It contains one Miltonic shot, made from a plane, in which a struck bomb, detonated in flight, reaches out an arm of explosion from perhaps a mile away, and as broad as a boulevard, which with a speed that pulls you out of your chair approaches and fills the screen.

December 16, 1944

Farewell, My Lovely, as Raymond Chandler wrote it, combined about equal parts of poetic talent, arrested-adolescent prurience, and the sort of self-pity which, rejoicing in all that is hardest-boiled, turns the two former faculties toward melodramatic, pretentiously unpretentious examination of big cities and their inhabitants. The picture preserves most of the faults and virtues of the book. I suppose a lot that I like about it is not really good except by comparison with the deadly norm, from the astuteness with costuming and sets—over-attentiveness to secondary levels of realism buying off sharp enough attention to primary—to the rather adventurous but rather arty photography. Nevertheless, I enjoyed the romanticism of the picture, and its hopefulness and energy, and much of its acting —that of Miles Mander, Claire Trevor, Ralfe Harald, and Dick Powell especially. Even its messiness and semi-accomplishment made me feel better about it than about the much better-finished, more nearly unimpeachable, but more academic and complacent *Double Indemnity*.

The Man in Half Moon Street, played by Nils Asther, whom

I have always liked and am glad to be seeing again, is ninety years old, looks thirty-five, and is eager to keep up that appearance forever, if possible, at the expense of the young men whose glands he and another medical friend (well-played by Reinhold Schunzel as Albert Bassermann) confiscate. Most of the movie tries, with uneven success, to be polite about its tenseness, but the scene in which Mr. Asther's years catch up with him—a really remarkable job of make-up, lighting, and I guess a sort of acting—is much more interesting and scary than one had reason to expect.

Jamming the Blues, a hot-jazz short by the *Life* photographer Gjon Mili, is exciting quite a few people around Hollywood, and has some right to, for it is one of the few musical shorts I have ever got even fair pleasure out of hearing, and the only one, barring the jam scene in *Phantom Lady*, which was not a killing bore to watch except as a heartsick attempt on the part of the makers to act as if this were the gayest, most provocative film assignment in the world. Yet I don't really care much for the picture. It is too full of the hot, moist, boozy breath of the unqualified jazz addict, of which I once had more than enough in my own mouth; and I thought the two effects which wholly compose it—chiaroscuro and virtual silhouette—too pretentious and borrowed and arty, despite their occasional good service, to be taken in a wholly friendly spirit, let alone an enthusiastic one. There are few things in any art or art-industry more discouraging to think of, more inimical to the furtherance of good work or to the chance to attempt it, than the middle-brow highbrows. Half a brow is worse than no head.

December 23, 1944

Frankly, I doubt I am qualified to arrive at any sensible assessment of Miss Elizabeth Taylor. Ever since I first saw the child, two or three years ago, in I forget what minor role in what movie, I have been choked with the peculiar sort of adoration I might have felt if we were both in the same grade of primary school. I feel I am obligated to this unpleasant unveiling because it is now my duty to try to review her, in *National Velvet*, in her first major role.

So far as I can see on an exceedingly cloudy day, I wouldn't say she is particularly gifted as an actress. She seems, rather, to turn things off and on, much as she is told, with perhaps a fair amount of natural grace and of a natural-born female's sleep-walking sort of guile, but without much, if any, of an artist's intuition, perception, or resource. She strikes me, however, if I may resort to conservative statement, as being rapturously beautiful. I think she also has a talent, of a sort, in the particular things she can turn on: which are most conspicuously a mock-pastoral kind of simplicity, and two or three speeds of semi-hysterical emotion, such as ecstasy, an odd sort of pre-specific erotic sentience, and the anguish of overstrained hope, imagination, and faith. Since these are precisely the things she needs for her role in *National Velvet*—which is a few-toned-scale semi-fairy story about a twelve-year-old girl in love with a horse—and since I think it is the most hopeful business of movies to find the perfect people rather than the perfect artists, I think that she and the picture are wonderful, and I hardly know or care whether she can act or not.

I am quite sure about Mickey Rooney: he is an extremely wise and moving actor, and if I am ever again tempted to speak disrespectfully of him, that will be in anger over the unforgivable waste of a forceful yet subtle talent, proved capable of self-discipline and of the hardest roles that could be thrown it. (I suggest it jealously, because I would so love to make the films rather than see them made; but if only a Studs Lonigan for the middle period could be found—the two I will mention might conceivably overlap it—and inter-studio entanglements could so be combed out that both Rooney and James Cagney—from whom Rooney has learned a lot—were available, they could find in Farrell's trilogy the best roles of their lives; and those novels, done as they should be, could become three major American movies.)

There are still other good things about *National Velvet*: the performance of Anne Revere as the girl's mother and of Donald Crisp as her father (except for their tedious habit of addressing each other as "Mr. Brown" and "Mrs. Brown," and some conventional bits of business which I suspect were forced down Crisp's throat); the endearing appearance (I don't suppose one can really call it a performance) of Jackie Jenkins; and a number of gently pretty "touches," mainly domestic, which may have been Clarence Brown's, who directed, or may have been in the script, or for that matter in Enid Bagnold's novel. And there are few outright blunders, like the silly burlesquing of one adolescent love scene.

Yet in a sense—the sense of all the opportunities, or obligations, which were either neglected, with or without reason, or went unrealized—almost the whole picture is a blunder mitigated chiefly but insufficiently by the over-all charm of the story and affectionateness of the treatment, by Rooney's all but unimprovable performance (I wonder only about his very skilful but stylized use of his hands in his impressive drunk scene), and by a couple of dozen piercing moments—which may have transfixed me exclusively—from Miss Taylor.

The makers of the film had an all but ideal movie: a nominally very simple story, expressing itself abundantly in visual and active terms, which inclosed and might have illuminated almost endless recessions and inter-reverberations of emotion and meaning into religious and sexual psychology and into naturalistic legend. But of all these reins, all of which needed so light, hard, clear a hand, they seem to have been conscious only of the most obvious; and they have bungled even their management of those. Far from understanding and valuing their story for all it is worth, they don't even tell its surface half well enough.

To take just two samples of this: the sequence during which the horse is trained for his race gives you little more than generalized pretty-pictures instead of a précis of the pure technical detail which must have deeply excited, instructed, and intensified the girl, and so could and should have done the same for the audience. As for the race and the immediate preparations for it, they are only the more sadly flunked because, again in a secondary, generalized way, they manage to make you half forget the fact by being quite fairly exciting. If the audience could have experienced what the girl experienced, with anything like the same razorlike distinctness of detail and intensity of action and of spirit, they would have been practically annihilated. But they not only never have a chance to identify themselves with the girl or her horse; they hardly even get a good look at them, during the whole course of the race. The jockeys, moreover—and again their horses—are not only not characterized, and play none of their professional tricks on each other or the amateur; by some horribly misguided desire to enhance the contrast between their mature masculinity and the heroine's frightened nubility, they are selected to look less like jockeys than like guards on All-American. Such neglect amounts to a dereliction, not of art, if Hollywood fears and bridles at the word, but of the most elementary common sense, which amounts to the same thing. If a man wrote a piece of music so full of chowf-chowf, people would hardly bear to listen to it (unless it were given some such title as "The Four Freedoms," or perhaps "The Seven Against Thebes"). But that is not going to make a flop of *National Velvet*. I expect to see it again myself, for that matter.

January 6, 1945

WHILE I was watching *The Keys of the Kingdom*, and for a few days afterward, I liked it quite well for its sincerity and for what then seemed its reasonably clean effort to present a hero whose heroism is moral. As I think it over, much of the sincerity and of the ethics seems beefy, over-comfortable, love-your-fellow-mannish, and in general rather uninteresting. I think it cheap to convince the audience that a priest's a male for all that by giving him a sweetheart, then knocking her off in order to provide him with manly rather than godly reasons for spending the rest of the show in a cassock. The relationship between the priest and a handsome mother superior is unusual for films and brings a couple of good scenes, but I disliked its being fed the audience as a sort of loveless love interest. It seems a little weak, for that matter, to spend most of your two hours in China in order that those who can't take their moral conflicts, such as they are, neat can always chase them with something pleasantly exotic. I wonder, too, why I thought Gregory Peck a particularly gifted actor. Now, it seems to me that he probably has talent, in a still semi-professional stage, and that I was moved and misled rather by his newness, his unusual handsomeness, and his still more unusual ability to communicate sincerity. There are, however, some fully unquestionable pieces of acting—a beautiful one by Sir Cedric Hardwicke, a good if broad one by Vincent Price, a disciplined, highly charged one by Rosa Stradner, and I imagine a good one by Edmund Gwenn; I can't wholly like or trust my judgment of the sort of mellow old man he plays here. Actually, I suppose it's a pretty good movie all around, but I feel about it as I might if I were given the original novel, bound in veal, for Christmas, and felt I had to read it with care. I am, incidentally, getting a little tired of seeing movies thought of as "religious" which carry not much more religious meaning or insight or adventurousness than a bourgeois's good intentions at New Year's. Not that priests would be by any means necessary to a good religious picture. I can't help noticing that they have never yet been shown on the screen at their real business, public or private; just as screen lovers are seldom shown to be capable of love.

Winged Victory has some briskly interesting and well-assembled material about the training and testing and rejecting phases of Air Force life. Aside from that I suppose it is all right, but I don't enjoy having anyone try to persuade me, so cheerfully and energetically, that the Air Force personnel is without exception composed of boy scouts old enough to shave. *Here Come the Waves* is an almost totally negligible musical, which does, however, involve Bing Crosby, Betty Hutton (in a double role), and Sonny Tufts. I would enjoy Crosby even if he did not amusingly kid Sinatra, and probably even if he did nothing but walk across a shot; I may begin to tire of Betty Hutton's violence some day, but I haven't yet; and though Sonny Tuft's work is almost wholly composed of "natural" mannerisms, I think most of them natural and entertaining. *Can't Help Singing* miscarries Deanna Durbin, a Jerome Kern score, and a trip across North America in 1849. It seems to me this could have been a beautiful and gay picture; unfortunately it is made without much feeling for either beauty or gaiety. *Music for Millions* so uses Margaret O'Brien and Jimmy Durante and June Allyson and Jose Iturbi and a symphony orchestra and God only knows how many dollars as to get close to the least good possible out of any of them. *Hollywood Canteen* tempted two Albany bank presidents each to buy $10,000,000 (ten million dollars) of war bonds in order that one might "stand in" for Errol Flynn and the wife of the other for Bette Davis at a "Proxy Première" in that city. Buy a war bond and a ticket to the show—the proceeds go to the real Hollywood Canteen—but take care to invest in a bar of nose candy on your way through the lobby.

January 20, 1945

If you compare the moving pictures released during a given period with the books published during the same period—or with the plays produced or the pictures painted or the music composed—you may or may not be surprised to find that they stand up rather well. I can think of very few contemporary books that are worth the jackets they are wrapped in; I can think of very few movies, contemporary or otherwise, which fail to show that somebody who has worked on them, in front of the camera or in any one of many places behind it, has real life or energy or intensity or intelligence or talent.

But you have only to compare the best of last year's films with the best that have been made or in your conception could be made, and the best that have been made with the best work you have known in any other art you choose, to know that those who make or care for moving pictures have great reason to be angry, for all that is frustrated, and still greater reason to be humble, for all that is fallen short of, frustration or no. And if you foresee how few years remain before the grandest prospect for a major popular art since Shakespeare's time dissolves into the ghastly gelatinous nirvana of television, I think you will find the work of this last or any recent year, and the chance of any sufficiently radical improvement within the tragically short future, enough to shrivel the heart. If moving pictures are ever going to realize their potentialities, they are going to have to do it very soon indeed. Aware of that, and aware also of the works of genius which have already been achieved in films, I have no patience with the patient and patronizing who remind us mellowly that it took centuries to evolve an Aeschylus or a Joyce.

The sickening thing is that nearly everything that has virtue or hope at all is lukewarm or worse. We are learning better and better all the time, for instance, how to make films beautifully, elegantly, patiently, perfectly—so long as nobody severely questions the nature of the beauty, the quality of the elegance, the focus and result of the patience, the meaning and value of the perfection. In this sense I suppose *The Song of Bernadette* is a nearly perfect picture. I would about as soon see all that kind of skill and devotion used in embroidering the complete text of the Solemnization of Matrimony on a pair of nylon drawers. It is as if all the power and resource of the English language were to culminate in the prose of Donald Culross Peattie.

This suffocating genteelism, this suicidal love for and pride in the utterly controlled and utterly worthless effect, has become as grim a threat to movies as the rankest commercialism that could ever be reputed of Hollywood. Needless, perhaps, to add, it is the one aesthetic logically available to the commercial mind; such minds can hardly be blamed for indorsing a kind of beauty they genuinely care for, to the detriment of kinds they have to accept or indorse, if at all, on faith.

Or consider *With the Marines at Tarawa*, the best of the four or five film records of war which I consider the best films of the year. I profoundly respect their craftsmanship, which is not only good but well used, and their good taste. And I grant that short of a tremendously forceful, daring, and sure creative intelligence, craftsmanship and taste are the best available two hands with which to work at such material. Yet it seems a sorry year in which decent grammar and a modest sense of one's subject, honorable as these are, have earned higher honor than any other achievement.

The best fiction films of the year, *The Curse of the Cat People* and *Youth Runs Wild*, were made by Val Lewton and his associates. I esteem them so highly because for all their unevenness their achievements are so consistently alive, limber, poetic, humane, so eager toward the possibilities of the screen, and so resolutely against the grain of all we have learned to expect from the big studios. But I am afraid there is no reason to be-

lieve that the makers of these films, under the best of circumstances, would be equipped to make the great, and probably
very vulgar, and certainly very forceful revolutionary pictures
that are so desperately needed. Indeed, I suspect that their
rather gentle, pleasing, resourceful kind of talent is about the
strongest sort we can hope to see working in Hollywood with
any consistent, useful purity of purpose; and the pictures
themselves indicate to what extent that is frustrated.

If only a half-dozen properly placed men in Hollywood realized and knew how to apply the lessons in *Going My Way*, they
might be assured of almost any number of hits, and we might
be assured of an equal number of more or less good films. The
lessons, if I read them right, are that leisureliness can be excellent, that if you take a genuine delight in character the universe
is opened to you, and perhaps above all that a movie, like any
other work of art, must be made for love. But I am ready to
bet that the chief discernible result, if any, of *Going My Way*
will be an anxiety-ridden set of vaudeville sketches about Pat
and Mike in cassocks; and on that bet, with enough takers, I
could set up a studio of my own.

It seems to me that when an intelligent director and an intelligent boss work smoothly together, you can expect pictures
like *Double Indemnity*. It is a neat picture, and it brings back
into movies a lot of acid things which ought to be there. But it
brings no new ones, and it does not handle the old ones, I
would say, with any notable ingenuity or interest in taking a
risk. Rather, it is strictly expert—a good thing of itself perhaps;
but it looks to me as if the expertness were always as sharply
controlled by what is dead sure at the box-office as by what is
right. I imagine that in this limited sense we can hope for more
from Billy Wilder, in the immediate future, than from anybody
else around.

But is it anywhere near enough? I feel more hope, on the
whole, in the climate of such a studio as Metro, which gave us
last year the very generous and pretty *Meet Me in St. Louis* and
the very likably earnest, dogged *30 Seconds Over Tokyo*. But I
would hardly say that either of these films gave me any hope
that next year, or the year after, their makers might bring out
one that you could never forget; indeed, both were rich in
guaranties that nothing of the sort will happen.

As for the films of Preston Sturges, which are of course among the best and most gifted of the year, I will be more at rest in my liking for them when I am thoroughly convinced that Sturges is not rejecting half his talents; or that there is nothing on earth he is temperamentally able to do about it. I will probably always like the films of David Selznick better than reputedly condescending aesthetes like me are allowed to like such things; for I think that more than most things that come out of Hollywood they show both genuine talent, as distinct from mere professionalism, and a genuine love for movies, as distinct from mere executive concentration on them. But I am afraid they also show, and probably always will, an equally genuine love for commercial success, and a weakness for emotional and aesthetic and philosophical attitudes which belong, if anywhere, to soap opera.

In some respects I admire Arthur Ripley more than anyone else who released a picture during the past year—for his *Voice in the Wind*, which was made relatively far outside the mill, on very little money, in very little time. His film showed an unequivocal and reckless passion for saying the best things possible in the best way possible. In nearly every other respect, I must admit, I thought it poor. But it is only in that kind of passion and disinterestedness, joined with adequate talent, that I see any hope. Name five men who have or have ever had it, and their position in Hollywood. And try to conceive what difficulties they would encounter, in raising the capital, in making the films, in getting them distributed, if they or any men of their order tried to do the work outside.

When an art is in good health, mediocrity and amorphous energy and commercialism and hostility toward disinterested men become more than forgivable, as lubricants and as stimulants, and the men of skill, or of affable or gentle or charming or for that matter venal talent, are more than welcome to exist, and to be liked and rewarded. When an art is sick unto death, only men of the most murderous creative passion can hope to save it. In either condition it is generally, if by no means always, this dangerous sort of man who does the great work. I wonder whether it is any longer possible, anywhere on earth, for such a man to work in films. I am almost certain it is not possible, and is not ever going to be, in this country.

February 3, 1945

T HE title *Sunday Dinner for a Soldier* suggests to me a movie that could be made in a dozen or a thousand versions, all of them good; but the version that has been made is not one of them. The family which stages the dinner lives on a house-boat near Tarpon Springs, Florida. The nominal head of the family is Charles Winninger with white whiskers; everybody calls him Grandfeathers. The actual head is Anne Baxter; she is wondering whether or not to marry a rich young man who can't understand why she dances all alone (to the music of a large invisible orchestra and chorus) in the sand-foundered ballroom of a derelict hotel. Other members of the family are a pretty little sister who loves a hen named Miss Easter, and two little brothers, one of whom says of a flower, "It stinks swell." These are represented as nice people, but very poor and, in their poverty, ever so whimsical and lucky. John Hodiak, the soldier who turns up for Sunday dinner, comes of nice people too, in a social and money sense, but his parents were divorced when he was twelve and he ran away when he was fourteen and worked in factories; so he too enjoys the advantages of all the classes and suffers the disadvantages of none. One of the ads for the film says of his romance with Miss Baxter, "Their eyes met! Their lips questioned! Their arms answered!" and though both players try to be reasonable about it, that is not much of an over-simplification.

I sat through the picture in a misery of embarrassment, which intensifies as I try to write about it. I feel embarrassment rather than simple anger because most of the people who worked on the show appear to have loved it, believed in it, and had great hopes for its originality and worthiness. The con-fused but genuine sweetness of their intention is as visible through all the mawkish formulas, and as disturbing, as a drowned corpse never quite surfacing. I cannot bear to say in detail why I found the film so distasteful. To do so would be like spending a self-controlled day with an innocently awful family, then sneering at all that was painful to you but dear to them.

Shanghai Drama was the last movie G. W. Pabst made in France before he went over to the Nazis. I understand that it was heavily censored by the French (including this American print), but it is hard for me to imagine that that can have made much difference. Shot by shot, some of it is interesting and nostalgically satisfying; even at his best Pabst is heavy as lead, but even at his worst he is also gifted. But the story—White Russians forced to work for Black Dragon agents—is like Malraux redone for the pulps. The worst we can do can hardly match the Europeans when they take their trash seriously.

February 10, 1945

WHAT films I will manage to discuss at anything like proper length when space next becomes available already puzzles me; I am snowed under by possibilities, some worthy, others quite as relevant through conspicuous unworthiness. For the time being I will say briefly that I enjoyed *On Approval*, an English-made film with Beatrice Lillie and Clive Brook, so thoroughly that I have to fight off superlatives; that *Hangover Square* is a better than average horror picture up to, but not including, its wildly overloaded climax; that *A Song to Remember* contains a good deal of nicely played Chopin, and is as infuriating and funny a misrepresentation of an artist's life and work as I have ever seen; and that judging by *The Three Caballeros*, a streak of cruelty which I have for years noticed in Walt Disney's productions is now certifiable. I should add fair warning about *On Approval*: it is a studied, dead-pan, parodistic, late-Victorian setting of a Lonsdale drawing-room comedy, and practically every good thing about it is extremely specialized. A popular hostile synonym for that is "precious." Trivial as it is, I would be grateful for a lot more preciousness of the same sort; *On Approval* itself could use more.

February 17, 1945

NEVER having read the novel, I can consider *A Tree Grows in Brooklyn* only in its movie version. I think it a more interesting and likable movie than most. It concentrates on poverty, on some crucial aspects of early puberty, on domestic relationships, and on life in a big city, which are rarely undertaken on the American screen, with considerable enthusiasm, tenderness, discipline, and intelligence. It even presents and accepts the idea, unpopular enough even in contemporary fiction, that some antagonisms and inadequacies are too deeply rooted to be wholly explicable or curable. It also develops its main love interest between a little girl and her father, and it presents a drunkard, the father, for once without moralizing about him or reforming him. (The agencies concerned about this are doubtless satisfied with his death.) The film is so interested in taking its proper time, with and between each scene, that a number of important scenes had, I infer, to be dropped for length; I don't otherwise understand such a thing as the barely illustrated relationship between mother and son, in a screen play so obviously careful—not to mention the virtual absence of the symbolic tree of the title, which could have been accounted for in about three extra shots.

The tenement sets and city streets of the movie are as lovingly and exhaustively detailed and as solid-looking as any I can remember. Most of the players, like those in the same studio's *Ox-Bow Incident*, clearly believed they had special duties, opportunities, and privileges. I was especially moved and impressed by James Dunn as the father and by the ways, visible and sometimes stammering though they were, in which Peggy Ann Garner and the director Elia Kazan handled what I take to be her rigidity as an actress, turning it into a part of her personal and visual charm, and of the role she is in those respects so well suited for. *A Tree Grows in Brooklyn* also contains single moments or shots so extraordinarily good that they make me wonder why the rest, granted the same eye that made or saved these, need have fallen short. There is a shot of the girl hesitant on a curb which has the lovely authenticity of a wild animal startled by a flashbulb—or of the same shot made by a concealed camera in a real street. There is a shot of Dunn, ghastly drunk in his inky waiter's suit, so painfully malappropriate to daylight, being shoved and shouted along his home street, which is as poetic and individualized an image of a state beneath humiliation as I have seen. There is a shot of Joan Blondell's bent hustling back, the thin dress propped and ridged through her underwear, as she goes in to help deliver her sister of a baby, which is equally successful in its evocation of women in a special and final class and world and predicament.

Yet *A Tree Grows in Brooklyn* is as much a disappointment—even an annoyance—as a pleasure. My heart goes out to the people who reproduced the Brooklyn streets—I could probably lose every other interest in life in the love for just such detail—but try as they will, they only prove, more convincingly because more masterfully than I have seen it proved before, that the best you can do in that way is as dead as an inch-by-inch description or a perfectly naturalistic painting, compared with accepting instead the still scarcely imagined difficulties and the enormous advantages of submerging your actors in the real thing, full of its irreducible present tense and its unpredictable proliferations of energy and beauty. I regret too that with sets even as good as they had they gave only token shots of the city for its own sake, free from the advancement of the plot or the complications of a character; what a wonderful chance they missed to take fifteen or twenty minutes' vacation from the story for, say, the free-gliding, picaresque, and perfect eye for a Saturday schoolchild's cruising of the city. I'm afraid too that they were too calculated in their use of offscreen noise and music, and in those scenes for which there were no accidental offscreen noises.

For the rest, trusting what friends who have also seen the film tell me of the novel, one must be dubious of both, if not with such full hatred, still with some of the same distaste which is inspired by an advertising artist's use of everything that was sweated out from Cézanne on. Ever since certain kinds of sexual sophistication began to qualify for the big-money market in *Anthony Adverse*—very likely it began before that—I have been bothered by how easy it was, cynically or in Miss Smith's case I would believe innocently, to make palatable to the irredeemable enemies of all courage and adventurous perception matters which they had helped crush more original artists and scientists for daring, however unprofitably, to take notice of. *A Tree Grows in Brooklyn* is "realistic" in a way which would have been loathed by the people who will now accept it if they had lived even a short while ago; and if a measure of its still fundamental cautiousness is needed, you can be sure they would still loathe *Greed*, for with all its own faults *Greed* never in the least degree tempered its wind to any part of its public.

A Tree's attention to poverty and need, though frank as such things go in films, is also temperate compared with the staring facts of poverty and need; the comfortable have always been able to lick their chops over the hunger of others if that hunger is presented with the right sort of humorous or pathetic charm; if certain Christian or Marxian glands are tactfully enough stimulated, they will drool as well. The father-daughter, mother-son relationships in the movie follow a classic Freudian pattern and for once make no phony scientific capital of the fact, but I found the classicism even more pat than it sometimes looks in Freud, and a lot more safely dressed up. The characters themselves bother me most, but here I have an even harder time defining my mistrust of them. It is, roughly, that the imagination has been used a little too glibly to blow up and trim off the presumptive originals of these characters into very comfortably readable, actable, easily understandable creatures, whose faults and virtues are all tagged or neatly braided. I don't forget mentioning that within themselves and in their relationships they are more complex and intransigent than is usual now—and far less vulgarly designed to expound some sociological or political or psychological doctrine. But even this, the respectable beginning at least of a return toward trying to represent human existence, can be so handled as to make it one more asset of a piece of fool-proof entertainment—like those novels whose authors go through half the pockets of the astounded Christian world merely by writing a few hundred pages housebreaking ten lionlike words from the New Testament.

For reasons such as these—or because, like me, they have automatically neglected to read a best-seller—I won't wonder if a good many intelligent people pass up this movie or, even if they see it, dismiss it. For all I regret or dislike about it, I don't think it is to be dismissed.

February 24, 1945

Objective Burma is the story of a group of American para-chutists who, after locating and destroying a Japanese radar station, try to walk out, through difficult country thick with the enemy. I can see no unconquerable reason why this shouldn't have been a great movie. But there are plenty of reasons why it isn't.

The main reason is that the players, by always saying the apt line at the apt moment and by almost every other means possi-ble, continually remind you that they are, after all, just actors, and that none of this is really happening. I must also mention the simple lack of the sort of talent which would have made it possible to tell wonderfully well, in an hour or so, what is here pretty well told in two hours and twenty-two minutes. Lack of adequate talent is of course all the more irrelevant to criticism when the makers of a film are so clearly and honorably doing the best they know how. But it is hard to understand why such sincere and generally skillful people stop so far short of the chances for improving their work which are open to people of every degree of talent. I am embarrassed that it is necessary for an amateur to offer the following suggestion.

However good they may be, known actors in this sort of semi-documentary film inevitably blunt the edge of your best hopes and intentions. If you are forced to use actors, known or unknown, at least put them, and yourself, and everyone else involved in making the movie, through an inch-by-inch study of the faces and postures and total images of actual warfare, as they appear in record films of the war. If, in spite of such study, you find that your actors—for instance—or you yourself can-not recognize or cannot very greatly narrow the innumerable and great differences between the real thing and the well-meaning, over-professional, over-expressive imagination of it, you are most thoroughly to be respected if you give the whole project up.

The people who made *Objective Burma* are by no means specially to be criticized on these grounds; the criticism applies with equal justice to every American fictional war film I have seen. Indeed, *Objective Burma* is one of the best of them. Its actors are always actors; but in their actorish idiom they play, generally, with restraint. In the storytelling there is more than usual recognition of the value of detail and process; there is also some good sense. Often the camera prowls and veers along façades of vegetation which are freighted with the threat of imagination and possibility but which properly seldom turn out to contain any actual danger. And at the climax, a night attack, the screen is nearly dark enough and, during the build-up, nearly quiet enough, to give the audience an adequate sense of ignorant, strained, globular anticipation. Even better, it is obvious in one shot after another that the people who made the picture are using every resource they have. This sense of the whole heart and hope involved, rather than merely the assignment, and salary, and reputation, can of itself give fulness and even a kind of nobility to a piece of work, especially during a time of artistic cowardice and cynicism and despair. It makes this picture moving and good, for all its outright faults and sorry limitations.

Roughly Speaking is, I fear, a faithful history of the American middle class. It glories in the idea that this is still a country where you don't get shot for dreaming. The one dream worth about ninety per cent of its footage is the making of money. The most nearly respectable object of all this dreaming is to make sure that the boys get to Andover and Yale. The whole thing depresses me beyond words. Jack Carson, however, is likable, as he always is.

The Thin Man Goes Home and *Having Wonderful Crime* are harmless comic detective stories. It is physically easier to read such things in bed; it is less boring to watch them on the screen. I can't see that anything is to be gained, either way; but I realize, from a great deal too much personal experience, that gain is no part of the idea. The real point, I presume, is to find your own special hermetic nirvana of boredom.

In an adults-only theater, recently, I saw two elderly movies, *The Lash of the Penitentes* and *Glamor for Sale*. The former contains some genuine and interesting shots, suspended in an aspic of terrifyingly pitiful and funny ineptitudes. The latter, a melodrama about the female escort business written by John Bright, is worthless and crisply nostalgic.

I want a bit tardily to recommend March of Time's *Report on Italy*, which contains the mobbing of Caretta, the execution of Caruso, and enough suffering and unaccusable faces of human beings who happen to be Italians to blast the brains out of a script twice as stern as this one is, with its talk about "the Italian penance." If people of the peace-making sort knew or cared in the least how to look at faces—or dared to—the exhibition of such films at the peace conference could supply more valuable evidence, and hope for the future, than anything else I can think of. But like most of the two billion people who will suffer the effects of the post-war arrangements I am, I must grant, an amateur.

March 3, 1945

Betrayal From the East, a spy melodrama about an ex-soldier who pretends to get for Japanese agents the plans for the defense of the Panama Canal, is supposed to be a true story. I am perfectly willing to believe it is, but my willingness is seldom encouraged by the way it is presented on the screen. If two Japanese spies employed in an American newspaper office in Tokyo are settling down to their daily eavesdropping, surely they don't bother to exchange a glance of villainous complicity. If an experienced reporter has to try to get back alive to the States with some mortally red-hot information, surely the idea of memorizing it doesn't elude his intelligence for a couple of hundred feet or, when at last he thinks of it, strike him as remarkably brilliant or brand-new. If two Army Intelligence agents meet in a hotel room to feed false dialogue to a planted enemy dictaphone, surely, once they are dead certain that no hidden camera or slanteye is trained on them, they stop trying to suit their actions to their words. If still another agent is being steamed to death in her Nazi ex-lover's beauty parlor, surely she would take prompt care, on principle or by instinct if for no better use, to get next the floor, where breathing lasts longest and the heat is least oppressive. If such minor oversights were rectified in advance of release, stories much less plausible than this one could be made to seem true, and even interesting. There is, on the other hand no sort of harm in the movie, and it is a pleasure to see Lee Tracy again, and Nancy

Kelly's famous shoulders. I may be presumptuous with that adjective, but they have always been famous with me.

Bring on the Girls is a hard-polished color musical about a susceptible millionaire (Eddie Bracken), his bodyguard (Sonny Tufts), and a predatory woman (Veronica Lake). It isn't much, I suppose; but I enjoyed a skit by a couple of subhuman quacks (Porter Hall and another very good, familiar face whose name I can't remember); Eddie Bracken is so likable, and knows his work so well, that he can't even walk out on a diving-board without getting sympathy and a laugh; and Sonny Tufts sings well. I have an idea he could become almost as good as Crosby, on almost as broad a range.

Pan-Americana is another of those buckets of good-swill that make me wish some Latin American movie people would come north, for a change, and take fair vengeance on the United States; a job at which I would be only too happy to help out. In some other respects, however, I rather liked the picture. There is a general air of casual lousiness about it—the aching dreariness of the climactic stage tableaux for instance—which seems very friendly and fresh compared with the high-finished pink granite gravestones which are normally released as musical comedies. The song-and-dance numbers are mainly poor, but with the fierce unembalmed poorness of the real thing, as you see it in night clubs. The love story is a classically heartless record—set up as merely cute—of fifth-rate conduct between a professional seducer and an even less scrupulous nice girl; but some of it is written and directed, and is played by Philip Terry and Audrey Long, as if such a relationship were worth honest observation, as indeed it is.

March 10, 1945

A GOOD movie might have been made from *The Picture of Dorian Gray*. Albert Lewin's version is respectful, earnest, and, I am afraid, dead. Lowell Gilmore is close to the mark as Basil Hallward, who tries to be artist, Christian, and bourgeois all at the same time, and I very much like Angela Lansbury as Sibyl Vane. Some people are liable to laugh at her and to think of her as insipid, but I think she is touching and exact in her defenseless romanticism and in a special kind of short-lipped English beauty, appropriate to the period and to Sibyl's class, and evocative of milkmaids in eighteenth-century pornographic prints. In general, too, Mr. Lewin's modifications of the story and his outright inventions seem sensible, and I feel, sympathetically, that he has tried very hard to transfer the tone of the novel to the screen. Yet for all its oddity and outright weakness the novel—which I thank Mr. Lewin for causing me at last to read—is distinguished, wise, and frightening; whereas the movie is just a cultured horror picture, decorated with epigrams and an elaborate moral, and made with a sincere effort at good taste rather than with passion, immediacy, or imagination.

As Oscar Wilde's proxy, Lord Henry Wotton, George Sanders delivers the epigrams almost too expertly. They will doubtless panic the public they were intended to pulverize, as I gather Wilde's epigrams, and most other good ones, always have; but they sound too purely like the nervous merciless rattle of cellophane. In tone and pace that could be good; but it isn't good here, because the shallow clatter completely fails to reveal Sir Henry's boredom and melancholy or his stature as an intelligence and as a moralist. Within these limits I think Sanders very capable, but two better men for the role would have been Robert Morley and the late Laird Cregar; and I suspect Henry Daniell or Alan Mowbray might have done better, for that matter. Nobody can be blamed very severely for the failure to cast Dorian Gray adequately; the only proper actor I can think of is John Barrymore in his early twenties. I realize that Hurd Hatfield represents a most unusually hard try at good casting, and once cast he certainly tries as hard as the wrong man can; but it is sad, like watching an understudy fall short with the chance of a lifetime. My main over-all regret about the movie is its failure to reveal in these two characters the depth and force and meaning that are in each, and to develop between them the philosophical tension and the sense of irresistibly challenging, ambiguous moral vortex without which their story is just an ornately naive tract.

I wish somebody would take book lovers like Mr. Lewin aside and explain to them, once for all, that to read from the text of a novel—not to mention interior monologues—when people are performing on the screen, while it may elevate the literary tone of the production, which I doubt, certainly and inescapably plays hell with it as a movie. I also regret the choice of Ivan Albright—and his brother Syzygy too, if both are responsible—to work out Dorian's portrait in its later stages. I no longer loathe the work of the Albrights as I used to before I realized how innocent it is; but I can't see Dorian Gray, even at his ripest, as a cross between Ivan Albright and the Wild Man of Borneo. I can't see either why Dorian's sinning—aside from the harm he does others—should culminate in a couple of visits to a dive where an old man plays Chopin. I can understand least of all why Mr. Lewin and his associates passed up the best movie chance of all: to let the portrait change before your eyes, rather than bringing it on, changed, at set intervals. At the end, to be sure, it goes through a climactic welter and emerges in its original state. But Hays office or no Hays office, if the camera had kept steady watch over the painting while Dorian was off about his distributable business, it could have put the audience through the whole thesaurus of evil, and scared them stiff into the bargain. Since practically nobody thinks it civilized, or in the interests of the common weal, to believe that there is such a thing as evil any more—in the bright lexicon of youth there are only war criminals, vitamin deficiencies, and similar social diseases which a little common sense will cure—this failure of opportunity is all the more to be regretted.

March 17, 1945

IN A newsreel theater not long ago I saw a version of the Crimea Conference which was so well photographed and so quietly, sensitively, leisurely cut that I wished I might know whose work, or even which company's, it was. It had a feeling for weather and light and space, for the proper insertion of side detail, and for personalities and their proper timing, progression, and juxtaposition, which I am tempted to compare with the clean-water physical absoluteness of Tolstoy's writing. Actually, there was nothing about it of that grand order except in the event, even so much of it—a good deal—as one could read in glimpses of the faces; the way it was handled by cameramen and cutters was merely right, which is a rarity and somewhere near a God's plenty. I would like especially to suggest that the shots of President Roosevelt, which I thought extremely moving, may turn out to be the most crucial and revealing portraits of him we are ever likely to get.

The other current movies are so tired-out and bleak that I can hardly write of them. *Hotel Berlin*, the most heavily routine of Warner Brothers' political melodramas, is stuffed with sympathetic veterans like Peter Lorre and Henry Daniell and George Coulouris and Raymond Massey, and with sympathetic and understandably more eager young people like Andrea King and Faye Emerson and Kurt Kreuger, but the only thing that had even a chance for any pure quality was a bit by Helene Thimig. *Thunderhead, Son of Flicka* has some beautiful horses, especially a heart-stopping, blue-eyed, pure-white stallion whom I would love to see in any adequately fierce movie about Pegasus or the Houyhnhnms or, for that matter, in any really appreciative story about plain horses. This is not such a story. Whenever the horses are busy, it is pleasant to look at; but so are moving clouds, or water, without much credit to their recorder. The picture gets very little even out of the mild drama it allows itself; nothing whatever of the power and glory there could be in a properly unhuman film about wild and half-wild animals.

Two pictures that I can recommend you are unlikely to get a chance to see—even, I'm afraid, if you live within reach of the small "art" theaters which alone handle nearly all great or even half-good films, along with so much false art and simple trash. *Break the News* was made in England by René Clair, with Jack Buchanan and Maurice Chevalier. It isn't at all on the level with those Clair films of which the mere recall can bring me tears of admiration and of a detached sort of pride; but it is full of ease and fun and extravagant but unstrained irony, enjoyable of themselves, and worth watching too because they so clearly indicate that, though England was not a good place for Clair to work, it was not, like this country, a hell on earth. *I Met a Murderer* interests me particularly because I am forced more and more to the narrow, dismal hope that if good movies are to be made any more at all, in this country anyhow, they will have to be made on shoestrings, far outside the industry, and very likely by amateurs or at best semi-professionals. This one was made in England, several years ago; the only person involved in it whose name I know is the actor James Mason. An unpretentious murder story including a romance and a chase, and strongly influenced by Hitchcock, it seems obviously to have been made in the hope that it could get commercial distribution. And that on the whole I trust, believing that most though not all good films get much of their vitality and resonance by being designed for a broad mixed audience, whether or not they turn out to satisfy such an audience. Though it tries almost too hard for its own artistic good—and often with remarkable smoothness—to look "professional," the picture is streaked with enough amateurishness to pretty well guarantee its commercial failure. There are also some downright poor things in it, some undigested-arty, others catchpenny flops. Often, too, when it might be very exciting—as when the hunt for the killer and the hunt for a fox interinvolve —the picture fails in most of those establishers of casual reality, and oblique cutting-edges of ironic or sensuous detail, by which Hitchcock, for instance, would have absolved or even transfigured and reinforced the over-obviousness of the parallel. In such passages I have to admit that any professional would have got it by the audience better than any amateur, though probably more emptily; and that only a thorough artist with a thorough professional training could really hope to make it come right.

Yet this is one of the fairly few movies I have seen in years in which it was clear that its makers knew and cared and in general had lively, sensible ideas how each shot should follow the next, and what in the way of emotion, atmosphere, observation, and psychological weight and progression each shot and each group of shots should contain. I also thought it graceful, gallant, resourceful, and in every way satisfying and encouraging in its broken-field run through the problems of cost. It is certainly not a great or even a memorably good movie, and in any ultimate sense I doubt that it was particularly worth the trouble to make: except that every such difficult undertaking, even half so well planned and carried out, seems of itself a worthier and more heartening achievement than any save the best films made under whatever circumstances. Without all these special prejudices in its favor, for that matter, I think it better and more enjoyable than most studio pictures.

THE Paramount newsreel issue about Iwo Jima subjects the tremendous material recorded by Navy and Marine Corps and Coast Guard cameramen to an unusually intelligent job of editing, writing, and soundtracking. I noticed with particular respect a couple of good uses of flat silence; the use of a bit of dialogue on "intercoms," recorded on the spot, in a tank; and the use, at the end, of a still photograph down whose wall the camera moved slowly. Still photographs of motionless objects have a very different quality from motion-picture photographs of motionless objects; as Jean Cocteau observed, time still moves in the latter. The still used here was of dead men, for whom time no longer moved. The device is not a new one; Griffith (or William Bitzer) used it for the same purpose at the end of a battle in *The Birth of a Nation*, and René Clair used stop-shots for a somewhat related purpose in *The Crazy Ray*. But it is a device too basic to poetic resource on the screen to discard as plagiarized, and I am glad to see it put back into use so unpretentiously and well.

The Fox version of the same battle—the only other version I could find—drew on the same stock, and is interesting to compare with the Paramount. In one way it is to its credit that it is much less noisy and much less calculated to excite; it is in other words less rhetorical, and the temptations to rhetoric must be strong in handling such material, and usually result in falseness. But in this Paramount issue it seems to me that rhetoric was used well, to construct as well as might be in ten hours' work and in ten minutes on the screen an image of one of the most terrible battles in history. And that is not to mention plain sense: the coherent shape of violence in the Paramount version, which moves from air to sea to land; its intact, climactic use of the footage exposed through a tank-slit, which in the Fox version is chopped along through the picture; and its use of the recorded dialogue, which Fox didn't even touch.

The Fox version does on the other hand have two shots—a magically sinister slashing of quicksilvery water along the sand, and a heartrending picture of a wounded Marine, crawling toward help with the scuttling motions of a damaged insect—which I am amazed to see omitted from a piece of work so astute as Paramount's.

Very uneasily, I am beginning to believe that, for all that may be said in favor of our seeing these terrible records of war, we have no business seeing this sort of experience except through our presence and participation. I have neither space nor mind, yet, to try to explain why I believe this is so; but since I am reviewing and in ways recommending that others see one of the best and most terrible of war films, I cannot avoid mentioning my perplexity. Perhaps I can briefly suggest what I mean by this rough parallel: whatever other effects it may or may not have, pornography is invariably degrading to anyone who looks at or reads it. If at an incurable distance from participation, hopelessly incapable of reactions adequate to the event, we watch men killing each other, we may be quite as profoundly degrading ourselves and, in the process, betraying and separating ourselves the farther from those we are trying to identify ourselves with; none the less because we tell ourselves sincerely that we sit in comfort and watch carnage in order to nurture our patriotism, our conscience, our understanding, and our sympathies.

March 31, 1945

IN the English-made *Colonel Blimp* David Low's lovingly malicious archetype—and by implication, every Tory—has been relieved of all selfish motives for his actions and of nearly all dangerousness or even obstructiveness in those actions. This is annoying, and worse; but at the same time the movie's characterization of an innocent, brave, honorable, and stupid man is, within its own limits, so persuasive and so endearing, and so rare to movies, that I am at least as grateful as I am annoyed. If Low's and the movie character were blended, Blimp would be a great tragicomic character. Lacking that, I wish that some publisher would get out a twenty-five-cent volume of the cartoons, to brace and extend the picture among the many people who otherwise will get their only idea of Blimp through the gentlest kind of Technicolor. There is nothing brilliant about the picture, but it is perceptive, witty, and sweet-tempered, and it shows a continuous feeling for the charm and illuminating power of mannerism, speech, and gesture used semi-ritually, rather than purely realistically, which owes a good deal to Lubitsch in the good second-best of his comedies. I very much liked the performances of Roger Livesey as the Colonel, Deborah Kerr as his imago in three instalments, and Anton Walbrook as his German friend.

In *God Is My Co-Pilot* the Flying Tiger hero, Dennis Morgan, tells a priest, Alan Hale, that he has killed a hundred men that day; he obviously feels deeply troubled by the fact, and is asking for spiritual advice. Since the priest does not answer him in any way about that, but pretends to by commenting comfortably on a quite different and much easier perplexity— *every* death makes a difference to God—it is regrettable, not to say nauseating, that they bothered to bring up the problem at all. Aside from these religious conversations, any one of which would serve to unite atheists and religious men in intense distaste for the lodgers in the abyss which separates them, there is a good deal of air combat on process screens, obstructed by the customary close-ups of pilots smiling grimly as they give or take death in a studio, for considerably more than soldiers' pay, a yard above the ground. The picture is not as bad, I must admit, as I'm making it sound; but it is not good enough to make me feel particularly sorry about that. God is my best pal and severest critic, but when He asked for this touching March afternoon off, I didn't have it in my heart to refuse Him.

I would like to be able to make *The Affairs of Susan* sound half as bad as it is, but I know when I'm licked. In this interminable film, which might be described as a Make's Progress, Joan Fontaine is photographed as Joan of Arc; the Maid looks as if she were testifying, for a handsome fee, to every nice thing the Voices told her about Lysol. Miss Fontaine also appears as a lake-shore innocent, in trousers and a thinly knit jersey; in a series of gowns and negligees which are still more earnestly calculated to refute the canard that, if the Hays office permitted, she would be ashamed to make a clean breast of her "development" (I think the word is); and in a collusion of horn-rims, tight hair, ties, and sharp tailoring which, if they suggest nothing admissibly human, may at least roughly approximate Mayor LaGuardia's mental image of *Trio*. This sort of thing makes me all the angier because Miss Fontaine has proved that she is an actress worth building a good picture around—or even worth using in one which doesn't build around anyone. About Dennis O'Keefe's characterization of a writer, I feel less kind. He achieves it purely by letting his hair get rather long behind the ears. In objecting to this, I am probably the only living writer who has to cast his stone through a glass house; and much as I loathe haircuts, I have been trying ever since I saw the picture to brace myself to enter a barber shop.

April 7, 1945

Practically Yours is an interestingly nasty Colbert-MacMurray comedy about a war hero on leave, a girl who gets the mistaken impression that he loves her, and some of their misadventures with her boss, her white-collar suitor, the newsreels, the radio, bond selling, a commercial photographer, and a war wife played straight. In a roughly typical scene the leads watch what has been done to them on the screen in the darkness of a newsreel theater, the hero cannot keep his disgust to himself, and an inflamed civilian turns and busts him in the jaw. In another they are aboard a rush-hour subway car when, by nightmarish chance, his emergency life-raft inflates. It is one measure of the movie quality of these and many more scenes and bits of business and detail in the picture that—though few of them are done as well as they might be—they are much better on the screen than they can be made to sound in words. Taken as a whole, the picture doesn't amount to much; the same cynicism which is responsible for most of its good points has helped take care that it won't. But lurking in a great many odd corners of the show there is a really remarkable amount and variety of coldly perceptive hatred.

Without Love is a satiny translation of a Philip Barry play; I like it all right and have very little to say for or against it. Unlike Mr. Barry, I don't find the expression "by gum" charming on lips which use it for charm's sake, and enjoy even less the heroine's recalling, of her dying husband, that he "grinned that grin of his." But a good deal of the dialogue is happy to hear and happier in its skill; Katherine Hepburn and Spencer Tracy are exactly right for their jobs; it is good to see Lucille Ball doing so well with a kind of role new to her; and I have a hard time breaking myself against the idea that Keenan Wynn is the best actor in Hollywood, rather than just a very good one indeed.

I am of that majority opinion about Tallulah Bankhead which will forgive her anything, and likes her so well that that seldom comes into question; but in spite of her randy impersonation of Catherine the Great, I did not much enjoy *A Royal Scandal*. Possibly I am too owlish a democrat to be sufficiently thrilled by the thought that queens and the women in the windows are centaurs under the skin; and probably I take too seriously the fact that bawdiness, especially "sophisticated" bawdiness, bores and annoys me beyond mailable description unless it is handled with enough style or energy to absolve it, through heart or magic, of its infantilism. But so far as I know, it's just that nothing was one-tenth well enough done, and that all the laughs are played for at their cheapest, far down the ramp. I suspect that if I saw Ernst Lubitsch's original version of this story, *Forbidden Paradise*, again, I might think a good deal of his pantomime just as tiresomely prurient at its roots; but I am almost certain it would stand up even so as a much more delicate and forceful and amusing version. I wish this twenty-year-old show were revived, both for its own sake as I remember it, and because between the two versions I believe you could get a pretty good measure of the difference between talking and silent pictures. I realize, of course, that talking pictures can be better than *A Royal Scandal*, and as good as anything silent, and conceivably even better; but in order even to try to be so, they have to know the value of pantomime, and they have to know when to shut up.

Very late in the nth day after any proper one, I want to add to Manny Farber's, and Orson Welles's, my own respect for the Monogram melodrama *When Strangers Marry*. The story has locomotor ataxia at several of its joints, and the intensity of the telling slackens off toward the end; but taking it as a whole

I have seldom, for years now, seen one hour so energetically and sensibly used in a film. Bits of it, indeed, gave me a heart-lifted sense of delight in real performance and perception and ambition which I have rarely known in any film context since my own mind, and that of moving-picture making, were both sufficiently young. Thanks to that, I can no longer feel by any means so hopeless as I have, lately, that it is possible to make pictures in Hollywood that are worth making. When I think even no farther than of the people who made this, and of the Val Lewton contingent, and of the various journeymen who put so much venom into *Practically Yours*, I know there are enough people out there of real ability to turn the whole place upside down. I doubt they will ever do it, partly because I doubt it could be done without a good deal of gunfire, and that on no parochial scale. But quite a few of them mean business, and some of them are wedging out small ways, at least, of doing it.

April 14, 1945

The Enchanted Cottage is the famous old Pinero valentine—brought up to date and from England to New England—about a homely spinster and a disfigured veteran who, because they are in love, look beautiful to each other until people who are not involved in their illusion rudely shatter—I believe one should say—their frail dream world. When I saw Richard Barthelmess and May McAvoy play it, in the early fourteenth century, I was so transfigured by it that for some weeks afterward, behind locked doors, I alternated my imitations of Mr. Barthelmess's work, with his cane and his wrung shoulder, with sculptural replicas of Miss McAvoy's hooked nose and protruding teeth. I can recommend the new Robert Young–Dorothy McGuire version to susceptible adolescents of any age, but I doubt that I can give it—or could now give the old one—a fair review, for everything about it embarrasses me too painfully for clear thought: its solemnly whimsical good intentions, its slushy philosophy and still slushier dramaturgy, the little kernels of truth which it turns into so much molasses-dipped popcorn, and the impressive variety of whimpers, snorts, eyedabs, and frantically salvaged sobs which it tickled, pleaded, pressed, shanghaied, kicked, clubbed, and above all blackmailed out of me. I have no objection to tears when they are honest ones honestly extracted—quite the contrary; and very possibly some of these were of that sort, but if so I will never know. I had too constantly to be preoccupied with the feeling that my spiritual pockets were being picked by people with sad sweet smiles who, worse still, believed in both the smiles and the thieving.

As well as I could see, however, through fears generated chiefly by helpless rage against myself and my merciless assailants, the movie was done quite well for the delicately vulgar sort of thing it is, especially by Robert Young and Dorothy McGuire. I can hardly imagine, for that matter, being seriously offended by Mr. Young; whatever he does, he is honest and sympathetic beyond offensiveness. Although I am happy to have to respect Miss McGuire's sensitiveness and proficiency, I can't help feeling sorry to see her use such coarse, all but village-idiot bids for pity-please as the worst she uses to communicate the heroine in her humbler phase. It is possible to get any amount of popular acclaim as an artist, in the kingdom of the blind, by relaxing to a level of acting once admired in character roles in little-theater productions; but it is deplorable and very dangerous as well, and Miss McGuire surely knows, can do, and wants, better.

I have always felt that one of the most profound and moving of relationships is that which can develop between a teacher and pupil, provided that both are alive; so I think less well of *The Corn Is Green*—which does that once over lightly, with exotic and proletarian trimmings—than I might have if I had come to it unprejudiced. I did come to it unprejudiced in another sense, for I never saw Ethel Barrymore play it. Trustworthy people tell me that she would have left me with my tongue hanging out, and by my own experience of Miss Barrymore I can find no reason to doubt it. Bette Davis left me with my tongue in my head, and I hope I can make it a civil one. I like and respect Miss Davis as a most unusually sincere and hard-working actress, and I have seen her play extremely well; but I did not find much in this performance to bring one beyond liking, respect, and, I am afraid, a kind of sympathy which no healthily functioning artist needs. It seems to me she is quite limited, which may be no sin but is a pity, and that she is limiting herself beyond her rights by becoming more and more set, official, and first-ladyish in mannerism and spirit, which is perhaps a sin as well as a pity. In any case, very little about her performance seemed to me to come to life, in spite of a lot of experienced striving which often kept in touch with life as if through a thick sheet of glass. To be sure, the role is not a deeply perceived or well-written one, and the whole play seems stolid and weak. I have a feeling that Miss Davis must have a great deal of trouble finding films which seem appropriate, feasible, and worth doing, and I wish that I, or anyone else, could be of use to her in that. For very few people in her position in films mean, or could do, so well. But I doubt that anything could help much unless she were willing to discard much that goes with the position—unless, indeed, she realized the absolute necessity of doing so.

April 21, 1945

FRED ALLEN'S picture *It's in the Bag* is the story of a flea impresario named Floogle (Mr. Allen) who inherits a fortune and in the process of getting hold of it runs into Jack Benny, Minerva Pius, Robert Benchley, Jerry Colonna, Binnie Barnes, William Bendix, John Carradine, and others, often very amusingly, sometimes not, knocking off enough sparks of satire in the process to destroy and fulfil a much worse civilization than this one if their molecular energy were organized into their ultimate, collective, bomblike meaning.

The Unseen, a story about a governess and some rather provocative children who live next a portentous deserted house, is done with quite a bit of intelligence and sophistication (it was produced by John Houseman and directed by Lewis Allen), but unlike Allen's *The Uninvited* it only generates sporadic wincing qualms of excitement without ordering them into anything constant and cumulative.

Molly and Me is the sort of story you might run across in its fifth buckram binding, illustrated, along the General Fiction shelves of a provincial public library: ex-theatrical housekeeper sweetens up rich old griper; London; turn of the century. It is a tame, oldfashioned, charming, worthless picture, very prettily done, with an admirably intense performance by Doris Lloyd, a likable one by Monty Woolley, and a perfectly beautiful one by Gracie Fields. I think Miss Fields is about as nice a woman over forty as I have ever seen; I have certainly never seen anyone in movies to approach her in that age bracket. I recommend her highly to anyone who has ceased to believe it is possible to grow decently into middle age.

April 28, 1945

THE moving pictures of President Roosevelt made at Teheran and at Yalta and when he reported to Congress after Yalta are, I believe, the best records we have of him. In the first I had fully and with sympathy and deep respect realized, however belatedly, how much that had seemed frivolous and even silly in Roosevelt was the high-pitched nervousness of a vivid, sensitive intelligence, and was inextricable from an extraordinary gallantry, in part created by background and in part limited by it, which I have always venerated. In the Yalta pictures there is not only the frightening thinness and sickness, or portent of sickness, but also much more. President Roosevelt had long been a great and fascinating figure for reasons which seemed mainly external, historical; now beyond any question, it seems to me, he was himself becoming a great man. An exceedingly complex and in many ways devious personality was undergoing profound and very rapid change. It was becoming integrated on a level it had scarcely before approached. In the plainest, simplest senses of the words that I can think of, his face was becoming the face of a religious, even of a seer, without loss of its adroitness and worldly resourcefulness and its singular, triumphant, essential gaiety. I felt in the face an intimacy with death and with tragedy which I had never seen in it before, and through that quiet and resolute, cheerful intimacy, a wonderful kind of recklessness, of all save the best that might be perceived and endeavored for the good of all other men. In this curiously light, shining, calm recklessness, this sense that all personal scores were settled and dismissed, in this quality of heroism emergent at last upon its highest level and its grandest prospect, I felt hope of a kind it was impossible to feel in any other living man, and reverence, regardless of how sure I felt that the best hopes must be proved idle. In the moving pictures made when the President addressed Congress, I saw all these same newly crystallized qualities at ease within the gentleman, and was convinced that nothing could destroy them. Their only impermanence was in their great possible increase; now this possibility has been ended. I will not try to describe with what glacial implacability this fact and the following days corroborated and enhanced my impressions.

If there is any possible excuse for my writing so subjectively, beyond the fact that I can hardly write or think of anything else, it lies in the fact that I was and remain fairly close to political agnosticism; and that if a person of my kind can be so moved by such a man, and such an event, that may be one more measure and one more expression of what the man and the event mean to those who have and who practice political hope and faith. For my own part I continue without much hope. But I doubt that I can ever again think of a man who works in politics, if his effort seems truly disinterested, without deepest respect.

So, too, I think of the new President. It is hard to imagine that history can ever have brought any man into a more terrible predicament. I realize too, as he does and as everybody does, that, forced to stand up and work his best under pressures which would fill the greatest and wisest of men with an annihilating sense of inadequacy, he is not very far, if far at all, from what we too contemptuously describe as mediocrity. But here again I am a sample of alteration which I assume applies still more powerfully in others. I have always believed, and still believe, in gifted individuals, and have trusted chiefly in their performance. But I have also always believed that the best that is in any ordinary man is illimitable; and now when that kind of faith is to be so severely tested, in the President and, just as acutely, in millions of others, I find it greatly fortified. Partly, it is because I know that greatness can emerge only under adequately difficult circumstances and that most people, including the great President who has died, find in themselves not the circumstances but merely the intellectual or still more important the moral adequacy to circumstance if it arises. Just as much, it is because sympathy, responsibility, love, magnanimity, resoluteness, and the obligation to selflessness, now more clearly than before, rest with great and equal weight upon all human beings who can so much as apprehend their existence. The wish that one might be of use is as great at least as the dismay, the shock, and the sorrow. The ways by which ordinary men can be of use are tragically limited, even in a democracy. To a great extent one is forced to fall back on a metaphysical yet very literal faith in unanimity and massiveness of spirit. I believe that this exists, and that if it is known to exist it can have very great power.

May 12, 1945

THE script of *Counter-Attack* was written by John Howard Lawson, and the picture was directed by Zoltan Korda, who wrote and directed *Sahara*. Barring the beginning and a few shots which show the Russians building and crossing an underwater bridge, it is one of those specialized pictures, like *Lifeboat*, in which the problem is to keep a movie alive and exciting in limited space. (Here two Russians and eight Germans, trapped in a shelled basement, with limited light, wrestle out their national and class traits.) It isn't really such a hard problem as might offhand be imagined, since rigorous form and self-denial furnish their own tensions and suggest many of their own solutions. It seems to me for that matter rather a ham one. But the director and writer and cameraman (James Wong Howe) and most of the cast are to be complimented on solving it, most of the time, very intelligently, without much resort to trick incident or emotional balderdash. The Germans, indeed, like all the supporting players in *Sahara*, are out of a class with anything you can ordinarily see in a contemporary American-made fiction film; so is Korda's handling of them except when each steps forward and does his histrionic equivalent to the old cliché in which each girl in the chorus line executed a solo Charleston—but it looks as if that should be blamed chiefly on the script. These enemies, incidentally, are presented as individuals, not as congenital criminals; one of them even comes over to the Russian side, and does so without any blathering about repentance. Paul Muni, excellent in his quieter moments, is too often an over-generalized, stagy embodiment of Russia. There is a certain amount of complacent formula about the picture, of a kind nearer Russian than American (the original story is Russian), but there is a lot of aesthetic and psychological good to it, too. I think it is worth seeing; and I expect that any Lawson-Korda picture is going to be.

Greer Garson has kinds of vitality and resource which might do very good kinds of work, but ordinarily they are turned into wax. She is waxen in stretches of *The Valley of Decision*, and embarrassingly actressy in some others; but often too, as an Irish servant in a rich Scottish household, she is alive, vivid, and charming, and suggests how really good she might be under better circumstances. If she were not suffocated and immobilized by Metro's image of her—and, I'm afraid, half-persuaded of it herself—I could imagine her as a very good Lady Macbeth. I could still more easily imagine her as a wonderful Elisabeth Ney (the half-sane sculptress who reduced Schopenhauer to a drooler and left the court of Ludwig of Bavaria for a rotting estate in Texas). But I suppose the best she will ever be allowed is this sort of short trot in pre-conditioned open air. Tay Garnett's direction is good, too good to be wasted on big, solemn, expensive trash-collections like this.

May 19, 1945

THE recently released films which show Nazi atrocities are only part of what is rather clearly an ordered and successful effort to condition the people of this country against interfering with, or even questioning, an extremely hard peace against the people of Germany. The simple method is to show things more frightful than most American civilians have ever otherwise seen, and to pin the guilt for these atrocities on the whole German people. I am judging this to be so by what I have seen and read in the press and by the effect of the atrocity press and the atrocity films as it can be observed in everybody, by everybody. I have not felt it necessary to see the films themselves. I don't agree with those who will feel that this deprives me of the right to have some reactions and ideas of my own, in relation to the general matter; or that they are necessarily, for that reason, not worth putting on paper.

I cannot get my thoughts in order, yet, to write what I think needs writing, about such propaganda and the general reaction to it. But I do want to go on record against it, as I believe many other people would like to, before our voices become indistinguishable among those of the many confused or timid or villainous people who are likely after a while, when the shock wears off—and when it is safe or even stylish—to come somewhat to their senses. Briefly then: the passion for vengeance is a terrifyingly strong one, very easily and probably inevitably wrought up by such evidence, even at our distance. But however well aware I am of its strength, and that in its full immediate force and expression it is in some respects irrelevant to moral inquiry, I doubt that it is ever to be honored, or regarded as other than evil and in every direction fatally degrading and destructive; even when it is obeyed in hot blood or in a crisis of prevention; far worse when it is obeyed in cold blood and in the illusion of carrying out justice.

I think it has taken such strong hold on so many of us most essentially because we suspect the passion itself, and know that even if the passion were a valid one to honor there would be no finding victims, or forms of vengeance, remotely sufficient to satisfy it. We cannot bear to face our knowledge that the satisfaction of our desire for justice, which we confuse with our desire for vengeance, is impossible. And so we invent as a victim the most comprehensive image which our reason, however deranged, will permit us: the whole of a people and the descendants of that people: and count ourselves incomparably their superiors if we stop short of the idea of annihilation. And we refuse to grant that this war has proved itself lost—if indeed it ever could have been won—as surely in our own raging vengefulness as in that of the mob in the Milan square. Indeed, we are worse than they and worse, in some respects, than the Nazis. There can be no bestiality so discouraging to contemplate as that of the man of good-will when he is misusing his heart and his mind; and there can be no trusting him merely because, in the long run, he customarily comes part way to, and resumes his campaign for, what he likes to call human dignity.

May 26, 1945

San Pietro is the record of the part which one regiment of infantrymen took in one of several fights which resulted in the capture of one village, the key to an Italian valley. At the end of the fight the seven-hundred-year-old village was chaos, and the regiment required 1,100 replacements. *San Pietro* runs only half an hour, and still leaves much of a world open to the most highly imaginative use of its kind of material. But it is in every way as good a war film as I have seen; in some ways it is the best.

It was made by six Signal Corps cameramen under the command of Major John Huston, who also designed the scenario and wrote and spoke the narration. Most of these men were veterans. That fact presumably helps to explain a number of things: how they all lived through the shooting of the film; how deep inside the fighting some of it was made; how well they evidently understood what to expect, how to shoot it, what it was good for, and its weight and meaning in the whole picture. But remarkable as the cameramen evidently were, it is fairly clear that the main credit for the picture goes to Major Huston. He moved continually from one of his men to the next, showing them what he wanted and where to go for it; he kept planning and revising his scenario and his narration in spare time during the days and nights of fighting; he had to work blind, for the film was developed and printed in Washington and he saw nothing he had—or had lost—until he got back to this country. Yet Huston and his cameramen understood so well what they were after that when he did return, to assemble the film, he had to make very few changes in his narration.

The attitudes which have pervaded most of our combat films are seldom questionable and usually something to be proud of; but there is a major advance here. It is clear that Huston understood what he was recording, and how to record it, with a wonderfully vigorous and whole maturity, at once as a soldier and an artist and a man. No war film I have seen has been quite so attentive to the heaviness of casualties, and to the number of yards gained or lost, in such an action; none has so levelly watched and implied what it meant, in such full and complex terms—in military terms; in terms of the men who were doing the fighting; in terms of the villagers; and of their village; and of the surrounding country; and of the natural world; and of human existence and hope.

Huston's narration is a slightly simplified technical prose, at once exact and beautifully toned and subtly parodistic; it is spoken with finely shaded irony, equally free of pompousness and optimism and mawkish generalizations and cheap bitterness. Against the images he has chosen, their always satisfying arrangement, and their beautiful over-all plan and implication, this text points itself so richly and flexibly that for once wordiness in a film more than earns its way. As for the over-all plan and implication, I don't see how that of any postwar film is going to improve on it, and I rather doubt that any will come quite up to it. For at one and the same time, without one slip along the line, from the most ticklish fringes of taste to the depths of a sane mind and heart, it accepts the facts and treats them as materials relevant to anger, tenderness, pride, veneration, and beauty. Somewhere close to the essence of the power of moving pictures is the fact that they can give you things to look at, clear of urging or comment, and so ordered that they are radiant with illimitable suggestions of meaning and mystery. Huston's simple, wordless use of children, toward the end of this film, does that, and seems to me the first great passage of war poetry that has got on the screen. In emphatic agreement with some recent comments by Bernard Haggin, however, I do want to object to one thing; music can only vitiate this kind of film. Here, with all words and irony at last withdrawn, as you watch the faces of the children, each one unimaginably beautiful and portentous, and ordered and timed into their culmination as nobly as the words in a great tragic line, it is as infuriating to have to fight off the emotional sales pressure of the Mormon Choir as it would be if all the honored watches and nasal aphrodisiacs insisted on marketing themselves against a Toscanini broadcast.

Music can be well used in movies. It was wonderfully used in Dovzhenko's *Frontier*, for instance; for another kind I like the naive, excitable, perfectly appropriate score of the sound-tracked version of *The Birth of a Nation*; and indeed I think the greatest possibilities have hardly yet been touched. But music is just as damaging to nearly all fiction films as to nearly all fact films, as it is generally used in both today. Its ability to bind together a succession of images, or to make transitions between blocks of them—not to mention "transitional" and "special-effect" and "montage" passages—inevitably makes for laziness or for slackened imagination in making the images and setting them in order, and in watching them. Still worse, it weakens the emotional imagination both of maker and on-looker, and makes it virtually impossible to communicate or receive ideas. It sells too cheaply and far too sensually all the things it is the business of the screen itself to present. The rough equivalent might be a poet who could dare to read aloud from his own work only if the lights were dimmed and some Debussy was on, very low.

One of the best scenes in Vincente Minelli's new picture, *The Clock*, is a good example. In this scene a soldier (Robert Walker) and a girl (Judy Garland) walk, as if hypnotized, into their first embrace. A kind of sentimental mysticism is tried for here, and more than achieved; moreover the timing of their walk and of the several shots is boldly and successfully unreal-istic; the increasingly large close-ups and the gravity, the sug-gestion of death, which grows in the soldier's face achieve at once a remarkably deep and pure power of the moment and of the individuals, and a kind of generic pity and majesty. But all this time, with the dirtiest and most merciless kind of effi-ciency, a full orchestra and hyped-up soprani are working at you, below the belt. How much better the same scene would play silent, or at least without music, I cannot gauge; but I am reasonably sure of two things. It would play much better; and if Minelli had not been assuming soft-salty horn-choirs and other questionable kinds of assistance—he was anyhow well content with them once they were glued on—he would have exerted himself to make the scene still more powerful. (A sudden reduction of the sounds of the city, to which they had just been listening, would have been good enough; but those sounds are as unimaginatively worked out as the music itself.)

The whole of *The Clock* suffers in every field from equivalent kinds of softness. It is strictly a romance, and in every essential respect a safe one, safely told, disappointing and angering in the thought of the great film it might have been. (The very simple story of a soldier's two days in New York, it had every right to be as good in its own very different way as *San Pietro*.) But within its softly chosen terms it is also quite charmingly and sometimes beautifully told. Emotionally, it is perceptive, detailed, and sweet, and there is more ability, life, resource, and achievement in it than in any fiction film I have seen for a long time. The script by Robert Nathan and Joseph Schranck is very shrewd; but the man who pours it so full of gifts is Minelli. Considering the breadth and variety of his talents, his eye and feeling for the city itself are surprisingly dull; but his extras and their gaits and groupings and clothes, and their stammering collisions and multiplicities of purpose and aimlessness, beat anything I can remember out of Hollywood; and while I don't wholly care for his passion for elastic boom-shots and for the curiously pelvic rhythm he gives this picture, I can certainly respect the achievement. Minelli appears, too, to know better than most directors just how to use his individual players: to turn the show over to Keenan Wynn for his alcoholic cadenza; to retract slightly James Gleason and to leave his wife Lucille a long tether; to develop in Robert Walker his singular gentleness and pathos and to rid him of infantile mannerisms; and to prove for the first time beyond anybody's doubt that Judy Garland can be a very sensitive actress. In this film Miss Garland can handle every emotion in sight, in any size and shape, and the audience along with it. Incidentally, the dress she wears during most of the film is about the most appropriate prop I can remember since McTeague's checked cap in *Greed*.

By what I can see in the film, and have heard, Minelli does not discriminate very clearly between the good in his work and the not-so-good or the downright bad which in part he puts into it and which in part is forced on him. Much as I regret that, it may on the whole be just as well. If he knew better, he might be either much more of an artist or much less of one; in either case he would have a much harder time working in Hollywood. I suspect I may overrate this best of his films; but I also suspect that twenty and fifty years from now, however embarrassing a lot of it is, it will be remembered.

June 9, 1945

WHEN a good man gets a real chance in Hollywood it is not only news; the least one can do is salute those who, aware of the gamble, gave him the money and the chance and protected him in it. So, with pleasure, I salute David Loew and Robert Hakim, thanks to whom Jean Renoir has made *The Southerner*, his own adaptation of George Sessions Perry's *Hold Autumn in Your Hand. The Southerner* is an attempt to tell the story of a year in the life of a family of cotton tenant farmers. Though its people are exceedingly poor, this is not a political or social "exposure" of the tenant system, nor does it pay any attention to class or racial friction. It tries simply to be a poetic, realistic chronicle of a farm year's hope, work, need, anxiety, pride, love, disaster, and reward—a chronicle chiefly of soil, seasons, and weather, the only other dramatic conflict being furnished by a pathologically unkind neighbor. About sixty per cent of the film was made on location—in California not Texas; most of the time the rest is so well done that you can't tell the difference. Physically, exclusive of the players, it is one of the most sensitive and beautiful American-made pictures I have seen. There is a solemnly eager, smoky, foggy 'possum hunt which may have been studio-faked for all I know; it gets perfectly the mournful, hungry mysteriousness of a Southern country winter. There is an equally good small-town street; I have seldom, in a movie, seen the corner of a brick building look at once so lonely and so highly charged with sadness and fear.

Yet warmly as I respect the picture's whole design and the many good things about it, I saw it with as much regret as pleasure. The heart of this kind of living is work, and the picture should have made the work as immediate to the watcher as to the worker in all its methods, meanings, and emotions. It offers instead, mere token shots of work; and in these, too often, the clothes aren't even sweated. Just as unfortunate and more constantly disappointing, most of the players are wrong, anywhere from a little bit to a whole world wide of the mark. I don't so much mind that the dialect is very much thinned out, or even that it lacks uniformity. The thinning, to the point of general intelligibility, is a convention I would accept, though I'd put my money on handling it straight. The lack of uniformity, though far less defensible, I would accept if only the people were right in other respects—which in that case would be unlikely. But most of the people were screechingly, unbearably wrong. They didn't walk right, stand right, eat right, sound right, or look right, and, as bad or worse, behind the work of each it was clear that the basic understanding and the basic emotional and mental—or merely human—attitudes were wrong, to the point of unintentional insult.

To cast and realize such a film correctly would be, I must grant, one of the hardest conceivable jobs; but when has that stopped being an artist's responsibility? The one person in the film who for all his minor mistakes is basically right, in everything from cheekbones and eyes to posture to spiritual attitude, is Zachary Scott; he was born in Texas. J. Carroll Naish is no Texan, but he is such an observant, disciplined, and clear-spirited actor that he comes close to making up the difference. I have no desire to go into unkind detail about other players such as Beulah Bondi, Betty Field, Percy Kilbride, Blanche Yurka, Norman Lloyd, and two dreadfully miscalculated children, but I'll have to a little, to make my point at all clear. Percy Kilbride is a wonderful player of certain rural types, but it is hard to imagine him much south of Connecticut or much west of the Hudson. Betty Field clearly and deeply cares for the kind of regional exactness I too care for; but her efforts to disguise the fact that she is an intelligent, sincere young artist who feels sympathy and respect for a farmer's wife are as embarrassing as mine would be if I tried to play Jeeter Lester. Beulah Bondi, an actress I generally admire, demonstrates merely how massively misguided, and how swarmed with unconscious patronage, the whole attitude of the theater has always been toward peasants. I don't want to go on. I am afraid that in my objection to this kind of inaccuracy there are streaks of parochial pedantry and snobbery. But mainly, so far as I know, my objection comes out of a respect for people. If you are going to try to show real people, in a real place, I think that you have to know how their posture and speech and facial structure can alter even within the width of one county; that you have to communicate the exact beauty of those minute particulars without their ever becoming more pointed to the audience than to the people portrayed, and without a single false tone; that if you don't you are in grave danger of unconscious patronage, you don't see or appreciate or understand your subjects as well as you think you do, you stand likely therefore to be swamped by your mere affection or respect, and so perhaps should give up the whole idea.

August 11, 1945

I SEE no reason why any of the following films should be reviewed at length. *Anchors Aweigh*, a musical about two sailors, a girl, and José Iturbi, is thoroughly happy-spirited and enjoyable; but once I have paid my particular respects to Gene Kelly, who dances and acts excellently, and to Frank Sinatra, a singer, I might as well move on. The March of Time's issue about teen-age girls is worth seeing in the sense that one might examine with interest a slide of cancer tissue. These girls may be no worse than the teen-age girls of any other country, class, or generation, but I would be sorry really to believe that, and am sorrier still to imagine their children.

Another powerful horror short, *The Fleet That Came to Stay*, is a record of Kamikaze, cut for thrills, but productive rather of dread, pity, and awe in any imaginative spectator. (I felt uneasy, by the way, not to say disgusted, when the narrator dismissed the Japanese fliers as "the men who want to die.") *Captain Eddie* combines some unpersuasive suffering aboard the Rickenbacker raft with extensive flashbacks to Rickenbacker's youth. These contain some pretty uses of detail and evocations of atmosphere, but the picture is at its mild best in its obsession with the comedy of pre-Pershing popular tunes, dance steps, and ground and flying machines.

The heroine of *Incendiary Blonde* bears the name of Texas Guinan, and at least once she shouts an obligatory "Hello, Sucker." From then on out the picture successfully ignores every one of the thousands of fine possibilities offered by its nominal subjects, in favor of entirely conventional noise and music. Betty Hutton just about saves it, but no more, for those who like her and I do. *Jealousy*, a Republic picture, was made by Gustav Machaty, who made *Ecstasy*. The story is of domestic misery, involving a disinterested refugee, and developing into murder melodrama. It is intelligently cast, and well played by Nils Asther, the extremely attractive Karen Morley, a fine, warm-hearted actor named Hugo Haas, John Loder, and Jane Randolph. The music is by Hans Eisler. I doubt that *Jealousy* will have any great success, either critical or commercial; but it is a sympathetic film, and in spite of its over-all failure, contains enough sincerity and enough artistry to make most of the other films mentioned here look sick.

I must catch up, too, on some more of the older films I have failed to review.

A Medal for Benny, after a rather mawkish start, turns into a broad but furious and well-filmed piece of invective against the attempt of some small-town boosters to exploit the death of a proletarian war hero. There is a first-rate performance by J. Carroll Naish. *Wonder Man* has little good in it beyond Danny Kaye—who, however, is almost continuously on screen. At his best Kaye suggests that he might be a much better comedian than he has yet become; at his loudest and blurriest he suggests that he may never become that good; but even at worst he is more than good enough. *Conflict*, another domestic murder piece (Humphrey Bogart and Rose Hobart), is quite well done, but its story is so fancy that it becomes tiresome. *Those Endearing Young Charms*, the story of a habitual seducer and his Waterloo, is well played by Robert Young and Laraine Day, well directed by Lewis Allen, and not quite interesting enough to be worth the time it takes. *Where Do We Go From Here?*, a fantasy in which Fred MacMurray strolls through American history to music by Kurt Weill and lyrics by Ira Gershwin, is nine parts heavy facetiousness to one part very good fun. *That's the Spirit*, a fantasy in which Jack Oakie, a ghost, leaves heaven to watch over his daughter Peggy Ryan, is clumsy but mildly enjoyable. I will not bother to speak of *The Singing Fool* or the latest Annette Kellerman waterwing, on the assumption that they are no longer in circulation.

It may be unforgivably decadent of me, but I cannot get much excited about incest, nor do I feel that any great victory has been won because a story about incest, *Uncle Harry*, has escaped from the Hays office in still fairly recognizable condition. I am, however, definitely excited by watching characters in conflict with themselves and with others; by the beauty, intelligence, and ability of Geraldine Fitzgerald; and by seeing her after years of criminal neglect in a role which, though not by a long way good enough for her, does give her room to move around in and things to do, and ought to guarantee her roles as good or better, from now on. Though he bats his eyes too often, as a sign that he is a simple soul, George Sanders is generally good as Miss Fitzgerald's infantile brother. Ella Raines is very handsome and effective as the woman who tries to make him grow up. I also like Angela Lansbury's mother, Moyna Maggill, as the gentler sister. The small New England town and its inhabitants are well-detailed, too—especially a set of witnesses at the murder trial, and the perfect dressing of Miss Raines' semi-permanent room in the hotel. I imagine the two people most to be thanked for so intelligently casting, specifying, and bringing to life this generally superior movie are the producer, Joan Harrison, and the director, Robert Siodmak. Nobody is to be thanked for the asinine ending. But if you will take care to hurry for the nearest exit as soon as Miss Fitzgerald tells her brother that that is the way things are, *Uncle Harry* can be recommended.

Over 21 is Ruth Gordon's story of the liberal newspaper editor who joined the army and was joined by his wife and his former boss in a crowded and flimsy Miami cottage. Some of the congestion and despair is amusing, especially a catastrophic cocktail party at which the ex-editor tries to entertain his Colonel and the Colonel's two ladies. I don't feel that Irene Dunne has quite the right kind of humor to play the wife, but Alexander Knox is very proficient as the editor, even when he is required to be impossibly silly. Toward the end of the film, resuming his impersonation of Wilson, he reads a most sincere editorial in which the creation of the postwar world is compared with the creation of an apple pie. In either undertaking, if disaster is to be averted, all the ingredients have got to be good. Since all the world is not apple pie, but is composed of atoms which have just begun to learn that they are many, and that we are few, I found this editorial unbearably discouraging.

Bewitched, which is derived from an Arch Oboler radio play, is Oboler's first movie. It is a melodrama about double personality, and uses mental voices and dialogue as profusely as if it were on the air. When these interior voices are expressive, carefully timed, and counterpointed with any discretion whatever, Oboler manages the first persuasive imitations of stream of consciousness I know of in a movie. Much more often, he bores to desperation with the vulgarity and mere violence of his "effects." As a moving picture *Bewitched* is at moments vigorous and at all times essentially lifeless. But the sensitiveness and charm of Phyllis Thaxter and the honesty and force of Horace McNally make it worth seeing.

I must apologize for postponing even the attempt to review *The Story of G.I. Joe*; the secondary radiations of the atomic bomb render me still unfit to consider a piece of work I so deeply admire. My apologies also for careless proof-reading, meaning none at all. The Nils Esther mentioned in the issue of August 11 is, of course, Nils Asther.

September 15, 1945

A GREAT FILM

WILLIAM WELLMAN and the others who are responsible for *Story of G.I. Joe* obviously did not regard their job as an ordinary one. They undertook a great subject. It is clear that they undertook it in a determination to handle it honestly and to make a masterpiece. A wonderful amount of their achievement measures up to their intention. If their picture had been made under the best of circumstances, in a time when everyone who had the heart and the talent was free to make the best pictures possible, it would still be among the best. Coming as it does out of a world in which even the best work is nearly always compromised, and into a world which is generally assumed to dread honesty and courage and to despise artistic integrity, it is an act of heroism, and I cannot suggest my regard for it without using such words as veneration and love. Many things in the film itself move me to tears—and in none of them do I feel that I have been deceived, or cynically seduced or manipulated, as one usually has to feel about movies. But not even the finest of the picture's achievements are more moving than the angry, bitter nobility of the intention which is implied behind the whole of it.

The authors of the screen play, Leopold Atlas and Guy Endore and Philip Stevenson, have not only avoided writing a story, in any traditional sense; they have also developed a rather original narrative style, dry, keen, sober, and visually very imaginative. This style seems to be based to some extent on that of Hemingway; but it is freer than some of Hemingway's less good writing of self-pity, over-insistent masculinity, and the musical gift which sometimes blurs even the most beautiful things Hemingway observes into one kind of Irish croon. Many of the scenes end abruptly; some are deliberately deflated or interrupted or made to end flat or tonelessly. All these devices are artful or, if you like, artificial, but on one seeing, anyhow, not one seemed dishonest either aesthetically or morally. It is about as taciturn a picture as I have seen; but not a verbal or speechless stretch in it seems forced or ineffective. Much use is made of a commonplace of good movie making which most American studios reject: that you can show a wave of action, even very complex and cryptic action, more excitingly and instructively rather than less if you don't pause continually to explain it to the audience, and if you don't delete the inexplicable. There is a wonderfully discreet and powerful use, for that matter, of purely "meaningless" bits—such as a shot in which Ernie Pyle (Burgess Meredith) sits by the road while some soldiers straggle past—which have as great meaning as anything could have, being as immediate and as unlimited by thought or prejudice as what the eye might see on the spot, in a casual glance. And visually there are some of the most eloquent and simple things ever put into a movie—the scene, for instance, in which the worn-out captain and the wretched young replacement private, silently and in great tension and shyness, watch and approach each other, and are interrupted by the sudden violent mental breakdown of a third soldier.

Many of the best things in the film are done just as exactly and unemphatically. With a slight shift of time and scene, men whose faces have become familiar simply aren't around any more. The fact is not commented on or in any way pointed; their absence merely creates its gradual vacuum and realization in the pit of the stomach. Things which seem at first tiresome, then to have become too much of a running gag, like the lascivious tongue-clacking of the professional stallion among the soldiers (Wally Cassell) or the Sergeant's continual effort to play the record of his son's voice, are allowed to run their risks without tip-off or apology. In the course of many repetitions they take on full obsessional power and do as much as anything could to communicate the terrific weight of time, fatigue, and half-craziness which the picture is trying so successfully to make you live through. The characters are just as unobtrusively introduced and developed—so quietly, in fact, that it is misleading to speak of "development" in any traditional sense. One of the most terrible things in the movie is the silent uninsistent notice of the change in the face of the youngest of the soldiers, after his first battle, from that of a lonely, brave, frightened boy to something shriveled and poisoned beyond suggesting by words. And the development of the character of the Captain is so imperceptible and so beautifully done that, without ability to wonder why, you accept him as a great man in his one open attempt to talk about himself and the war, and as a virtual divinity in the magnificent scene which focuses on his dead body. This closing scene seems to me a war poem as great and as beautiful as any of Whitman's. One of the glories of the over-all style and tone of the film is its ability to keep itself stopped down so low and so lucid, like a particularly strong and modest kind of prose, and to build a long gently rising arch of increasing purity and intensity, which, without a single concession to "poetic" device, culminates in the absoluteness of that scene.

In a film so excellent there are so many things to honor, and to comment on, that I feel incapable of clearness even on a few, much less of completeness or order. The picture contains, for instance, the first great triumphs of the kind of anti-histrionic casting and acting which I believe is indispensable to most, though by no means all, kinds of greatness possible to movies. It would be impossible in that connection to say enough in praise of the performance of Bob Mitchum as the Captain and Freddie Steele as the Sergeant, or of Wellman for his directing and, I suppose, casting of them. It is also the first great triumph in the effort to combine "fiction" and "documentary" film. That is, it not only makes most of its fiction look and sound like fact—and far more intimate and expressive fact than it is possible to record on the spot; it also, without ever inflating or even disturbing the factual quality, as Eisenstein used to, gives fact the constant power and meaning beyond its own which most "documentors"—and most imaginative artists as well—totally lack feeling for. I don't insist on the word if you feel it is misleading, but most of this film is good poetry, and some of it is great poetry, and all of its achievements, and even most of its failures, are earned in terms purely of moving pictures. The sudden close-up, for instance, of a soldier's loaded back, coldly intricate with the life-and-death implements of his trade, as he marches away from his dead captain, is as complete, moving, satisfying, and enduring as the finest lines of poetry I know.

This is not a faultless movie. Most of its scenes are perfectly and often originally fitted together, but one of the major transitions—between Africa and Italy—is diffuse, generalized, and conventional, and another—the fight for Cassino—remains rather a disappointing and somewhat leaky transition, not the climactic release of energy that was needed and I believe intended. Indeed, though I am aware of my limited right to an opinion, it seems to me that the movie does fail in one important thing: to give adequate direct impressions—indirectly, it gives any number—of the individual's experience of combat. Even when shots from *San Pietro* are used, in the last fight, the reality to the individual does not come through; and when the Captain and the Sergeant outwit German snipers in a ruined church, the episode seems brilliant, highly specialized, and almost literary, rather than something common to the experience of many infantrymen. If people as good as these can't communicate that experience, I am about ready to believe it has been proved inexpressible; but I still wonder what might have been done if during one combat sequence the camera had worked inside some individual as well as outside. Much of the picture is very somber in lighting and slow in movement—it has drawn as intelligently on Mauldin as on Pyle—but some of this darkness seems a little sumptuous and studioesque; and some of the outdoor sets, diligent and good as they are, seem over-prepared, with nothing left to chance, like the groundwork of a first-rate diorama—as if the mud had been churned up inch by inch by union labor, before the actors took over. But these are about the only faults worth mentioning; and if by any chance *Story of G.I. Joe* is not a masterpiece, then however stupid my feeling is, I cannot help resenting those films which are.

I imagine that some people, better educated than the infantrymen in *Story of G.I. Joe*, will wish to point out that for all its courage and intelligence "as far as it goes," the film is not, in the sense they understand it, "an indictment of war." Nobody is accused, not even the enemy; no remedy is indicated; and though every foot of the film is as full an indictment of war as I ever expect to see, it is clearly also demonstrating the fact that in war many men go well beyond anything which any sort of peace we have known, or are likely to know, makes possible for them. It seems to me a tragic and eternal work of art, concerned with matters which I know are tragic and which I suspect are as eternal, anyhow, as our use of recent scientific triumphs will permit. Both the film and I may be wrong about this, but I am afraid the burden of proof rests with the optimists.

September 29, 1945

THE following are more or less recommended:

The True Glory. Official war film, invasion of Normandy to German surrender. Bold, welcome, but inadequate use of blank verse; much more successful use of many bits of individualized vernacular narration, unusually free of falseness. Very jab-paced, energetic cutting; intelligent selection of shots, of which several hundred—so it seems—are magnificent. Lacks the greatness of the best short war films, but for the hugely complicated kind of job it is, it could hardly have been done better, on a fact-telling plane anyhow.

Pride of the Marines. A true story of a blinded Marine. Very good performances by John Garfield and Dane Clark. An exciting combat sequence, unusually persuasive of authenticity, at least to this layman. Considerable liberalizing about racial and postwar problems, most of it a pleasure to hear, some of it rather mouthily over-optimistic (don't crab—if we fight for our rights and needs we're sure to have nothing to crab about). Long drawn out and never inspired, but very respectably honest and dogged, thanks considerably, it appears, to Albert Maltz's screen play.

Isle of the Dead. Val Lewton–Mark Robson horror film, with Karloff, Katherine Emery, Helene Thimig especially effective. Tedious, over-loaded, diffuse, and at moments arty, yet in many ways to be respected, up to its last half-hour or so; then it becomes as brutally frightening and gratifying a horror movie as I can remember. (More self-contained, and more pleasingly toned and told, is Lewton's recent *Body Snatchers*, with Karloff, Lugosi, Henry Daniell. It too, for all its charm and talent, is a little dull and bookish; but it explodes into an even finer, and a far more poetic, horror-climax—which, however, is sustained for only the last few minutes.)

State Fair. Rodgers and Hammerstein adaptation of the Phil Stong novel; nice performances by Jeanne Crain, Dana Andrews, Henry Morgan; pretty tunes, graceful lyrics. Otherwise lacking any real delicateness, vitality, or imagination, and painfully air-conditioned-looking, for a bucolic film; it is nevertheless good-natured and pleasant.

Our Vines Have Tender Grapes. Life on a Wisconsin farm with Margaret O'Brien, Edward G. Robinson, Agnes Moorehead, who perform exceedingly well. Here too a lack both of rural redolence and of fresh air; in stretches almost as indigestible as its title. But some of the willful leisureliness comes properly to life, and several scenes and many details are as gracious and touching as the intention of the whole film.

Love Letters. A story so inconceivably factitious that only a poet-moralist or a romancer of genius could have been wisely attracted by it, or could have brought it above the sill of absurdity. But Lee Garmes's lighting and photography are wonderful, in a romantic way I do not personally care for; and his—or William Dieterle's—camera set-ups and shot-series and

Dieterle's directing are like a highly skilled piece of wrestling. Most of the acting, especially that of Ann Richards (in a rather easy role), has unusual intensity and style.

Considerably less commendable is *Her Highness and the Bell-Boy*, a would-be Modern Fairy Story told with incredible heaviness and made only sporadically enjoyable through the friendliness of Robert Walker and Rags Ragland, the beauty of Hedy Lamarr, the sincerity of June Allyson.

October 13, 1945

Mildred Pierce. Nasty, gratifying version of the James Cain novel about suburban grass-widowhood and the power of the native passion for money and all that money can buy. Attempt made to sell Mildred as noble when she is merely idiotic or at best pathetic; but constant, virulent, lambent attention to money and its effects, and more authentic suggestions of sex than one hopes to see in American films. Excellent work by Joan Crawford, Jack Carson, Zachary Scott, and a little girl whose name I can't find who is as good an embodiment of all that is most terrifying about native contemporary adolescence as I ever hope to see. John McManus of *PM* and doubtless many others regard the film as a bad advertisement for this country abroad. As movies go, it is one of the few anywhere near honest ones, if that is of any importance; and should be signally helpful in holding down immigration to the kind of people we appear to want—people like the immeasurably swinish German family in *Girl Number 217*.

Girl Number 217. Russian story of a German family and its wartime slave. Insists, infuriatingly, that these are average Germans, implying—finally even stating—that all Germans are equally bestial and guilty. They are not average anything, but they are intelligent, powerful caricatures of the worst that can be expected of the petty bourgeois, anywhere (see above), even in Russia, where presumably they go by some other class name. Passionately acted and in general well conceived and well done; a little like Flaubert rewritten with hammer and sickle.

The House on 92d Street. Semi-fictional telescoping of several FBI espionage jobs. Unconvincing brouhaha to the effect that this could not be released prior to Hiroshima. Convincing inadvertent suggestion that the FBI functions efficiently less through intelligence than through doggedness plus scientific equipment. Extensive and gratifying use of actual-spot shooting and reenactment. Effective pseudo-naturalistic performances by Lydia St. Clair, Gene Lockhart, William Eythe, and others, none of whom, however, manage to suggest how spies, counterspies, and traitors who look and act like that are not identifiable to those interested at five hundred paces. Unpersuasive, often skilled, generally enjoyable.

October 27, 1945

Early in *Kiss and Tell* Shirley Temple's screen mother is horrified to find the child stepping up her sales of guest towels to soldiers, at some kind of patriotic ice-cream supper, by throwing in kisses. This is so played that one half expects the injured innocent to squawk suddenly, "But *jee*pers, Mommy, it was only for *mon*ey," and to be snatched-to-bosom and cooed over forgivingly for the quintessence of clean-limbed American nubility she is. But that would have given too quick and conscious a happy ending; the authors have hours more of the same and worse up their sleeves. There is, for instance, a lump of calf love from across the lawn who, when he is not too busy bumping into properties, expresses himself all but exclusively through several thousand exclamations of "*ho*-ly *ca*-ow!" not too mercifully varied, now and then, by "*don't* be a *dree-yup*!" There is a Horrid Little Brother whose own favorite aria is a withering "persnly I think it's all *ve*-ry *dumb*." There is an hour or so during which the audience, pimpishly helped out by the camera, which develops an almost pathological interest in the girl's hind quarters, may tickle itself with the thought that most of the other players think that Shirley—yes, little tiny *Shir*-ley—is pregnant and, for a while, even unmarried. There is a plot held together only through the enormous stupidity, cowardice, and mean-heartedness of as ugly a bunch of suburban parents as have never yet got themselves done up brown, in any treatment worthy of them. It is all brilliantly characteristic of the worst anyone could think of American family life, and it is all clearly presented on the assumption that you will find it charming, and sympathetic, and funny, because everyone in it is so exactly like you. I like Shirley Temple, and I rather like this movie, but I can't accept a foot of it, I'm afraid, in quite the spirit it is offered in.

Blithe Spirit. Noel Coward's smooth color production of his play about the ghostly wife who returns to make mischief with the kind of second marriage generally insisted on in the dangerous words "perfectly happy." The ghost, who faintly suggests a *bidet* out of repair, is very entertaining. Whenever Margaret Rutherford is on screen, as the medium who starts and tries to control the trouble, the picture is wonderfully funny.

And Then There Were None. René Clair–Dudley Nichols version of the Agatha Christie round-robin. Might better have been played for fear as much as for taste and laughs. Skillful cast, stretches of pretty Clair adroitness; almost devoid of feeling; a smooth, cold, amusing show.

Duffy's Tavern. The radio characters and a variety show including everyone in Paramount—except maybe Y. Frank Freeman—who was not overseas, in hiding, or out to lunch. Most of their turns are about as incisive as a Mozart sonata played through a catcher's mitt; but Ed Gardner and Victor Moore are very likable and sometimes quite funny.

Paris Underground. Constance Bennett production of the Etta Shiber noble about two women who helped innumerable grounded airmen get back to England. Good performance by Bennett except in any attempt to portray actions requiring a heart. Excellent performance by Gracie Fields. Otherwise mainly trash, involving enough handsome young men, in various postures of gallant gratitude, to satisfy Mae West in her prime.

November 10, 1945

Confidential Agent is a surprisingly serious translation of Graham Greene's thriller about a Spanish Republican who came to England to negotiate a coal deal for his government and ran into a kind of nightmare cartoon of the cruelty, treachery, stupidity, and hopelessness of the period. The film's intre-

pidity in calling Sp—n, and even F–sc–sm, by their full right
names would have been easier to appreciate in 1938 or so. Yet
this is in some ways an exciting and good picture, the best attempt yet, though still inadequate, to make the most of a
Greene novel. Charles Boyer, imaginatively cast, gives the agent
a proper balance of incongruous frailty, incompetence, tragic
responsibility, and moral courage; Lauren Bacall is still amateurish and she is about as English as Pocahontas, but her very
individual vitality more than makes up for her deficiencies. The
various capitalists, workers, fascists, thugs, scientific idiots, ide-
alistic imbeciles, and perfidious undergrounders of Greene's
fable are played with unhoped-for edge and earnestness, with
especially vivid performances by Katina Paxinou, Peter Lorre,
and a young girl, new to me, named Wanda Hendrix. Even
Greene's somewhat mawkish metaphysic of universal mistrust
is undertaken rather than discarded. In several scenes—Lorre's
ugly aria of fear, Hendrix's death, Boyer's horrible parting
scene with Paxinou—the players bear down and the camera
bores in with an intensity which suggests the sense of liberty,
even in matters irrelevant to censorship, which freedom from
the Hays code can bring. The most interesting failures in the
movies are failures in pace, atmosphere, and visual brilliance. It
should have been possible to tell the story in about two-thirds
the time taken, without skipping or slighting anything or
seeming at all to hurry; and in spite of some very good sets and
a number of beautiful shots, Greene's greatest talent—which
is, I think, with the look and effluence of places, streets, and
things—is not once even approximated. This is odd, because
in these respects Greene achieves in print what more naturally
belongs in films, and in a sense does not write novels at all, but
verbal movies. I don't entirely like to think so, but he may
have proved that certain kinds of movies anyhow are better on
the page than they can ever be on the screen.

Spellbound. Alfred Hitchcock's surprisingly disappointing
thriller about psychoanalysis, is worth seeing, but hardly more.
A psychiatric adviser appears among the credits, and with
enough toe-dancing through the labyrinthine rationalizations
of dramatic (and box-office) license, it is possible to imitate the
faint ways in which the advice may have been followed. But I
felt that the makers of the film had succeeded in using practi-

cally none of the movie possibilities of a psychoanalytic story, even those of the simplest melodrama; and that an elaborate, none-too-interesting murder mystery, though stoutly moored to the unconscious, merely cheapened and got in the way of any possible psychological interest. To quite an extent the psychological pretensions cluttered up the murder mystery too. Ingrid Bergman plays the scientist and wears glasses to prove it; Gregory Peck is the troubled layman. Both are ornamentally effective-looking—so much so that in spite of some bits of pretty good playing it was impossible to disidentify them from illustrations in a slick-paper magazine serial, and more hopeless still to identify them with living people. There are some frightening shots of the kinds of striated whiteness which mysteriously terrifies the patient—the mark of fork-tines on a table cloth, for instance; the remembrance of the initial trauma is excitingly managed; and in one crisis of mental dereliction, in which the camera flicks its eye forlornly around a bathroom, you get a little of the unlimited, cryptic terror which can reside in mere objects. But these are practically the only suggestions of the hair-raising movie this had every right and obligation to be. As for the dream designed by Salvador Dali, it is as frankly irrelevant to dream reality, and so to criticism for its lack of reality in that direct sense, as Markova is for not growing a four-foot larynx for *Swan Lake*. The trouble is that this decision in favor of unreality was mistaken in the first place. In the second, the dream is none too good in its own terms. James Cruze did one many times better, twenty years ago, in *Hollywood*, probably without even considering calling in an outside specialist, far less a psychiatric adviser. But then I doubt that they could have thought of hiring Dali in the first place if they had been at all wise to the possibilities of their subject. *Spellbound* is just so much of the Id as could be safely displayed in a Bergdorf Goodman window.

November 24, 1945

The Last Chance was made by Lazar Wechsler, in Switzerland, during the war. It is the story of the attempt of some derelict English and American soldiers to shepherd a polyglot group of refugees across the mountains from Italy to Switzerland. Most of the players are amateurs; some of them virtually reenact their living roles as refugees. With minor exceptions the performances, or the ways in which nonperformances are put to good use, are excellent. Some of the character conceptions, symbolizations, and melodramatic passages are over-obvious, high-flavored, and stagy, but none of the weaknesses of the film more than superficially vitiate its desperate courage, humaneness, and intensity, or its over-all eloquence. Nor does it strike me as dated: the world it tries to epitomize has changed, since the film was made, more for the worse than for the better. I am therefore more interested in Metro-Goldwyn-Mayer's attempt to give it regular feature-film circulation; I only wish I could believe that it will please, and arouse, any sufficient part of the general American audience.

Glad as I am, in some respects, that Metro plans to put a number of European films into broad circulation, I feel it may turn out to be a mixed blessing. I don't know, but think it reasonable to assume, that the effort is being made as one part of breaking down European tendencies to lock theaters against American films. If this is so and the reciprocal circulation gets going at all strong, I am afraid we shall have to expect more harm than good; that American films will become, more than ever before, vapid, safe advertisements of our well-known way of life—even touched up or supervised, perhaps, by the State Department; and that European films will become more and more "American" in style and content; and that it will on the whole become harder than before, not only here but in Europe, to make films that are worth making. I agree with anyone who insists that movies can be international in style and content; but for every good foot of internationalization I would expect a hundred bad, and would expect it even if that were not the way the money is stacked. Moreover, since intimate specification is even less dispensable to most good art than generalization, I believe that most of the best films, like most of the best of any other art, are and would always have to be developed locally, and primarily for local audiences.

My Name Is Julia Ross, a mouse-among-cats thriller, shows bewildered Nina Foch, who thought she was merely a new secretary, trying to escape from Dame May Whitty and George

Macready, who insist that she is respectively their daughter-in-law and wife, and who do their best to drive her to madness and suicide. The film is well planned, mostly well played, well directed, and in a somewhat boom-happy way well photographed—all around, a likable, unpretentious, generally successful attempt to turn good trash into decently artful entertainment. I have to add that I was not scared or even excited nearly so often as it was obvious I should be; but I suspect the deficiency was not the film's, but was temporary, and my own.

December 22, 1945

WHILE I watched the movie which Billy Wilder and Charles Brackett have made out of Charles Jackson's story about alcoholism, *The Lost Weekend*, I was pretty consistently gratified and excited. When I began to try to review it, I could not forget what Eisentein said, years ago, when he was asked what he thought of Lewis Milestone's *All Quiet on the Western Front*. He said he thought it was a good Ph.D. thesis. I am afraid that applies to *The Lost Weekend*, too. I don't mean that it is stuffy: it is unusually hard, tense, cruel, intelligent, and straightforward. But I see nothing in it that is new, sharply individual, or strongly creative. It is, rather, a skillful restatement, satisfying and easy to overrate in a time of general dereliction and fatuousness, of some sound basic commonplaces.

On that scale, of course, excellent things can be done. I don't see how the drunkard's first experience of the d.t.'s could be improved on by any means except possibly a dragging-out and brutalization of its climax. Frank Faylen's performance as a male nurse is fully as right and powerful; so is a shrieking free-for-all in an alcoholic ward—which is fought, however, by an incredibly mistaken use of "background" music. Ray Milland's performance as the alcoholic Don Birnam is debatable at first, but so absorbed and persuasive as the picture moves along that he all but wins the picture and the doubters over. There are also some first-rate re-creations of place and atmosphere—a soft-leather, soft-noised cocktail lounge, and a perfect setting of the Birnam apartment, and some shots of

New York streets and times of day. At best there is a purity of tone and an acuteness about a city and the people in it which belong high in the movies' great classical strain of unforced, naturalistic poetry. While you watch it, it entirely holds you.

Thinking it over, though, there are curious and disappointing things about the picture. Good as he is, Milland is too robust for the best interests of his role; and in the earlier reels, when he is still sober enough to be assessed as a normal human being, it seems clear that neither he nor the director happens to know very much about the particular kind of provincially born, genteelly bred failed-artist Milland is supposed to be playing. None of the other players seem thoroughly at home, either, in the commonplace yet extremely specialized kind of apartment they use, though Philip Terry's gentle performance as the brother is of itself good, and Jane Wyman is knowingly cast as a *Time* researcher. Howard de Silva plays the ambiguous bartender well and with force, but the force and his face, in this context, turn it into ambiguity for little tots. The players miscast as Miss Wyman's ultra-bourgeois parents are probably not to blame, but they turn a sequence where intelligence and restraint would have been particularly gratifying into heavy caricature.

The causes of Don Birnam's alcoholism were not thoroughly controlled or understood, I thought, in the novel. In the movie they hardly exist. It may have been the better part of valor not to try to tackle them, and not to dabble in streams of consciousness, but when you add to this the fact that Mr. Milland cannot convincingly put before you this particular kind of thirsty man, you can see that the picture is bound to lack certain important kinds of depth, warmth, and intensity, not to mention plain dramatic interest. It becomes, too much of the time, just a virtuoso piece about a handsome, practically unidentified maniac. In one or two scenes you get with some force the terrible humiliation which is one of the drunkard's experiences; but considering the over-all quality of the film, it is remarkable how much you seem to have been given, and how little you actually get. There is very little appreciation, for instance, of the many and subtle moods possible in drunkenness; almost no registration of the workings of the several minds inside a drinker's brain; hardly a trace of the narcissism and self-deceit which are so indispensable or of the self-loathing and self-pity which are so invariable; hardly a hint, except through abrupt action, of the desperation of thirst; no hint at all of the many colorings possible in the desperation. The hangovers lack the weakness, sickness, and horrible distortions of time-sense which they need.

It is irrelevant to the carefully developed, finely photographed, wholly objective scheme of the movie, but I cannot help suggesting that many of these failures might have been avoided if the work had been done from a little farther inside. In some respects the method would still have been objective. A few minutes of dead-silent pantomime (*without music, please!*) of deadly weakness, in hangover, for instance, might have made definitive a good deal that is here only sketched; it should be the kind of weakness in which it is virtually unbearable to lift a hand, and for some reason necessary to do much more than that. Much of the wrestling of minds and moods too, I suspect, could have been registered from outside, through lines, business, mere close-up, and posture: Chaplin, after all, has made incredibly complicated things articulate in pantomime. Surely, for one simple instance—most obviously perhaps after the dawn escape from the hospital—it would have been possible to show the abject shattering coldness to which even temperate men are liable; and perhaps also to capture, through it, the sudden annihilating loneliness and fear of God—or whatever more terrifying it may be—which are so common, if peculiar, an experience. For certain other things you would have to take your camera and soundtrack part way inside the mind. Not to mention the curious enhancements and dilations which the outside world takes on for a drunken man—and I don't mean distortions in any "artistic" or "fantastic" sense but only such qualities as withering, euphoria, and tumescence. In the aftermath of drunkenness one is liable to be excruciatingly oversensitive to things touched, and to sound, and to light. Touch would have had to be carried by business—and might surely have been used to convey feverishness as well. Sound and light peculiarities could have been impacted in the film and track by appropriate, dry exaggerations. A knocking radiator, an abrupt auto horn, coupled with the right kind of playing, might have told the audience as much in an instant as an hour of pure objectivity could. The light equivalents of flashing traffic on a sunny autumn day, as Birnam would experience them, might drive an audience moaning from the theater, unless their exact realism were modified into art.

I undershtand that liquor interesh: innerish: intereshtsh are rather worried about thish film. Thash tough.

January 5, 1946

*T*he Bells of St. Mary's, like *Going My Way*, is distinguished for leisure and spaciousness, for delight in character and atmosphere, for its use of scenes which are inserted not to advance the story but for their own intrinsic charm. One such set-piece —in which primary-school children rehearse a Christmas play —is almost magically deft and pretty; and the picture is full of shrewd and pleasant flashes. It is also fascinating to watch as a talented, desperate effort to repeat the unrepeatable. But on the whole it is an unhappy film. Bing Crosby's priest, who was so excellent in the earlier picture, at times looks just bored, cold, and sly, as if he knew that this sort of thing had gone on too long for the good of anybody's soul, his own first of all. Ingrid Bergman replaces Barry Fitzgerald and, for my money, cannot compete with him in sex appeal, though she has and uses a lot too much to play a Mother Superior, comes painfully close to twittering her eyes in scenes with Crosby, and in general, I grieve to say, justifies a recent piece of radio promotion which rather startlingly describes a nun: "Ingrid Bergman has never been lovelier, hubbahubbahubba."

I find very objectionable the movies' increasing recognition of the romantic-commercial values of celibacy. I like hardly better a little boxing lesson in which Mother Bergman shows one of the schoolboys how not to lead with the other cheek. I am just plain horrified by the way in which the sisters hound an old nabob into beneficence. And though I was amused both by a kitten which got fouled up in Fr. Crosby's famous straw hat, and by a mongrel which got a fit of yawns while Henry Travers was trying to pray, I think that too much of a good thing is more than enough. The trouble is, the whole picture is more than enough, and anyone of Leo McCarey's talent would have been wise to use the talent on something entirely new instead. But it looks as if Father O'Malley, like Andy Hardy, is set to go on and on. In case there is any doubt about a subject, I suggest that the priest become a fixer, next time, for the Little Brothers of St. Dismas—if only in order that he may sing the theme song (which I will gladly furnish on request) "Take It on the Lam of God."

For what seems at least half of the dogged, devoted length of *They Were Expendable* all you have to watch is men getting on or off PT boats, and other men watching them do so. But this is made so beautiful and so real that I could not feel one foot of the film was wasted. The rest of the time the picture is showing nothing much newer, with no particular depth of feeling, much less idea; but, again, the whole thing is so beautifully directed and photographed, in such an abundance of vigorous open air and good raw sunlight, that I thoroughly enjoyed and admired it. Visually, and in detail, and in nearly everything he does with people, I think it is John Ford's finest movie. Another man who evidently learned a tremendous amount through the war is Robert Montgomery, whose sober, light, sure performance is, so far as I can remember, the one perfection to turn up in movies during the year.

A Walk in the Sun is often very alive and likeable, thanks to several of its players, particularly Herbert Rudley, Richard Conti, Lloyd Bridges, and Dana Andrews. The gradual increase of daylight which opens it is atmospherically and technically wonderful; you can seldom get your eyes hurt, as I did here, by the manipulation, against dark contexts, of a little bit of cloudy light on a screen. In motion and shooting, much of the film is worked out with very unusual vitality and care—much of which, unfortunately, is related more nearly to ballet than to warfare. But mainly, I think, it is an embarrassing movie. The dialogue seems as unreal as it is expert. Most of the characters—as distinct from the men who play them—are as unreal and literary as the dialogue. The aesthetic and literary and pseudo-democratic preoccupations are so strong that at times all sense of plain reality drops out of the picture. At the end, for instance, with their farmhouse captured, various featured players are shown completing the gags which tag their characters—chomping an apple, notching a rifle-stock, and so on—while, so far as the camera lets you know, their wounded comrades are still writhing unattended in the dooryard.

BEST OF 1945

On two previous occasions I have conducted something of an open wake, here, over the best films of the year just ended. I see no point in going through with it again. The past year was distinguished by two extremely fine pictures, which I expect to hear respectfully mentioned twenty years from now, if anyone is at that time free to express an honest opinion, or alive to express any opinion at all. Aside from these two pictures I see nothing to get particularly hopeful about—or any more despondent about than usual, for that matter.

Major John Huston's *San Pietro* was the finest of the several movies made during the course of the war which have proved what men of talent, skill, and courage can do if even one hand is untied from behind their backs. It is worth remembering, however, that this film was released to the civilian public something like a year late, and was censored at that; was then slowly and so far as I have heard thinly accepted by exhibitors; and was neglected by such sincere and intelligent people as the members of the National Board of Review's Committee on Exceptional Films, in favor of the showy, skillful, far less fine *The True Glory*, which was called the best film of its year.

The war is over now; I doubt that we shall see many more American factual films of anywhere near the quality of *San Pietro.*

Even more wonderful, in a sense, was William Wellman's less nearly perfect film, *Story of G.I. Joe*, for it proved what can be done, even now, in the middle of Hollywood, when men adequate to a noble subject are not drawn and quartered by their bosses. But it proves nothing, of course, about the chances a hundred other able people are going to get.

Neither does Jean Renoir's *The Southerner*, though it too is a film which could hardly have been made except by grace of unusually disinterested producers. If I were a "constructive" critic—that is, able to believe that *A Song to Remember* is a film to be praised because it brings Chopin to the juke-boxes—I might see in these two films what is called a hopeful trend. I will wait, instead, and see how many producers and investors allow how many good artists to do work worth doing in 1946. And I will remember that although Haydn was almost too well fixed with the Esterhazys for his own best interests, that was no help to Mozart.

I won't try to go on with this discussion, even in this super-ficial way. Among the other best films of 1945 I would particu-larly mention, in roughly the following order of preference, the very pretty, very talented, rather velvety *The Clock*; the very hard-surfaced, bright, superficial *The Lost Weekend*; the hard-worked, exciting *Objective Burma* and the equally hard-worked, more doggedly humane *Pride of the Marines*; the charming but equivocal and overrated *Colonel Blimp*, now cut to bits; the fitful, sometimes very encouraging *A Tree Grows in Brooklyn*; the cellophaned aspidistra *On Approval*; John Ford's visually beautiful, otherwise not very interesting *They Were Ex-pendable*, with Robert Montgomery's unimprovable perform-ance; the somewhat poky yet very able *The Way Ahead*; the sometimes corny, always impassioned *The Last Chance*. Other good pictures to see, and some of them better than that, are the tawdry, bitter *Mildred Pierce*, with Joan Crawford's return, and her best performance; Herman Shumlin's intense, faithful *Confidential Agent*; the clever, nasty little comedy *Practically Yours*; some angry, hard-focused scenes in *A Medal for Benny*; the easy, sunny *Anchors Aweigh*; *State Fair*, for pleasant tunes and a few pleasant scenes; Val Lewton's *Body Snatchers* and *Isle of the Dead*, too pedagogic and verbal at times, but still showing some of the most sensitive movie intelligence in Hol-lywood; Robert Siodmak's visually gifted melodrama *The Sus-pect*; *Fighting Lady*, a well-made and spectacular film which looks to me more and more like a magnificent box of choco-lates filled with plasma; the bustling *True Glory*, which also loses value in retrospect; and Fred Allen's rowdy *It's in the Bag*. To people who share my near-adoration of the intricately wrong I also commend *Kiss and Tell*, *The Three Caballeros*, and *A Song to Remember*, high among the unforgettable films of the year. While I am about it, too, I had better place near the top of the year's list *Salome Where She Danced*. I merely enjoyed it when I saw it, and was slow to realize how much of it must have been meant for that kind of enjoyment. I now gratefully salute it as the funniest dead-pan parody I have ever seen; and if by unlikely chance any Merton Gills are hurt by this, I am much sorrier than I know how to say.

If you are content to be merely realistic about it—to use a strangely perverted word in the only meaning it seems to carry today—I suppose that it wasn't exactly a bad movie year. Those who are satisfied with it are welcome to it. So far as I am concerned, I am grateful that a few of the many people of ability and integrity who work in Hollywood managed, with God knows what bloodshed and heartbreak, to get *on* the screen something more than a split-second glimmer of what they have in them to put there. And I am grateful for hundreds of split-second glimmers, which I wish I had room to specify. But the desire of any critic, like that of any artist, who has a right even to try to defend or practice an art—as perhaps of any human being who has a right even to try to defend or practice living—cannot be satisfied short of perfect liberty, discipline, and achievement, though the attempt may be wholly loved and honored.

I see little if any more to love and honor for the attempt, in films, and little if any more substantial chance even to make the attempt, than at any other time during the past fifteen years.

February 16, 1946

SINCE last fall a change of job has made it impossible for me to see more than a few of the movies which, as a reviewer, I have wanted and felt I ought to see and review. I should have spoken of this months ago, but until lately I was unable to resign myself to the impossibility. Until further notice, then—and of that I see no prospect—anything like adequate coverage is out of the question, and I may be late, as herewith, even with those films which most obviously require reviewing. Just as I was slow to realize that there was nothing I could do about my new situation except describe it, I shall probably be slow to realize whether or not, under these circumstances, I can write a column useful enough to justify my going on with it. That my editor and my readers will have as much to do with that as I will goes without saying.

Of current films the two best I have seen were already weeks at large before I got to them, and for both reasons deserve priority now.

It Happened at the Inn (*Goupi Mains Rouges*) should have gone high on my selection of last year's best films. I kept putting off seeing it because, stupidly, I was as usual set on edge by the kind of finishing-school, French-table, cultural chitchat to which so many American enthusiasts are aroused by anything from France. This film should teach me better sense, if anything since Clair's best films can. Whether or not I like my company, I have a standing love affair with a good deal that is French—particularly the French mass as understood by the least affected of the French intelligentsia—and this film reawakened me to the fact.

"Goupi" is a comic melodrama—or perhaps a lightly tragic farce—about a family of wrangling, innocently cruel, frustrated, strongly individualistic peasants. Some of the characters are as salient as those of comic strips; none lose truthfulness or depth through this; all are with tender, sober adroitness graded, controlled, and modulated between different levels of caricature and of limpid, always poetic realism. Like most French films, this one is basically nearer literature than movie; but, like many, it is always supple, quick, and expressive visually and in its use of dialogue and sound; and, again like many, it makes even the best American work look childish so far as reverence for and skill with character and background and atmosphere are concerned. At times the picture goes so wild that it suggests Gogol or Erskine Caldwell—or, simply, that rural life is at once the most localized and the most universal, and that its pine-knot paroxysms of grotesqueness are among the most endearing, even noblest, of its characteristics. But as a whole, and more intensely, gently, and richly, it embodies France. There is no evidence, good or bad, that Pierre Very, who wrote the picture, or Jacques Becker, who directed it, were trying to do anything "great." Perhaps for that reason, among many others, I thought it wiser, more beautiful, and much more fun than nine out of ten masterpieces, written or filmed.

Murder, My Sweet should have been mentioned in last year's listing, too. So should Edward Dmytryk's next picture, *Cornered*. *Murder, My Sweet* gave a Raymond Chandler story the combination of skinned knuckles and big-city sentience proper to it; *Cornered*, without losing much if any force as melodrama, is much more elaborate, self-assured, and ambitious. I have never been in Buenos Aires, and I have known few fascists or even people who pretended to be or thought they were—though I know any number who think they aren't—but in casting, business, setting, and, with few exceptions, writing and costuming the picture consistently convinced and excited me. One beautiful little bit, of an old waiter's silent reaction when he is questioned too closely for his own safety, suggests that the only serious problem about intelligence, even subtlety, on the screen, is inventing it; for it got a yell of understanding and joy from an audience at the Palace. Dick Powell, with a Bogart haircut, sometimes works a little too conspicuously at being The New Dick Powell ("rougher, tougher, and more terrific," as the billboards not very helpfully insist). But on the whole, perhaps because he still looks less official, less highly paid to look small-bracket, and less superhuman and bound-to-win-out, I think he is even better, just now, for this sort of role, than the Founder himself.

March 2, 1946

ANYONE who wants to make creatively interesting movies in this country today gets stuck in one of three, or at the outside four, ways, all of them too familiar to require more than mention. If he works in Hollywood, it is unlikely that he will get more than a fraction of his best ability on to the screen; and that is not to mention the liability of resignation to compromise, and of self-deceit. If he works on his own, he is unlikely to get his films distributed or even sporadically shown; and that is not to mention either the difficulty of getting the money and equipment to make the movies or the liability of self-deceit in the direction of arrogance and artiness—the loss of, and contempt for, audience, which can be just as corrupting as its nominal opposite. If, on the other hand, the would-be artist goes abroad to work, he is likely to find, in future, that the advantages are not so clear by a good deal as they were in the past; and unless he is a very specialized—and perhaps also a very limited—artist indeed, he is certain to suffer as profoundly by a change of country as he would, if he were a writer, by a change of language. The fourth possibility is paralysis, or resignation to the practice of some more feasible art. Either of these is perhaps preferable to literal suicide, but not practically so as far as the movie artist and the movie art are concerned.

Maya Deren and Alexander Hammid have made three short films on their own. These are getting no kind of formal distribution, but they were shown recently in New York at the Provincetown Playhouse, and presumably will be shown again when and as that is possible. I can only suggest that those interested keep their ears open.

Of the three films one, which I have not seen, is called *A Study in Choreography for Camera*. The other two, *Meshes of the Afternoon* and *At Land*, can be roughly classified as "dream" films and also approach, as Parker Tyler has said, "a type of personal expression in cinema analogous to the lyric poem." Their quality seems to me to be impaired by Miss Deren's performance in the central roles, which strikes me as showing the emotional characteristics that make so much of "modern" dancing, for instance, not only unedifying to watch but radically mistaken and hostile in its relation to the nature of good art. There are many satisfactions of mood and implication and image in the movies, of kinds which are the unique property of the movie camera, and which are hardly even hinted in studio productions. Yet I cannot feel that there is anything really original about them—that they do anything important, for instance, which was not done, and done to an ill-deserved death, by some of the European avant-gardists, and especially by the surrealists, of the 1920s. At worst, in fact, they are solemnly, arrogantly, distressingly pretentious and arty. Nevertheless, I think they are to be seen, and that there is a good deal in them to be liked, enjoyed, and respected. I don't at all agree with Miss Deren that "reality," in its conventional camera sense, cannot be turned into a work of art without being turned also into a fantasia of the unconscious; but if you have to believe that in order to try to do it—which I doubt—then I am glad that she does. For I certainly believe that it is worth doing; and I know of nobody else in films, just now, who is paying any more attention to that great universe of movie possibility than to make safely conducted little tours of the border villages.

I must again postpone comment on several current films because none of them interest me as much as these. Meanwhile, with degrees of fervor ranging from able to take nourishment to unlikely to last out the night, I can recommend *Three Strangers*, *Scarlet Street*, and *Road to Utopia*. I don't think there will be any trouble finding them.

March 23, 1946

Recently I saw a moving picture so much worth talking about that I am still unable to review it. This was the Italian *Open City*. For the moment I can say only that I am at once extremely respectful and rather suspicious of it, and that I recommend it very highly, with a warning, however, to those who are particularly sensitive to scenes of torture. I will probably be unable to report on the film in detail for the next three or four weeks. Meanwhile, here are briefs on a few current films.

Bedlam is an elaborate improvisation, but not an improvement, on one of Hogarth's engravings. Boris Karloff has charge of the madhouse, prior to its reform. A Quaker and a spirited young woman are also involved. There is enough metaphoric moralistic pedagogy to carry a story a dozen times the weight; more than enough verbiage for the same; enough taste, and movie feeling, as well. There are also some nasty thrills, which are too often obscured by the foregoing. This is a Val Lewton production. I hear I have been accused—it has not been done to my face—of favoring Mr. Lewton, for reasons presumed to be underhand. The actual reason is underhandedness epitomized: I think that few people in Hollywood show in their work that they know or care half as much about movies or human beings as he does. Of such people I will always write with friendliness and respect. I am afraid that this particular film is a careful, pretty failure, and I regret and somewhat fear Lewton's recent interest in costume movies, which seem to draw on his romantic-literary weaknesses more than on his best abilities, which are poetic and cinematic. But Lewton and his friends would have to make much less sincere and pleasing films than this before I would review them disrespectfully.

The Spiral Staircase may be better fun to see than *Bedlam*, but I feel it has been overrated. It entirely lacks the mental excitement which *Bedlam* at least tries for. Even though she plays it well, I am not impressed by Dorothy McGuire—or anyone else—stunting along through several reels as a suffering mute; nor am I willingly hornswoggled by Ethel Barrymore's unprincipled use of her lighthouse eyes, wonderful as they are. Still, the movie is visually clever; and until some member of the Screen Writers' Guild takes care to correct me—neglecting, as I am doing, such nonentities as the set designer, cameraman, and editor—I will mainly credit Robert Siodmak for that; he merely directed the show.

A director I had never expected to praise is Jean Negalescu, who has always made me think of Michael Curtiz on toast. (Mr. Curtiz, in turn, has always seemed like Franz Murnau under onions.) I may be wrong in praising him now, since *Three Strangers* was smartly written by John Huston and Howard Koch and is still more smartly played by Geraldine Fitzgerald, Peter Lorre, Sidney Greenstreet, Rosalind Ivan, and Joan Loring. But this rather silly story of three blemished people buzzing around a sweepstakes ticket is told with such exactly fancy terseness, even in casual street scenes, that I think nobody should be left out. It is one of few recent movies you don't feel rather ashamed about, next morning.

Vacation from Marriage is the story of a lower-middle-class English couple (Robert Donat and Deborah Kerr), peacetime dimouts who are transformed by history. During the early reels they look as abject as gray greasepaint and a nice burlesque of stultified timidity can make them; and, in a comic-strip way, develop a good deal of pathos and quite a fierce little indictment of the kind of world which can evolve such creatures. Later on, in an easy travesty of a generally uneasy problem, they confront each other looking like movie stars. War is supposed to be the catalyst, the sportsman's bracer; and the film's chief weakness is its failure to show the briefly exalted couple sinking back, uncontrollably, under their peacetime stone. That might be an unbearably depressing movie, this one is unbearably inspiriting. Even without qualifiers or full honesty, it is good to see war credited with one of the few things it can possibly be credited with. But the real logic of the picture is that a large part of the human race is hardly fit for existence under any other circumstances. My chief objection is that this logic is not shown to be either inescapable or changeable.

April 13, 1946

Open City is a story of underground resistance during the late phases of the German occupation of Rome. The heroes are an underground leader; a co-worker and friend of his who hopes to marry a widow, pregnant by him; a priest who, generally at great risk to himself, is eager to help all of them. The villains are an epicene Gestapo officer; his Lesbian assistant; and a rudderless young Italian girl, misled by dope, sex, poverty, and easy money into betraying the patriots. The widow is shot down in the street. The leader dies under torture, without denouncing his comrades. The priest, who has to witness the torture, does so without pleading with the victim to give in and without ceasing to pray for his courage; then he is executed. The widow's lover survives; so does her eight-year-old son, who is active, with other children, in an effective underground of their own.

I have no doubt that plenty of priests, in Italy and elsewhere, behaved as bravely as this one. Nor do I doubt that they and plenty of nonreligious leftists, working with them in grave danger, respected each other as thoroughly as is shown here. I see little that is incompatible between the best that is in leftism and in religion—far too little to measure against the profound incompatibility between them and the rest of the world. But I cannot help doubting that the basic and ultimate practicing motives of institutional Christianity and leftism can be adequately represented by the most magnanimous individuals of each kind; and in that degree I am afraid that both the religious and the leftist audiences—and more particularly the religio-leftists, who must be the key mass in Italy—are being sold something of a bill of goods. I keep telling myself that the people who made the film were still moved to reproduce recent experience and were in no state of mind and under no obligation to complicate what they had been through; I recognize with great pleasure how thoroughly both the priest and the partisans are made to keep their distinct integrities; and the fire and spirit of the film continually make me suspicious of my own suspicions. Nevertheless, they persist; so I feel it is my business to say so. If I am right, as I hope I am not, institutions of both kinds are here, as so often before, exploiting all that is best in individuals for the sake of all that least honors the individual, in institutions.

One further qualifier, which I mentioned a few weeks ago, no longer applies; some especially close details of torture have been cut, with no loss I feel, considering the amount of backstairs sadism any audience is tainted with. I have another mild qualifier: *Open City* lacks the depth of characterization, thought, and feeling which might have made it a definitively great film.

From there on out I have nothing but admiration for it. Even these failures in depth and complexity are sacrifices to virtues just as great: you will seldom see as pure freshness and vitality in a film, or as little unreality and affectation among the players; one feels that everything was done too fast and with too fierce a sincerity to run the risk of bogging down in mere artistry or meditativeness—far less the WPA-mural sentimentality and utter inability to know, love, or honor people to which American leftists are liable. The film's finest over-all quality, which could rarely be matched so spectacularly, is this immediacy. Everything in it had been recently lived through; much of it is straight reenactment on or near the actual spot; its whole spirit is still, scarcely cooled at all, the exalted spirit of the actual experience. For that kind of spirit there has been little to compare with it since the terrific libertarian jubilation of excitement under which it was all but inevitable that men like Eisenstein and Dovzhenko and Pudovkin should make some of the greatest works of art of this century.

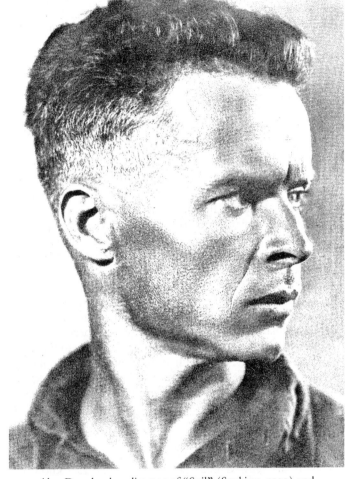

Alex Dovzhenko, director of "Soil" (Sovkino, 1930) and other movies.

Roberto Rossellini, who directed this film, and Sergio Amadei, author and script writer, are apparently not men of that order of talent; but they are much more than adequate to that spirit and to their chance. They understand the magnificence of their setting—the whole harrowed city of Rome—as well as the best artist might and perhaps better, for though their film bristles with aesthetic appreciation and eloquence, these are never dwelt on for their own sake; the urgency of human beings always dominates this architectural poetry; nor are the human beings or their actions dwelt on in any over-calculated way. The raid on the bakery, the arrest of the priest and the partisan leader, the rescue of partisan captives, and a sequence during which all the inhabitants of a tenement are hauled down into a courtyard by a German searching party are as shatteringly uninvented-looking as if they had been shot by invisible newsreel cameras.

The scene which shows the violent death of the widow and the violent reaction of her son—in cassock and cotta—has this same reality, plus a slammed operatic fury of design which in no way turns it false. There are quieter scenes which I admire fully as much—a family quarrel, an apartment scene involving two men and two women, and a casual little scene between the underground leader and the widow in which anyone of even my limited acquaintance with underground activity will recognize the oxygen-sharp, otherwise unattainable atmosphere, almost a smell, of freedom. The performances of most of the Romans, especially of a magnificent woman named Anna Magnani, who plays the widow, somewhere near perfectly define the poetic-realistic root of attitude from which the grand trunk of movies at their best would have to grow; and the imitations of Germans seem better than our best imitations because they are more strongly felt and more poetically stylized. The picture is full of kinds of understanding which most films entirely lack, or reduce to theatricality. I think especially of the sizing-up look and the tone and gesture with which the Gestapo officer opens his interview with the newly captured, doomed partisan leader. In art only Malraux and Silone, so far as I know, can equal that in experienced, unemphatic astuteness.

Open City was made during the distracted months just after the Allies took Rome over. It was made on a good deal less than a shoestring; mainly without sets or studio lighting; on varying qualities of black-market film. All sound, including dialogue, was applied later. The author and director had a good deal of movie experience; nearly the whole cast was amateur. The result is worthless to those who think very highly of so-called production valyahs, and plenty of people in Hollywood and elsewhere will doubtless use that fact twice daily, like Mothersills. Others may find this one of the most heartening pictures in years, as well as one of the best. Not that anything it proves will come to them as a revelation. The Hollywood cameraman Karl Brown made his excellent, pitifully titled *Stark Love*, a story of Southern mountaineers, about twenty years ago, on about $5,000. And most of the great Russian films used amateur players—and surroundings—on budgets which would probably not pay for an American singing Western today. But plenty of people realize a point that many others will never understand and that there is no use laboring: some professional experience is exceedingly useful and perhaps indispensable, but most of the best movies could be made on very little money and with little professional experience. Judging by *Open City* they can be made a great deal better that way.

April 27, 1946

AFTER the late Wendell Willkie returned from his trip around the world, I felt that his sincerity was entirely to be respected. Before the trip I am sure he was as sincere as he knew how to be, but the meaningfulness of the sincerity seemed measurable in the kind of Jackie Cooper pout he used for the more "human" moments in his speeches. I respect the sincerity of *From This Day Forward* just about as much, neither denying nor decrying it, but believing it has a lot to learn. *From This Day Forward* is a story about young married love up against the worst that a bad economic system can do and send an audience home comfortable. Its message seems to be that in the long run ardor and courage—neither of which is seriously embarrassed by any difficulties—will hold their fort, and better.

Movies so seldom even try to be honest or sympathetic about such problems of working-class life as -n-mpl-ym-nt, sh-lt-r, and b-b–s that the least one can do is to honor the attempt with further honesty. In this intention I must regret two kinds of miscarriage of sincerity which between them use up most of the film. One kind is most fully represented by Joan Fontaine as the wife. Quite aside from her efforts to be at once a serious actress and a fan-magazine star, she has, for all her good intentions, about the understanding of her role that an heiress might have who was advised by her analyst to take up social work in order to work off her guilt about her income. The other kind is best embodied in bits by a resentful intellectual who slaps some books off a counter, and by the clerk at an orange-drink stand who sharply communicates the meanness and snobbery with which members of the same class can treat each other. Both bits, like an ugly scene in court, are neat and authentic beyond the picture's ability to communicate more pleasant aspects of underprivileged city life; yet all three, I feel, are false in their own way. They supplant the unrealism of most movies with a slick kind of pseudo-realism, rather special to New York, which has been most clearly developed in the less good mannerisms of the Group Theater and in the more serious *New Yorker* stories. *From This Day Forward* is an unusually serious and respectable film, but very little in it is free from one or the other of these kinds of falseness.

Deadline at Dawn, a melodrama about an ingenuous sailor's effort to clear himself of murder, is Harold Clurman's direction of a script by Clifford Odets. Some of Clurman's direction is pure stage—some of which comes through very well; some of Odets's writing is pure ham. At its worst the picture is guilty of worse pseudo-realism and pseudo-poetry about the lost little people of a big city than the poorest things in *From This Day Forward*. But on the whole I think it is a likable movie. Odets apparently cannot either separate his weakness and strength or greatly change their proportions, but even in this rather pretentiously unpretentious little job the strength is there; he is obviously one of the very few genuine dramatic poets alive. And his good bits, to say nothing of his bad, are handled competently by Susan Hayward, disarmingly by Bill Williams, and beautifully by Paul Lukas.

The Green Years has been described in the ads as "wonderful" by practically everybody within Louis B. Mayer's purchasing power except his horses; so I hesitate to ask you to take my word for it: the picture is awful. I know: it is made with all the loving care that an Idaho housewife puts into a first novel that is going to win the Grand Prize at Biarritz; Shakespeare can never have been a thousandth as high-minded. I know: it deals with large, grave, stylish matters of religious faith, etc., in a manner to make me want to turn the handiest penitential novena into a five-alarm call for the vice squad. I know: it is stuffed to the scalp and well beyond with "characters," all of Dickensian proportions if only A. J. Cronin were Dickens and if only Dickens were writing soap opera. I know too, to my misery, that this must have been regarded, around the Metro lot, as a great and disinterested dedication to art, and it is no pleasure to sneer at those who so regarded it. But until a worse example comes along, this one will serve very nicely as an apotheosis of all that has gone most deadly wrong with movies since the people with the money learned to believe that the medium could aspire to what is printed on slick paper, and could read it right side up, even without illustrations.

(Note: In my review of *Open City* Einstein should have read Eisenstein, and "shammed operatic fury of design" should have read "slammed," etc. The misspelling of "illustrations," here, is intentional.)

Devotion is a story about the Brontë sisters, about whom I know little. By what little I know, I gather that they might have served as basis for a very good movie. Whether it would be more or less faithful to fact than this one, I care only this much: that here faithfulness to essential truth—that is, truth of mood and psychology—might have exceeded even the best dramatic imagination. So far as I know, this film is reasonably faithful to nonessential truth; it is also about as vapid, considering the subject matter, as you—or rather, they—could possibly imagine. The drunken brother Branwell carries some hint of the force the truth might have had. Charlotte, almost purely fictional in characterization, is the only roundly realized human being in the show. I know nothing about the authenticity of Odette Myrtil, in her small role as the wife of the Brussels schoolmaster, but in relation to the rest of this film she is like a court dagger dismembering a tomato surprise.

Destruction sickens, but less than I do, as I move on to Walt Disney's *Make Mine Music*. I try to realize that it is a perfectly harmless, innocent, proficient, appropriate attempt to set several pieces of popular music, but that helps my sense of proportion little if at all. I know that much of the best in Disney's films comes of his ruralness, and I respect it. But toward some aspects of rural taste the best I can muster is a polite but nauseated smile. Of such, this picture is a reasonably definitive anthology. There is an infinitely insulting animation of a hill-billy ballad which I cannot doubt that many hill-billys will love, a fact which grieves me all the more because I have hill-billy blood myself. There is a friendly number about adolescent lovers of corrupted jazz which forces me to suspect that, next to a really thorough chain reaction, the best hope of the human race lies in segregation of the sexes up to the age of perhaps ninety. There are "pretty" numbers which in their aptness toward the rural aesthetic instinct which Tolstoy venerated make such classics as "A Reading from Homer," "Hope," "The Country Doctor," "A Little Bit o' Heaven," "The End of the Trail," and tinted photographs of Aunt Eula and the Grand Canyon look as contemptibly inaccessible, to the pure in heart, as Van Gogh prior to his Department Store period. I realize that Disney and his associates must have aimed for this kind of charm with a good deal of honest affection, and I am in part taken in by it, not only as a record and achievement but also through my own less honest affection for the tacky; but to use an over-used word, my affection for the tacky is highly ambivalent. So absorbingly so, that I almost neglected to mention that there is also enough genuine charm and imagination and humor in the film to make up perhaps one good average Disney short.

May 11, 1946

The Postman Always Rings Twice is mainly a terrible misfortune from start to finish. I except chiefly the shrewd performances of Hume Cronyn and Leon Ames, as lawyers. I say it with all respect for the director, Tay Garnett, and with all sympathy for the stars, Lana Turner and John Garfield. It looks to have been made in a depth of seriousness incompatible with the material, complicated by a paralysis of fear of the front office. It is, however, very interesting for just those reasons—it is what can happen, especially in Hollywood, if you are forced to try both to eat your cake and have it, and don't realize that it is, after all, only good pumpernickel. It is also interesting as the third current movie—the others are *From this Day For-ward* and *Deadline at Dawn*—which represents the Law as an invincibly corrupt and terrifying force before which mere vic-tims, whether innocent or guilty, can only stand helpless and aghast. Of course this could at a moment's notice shift over to the one about the state being far greater than the individual, because stronger, smarter, and more inscrutable; and I sup-pose that before we know it, if not sooner, we shall have it that way. But so far the attitude is almost 100 per cent contemptu-ous of organized justice and is accepted as such, with evident pleasure, by the audience. I could almost believe that this indi-cates a Trend. I hope so.

Hymn of the Nations is a film record of Toscanini, conducting also another work of Verdi's, the overture to "La Forza del Destino." Much of the time the camera shows Toscanini close to. I could not hear the voice, though it is visibly at work in many parts of the performance, but the face is as good a record of human existence somewhere near its utmost as we are likely to see.

Days and Nights is about as close as Russian movies get to Hollywood; which is too close for anybody's comfort. There are, however, some excellent and well-arranged shots of the siege of Stalingrad; the girl is very sweet; most of the men are admirable. I didn't read the novel, but to judge by the movie it was apotheosized by the Book-of-the-Month Club for more than merely courteous reasons.

Portrait of a Woman presents Françoise Rosay in four roles, all directed by her husband, Jacques Feyder. She is good in all of them, and the picture is obviously controlled by a man of talent and high principles; but the story is like a Frenchified drugstore version of a Samuel French Co. play, and there is a pathetic, marking-time seediness about the whole film which made me both like it and want to forget it.

I have almost never mentioned, much less written, movie news here; but I think a few things are worth calling to your attention.

Chaplin will start shooting his comedy about Landru this summer; this I regard as the best piece of news in some time.

David O. Selznick has "registered" the titles of seven (7) plays by Shakespeare; which, unless I overestimate the power of law, means that nobody else in this country can make movies of them before he does. No comment.

A French film, *The Virtuous Vivi*, has been banned by the New York censors. Since it is played straight down the censors' throats, in reckless amusement over their kind, that was only to be expected. It is in spots cruel, and questionable—I don't entirely like making fun of an imbecile, even in fun; it also tends, as I think they say, to undermine morals. For that reason, and because it is very funny, touching, and skillful, I urge everyone to protest the ban, whether it does any good or not.

John Huston's *Let There Be Light*, a fine, terrible, valuable non-fiction film about psychoneurotic soldiers, has been forbidden civilian circulation by the War Department. I don't know what is necessary to reverse this disgraceful decision, but if dynamite is required, then dynamite is indicated.

May 25, 1946

APPARENTLY you never know when you are seeing the last of the Marx Brothers; so it is unnecessary to urge anyone who has ever enjoyed them to see *A Night in Casablanca*. It is also beside the main point to add that it isn't one of their best movies; for the worst they might ever make would be better worth seeing than most other things I can think of. Many of the things in this one which by substance and look should be level with their best fall somehow flat. The only two reasons I can get wind of are the manufacture of repetition and the fact —they work too well for it to show obviously—that after all these years the Brothers are tired. But to anyone who likes them much I don't think that will get in the way. Chico is still the same as ever, which could suit me better only if he got into more entanglements like the viaduct-why-a-duck-vy-a-dock business in I forget which movie. Harpo has happily dropped his pied-piper, Jewish-Pan pretentiousness and regrettably dropped his erotic ravenousness. He is used more centrally than I remember seeing before. I think this is his best performance. Of the three he shows his age most. He is sadder than before, more acid, more subtle; he looks uncannily like Charlie Chaplin out of character.

Only a mash-note, or the work of several weeks, could contain my regard for Groucho. He is not, I suppose, one of the great comedians, but I can't think of anyone who has given me greater pleasure. My only regret is that, so far as I have seen, he has never yet been in a position to use everything I think he has. Most good comedians, probably all the great ones, require a very broad audience; Groucho, working with extremely sophisticated wit rather than with comedy, has always been slowed and burdened by his audience, even on the stage. He needs an audience that could catch the weirdest curves he could throw, and he needs to have no anxiety or responsibility toward even a blunter minority, let alone majority. I think of night clubs. But no American night-club audience I have seen would be up to the best of it; and to imagine him at work in a European literary cabaret, if I'm right about its mental snobbery and sententiousness, is far from satisfying too. If you have to choose between fun for brain's sake and fun for fun's sake, I certainly prefer the latter, local brand. But because there is no sufficient audience for the use of the brain for fun's sake, I suspect that we lose, in Groucho, the funniest satirist of the century.

I wish I had seen Danny Kaye as a night-club entertainer, too. Most of the best things I have seen him do—all in movies —belong there, and are evidently blunted on the screen. I think he may still become a fine screen comedian; quite possibly more than that. Meanwhile he is mainly very likable, unarguably gifted, sufficiently amusing to carry otherwise dead shows, and only by flashes brilliantly or deeply funny. But I suspect that if he ever comes through to his best, it will be not as a patter-man and parodist but as a comic archetype, as rooted in human character and as unvarying from show to show as Chaplin or Keaton. And I know that if he does, his own comic ideas and those surrounding him will have to be worked out —without, of course, losing at least their appearance of spontaneity—to the last ten-thousandth of an inch, instead of being roughed-in like an after-dinner speaker's badly told joke, as they generally are in *The Kid from Brooklyn*. Screen comedies used, after all, to be machines as delicately, annihilatingly designed for their purpose as any machines that have ever been constructed out of words or tones; the only things today that have anything approaching that mechanical and psychological perfection are some of Disney's slapstick shorts. It may be that the day for comic archetypes passed, with the loss of silence, beyond the recovery of any merely individual intuition; it certainly looks as if nobody in Hollywood any longer knew or cared how really to strip the last drops out of even a verbal joke, not to mention a piece of comic pantomime. Not even the Marx Brothers succeed in it often, in their new movie.

June 8, 1946

IN *The Blue Dahlia* a newly discharged veteran, Alan Ladd, spends a busy night raking the Hollywood half-world for the killer of his wife, whom he didn't much want anyhow. He becomes involved with a motel house dick, the deskman of a mean hotel, a couple of gunmen, a night-club proprietor, some detectives, and Veronica Lake, among others; and they and the sets and moods they move through all seem to me convincing and entertaining in a dry, nervous, electric way. John McManus of *PM* has recently objected to this and similar seamy melodramas, accusing Hollywood of neglecting to make films which can possibly interest, open, or influence honest minds on any social or political issue. I agree that the job has been neglected, and there is a good deal in that line that I wish was being done. But I don't think that is a criterion for good movies; I feel there is at least as much to be dreaded as desired in American films taking up such editorial "responsibilities" instead of just leaving it to Harry Warner and Eric Johnston to sound off about them; and I hope there will be more films of the quality of *The Blue Dahlia*, rather than fewer. The picture is as neatly stylized and synchronized, and as uninterested in moral excitement, as a good ballet; it knows its own weight and size perfectly and carries them gracefully and without self-importance; it is, barring occasional victories and noble accidents, about as good a movie as can be expected from the big factories. In its own uninsistent way, for that matter, it does carry a certain amount of social criticism. For it crawls with American types; and their mannerisms and affectations, and their chief preoccupations—blackmail and what's-in-it-for-me—all seem to

me to reflect, however coolly, things that are deeply characteristic of this civilization.

Her Kind of Man is the same kind of thing, done, however,
with much less taste and style, an ounce or two of uninteresting interest in cause and motive, and an apparent desire, in
which to a mild extent it clumsily succeeds, to present the world
of gambling and show-business of the Year of Repeal as both
attractive and repellent.

Cluny Brown is a comedy about English snobbism on three
levels; county family, backstairs, and lower middle class. For
good measure there is also a plumber who, despite his loyalty
to the labor ticket, wears a bustle on his brain. There are also a
couple of patrician liberals, fatuously melodramatic in their eagerness to protect an anti-fascist refugee, Charles Boyer, from
assassination. I would think better of the pasting of this kind of
liberal, richly deserved as it is, if it had been done at a less safe
time. All this social kidding turns on a housemaid, Jennifer
Jones, who can never remember for long what is meant by
knowing one's place. One main difficulty is that comedies
about snobbism seem, as a rule, to depend on stimulating
and playing up to, rather than shriveling, the worst kinds of
snobbism in the audience. In spite of this, Ernst Lubitsch's
direction—always, at its best, so shrewd about protocol—
makes the film more amusing than there was any other reason
to expect; and Richard Haydn's performance as a prissily bullying, mother-bound druggist is very nice caricature.

In *Without Reservations* Claudette Colbert, another kidded
liberal, learns more about life in the course of a transcontinental romp with a couple of men in uniform, John Wayne and
Don DeFore. Messrs. Wayne and DeFore have kinds of hardness and conceit, in their relations with women, which are a
good deal nearer the real thing than movies usually get. A
predatory toots is repeatedly spoken of as a beetle, a good
word for the kind which I had heard of, before, only as German slang. Miss Colbert does another of those tipsiness acts of
hers which do more toward reducing me to Pepsi-Cola than
any number of Lost Weekends ever could. The whole business
is fairly smooth and spirited without attaining to any of the
charm, or for that matter much of the corn, of *It Happened
One Night*. One thing I really enjoyed in it was the flooding

of landscapes past the train windows, which were the most satisfying—if not nearly satisfying enough—that I remember seeing in an American movie. I was also glad to see Mervyn Leroy destroy the Hollywood convention which forbids shooting such things as a scene in a railway coach in such a way that the landscape moves now left-to-right, now right-to-left. And late in the film Louella Parsons appears, in person, at her microphone, also in person, with all the bewildering force of a chenille sledgehammer.

June 22, 1946

Orson Welles's new movie, *The Stranger*, is a tidy, engaging thriller about a Nazi arch-criminal (Mr. Welles) who hides out as a teacher in a New England boys' prep school. It seems to have raised the question, in the minds of some people, whether Welles has any right to make movies at all. I think I understand why it raises such a question. For years Welles was fatuously overrated as a "genius," boy and otherwise; possibly, for that matter, he overrated himself. In any case, many people who overrated him and many others still who, knowing better and annoyed by all the talk, stupidly blamed Welles for it and underrated him—as I did for a while—are now so eager to think ill of him that they will hardly bother to look at what is before them. I am perfectly willing to agree with anyone who points out that this is "only human" if such people are equally willing to accept my synonyms for that, which are that it is also contemptible and, in its genteel way, criminal. So far as I can make out, Welles never was and never will be a genius, but he is just as gifted as he ever was. In this film he is not using the most adventurous, not to say florid, of his gifts, but neither is he indulging any of his weaknesses. There is nothing about the picture that even appears to be "important" or "new," but there is nothing pretentious or arty either, and although I have occasionally seen atmospheres used in films in far grander poetic context, I don't think I have seen them more pleasantly and expertly appreciated. In a quite modest way the picture is, merely, much more graceful, intelligent, and enjoyable than most other movies; and I think that anyone capable of looking at it without bias will find plenty of reason to be glad that Welles is back at work.

Although Mr. Welles takes a reasonable amount of care not to insist on it, *The Stranger* is an "art" movie; Ben Hecht has been rather less cautious, in both good and bad ways, in making his thriller about an insane ballet dancer, *Specter of the Rose*. There is little if anything unprecedented in the way he has gone about making it, but it happens to be one of the very few right ways that are conceivably available in Hollywood. He persuaded Republic Studios that it might well be worth risking the cost of a B picture, $200,000, on a serious film for a limited audience; and that he should be let alone in making it. His juvenile leads combined two great advantages in being both new to movies and cheap; two of his supporting players are Michael Chekhov and Judith Anderson. He shared production and direction with his highly experienced cameraman, Lee Garmes. A great deal of rehearsing was done outside the studio. The only thing that went wrong was the movie itself—or enough of it to do bad harm to all the good that is in it. But enough of the movie went right to make it clear that under those circumstances it is not inevitable that such movies go wrong—though it is possible that men of surer taste than Mr. Hecht's could not raise the money and get the hands-off agreement. Hecht's taste is—if I can trust, as I have to, my own palate—so often rancid that I can commend only his intention and his method, and the generic good sense of the Republic executives, with a whole heart. Yet much in the film is worth seeing. I was delighted by Chekhov's performance as a sweet androgyne; by the fresh air of hope, pleasure, and freedom in which the picture moves because it was made that way; by a beautiful after-dinner speech delivered by a small-time patron of the arts; and by a good deal of the athletic innocence of backstage ballet. Republic has tried this sort of thing before—notably with Gustav Machaty's *Jealousy*—and plans, I gather, to keep on trying. Regardless of the uneven qualities of the films, I feel that Republic is heartily to be respected and thanked, and I hope they make enough money out of such pictures to develop—and spread—a policy. For sooner or later, under this kind of arrangement, some first-rate things are going to be done; and the chances look very slim that they will get done in any other way, in this country.

July 6, 1946

LILLIAN HELLMAN'S *The Searching Wind* is a study of the characteristic inability of Americans of good family and responsible position to admit what stares them in the face or, admitting it, to try to do anything about it. The personal and political aspects of the drama get in each other's way and, perhaps inevitably, lose in drive and shape by being staged to cover practically every major political crisis between the March on Rome and the immediate past. But the people themselves and the way they talk and think reveal many painful variations of our particular national brands of well-bred cowardice—political, emotional, and moral; and those who are more conscious and brave are given the limitedness, self-righteousness, and monotony which, unfortunately, are so often typical of them. People as highly civilized as these are seldom seen in the movies, and are still more seldom played with understanding. They are very firmly played here—though with touches perhaps of highly civilized ham—by Dudley Digges, Robert Young, Sylvia Sidney, Ann Richards, and Albert Bassermann. Their actions are very sumptuously and very well set, lighted, and dressed. And they are directed with his usual controlled intensity by William Dieterle. I can't feel that the picture will do any good, at this late hour, any more than it might have at an earlier one; nor, I fear, would any kind of dramatized self-criticism, no matter how deeply searching. But it is a careful, angry, honest film, and nothing it says is less apposite now than it would have been ten years ago, or twenty.

I did not read *Anna and the King of Siam*; after seeing the movie I am, to my pleased surprise, tempted to. I am not among those who take to Irene Dunne—as a rule she makes my skin crawl; nor do I wholly enjoy Rex Harrison's highly skilled, generally restrained horsing as the naively intelligent monarch whose good intentions enthrone him in a pratfall between his ancient and our modern world. There is indeed a good deal of high-polished and expensive cuteness about the whole production which stands, I suppose, as an apology for venturing to film a story that fits none of the formulas. But in spite of and through all this, the relationship between the rattled, irascible king and the English widow is often real, clear, and delightful, and occasionally very touching.

I cannot recommend *To Each His Own* highly enough to those who can still bear to be interested in what goes on in the cerebral powder-rooms of middle-class American women; or who still care to measure the depths to which some professionals will dive, self-deluded or otherwise, in the effort to profit by the pathological appetites of such women. In these terms it is an extraordinarily illuminating and skillful movie. It is skillful, in fact, however you look at it. But if you lack my all but necrophilic kind of interest in such stuff, you have fair warning. As for skill, any scientist can tell you what that is good for, irresponsibly employed.

Of course it is still possible to put it to work honorably; the results of that are so admirable in Laurence Olivier's production of *Henry V* that I must postpone any attempt to do the film honor until I have more space.

July 20, 1946

THE press on Laurence Olivier's production of Shakespeare's *Henry V* has been exceptionally warm and friendly, as seems no more than proper. Although the press is not to blame for it there is also a rumor, credited apparently by a good many, that it is the best movie ever made. Through some people I have talked with I gather that it is also possible for intelligent people to be disappointed, displeased, or even bored by the film. Indeed I will not be greatly surprised if a sort of highbrow underground develops, devoted to spoiling the fun of relatively easy-minded enthusiasts. Let me therefore first appease the more demanding among my readers, insofar as may be, by getting off my chest all I can possibly find to object to.

Henry V is by no means the best movie ever made; it is a re-creation of an old dramatic poem, not the creation of a new one. Nor is it the best of Shakespeare's plays; it is merely a very good and vigorous and at times very moving and beautiful one which, among all his plays, is one of the most obviously amenable to movie treatment and which was for obvious reasons particularly germane at the time it was planned and made. The movie treatment, in turn, is by no means as adventurous as it might have been. No attempt is made to develop a movie style which might in poetic energy and originality work as a cinematic counterpart to the verse. The idea is, rather, to make everything on the screen and soundtrack serve the verse, as clearly and well and unobtrusively as possible. Within this relatively modest and, I think, very wise and admirable intention, moreover, the success is not complete.

Much as I like most things about the opening sequence, in the Globe Theater, and skillfully as I think it is used on the whole, to accustom many levels of the contemporary audience to Shakespeare's style and skill, I am sorry about the subtly patronizing way in which a good deal of it was done. We have a right to assume that the Elizabethan stage at its best was in its own terms as good as the theater or the screen can ever hope to be, and I wish this might have been suggested—as it is in flashes by Olivier—without even the faintest suggestion of *Murder in the Old Red Barn*, or of "life ran very high in those days." The gradual transference from theater to screen seems to me good or better than good in each single idea, but a little heavy and balky taken altogether, and in spite of shrewd editing and, within each single scene, exquisite pacing the movie is during its first hour or so almost as fitful and choppy as the play. I very greatly like the anti-naturalistic, two-and-a-half-dimensional effect that is got by obtunding shallow perspectives in painted drops, and these drops are very pretty and clever; but too many of them are pretty and clever in a soft, almost travel-poster way which to some extent conflicts with and lets down the foregrounds. The night sequence in the English camp might, I think, have been still better if it had taken more of its country-night poetic atmosphere straight from nature, and had wholly avoided the smell and look of a good, semi-naturalistic studio set. The shooting of the battle is fine in its main design; I have an idea that here again sharp naturalism and sharp detail would have improved it and would only have intensified its poetic quality. Shakespeare, after all, was exceedingly rangy in his diction; the movie diction of these good but lesser poets is a little too resolutely "poetic."

I personally enjoyed—and even heard and understood—nearly everything that was done by the comics and semi-comics—especially Robert Newton as Pistol—but well played as they mostly were, I'm not convinced that they survive three hundred years with enough vitality to make them honestly and generally amusing, without a sort of "cultured" over-generosity toward them which I rather dislike in any context and find particularly distasteful in humor. They were not up to giving the narration of Falstaff's death any of the dizzying blend of comedy and noble piteousness it has in the text, nor can I imagine any human beings who would be; and although the actress who played Mistress Quickly gave her lines much tenderness and thought, she was, barring the Irish comic—with his unplayable role—the only embarrassing bit of amateurishness in the show.

I have, I must confess, a glimmer of the kind of unhappy premonition which sometimes signals a change of heart—a feeling that with many more seeings, and a good deal more remembrance, much that now seems highly satisfying, visually, will come to seem too much like conventional illustration to be quite so happy; and that a good deal of the casting, which now seems as nearly perfect as any I have ever seen in a film, and incomparably the best I have seen in a Shakespearian production, will seem perhaps no less good, so far as it goes, but a little predictable, even stodgy. I fear particularly that elements in Renée Asherson's performance as the French princess, which now seems to me pure enchantment, will in time look a little coarsely coy. But if this time ever comes I fear also that I will have lost a certain warmth of spirit, and capacity for delight, which this film requires of those who will enjoy it, and which it asks for, and inspires, with a kind of uninsistent geniality and grace which is practically unknown in twentieth century art, though it was part of the essence of Shakespeare's. I don't have the feeling that any extraordinary fresh creative force is at large in the film except that of Shakespeare, though the film itself swarms with the evidence of creative intelligence of a gentler and still highly honorable kind, and with evidence also of a quality of taste which is far too good and too sure of

itself to need to scorn the great middle audience. It is not, I repeat, the most exciting or inspiring or original film I have seen.
But I cannot think of any that seems to be more beautiful,
more skillfully and charmingly achieved within its wisely ordered limits, or more thoroughly satisfying.

Such are my objections; I could with pleasure fill twenty
times this space with a mere listing of specific excellence, without more than beginning to express my esteem for the film
and its makers. But what little of that there will be room for
will have to wait a couple of weeks.

August 3, 1946

It seems impertinent to discuss even briefly the excellence of
Laurence Olivier's production of Shakespeare's *Henry V* without saying a few words, at least, about the author. If Shakespeare had been no more gifted with words than, say, I am, the
depth and liveliness of his interest in people and predicaments,
and his incredible hardness, practicality, and resource as a craftsman and maker of moods, rhythms, and points, could still have
made him almost his actual equal as a playwright. I had never
realized this so well until I saw this production, in which every
nail in sight is so cleanly driven in with one blow; and I could
watch the film for all that Shakespeare gave it in these terms
alone, and for all that in these terms alone is done with what
he gave, with great pleasure and gratitude. But then too, of
course, there is the language, of a brilliance, vigor, and absoluteness that make the craftsmanship and sometimes the
people and their grandest emotions seem almost as negligibly
pragmatic as a libretto beside an opera score. Some people,
using I wonder what kind of dry ice for comfort, like to insist
that *Henry V* is relatively uninteresting Shakespeare. This uninteresting poetry is such that after hearing it, in this production, I find it as hard to judge fairly even the best writing since
Shakespeare as it is to see the objects in a room after looking
into the sun.

The one great glory of the film is this language. The greatest credit I can assign to those who made the film is that they
have loved and served the language so well. I don't feel that

much of the delivery is inspired; it is merely so good, so right, that the words set loose in the graciously designed world of the screen, like so many uncaged birds, fully enjoy and take care of themselves. Neither of the grimmest Shakespearian vices, ancient or modern, is indulged: that is to say, none of the text is read in that human, down-to-earth, poetry-is-only-hopped-up-prose manner which is doubtless only proper when a charter subscriber to *PM* reads the Lerner editorial to his shop-wise fellow traveler; nor is any of it intoned in the nobler manner, as if by a spoiled deacon celebrating the Black Mass down a section of sewerpipe. Most of it is merely spoken by people who know and love poetry as poetry and have spent a lifetime learning how to speak it accordingly. Their voices, faces, and bodies are all in charge of a man who has selected them as shrewdly as a good orchestrator selects and blends his instruments; and he combines and directs them as a good conductor conducts an orchestral piece. It is, in fact, no surprise to learn that Mr. Olivier is fond of music; charming as it is to look at, the film is essentially less visual than musical.

I cannot compare it with many stage productions of Shakespeare; but so far as I can they were, by comparison, just so many slightly tired cultural summer-salads, now and then livened, thanks to an unkilled talent or an unkillable line, by an unexpected rose-petal or the sudden spasm of a rattlesnake: whereas this, down to the last fleeting bit of first-rate poetry in a minor character's mouth, was close to solid gold, almost every word given its own and its largest contextual value. Of course nothing prevents this kind of casting and playing on the stage, except talent and, more seriously, the money to buy enough talent and enough time to use it rightly in; and how often do you see anything to equal it on the Shakespearian stage? The specific advantages of the screen are obvious, but no less important for that. Microphones make possible a much more delicate and immediate use of the voice; reactions, in close-up, can color the lines more subtly and richly than on the stage. Thus it is possible, for instance, to get all the considerable excellence there is out of an aging player like Nicholas Hannen, who seemed weak in most scenes when, on the stage, he had to try to fill and dilate the whole Century Theater with unhappy majesty; and the exquisiteness of Renée Asherson's reactions to Olivier's spate of gallantry, in the wooing scene, did as much as he did toward making that scene, by no means the most inspired as writing, the crown of the film. When so much can be done, through proper understanding of these simple advantages, to open the beauties of poetry as relatively extroverted as this play, it is equally hard to imagine and to wait for the explorations that could be made of subtler, deeper poems like *Hamlet, Troilus and Cressida*, or *The Tempest*.

Speaking still of nothing except the skill with which the poetry is used in this film, I could go on far past the room I have. The sureness and seductive power of the pacing alone and its shifts and contrasts, in scene after scene, has seldom been equaled in a movie; the adjustments and relationships of tone are just as good. For just one example, the difference in tone between Olivier's almost schoolboyish "God-a-mercy" and his "Good old Knight," not long afterward, measures the King's growth in the time between with lovely strength, spaciousness, and cleanness; it earns as craftsmanship, the triumph of bringing off the equivalent to an "impossibly" delayed false-rhyme; and psychologically or dramatically, it seems to me—though my guess may be far-fetched—it fully establishes the King's coming-of-age by raising honorable, brave, loyal, and dull old age (in Sir Thomas Erpingham) in the King's love and esteem to the level of any love he had ever felt for Falstaff.

Olivier does many other beautiful pieces of reading and playing. His blood-raising reply to the French Herald's ultimatum is not just that; it is a frank, bright exploitation of the moment for English ears, amusedly and desperately honored as such, in a still gallant and friendly way, by both Herald and King. His Crispin's Day oration is not just a brilliant bugle-blat: it is the calculated yet self-exceeding improvisation, at once self-enjoying and selfless, of a young and sleepless leader, rising to a situation wholly dangerous and glamorous, and wholly new to him. Only one of the many beauties of the speech as he gives it is the way in which the King seems now to exploit his sincerity, now to be possessed by it, riding like an unexpectedly mounting wave the astounding size of his sudden proud awareness of the country morning, of his moment in history, of his responsibility and competence, of being full-bloodedly alive, and of being about to die.

This kind of branching, nervous interpretive intelligence, so contemporary in quality except that it always keeps the main lines of its drive and meaning clear, never spiraling or strangling in awareness, is vivid in every way during all parts of the film.

It is tantalizing to be able to mention so few of the dozens of large and hundreds of small excellences which Mr. Olivier and his associates have developed to sustain Shakespeare's poem. They have done somewhere near all that talent, cultivation, taste, knowledgeability, love of one's work—every excellence, in fact, short of genius—can be expected to do; and that, the picture testifies, is a very great deal. Lacking space for anything further I would like to suggest that it be watched for all that it does in playing a hundred kinds of charming adventurousness against the incalculably responsive sounding-boards of tradition: for that is still, and will always be, a process essential in most, though not all, of the best kinds of art, and I have never before seen so much done with it in a moving picture. I am not a Tory, a monarchist, a Catholic, a medievalist, an Englishman, or, despite all the good that it engenders, a lover of war: but the beauty and power of this traditional exercise was such that, watching it, I wished I was, thought I was, and was proud of it. I was persuaded, and in part still am, that every time and place has since been in decline, save one, in which one Englishman used language better than anyone has before or since, or ever shall; and that nearly the best that our time can say for itself is that some of us are still capable of paying homage to the fact.

August 17, 1946

IN *Caesar and Cleopatra* large million-dollar chunks of ancient Egypt are tossed around under Shaw's lines as casually as so many rehearsal campstools. They are often pleasantly gaudy, sometimes beautiful, and never, I think, primarily objectionable; yet to some extent, by their massiveness and their violence of complexion, they cloy one's attention and thus slow up the mind and the dialogue. The movie could have been as good, I am sure, and perhaps better, if the budget had been adequate only to take care of the players and their costumes, and their background had, with proper wit, been suggested and sketched in. But even as it stands, the show is exceedingly good at the core, if you enjoy Shaw. Over that I am in no position to argue. I know of very little writing and not much music, for that matter, more pleasing than his work; nor do I expect to see his dialogue better used or his insights better understood than by most of the people in his cast, particularly Claude Rains and Vivien Leigh in the leading roles. Shaw's study of genius in Caesar, incidentally, makes most political leaders, and most studies of them, look about as well house-broken as a high-school debating society.

Caesar and Cleopatra was, I gather, generally panned in England. I can't see why. *Dead of Night*, which was also made in England, got raves here. I think I do see why. The film is made up of three amusing, rather old-fashioned, cryptic little episodes which might be supernatural or might just be elaborately "psychological." If you wholly reject the non-rational, the picture is no fun. But if you are by habit over-rational, a film so persuasive as this, suavely presenting as accomplished fact so much that you have refused to regard as even faintly conceivable, can profoundly disturb and excite you. This is, of course, an important and serious event, but the disturbed person has chiefly himself to thank for that, not the picture. Two excited reviews of the film seemed to me as sympathetic, yet naïve, as the reactions of certain friends of mine who heard Willkie talk just after his world tour and who, because for once they were sure they had found a sincere man, were sure they had found a great one. For such reasons, among others, any further development of America's so-called religious so-called revival is deeply to be dreaded, though no more so than most of those who dread or scorn it. If anyone can be trusted to hold his liquor, it is the habitual drinker. All this aside, *Dead of Night* is in every way made with exceptional skill and wit; as intelligent light entertainment it could not be better; and its famous last shot, whether one has foreseen it or not, is one of the most successful blends of laughter, terror, and outrage that I can remember. Even so I think it would be still better if "The End" were not superimposed on it, and if it ended with the first full close-up of its character.

Notorious lacks many of the qualities which made the best of Alfred Hitchcock's movies so good, but it has more than enough good qualities of its own. Hitchcock has always been as good at domestic psychology as at thrillers, and many times here he makes a moment in a party, or a lovers' quarrel, or a mere interior shrewdly exciting in ways that few people in films seem to know. His great skill in directing women, which boggled in *Spellbound*, is functioning beautifully again: I think that Ingrid Bergman's performance here is the best of hers that I have seen. One would think that the use of the camera subjectively—that is, as one of the characters—would for many years have been as basic a movie device as the close-up, but few people try it and Hitchcock is nearly the only living man I can think of who knows just when and how to. He is equally resourceful, and exceptional, in his manufacture of expressive little air-pockets of dead silence. He has a strong sense of the importance of the real place and the real atmosphere; the shots of Rio de Janeiro are excellent and one late-afternoon love-scene is equally remarkable in its special emotion and the grandeur of excitement it gets away with, and in communicating the exact place, weather, and time of day. Hitchcock also knows the movie value of the special tones and looks of people with special backgrounds, at special jobs. Gary Grant, as an American agent, has almost precisely the cultivated, clipped puzzled-idealist brutality of a man whom I know in a roughly equivalent job; and Louis Calhern, as his boss, reminds me even more forcefully that, for what little good it gets us, there are considerable depths of specifically native sophistication at work, in and out of Washington. There is perhaps no telling how much of all this should be credited to Ben Hecht's screen play; but it seems safe to credit a good deal of the sharpest movie sense, and of a cool kind of insight and control which suggests a good French novelist, to Hitchcock. The story by the way, shows Miss Bergman, a Nazi's daughter and a quondam tramp, doing State Department fingerwork among postwar German plotters in Brazil. Among her more painful duties is marrying Claude Rains, who is no less good as one of Hitler's unhappier orphans than as Bernard Shaw's coldly genial prototype of all dictators.

August 31, 1946

Brief Encounter, an expansion of a one-act play by Noel Coward, is a story about two decent middle-class people who fall in love outside their marriages and, beset by guilt and unable to stomach the enforced deceit and humiliation, give each other up. It is my impression that the same story, with fancy variations, is told once or twice in every issue of every magazine for housewives—often with a certain amount of sincerity, almost never with enough insight, detachment, style, or moral courage to make it better than wretched. Here, I must grant, there are several tricks of over-artifice and some of ham. But because in this case the story is written, filmed, and acted with a good deal of the positive qualities I mentioned, the picture is both a pleasure to watch as a well-controlled piece of work, and deeply touching. Even an unforgivable formula such as the lover's Looking Like A Little Boy when the woman's attentiveness reawakens his idealism, becomes remarkably real when it is handled tenderly and cleanly. I particularly like the performances of Celia Johnson and Trevor Howard as the lovers, and the things that are done with their faces and with the various ways they walk, at various stages of the affair. If, in my opinion, the movie at its best suggests merely all that woman's-magazine fiction might be at its own best, that is not intended as a back-handed compliment. For it seems to me that few writers of supposedly more serious talent even undertake themes as simple and important any more: so that, relatively dinky and sentimental as it is—a sort of vanity-sized *Anna Karenina*—*Brief Encounter* is to be thoroughly respected.

The Big Sleep is a violent, smoky cocktail shaken together from most of the printable misdemeanors and some that aren't —one of those Raymond Chandler Specials which puts you, along with the cast, into a state of semi-amnesia through which tough action and reaction drum with something of the nonsensical solace of hard rain on a tin roof. Humphrey Bogart and several proficient minor players keep anchoring it to some sufficient kind of reality. The picture is often brutal and sometimes sinister, and *PM* is probably correct in rating it as a new high in viciousness; but I can't bring myself to mind this sort of viciousness, far less to feel that it shouldn't be shown. I know it's a dream world, and doubtless it stimulates socially undesirable appetites in me and in others, but beside the really bottomless vileness of films like, for instance, *To Each His Own*, which walk the streets unchallenged and never even pass a serious medical inspection, it seems to me about as toxic as a package of Tums.

Two Years Before The Mast would be fair enough as a piece of straight sea-melodrama. The performance of Howard da Silva as the Captain and the presentation of the claustrophobia that is developed aboard ship—made in wartime, entirely ashore, the film grants few relieving views even of a process wave—are better than fair. What I object to is Paramount's presenting this heavily hopped-up picture of what a merchant seaman was up against, a century ago, as if it were historical fact, vouched for in Richard Henry Dana's book. Dana, if they'd care to tell the truth about it, said that he would have hated to command a crew of that sort unless the law gave him flogging-rights.

Monsieur Beaucaire turns Booth Tarkington's story inside-out and dresses Bob Hope in it. Some of it seems to me such rock-bottom Hope formula that whether you yawn or rather wearily laugh depends chiefly on your chance state of mind. Bits of it, however—Hope's reception in the Spanish court, his minuet, and his duel with Joseph Schildkraut—seem funny enough to take anyone, regardless of state of mind. And for what the minor role is worth, Schildkraut understands how to make and control his points, in this sort of show, much better than the star does.

In an elevator the other day—a hell of a place to bring such a thing up—an acquaintance rebuked me for liking *Caesar and Cleopatra*. As it turned out, he simply doesn't like the play much, whereas I simply do; and he minded the gaudiness, whereas I still don't; but I found I was close to agreeing with him about Claude Rains. He flatly thought Rains was a ham. I think he is, but has a saving ironic understanding of his hamminess; I also think Shaw's Caesar is, among other things, a conscious ham. Watching Rains again as Caesar, I realize that he plays nearly everything much too broad, to be as right for the role as I had thought. I now think he was adequate, and skillful, and amusing, but in second gear.

I speak of this now partly out of my duty toward myself, my

God, and my neighbor, chiefly because I was unable to do anything but mumble about it in the elevator. Ground floor.

THE idea keeps nagging at me that more and more people who think of themselves as serious-minded, and progressive, thoroughly disapprove of crime melodramas. They feel that movies should be devoted, rather, to more elevated themes such as a biography of George Washington Carver, omitting nothing down to the last peanut, or a good faithful adaptation of *Adam Bede* in sepia, with the entire text read offscreen by Herbert Marshall, or the story of how the way to atomic control and the brotherhood of man has been pointed out by egg cooperatives. They seem not to remember or not to care that in Germany, a few years ago, movies had to be constructive; stories of crime, and of troubled marriage, for instance, were strictly forbidden. For many years so much has been forbidden or otherwise made impossible in Hollywood that crime has offered one of the few chances for getting any sort of vitality on the screen. The three following movies are crime melodramas, factory-made. I can't say much for them, except that they are better to watch than most other factory products and, I suspect, better still to watch than the bracing, informative, constructive films which are the only kind these progressives would allow, if they were given half a chance.

The Killers starts off with Ernest Hemingway's brilliant, frightening story, then spends the next hour or so highlighting all that the story so much more powerfully left in the dark. The results aren't quite what might be expected. The story is well presented, but Hemingway's talk, which on the page used to seem so nearly magical and is still so very good, sounds, on the screen, as cooked-up and formal as an eclogue. From there on out the dialogue, though generally skillful and talented, isn't within miles of Hemingway's in quality, but it is made to be seen as well as heard, so, coming out of pictures, it sounds more nearly real. The story, from where Hemingway leaves off, is also a comparative letdown, but it too is better movie—good bars, fierce boxing, nice stuff for several minor players, and the kind of calculated violence and atmosphere in the filming of a robbery and of the last two sequences which was commonplace in old gangster films and is now so rare that in a good sense as well as a bad it is almost museum material. There is a good strident journalistic feeling for tension, noise, sentiment, and jazzed-up realism, all well manipulated by Robert Siodmak, which is probably chiefly to the credit of the producer, Mark Hellinger. There is nothing unique or even valuable about the picture, but energy combined with attention to form and detail doesn't turn up every day; neither does good entertainment.

Black Angel is pretty good entertainment too, on a humbler level. Taken casually, it is about like a better-than-average mystery reprint; pleasant to read yourself to sleep with. Taken as it deserves, it is better than that. Most movies of this inconspicuous, limited kind are made on a level of pure hack competence, or practically sleepwalking. Most of the people who wrote, directed, photographed, and played in this one have worked as if they believed that no job is so trivial but what it deserves the best you have. I particularly liked Dan Duryea's performance.

I finally caught up with *The Dark Corner*—not, I must confess, so badly out of breath as duty tells me I should have been. I enjoyed seeing it. I think everyone was right who pointed out that it is a shameless combination of formulas—of the murder-in-aspic, *Laura* sort of thing with the deep-city, Chandler kind which the existentialists will probably start discovering, and explaining, and imitating, almost any year now. But once in a while slickness and derivativeness persist so far in their folly that they develop a kind of vitality of their own—not to mention the fact that in movies, especially, people of real talent have sometimes either to succumb wholly to those vices or to use them as still another kind of leverage for surreptitious quality. There is no point in recommending *The Dark Corner* at all highly; but a great deal of intelligence and a fair amount of talent not only went into it, as they do into most movies, but manage—as they do in few—to remain visible. This, I thought, kept the show alive and fairly interesting.

A better show than any of these, and the funniest thing I have seen since the decline of sociological dancing, is *Rhapsody*

Rabbit. It is incredibly simple-minded: Bugs Bunny, interrupted by carrots and a mouse, gives a cut yet definitive performance of the most familiar of Liszt's Hungarian Rhapsodies —I forget which number. Some of it is as flatly brutal as Spike Jones, but I have never heard Jones within light-years of it except in parts of "You Always Hurt the One You Love." The best of it goes two ways: one, very observant parody of concert-pianistic affectations, elegantly thought out and synchronized; the other, brutality keyed into the spirit of the music to reach greater subtlety than I have ever seen brutality reach before. I could hardly illustrate without musical quotation; but there is a passage in which the music goes up with an arrogant wrenching of slammed chords—Ronk, *Ronk*, RONK (G-B-E) —then prisses downward on a broken scale—which Bugs takes (a) with all four feet, charging madly, scowling like a rockinghorse late for a date at stud, (b) friskily tiptoe, proudly smirking, like a dog toe-dancing through his own misdemeanor or the return of an I-Was-There journalist, a man above fear or favor who knows precisely which sleeping dogs to lie about. It killed me; and when they had the wonderful brass to repeat it exactly, a few bars later, I knew what killed really meant. Perhaps I should warn you, however, not to expect too much— not to expect anything, if possible. I usually loathe these hearty burlesques of good ham art; chiefly because most of them are made in hatred of all art, and in a total lack of understanding of the thing they are burlesquing. But a good musician must have worked on this art. Barring Beatrice Lillie I have never seen anything done from so deep inside the ham; I also had the great advantage of seeing it without warning. Perhaps I can put it this way. I have always very much liked this particular eruption of Liszt's, and though it made me laugh, the laughter was without patronage, far less scorn. After seeing its guts torn out in this movie short I knew more about it, and liked it better, than ever.

September 28, 1946

IF I were to review the English-made *The Notorious Gentleman* fairly, I could say in its favor that it contains a well-filmed rescue from drowning; that a new girl whose name I missed but who is, I gather, the wife of the star, Rex Harrison, is unusually lovely in her role as a Viennese refugee and is quite sensitive and quite possibly an actress as well; and that there are funny moments on a British coffee plantation and during the course of a quarrel between an adulterer and a cuckold. I could add that an attempt was made here, unusual only inasmuch as it is seldom carried so far in movies, to make the old-fashioned cad interesting and attractive—a job which was done better in *The Scoundrel*—and to use him as an instrument, crowbar rather than scalpel, for social comment. I would have to add that nothing about this attempt seemed to me as interesting as the fact that it was made; that that fact, in turn, did not interest me much; and that the comedy and satire and social comment, such as they are, seemed to me to struggle as in a rip-tide against crude writing, cruder pantomime, and the almost ethereal complacency of the film's low-grade sophistication. I would say, too, that except for the way he overrates it, Mr. Harrison is good at his job.

Having written what seems to me a fair review, if only in the subjunctive, perhaps I ought to let it go at that. But I can't. Most of the people I know who have seen the film in preview think so well of it that I am all but sure it will get a reputation it doesn't deserve. Although, as is perhaps immodest to point out, the whole of the movie world waits trembling from fortnight to fortnight to learn from this column what should or should not be done next, I am afraid I can't prevent the development of this false reputation; that will occur mainly among intellectuals. But at least I can throw spitballs.

The film tells the story of one of those irresistibly forgivable and seductive top-drawer skunks, worthless in all of an interminable series of relationships and dangerous in some, who turns out to be just what our side needs once he gets into a war. It is even strongly suggested that the war couldn't have been won without his kind; and it is more slyly suggested that it is the glory and the all-sufficient vindication of the upper classes to have bred such queen-bees. Well, I doubt it. For one thing, this type is international, including the enemy nations, and so might be supposed to cancel out in battle, like love of home and family, and God, who backs every horse if you ask the horse's opinion, and adoration of those lofty principles for which all nineteen sides and all seventy-one satellites are so devoutly bashing each other's brains out. Then, too, if the opportunities for enlightened self-interest are anything like as handsome in war as in peace, most men of this kind can be particularly well counted on to take advantage of them: for if they have a single virtue which distinguishes them from the cloddish bulk of the race, it is that, having nowhere to go that is more comfortable, they seldom betray their own natures. Then again it is popularly assumed, for heaven knows what self-accusatory reason, that whatever crimes they commit one has to like these scoundrels, because they are so devilishly charming. I doubt that too. They might have all the charm of Lucifer asking to stay up till nine, and one need not—must not—go cross-eyed over their innocent little cruelties; but do they really have charm? It may be that most people of extravagant charm are to some extent criminal; but few criminals, even of the type whose chief weapon is charm, have more of the genuine faculty than it takes to give themselves animal self-confidence enough to knock over the next victim. They may deceive themselves and this victim—not to mention their author. But unless the author is on to them—as he isn't in this movie—I find their crimes and their overrating of themselves as far from charming to watch in fiction as in actual life. Or yet again it is generally assumed that these hypnotists are as a rule well born, whereas the most efficient fake ones I have seen, and one or two of the real ones, are diamond-eyed, ravenous, climbing snobs—generally homosexuals manqués—whose fiercest compulsion is explained by their origin in the lintiest, most respectable under-bed obscurities of the lower middle class. And even if all I have argued were wrong, and the upper classes did indeed breed these indispensable men, I would not feel that that vindicated either the class or the fatuous and cruel peacetime career or, for that matter, even the stupid glory of murdering supernumeraries of some other camp. I would feel rather that considering all that this class had done toward and in indifference to the rest of us, in peace, in war, and in helping the world over the low hump from one to the other, breeding saviors who weren't even saviors would be the very least that might be expected, and an apology that no gentleman would make, at that. Nor could I be dissuaded if the film pointed out to me, as this one tries to, the deadly blockishness of the merely plebeian and serious-minded. I know much more about that than they know how to show, being myself plebian and, much as I regret it, rather too serious-minded as well. When I see intelligent people missing these points and deceived by this film, and remember that most of them have been involved in the past seven years much more intimately than I have, I wonder more wistfully than ever about substitutes for Byrnes and Truman, or what rude beast could possibly be rude enough to suspect what time of day it really is.

I feel all the more annoyed about all this because I do recognize that at its best the Don Giovanni type is one of the most wonderful kinds of human being. Such a man is as a rule, though not invariably, well born and even better bred. He is, as a rule, one of the few excuses that his own class or any other can make for itself—rarely though it avails itself of that privilege. And he has genius for careless, skillful, and gallant action which is most often exercised on the way to bed with some unfortunate or, more rarely, in a work of art or politics, but which I presume must in a very few individuals find its most brilliant expression in war. (In war, the conventional or even the stuffy aristocrat is probably just as often just as good—and there are lots more of them.) If such a man were adequately presented and explored in a movie, and if the merely sincere or scientific or humanitarian man were measured against him, the world would have at hand so much useful knowledge that, if only it knew how or dared to use it, I would not be reading it, nor would any of those who were about to decide it would be criminally insane to invent the wheel and the lever care whether or not the foregoing clause is anticlimatic. But it takes a great artist to present such a man (I remember no example of the full, contrasting job): Mozart presented him in *Don Giovanni* and Byron, more spottily, in *Don Juan*; on a high, though less inspired level Shaw has been doing it most of his life. But smaller people seldom get away with it. Waugh did, by reducing the type to pure meeching horror in *A Handful of Dust*, but the reality of Basil Seal becomes as arguable as the uses he is put to in *Put Out More Flags*. The people who made *The Notorious Gentleman* are much farther below Waugh than he is below Mozart or even Byron. Considering how supremely this job has been done a few times, and how often it has been done much better than here, how can anyone care for this version? As the makers of this film miscalculate their materials, every truth becomes an annoying half-truth, and every half-truth a clumsy lie, and only the very generous and the very hungry can mistake the scarcely understood intention for the generally boggled deed. They fell so far short of their best intentions that some of the enthusiasts I have argued with think of the whole show as just an amusing lot of froth. Discounting the adjective, they are probably right. Froth on a pool that beasts would cough at; but profounder, thirstier people, who surely know better, whoosh it aside, and drink deep.

October 12, 1946

The Raider, an English film once called by the beautiful title *Western Approaches*, is the story of the convergence in mid-Atlantic of a U-boat, an English lifeboat, and an English ship which has strayed from convoy. The men in the lifeboat realize that the Germans are using them as a decoy; they are determined to warn off the rescuing vessel, if need be at the cost of their lives. The rescuers are torpedoed all the same, but manage to outwit and sink the submarine. The submarine crew, so far as I could make out, is left to drown; the English derelicts are taken aboard at last.

This very broad, strong, simple story, which suggests many of the good things about Kipling or even Tolstoy, is, I gather, true, or is anyhow a composite of true incidents. It is played entirely by nonprofessional actors, sailors, and we are told that they are reenacting their experiences. The picture is directed by Pat Jackson, who also wrote the scenario and the dialogue for the semi-fictional scenes of reenactment.

The Raider reaches this country very late, after a muffle of delays I would be curious to see explained. It is a war film and was made to be seen in wartime; but it is also one of very few war films which can be seen without blushing at any time, and which is, I think, permanently to be respected.

It is not, to be sure, in any sense a morally or politically searching or a psychologically exciting piece of work. The predicament is a deadly simple, physical one, and the reactions are no less simple and physical. There is little exploration of development of character: the men in the lifeboat, for instance, know each other well to begin with and get to know each other even better in the course of a couple of weeks' exposure, but the audience gets no illusion of knowing them better; it is merely privileged to rubberneck. But it is looking at the surfaces of people of extraordinary strength and authenticity; moreover, the Germans, especially the U-boat captain, are no less full-blown as personalities than the English. Most attempts to make the enemy "human" have gone as fishy as the still more conventional attempts to make him a devil, a brute, a clown, or at very least a foot-fetishist; here, more successfully than in any other film I can remember, he is merely made up of another bunch of people who are very deeply absorbed in a life-and-death predicament and as deeply interested in their jobs. It is an obvious point, of course, but you have to see it really done, for once, to realize fully the childish shallowness of any other way of "indicting" war. By a characteristically good and unobtrusive bit of writing the only Englishman who expresses hatred for the Germans for using them as bait is also the only one who has opposed his captain's determination to warn off the rescuers. Another fine little bit is the submarine captain's red-bearded patriarchal smile as he says that they'll just turn loose their last couple of torpedoes and then—home.

It is this same hale, sane, uncomplicated, and unquerulous sense of reality which gives the whole picture its finest qualities. To use nonprofessionals well in this semi-fictional kind of work requires a particularly warm, quick, and flexible understanding of people—of when to direct and when to leave alone, of how to combine several degrees of both harmoniously, and of what, artistically, is more "real" than the actual and what is less real. It is a rare and potentially very important kind of creative faculty, called for by movies and by still photography as by no other kind of art. I have seen some very good things done with it, chiefly by the English; and the Russians have often used it very powerfully—though less perceptively in a purely human way—by, for instance, cutting nonprofessional faces into intense poetic or rhetorical contexts. But I don't remember seeing anyone use non-actors so extensively, with such respect and understanding and thorough success, as Mr. Jackson has used them here. Anyone who wants, for instance, to see the varied awkwardness of nonprofessionals used to perfection can study over and over the little scene in New York in which the convoy captains are briefed. Or for a sample of directing neither too much nor too little, so that art and actuality work on each other like live chemicals, there is the exchange of smiles between the radio operator and the adolescent boy in the lifeboat, at the moment when everyone first has good reason to give up hope. Or for a quietly definitive illustration of the quality free naturalism can have when a man with the right poetic instincts is in charge, watch the variety of manner in which the sailors transfer from the lifeboat to the ship, and compare the unlimited beauty and touchingness of this little scene with the also touching, skillfully predigested and packaged quality of the realism in the scene in which crew and captain part in *In Which We Serve.* Or to check the film against something with which you may have been familiar, see what has been done with shots of the New York mid-war waterfront. The most ordinary "documentary" material in this film is always used with so deep and unpretentious a sense of its human meanings that without rhetoric or comment it becomes automatically poetic; and all that is necessarily fictional is anchored as short as can be managed to what is known to have been so. That combination sounds like and perhaps is the minimum of common sense for this type of film; it is not often attempted, however, and almost never achieved.

This same sort of purity of plain good sense at its best must help, I think, to account for the excellence of the transitions and of the cutting, which never use artily, or point up, or intrude on, but are always made part of the hypnotic leavening of, the noble prevailing rhythm of the film, which is simply that of ocean water. It must have taken the same good sense to foresee that such a film could and should be made in color; that the imperfections of color film, as a rule so deadly under studio control, greatly enhance both immediacy and beauty when they collaborate with the imperfections of unaffected people and of open nature. And it took a kind of flat plain sense—far beyond that of the mere realist—which I have never seen get so far on the screen before, to realize that you have no right to record the sufferings and honor the fortitude of men exposed in a lifeboat unless you make those sufferings at least real enough, in swollen features and livid coloring, feebleness of motion and obvious crushing headache, to hurt an audience, and hurt it badly.

It seems to me striking that in this film and in others the English have done so well in their handling of real people in films, and that we as a rule have done so very badly. (One must, thank heaven, except several of our war record films.) The chief reason, so well as I can understand it, is an ugly one. Few Americans either behind or in front of our cameras give evidence of any recognition or respect for themselves or one another as human beings, or have any desire to be themselves or to let others be themselves. On both ends of the camera you find very few people who are not essentially, instead, just promoters, little racketeers, interested in "the angle." I suspect it will some day be possible to deduce out of our nonfiction films alone that the supposedly strongest nation on earth collapsed with such magical speed because so few of its members honored any others, or even themselves, as human beings.

October 26, 1946

IT is interesting to compare Marcel Pagnol's *The Well-Digger's Daughter* with the popular American film *To Each His Own.* Both examine at some length the consequences of having an illegitimate child, and both, in their very different ways, are highly designed and artificial. But the American film, for all its polish as a production and in spite of a good many glints of secondary reality, struck me as one of the most false and unpleasant movies in years; whereas the French film, pitifully raw as a production—it was made during the German occupation—and showing its own fair quota of worse faults than that, has about it a very remarkable amount of truth and beauty.

To Each His Own is so little worth talking about that I will make few more comparisons: let it suffice that from the moment the girl knows she is pregnant she acts like the moral coward nearly everyone in Hollywood and in the audience requires her to be, and that every plot complication and tearjerk from there on proceeds from, and exploits, premises of cowardice, cynicism, and the rottenest kinds of sentimentality. In *The Well-Digger's Daughter* it never once occurs to the girl, or to her father, or to anyone else that she must avoid the consequences or be tricky about them, and most of the rest of the picture, proceeding from this simplicity, remains equally real and touching. There is a beautiful scene, for instance, in which the girl tries to tell her casual lover of her sadness in being no longer a virgin, of her sense of separation from her family. There is a very painful scene in which the workman brings his pregnant daughter—and her five younger sisters—before the parents of the young man; these parents, true to their shopkeepers' mentality, cannot conceive that he has come for anything but blackmail, and manage to infect the father with their own assumption that the girl is a promiscuous liar. And there is a wonderful scene in which these parents, who have just learned that their son has died in the war, first see and desire to help their grandchild. Such scenes as these are written and played with a gentle and pure feeling for outrightness and comedy which makes all that is most serious in them extremely unaffected and poignant. In later scenes, significantly, when the story goes questionable—with the son's unexpected return, and eagerness to marry the girl—the acting goes rocky too. Even the late Raimu, as the girl's father, an actor with matchless discretion, as a rule, about when to neutralize the sentimentality with something dry, hard, and practical, puts on an old-fashioned gagging smirk which must now cause his ghost one of the few blushes it ever need suffer. And the delightful clown Fernandel, who has been finely sympathetic as the second-string suitor, shoves his head in the window for the punch-line with all the quality that used to be got by making Buck Jones's horse flare his lip and cross his fore hoofs at the final clinch.

In at least half of this film, however, it is so happy to see people behaving like human beings in a basic, moving, difficult situation that I thoroughly understand and like what Archer Winsten means when he writes that such a film can be made only by the pure in heart. And mainly I agree. But to an extent even much that I like in this film, and in its whole French kind, makes me uneasy. I'm not too fond of the fondness for nature symbolism—the bread in *Harvest*, or here, the contrast-collaboration between aviation and well-digging. But I could let that be. What bothers me more is that something goes a little fishy about the purity of attitude in which the people are seen—good and true as it is, essentially. This sense of honoring the basic needs and experiences and values, of delighting in the animal innocence of unspoiled people, is hard though I hope not impossible to have without some taint both of sophisticated patronage and of snobbish, pseudo-respectful sentimentality, and without depending upon and stimulating those attitudes, however obscurely, in the audience. At its queasiest the attitude seems to read: "We're all just more or less good animals—or anyhow *they* are, and how we like and envy them." It is more worldly wise and more genuinely humane, but it makes me think of the attitude of the nicer Southern people toward "darkies"; it even sets some faint bells blurring over in the Hitler corridor, where all such simplicities are, I gather, sincerely yet perversely venerated. I think there is much in these simplicities that requires our veneration, but that for people sophisticated enough to feel the veneration, there are many hidden traps.

November 9, 1946

The Dark Mirror is a smooth and agreeable melodrama about twin sisters (Olivia de Havilland, sweet and dry), and a psychiatrist (Lew Ayres) and a detective (Thomas Mitchell) who find out which one is an insane murderess. The detective work involves ink-blot and word-association tests and an amusingly sinister tandem of oscillating pens which register concealed emotions as one of the sisters talks. The picture could have been more exciting if Nunnally Johnson and his colleagues had risked more subtlety and puzzlement in the psychologizing, the situations, and the everyday performance of the sisters, but it is fairly clear that they were worried about just such risks and decided to eat-and-have only bits of the frosting instead of the whole cake. As far as they go with it, they do it very intelligently. I like the illusion of relaxation Mr. Johnson can create in dialogue which is actually very tightly designed, and I very much like Olivia de Havilland's performance. She has for a long time been one of the prettiest women in movies; lately she has not only become prettier than ever but has started to act, as well. I don't see evidence of any remarkable talent, but her playing is thoughtful, quiet, detailed, and well sustained, and since it is founded, as some more talented playing is not, in an unusually healthful-seeming and likable temperament, it is an undivided pleasure to see. I wish I could speak as respectfully of Mr. Ayres's performance, in his first film since the war, as I feel toward his performance during the war, but it seemed to me to be done wholly from the outside. Although I can remember very good work of his, perhaps he was never vocationally an actor; now, in any case, he seems no longer to be doing work he can care for: a predicament in which I and probably most of two billion other people can sympathize with him profoundly, without being eager to watch a sight so unhappy and so familiar.

I can't understand the excitement over *The Jolson Story*. Without for a moment thinking they had anything to do with jazz, I have always liked Jolson and his style and most of his songs, and I still like hearing them on the soundtrack; and I suppose Larry Parks does about as well, as the visual Jolson, as anyone except the original would be likely to. Evelyn Keyes has always seemed to me one of the more attractive and capable girls in Hollywood, and one of the most neglected, and it is good to see her again, even in a role which can use so little of what she has, and which misuses most of that. I would probably enjoy William Demarest as Little Eyolf; so I had no great trouble liking him here. In fact, I have nothing in the world against this picture except that at least half of it seemed to me enormously tiresome. The other half is pleasant enough, but no more. The trouble is, it is here nearly as hard to separate the pleasant from the boring as to get the cream out of homogenized milk.

The Museum of Modern Art is screening a gigantic historical anthology of movies; the program started the middle of last September and will finish a year from next December. I could, and in the course of time may, regret and criticize quite a few omissions and inclusions, and some of the ways of classifying the films—for instance, the bewildering inclusion of *Der Dreigroschenoper* under the rubric *Pabst and Realism*. And I feel that when the historians get to work on anything, arteries begin to harden, in the subject and in the people interested. Yet there is hardly a program in the bunch that doesn't offer some film I have seen and would highly recommend for re-seeing, or to anyone who missed it; or some film I want to see because through incarceration in one school or another, or inability to milk or steal the price of admission, I had to miss it myself. During the next two weeks I particularly recommend the following to those within radius: Von Stroheim's *Foolish Wives*, Flaherty's *Nanook of the North*, *Wild Bill Hickok* with William S. Hart, Thomas Ince's *The Last Card*, James Cruze's *The Covered Wagon*, *Grandma's Boy* (Harold Lloyd), and *Sherlock, Jr.* (Buster Keaton). *Foolish Wives* is fiercely trashy, but along with the trash there is some brutally shrewd atmosphere and sexual realism and comedy. *Nanook* has a beautiful simplicity, cheer, and hardiness which no subsequent documentary has improved on and which most have lost or perverted. I missed *Wild Bill*, but I didn't miss the late William S. Hart, and I think that at his best he was in his face and his way of handling himself almost as mythically and finely racial—or I suppose I have to say national—as Lincoln. Hart is in *The Last Card*, too, which I also missed, and that is the only film by Ince, who was as great in his way as Griffith, that the museum is able to show. Some of *The Covered Wagon* looks pretty embarrassing now, though I still think the frontier-comic work of Ernest Torrence and Tully Marshall has grandeur, for all that it is corny; but all that is massive and detached from characters and character-plot is tremendously strong, moving, and beautiful. The chase and fight in *Grandma's Boy*, as I remember them, are a high point in melodramatic slapstick, thanks importantly to the terrifying face of Dick Sutherland as the villain; and Grandma's Civil War flashback is achingly funny. *Sherlock, Jr.* is not one of Buster Keaton's funniest—none of his full-length films were—but it is about a hundred times as funny as anything made today. Some of the houses, yards, and streets are even more beautifully photographed than was usual in the old comedies. And one chase gag, involving a motorcycle and a long line of ditch-diggers, is hair-raising both in its mechanical perfection and as a piece of better-than-conscious surrealism. I am sorry the museum isn't showing Lloyd's finest comedy, his paralyzing first version of *Safety Last*, a piece about a human fly which is as staggeringly fast as machine-gun fire. I'm even sorrier that the museum, or some dime theater, isn't showing every short film Keaton ever made, night and day, over and over. Barring only the best of Chaplin, they seem to me the most wonderful comedies ever made.

December 7, 1946

WHAT HOLLYWOOD CAN DO

The Best Years of Our Lives, a misfired title, seems to have started as a gleam in Samuel Goldwyn's eye when he saw in a mid-war issue of *Time* a picture and article about returning veterans. At a later stage it was a verse novel by MacKinlay Kantor called *Glory for Me*—not a very good title either. Robert E. Sherwood turned this into a screen play; the director William Wyler and the cameraman Gregg Toland and a few hundred others turned the screen play into a movie. The movie has plenty of faults, and the worst of them are painfully exasperating; yet this is one of the very few American studio-made movies in years that seem to me profoundly pleasing, moving, and encouraging.

The story is of a sort that could have been, and often remains, just slick-paper fiction at its most sincere, and that could also have become, and occasionally suggests, a great and simple, limpid kind of fiction which few writers of serious talent seem able to attempt or even to respect, at present. An ex-bombardier (Dana Andrews), an ex-infantry sergeant (Fredric March), and an ex-sailor (Harold Russell) meet for the first time as they return to their home city, part to undertake the various pleasures and problems of their return, and meet again at various subsequent times as their lives and relationships shake down into new shape.

The bombardier, a highly intelligent proletarian, can find nothing better in the way of a job than his old place in a drugstore. He finds, too, that he and the girl he married just before he went overseas no longer get along. The sergeant, who was once the kind of nervously well-married, vocationless, rather sensitive business man, too good for his job, who tries to sweep along his uneasiness in a momentum of alcohol, clowning, fairly sophisticated wit, and his real but seldom focused affections, finds that none of that has changed for the better. He is made vice-president of his bank, in charge of G.I. loans, and spends a good deal of his time drunk. The sailor, who has lost both hands and has learned to use a pair of hooks quite well, returns to the gentlest and most touching depths of the lower middle class. His chief problem is the girl he had always expected to marry; another is his extreme uneasiness about everybody's attempt to be good about his hooks; a hideous complication is that he is at once intuitively very perceptive and sensitive, and hopelessly inarticulate, and that most of the people he returns to are equally well-meaning and unsophisticated.

At its worst this story is very annoying in its patness, its timidity, its slithering attempts to pretend to face and by that pretense to dodge in the most shameful way possible its own fullest meanings and possibilities. Perhaps one shouldn't kick too hard at a "mere" device, but I feel very dubious about the invention of a nice bar in which the veterans keep meeting each other, perhaps because I suspect that one of the dodged truths is that, once they become civilians again, most men of such disparate classes or worlds would meet seldom, with greater embarrassment than friendliness, and that the picture is here presenting, instead of the unhappy likelihood, a hopeful and barely plausible lie. I feel a good deal of interest in the love affair that develops between Andrews and the banker's daughter, played by Teresa Wright, but again they have made it easy for themselves by showing Andrews's wife to be a bag, and they atone for this convenience only in part by making her as well-meaning and sympathetic and essentially innocent as, in terms invented for her, she could be. Thanks to much of the writing and all of the playing, this illicit affair is by implication remarkably real and mature; but in action, in the good old inevitable Sunday School way, the extra-marital activities are limited to a single Andrews-Wright kiss and a boy-friend, for Andrews's wife, lolling in his shirtsleeves; and it is the wife who asks for a divorce.

Or again, they pretend to hit the banker's predicament

between the eyes, and allow him to tell off his careful world which doesn't want to make loans to veterans without collateral in a speech which, on the movie scale of things, is reasonably bold. They even have the firmness to let March have the last word on that issue; he says that with nearly every loan without collateral he will have to put up the same fight all over again. Yet one is emotionally left with the impression that he has cleverly and lovably won his fight and will win it on every subsequent occasion, and the hints that his own bread and butter are and will be increasingly in jeopardy if he keeps his courage are so discreet as to be all but inaudible. As a footnote to this his boss, played by Ray Collins, is represented, not with the cool realism which could here have been so good and so nearly unprecedented in an American movie, but in the kind of skillful caricature which, like so much of Gilbert and Sullivan, makes every punch a kind of self-caress.

The only boss types represented cruelly are the manager and floor-walker of a chain drugstore—that is, men in a job predicament in which they are as much bullied as bullying; and it is not shown that they are bullied. The only business type who is represented with what seems like perfect justice is the father of the sailor's sweetheart, a specialized, fussy, feminine little man who nervously tries to badger the sailor about his plans for the future. Or for still another major fault—and here direction and playing are as much to blame as the script—the very interesting and, for movies, new character of the banker is only hinted at, not solidly presented. Only the psychologically sophisticated can gather from the film that his marriage is only nominally happy and is actually precarious, and that the people who made the movie may possibly be on to this; and March's benders, though extremely well done in their way, are staged with all but frantic gratitude as broad comic relief, as if professional entertainers who were also good artists were on these occasions very glad to betray their responsibilities as artists for the sake of getting a little bit of sure-fire—and commercially much-needed—fun into the show.

In fact, it would be possible, I don't doubt, to call the whole picture just one long pious piece of deceit and self-deceit, embarrassed by hot flashes of talent, conscience, truthfulness, and dignity. And it is anyhow more than possible, it is unhappily obligatory, to observe that a good deal which might have been very fine, even great, and which is handled mainly by people who could have done, and done perfectly, all the best that could have been developed out of the idea, is here either murdered in its cradle or reduced to manageable good citizenship in the early stages of grade school. Yet I feel a hundred times more liking and admiration for the film than distaste or disappointment.

[*Mr. Agee's review of "The Best Years of Our Lives" will be concluded next week.*]

December 14, 1946

[*This is the concluding section of Mr. Agee's review of "The Best Years of Our Lives." The first half was printed last week.*]

IT SEEMS to me that the movie's basic weaknesses are in the script—or are more likely, in the writer's knowledge of all that he would have to go easy on as a part of the rather remarkable bargain by which he got away with all that he managed to. Yet this is a most unusually good screen play. Although the dialogue has a continuous sheen of entertainment slickness it is also notably well-differentiated, efficient, free of tricks of snap and punch and over-design, and modest in its feeling for how much weight it should carry on the screen; and most of the time there is an openness about the writing which I don't doubt every good screen writer tries for but which few achieve. By openness I mean simply that the scenes are so planned, and the lines so laid down, that every action and reaction, every motion and everything that is seen, is more centrally eloquent than the spoken lines. The movie thus has and takes its chance to be born in front of the camera, whereas the general run of screen plays force what takes place before the camera to be a mere redigestion of a predigestion.

With a director and camera man in charge so gifted as Messrs. Wyler and Toland it is impossible to guess which of them, or Mr. Sherwood, is most to be thanked for the great force, simplicity, and beauty of some of the scenes and countless of the camera set-ups; so it is purely my hunch, with apologies in advance, that the real heroes in this film are Wyler and

Toland, with invaluable assists credited to the set designer and art director, who provide some of the best stages for the action that I have ever seen in a movie. I can't think of a single shot of Toland's that doesn't show the amount of will, creative energy, and taste, and doesn't add with perfect power and modesty its own special kind of expressiveness, which of course ought to be evident in every shot in every good movie, and which of course plenty of people try for without more than spasmodically achieving. I can't remember a more thoroughly satisfying job of photography, in an American movie, since *Greed*. Aesthetically and in its emotional feeling for people and their surroundings, Toland's work in this film makes me think of the photographs of Walker Evans. Toland either lacks or subsumes any equivalent intellect, irony, and delight in the varieties of texture, edge, meaning, mystery, and shape in clothing and in all inanimate things; but it is a question how much such powers of perception could be used in telling a story in motion.

William Wyler has always seemed to me an exceedingly sincere and good director; he now seems one of the few great ones. He has come back from the war with a style of great purity, directness, and warmth, about as cleanly devoid of mannerism, haste, superfluous motion, aesthetic or emotional overreaching, as any I know; and I felt complete confidence, as I watched this work, that he could have handled any degree to which this material might have been matured as well as or even better than the job he was given to do. His direction of the nonprofessional, Harold Russell, is just an exciting proof, on the side, of the marvels a really good artist can perform in collaboration with a really good non-actor; much more of the time it was his job to get new and better things out of professionals than they had ever shown before. One conspicuous failure—good as it is in its regrettable way—is March in his drunk scenes; and Myrna Loy, as his wife, is surprisingly uneven. But March is far outside his normal habits, and very good indeed, in, for instance, his interview with Dana Andrews over the question of the March daughter. And such a scene as that in which the sailor's father helps him get ready for bed seems to me so quietly perfect that I would set it in the world with the best fiction, or poetic drama, or movies that I know.

Almost without exception, down through such virtually noiseless bit roles as that of the mother of the sailor's fiancée, this film is so well cast and acted that there is no possible room to speak of all the people I wish I might. I cannot, however, resist speaking briefly, anyhow, of Teresa Wright. Like Frances Dee, she has always been one of the very few women in movies who really had a face. Like Miss Dee, she has also always used this translucent face with delicate and exciting talent as an actress, and with something of a novelist's perceptiveness behind the talent. And like Miss Dee, she has never been around nearly enough. This new performance of hers, entirely lacking in big scenes, tricks, or obstreperousness—one can hardly think of it as acting—seems to me one of the wisest and most beautiful pieces of work I have seen in years. If the picture had none of the hundreds of other things it has to recommend it, I could watch it a dozen times over for that personality and its mastery alone.

I can hardly expect that anyone who reads this will like the film as well as I do. It is easy, and true, to say that it suggests the limitations which will be inevitable in any Hollywood film, no matter how skillful and sincere. But it is also a great pleasure, and equally true, to say that it shows what can be done in the factory by people of adequate talent when they get, or manage to make themselves, the chance.

December 28, 1946

STUFF the following with sage and serve hot, with soda-mints, to men of sufficiently good will:

It's a Wonderful Life, Frank Capra's first film since those he made for the army, is one of the most efficient sentimental pieces since *A Christmas Carol*. Often, in its pile-driving emotional exuberance, it outrages, insults, or at least accosts without introduction, the cooler and more responsible parts of the mind; it is nevertheless recommended, and will be reviewed at length as soon as the paralyzing joys of the season permit.

Wanted for Murder, an English melodrama, stars Eric Portman as a middle-class mother's boy who can't keep his hands off the throats of working girls, of whom he strangles several

before Scotland Yard catches up with him. To have held out so
long, he is remarkably careless at his work, dropping a marked
handkerchief near one corpse, a shard of cigar near another,
and the balance of the cigar in Inspector Conway's ash-tray.
He even knocks the head off his late, mad uncle, "The Happy
Hangman," who is on exhibit at Madame Tussaud's and under
whose influence the hero does his killing. Neck-deep as he
stands in a blizzard of such manna, Roland Culver manages to
make the Inspector seem capable and subtle as well as likable.
Mr. Portman, who suggests a cross between Paul Henreid
and Louis Calhern, gives the maniac a dangerous, melancholic
grace. Both men seem to me considerably more persuasive than
most of the bench-dogs who are paid to charm women in
American films; but not being a woman—not even an American woman—I am ill-qualified to judge. This is a pleasant, unpretentious thriller of the second or third grade, with oddly
contradictory streaks of good and crude directing, and some
beautifully exciting shots of Hyde Park as a police cordon
clears away the rattled crowds and closes, through the twilight,
for the kill.

Till the Clouds Roll By is a little like sitting down to a soda-
fountain de luxe atomic special of maple walnut on vanilla on
burnt almond on strawberry on butter pecan on coffee on rasp-
berry sherbet on tutti frutti with hot fudge, butterscotch,
marshmallow, filberts, pistachios, shredded pineapple, and rainbow sprills on top, go double on the whipped cream. Some of
the nuts, it turns out, are a little stale, and wandering throughout the confection is a long bleached-golden hair, probably
all right in its place but, here, just a little more than you can
swallow. This hair, in the difficult technical language of certain members of the Screen Writers' Guild who exult in my
nonprofessionalism—political as well as cinematic—would, I
suppose, be called the "story-line." The story is enough of the
life and not very hard times of the late Jerome Kern to make
you want either not to hear any of it at all or to get the real
story instead. Besides the story, however, the picture contains
something over twenty stars and featured players, many of
them nice people, and they sing no less than twenty-two of
Kern's songs. If, as I do, you like a good deal of his graceful,

nacreous music, the picture is pleasantly, if rather stupefyingly, worth all the bother. The songs are nearly all sung with care and affection, though not one that I have heard before is done here quite as well as I have heard it elsewhere. The most surprising defection is the failure twice around, to give "Old Man River" any of the pulse and momentum which go so far toward making it Kern's best song. Both Sinatra and a colored singer do it, instead, with all misplaced reverence, is if they were re-translating at sight, out of Tacitus, the Emancipation Proclamation. This I realize is called *feeling* the music; for that kind of feeling I prefer W. C. Fields's cadenza on the zither, which was rendered in sparring-gloves.

January 25, 1947

MOVIES IN 1946

Of the films of 1946 that I saw—I missed a number of likely candidates—I liked most *The Best Years of Our Lives*, *Brief Encounter*, *Henry V*, *Let There Be Light*, *Open City*, and *The Raider*.

The Best Years is equivocal in story, but in front of the camera—and this is still more important—it is done about as well as a movie can imaginably be, made among the frustrating facilities of a contemporary American studio.

Much of *Brief Encounter* is very likable and affecting; it seems to me the best romance since *Mayerling*. It is a shriveling commentary, though, on the reality of the run of films, that so many people have spoken of this one almost as if Noel Coward had personally invented realism—and wholly as if the realism in this film were of an adventurous or even a high order. It seems to me, instead, a particularly neat sample of how to *package* realism, astutely modifying everything that might make the package fit clumsily into a lady's handbag.

In making *Henry V* Laurence Olivier and his associates chose to serve Shakespeare rather than to compete with him— and served him with honor, ingenuity, and grace. The bolder attempt would even in principle have excited me more; great movie poetry, deliberately or intuitively undertaken from scratch, without benefit of hindrance of a classic, I think still better of than that. But neither preference qualifies my admiration or my love for this beautiful film as it stands; nor am I terribly disturbed because it is a patriotic film, finds a good deal of good in war, and tells sympathetically of a cynical invasion.

Let There Be Light, John Huston's intelligent, noble, fiercely moving short film about combat neurosis and some of the more spectacular kinds of therapy, will probably never be seen by the civilian public for whose need, and on whose money, it was made. The War Department has mumbled a number of reasons why it has been withheld; the glaring obvious reason has not been mentioned: that any sane human being who saw the film would join the armed services, if at all, with a straight face and a painfully maturing mind. In a nation with half its forebrain left and a thousandth of its moral intelligence, even such a little suppression as this would cause a monstrous scandal, and an adequate fight. But in such a nation the general reaction to a good many more disastrous bits of crime and cowardice would long ago have had such effect that by now you would hardly recognize the place, and might not even need to be ashamed to be a part of it.

Of the films I have seen this year *Open City* is by all odds the best; and I beg leave—of those who don't dare admit they are ever capable of an opinion before they examine a piece of work—to doubt that *The Razor's Edge* or even *The Strange Love of Martha Ivers* is likely to be as good. *Open City* goes far in what I believe is the best general direction movies might take, now and within the discernible future. By this I don't mean they need be socially or politically hot under the collar—though much of the spirit and grandeur of this film come of that kind of heat. I do mean that the theme or story needs to be passionately felt and intimately understood, and that it should be a theme or story worthy of such knowledge and passion. I also put my deepest hope and faith in the future of movies in their being made on relatively little money, as much at least by gifted amateurs as by professionals, in actual rather than imitated places, with the binding energy, eye, conviction, and delight in work which are fostered in good-enough people by that predicament and which are at best hindered by commercial work in studios. As I saw to some extent when I reviewed the film and as an article by James T. Farrell has made much clearer to me, the film is among other things Communist propaganda. I don't enjoy this fact; but that cannot prevent my thinking *Open City* the best movie of its year and one of the best and most heartening in many years. It seems to be time, after many centuries of flagrant proof, to get used to the fact that by no means all one's enemies, or friends, for that matter, line up comfortably in the same camp, however the lines are drawn; and that no one group, however well accredited, has a monopoly on the human or the creative soul.

Like *Open City*, *The Raider* put amateurs through a reenactment, mainly, of actual events. Like *Open City*, it triumphantly demonstrates how well that can be done. It is less furiously felt and more honest; its theme, if less grandiose, is nevertheless a fine one. Since I think so highly of both films I should take special care to make clear that this is not *because* they use non-actors, or are semi-documentary, or are "realistic." It is, rather, that they show a livelier aesthetic and moral respect for reality —which "realism" can as readily smother as liberate—than most fictional films, commercial investments in professional reliability, ever manage to. If they are helped to this—as they are —by their concern for actual people and places, that is more than can be said for most documentaries, which by average are as dismally hostile to reality as most fiction films. The films I most eagerly look forward to will not be documentaries but works of pure fiction, played against, and into, and in collaboration with unrehearsed and uninvented reality.

A few notes at random.

We saw last year about the last of films made during or directly inspired by the war: it is clear that many gifted people, such as William Wyler (*The Best Years*), and Olivier, and Huston, and John Ford, grew greatly during the war. From now on we shall see what they can do with this new maturity during the next interval of peace. My best wishes, God knows, are with them; my bets are against them. Once in a while, quite certainly, a good film is sure to get made: but my bet is that the next ten years or so will be even harder for good people to work through than the last; that soon there will no longer be a place on earth where honest talent will be allowed to break loose from the asylum for more than a male nurse's afternoon off.

It is said of J. Arthur Rank, under whom three of the listed films were made, that he intends to continue shooting for big money with one hand and backing small-audience talent with the other. I hope so; and will bet that within five years—three if you like—it will be as hard to make a good film in England as in Hollywood; and that Mr. Rank will be chiefly responsible. My reason? I suggest that you consult both God and Mammon on which is the more successful in coping with the servant problem.

I have the same doubtful hope and best wishes for Republic's low-budget investment in such films as Ben Hecht's *Specter of the Rose* and—in 1945—Gustav Machaty's *Jealousy*. I hope the policy will be continued; I wish it would be extended. But that will be useless unless such opportunities are sought by, and given to, people who are capable of taking mature advantage of them.

This was the year during which Sergei Eisenstein once more got it in the eye. Part Two of *Ivan the Terrible* will never be released: Part Three will never even be made; Eisenstein was once more called a bourgeois and a formalist, and other words almost as dirty. Civilization has come a long way since the days when in Vienna, the High Altar of western music, Mozart and Schubert could die so young, largely for want of mere patronage. Today we appreciate our men of genius. In Russia we make corpses of them, living or genuine; here we drown them in cream.

The Hays office became the Johnston office. It remained possible, as before, to say almost anything if it was prurient, childish, or false enough in the first place and sneakily enough said in the second. It remained impossible, as before, to say anything whatever, without sneaking it, which might move or interest anyone past the moral age of five.

Quite a few Hollywood people amused themselves as best they could in their captivity by making such nostalgic and amusing, if far from original melodramas as *The Killers*, *The Big Sleep*, and *The Dark Corner*. Such harmless little slumming parties were treated by a number of critics, reviewers, and editorial writers as if they were a sinister mirror of American morals, psychology, society, and art. Since practically every movie is, to quite some extent, I can't insist that these were happy exceptions, except in so far as they were relatively intelligent, accurate at least to something in this world, and entertaining. I realize also that on its most careful level, as practiced by Dr. Siegfried Kracauer or Barbara Deming, this sort of analysis is of interest and value, dubious as I am about a good deal of it. But to me, the most sinister single thing that happened during the movie year was the emergence of just this kind of analysis—or rather, was the way in which it was indorsed by those incapable of it. I have long postponed writing on this difficult subject and must now again postpone: but briefly, for reasons which transcend movie boundaries, I am deadly alarmed to find that the function once performed, harmfully enough, by clubwomen and the nastier kinds of church pressure groups is now taken over, without a murmur or even a sign of divided consciousness, by the kind of people who used most earnestly to oppose priggishness.

Most lists of "the ten best" this year, including my own list of six, went very thin on Hollywood; and many reviewers commented on the fact, rather as if Hollywood had hit the nadir. It seems to me unjust to single out for sudden vilification one particular Hollywood year when every year for so long a time has been so very moderately fresh an egg.

February 3, 1947

Nonpolitical or essentially "humanistic" movie artists have made many unbeatable comedies and quite a few good dramas; but with exceptions so rare I can scarcely think of them, the only movies whose temper could possibly be described as heroic, or tragic, or both, have been made by leftists. This fact agrees neither with my wishes nor with my deepest convictions as to the source of great tragic art, nor am I persuaded of any merely "historical" explanation of it; but I do think it needs to be remembered, and questioned at length, as I cannot question it here, by those who like myself trust only the individualist in art, and who tend automatically to dismiss all political and propagandist art.

The latest example of what I mean by a great leftist film, and one of the finest, is André Malraux's *Man's Hope*, which was made during the last days of the Spanish civil war and is only now released in this country. It is clear that this film is not going to lack for an audience, if probably a small one; but I suspect that its appeal will be chiefly political, and that even those among this political audience who are particularly interested in films will overlook, or undervalue, some of its most important qualities as a film.

I will accordingly by-pass a good deal that is the heart and soul of the movie—that it is, including and far beyond its political intensity, one of the few wonderful film records of men in courage and sorrow—as so clear and so compelling that it needs no detailed comment. I prefer to use this space to defend things about the film that I have heard talked of as weaknesses and imperfections.

I will not worry about, or argue with, those who may regret the use of amateurs as actors. So far as I am concerned, the film merely emphasizes, even more sharply than most of its kind, the superiority of amateurs over professionals for a large and crucially hopeful part of achievement and possibility in films. The people in this film—Spaniards and members of the International Brigade—do and *are* things, over and over again, which are beyond acting and utterly different from it; and the one considerable piece of acting that is required—a peasant's face as, in avalanching despair, he tries to locate a Fascist flying field from the unfamiliar perspective of a Loyalist bomber—is as inspired a blending of reality with imagination as I remember to have seen. Of course it adds immeasurably to the force, poignancy, and realness of these players that they were not merely amateurs but also fighters, in the last ditch of a lost war, whose "reenactments" here were hardly that, pinched as they were into spare moments between actual work and actual war.

The early scenes, of staff conferences and small interlocking missions, are fitful, nervous, ragged in pace and series and apparent aim; compared with more traditional films they seem repetitive and undramatic. But they seem to me an original and important achievement. Barring a few literary touches they go dead against every one of the graces of art, including the good ones; and instead of those graces they achieve scrawny kinds of pace, immediacy, and personal detail which I have never before seen art attain. In their over-all shape and linkage, moreover, even in their near-repetitiveness, these scenes communicate with sharp success the lost, near-blind, yet intensely alive and responsible experience of men as individuals and, at the same time, the desperate interdependence of their efforts. They are also filled, in fantastic paradox to all that is hostile to liberty in left-wing politics, with that strange nascent-oxygen vitality, the very quintessence of liberty, which so far as I can make out is an ambience peculiar to dedicated revolutionists.

It is in these scenes, moreover, that Malraux does his most interesting things with "excess of energy" and with his sound-track. By excess of energy I mean his interest—which he may have learned from Eisenstein—in letting things and movements into his frame which have nothing to do with the central action or which enhance it only queerly and surprisingly—a guerrilla's sudden skipping change in step and his sudden hand to his sweating neck; or a dog wandering in from one corner of a street scene while a ball maunders in from another —little things which brilliantly lock men and their efforts and feelings into the exact real place and time of day. Some of these devices remain "studies"—the work merely of a highly gifted beginner in films—in a not wholly satisfying way; but generically I believe in them and in the few people who use them rather than trying their best to keep their films tidily to one nicely shaped and euphonious event at a time. Malraux's sound-track is more successful: blendings and counterpointings, along an echoing street, of the bawling of cattle and a rooster's shout, against the metal, vindictive language of modern war's stupendous guitar.

A little later Malraux dares, as few others would, so to extend a night drive through deep country in search of the automobiles needed to headlight the bombers' night take-off that for once the hypnosis, exhaustion, sadness, and beauty of such a task, and the passage of hours, are utterly communicated, not just comfortably suggested. I may as well mention here as anywhere else the remarkable thoughtfulness and beauty of *form* in this picture: the jagged, scratchy, miscellaneous scenes of exposition, almost an orchestra's tuning-up, first swept up and bound into a sheaf by the poring motion of this night drive—catapulting the film into the air and its wildest action—which in turn drains down a mountainside in one of the most ambitious codas ever designed in a film. It is a commonplace that movie and musical form are closely related, but films which show any creative reverence for the relationship are not so common.

Malraux's climax—the Loyalists' attempt to bomb a flying field and a bridge against impossible odds, and their dependence on the eyes of a peasant who has never been off the ground before—is more clearly within movie dramatic tradition. I need say of it only that it is so powerful in emotion and meaning, and so beautifully done, that as pure accomplishment it excels every other excellence in the film, and stands with the few great classical passages which have been achieved, in films, through the perfect identification of melodramatic suspense with meanings which are normally far above the proper use of melodrama.

Once the Loyalist fliers have crashed, Malraux begins his closing movement: the slow and painful bringing down of the dead and wounded from mountaintop to valley, assisted and attended by more and more peasants. I am not sure that this sequence is wholly successful; I am sure only that I was so deeply moved by all I saw, and by Malraux's confidence in the grandeur of the interlocked fact and symbol, and by his determination to build this wonderful symbol through a virtually endless series of near-repetitions into a colossal dirge for heroes, that for me it towered above most successes, and most attempts, that I have ever seen in films. A man of poetic genius, say an Eisenstein, would, I am sure, have adorned his central meaning with many and brilliant smaller symbolic perceptions; and this, I suppose, would have been even better. But I revere the way Malraux has done it as much for its nakedness as for its nobility.

Last week, speaking of *Henry V*, I said that I prefer to see great poetry attempted on the screen from scratch. *Man's Hope* is a glorious example of what I mean. The heartsick peasant in the disastrous plane is great movie poetry. The descent of the broken heroes from the desperate stone crown of Spain, as from a Cross, to the maternal valley, a movement so conceived that a whole people and a whole terrain become one sorrowing and triumphal Pietà for twentieth-century man, falls possibly short of its full imaginable magnificence, considered syllable by syllable; but in its mass it is poetry even greater. Homer might know it, I think, for the one work of our time which was wholly sympathetic to him.

March 1, 1947

13 Rue Madeleine is doing astonishingly well at the box-office. I wish I knew how much of this, even in the semi-conscious part of the audience mind, could be credited to the use of uninvented backgrounds, in and around Quebec. These are selected and photographed with such intelligence, and give the film such vitality, that the good performances of James Cagney, Richard Conte, and Annabella and a generally smart piece of movie-making look weak by comparison. The story tells of the training and work of a group of OSS men. At its best it is briskly informative without informing you of much. At its silliest it assigns an OSS boy with a face as transparent as a bent-glass display window to keep tabs on his best friend, who has been found out as a Nazi spy. The whole success of the Norman invasion is made to depend, for a while, on his hiding his feelings about this friend from the friend. OSS is also called O-77, for reasons of security which no patriotic American will question, though some people may never sleep well again if they once reflect that such a gnat was strained when the aforementioned brontosaurus was tossed down without even causing a hiccup. But the backgrounds more than make up for this kind of tarradiddle. Louis de Roche-mont, the producer, is not the only man making movies in this country who knows the great value of getting outside the studio and shooting in highly specific places; but he is getting more of it done, more effectively, than anyone else, and if the idea spreads, and becomes a practice, I expect that most of the credit will be due to him.

The substitution of "O-77" for "OSS" as a supposed security measure is child's play compared with what has been done to make *The Beginning or the End*, which is the story of the atomic bomb, safe for democracy and points right and left. You learn less about atomic fission from this film than I would assume is taught by now in the more progressive nursery schools; you learn even less than that about the problems of atomic control; and you learn least of all about morals. There is to be sure a young scientist, played with sincerity by Tom Drake, who suffers from scruples; but his conscience is neatly canceled by the posthumous letter in which it is he and he alone who realizes, discarding his worries like last summer's sand fleas, that in God's own time transcontinental commuting, better complexions, and the millennium itself will be achieved on the power generated from an old hat check.

Oh, yes, the movie. Well, there is very little to say. The bombing and the Alamagordo test are effectively staged, though hardly adequate to one's information, let alone one's imagination of how to handle that information creatively. For the rest it seemed to me surprisingly bad even though I rather expected it to be bad, for a good reason: only people of first-rate talent stand even a chance of not being paralyzed, for a long time, by a new subject; *Wake Island*, the first American movie about the last war, was hardly better than this. The film is also a horrifying sample of what American movies will be like if the state interferes with them much; it gives me unexpected respect for those who, under such circumstances, do so much better even with the worst of the Russian movies which get over here. Barring the two bits of staging I mentioned, which are to the credit of light-technicians, the whole show could as well be called *Tom Swift and His Giant Ego*—which, for that matter, could go for practically everything to do with the development of the bomb in fact.

Postscript: One seldom has the pleasure of expressing a hope and being thankful for its fulfilment in virtually the same breath. In reviewing *13 Rue Madeleine*, above, I spoke respectfully and hopefully of its producer, Louis de Rochemont. I have just seen Mr. de Rochemont's *Boomerang!* It is too late to say more about it in this issue than that it enlarges my respect for him and exceeds my hopes.

—

Correction: I recently referred, in this column to Archbishop Spellman. Is his hat red!

March 22, 1947

I SHOULD review several of the films mentioned below at some length, and I hope that at length I will. But I have left so many films unreviewed, some of them weeks or months old by now, that I can begin to catch up only by reviewing them now, somewhere near as briefly as possible.

The Adventuress, an English film, stars Deborah Kerr as a patriotic Irish innocent who helps Nazi spies until she learns better. It is a try at comedy melodrama and in both ways is sometimes clever. More often, the styles go thin or conflict, or lose themselves in rather unpleasant bids for general American liking. A good deal has been derived from Hitchcock, but little of the intensity and conviction which made his English films so good. There is some grace, intelligence, and fun here, but essentially this seems to me a supercilious drama, as if it had been made by bright young men who had decided to package and toss a bone to the groundlings.

The Angel and the Bad Man, John Wayne's first production, mixes up Quakers with gun-bearing cowboys. The result is unpretentious, sweet-tempered, and quite likable.

Before Him All Rome Trembled tells the story of *La Tosca* in a sort of double exposure; the principals sing the crisis of the opera and go through a similar offstage crisis in Nazi-dominated Rome. This is all likably mediocre except for Anna Magnani of *Open City*, whom I could watch for any length of time for her square-handed operatic gestures alone. She has never yet been used for anything like all she has, or promises, and I suppose never will be, now that she is coming to Hollywood, which is a pity, for both as a woman and as a movie actress she is magnificent—the nearest thing to an absolute that I have seen in films since the silent Garbo movies. Incidentally I hope that the Pope, at least, will sooner or later get around to admitting that he took no very active part in the anti-Nazi underground; judging by Italian films, practically everyone else in Italy did.

Blaze of Noon is a story about four flying brothers and the anxious girl one of them marries. So long as it sticks to stunt-flying and mild comedy it is pleasant enough, but the last half, during which the obsessed brothers come one by one to grief and the little woman waits it out, gets pretty monotonous.

Boomerang!, produced by Louis de Rochemont and directed by Elia Kazan, is the story of a real-life murder and the resultant police and political work. This is still only March, but I won't be surprised if it turns out to be the best American film of its year, barring only Chaplin's. It was made in Stamford and White Plains; it is notable for Dana Andrew's best performance to date; a large cast mainly of Broadway actors, inspired perhaps by their surroundings, the nonprofessional actors, and the highly intelligent general intention, turns in the most immaculate set of naturalistic performances I have seen in one movie. The script and photography are exactly what they should be. *Boomerang!* never tries to get beyond the very good best that good journalistic artists can do, but on that level it is a triumph, a perfect job, and I very much hope a springboard for many more films of its kind.

A Cage of Nightingales, a French film, reminds me of *Mädchen in Uniform* and of the fantastically original and inspired *Zero de Conduite*, both of which were about the treatment and maltreatment of schoolchildren. This time the talented teacher, the healer (the comedian Noël-Noël), reforms the boys in a reform school, largely through getting them interested in choral music. Both he and the children are very charming. I like these demonstrations of what even a reasonable amount of kindliness, common sense, guile, and self-reliance can do against brute authoritarianism, and I know they are still apposite and always will be. But I would like still better to see any sufficiently intelligent attack on the new kinds of soul-destroyer—those heirs of the healers of the recent past who have learned the words ever so earnestly but, lacking the remotest ear for the tune, do their work by the book. (I'm told that one of the newer books on child-raising tell you that it's all right, indeed altogether well-advised, to smile at your baby.) They are the most deadly enemies, in our particular time, and they are still hardly even suspected, much less assaulted, except by the neo-lithic types they have to some extent supplanted.

I will be back at this remnants counter as soon as possible. Meanwhile I must digress briefly to say a few words about the clergy.

In the current issue of *Motion Picture Magazine* are three articles about divorce in Hollywood, signed by Monsignor Sheen, Rabbi Goldstein, and Dr. Fosdick. They say a good deal about marriage and divorce and about the relationship between the strength of a civilization and the integrity of the family, with which I agree, whether I want to or not. They also wish to require of the Hollywood stars that they serve as a good example rather than a bad one to the mere human beings who make up the stars' general audience; one even demands that the industry see to it that these employees behave themselves. In my opinion such moralists are impudent enough in horning in on what appears on the screen without assuming it is their right and duty, as well, after the stars' working hours, to get into bed with them. I would like to know, moreover, what a few people whose moral sense has reached the shaving age think of arbiters of morals who still believe in the obligation of the prominent to set a good example; who still believe in exerting pressure on them in order that they shall exert pressure on others; and who feel so profound a contempt for the souls and minds of people in general as to dare to approach them through force and through example.

I have an unsolicited apology to make. I recently referred to Cardinal Spellman in this column in a way which now seems to me to have been over-personal and otherwise vulgar. I lose no love to the Cardinal or to the clergy in general, of whatever denomination, but I am ashamed to have expressed my dislike in the way that I did.

April 12, 1947

A FEW more splinters off the backlog.

Children of Paradise, which Jacques Prévert wrote and Marcel Carné produced and directed in France during the war, is close to perfection of its kind and I very much like its kind— the highest kind of slum-glamor romanticism about theater people and criminals, done with strong poetic feeling, with rich theatricality, with a great delight and proficiency in style, and with a kind of sophistication which merely cleans and curbs, rather than killing or smirking behind the back of its more powerful and vulgar elements. All the characters are a little larger and a good deal more wonderful than life—a mime of genius, a fine florid actor, an egomaniacal criminal, a cold great-gentleman, and the hypnotic gutter-beauty whom they all pursue and, after their varying fashions, possess. The story has a similar slight over-ripe grandiloquence—a many-triangled study of love and love's numerous poor-relations, it works the world-as-stage-and-vice-versa cliché for all it is worth and does so always with as much elegance and irony as intensity and commitment. The Chaplinesque mime (Jean Louis Barrault) is the only depiction of an artist, on the screen, which has fully convinced me of the genius he was supposed to have. Arletty, who plays the female beanbag, is almost as good at making that symbol definitive. The great actor is a little short of size; so is the criminal; so perhaps is the sporting nobleman al-though he outdid anyone else I have ever seen try it; but on their slightly smaller scale they too are perfect, as is the woman who wrecks the mime's life through her "selfless" love for him —and I suspect that this scaling-down was calculated exactly as it turns out. The miming itself is breath-taking, and there is some flirtatious repartee which delighted me more in its way than anything since the fruitier exchanges in Dumas when I read them at the age of eleven; indeed the whole sexuality of the picture, which assumes that the audience knows all about where babies come from and a good deal about how uniquely dangerous the preliminary activities can be, makes one want to forage through Hollywood and various censors' offices as a sort of improved, not to say dedicated, Jack the Ripper. I do suspect that unless you have a considerable weakness for ro-manticism, which I assume includes a weakness for the best of its ham, this will seem just a very fancy, skillful movie. But if you have that lucky weakness, I think the picture can be guar-anteed to make you very happily drunk.

The Fabulous Dorseys—meaning Jimmy and Tommy—is one more musical biography. It has very little to recommend it ex-cept that the musicians look and act a little more than usual like musicians.

The Farmer's Daughter is a very stale story—the country girl who comes to the metropolis, plants her housemaid's-knee firmly in the sweetbreads of high society, and makes the most of her advantage. This time, however, the bluebloods are also the people who run politics in their state. The story seems surprisingly fresh because everyone involved in making the movie appears to know and care for the sort of people the story is about. Patricians, politicians, even peasants, are portrayed with unusual perception and wit, and Ethel Barrymore, as the head of the house and of her political party, suggests very excitingly what she could do with a similar role written to her size.

It Happened in Brooklyn features Frank Sinatra, whom I like, Jimmy Durante, in comparison with whom I would, I am sure, find the millennium a rather chilly formal dance, and a great many affectionate japes about Brooklyn, which I could be much happier without. Aside from Sinatra and Durante the show amounts to practically nothing, but there is a general kindliness about it which I also enjoyed.

I will try briefly to discuss Eisenstein's *Ivan the Terrible* in the next installment.

April 26, 1947

WHEN he made *Alexander Nevsky*, Sergei Eisenstein deprived himself of practically everything that had been most wonderful in his original style and developed a new and less exciting one—a kind of speeded-up, fluent, basically operatic style which was like watching a handsome, well-organized funeral cortège carry his free genius to its grave at a cheerful forty miles an hour. Relatively conventional as the film was, it was also highly charged, in nearly every shot, with Eisenstein's unique blend of poetic, intellectual, and purely animal energy. In *Ivan the Terrible*, Part I, Eisenstein has deprived himself even of the speed, flow, and shape which helped give *Nevsky* grace, and most of his peculiar energy has become cold, muscle-bound, and somber. Yet *Ivan* is a bolder, more adventurous, more interesting film; for a while I felt even more admiration for it than grief over it.

Eisenstein's theme is more deeply involved in an individual

and his development, and is in many ways greater, than any he has undertaken before. It is a study, on a scale as ambitious anyhow as that of Shakespeare in his political plays—and more politically knowledgeable and incomparably hotter to handle —of an able man in whom two obsessions collide and become all but identical: love for an idea (his country's strength) and, however discreetly suggested, love of power for its own sake. It is a study of what such a fanatic becomes, given unprecedented power and opportunity, under the impingement of constant danger, treachery, and intrigue. Ivan, as Eisenstein presents him, is a fair parallel to Stalin; but he is still more suggestively a symbol of the whole history of Russian communism. Eisenstein has, for Ivan, a magnificent looking actor, Cherkassov, who can handle the utmost grandiloquence of manner; he causes him to suggest some of the superhuman complexities of Stavrogin, and it may not be accidental that he makes him up with a chin and cranium which becomes ever more pointed, like John Barrymore as Mr. Hyde. He seems all but desperately absorbed in communicating political ideas and vindications, especially parallels to Stalin and his regime. Ivan's siege and defeat of Kazan, to choose one of the simpler examples, becomes an interesting text on dealing with a foreign enemy: while the enemy watches the army which threatens their walls, you tunnel beneath their city, roll in kegs of gunpowder, and blow it to kingdom come, meaning *your* kingdom. (It is made clear, moreover, that this stratagem is strictly Ivan's idea, that his lieutenants prefer the old-fashioned cavalry charge, and that his sappers never quite realize what they're up to.)

Eisenstein is very acute with his research, very excitable over architecture and decoration, costume and ritual, and very astute and forceful in his use of them. He is evidently much interested in finding out how little a movie can be made to move and yet move at all, and in giving each movement legendary grandeur—as in the marvelous shots, at once comic and sinister and full of glory, in which the kneeling Ivan's rising hands accept the orb and scepter. He goes boldly and successfully against naturalism and even simple likelihood: in his poisoning scene only opera singers could be so blind to what is happening in plain sight, and in one fine close-up Ivan's wife, his arch-enemy, and his treacherous best friend huddle their heads into the intimacy of one frame as they would never do in a court obsessed with intrigue and suspicion. Depriving himself of a good 99 per cent of all he believes in and is capable of as a cutter, Eisenstein nevertheless demonstrates what exquisiteness and power can be accomplished, even conventionally, by rhythm and series alone. The film is already famous for its lavish use of prodigious close-ups and of exorbitance in gesture and in facial expression, and I would like to make a particularly unprintable gesture toward those who can feel that in his use of these one of the most sophisticated artists of the twentieth century has been naive.

I have only faintly suggested a few of the things about *Ivan*, and behind it, which make the film fascinating to watch; but I will have to move along. Interesting as the film is, the longer I reflect on it the unhappier I feel about it. I can't remember a foot of it which doesn't give evidence of a first-rate creative intelligence at work; but there is hardly a foot in which that intelligence is working on anything anywhere near sufficiently worthy of it. The picture is splendid to look at; yet there is little that is superior to, or much different from, Russian operatic and theatrical mannerisms which must have been over-rich and over-digested a generation ago. It is as if Picasso were to spend several years crowding all the sophistication that would fit within the conventions of nineteenth-century chromos. And considering the illusion Eisenstein manages to create of expressing many complex ideas, densely and continuously, it is remarkable how little actually gets expressed, and how commonplace most of it is.

I even have to wonder whether Eisenstein perversely or perforce intended this doubleness. I wonder, for that matter, whether he may not be split between a compulsion to choose the most dangerous theme possible, and virtual paralysis in its development: a paralysis which might be a natural effect of being unable, on pain of death, to say honestly, or even surreptitiously, what you really believe. There is a kind of frozen, catatonic deadness about the particular intensity and rigidity of style developed for this film—as if the intelligence, great as it is, could liberate only a very little of itself in the actual images of the film. The kind of liberation I mean occurs just twice in this picture, in the opening, coronation scene; a deacon's hair-raising intonation of a royal benediction (and his wonderful face as he sings), and the moment at which Eisenstein cuts from the ritualistic pouring of gold coins over the new Czar to the faces of young women, watching the sleeting gold and the monarch's tumescent face through it and blossoming into smiles of sexual delight. In their suddenness, beauty, and wildness, and in their ability to enrich the film with whole new trains of ideas and reactions, these two moments are of a different order from any others in *Ivan*. They would have been memorable in any of Eisenstein's early films; but there, ideas as good swarmed and coruscated upon his new-found, new-crowned poetry as abundantly as the anointing storm of gold itself.

For years, as everyone knows, Eisenstein has been working as if in a prison, under the supervision of jailers who are not only peculiarly dangerous and merciless but also as sudden to change their minds as minnows their direction. It goes without saying that this has interfered monstrously with his work. Just how, and just how much it has shaped his work and his mind, I see no use whatever in trying to guess, for I fear it is impossible to guess how much he agrees with his jailers, even in their treatment of him, and how much, quite aside from that, his own nature may have been predisposed to this sort of hardening and change. No mind and spirit stand still, least of all the mind and spirit of a great artist. Even discounting outside pressures, there is no guaranty that the development will be for the better, and heaven knows they cannot be discounted in Eisenstein's case. Everything that is meant by creative genius and its performance, and everything that that signifies about freedom and potentiality in general, is crucified in Eisenstein, more meaningfully, and abominably, than in any other man I can think of. I hardly know which seems the more tragic: the possibility that he is still essentially a free man, his own master, doing the best he can under annihilating difficulties; or the possibility that he accepts the crucifixion and has even helped drive such nails as, in that predicament, he could manage.

Wɪᴛʜ deep regret I must postpone my attempt to review Chaplin's *Monsieur Verdoux*. I cannot hope to do it justice, but I do prefer to discuss it a little more coherently than I have been able to, to date. In case this leaves any doubt of my opinion of the film, let me say that I think it is one of the best movies ever made, easily the most exciting and most beautiful since *Modern Times*. I will add that I think most of the press on the picture, and on Chaplin, is beyond disgrace. I urge everyone to see *Monsieur Verdoux* who can get to it.

Well, to resume my skulk through the alphabet. I was down through *I* as in Ivan. Meanwhile a *B*, three *C*'s, and a particularly fragrant *E* have sprung up behind me.

The Barber of Seville is Rossini's opera, as sung and played by Ferrucio Tagliavini (Almaviva), Tito Gobbi (Figaro), Italo Tajo (Basilio), and other competent and attractive Italians. The sets are rather pathetically flea-bitten, the sound is not awfully good, the lighting is drab; you watch the conventions of opera through the most transparent of movie conventions. I suppose it is rather dull, but I liked it.

Carnegie Hall is about the thickest and sourest mess of musical mulligatawny I have yet had to sit down to, a sort of aural compromise between the Johnstown flood and the Black Hole of Calcutta. I have an idea that some of the music was well done, but I was so exhausted by suffering and rage that I can't possibly be sure of what. However, as a gnarled mirror of American musical taste at its worst, and as a record of what various prominent musicians look like under strange professional circumstances, it is a permanently fascinating and valuable show. There is, for a single instance, the protracted spectacle of Stokowsky—shot from the floor—who seems to be undergoing for the public benefit an experience, while conducting a portion of Tschaikowsky's Fifth Symphony, which men of coarser clay wish exclusively on women, or perhaps on albums of prefabricated trade-union folk songs. I am sorry to be writing this way about *Carnegie Hall*, for I can't avoid feeling that some rather good intentions were involved in it. But then I can't doubt that Hitler had good intentions. He and I just didn't see eye to eye.

The Captive Heart, a British movie about prisoners of war, has been greeted as a masterpiece by some of the reviewers who, only too literally, couldn't "see" *Monsieur Verdoux*. So now we know what a masterpiece is: something that isn't either really bad or by any generosity really good; another of those group-as-hero stories, a dangerous cliché in the first place, in which each member of the group is just one more cliché; and something truly creative for Michael Redgrave, a Czech who for self-protection is forced to take on a dead Englishman's identity and to write the widow love letters—with his left hand, of course, in order not to tip his mitt. This decent, mediocre film is sincerely but often cornily written and is in general honestly acted. It all takes its measure—about ankle high—against a number of beautiful shots which were made in a camp in North Germany. These shots are made in a style closely related to the style which is called archaic, or worse, when Chaplin uses it; and Chaplin uses it all the time, for incomparably richer and subtler purposes.

Carnival in Costa Rica is a Technicolor musical with a score by Lecuona. I liked the score, some fine Costa Rican backgrounds, a medium-good solo by Massine, who designed the generally uninteresting dances, and the dancing and acting of Vera-Ellen. I even liked Dick Haymes. I was also interested to see that Ann Revere, as a Kansan, was shown to be happily married to J. Carroll Naish, as a thoroughly Costa Rican coffee planter. If this sort of un-American propaganda takes decent hold in Hollywood, the day will come when the husband of a high-bridged daughter of the Confederacy will shag into the scuppernong arbor playing ootchmagootch to a slice of watermelon and reciting *Ballad for Americans*, between spat seeds, in an Oxford accent.

The Egg and I asks you to believe in, and laugh at, Fred MacMurray and Claudette Colbert as nauseatingly clownish city people who try their hands at poultry farming. Marjorie Main, in an occasional fit of fine, wild comedy, picks the show up and brandishes it as if she were wringing its neck. I wish to God she had.

May 31, 1947

MONSIEUR VERDOUX — I

ALTHOUGH I have been granted extra space, and propose to discard most other considerations for brevity's sake, I can say here only a few of the things that I feel need to be said about Mr. Chaplin's new film. I can only hope that these notes may faintly suggest the frame-by-frame appreciation, the gratitude, and the tribute which we owe this great poet and his great poem; and may help some readers to enjoy more of what he has done than they otherwise might.

The skeletal story: Henri Verdoux, a French bank teller of the thirties who has lost his job in a depression, works out a business of his own whereby he can support his crippled wife (Mady Corell) and their little boy. He becomes a professional murderer of women of means. He courts them, marries them, finesses their little fortunes into his possession; murders them and eliminates their corpses; plays the market with the whole of his profits. We see him at work on four such women. One is going up in smoke when Verdoux first appears. One is a socially prominent widow (Isobel Elsom) whom he woos industriously through most of the film; she takes him for a boulevardier. One is a sour old small-town dame (Margaret Hoffman) whose money he cajoles by stop-watch and whom he promptly murders; she thinks he is a globe-trotting civil engineer. One is a half-daft ex-tart (Martha Raye) who has hit luck in a lottery. She takes him for a sea captain. His efforts to kill her are almost the only passages of pure slapstick in the film.

A very busy little man—his business dashes him all over France and from top to bottom of society—Verdoux can visit his true home seldom. Even when he does he is likely to mix business with the pleasure. He learns from a druggist friend (Robert Lewis) about a new poison, painless and untraceable. He picks up a friendless young woman (Marilyn Nash) to try it out on, but spares her when he realizes that she, like himself, "could kill for love." When he meets her later, by accident, he cryptically brushes her off. Late in the film, long after he has retired from business, they meet again. But just then and there he is recognized by relatives of a former wife. After showing how effortlessly he could have escaped, he deliberately puts

himself in the way of arrest. The film ends with the famous
scenes in which Verdoux hears his sentence and explains himself, more or less, to the court and the world; pays his equally
cold respects to journalism and to God; and walks to the
guillotine.

Disregard virtually everything you may have read about the
film. It is of interest, but chiefly as a definitive measure of
the difference between the thing a man of genius puts before
the world and the things the world is equipped to see in it.
There is room neither to analyze nor to argue much about this
peculiar criticism; yet in all conscience a few points must be
mentioned. The ruck of these reviewers have said, for instance,
that the film isn't funny; is morally questionable; is in bad
taste; that Chaplin should never have stopped playing the
tramp; that Raye steals her scenes with Chaplin; that Chaplin is
no good at casting, writing, directing, producing; that he
should have hired people, for all these jobs, who knew the techniques which have been developed since talkies began. Some
brief replies:

Not funny. Not much of it is, unless you have an eye and
mind for the far from cliché matters which can be probed and
illuminated through poetically parodied cliché; an appetite for
cold nihilistic irony; respect for an artist who subdues most of
his outrageous fun to the grim central spirit of his work.

Morals. For later discussion. I could take more seriously
those who have objected on these grounds if any of them had
shown himself capable of recognizing an act of moral and
artistic heroism when he saw it. Not one did.

Taste. *Verdoux* is in bad taste if death is, as so many Americans feel; and if it is in bad taste to treat a serious matter seriously, and to make comedy cut to the bone.

The tramp. Very young children fiercely object to even
minor changes in a retold story. Older boys and girls are not,
as a rule, respected for such extreme conservatism.

Raye. Verdoux cannot properly get many of the big laughs;
that is what Raye is there for. She does her job beautifully, and
Chaplin feeds her and foils her beautifully. One of the finest
aspects of his miraculous performances is his quiet skill and
graciousness, in these and many other scenes, as a feeder, a sardonic ringmaster, an inspired emcee.

Casting. Raye's mere presence disproves that. So does Marilyn Nash; name one trained actress who could give that role, besides her lovely demeanor, her exactly right spirit, vitality, and freshness. So does every player and bit player in the cast. Chaplin is the most perceptive, imaginative, exact man alive, at casting; these reviewers are less so.

Writing. Verbally most of *Verdoux* is inferior to its visual achievements—that is to say, it is only one of the most talented screen plays ever written. Chaplin also wrote the story and its subtleties; designed one of the few really *formed* movies in years; invented at least twenty-five characters who live very keenly both as social types and as individuals; and reproduced, just as cleanly and quietly, that entire grand façade of a society which was germane to his theme. (The significant omissions are farmers and industrial workers; the world of *Verdoux* is the world of gain, gotten ill, by chance, by heritage, by crime.)

Directing. He directed this film—all the people mentioned and successes suggested above, and still others as great and greater, handling a munificent complex of characters, ideas, milieux, and tributary styles and tones with all but perfect visual wit and expressiveness and with an all but unblemished grace, force, and economy. For directing as brilliant I refer you to his own *Modern Times* and to Dovzhenko's *Frontier*; there has been none since.

Production. Is criticized as stingy, and as unlike France. Instead, it is a manifesto against a kind of vulgarity in which Hollywood is drowned—the attempt to disguise emptiness with sumptuousness. It looks hand-made, not machine-turned. Like the casting and acting and directing it is poetic, not naturalistic, though naturalistic elements are finely used poetically. Verdoux's France is a highly intelligent paraphrase, far more persuasive of its place—half in the real world, half in the mind —than most films are of their supposed place, foreign, native, or imaginary.

New techniques. They are on the whole weakened derivations from styles developed before sound came, in Russia, Germany, and, in this country, by Chaplin among others; virtually nothing has been done with sound. Such as the new style is, it can be used decently; that is proved by *The Best Years of Our Lives*. But in the average well-made movie, such as these reviewers praise, it signifies just this: the art of moving pictures has been so sick, for so long, that the most it can do for itself is to shift unceasingly from one bedsore to the next. Chaplin, by contrast, obviously believes that if you can invent something worth watching, the camera should hold still and clear, so that you can watch it. That is still, and will always be, one of the best possible ways to use a camera; Chaplin is the one great man who still stands up for it.

To be sure, you have to be competent to see what he puts before you; and thanks to the depravities of the latter-day "style," most of us have spoiled eyes. We cannot appreciate swiftness and uninsistence; nor the bracing absence of fancy composition and prettiness; nor Chaplin's genius for "mood" when that is important (the first great shot of Verdoux's closed garden); nor for atmosphere, authenticity, and beauty in mock formlessness (some wonderful loose group shots, full of glass, gravel, gray sky, pale heads, and dark clothing, at the garden party); nor for visual wit (the astoundingly funny long shot of the lake, with the murder boat almost imperceptibly small). We are just smart enough to recognize a cliché; never enough to see how brilliantly a master can use it. So we sneer at Chaplin's frequent use of locomotive wheels, charging ever more desperately across the screen, this way and that, to mark another business trip or return; saying that he tries thus, unimaginatively, to bind together his formless continuity. But in fact these wheels do a lot at once. They are in the best sense economical; they are cumulatively funny; they cumulatively express Verdoux's ever more frantic busyness; and they wind the film up like a tight spring.

(To be continued)

June 14, 1947

MONSIEUR VERDOUX—II

CHAPLIN'S performance as Verdoux is the best piece of playing I have ever seen: here, I cannot even specify the dozen or so close-ups each so great and so finely related and timed that withdrawn and linked in series they are like the notes of a slow, magnificent, and terrifying song, which the rest of the film serves as an accompaniment. I could write many pages, too, about the richness and quality of the film as a work of art, in fact, of genius; and as many more trying, hopelessly, to determine how Chaplin's intellect, instinct, intuition, creative intelligence, and pure experience as a master artist and as a showman, serve and at times disserve one another: for intellectually and in every other kind of self-exhaustion this seems incomparably his most ambitious film. And since the film is provocative of so much that cannot be examined as fun, I wish I might also use the many thousands of words I would require to do it adequate honor, purely as fun. And all the more because I love and revere the film as deeply as any I have seen, and believe that it is high among the great works of this century, I wish I might discuss at proper length its weaknesses as a work of art and of moral understanding. I have reluctantly chosen, instead, to suggest a single aspect of its meaning, which seems to me particularly important. And this itself, I fear, I may have reduced beyond usefulness.

Chaplin's theme, the greatest and the most appropriate to its time that he has yet undertaken, is the bare problem of surviving at all in such a world as this. With his usual infallibility of instinct he has set his story in Europe; Europeans are aware of survival as a problem, as we are not. As rightly, he has set aside the tramp, whose charming lessons in survival are too wishful for his purposes, for his first image of the Responsible Man, and of modern civilization. (For Verdoux embodies much of the best that can be said of modern civilization, whether democratic-capitalist, fascist, or communist: whatever he may lack in the way of conscience, he does have brains; and whatever crimes he commits, they are committed, or so he believes, out of compassionate love and in uncompromising discharge of responsibility.) The tramp is the free soul intact in its gallantry, innocence, eagerness for love, ridiculousness, and sorrow; we recognize in him much that is dear to us in ourselves. Verdoux is so much nearer and darker that we can hardly bear to recognize ourselves in him. He is the committed, dedicated soul, and this soul is not intact: we watch its death agonies. And this tragic process is only the more dreadful because it is depicted not gravely but briskly, with a cold savage gaiety; the self-destroying soul is rarely aware of its own predicament.

The problem of survival: the Responsible Man. Chaplin develops his terrible theme chiefly as a metaphor for business. But the film is also powerful as a metaphor for war: the Verdoux home as an embattled nation, the wife and child as the home front, Verdoux as expeditionary force, hero in the holiest of causes, and war criminal. But it is even more remarkable and fascinating as a study of the relationship between ends and means, a metaphor for the modern personality—that is, a typical "responsible" personality reacting to contemporary pressures according to the logic of contemporary ethics.

In the terms of this metaphor the basic cast is small. Verdoux, his wife, and their son are differing aspects of a single personality. Verdoux is the master, the intelligence and the deep unconscious; he has estranged his soul and his future. He has made the assumption that most people make, today—one of the chief assumptions on which modern civilization rests. That is, that in order to preserve intact in such a world as this those aspects of the personality which are best and dearest to one, it is necessary to exercise all that is worst in one; and that it is impossible to do this effectively if one communicates honestly with one's best. Accordingly the personality which, until the world struck that living down, lived in poverty and docility, but happily, is broken and segregated.

The wife and child are shut away in a home which is at once a shrine and a jail; and there, immobilized, and cut off from the truth, they virtually cease to exist as living objects of love; they become an ever more rigid dream. For when the worst and the best in the personality are thus segregated, and the worst is thus utilized in the nominal service of the best, it is inevitably the good which is exploited; the evil, which thinks of itself as faithful slave, is treacherous master; and evil, being active and knowledgeable, grows; and good, rendered motionless and denied knowledge, withers. Like most men obsessed with the world's ruthlessness, Verdoux carries his veneration of innocence to the extreme; he is determined that it shall never be touched, shall never change (the song of how many million homesick soldiers: "We want to find everything at home just as we left it"). But change is inevitable, and uncontrollable.

Ruthlessness and the murderous adoration of static innocence enlarge each other; and the ruthless man becomes the more ruthless because he has broken all communication with innocence. And innocence itself is altered. At the moment Verdoux tells his wife that they own their home at last, she dares to remember sadly that they were happier when they were poor. Her face shows the terrible drugged passiveness of the over-sustained, the still more terrible intuitive guilt that comes of all that is uneasily apprehended, untold, and unasked. Small wonder that she has become a cripple; the wonder is that she continues to breathe. Passiveness was forced on her, truth was destroyed, love was undermined, her own love became pity, as surely as her husband's, and in pity and in fear she failed to question what was being done. As is so often true, it was not she who wanted to be so well provided for; that was her husband's desire, the one desire he might hope to satisfy; so she let him satisfy it.

As for Verdoux, he is irreparably committed. All the heart he has left prevents his confessing to his wife, and prevents his changing trades. He could only have chosen his course through defect of love—vengefulness and self-pity masked as pity, pity masked as love; the love-destroying, monstrous arrogance it requires to make the innocent answerable for your guilt—and the constant necessity of deceiving love has damaged love still more profoundly. Like many business men who feel unloved, or incapable of full enough love, he can only propitiate, and express, his love by providing for his family as handsomely as possible. (He can desire this of course, rather than the bare subsistence his wife prefers, only because he respects the standards of the world he thinks he despises. During his docile years, remember, he served at the high altar of modern civilization, breathing year in and year out The Bank's soul-dissolving odor of sanctity, all day, every day, touching the sacred wealth he must never dare touch with his conscious desire. When he was thrown out of his job, this ruthlessness released the tremendously impounded ruthlessness in him.) But that is never well enough to satisfy him—and only *his* satisfaction really counts, in this household—for his wife and child scarcely exist for him except as a self-vindicating dream, which he must ceaselessly labor to sustain, improve, perfect, be worthy of. A vicious cycle is established. Only through the best good-providing possible can Verdoux at once express his love, quiet his dying intuition that his love is defective and that he is wrong even in the little that he believes to be right, sustain the dream that is all that remains of love, require of himself ever more obsessive industriousness in crime, and silence his wife.

As good, by his will, is ever more stonily immobilized, evil becomes ever more protean in disguise and self-disguise, ever more mercurial in its journeyings. (The personality is also a constant metaphor for modern civilization—in which, for one instance, creative power is paralyzed except in the interests of gain and destruction; in those interests it is vigorous as never before.) Verdoux cannot bear to sit still, to stop work, long enough to realize his predicament. He cannot feel "at home," at home. He has to act his roles as perfect husband and father, dearly as he wants merely to *be* both, just as he acts all his other roles. All that he loves is saturated in deceit; and he in self-deceit as well. He gets home seldom, apparently never longer than overnight; the divided spirit can only assert its unity, even its illusion of unity or its desire, in twilight contemplation or in dreams; and the pressure of business is always on him. The pressure of business indeed! Verdoux's family is almost lifeless; such piteously cherished life as it retains, he is hopelessly estranged from. All that requires his intelligence, skill, and vitality, all that gives him life, is in his business. He is the loneliest character I know of: he can never be so desperately lonely as during these hours among those dearest to him, when he must deceive not mere victims, or the world at large, but those he loves. The only moments during which this appalling loneliness is broken, during which he ever honestly communicates, however briefly, with other human beings, are those few moments during which he can know that his victims realize they are being murdered. No doubt he loves his wife and child—there are two of the most heart-stopping, beautiful close-ups ever made, to prove that—but in the fearful depths into which he cannot risk a glance he loves only their helplessness; and deeper, only the idea of love; and that only because it consecrates his true marriage, which is to murder.

(To be continued)

June 21, 1947

MONSIEUR VERDOUX — III

(Monsieur Verdoux *has been withdrawn and will be re-
released only after a United Artists' build-up which will, I
hear, try to persuade people that they will kill themselves
laughing. I will take care to notify readers of this column of
its return, and of changes, if any are made. I am grieved to
be so late—or early—with this review, but not very; this film
has too long a life ahead of it. It is permanent if any work
done during the past twenty years is permanent.*)

THE most mysterious line in the film, Verdoux's reference to
having "lost" his family, becomes clear if the three are seen as
members of a single personality. The wife whom segregation
and deceit so inevitably paralyzed was dying a slow death from
the moment she became uneasy and failed with her own kind
of misguided tenderness, to beseech her husband's confidence;
and the child could not long have survived his mother.

With their death Verdoux all but dies himself. He becomes
old, bent, sore, stiff, not only through heartbreak or because
all that he most cherished in his nature is destroyed, but because their death has deprived him of the one motive he would
recognize for his criminality. The third meeting with Miss
Nash, for all its handsome prospects, revives him only to an
old man's charming glimmer; but as soon as danger once more
requires work of him and, after showing how effortlessly he
might escape, he casually surrenders himself to society's vengeance, he limbers up and shines like a snake which has just cast
its winter skin. All that remains now is memory and the pure
stripped ego, the naked will to survive which discovers, with
ineffable relief, that there is no longer any point in surviving.

With his soul dead at last, it is no wonder that Verdoux
asserts himself so proudly, in the courtroom and death cell, in
terms of his dream of himself. He would have explained himself less proudly and with greater moral understanding to his
wife, but he had successfully avoided that possibility, at the
cost of their marriage and her life. His dream of himself is urgently challenged only once, by the girl whose life he spares;
and he successfully resists that challenge in the strangest and, I
think, most frightening scene ever filmed.

I had expected this film to be the last word in misogyny; but although there is a good deal of it about, Verdoux's handling of his victims is in general remarkably genial and kindly. The one really hair-raising moment of that sort is the chance second meeting with the girl, the scene in which he brushes her off. After all, Verdoux risks nothing against the poor frumps he kills or tries to kill, except his life. But the girl is infinitely more dangerous. She is the one human being with whom he holds in common everything he regards as most important. Both have known love as passionate pity for the helpless, both could kill for love; both would be capable of maturer love, if at all, only with their own kind. The girl is much closer to Verdoux than his own wife, or his murdered wives; in sparing her he has betrayed both his marriage and his vocation. Since he is above all else a family man and an artist, she threatens the very structure of his soul. But the deranged and deadlocked will which has made and sustained Verdoux is never so strong or so ruthless as when it faces the threat of cure; and I know of no moment more dreadful or more beautifully achieved than that in which Verdoux veers from the girl, the sun on his suddenly shriveled cheek, and mutters in the shriveled, almost effeminate little voice of more than mortal hatred and terror: "You go on about your business."

But *why* does Verdoux become a murderer? One good answer is: why not? Verdoux is a business realist; in terms of that realism the only difference between free enterprise in murder and free enterprise in the sale of elastic stockings is the difference in legal liability and in net income. And if the film is regarded as a metaphor for war, we may blush to ask Verdoux *why*; or if it is regarded as a metaphor for the destruction of the soul, murder is almost too mild a vocation. Yet we may still ask why, and wonder why Chaplin's only direct statements, most of which are made through Verdoux, are so remarkably inadequate. Verdoux, to be sure, is grandly in character in holding "society" accountable and in absolving the individual; but is this all that Chaplin knows? If so, he is as surely a victim and dupe of evil as Verdoux or the civilization he excoriates, and all that goes deeper in the film is achieved intuitively, as if in a kind of waking dream. If he knows better, then he is gravely at fault, as artist and moralist, in making clear no more than he does, still worse in tossing the mass-audience so cynical and misleading a sop; and one of the purest and most courageous works I know of is, at its climax, pure and courageous only against the enemy, not in the face of the truth. For the answers to why and how criminality can be avoided, we can look inward more profitably than at the film; for all that is suggested in the film is operant in each of us. If Chaplin had illuminated these bottom causes more brightly than we can see them in ourselves, *Verdoux* would be a still greater work of art than it is. But in proposing so richly suggestive an image of process and effect in the world and in the personality, and in proposing it so beautifully, the film, with all its faults, is one of the few indispensable works of our time.

It even contains and implies the beginning of the answer. Good and evil are inextricable, Verdoux insists. But his fatal mistake was in trying to keep them apart. If the film is regarded as a metaphor for the personality, and through that metaphor, as a metaphor for the personality as the family as business as war as civilization as murder, then this is certain: if the man and wife had honored their marriage with more than their child, the murders would never have been committed, the paralysis would never have imposed itself or would have been dissolved, and the wife and child would never have been shut into that exquisite tabernacle of a closed garden, but all three would have lived as one in that poverty for which the wife was forlorn, in the intactness of soul and the irresponsibility of that anarchic and immortal lily of the field, the tramp, the most humane and most nearly complete among the religious figures our time has evolved; whom for once in his life Chaplin set aside, to give his century its truest portrait of the upright citizen.

July 5, 1947

I F you regard all experiment as affectation and all that bewilders you as a calculated personal affront, and if you ask of art chiefly that it be easy to take, you are advised not to waste your time seeing Jean Vigo's *Zero de Conduite* and *L'Atalante*; go on back to sleep, lucky Pierre, between the baker's wife and the well-digger's daughter, if you can squeeze in among the reviewers who have written so contemptuously of Vigo's work. If you regard all experiment as ducky, and all bewilderment as an opportunity to sneer at those who confess their bewilderment, and if you ask of art only that it be outré, I can't silence your shrill hermetic cries, or prevent your rush to the Fifth Avenue Playhouse; I can only hope to God I don't meet you there. If, on the other hand, you are not automatically sent either into ecstasy or catalepsy by the mere mention of avant-gardism, if your eye is already sufficiently open so that you don't fiercely resent an artist who tries to open it somewhat wider, I very much hope that you will see these films. I can't at all guarantee that you will like them, far less that you will enjoy and admire them as much as I do, for they are far too specialized. I can only be reasonably sure that you will find them worth seeing.

Zero de Conduite is a forty-minute movie about a French boys' boarding-school. It is hard for me to imagine how anyone with a curious eye and intelligence can fail to be excited by it, for it is one of the most visually eloquent and adventurous movies I have seen. But its fullest enjoyment depends rather heavily, I believe, on subjective chance. I happen to share a good deal of Vigo's peculiar kind of obsession for liberty and against authority, and can feel this in particularly clear emotional focus, as he does, in terms of the children and masters in a school. So the spirit of this film, its fierceness and gaiety, the total absence of well-constructed "constructive" diagnosis and prescription, the enormous liberating force of its quasi-nihilism, its humor, directness, kindliness, criminality, and guile, form for me as satisfying a revolutionary expression as I know.

On one seeing, anyhow, the film is quite bewildering, even if you understand its main device, as I was slow to do; but if you know the device, and accept it, the bewilderment itself becomes essential to the poem, and to your pleasure in it. As I see it the trick is, simply, that Vigo gets deeper inside his characters than most people have tried to on film, is not worried about transitions between objective, subjective, fantastic, and subconscious reality, and mixes as many styles and camera tricks, as abruptly, as he sees fit—always, so far as I can see, using the right style at the right moment, and always using it with force, charm, and originality. I assume that he intended, as one of his main points, to insist that these several levels of reality are equal in value, and inter-penetrative; and I would accept this aesthetically for its enrichment of poetic perception, metaphor, and device, even if I rejected it intellectually.

It seems clear to me that on the wild level of *Zero*, and on levels less adventurous, the unprejudiced eye could learn its way around such intricate treatment as naturally as it learned to link the many disparities which make up the basic vocabulary of conventional movies. Most movies, including many of the best, have been made timidly and under great handicap, with fragments of the movie alphabet which were mostly shaped and frozen by around 1925. In an important sense Vigo is far from "unconventional"; he is merely making much of the rest of the alphabet available. He has gone as far in this, I think, as Eisenstein or Dovzhenko—in a very different direction, of course—and a great deal that he has done in this film, bold as it is, should be regarded less as inimitable experiment than as the conquest of more of the full ground on which further work can be done. It is as if he had invented the wheel. Many others were fumbling at it; some still are; but nobody of anything remotely like his ability is trying to find further uses for it; and one is sure to be branded as a solemn snob, incapable of "enjoying" movies, if one so much as dares to speak in favor of these elementary devices by which enjoyment could be enlarged.

The boys in *Zero* are seen as they see each other; the audience is one of them. Although they are much the hardest, most happily perceived children I have seen in a movie, in one sense they are sentimentalized. They have the aloof, dangerous beauty of young, wild preying animals; whereas some of the schoolboys I knew were merely unnoticeable, others were sick, others gentle or timid, and still others were safe-playing, sycophantic dolts from the day they were born—faculty members already. I wish they had been shown in this variety, however it might have complicated Vigo's child-worship and his anarchic fury. The teachers, however, are perfect. Seen as the boys see them or hope to see them, they are masterpieces of caricature, mainly ferocious, one coldly compassionate, one in the

hyperboles of admiration. The sympathetic teacher who inspires them to revolt is a sort of lay Chaplin; another, an inspired epitome of the snoop, suggests Groucho Marx or, still
more, a tiptoeing lobster dressed in an undertaker's suit; the
headmaster is a pompous, murderous, shrieking midget.

There are so many wonderful scenes that I can mention only
a few: the silent, mysterious opening, in which two boys in a
railway compartment play out the most beautiful white-magic
I have ever seen, with toys, tricks, and suggestions of competitive vice; a blood-slowing capture of paralysis of time on a Sunday, and on the carpet of the headmaster's office; a dormitory
riot and procession, bearing a crucified teacher through a
slow-motion storm of pillow feathers, which combines Catholic
and primordial rituals and as an image of millennial, triumphal
joy has only been equaled on film, so far as I know, by newsreel
shots of the liberation of Paris. Vigo does some beautiful
things, too, with subtly *slurred* rather than slow motion; and
the stripped, mean sets and the occasional glimpses of pure
naturalistic action are grim and firm as stone outcrops. Maurice Jaubert's score seems good but nothing extraordinary as
music, but fitted with the film I like it as well as any outside
Dovzhenko's *Frontier*.

(To be continued)

July 12, 1947

Of the two films by Jean Vigo at the Fifth Avenue Playhouse, *Zero de Conduite*, which I commented on last week,
seems to me all but unblemished inspiration, moving freely
and surely in its own unprecedented world from start to finish,
one of the few great movie poems. I admire *L'Atalante* less; it
is only the best French movie since the best of René Clair. *Zero*
seems to have been made, as all the best work has to be, from
the inside out; *L'Atalante*, on the whole, is put together from
the outside inward. It is very good, spasmodically great poetry
applied to pretty good prose; a great talent trying, I judge, to
apply itself so far as it can stand to, conventionally and commercially.

The story, which Vigo adapted rather than invented, could

almost be one of those pseudo-simple, sophisticated-earthy things which several French movie-makers handle gracefully, to the delight of cultivated Americans who will despise Vigo's work; the sex life of a jealous barge captain and his restive peasant bride; the crawling of the claustrophobic, ironically christened barge along the Seine; a couple of weird flirtations; estrangement; reunion. But Vigo's treatment shows up the French movie "classics" of this sort for the genteel literary exercises they really are. The old familiar "civilized," "Gallic" smirk is strictly outlawed; these are horribly serious, instinctual, brainless people, presented with a naked directness that is beyond patronage or gentle laughter up the sleeve, beyond even any particular show of sympathy. The "atmospheres" which in later films of this sort are sketched in so prettily are not pretty here but gravely monumental, and all-pervasive. The ordinary clever use of props in French films is here no tender exhibition of naive trinkets before the comfortable but a solid drench of inanimate objects, passionately, all but mystically, respected for what they are, and mean to their owners.

At its best *L'Atalante* is sensuously much richer and more beautiful than *Zero*—in spite of the somewhat damaged prints it is clear that Boris Kaufman's camera work in both films should have an article to itself—and once in a while the picture breaks free into Vigo's half mad, strangely majestic kind of poetry. The bridal procession from church to barge, which opens the film, is a great passage, forlorn, pitiful, cruelly funny, and freezingly sinister; Dita Parlo (the bride) is the fullest embodiment of sub-articulate sex that I have seen; the trinket salesman with whom she flirts is an astonishing cross-breed of slapstick with a kind of jail-bird Ariel; and Michel Simon, as a pre-mental old man, is even more wonderfully realized as a poetic figure, a twentieth-century Caliban. Vigo was a more experienced director by the time he made *L'Atalante*, and the picture shows gifts fully as great as those shown in *Zero de Conduite*. But for all its quality *L'Atalante* suggests the strugglings of a maniac in a strait-jacket; whereas in *Zero* he moves freely, and it turns out that he is dangerous only to all in the world that most needs destroying.

It is clear that Vigo picked up a good deal from German films of the early twenties, from Clair and Chaplin, and from the whole creative brew of the Paris of his time. On a foggy day, indeed, or with a prejudiced eye, it would be possible to confuse his work with the general sad run of avant-garde movie work, as several reviewers, including some whom I ordinarily respect, have done. But Vigo was no more a conventional avant-gardist than he was a Hollywood pimp; he was one of the very few real originals who have ever worked on film. Nobody has approached his adroitness in handling reality, consciousness, and time on film (in *Zero*); or has excelled his vivid communication of the animal emotion, the senses, the inanimate world, and their interplay (in *L'Atalante*); nor have I found, except in the best work of the few masters, a flexibility, richness, and purity of creative passion to equal his in both these films.

Here is the little I know about him. He was the son of a Basque revolutionist, and learned to walk in the prison in which, as Vigo put it, his father was suicided. Perhaps that helps explain why he never so much as tried to learn to put his best foot forward. He began his career as an artist in a photographer's studio in Nice. He became an assistant movie cameraman, helped organize a film society, and made *A propos de Nice*, which was, I gather, a short and extremely sardonic film, nominally in the "documentary" manner. In Paris he made *Zero de Conduite* in 1933 and *L'Atalante* in 1934. He planned several other films, including one about tennis (with Cochet) and one about the French penal colonies; but all arrangements for financing these schemes fell through. When Paris censors saw *Zero* they forbade its release; even at a press screening it caused a near-riot. He was luckier with the more conventional *L'Atalante*. The miseries of dying, of tuberculosis, at the age of twenty-nine, with most of his abilities still unused, were exacerbated in Vigo by his knowledge that now that he was helpless to interfere, movie tradesmen were making little improvements on the picture.

Today, according to the Hollywood *Quarterly*, from which I got most of this information, both films are playing the French neighborhood theaters. It is not said whether they are popular.

Great Expectations does for Dickens about what *Henry V* did for Shakespeare. That is, it indicates a sound method for translating him from print to film. The method is not one of the most exciting that could be imagined, nor in its own terms is it used as excitingly as could be imagined; but the film is almost never less than graceful, tasteful, and intelligent, and some of it is better than that. The first few reels, on Pip's childhood, are especially well done, one strangeness and surprise unfolding from the center of another without flurry or overemphasis, with something of the cool enchantment there has always been in sped-up shots of the blooming of a flower. It looks as if the director, David Lean, and his associates have understood Dickens's novel as a work of literature and as a literary but good moving picture and also with the help of Freud and perhaps to some extent of Marx, and have had the wisdom not only to get guidance and leverage from these kinds of knowledge but also never to urge them on to the screen or the audience. Whether or not they went about it in this way, the picture has a good deal of the tone and the extra resonance of dreams, legends, or fairy tales. I thought it very provocative, for instance, as a symbolized intuitive image of nineteenth-century England, with the century (Pip and Estella) moving as if hypnotized by the vengefulness, gratitude, and deviousness of great ancestral forces: Magwitch as the archetype of the nameless swarm; Miss Havisham as the embittered Virgin Queen; the sinister-benign Jaggers as Law and Government.

Nearly all of the casting and playing is so good that it is useless to clog a lot of space trying to list preferences, but it should be said that Anthony Wager, as young Pip, is so extraordinarily fine that it is a great pity he was not used more often before he outgrew childhood roles; and that good as she is, Jean Simmons, as young Estella, seems affected in a wrong way, on a second seeing. I regret with the English reviewer Dillys Powell that more minor characters were not sketched into the background; as she observes, a great deal more of this could have been dared, for the screen can communicate in a second or two what may require pages in print.

I also wish that the Dickens illustrations had been studied

still more faithfully and imaginatively—that the whole tone of the film had had a kind of india-ink darkness, psychologically as well as visually: for it seems to me they had hold of a story much more cruel and mysterious than the one that got told. If this had been felt, the picture would not only be darker; the whole smooth, middle-distance narrative style, which so often merely illustrates the story nicely, would have been contorted into a style much more subjective and more visually expressive. I doubt that such a film would have been so popular as this one, and I am sure it could not have been so charming. All I can say for it is that it would have been still more faithful to Dickens—or my idea of him, anyhow—and at the same time less subservient; that it would have been a really original movie, a transfiguration rather than a translation; that it would have run the risks that are always run when primary creative intelligence rather than the best that good taste can do is turned loose on the screen. It is depressing to realize how many people feel that *Great Expectations* is about as good a job as the screen can do; how can people who believe that, think they really know or care much of anything about movies? But that is the prevailing taste, and I will admit that in its relatively mild terms this is a very good and enjoyable piece of work.

I enjoyed *Great Expectations* more than Carol Reed's *Odd Man Out*, but I was more interested in Reed's film, and liked it more. Essentially, though not on the whole in effect, it is a much more difficult and ambitious film, aimed in a more useful direction. The hero, a murdering and fatally wounded fugitive revolutionist, is an image of much of the best in contemporary mankind. The picture tells the story of his flight through the night streets of Belfast. This night city is civilization; on that intricate stage a wide variety of people try to help or hinder or capture the fugitive. Many of them are selfless in relation to some idea or passion or conception of duty of their own; not one is capable of the selfless charity it would require to deal with this hounded, doomed soul purely for its own sake. This seems to me a just image and useful diagnosis of the world, and an exceedingly good idea for a film; but quite a bit falls short in the making.

The early reels are exciting and beautiful—purely in movie terms, they are the best—yet they fail all but entirely to communicate the revolutionary edge that is so well got in F. W. Green's novel; in that respect John Ford's *The Informer* was better; and even some of the best purely movie details that Green wrote down are surprisingly omitted from the film. In the later reels the film, like the novel, tries for broader and broader allegory and phantasmagoria, but much as I respect this boldness, I don't think it succeeds. The story seems merely to ramify too much, to go on too long, and at its unluckiest to go arty. Most unfortunately the central character, effectively yet monotonously played by James Mason, is given too little remaining life of his own. He has virtually no will or mind or strength left but almost from the beginning is just a football, deflated so far that even its kicking around by the rest of the cast is rather soggy. So, as an image and allegory, the whole film loses much of its possible force: it is not a tragic poem but a series of passive elegiac tableaux with a certain suggested relationship, generally inferior, to the Stations of the Cross. The tone of pity for man is much too close to self-pity.

Yet detail by detail most of *Odd Man Out* is made with great skill and imaginativeness, and with a depth of ardor that is very rare in contemporary films. In fact, the kind of creative energy is at large here that is lacking in *Great Expectations*; and even the mistakes made by that kind of energy are more moving and more admirable than the gentler kinds of success. It does strike me, though, that *Odd Man Out* is at its weakest with its most important ideas, and next weakest with its most important characters, and is at its best with the inanimate world and with people as denizens of that world, not as self-responsible salients. If the world should end tomorrow, as this film rather substantially suggests that it must, and may as well, this film would furnish one of the more appropriate epitaphs: a sad, magnificent summing up of a night city. Movies have always been particularly good at appreciating cities at night: but of a night city this is the best image I have seen.

August 2, 1947

Crossfire is a gruesomely exciting story about some soldiers, one of whom murders a Jew. It is extremely well played by

Roberts Young, Mitchum and Ryan, very notably Ryan; by Sam Levene and Paul Kelly; and by practically everyone else in the cast. It is excellently written and directed by John Paxton and Edward Dmytryk, respectively. In part, I don't doubt, because the picture is *about* something, which everyone making it can take seriously, it is, even as melodramatic entertainment, the best Hollywood movie in a long time. (Chaplin doesn't make Hollywood movies; he makes Chaplin movies.) Much of its more serious stuff, about Anti-Semitism, is very good and very heartening too, but I think the following qualifiers must be recognized: 1) In a way it is as embarrassing to see a movie Come Right Out Against Anti-Semitism as it would be to see a movie Come Right Out Against torturing children. 2) Few things pay off better in prestige and hard cash—granted you present it in an entertaining way—than safe fearlessness. 3) This film is not entirely fearless, even within its relatively safe terms. They have the sardonic courage to preach the main persuaders to a Southern boy, taking painfully embarrassing care never to mention Negroes; but they lack the courage to make that omission inescapably clear to the audience.

Largely because of this film and his recent statement that he believes in making other movies that take chances, RKO-Radio's vice-president in charge of production, Dore Schary, is likely to be regarded by many people as a white hope and a hero. I do not question the goodness of his deepest motives, and I certainly wish him well; but it may as well be remembered that, at best, Hollywood's heroism is calculated to land buttered side up. Movies about Anti-Semitism aren't so desperately chancy, after all. Millions of people will look forward to them if only for the questionable excitement of hearing actors throw the word "Jew" around; Fox and Goldwyn are coming out, respectively, with *Gentleman's Agreement* and *Earth and High Heaven*, and Goldwyn has astutely postponed production, not to be snowed under by his competitors. The murdered Jew in *Crossfire* was a murdered homosexual in the original novel, Richard Brooks's *The Brick Foxhole* and I learn from a reliable source that this quick shift was made, and *Crossfire* was rushed through, in order to jump the gun on the two more pretentious films. I am sorry to spend so much time on such matters, but I suspect they will be generally neglected in the pleasure of awarding Hollywood a sprinting-prize for taking Baby's First Step; and they shouldn't be neglected. All that aside, however, *Crossfire* is an unusually good and honest movie and may—I hope, will—prove a very useful one.

The Hucksters comes right out against radio advertising, and in the Hollywood scheme of things this is doubtless much more heroic than attacking Jew baiters, who are not so well organized as advertising men to fight back. Some of the singing commercials are very funny, and some of the minor characters are drawn with medium shrewdness. Clark Gable seems well at ease, most of the time, but something soft and unfortunate has happened to his mouth; Deborah Kerr struggles prettily but, I'm afraid, rather compliantly, against a thorough job of packaging. I dislike the movie as I disliked what little I could read of the book: for I find uniquely nauseating the spectacle of incurable corruption laboring under delusions of honesty.

I agree with Shirley O'Hara of the *New Republic* that the period of the original *Perils of Pauline* is good for a lot more than patronizing laughter. I am also astonished that so many people find the new *Perils* so howlingly funny. People who can accept such stuff as solid gold have either forgotten a lot, or never knew first-rate slapstick when they saw it, twenty to thirty years ago, when it was one of the wonders of the world.

I am with Miss O'Hara again, and everyone else who knows what a beautiful film could be made about jazz. For years, I wished I might make a movie about New Orleans, centered on Louis Armstrong and his colleagues. I like *New Orleans* because, barring Gjon Mili's rather too alligatorish short, it is the only movie ever to show any real feeling for jazz; and because the Negro musicians are much more nearly at ease than is usual in movies; and because of Armstrong, who seems to me one of the most likable people in the world, and certainly as fine a musical talent as this country has ever had. (Some unknown Negroes and whites have developed music even finer.) All the same, the movie is a crime. Not only is it horribly inept and unimaginative in everything that does not center on jazz; the jazz itself is too often cut short, or smothered as background for pictures which fail to carry it out; and as the ultimate triumph, jazz wins over a full-dress audience—which is a little as if St. Francis and his Fifty Thousand Feathered Friends became headliners at the Bronx Zoo.

The Unfaithful comes out against inadequately premeditated divorce and even suggests that a cuckold should try to understand and forgive his wife's adultery. It does not suggest, however, that *he* should ask *her* forgiveness for his far more contemptible failure to discipline his jealousy. And it dresses up what might have been good and plain, if rather immature, drama in some of the most superfluous plot-complications in years.

Ivy is an unusually ornate melodrama about an Edwardian murderess; it stars Joan Fontaine, who pops her eyes, coarsens her jaw, and wears her elegant clothes very effectively. The real star is whoever was chiefly responsible for the dressing, setting, lighting, and shooting, and that, I infer from past performance, is the producer, William Cameron Menzies.

Moss Rose is also English-turn-of-the-century, ornate, and about murder. It is not by a good deal as good of its kind as *Ivy*. But Peggy Cummins is famishingly pretty; and Ethel Barrymore, in an even sillier role, has moments, when her sardonic slip shows, and others of such pure, gentle splendor that they make Gainsborough look like Varga.

A CHECKLIST on some new and recent movies:

Life With Father. Rich, careful, rather heavily proficient. Fun, I suppose; but I can't really enjoy laughing at tyrants, least of all tyrants who are forgiven because of their innocence. William Powell acts, rather than is, Father rather well, but it's strictly an impersonation. Irene Dunne is painfully miscast as Mother; she would probably keep her tongue in her cheek uttering the Seven Last Words.

The Secret Life of Walter Mitty. By no means what it might have been if it had used what James Thurber's story offered it, but quite an entertaining movie. I am getting a little wan about Danny Kaye's tonsil-juggling numbers, but there are good bits of henpecking and office life, and at moments during the day-dreams Kaye is wonderful. He is so good at his best that it is hard to forgive—or even believe—all that he mishandles. I am sorry that the dreams are set and dressed as fantastic musical-comedy numbers; they would have been much funnier if Mitty had dictated every square inch of his surroundings. The Goldwyn-Thurber correspondence in a recent issue of *Life*, by the way, makes very interesting reading.

Down to Earth. And so far as I'm concerned, six feet under it. Mr. Jordan, dry-ice mist, and heaven too.

A Broadway musical called *Swinging the Muses.* Terpsichore (Rita Hayworth) intervening to turn this rotten piece of commercial entertainment into still worse high art. There are, however, some prettier than average tunes, and a few glimpses of Miss Hayworth are also prettier than average.

Black Narcissus. Several nuns get upset by the strange atmosphere of, and surrounding, their new convent, which was formerly a Himalayan harem. (Quite an idea for a musical, that. Take it away, Rita.) One (well played by Kathleen Byron) falls for a local Englishman (David Farrar) and fails to renew her vows. The head nun (Deborah Kerr) just makes Sisterly sheeps' eyes at him as he lunges around the sanctuary in his shorts (he is not, one gathers, a Believer). There is also a local Holy Man, staring at a peak, and a great deal of talk about the wind and the strangeness of it all. After a while the Sisters give it up as a bad job. It is all intended to be very "psychological," "atmospheric," "rueful," and "worldly-wise." I suspect that the worst faults lie in Rumer Godden's original novel; that Michael Powell and Emeric Pressburger were badly mistaken in trying to make a movie of it at all. There is some unusually good color photography, and as movie-making some of it is intelligent and powerful. But the pervasive attitude in and toward the picture makes it as a whole tedious and vulgar. P.S.: Barring perhaps one in any hundred who willingly practice it, I think celibacy is of itself faintly obscene; so I admire still less the dramatic exploitation of celibacy as an opportunity for titillation in the best of taste.

Frieda. Are *all* Germans Guilty? This English film spends a long time earnestly telling you that some aren't, entirely, and some are, and that time heals, respectively, all wounds and none. It appears that the only thing open to a German who wants really to convince one of a willingness to be reeducated is a sincere attempt at suicide. Mai Zetterling, who was very good in the Swedish film *Torment*, is still pretty good in this, but the face and the talent are freezing; unless she is smart and careful, Hollywood will finish her, directly or indirectly. David Farrar, who sets the nuns a-flutter in *Black Narcissus*, is also in this one. He might easily become a matinee idol, and he might possibly become something better than that.

The Long Night. A long, loud, ambitious film, Anatole Litvak's first since the war, about a simple man (Henry Fonda) who is driven to murder by the calculated confusions of a very corrupt man (Vincent Price). It would be interesting to see it on a double bill with its original version, the French *Daybreak*. Both films obviously rate themselves as tragedies; both are merely intelligent trash. But the old one is much more discreet with its self-pity and much more sharply edged. The new one depends too heavily on crowd-commotion; noise (there are gruesome distortions of the slow movement of Beethoven's Seventh Symphony); huge, lugubrious close-ups of Fonda looking adenoidal; and class-angling. It is, however, much better than the run of contemporary movies.

Thunderbolts. Made by William Wyler during the war too late for release, released now as a recruiting incentive. A record of the bombing and strafing operation which cut off the Germans in Italy from their supplies. A good many incredibly fine air shots, well organized; by a long shot, the best of the movies reviewed above.

Some older movies that are worth seeing, or mentioning anyhow:

The Macomber Affair. Best movie job on Hemingway, to date. I persist in believing that Zoltan Korda is one of the best directors in Hollywood. *The Woman on the Beach.* An exceptionally evocative melodrama, directed by Jean Renoir. *Copacabaña.* Groucho Marx with a new mustache and a modified style. *The Red House.* Back-country melodrama well written and directed by Delmar Daves, who makes good use of his location and of some adolescents. *Torment*. The first half is a fine, ardent movie about a schoolboy, a deranged teacher, and a terrified working girl; thereafter it fritters out into pretty good horror melodrama and pale conclusions. *Miracle on 34th Street*. Santa Claus (well played by Edmund Gwenn) comes to Herald Square and wraps up the millennium in one neat package. Clever, and pleased with itself, and liked by practically everybody; but since I have always despised the maxim "Honesty is the best policy," I enjoy even less a statement of the profits accruing through faith, loving kindness, etc. I expect next a "witty, tender little fantasy" presenting the Son of God (Sonny Tufts) as God's Customers' Man.

September 13, 1947

THE Italian-made *Shoeshine* is about as beautiful, moving, and heartening a film as you are ever likely to see. I will review it when I am capable of getting any more than that into coherent language and feasible space.

I Know Where I'm Going is a very pleasant English film by Michael Powell and Emeric Pressburger. It is the story of an imperious young Englishwoman (Wendy Hiller), about to marry for money, who is delayed among the natives of one of the islands off the coast of Scotland and there learns better things about herself and about life in general than she might have expected to. Some of this story is told, and charactered, with slickness and whimsy as well as genuine lightness; I kept realizing, as I watched and enjoyed it, how shallow and shabby it would probably seem in print. But there are engaging performances by Miss Hiller and Roger Livesey; the sensitive photography and the intelligent if not very imaginative use of sound do more than enough to make eloquent the influence of place on people; and the whole thing is undertaken with a kind of taste and modesty whose absence did much to harm Messrs. Powell and Pressburger's *Stairway to Heaven* and *Black Narcissus*. Theirs is a gentle sort of talent at last, but at times they know very well how to use it, without much concession to their liabilities—inordinate ambition, bumptiousness, and a general unevenness of judgment.

Kiss of Death, which sketches the embarrassments of a burglar who becomes a stool-pigeon, is another of Hollywood's "locale" movies. (Possibly that word will do: what I mean by it is that the picture is shot mainly or wholly in actual places; the story, as a rule, is based on fact, though that seems to me less important.) It is written, coldly and convincingly, by Ben Hecht and Charles Lederer. It is directed by Henry Hathaway and photographed by Norbert Brodine. The script, though expert, is certainly not inspired, and I can't believe that the director and cameraman are better than thoroughly competent, either. All of which makes *Kiss of Death* the more striking, for apparently if good technicians pay careful attention to the actual world, they can hardly help turning out a movie that is worth seeing; and the actors who have to play up to this world are greatly stimulated and improved by their surroundings, too. I don't care as much for this film as for the much more lively *Boomerang*, but in its own way it is nearly as good a job. Victor Mature is good as the burglar. I have always wished I might cast him right; he is well cast this time. In any adequate production of the picture he would be still better in a still better role: as Diomed in Shakespeare's *Troilus and Cressida*.

The Roosevelt Story is interesting to see, chiefly because it includes a good many revealing portraits of the late President, and because in most other respects it is so archetypically awful. It claims to be nonpolitical, which is as absurd as if one put out a biography of Babe Ruth, taking care to avoid the hot subject of baseball. Its commentary approaches the low, to date, in pseudo-common-mannishness (and that is a pleonasm if ever I perpetrated one). You can't help realizing as you watch it, still more as you listen to it, that a terrifying number of Americans, most of them in all innocence of the fact, are much more ripe for benevolent dictatorship—and every dictatorship is seen as benevolent by those who support it—than for the most elementary realization of the meanings, hopes, and liabilities of democracy. It is doubtless an exceedingly well-meant film, but that doesn't exactly reduce its power to sadden and to disturb. It includes a good many shots of the dead-march in Washington. These are some of the most beautiful shots ever put on film and, properly arranged, could be as great and as moving, in their far more complex and qualifiable way, as Whitman's threnody. They were very well ordered in the newsreels just after Roosevelt's death. Here they are so used as binders, and as springboards for flashbacks, that most of their possible power is thrown away. But even in this mangled state some of the single shots are enough to stop the breath.

The Devil's Envoys is the work of Jacques Prévert and Marcel Carné, who made *Children of Paradise*. The pretentious, hammy, romantic symbolizing and oblique philosophizing of the latter bothers me more than it used to, but I still very much like the picture; it does have style and glamor. *The Devil's Envoys* has style and glamor too, but not of a kind I can care much for. The effort is to make a movie equivalent of one of those medieval romances which have always seemed to me as overrated as they were interminable; and to lace this sleepy posset with a lot of heavy allegory about Love as Evil and Love versus Evil. Quite a bit of it is elaborately beautiful; but I was forced to realize anew, as I watched it, just how boring unalleviated beauty can be. Once in a while this trance-like ballet of beauty and black magic permitted, almost as if by accident, a glimpse of what the actual Middle Ages must have felt and looked and smelled like. At those moments the picture became wonderful, magic and beauty and even allegory included. But most of it is like a required reading of *Aucassin and Nicolette*, translated into Middle High Marshmallow. It is a discouraging sign of the times that *The Devil's Envoys* won a French Critics' award. That goes far toward helping explain why the best movies in the world, and in many years, are being made in Italy.

I was astounded to hear that some knowledgeable people think of *Brute Force*, a movie about men in a big jail, as a happy return to the melodramas of the early thirties. Maybe so, in some of the jab-paced, slickly sadistic action sequences. But there isn't a line in it, or a performance, or an idea, or an emotion, that belongs much later than 1915, and cheesy 1915 at that. And terrible as the movie is, that is its considerable charm. I suspect, without malice, that the ideal audience for O'Neill's *The Iceman Cometh* is in some non-temperance Old Men's Home along the Bowery—it is in that sense a genuine and likable folk-play. I also suspect that the ideal audience for *Brute Force* is among men who have been shut off from the world, paying their debts to society—as society laughingly puts it—since Pershing was a pup. I am sure they were never like the men in this picture, even in their youth; but I'm also reasonably sure that they think they were, and think people still are. If you have ever seen a country audience taking *The Old Homestead* for Gospel, you'll know what I mean.

September 27, 1947

The Great Dawn is a quasi-biography of the Italian musical prodigy Pierino Gambina, starring Pierino Gambina. Now and then the picture faintly promises to show how a prodigy is really manufactured and sold; and Pierino, a haunted-looking little boy, looks as if under wise direction he could carry whatever they handed him, of that sort. But the promise never pays off, whether because this is a highly "authorized" biography, or because of everybody's genuine affection and admiration for the child, or because this particular prodigy is as lucky in life as he is on film, I don't know. What you get here is a simple little story about a gifted child; his pretty mother, a runaway bourgeoise; his musician father, who runs away from her; her solid father, who detests "artists"; and an engaging, slaphappy priest, who rather suggests Keenan Wynn and who is chiefly responsible for developing and placing the boy's talent. In many respects the whole business is rather thin, even silly, but there are redeeming features which make the picture, at worst, pleasant to sit through. It is done more like a charade than a would-be work of art or even of professional entertainment, with quite a nice sense of comedy, and with little jets of that free talent and fearless vitality which seem to abound today in Italy. I couldn't be sure, thanks in part either to flaws either in the sound-track or in the theater's equipment, whether Gambina is a good conductor or a madly overrated one. I am sure that the strings catch fire nicely in one passage in the William Tell Overture, that the well-known Four Notes in Beethoven's Fifth Symphony should not be performed as if they said Fee Fie Fo Fum, and that unless movie people can manage to present pieces of music whole rather than in bloody gobbets, they'd better not try at all.

The Tawny Pipit is an English pastoral comedy about bird-lovers, both lay and professional, and what happens to them when, in mid-wartime, a pair of very rare birds decides to breed in an English pinfold. The English reviewer C. A. Lejeune was rather chilly about this film. I think she was right, and that a good many other Englishmen must agree with her; for what might, with sharper treatment, have been a real beauty of a comedy is blunted by that special simpering affection which some of the English are so ready to feel for themselves. It is an almost unimaginably genteel picture, and if you had, as it were, to sit in the same parlor with it, you would probably suffer a good deal. But at this comfortable distance in blood as well as space I was able, rather to my dismay, to take all this extreme Englishness almost in the spirit in which it was offered. For one thing, the picture is so obviously a labor of love, and the job of a lifetime, for Bernard Miles, an actor who has always seemed to me a particularly nice guy; he not only acts in this—rather badly—but co-wrote and co-directed it, with Charles Saunders. For another, in spite of its profuse cuteness and genteelism, it has a good deal of genuine charm, humor, and sweetness of temper.

October 11, 1947

THE elementary beginning of true reason, that is, of reason which involves not merely the forebrain but the entire being, resides, I should think, in the ability to recognize oneself, and others, primarily as human beings, and to recognize the ultimate absoluteness of responsibility of each human being. (I can most briefly suggest what I mean by a genuine recognition of human beings as such by recommending that you see the Italian movie *Shoeshine* and that you compare it in this respect with almost any other movie you care to name.) I am none too sure of my vocabulary, but would suppose this can be called the humanistic attitude. It is still held, no doubt, by scattered individuals all over the world, is still nominally the germinal force of Western civilization, and must still sleep as a potential among almost unimaginably large numbers and varieties of people; but no attitude is more generally subject to disadvantage, dishonor, and misuse today, and no other is so nearly guaranteed extinction. Even among those who preserve a living devotion to it, moreover, few seem to have come by it naturally, as a physical and sensuous fact, as well as a philosophical one; and fewer still give any evidence of enjoying or applying it with any of the enormous primordial energy which, one would suppose, the living fact would inevitably liberate in a living being. I realize that I must be exaggerating when I think of it as hardly existing in a pure and vigorous form anywhere in contemporary art or living, but I doubt that I am exaggerating much: I know, in any case, that *Shoeshine*, because it furnishes really abundant evidence of the vitality of this attitude, seems to stand almost alone in the world, and to be as restoring and jubilant a piece of news as if one had learned that a great hero whom one had thought to be murdered or exiled or corrupted still lives in all his valor.

This is one of the few fully alive, fully rational films ever made. And one of the beauties of it is that its best intelligence seems to have operated chiefly on an instinctual level, forcing the men who made the film, who are I gather no more than very sincere and quite talented, to do better than the best their talents alone might promise them and better, I imagine, than they planned or foresaw. I suspect that all they intended in this story of two street boys who are caught almost by accident into the corrective machinery of the state, and are destroyed, was an effective work of protest, a work of social art; and that it was more out of the aroused natural honesty of their souls, and their complete devotion to their subject, that they went so much deeper. *Shoeshine* is all that a work of social art ought to be, would have to be to have any worth whatever, and almost never is. It is remarkably perceptive and compassionate in its study of authority and of those who embody authority, serve it, and suffer in and under it. It is also the rarest thing in contemporary art—a true tragedy. This tragedy is cross-lighted by pathos, by the youthfulness and innocence of the heroes, and I suspect that the makers of the film were themselves confused by pathos, but it is stern, unmistakable tragedy as well. The heroes would presumably not have been destroyed unless they had been caught into an imposed predicament; but they are destroyed not by the predicament but by their inability under absolutely difficult circumstances to preserve faith and reason toward themselves and toward each other, and by their best traits and noblest needs as well as by their worst traits and ignoblest needs. Moreover, the film is in no sense a despairing or "defeatist" work, as some people feel it is. I have seldom seen the more ardent and virile of the rational and Christian values more firmly defended, or the effects of their absence or misuse more pitifully and terribly demonstrated.

The film is almost uniquely moving and heartening for still another reason. Almost every minute of it has a kind of rashness, magnanimity, and deep, wise emotional directness which, I am convinced, can hardly if at all exist in a piece of work unless those who make it are sure they are at one with a large, eager, realistic general audience: in other words, very large parts of a whole people must have been moved, for a while at least, by the particular kind of aliveness which gives this film its peculiar radiance. When that is the case, men of any talent whatever can hardly help surpassing themselves. But when most of a people are in apathy, or sufficient anxiety to stun the spirit, every talent or hope, no matter in what spirit or attitude it may operate, is reduced to a fraction of its potentiality.

Great works of art, and the best hopes of good living, could come out of this quality of spirit, as out of no other. This film is not a great or for that matter a wholly well-realized work of art. It has some very considerable virtues besides those already mentioned: one of the few poignant and maturely perceived "love stories" ever to reach the screen; beautifully directed playing by all the boys, who are all amateurs, and by several naturalistic and a few well-chosen florid professionals; and an illusion of spontaneity which, considering that the director, Vittorio da Sica, had to put his amateurs through as many as thirty-nine takes for one scene, is one of the pure miracles of fifty years of movies. And in spite of some near-stock characterizations and situations, everyone in the film bulges with a depth and complexity of realness that is immeasurably beyond the hope of mere naturalism; because everybody is perceived as a complete human being, one feels at every moment that almost anything could happen, and that the reasons why any given thing happens are exceedingly complex and constantly shifting their weight. In playwriting, however, and camera work, and cutting, and sound, though it is eloquent, supple, unaffected, and uninhibited, even the very fine best of the film is seldom sharply inventive; one is very frequently moved and pleased, very seldom convinced that anything has been done definitively. Such feeling for form as there is, is more literary than cinematic. But the quality and energy of spirit are so compelling, pervasive, and valiant that I never felt, and cannot feel now, the pain or anger that is almost inevitable in seeing a good thing fall short of its best possibilities.

I gather that this spirit is already fading in Italy; that audiences are wanting and movie people are preparing costume dramas and screen operas. I suppose that it seldom holds a people strongly in focus, for long; it is a terrible pity that no men of genius were able to take advantage of this moment. But a moment which has made it possible for good, less gifted men to make such films as *Open City*, the still better *Shoeshine*, and a few others which, by their reputation, I hope we shall see soon has been by no means completely lost.

November 8, 1947

N*ightmare Alley* is the story of a cold young criminal (Tyrone Power) who starts as a carnival "mentalist," moves on to a Chicago night club, and is on the verge of the big time (pseudo-religion, with prospects of a personal "temple" and radio station), when two of the women he has used gum up his act. The picture goes careful just short of all that might have made it very interesting; I gather from the handed-out synopsis that a temple sequence was made which does not appear in the show. Even so, two or three sharply comic and cynical scenes make it worth seeing—Power's wrangle over "God" with his wonderfully stupid but not-that-stupid wife (Coleen Gray), a scene which has some of the hard, gay audacity of *Monsieur Verdoux*, and every scene in which Taylor Holmes impersonates a skeptical but vulnerable industrialist. In any mature movie context these scenes would be no better than all right, and an intelligently trashy level of all right, at that; but this kind of wit and meanness is so rare in movies today that I had the added special pleasure of thinking, "Oh, no; they *won't*

have the guts to do *that*." But they do; as long as they have
any nerve at all, they have quite a lot. The rest of the show is
scarcely better than average. Lee Garmes's camera work is lush
but vigorous.

Body and Soul, which gets very bitter and discreetly leftish
about commercialism in prize fighting, is really nothing much,
I suppose, when you get right down to it. But it was almost
continuously interesting and exhilarating while I watched it,
mainly because everyone had clearly decided to do every scene
to a finish and because, barring a few letdowns, scene after
scene came off that way. It is never as nervy as the best of
Nightmare Alley, but of its own kind it is more solidly made. I
like both pictures because in both there is quick satirical observation, a sense of meanness to match the meanness of the worlds
they are showing, a correct assumption of cynical knowledge
in the audience which relieves them of the now almost universal practice of drawing diagrams for the retarded, and a general
quality of tension and of pleasure in good workmanship, which
now all seem to me to have been commonplaces of American
movies of the early thirties and which rarely appear now without looking like cautious museum copies.

Song of Love takes the Liberty of Showing Johannes Brahms
declare his love for Clara Schumann; but at least things aren't
made easy for them by showing Robert having a petulant
shindy with Lola Montez, Franz Liszt, or a bottle. In fact,
Schumann reacts to the news like a gentleman, rather than a
stallion disputing a question of overtime; thereby giving the
movies practically their unique maturely intended scene on
that subject. Liberties are also taken with the music; even so
short a piece as Brahms's G-Minor Rhapsody is haggled to
bits. I don't like these kinds of license even when they are ex-
cusable, or unavoidable. But very much to my surprise I did
rather like *Song of Love*. All such inaccuracies and mutilations,
and some clumsy casting, and some wrongly styled acting,
were in my feeling more than counterbalanced by the real tenderness and quiet in which the picture was obviously undertaken. About Artur Rubinstein's back-screen performances, in
the manners of the various musicians, I don't feel competent
to judge. But whether or not it was in fact appropriate to Clara
Schumann, I liked the contained, splintering-crystal style that

was given her; thought Brahms gave a surprisingly subdued performance of his Rhapsody; and I think they would have been wise to call in Horowitz to double for Liszt's playing.

Ride the Pink Horse is practically revolutionary for a West Coast picture; it obviously intends to show that Mexicans and Indians are capable of great courage and loyalty, even to a white American, and can help him out of a hole if they like him. In a particularly gratifying scene the star-director, Robert Montgomery, escorts a young Indian girl, Wanda Hendrix, into the dining-room of the best hotel in a small New Mexico town, and the reactions of the diners and hired help are recorded with simplicity, accuracy, and courage. But she is shown also to be no serious threat in any traditional movie sense—a mere child with a crush on the white hero, not a possible sweetheart, and something of a little savage at that; and in spite of good intentions the chief Mexican, Thomas Gomez, is just a character actor. As for the central quarrel of the story, it is so carefully vague you can hardly follow it. Montgomery, for so many motives so dimly stated and so contradictory that you can believe in none of them, is trying to blackmail a war profiteer (well played by Fred Clark) whose exact crime, even whose business, we never learn. Whether it is dread of libel suits, the so-called international so-called style, or plain blind habit, few American films ever manage really to specify a character or a situation so that either can achieve personal life or general applicability; people merely dance their way, more or less ingratiatingly, through a sequence of windy generalizations. They are not by any fat chance intended to be confused with any persons living or dead or who might ever possibly have lived.

Monsieur Verdoux is again in circulation. Because I am leaving town for vacation, I haven't yet had a chance to check on the three "minor" cuts I hear have been made. If you can't get a vacation, by all means see it—and René Clair's *Man About Town*, a mainly delightful movie which I saw too late for inclusion in this review.

I haven't seen *Variety Girl*, but H. B. Darrach, of *Time*, has, and I think posterity should have the benefit of his definitive description of one of the players, Lizabeth Scott, as "a Milton Caniff version of the Mona Lisa."

December 13, 1947

Luigi Zampa's *To Live in Peace* is less thoroughly worked out and less acutely put on film than *Shoeshine* and *Open City*, but in some important respects it is even more remarkable. It is the story of what war meant to an infinitesimal Italian hill town and especially to a peasant family which, on pain of death, sheltered two American fugitives. I think that in spirit and basic understanding it is the wisest and most deeply humane movie of its time.

Its central characters are wholly unpolitical men, whose chief concern with history is to try to scrape it off their shoes. It is suggested that this is the ordinary condition of ordinary men, against which political men, good or bad, must take their measure; and that at best this measure is relatively puny. These central characters are what is known as simple men, a danger-ous kind for contemporary artists to fool with; I have never before seen simple men presented with so much kindliness, immediacy, understanding, and freedom from calculation and self-deceit. They are presented so richly in their weakness as well as their excellence that it is unimaginable that it occurred to anyone who worked on the film that they were doing a "balanced" job. The work is obviously done in that fundamen-tal innocence which comes from a genuine love for and realism about human beings; which is the natural air that any half-sane artist, or man, has to breathe; and which is breathed in most parts of the world, by now, about as freely as in the Black Hole of Calcutta. To choose only one of many examples, a Negro soldier, hidden in a wine-cellar while a German soldier visits the terrified peasants, gets stinking drunk and very noisy. This results in the death of the hero of the picture, and of the Ger-man. Archer Winsten of the *Post*, whose reviews, regardless of certain areas of disagreement, I warmly like and recommend, thought this action psychologically questionable. He wrote that it was impossibly inconsiderate and ungrateful of a soldier in that predicament. No doubt it was. But there is no evidence that the Negro, the peasants, or even the people who made the film ever looked at it in that light. To all of them it was, unfor-tunately, the most natural thing in the world; and one of the glories of the picture is the complete simplicity with which the whole thing is done and passed over, without any psychological or moral elaboration. As a native of this country, with more than enough experience both of the South and of non-Southerners who think they mean well by Negroes, I am like many other Americans particularly impressed by the whole treatment of the Negro; it is the only pure presentation of a man of his race that I have seen in a movie. As a human being, who would rather be a citizen of the world than of the United States, I am as deeply impressed by the treatment of the German; as for the peasant father, he is beyond "treatment," a great character and symbol.

This same fundamental innocence, coupled with a broad, almost operatic (and sometimes hammy) theatrical vitality, boldly clashes extremely discordant attitudes and styles, anything from desperate seriousness and majestic satire through passionately improvised slapstick. During the long climax these clashings blend in such a way that the picture, faults and all, soars along one of the rarest heights possible to art—the height from which it is seen that the whole race, including the observer, is to be pitied, laughed at, feared for, and revered for its delusions of personal competence for good, evil, or mere survival, as it sleepwalks along ground which continuously opens bottomless chasms beneath the edges of its feet. This seems to me one of the truest conceivable perspectives on the human predicament.

The man in the film who evidently understands it best, and who evidently realizes also the prodigious animal power to endure, and the limited fertility of the heart and spirit through which man is indestructible and victorious even in his downfall through this insanity, even in his absurdity, is Aldo Fabrizi, who plays the peasant, and who collaborated on the script. I infer that he understands it neither intellectually nor aesthetically, but so thoroughly that it does not even strike him as particularly interesting. This is the most mature way of understanding it that I can conceive of; and this healthy, casual, and unvalued wisdom so generally illuminates and invigorates the film that many of its inadequacies are transfigured and many others are made to seem negligible. I don't agree with those who talk of Fabrizi as a great actor. As an actor he seems thoroughly experienced, astute, uninhibited, and no more. His grandeur is as a man. His good luck is his solid equipment as an artist and his magnificent equipment, in face, and lowering head, and burly body, to make visible certain kinds of greatness. The performance is merely a very good one. The embodiment is heroic: one of the few towering archetypes I have seen on the screen. I wish that this tremendous character, so close to "type" yet so far beyond it, had been given material through which it could have been much more thoroughly explored and exhausted. But one of the wonderful things about the film is the casualness with which this figure is examined and tossed away, as if the sea were stiff with fish as good and better. It is. But how many fishermen, where else in the world, know it? And of those who know it, how many are competent to haul them in?

December 27, 1947

I T IS time and past time to add my own useless comments to all those which have been provoked by the recent relationships between Congress and Hollywood and by the Catholic Veterans' holy war against Chaplin. But I can say very little. I might manage an adequate salute to the Catholic Veterans and to a church which has forborne, with such unfathomable patience, to commend them to the rack; but this is made impossible by the postal laws. I am still less capable of adequately discussing the case of the ten men cited for contempt of Congress, and fired by their employers. For the nothing that it is worth, I cannot imagine how any self-respecting man could, under such circumstances, hold Congress otherwise than in contempt; such contempt naturally extends to include those who, with such eager and prissy abjectness, hastened to disown these men —thereby reducing the hopes of every honest man in Hollywood from a desperately achieved two per cent to sub-zero.

I believe that a democracy which cannot contain all its enemies, of whatever kind or virulence, is finished as a democracy. I believe that a vigorous and genuine enough democracy could do so. But I see no reason to believe that this democracy is vigorous or genuine enough by a good deal, or to hope that it can become so; nor am I thoroughly convinced that such a

democracy can ever exist except in the most generous and sanguine imaginations. It seems to me that the mere conception
of a vigorous and genuine democracy, to say nothing embarrassing about its successful practice, depends on a capacity for
faith in human beings so strong that on its basis one can dare
to assume that goodness and intelligence will generally prevail
over stupidity and evil.

This is, I would presume, the bravest and noblest faith of
which men, purely as such, are capable; but I cannot see that
this faith is any longer available, in the face of all the monstrous evidence to the contrary, except to one particularly obstinate kind of religious enthusiast; and I am convinced that a
religious enthusiast who is required, on pain of heresy, so recklessly to underrate the power of evil and stupidity is in a singu-
larly insecure, not to say insane, position. I think it would be
possible to proceed on this assumption in any hope of sanity
only among people who could share a minimum, however
humble, of veneration for individual human beings, and of an
ability to honor and trust each other's humanity, even in their
fiercest differences. But it seems to me that virtually nobody,
any more, chooses even to try to honor and trust even himself,
or even his best potentialities. Failing that, it is of course impossible to deal honorably or trustworthily with others; and we
have harrowing evidence what a peculiarly infernal mechanism
democracy inevitably becomes when it is manipulated by and
for people who no longer understand its meaning and purpose.
The Stalinists are by no means the only enemies of this reverence for single people, and of the possibility of mutual trust,
even among opponents; in that respect non-revolutionists of
every kind and class have already depraved themselves, this nation, and "democratic civilization" beneath any likely prospect
of cure. But among all these enemies the Stalinists are as ruthless as the worst of the others; are moved by the energy of
idealism, of a kind, rather than the naive self-cannibalistic self-
interest which is so ravenous here; and are the most intelligent,
coherent, and vigorous, the best equipped in every essential
way to turn all alternatives to their advantage, and to win. More
elaborately than any others they have developed a science of
contempt for present humanity, including themselves in their
own scruples as individuals, in the name of future humanity,

and a science for utilizing, and conquering, those who believe merely in each other, or merely in self-advantage.

Harmless therefore as these ten men seem to me as individuals—harmless and, some of them, a good deal better than that, and contemptible as those are who have fingered them out, or who have run from the opportunity to defend them and their own self-respect, it seems merely sensible to recognize Stalinists in general as particularly dangerous enemies and to settle as best one can the unhappy question whether or not one prefers, in the name of the brotherhood of man, to offer legal protection to a professional assassin in the practice of his vocation among the members of one's family. A secondary meditation might—or might not,—determine which members of the family are classifiable, not necessarily as human, or friends, but at least as enemies who can be lived with; and which of them can qualify even as watch dogs.

Yet the real crucial conflict is not between the Stalinists and the nominal democracies. It is between those who honor existence and so, necessarily, morality and those who honor either only in the hypothetical future, if at all. I have a few personal opinions as to who is who and how to know them apart; some Stalinists, I am sure, and even, believe it or not, a Congressman or two qualify more honorably than group-mad bigots can ever suspect as members rather than enemies of the human race. But to venture such opinions, of interest to few, of use to none, would be the more frivolous and impertinent for a reason somewhat more grave. Those whom I regard as friends and fellow-soldiers, many of them conscious and unimaginable millions of them never to become conscious, have already lost. And those whom I regard as enemies are already so securely in charge, throughout the governing of the world and throughout the so-called opposition groups, that one can care very little who fends off or dislodges whom, or which laws and principles, long insulted and injured, are at last officially put out of their misery—very little except in the tragicomic intelligence and in a small but acute personal way. I shall presumably die a so-called natural death if the civilization within which I live continues in anything roughly like its present form—unless, of course, I offend one of its idiotic machines. If it does not so continue, I assume that my death will be even less welcome and more terrible than the considerable talent of nature ordinarily provides. I doubt that it will continue. It has been rotting above ground, on its feet, legally classified as alive, for a long while already, and will destroy itself either by failure to shut out enough of its enemies, or by definitively violating its own nature in its primordial efforts to defend itself, or by shutting out, along with some of the more conspicuous of its enemies, all those who might conceivably preserve within it some last flicker of humanistic sanity. Whatever happens, I doubt that war will ever be joined on the only issue which sane men could whole-heartedly give themselves for.

January 10, 1948

A FEW notes about the best movies released in the United States during the past year.

The best was Jean Vigo's *Zero de Conduite*. It was the one film which worked deeply within pure motion-picture style, and it extended the possibilities of style and expression as brilliantly, and germinally, as the best work of Griffith, Chaplin, Eisenstein, Dovzhenko, and Murnau. It was made fourteen or fifteen years ago, and nothing so adventurous in terms of pure movie expressiveness has been made since.

Chaplin's *Monsieur Verdoux* is as adventurous in every other respect. It is not the best of Chaplin's films, but it is the most endlessly interesting. Beside it every movie since *Zero* and *Modern Times* is so much child's play. Incidentally, as two samples of the hundreds of things which I, or somebody, should have pointed out: the Verdoux character is obviously developed out of the first character Chaplin played in movies—the slick, shady little masher with Verdoux's own wicked mustache, who gradually refined into the tramp; and the name Verdoux means Mild Worm.

Vittorio da Sica's *Shoeshine* and Luigi Zampa's *To Live in Peace* were overrated by nearly everyone, flagrantly including me. I can think of two excellent reasons. Although there were many poor or not good enough things about both pictures, both essentially were made from the heart, and so touched the heart. The other reason is merely a paraphrase of that. They

were made in a creative generosity and fearlessness which
except in the best of jazz has been dead, or at best semi-
paralyzed, in art, so far as I know, since the death of Verdi. But
it is important to remember also, more coolly than I was able
to, that they are not completed works of art, or anywhere near
it, but are the raw or at best the roughed-out materials of art.

André Malraux's *Man's Hope* is probably a very fine and
moving film only for those who, like myself, bring special attitudes of mind to it. That is, I would have to grant that plenty
of competent critics who came to it cold would think it largely
a failure. Right or wrong, I care a great deal for work which
requires special attitudes of those who will fully appreciate it.
But I am bound to respect the judgment of the "cold" critics;
and I prefer them infinitely to those who patronize such a picture. A friend wrote me, not long after *Man's Hope* opened,
about a talk she had had with such a comfortable Friend of the
Cinema as Bennett Cerf, who said that it was really a surprisingly good picture, considering the difficulties under which it
was made—that is, on and near the war front in Spain, catch
as catch can, between fights. My friend observed that Mr. Cerf
and his kind would undoubtedly say of Jesus Christ that He
conducted a really remarkably effective crucifixion, considering that He was nailed to a cross.

John Ford's *The Fugitive* is a solidly pro-Catholic picture
about a priest, a creeping Jesus. My feelings about the Catholic
church are, to put it mildly, more mixed than Mr. Ford's; I
doubt that Jesus ever crept, and I am sickened when I watch
others creep in His name; I dislike allegory and symbolism
which are imposed on and denature reality as deeply as I love
both when they bloom from and exalt reality; and romantic
photography is the kind I care for least. Over all, I think *The
Fugitive* is a bad work of art, tacky, unreal, and pretentious.
Yet I think almost as highly of it as of the films mentioned
above, because I have seldom seen in a moving picture such
grandeur and sobriety of ambition, such continuous intensity
of treatment, or such frequent achievement of what was obviously worked for, however distasteful or misguided I think it.

Elia Kazan's *Boomerang* is a work of journalistic art, which
isn't necessarily a paradox, and of that kind is perfect. David
Lean's *Great Expectations* is an over-sunny transcription of

Dickens, and it seems to me primarily unimportant how well or ill somebody else's classic is brought to film; but it is a very pleasant piece of entertainment, and its first half unfolds as prettily as a Japanese paper flower on water. Carol Reed's *Odd Man Out*, like *The Fugitive*, uses allegory wrong end to, but has many incredibly beautiful images of a city. Eisenstein's *Ivan the Terrible* is pitiful to think of beside his finest work, but I was fascinated by his experiments in rigidity and grandiosity. Clair's *Man About Town* can stand comparison with his best work only in visual and structural charm, but it was a delight to see him at liberty again after all these years, and this is a quietly beautiful film: if it were not for *Man About Town* and *Verdoux*, one would have to believe that the highest kind of style, economy, and grace had died out of moving pictures. Cocteau's *Beauty and the Beast* seems to me no sort of miracle, but it is a thoroughly satisfying movie; I especially liked Christian Berard's costumes, and Cocteau's absolute directness and simplicity. Edward Dmytryk's *Crossfire* has been somewhat overrated, but it is a rather good melodrama. I have not yet seen *Gentleman's Agreement*; but, quite aside from its subject matter, I have come to expect very good work of Elia Kazan.

It is really quite a year for movies, even when one remembers —as one certainly must—that some of the best films released here during 1947 were made years before. It especially struck me that a great many people in Hollywood were working harder, more frankly, more hopefully, and more artfully, than they have had the heart or the chance to in many years. Nothing great or even extraordinarily promising came of this except *Verdoux*, which can hardly be counted as a Hollywood picture; but it was an exceedingly hopeful year for American movies. It is hard to believe that absolutely first-rate works of art can ever again be made in Hollywood, but it would be idiotic to assume that flatly. If they are to be made there, they will most probably develop along the directions worked out during the past year or two; they will be journalistic, semi-documentary, and "social-minded," or will start that way and transcend those levels. For I have no confidence that works of "pure art"—which doubtless means something—can ever be made in American studios. It is now an absolute certainty that every most hopeful thing that has been stirring in Hollywood is petrified more grimly than ever before. The firing of the Ten Contemptuous Men was merely the most conspicuous death spasm; I doubt that from now on—for how long it is impossible to imagine—anyone in Hollywood will dare even to breathe loudly.

January 31, 1948

SEVERAL of the best people in Hollywood grew, noticeably, during their years away at war; the man who grew most impressively, I thought, as an artist, as a man, in intelligence, in intransigence, and in an ability to put through fine work against difficult odds, was John Huston, whose *San Pietro* and *Let There Be Light* were full of evidence of this many-sided growth. I therefore looked forward with the greatest eagerness to the work he would do after the war.

His first movie since the war has been a long time coming, but it was certainly worth waiting for. *The Treasure of the Sierra Madre* is Huston's adaptation of B. Traven's novel of the same title. It is not quite a completely satisfying picture, but on the strength of it I have no doubt at all that Huston, next only to Chaplin, is the most talented man working in American pictures, and that this is one of the movie talents in the world which is most excitingly capable of still further growth. *The Treasure* is one of very few movies made since 1927 which I am sure will stand up in the memory and esteem of qualified people alongside the best of the silent movies. And yet I doubt that many people will fully realize, right away, what a sensational achievement, or plexus of achievement, it is. You will seldom see a good artist insist less on his artistry; Huston merely tells his story so straight and so well that one tends to become absorbed purely in that; and the story itself—a beauty —is not a kind which most educated people value nearly enough, today.

This story and Huston's whole handling of it are about as near to folk art as a highly conscious artist can get; both also approach the global appeal, to the most and least sophisticated members of an audience, which the best poetic drama and nearly all the best movies have in common. Nominally an adventure story, this is really an exploration of character as revealed in vivid action; and character and action yield revelations of their own, political, metaphysical, moral, above all, poetic. The story unfolds so pleasurably on the screen that I will tell as little as possible of it here. Three American bums of the early 1920s (Walter Huston, Humphrey Bogart, Tim Holt) run into lottery luck in Tampico and strike into the godforsaken mountains of Mexico in search of gold. The rest of the story merely demonstrates the development of their characters in relation to hardship and hard work, to the deeply primitive world these modern primitives are set against, to the gold they find, and to each other. It is basically a tragic story and at times a sickeningly harsh one; most of it is told as cheerfully brutal sardonic comedy.

This may be enough to suggest how rich the story is in themes, semi-symbols, possible implications, and potentialities as a movie. Huston's most wonderful single achievement is that he focuses all these elements as simply as rays in a burning-glass: all you see, unless you look sharp, is a story told so truly and masterfully that I suspect the picture's best audience is the kind of men the picture is about, who will see it only by chance.

But this single achievement breaks down into many. I doubt we shall ever see a film more masculine in style; or a truer movie understanding of character and of men; or as good a job on bumming, a bum's life, a city as a bum sees it; or a more beautiful job on a city; or a finer portrait of Mexico and Mexicans (compare it with all the previous fancy-filter stuff for a definitive distinction between poetry and poeticism); or a crueler communication of absolute desolateness in nature and its effect on men (except perhaps in *Greed*); or a much more vivid communication of hardship, labor, and exhaustion (though I wish these had been brutally and meticulously presented rather than skillfully sketched); or more intelligent handling of amateurs and semi-professionals (notably the amazing character who plays Gold-Hat, the bandit leader); or a finer selective eye for location or a richer understanding of how to use it; or scenes of violence or building toward violence more deeply authentic and communicative (above all in Huston's terrific use of listlessness); or smarter casting than that of Tim Holt as the youngest bum and that of Bruce Bennett as an intrusive Texan; or better acting than Walter Huston's beautiful performance; or subtler and more skillful collusions and variations of tempo (two hours have certainly never been better used in a movie); or a finer balance, in Ted McCord's perfect camera work, in every camera set-up, in every bit of editing, of unaffectedness, and sensitiveness. (As one fine example of that blend I recommend watching for the shot of Gold-Hat reflected in muddy water, which is so subtly photographed that in this noncolor film the hat seems to shed golden light.) There is not a shot-for-shot's sake in the picture, or one too prepared-looking, or dwelt on too long. The camera is always where it ought to be, never imposes on or exploits or over-dramatizes its subject, never for an instant shoves beauty or special meaning at you. This is one of the most visually alive and beautiful movies I have ever seen; there is a wonderful flow of fresh air, light, vigor, and liberty through every shot, and a fine athlete's litheness and absolute control and flexibility in every succession and series of shots. Huston shows that he is already capable of literally anything in movies except the profoundest kind of movie inventiveness, the most extreme kind of poetic concentration, artiness, soft or apathetic or sloppy or tasteless or excessive work, and rhetoric whether good or bad. His style is practically invisible as well as practically universal in its possible good uses; it is the most virile movie style I know of; and is the purest style in contemporary movies, here or abroad.

I want to say a little more about Walter Huston; a few thousand words would suit me better. Rightly or wrongly, one thing that adds to my confidence that the son, so accomplished already, will get better and better, is the fact that the father has done that, year after year. I can think of nothing more moving or happier than every instance in which an old man keeps right on learning, and working, and improving, as naturally and eagerly as a child learns the fundamentals of walking, talking, and everything else in sight until his parents and teachers destroy his appetite for learning. Huston has for a long time been one of the best actors in the world and he is easily the most likable; on both counts this performance crowns a lifetime. It is an all but incredible submergence in a role, and transformation; this man who has credibly played

Lincoln looks small and stocky here, and is as gaily vivacious as a water bug. The character is beautifully conceived and written, but I think it is chiefly Walter Huston who gives it its almost Shakespearean wonderfulness, charm, and wisdom. In spite of the enormous amount of other talent at large in the picture, Huston carries the whole show as deftly and easily as he handles his comedy lines.

There are a few weaknesses in the picture, most of which concern me so little I won't even bother to mention them. Traven's Teutonic or Melvillean excitability as a poet and metaphysician sometimes, I think, misleads him—and John Huston; magnificently as Walter Huston does it, and deeply as he anchors it in flesh and blood, the Vast Gale of Purifying Laughter with which he ends the picture strikes me as unreal, stuck-onto-the-character, close to arty; yet I feel tender toward this kind of cliché, if I'm right that it is one. One thing I do furiously resent is the intrusion of background-music. There is relatively little of it and some of it is better than average, but there shouldn't be any, and I only hope and assume that Huston fought the use of it. The only weakness which strikes me as fundamental, however, is deep in the story itself: it is the whole character of the man played by Bogart. This is, after all, about gold and its effects on those who seek it, and so it is also a fable about all human life in this world and about much of the essence of good and evil. Many of the possibilities implicit in this fable are finely worked out. But some of the most searching implications are missed. For the Bogart character is so fantastically undisciplined and troublesome that it is impossible to demonstrate or even to hint at the real depth of the problem, with him on hand. It is too easy to feel that if only a reasonably restrained and unsuspicious man were in his place, everything would be all right; we wouldn't even have wars. But virtually every human being carries sufficient of that character within him to cause a great deal of trouble, and the demonstration of that fact, and its effects, could have made a much greater tragicomedy—much more difficult, I must admit, to dramatize. Bogart does a wonderful job with this character as written (and on its own merits it is quite a character), miles ahead of the very good work he has done before. The only trouble is that one cannot quite forget that this is Bogart putting on an unbelievably good act. In all but a few movies one would thank God for that large favor. In this one it stands out, harmfully to some extent, for everything else about the picture is selfless.

It seems worth mentioning that the only thing which holds this movie short of unarguable greatness is the failure of the story to develop some of the most important potentialities of the theme. In other words, "Hollywood," for once, is accountable only for some minor flaws. This is what it was possible to do in Hollywood, if you were talented enough, had standing enough, and were a good enough fighter, during the very hopeful period before the November Freeze. God knows what can be done now. But if anybody can hope to do anything, I count on Huston, who made *San Pietro* and *Let There Be Light* as an army officer and *The Treasure of the Sierra Madre* as a Hollywood writer-director.

February 14, 1948

MIDWINTER CLEARANCE

Albuquerque. An actor, shot at, grabs his kneecap and falls down stairs. Within a few seconds he is able to explain, in a politely stoical voice, that he isn't badly hurt—just hit in the leg. This is a fair measure of how intimately most movies are acquainted with even the most rudimentary realities of experience. A good excruciating crack on every kneecap that needs it might be enough to revolutionize Hollywood. Even if it didn't, it would be a pleasure to deliver.

A Lover's Return. Louis Jouvet, in charge of a ballet troupe, gets back to Lyon after twenty years and torments the bourgeois types who did him dirt. The story is essentially sub-Montherlant trash, but it is acutely understood, easily filmed, and nicely played. Pleasant ballet stuff, backstage and on.

An Ideal Husband. Vincent Korda's sets are good, Cecil Beaton's costumes are mouth-watering, and most of the players are visually right. The composing and cutting of this fine raw material is seldom above medium grade. Wilde's lines are unevenly and in general too slowly and patiently delivered, and the whole production is too slow and realistic.

A Woman's Vengeance. Aldous Huxley's screen play of his *Gioconda Smile.* A rather literary movie, but most movies aren't even that; much less are they real movies. Sensitively directed by Zoltan Korda and generally well played, above all by Jessica Tandy.

Bush Christmas. Australian children hound horse thieves through some beautiful wilderness. A child's-eye movie, not imaginative enough, but simple and likable.

Captain from Castile. The first few reels have flow and a kind of boys'-book splendor; the rest is locomotor ataxia. The costumes of Montezuma's emissaries are as magnificent as any I have ever seen. They are utilized, for movie purposes, about as appreciatively as so many sack suits.

Furia. An Italian farmer's wife plays around with a Cornel Wilde-ish groom. This is filmed with a carnal and psychological frankness I am happy to see—and to thank the censors for saving a good deal of—and the picture is essentially sincere rather than pornographic. It is also rather childish in conception and inept as art. Good work by the two most prominent women in the cast.

Golden Earrings. Dietrich as a gipsy, Ray Milland as a British agent. Dreary comedy-melodrama; a good bit by Reinhold Schunzel.

Good News. I like the tunes and June Allyson. Joan McCracken makes me think of a libidinous peanut; Mel Torme reminds me of something in a jar but is, unfortunately, less quiet. If they had used the old George Olson arrangements on the tunes and had had any real feeling for the late twenties, this could have been a beauty.

If Winter Comes. In its essence this tearjerker is much better than the determinedly tearproof allow themselves to realize. From there on out it is pretty awful. Rather well played; an overdone but promising performance by Janet Leigh.

I Walk Alone. Good performances by Wendell Corey and Kirk Douglas; a sharp scene about an old-fashioned gangster's helplessness against modern business methods. Some better than ordinary night-club atmosphere. Otherwise the picture deserves, like four out of five other movies, to walk alone, tinkle a little bell, and cry "Unclean, unclean."

Mourning Becomes Electra. In my opinion a badly mistaken

play; so, a bad mistake to turn into a movie, especially a reverential movie. Within its own terms of mistaken reverence it seems to me a good, straight, deliberately unimaginative production.

The Paradine Case. Hitchcock uses a lot of skill over a lot of nothing. Some very experienced work by Laughton and Leo G. Carroll; better work by Ann Todd and Joan Tetzel, who is at moments very beautiful. Valli is something to look at, too. The picture never for an instant comes to life. This is the wordiest script since the death of Edmund Burke.

The Road to Rio. Hope, Crosby, Lamour. Enough laughs to pass the time easily and to remind you how completely, since sound came in, the American genius for movie comedy has disintegrated.

The Secret Beyond the Door. Because he thought his mother didn't love him, the poor fellow developed a terrible, but of course forgivable, compulsion to kill women. Fritz Lang gets a few wood-silky highlights out of this sow's ear, but it is a hopeless job and a worthless movie.

The Senator Was Indiscreet. Kaufman, MacArthur, and Nunnally Johnson put William Powell through some loosely adjusted political wringers. Most of it would seem feeble in print or on stage, but because of the generally vapid state of the movies it seems quite bold and funny on the screen.

T-Man. This is being over-promoted and overrated, but it is an enjoyable and energetic semi-documentary melodrama.

This Time for Keeps. Jimmy Durante; Esther Williams; some shiny bellowing from Lauritz Melchior; an attempt at off-beat locale work in Michigan; Metro's customary brats and goodwill; a lot of boring music; Technicolor. The money spent on this production might easily have kept Mozart and Schubert alive and busy to the age of sixty, with enough left over to finance five of the best movies ever made. It might even have been invested in a good movie musical.

Tycoon. Several tons of dynamite are set off in this movie; none of it under the right people.

You Were Meant for Me. That's what you think.

March 13, 1948

Farrebique was made on a farm in southern France by Georges Rouquier, who was born and raised in the neighborhood, left home and became a linotyper, and ultimately got into movie-making because he couldn't keep away from it. Rouquier had made only one short film before this, a documentary about the making of wine vats. Both the subject of the new film and the particular kind of movie treatment happen to be obsessions of mine; so I cannot hope that many other people will be as deeply excited and satisfied by this film as I am. On the other hand, it is clear to me that because of the same obsessions I would be more merciless toward any mismanagements and betrayals, of the subject or in the treatment, than most people would.

Rouquier's idea is simply to make a record of the work and living of a single farm family, and of the farm itself, and of the surrounding countryside, through one year. I cannot imagine a better subject, or one that is as a rule more degenerately perceived and presented. In a sense, all that can be said of Rouquier's treatment of it is that it is right. That means, among other things, the following:

He realizes that, scrupulously handled, the camera can do what nothing else in the world can do: can record unaltered reality; and can be made also to perceive, record, and communicate, in full unaltered power, the peculiar kinds of poetic vitality which blaze in every real thing and which are in great degree, inevitably and properly, lost to every other kind of artist except the camera artist. He is utterly faithful to this realization; and it is clear in nearly every shot that he is infinitely more than a mere documentor, that his poetic intelligence is profound, pure, and vigorous; and it is clear many times over that he has the makings, and now and then the achievement, of a major poet. There is not an invented person or thing in the picture, and the reenactments, and invented incidents, are perfect examples of the discipline of imagination necessary under these difficult circumstances. One could watch the people alone, indefinitely long, for the inference of his handling of them, to realize that moral clearness and probity are indispensable to work of this kind, and to realize with fuller contempt than ever before how consistently in our time so-called simple people, fictional and nonfictional, are consciously and unconsciously insulted and betrayed by artists and by audiences: it seems as if the man is hardly alive, any more, who is fit to look another man in the eye. But this man is; and this is the finest and strongest record of actual people that I have seen.

Rouquier's sense of the discretion and power of plot and incident, such as they are, is just as sure and as rare. Even more remarkable is his ability with all the small casual scraps of existence which are neither plot nor incident nor even descriptive, nor revealing of mood or character, but are merely themselves, and of the essence of being. He never imposes poetry or rhetoric or special significance upon these scraps, and they are never left half-dead and helpless, as mere shots-for-shots'-sake: they are incredibly hard stuff to organize, but he has so ordered them that they are fully and euphoniously articulate in their own perfect language. He knows as well as any artist I can think of the power and the beauty there can be in absolute plainness: his record, for instance, of the differing faces of three men and two women as they stand in their home for night prayer; or the mere sequence of bedding down the cows. Much of the picture, and much of the finest of it, has this complete plainness; but raised against this ground bass Rouquier's sense of device and metaphor is equally bold and pure. He develops a wonderful communication of the rooted past, the flowering present, and the ungerminated future in about three minutes during which the Grandfather tells the children the history of the farm and family, while the camera examines snapshots and mementos which are like relics from a primitive grave. He does a beautiful thing in showing the dreams of the old man, his son, his son's wife, wishes as touching and naive as those of a child: then hovers the dreamless face of the Grandmother. His use of analogy and metaphor is Homeric in simplicity and force: the terrifying blooming of a sped flower, as an image of childbirth; the sound of an ax and of a falling tree as the camera watches a man's pulse die. He uses stop-motion as I have always wanted to use it: very plainly, to show the motions of darkness and light and shadow; and with complete freedom and daring, in his orgiastic sequence on spring, to show the jubilant rending and pouring upward and blossoming of the

world. This sequence is as prescient and as primordially exciting as the *Pervigilium Veneris*. He also dares to add to it—
almost whispered, as it should be—a poem of his own; and so
well as I could hear, it is an extremely good poem. I'm not
sure the picture wouldn't be still better without it; yet it adds a
quality and full dimension of its own, and in principle I am for
it. In one sense this film is a kind of Bible which expounds not
only the grave kinds of discipline necessary to such work but
also the kinds, degrees, and tremendous reaches of liberty and
adventure which obedience to these kinds of discipline makes
possible.

Bosley Crowther of the *Times* has written that *Farrebique* is
"lacking in strong dramatic punch . . . not even a plain folk
triangle," and that it will have to depend for support upon
"the loyal, the very loyal." I don't feel that Mr. Crowther
means ill by the film—though there is a certain patronizing air
toward those who are poky and arty enough to admire it—and
I thoroughly disenjoy derogation by name; but when a great
work of art is dismissed so casually as not so good as "the classic French film, *Harvest*" (!), I find that I am loyal, very loyal.
By no means all the great poetry in the world, especially the
kind which is uniquely possible to moving pictures, is or can
stand to be dramatic; and this picture is not for cultists, but for
those who have eyes capable of seeing what is before them,
and minds and hearts capable of caring for what they see.
Others have complained that the film is repetitious. It is, exactly in the sense that the imitation and counterpoint and
recurrence in a Mozart symphony are repetitious, and somewhere near as satisfyingly.

Rouquier's film is so far above and beyond the fat-headed
"instructiveness" of most nonfiction films that I wish he had
shown that even "instructive" material can transcend its kind.
Even within his scheme as I understand it one should make
clear just what the family lives on and just how it gets its living:
but we don't know for sure, here, what is for subsistence and
what goes to market. I wish also that there was a fuller record
of the undomesticated natural year, as distinct from the farm; I
learn that Rouquier wished so too, tried very hard for it, and
could not get enough of what he was after—exactly the right
shots of a fox, the flight of a crow, and so on. On "inanimate"

nature and the differing lights of weathers and seasons, however, he was as right as it is imaginable to be. Whatever devices may have been used to help out the camera, they are used legitimately, that is, invisibly, and in order that the film may accept the exact light the world gives it; and in this the film is full of lovely achievements: subdued autumnal light in which the whole world is as scratchily distinct as trillions of little briars; the veiled shining of spring; the supernal light beneath impounded thunder; the holy light of snow. I would suppose, but am not sure, that with infra-red, or through stop-motion, luminous night images might have been had, of the woods and the open land, deep in the darkness—or throughout one night, condensed into a minute; of the luminousness of fallen snow in still, open woods during a cloudy night; of storming snow in the dark; of the stars. If these things were possible, I am very sorry not to see them here: sorriest, I guess, not to see what would have come of two shots: the stop-motion camera trained throughout one night upon the Pole Star, and upon the zenith on a moonless and starry night; so that in either case the whole sky turns, and bit by bit obliterates with morning. I think it is probable, too, that beautifully as the shots are articulated, and strong and rich as they are in poetry, they are seldom ordered into the definitive, unforgettable eloquence of the highest poetry which might have been made out of the subject. But it will take a good many seeings before I can be sure of that. I am sure already, however, of one thing. Whether or not this film is fully as great as it might have been, it is one of the finer works in the whole great line of rural art which extends backward through Van Gogh and Brueghel to the *Georgics* and to the *Works and Days*. It combines the cold deep-country harshness of Hesiod with a Vergilian tenderness and majesty; and its achievement is wholly of our time, through that reverence for unaltered reality which can be translated into a work of art only through the camera.

I had to choose between writing of this film, which indicates that the greatness of moving pictures is by no means over, and writing of the death and tragic life of Sergei Eisenstein, in whom so many of the greatest possibilities conceivable in the medium were for a long while imprisoned and tormented, and now lie buried. I ultimately chose the former, not in any sentimental favoring of life over death, but because Eisenstein was a great hero to me, and I found that I could not hope to speak of him as I wished to, in a thousand words or so. I would be thankful, for his sake, that his life is over; but since for years on end, under unspeakable provocation, he successfully resisted suicide and martyrdom and madness in order to serve his genius as best he still could, he cannot be congratulated, with a whole heart, upon an escape he never sought.

April 24, 1948

H ERE are twenty-five more of them.

All My Sons. The Arthur Miller prize-winner. A feast for the self-righteous; Ibsen for beginners; for the morally curious a sad bore. By the standards of the Screen Writers' Guild this sort of thing is the white hope of Hollywood. Entirely well-intended and sincerely acted; but not an interesting play, and certainly not a movie.

Angelina. A sloppy job from Italy, with a few fine flashes from Anna Magnani.

Bill and Coo. Over two hundred trained birds, complete with neckties, hats, etc., waddle around an anthropornithomorphic community called Chirpendale. By conservative estimate, the God-damnedest thing ever seen.

Call Northside 777. A rather dogged but otherwise competent fact-fiction movie; good camera work on Chicago slums; intelligent use of natural sound. Next to *Boomerang!* the best, so far, of its kind.

Crime and Punishment. A Swedish version; deeply felt, impoverished, intelligent, and uninspired.

Fanny. Pagnol, at it again: unmarried pregnancy. Some nice moments and some very nice acting, but much too wordy, slow, and smug.

The Idiot. A skillful, sensitive, intense reduction, with beautiful work by Gerard Philippe, Edwige Feuillière, and Lucien Coedel. The most satisfying movie version of a Dostoevski novel that I have seen. It was adapted by Charles Spaak and directed by Georges Lampin.

I Remember Mama. Much more love and talent are devoted

to this show than the basic show is worth. A beautifully shaded production; a good deal of skillful acting and direction; subtle outdoor work by the cameraman, Nicholas Musaraca. A mild but generally gratifying "family" movie.

Jenny Lamour. Jealousy, crime, and consequences among small-time Parisian entertainers, well acted by Jouvet, Bernard Blier, and the succulent Suzy Delair. The director, Henri-Georges Clouzot, has an uncanny flair for occupational detail; a Germanic eye; French pace. Of its kind—intelligent trash—nearly perfect.

Killer McCoy. A harmless, worthless movie about prize-fighting, almost old-fashioned enough to be nostalgically likable; a coolly magical performance by Mickey Rooney; good support from James Dunn and Ann Blyth.

The Miracle of the Bells. As pernicious a gobbet of pseudo-religious asafetida as I have been forced to sniff at, man and Sunday-school-boy. I hereby declare myself the founding father of a Society for the Prevention of Cruelty to God.

Mr. Blanding Builds His Dream House. How to go broke on $15,000 a year, efficiently demonstrated by Myrna Loy, Cary Grant, and Melvyn Douglas. A bull's-eye for middle-class middle-brows. For the low and the high not hard to take and just as easy to let alone.

The Naked City. With the Homicide Boys in Old Manhattan. Photographed by William Daniels—who shot *Greed*—with a lovely eye for space, size, and light. A visually majestic finish. Otherwise, mawkish and naive.

Out of the Past. Conventional private-eye melodrama. More good work by Musaraca, largely wasted. Kirk Douglas, wasted as usual. Bob Mitchum is so very sleepily self-confident with the women that when he slopes into clinches you expect him to snore in their faces.

Paisan. Italian-American wartime relationships, in six episodes. The director, Roberto Rosselini, is being overrated by most people, underrated by some. I see no signs of originality in his work; a sickening lack of mental firmness, of fundamental moral aliveness, and of taste; but at his best an extremely vigorous talent for improvisation, for naturalistic poetry, and for giving the illusion of the present tense. He is the best of the few good improvisers at work. The best of this movie is the best that has come out of Italy; highly gratifying and exciting; the worst is sycophantic, vulgar, lick-spittle stuff which could begin to be forgivable only in a man of, say, D. W. Griffith's size.

The Pearl. A poor Mexican fisherman finds a great pearl—the Wealth of Nations and the Hope of Man; he and his wife and child suffer the quasi-tragic consequences. These simple folk speak a kind of pseudo-Biblical Choctaw, by Steinbeck; most of the posing and camera work is earnestly luscious salon idealization. An extremely sincere and high-minded effort and, in my opinion, perfectly lousy "art." There's a lot of stuff like it, nowadays. It's all the contemporary equivalent, come to think of it, of Tennyson's *Idylls of the King.* The difference is that then the heroes were well-born people who had never existed and so were in no position to object. In our more democratic times the very salt of the earth is reverently changed into so much stale saccarin. And nobody objects. In both cases the artist's target is the big, soggy heart of the middle class, which doesn't know anything about art, that is, about objectivity and imagination, but which certainly likes what it knows.

The Raven. A poison-pen maniac upsets a French town. By no means as malign or as brilliant as it's cracked up to be but a sour, clever, amusing job, directed by Clouzot. Yes, yes, it was made in occupied France, by Frenchmen, for a German-controlled company; and what the hell of it?

Relentless. The careful, pretty production and the decent work of Robert Young and Marguerite Chapman are better than this Western story deserves.

The Search. A displaced mother and child seek and find each other in American Germany. Awfully well intended and sometimes sweet or touching, but pathetically mild and unimaginative, as if it had been made to interest American clubwomen in sending CARE packages—as indeed I wish they would. At one point, while starving children grab for bread, a lady commentator informs one that they are hungry, and that the bread is bread.

The Sign of the Ram. A vapid "psychological" melodrama in which Susan Peters polishes off a hearty histrionic banquet at her leisure while several other likable players—Phyllis Thaxter,

Diana Douglas, Allene Roberts, Alexander Knox—snap forlornly at scraps.

Sitting Pretty. Clifton Webb's prim snottiness is amusing in an otherwise expendable farce.

The Smugglers. A costume story about a coward, by Graham Greene out of maybe Stevenson. With more style this might have been rather good. Outside of life more private than I am normally party to I can't remember hearing so many men so often say, to other men, "I *hate* him!" "I *hate* you!"

Voyage Surprise. Jacques Prévert and his brother Pierre: a neo-neo-primitive, post-post-surrealist frisk in the Mack Sennett manner. Loose, lazy, and I fear fundamentally arty, but I enjoyed it. I am apparently the only man in North America who did. It is more essentially a movie than any other reviewed in this installment. That's one strike against it. Another: it is visual comedy, not verbal.

Where There's Life. Bob Hope and his Giant Concupiscence. Some laughs, all of them verbal; no harm in the word. *Voyage Surprise* is better than *that*, anyhow, damn it all.

May 22, 1948

By the time John McCarten's very favorable review of Carl Dreyer's *Day of Wrath* appeared in the *New Yorker*, the picture was through, at the Little Carnegie. It quite possibly wasn't liked during its short run; but it appears to have been killed at the outset by the daily reviewers. Only two of them, Rose Pelswick and Archer Winsten, reviewed it favorably; the next day Winsten—who also stood practically alone for *Monsieur Verdoux* last year—wrote a valiant, sore article in the film's defense, and in contempt for the degenerate taste of most of his colleagues. In the Sunday *Times* for May 9 Bosley Crowther took a swing, in turn, at Winsten, and wrote of the film: "The tax of [Dreyer's] slow and ponderous tempo upon the average person's time is a rather presumptuous imposition for any motion-picture artist to make. Maybe the cultists can take it. But is it justified? Is it art?"

Hearing the slow movement of Beethoven's "Archduke"

Trio, Mr. Crowther might find the tax of Beethoven's slow and ponderous tempo upon the average person's time—meaning, one supposes, *his* time—an equally presumptuous imposition, and might dismiss those who don't agree with him as "cultists," into the bargain; but he still would have said nothing which justified him in asking the rhetorical questions, "Is it justified? Is it art?" It is, after all, possible to use slowness as artfully as speed, in moving pictures as well as in music, and the reactions of the average person are seldom a good indication of how well or ill it has been used; and not even reviewers are necessarily any better qualified.

Winsten wrote me that he felt sure that if some exhibitor with a small overhead would reopen the picture, he could make a go of it. Crowther wrote much the same thing in his column: "Skeptics and outraged art lovers will have to catch it in the tea-spots"—by no chance, of course, to be confused with the Itsy-Bitsy Carnegie—"later on." No doubt they will go, and lap up the tea; meanwhile I suspect that a sustaining number of intelligent and unaffected human beings will wander in and enjoy the show. Winsten and McCarten think it is one of the best ever made. I don't care quite that much for it, but of the movies made during the past twenty years I think it is unquestionably one of the dozen or so best worth seeing. I'll write further of it, in the hope that *enough* favorable reviews may prompt some people to ask small-theater exhibitors about it, and may encourage some exhibitors to risk a few days of it, anyhow. I can at least guarantee them, and any prospective customers, that it is a hundred times better than the run of stuff that shows in the art theaters, genially indorsed by the reviewers who flick this one off their cuffs.

Day of Wrath, which is set in seventeenth-century Denmark, is a study of the struggle between good and evil as waged among—and within—witches, those who burned them, and the members of an old man–young wife–stepson triangle. Movies seldom contain any material, except by inadvertence or head-on outrage, which can interest the morally curious; this one contains a good deal, and none of it is inadvertent or outrageous. I particularly respect the film's interest in the deeply entangled interproductiveness of good and evil among several people and within single people; its steep, Lutheran kind of probity—that is, its absolute recognition of the responsibility of the individual, regardless of extenuating or compulsive circumstances; its compassion; and its detachment.

Originally this was a novel. As I watched it I had to realize that it could still as easily be a novel, or a play; nevertheless, Carl Dreyer has done a very hard job beautifully. He has not only preserved an amount of psychological and moral complexity which isn't popularly supposed to be possible in movies; he has also made them very clear visually, as a rule by very simple means. I don't ordinarily like stuff that is shot in the dark or that depends on very slow movement, because these are ordinarily the first resources of the merely solemn, or pretentious, or arty, when they have nothing of what it takes except ambition. Even less do I ordinarily care for "art" references in camera work—approximations, or reproductions, of famous paintings, or a style derived from painting. I'm not sure I can entirely take this in Dreyer's film, though in general his sense of how and why to use what he wants to take from Rembrandt and others seems very just, modest, useful, clear of "culturalism" or mere weakness of personal style; and his one conspicuous derivation—from Rembrandt's "Lesson in Anatomy" —lends more than mere ironic vitality to the watching clergymen in a torture scene.

Dreyer's lighting, and pace, and sound—including his use of dialogue—I wholly respect. My impression is that, short of absurdity, he wants to work close to their respective absolutes of darkness, stasis, and silence, and never to deviate from these absolutes beyond the minimum that is justified. I don't think this is the only good way to work or necessarily the best; but I suspect for instance that Gluck, and Beethoven, in some of their finest music, were acutely aware of silence. I'm not implying that Dreyer has done anything here to approach their work; I do mean that the style he has worked out for this film has a severe, noble purity which very little else in movies or, so far as I know, in contemporary art can approach, or even tries to. By one seeing, anyhow, I don't think there is a single excess in word or lighting or motion, or a single excessive stopping-down of any of these. Dreyer appears to know and to care more about faces than about anything else; it seems to me a sound preference; and since he is served at worst by very good actors and faces and at best by wonderful ones, the finest things in this film are his close-ups. They are held longer than anyone else except Chaplin could dare or afford to hold them; and as a rule they convey the kind of intricate subtlety, mental and spiritual, which one can ordinarily expect to find only in certain kinds of writing.

In these long close-ups, as in much else that he does, Dreyer goes against most of the "rules" that are laid down, even by good people, for making genuine and good motion pictures. In a sense I have to admit that he is far out at the edge rather than close to the center of all that I think might be most productive and original. But there is only one rule for movies that I finally care about: that the film interest the eyes, and do its job through the eyes. Few movie-makers do that, few even of those who are generally well esteemed. Dreyer has never failed to, and I cannot imagine that he ever will. For that reason alone, even if I did not also respect him as one of the few moralists, and classicists, and incorruptible artists, in movies, I would regard him as a master and this film as a quiet masterpiece.

June 19, 1948

I AM still trailing *Anna Karenina* and *Dreams That Money Can Buy* by several lengths, but I've caught up on a number of others:

Another Part of the Forest. Lillian Hellman's saber-toothed play about the new-born New South, ardently acted, and directed with sense and tension by Michael Gordon. Smart casting of instruments, musicians, and music, for a deep-provincial "musical evening." Some alert intercutting of reactions around a smoldering dinner table. Is unusually good hybridization of stage and screen drama.

Arch of Triumph. Some real talent, and a lot of desperate effort, lost in a picture God wisely forsook. If you haven't lived until you've seen Bergman love Boyer, you should have stood in bed.

The Big Clock. An overrated but slickly amusing melodrama, with many good bits of comic directing by John Farrow. A perfect performance by George Macready; the tilt of his jaw line and cigarette on his hearing that his boss has committed murder is one of the neatest moments of the season. A beautifully economical piece of cutting on a shot of an editorial conference, caught the split second before an hour's boring tension relaxes, with adjournment.

The Bride Goes Wild. Attractive June Allyson and ineffable Van Johnson in a farce so lazily done that it is lazily amusing.

The Brothers. Heavy breathing, heavier dialect, and any number of quaint folk customs on the Island of Skye. The island and its actual inhabitants are all right; the rest is Mary Webb with hair on her chest.

Casbah. The old reliable garbage of *Pépé le Moko* and *Algiers* turned into a likably unpretentious semi-musical. Disconcertingly straight work by Tony Martin and Yvonne de Carlo.

The Fuller Brush Man. Red Skelton and a fair amount of rough-hewn comedy.

Fric-Frac. Three good comedians—Fernandel, Arletty, and Michel Simon—work in second gear in a third-rate comedy about a jeweler's clerk who falls among thieves.

Green Grass of Wyoming. A white stallion and a black mare which are as magnificent as anything on the contemporary screen; and several considerably less magnificent human beings, who are around too much.

Hazard. Paulette Goddard and Macdonald Carey in perhaps an hour too much of the kind of edgy, intelligent worthlessness which Paramount turns out in its sleep.

The Iron Curtain. If it could be proved that there is any nation on earth which does *not* employ spies, that would be news. This is just the same old toothless dog biting the same old legless man. However, it is efficient melodrama, and fairly restrained in delivering its world-shaking message.

Melody Time. There seems to be an obvious connection between the Disney artists' increasing insipidity and their increasing talent for fright, but I will leave it to accredited sado-masochists to make the official discovery.

The October Man. A nice unobstreperous thriller, written and produced by Eric Ambler, starring John Mills.

The Pirate. Color worth seeing, and Gene Kelly's very ambitious, painfully misguided performance, by John Barrymore out of the elder Douglas Fairbanks. Judy Garland is good; and

Vincente Minelli's direction gives the whole business bulge and splendor. My sympathies are largely with them, for they're all really trying something—and in musical comedy, whose wonderful possibilities are too seldom realized by "artists," good or bad. Many people admire *The Pirate*, but it seems to me to have the death's-head, culture-cute, "mirthful" grin of the average Shakespearean comic.

The Sainted Sisters. Veronica Lake, Joan Caulfield, and a swarm of clichés, pleasantly kidded in a manner derived from Preston Sturges.

Scudda Hoo! Scudda Hay! Some very handsome mules, and enough reverent talk about them to turn their ears bright red.

So This Is New York. I still haven't read Lardner's *Big Town*, on which this is based; but in a quick, dry, unemphatic way this is a very entertaining movie, thanks especially to Henry Morgan, Dona Drake, and Rudy Vallee.

The Time of Your Life. Saroyan is an exasperatingly irreducible blend of Nehi and sacramental wine, and his play needs the live stage the way a fish needs water. The Cagney Brothers' loving production as nearly overcomes these handicaps as any I can imagine. James Barton's beautifully timed and pointed act is already famous, and deserves to be. In its own way James Cagney's controlling, self-effacing performance is fully as good.

They Are Not Angels. Well, who'd expect them to be; they're French parachute troops. Good in spots but very long and often next-door to tiresome.

The Woman in White. The Wilkie Collins novel, given the studious, stolid treatment ordinarily reserved for the ritual assassination of a Great Classic. This is not intended as a recommendation.

Carl Dreyer's *Day of Wrath* is now at the Fifth Avenue Playhouse; *Le Silence est d'or*, the original French version of René Clair's *Man About Town*, is at the Fifty-Fifth Street Playhouse; Garbo's *Camille* has been revived.

July 3, 1948

CINEMA 16, a film society founded in New York last fall, is not exclusively devoted to 16 mm. films. The idea is to show the best of the various kinds of documentary, pedagogical, experimental, and (sometimes) censorable movies which don't ordinarily get a showing in theaters, not even in the little theaters. Some of them do get shown around, more or less, in union halls, parish houses, schools; some others, I imagine, by societies of amateur movie-makers, or in the homes of friends, or, in a sort of extension of shop talk, among the people who made them in the first place. But in general the people who make such pictures have to work against the discouraging assumption that their work will never be seen by most of the people who might be most interested; let alone by a general audience. And, on the other end, those who might like to see such films seldom get a chance to. The only way I can imagine of getting these people and the films and their makers into any kind of healthy reciprocal acquaintance is through just this kind of subscription plan. There, I gather, the difficulties only begin: some of the distributors or owners of these movies refuse to "cooperate" at all; others make it as hard as possible rather than as easy as possible. But all this is likely to loosen up with time, and already a great deal of work, good and bad, is available.

So far as I know, Cinema 16 is the only society of its kind in the country. I only hope the idea will spread. I only wish it might spread well beyond the big key cities; for I have some idea how many interested people there are in smaller cities and small towns who never get a chance to see such films as these, or European films either. But in many communities there are probably so few of these people that they doubt they can ever develop or support any kind of subscription plan. Another difficulty is that at any distance from New York it becomes very hard to know whom to write to for information about available films, or how to begin. Alex Vogel, of Cinema 16, tells me that he has had between twenty and thirty inquiring letters from various parts of the country; so the spread is already beginning. The society will be glad to hear from anyone who is interested. The address is Cinema 16, 59 Park Avenue, New York 16.

All that is unfortunate about movies doesn't, of course, begin and end with Hollywood and the general Hollywood audience. One of the biggest mistakes that can be made and one which appears to be made remarkably often, is to assume that uncommercial or relatively uncommercial motives guarantee a good film or a good minority audience for it. Instead, such motives guarantee special temptations and liabilities, as grave at least as those imposed by rankest commercialism. Only too many documentaries make the very word seem a synonym for dullness. Only too much of the pedagogical and social content boils down to special pleading, dishonest thinking and perception, and again dullness. Only too often the experiments were not fundamentally experimental any more when movie people first borrowed them from other arts and to some extent from science back in the 1920s. And there are inevitable drawbacks about this kind of showing which so exclusively assembles the specially interested: the danger of a kind of churchy smell to the whole business which seems to me essentially much more hostile to vigorous work and vigorous enjoyment and criticism than the good honest stench of the average movie theater—the odor, if not of sanctity, of cold, arrogant, uncritical self-righteousness in the audience, in the pictures, and in those who make them. But that can't be helped, certainly not at this stage of the game anyhow. And it isn't by any means all you get. Some of the most honest, selfless, and talented people in movies work on such pictures; some of the best that can be hoped for will come from them if from anyone; and the audience is by no means all churchy. After all, there are a good many people who honestly enjoy movies, know the difference between good work and bad, and care a great deal about the difference. They are the people I hope, and assume, who will be most interested to learn more about Cinema 16.

July 24, 1948

*D*eep *Waters*. A lobsterman (Dana Andrews) and a social worker (Jean Peters) languidly dispute the future of an orphan boy (Dean Stockwell) who loves the sea. Very mildly pleasant, with good Maine Coast backgrounds, unfortunately drenched in sepia.

Dreams That Money Can Buy. A 16-mm. color movie made by Hans Richter, who made several avant-garde movies in

Germany during the 1920s. Among the contributors are Max
Ernst, Marcel Duchamps, Alexander Calder, John Latouche,
Man Ray, Darius Milhaud, John Cage, Libby Holman, Josh
White, Julien Levy. Some spirals by Duchamps are hypnotic
and attractive until they go hot-colored and pretend to be
eyes, googling desperately at a multiple image of a not-very
nude descending a staircase. Julien Levy is well cast as a sort of
middle-aged Julien Sorel. I rather liked the only music by John
Cage that I've heard, to date, though it doesn't sound as original as often advertised; more like Japanese court music simpli-
fied for an appreciation class. There is a sleek, easy ballad about
a girl with a prefabricated heart (a store-window dummy).
Much of the verbiage is so pitched that you can hear it if you
try, or take it as a sort of music if you prefer; I rather like this
idea. There is a good, scary suggestion of an octopus, by
Calder. Aside from these things the movie leaves me cold, and
some of it leaves me worse than cold. It seems at once arch,
snobbish, and sycophantic. It is about as genuinely "experimental" as a Chemcraft set, and not even its laziness is likable.
In its own terms it is as formula-ridden as the worst junk ped-
dled out of Hollywood, and I like it still less than factory junk
because it pretends to be much more than it is. I imagine that
those who made it excuse themselves a good deal on the
ground that they were trying to popularize the idioms they are
working in, as light entertainment. If so, they are excusing
themselves too easily. A fair amount of the picture is more
pleasant than average to see and hear, but against that one has
to fight off the depression of watching some talented men,
some sincere men of little or no talent, and some outrageous
fakes and hangers-on overestimating their abilities, and under-
estimating their audience and the difficult, considerable art of
really entertaining.

Easter Parade. Fred Astaire, Judy Garland, Ann Miller, and
several of Irving Berlin's old songs ought to add up to something better than this; but much of it is painless and some of
it—chiefly Astaire—is pretty good.

The Emperor Waltz. Bing Crosby, a Yankee drummer, loves
Joan Fontaine, a Viennese countess. Crosby's dog, a fox ter-
rier, loves Fontaine's dog, a poodle. The Emperor Franz Josef
himself at length declares that Americans are not merely just as

good as Austrocrats but better. That goes for their dogs too. At its best this semi-musical is amusing and well shaped, because Charles Brackett and Billy Wilder have learned a fair amount from the comedies of Ernst Lubitsch. In general it is reasonably good fun. At its worst it yaps and embraces every unguarded leg in sight.

Escape. John Galsworthy's play about a convict (Rex Harrison) who prefers freedom to security, rather nicely done by an American company in England. Apparently people a few years younger than I am are puzzled by the hero's preference. Considering the world they grew up watching, I don't wonder. But I can't help feeling it is their loss, and the world's, and about as grave a one as I can imagine.

Fighting Father Dunne. A dreary, hully-chee sort of piece about a St. Louis priest who builds a home for derelict newsboys. Pat O'Brien, an assortment of tiresome hellions, a good bit by Joseph Sawyer, and some better than average sets by RKO's Darrell Silvera and Company.

A Foreign Affair. Brackett and Wilder again, this time in American Berlin. A visiting Congresswoman (Jean Arthur), an ex-girl friend of a ranking Nazi (Marlene Dietrich), an American soldier (John Lund). Some sharp, nasty, funny stuff at the expense of investigatory Americans; then—as in *The Emperor Waltz*—the picture indorses everything it has been kidding, and worse. A good bit of it is in rotten taste, and the perfection of that is in Dietrich's song "Black Market."

Fort Apache. American soldiers and Indians shortly after the Civil War. Shirley Temple and her husband, John Agar, handle the love interest as if they were sharing a soda-fountain special, and there is enough Irish comedy to make me wish Cromwell had done a more thorough job. All this is entirely appropriate to the story, which is the kind that *would* have a heroine named Philadelphia Thursday. However, John Ford directed it, and the Indian parleys and fights and a good deal of the camera work which sneaks by as incidental are somewhere near worth enduring the rest for. Henry Fonda does well, if thinly, as a megalomaniacal martinet.

Give My Regards to Broadway. Vaudeville is dead; I wish to God someone would bury it.

—

CORRECTIONS. In the issue of June 19 I wrote, "Carl Dreyer's *Day of Wrath* is now at the Fifth Avenue Playhouse." It had been expected to open by that date. I now hear (July 13) that it is "definitely set for Friday, July 16"; same theater. I recommend it highly.

In the issue of July 3 I suggested that those interested in the movie subscription society Cinema 16 write the secretary, Alex Vogel, 59 Park Avenue. The name is Amos. I hereby apologize to Mr. Vogel and to you; and sadly join company with an aunt of mine who used to refer to Sacco and Vanetsi, and with all those who call me Aggie, Ad´ji, Adjee´, Uhjee´, and Eigh´ggeee´.

July 31, 1948

THE scene of *A Friend Will Come Tonight* is a rather lenient Franco-Swiss insane asylum during the war. Some of the inmates are sane patriots in disguise; when local German soldiers make trouble, you begin to find out which are which. This seems at best a cheesy idea, but parts of the early reels are done with enough irony and visual style to make it look weirdly good. Later on the picture is done so abominably that you wonder how the same crew could write and film both ends of it. With over half an hour to get there, and a maximum five minutes to walk, none of the patriots bother to walk it until the last possible moment, to disconnect a time-signal which guarantees their destruction. Michel Simon is quite amusing as a sort of house Jesus.

The Illegals, a film about the underground railroad through Europe to Palestine, was made on the spot, under heartbreaking difficulties, by Meyer Levin. Even the knowledge that I was watching actual participants in the actual exodus could seldom prevent me from feeling, sadly, that most of the picture is a bore. On shipboard, however, a new cameraman took over, and the whole thing came powerfully to life. No doubt the intrinsic material here was at once visually more eloquent and more thickly within reach of the camera; but I suspect that the presence of a talented eye made the main difference.

Key Largo. John Huston and Richard Brooks have almost

completely rewritten Maxwell Anderson's play, and I think that in almost every way they have sharply improved on it. Huston's directing is even better than the screen play: in some respects, because the starting materials are so much less amenable to movies and so much less promising anyhow, this picture demonstrates his abilities even more impressively than *Treasure of Sierra Madre* does. Some of the points Huston wanted most to make were cut out of the picture after he finished it, and I rather doubt anyhow whether gangsters can be made to represent all that he meant them to—practically everything that is fundamentally wrong with post-war America; so the picture is weak in the way it was obviously intended to be strongest. Even as a study of character under stress it is sometimes stagy and once or twice next door to hammy; and nearly all of it has the smell of the studio and of intelligent but elaborate and compromised artifice. But it is exceedingly well acted, and as picture-making most of it is as well worth watching as anything you will see this year. Huston manages kinds of vitality, insight, and continuance within each shot and from one shot to the next which are the most inventive and original, the most exciting and the hardest to analyze, in contemporary movies; everything that he achieves visually is so revealing of character, atmosphere, emotion, idea, that its visual and rhythmic rightness and beauty, and the freshness and originality themselves, generally overtake one as afterthoughts. There are a few others so good that I hesitate to say it, but Huston seems to me the most vigorous and germinal talent working in movies today.

So Evil My Love. A sinister artist tempts an innocent widow into passion and crime: still another of those lacy, overelaborated, psychosexual period melodramas by Joseph Shearing. Handsomely produced in England by an American company. Good enough work by Ray Milland; a nice minor job by one of the most attractive and neglected women in movies, Geraldine Fitzgerald; a professional and very likable performance by Ann Todd.

Vicious Circle. A movie about persecuted Jews in Hungary, based on an actual—and outrageous—trial of the 1880s. The writing and directing are so old-stage and so pitifully bad that even such good actors as Fritz Kortner, Reinhold Schunzel, and Conrad Nagel are as helpless as mice in molasses.

September 4, 1948
DAVID WARK GRIFFITH

He achieved what no other known man has ever achieved. To watch his work is like being witness to the beginning of melody, or the first conscious use of the lever or the wheel; the emergence, coordination, and first eloquence of language; the birth of an art: and to realize that this is all the work of one man.

We will never realize how good he really was until we have the chance to see his work as often as it deserves to be seen, to examine and enjoy it in detail as exact as his achievement. But even relying, as we mainly have to, on years-old memories, a good deal becomes clear.

One crude but unquestionable indication of his greatness was his power to create permanent images. All through his work there are images which are as impossible to forget, once you have seen them, as some of the grandest and simplest passages in music or poetry.

The most beautiful single shot I have seen in any movie is the battle charge in *The Birth of a Nation*. I have heard it praised for its realism, and that is deserved; but it is also far beyond realism. It seems to me to be a perfect realization of a collective dream of what the Civil War was like, as veterans might remember it fifty years later, or as children, fifty years later, might imagine it. I have had several clear mental images of that war, from almost as early as I can remember, and I didn't have the luck to see *The Birth of a Nation* until I was in my early twenties; but when I saw that charge, it was merely the clarification, and corroboration, of one of those visions, and took its place among them immediately without seeming to be of a different kind or order. It is the perfection that I know of, of the tragic glory that is possible, or used to be possible, in war; or in war as the best in the spirit imagines or remembers it.

This is, I realize, mainly subjective; but it suggests to me the clearest and deepest aspect of Griffith's genius: he was a great primitive poet, a man capable, as only great and primitive artists can be, of intuitively perceiving and perfecting the tremendous magical images that underlie the memory and imagination of entire peoples. If he had achieved this only once, and only for me, I could not feel that he was what I believe he is; but he created many such images, and I suspect that many people besides me have recognized them, on that deepest level that art can draw on, reach, and serve. There are many others in that one film: the homecoming of the defeated hero; the ride of the Clansmen; the rapist and his victim among the dark leaves; a glimpse of a war hospital; dead young soldiers after battle; the dark, slow movement of the Union Army away from the camera, along a valley which is quartered strongly between hill-shadow and sunlight; all these and still others have a dreamlike absoluteness which, indeed, cradles and suffuses the whole film.

This was the one time in movie history that a man of great ability worked freely, in an unspoiled medium, for an unspoiled audience, on a majestic theme which involved all that he was; and brought to it, besides his abilities as an inventor and artist, absolute passion, pity, courage, and honesty. *The Birth of a Nation* is equal with Brady's photographs, Lincoln's speeches, Whitman's war poems; for all its imperfections and absurdities it is equal, in fact, to the best work that has been done in this country. And among moving pictures it is alone, not necessarily as "the greatest"—whatever that means—but as the one great epic, tragic film.

(Today, *The Birth of a Nation* is boycotted or shown piecemeal; too many more or less well-meaning people still accuse Griffith of having made it an anti-Negro movie. At best, this is nonsense, and at worst, it is vicious nonsense. Even if it were an anti-Negro movie, a work of such quality should be shown, and shown whole. But the accusation is unjust. Griffith went to almost preposterous lengths to be fair to the Negroes as he understood them, and he understood them as a good type of Southerner does. I don't entirely agree with him; nor can I be sure that the film wouldn't cause trouble and misunderstanding, especially as advertised and exacerbated by contemporary abolitionists; but Griffith's absolute desire to be fair,

and understandable, is written all over the picture; so are degrees of understanding, honesty, and compassion far beyond
the capacity of his accusers. So, of course, are the salient facts
of the so-called Reconstruction years.)

Griffith never managed to equal *The Birth of a Nation* again,
nor was he ever to strike off, in any other film, so many of
those final images. Nevertheless, he found many: the strikers in
Intolerance—the realism of those short scenes has never been
surpassed, nor their shock and restiveness as an image of near-
revolution; the intercutting, at the climax of that picture, between the climaxes of four parallel stories, like the swinging
together of tremendous gongs; the paralyzing excitement of
the melodrama near the waterfall, in *Way Down East*; Paul
Revere's ride and the battle of Bunker Hill, in *America*; Dan-
ton's ride, in *Orphans of the Storm*; most subtle and remarkable
of all, the early morning scene in his German film, *Isn't Life
Wonderful?*, in which the ape-like Dick Sutherland pursues
Carol Dempster through a grove of slender trees. All these images, and so many others of Griffith's, have a sort of crude
sublimity which nobody else in movies has managed to achieve;
this last one, like his images of our Civil War, seems to come
out of the deep subconscious: it is an absolute and prophetic
image of a nation and a people. I will always regret having
missed *Abraham Lincoln*, his last film to be released: a friend
has told me of its wonderful opening in stormy mid-winter
night woods, the camera bearing along toward the natal cabin;
and that surely must have been one of Griffith's finest images.
Even in Griffith's best work there is enough that is poor, or
foolish, or merely old-fashioned, so that one has to understand,
if by no means forgive, those who laugh indiscriminately at his
good work and his bad. (With all that "understanding," I look
forward to killing, some day, some specially happy giggler at
the exquisite scene in which the veteran comes home, in *The
Birth of a Nation*.) But even his poorest work was never just
bad. Whatever may be wrong with it, there is in every instant,
so well as I can remember, the unique purity and vitality of birth
or of a creature just born and first exerting its unprecedented,
incredible strength; and there are, besides, Griffith's overwhelming innocence and magnanimity of spirit; his moral and

D. W. Griffith. Hollywood was his invention.

poetic earnestness; his joy in his work; and his splendid intu-itiveness, directness, common sense, daring, and skill as an in-ventor and as an artist. Aside from his talent or genius as an inventor and artist, he was all heart; and ruinous as his excesses sometimes were in that respect, they were inseparable from his virtues, and small beside them. He was remarkably good, as a rule, in the whole middle range of feeling, but he was at his best just short of his excesses, and he tended in general to work out toward the dangerous edge. He was capable of real-ism that has never been beaten and he might, if he had been able to appreciate his powers as a realist, have found therein his growth and salvation. But he seems to have been a realist only by accident, hit-and-run; essentially, he was a poet. He doesn't appear ever to have realized one of the richest promises that movies hold, as the perfect medium for realism raised to the level of high poetry; nor, oddly enough, was he much of a dra-matic poet. But in epic and lyrical and narrative visual poetry, I can think of nobody who has surpassed him, and of few to compare with him. And as a primitive tribal poet, combining something of the bard and the seer, he is beyond even Dov-zhenko, and no others of their kind have worked in movies.

What he had above all, his ability as a craftsman and artist, would be hard enough—and quite unnecessary—to write of, if we had typical scenes before us, or within recent memory; since we have seen so little of his work in so many years, it is virtually impossible. I can remember very vividly his general spirit and manner—heroic, impetuous, tender, magniloquent, naive, beyond the endowment or daring of anybody since; just as vividly, I can remember the total impression of various major sequences. By my remembrance, his images were nearly always a little larger and wilder than life. The frame was always full, spontaneous, and lively. He knew wonderfully well how to contrast and combine different intensities throughout an im-mense range of emotion, movement, shadow, and light. Much of the liveliness was not intrinsic to the characters on the screen or their predicament, but was his own vitality and emo-tion; and much of it—notably in the amazing flickering and vi-vacity of his women—came of his almost maniacal realization of the importance of expressive movement.

It seems to me entirely reasonable to infer, from the extraordinary power and endurance in the memory of certain scenes in their total effect, that he was as brilliant a master of design and cutting and form as he was a composer of frames and a director of feeling and motion. But I cannot clearly remember one sequence or scene, shot by shot and rhythm by rhythm. I suspect, for instance, that analysis would show that the climactic sequence on the icy river, in *Way Down East*, is as finely constructed a piece of melodramatic story-telling as any in movies. But I can only venture to bet on this and to suggest that that sequence, like a hundred others of Griffith's, is eminently worth analysis.

My veneration for Griffith's achievements is all the deeper when I realize what handicaps he worked against, how limited a man he was. He had no remarkable power of intellect, or delicateness of soul; no subtlety; little restraint; little if any "taste," whether to help his work or harm it; Lord knows (and be thanked) no cleverness; no fundamental capacity, once he had achieved his first astonishing development, for change or growth. He wasn't particularly observant of people; nor do his movies suggest that he understood them at all deeply. He had noble powers of imagination, but little of the *intricacy* of imagination that most good poets also have. His sense of comedy was pathetically crude and numb. He had an exorbitant appetite for violence, for cruelty, and for the Siamese twin of cruelty, a kind of obsessive tenderness which at its worst was all but nauseating. Much as he invented, his work was saturated in the style, the mannerisms, and the underlying assumptions and attitudes of the nineteenth century provincial theater; and although much of that was much better than most of us realize, and any amount better than most of the styles and non-styles we accept and praise, much of it was cheap and false, and all of it, good and bad, was dying when Griffith gave it a new lease on life, and in spite of that new lease, died soon after, and took him down with it. I doubt that Griffith ever clearly knew the good from the bad in this theatricality; or, for that matter, clearly understood what was original in his work, and capable of almost unimaginably great development; and what was over-derivative, essentially non-cinematic, and dying. In any case, he did not manage to outgrow, or sufficiently to transform, enough in his style that was bad, or merely obsolescent.

If what I hear is right about the opening scene in *Abraham Lincoln*, this incapacity for radical change may have slowed him up but never killed him as an artist; in his no longer fashionable way, he remained capable, and inspired. He was merely unadaptable and unemployable, like an old, sore, ardent individualist among contemporary progressives. Hollywood and, to a great extent, movies in general, grew down from him rather than up past him; audiences, and the whole eye and feeling of the world, have suffered the same degeneration; he didn't have it in him to be amenable, even if he'd tried; and that was the end of him. Or quite possibly he was finished, as smaller men are not, as soon as he had reached the limit of his own powers of innovation, and began to realize he was only repeating himself. Certainly, anyhow, he was natural-born for the years of adventure and discovery, not for the inevitable following era of safe-playing and of fat consolidation of others' gains.

His last movie, which was never even released, was made fourteen or fifteen years ago; and for years before that, most people had thought of him as a has-been. Nobody would hire him; he had nothing to do. He lived too long, and that is one of few things that are sadder than dying too soon.

There is not a man working in movies, or a man who cares for them, who does not owe Griffith more than he owes anybody else.

Undirectable Director

Of the directors whose work Agee most admired, John Huston was perhaps the one he was most personally drawn to. In the course of working on this article the two met for the first time. Subsequently they worked together on The African Queen. *This article appeared in* Life, *September 18, 1950.*

THE ant, as every sluggard knows, is a model citizen. His eye is fixed unwaveringly upon Security and Success, and he gets where he is going. The grasshopper, as every maiden ant delights in pointing out, is his reprehensible opposite number: a hedonistic jazz-baby, tangoing along primrose paths to a disreputable end. The late Walter Huston's son John, one of the ranking grasshoppers of the Western Hemisphere, is living proof of what a lot of nonsense that can be. He has beaten the ants at their own game and then some, and he has managed that blindfolded, by accident, and largely just for the hell of it. John was well into his twenties before anyone could imagine he would ever amount to more than an awfully nice guy to get drunk with. He wandered into his vocation as a writer of movie scripts to prove to a girl he wanted to marry that he amounted to more than a likable bum. He stumbled into his still deeper vocation as a writer-director only when he got sick of seeing what the professional directors did to his scripts. But during the ten subsequent years he has won both Security aplenty (currently $3,000 a week with MGM and a partnership in Horizon Pictures with his friend Sam Spiegel) and Success aplenty (two Oscars, a One World Award and such lesser prizes as the Screen Directors' Guild quarterly award which he received last week for his *Asphalt Jungle*).

Yet these are merely incidental attainments. The first movie he directed, *The Maltese Falcon*, is the best private-eye melodrama ever made. *San Pietro*, his microcosm of the meaning of war in terms of the fight for one hill town, is generally conceded to be the finest of war documentaries. *Treasure of Sierra Madre*, which he developed from B. Traven's sardonic adventure-fable about the corrosive effect of gold on character, is the clearest proof in perhaps twenty years that first-rate work can come out of the big commercial studios.

Most of the really good popular art produced anywhere comes from Hollywood, and much of it bears Huston's name. To put it conservatively, there is nobody under fifty at work in movies, here or abroad, who can excel Huston in talent, inventiveness, intransigence, achievement or promise. Yet it is a fair bet that neither money, nor acclaim, nor a sense of dedication to the greatest art medium of his century have much to do with Huston's staying at his job: he stays at it because there is nothing else he enjoys so much. It is this tireless enjoyment that gives his work a unique vitality and makes every foot of film he works on unmistakably his.

Huston seems to have acquired this priceless quality many years ago at the time of what, in his opinion, was probably the most crucial incident in his life. When he was about twelve years old he was so delicate he was hardly expected to live. It was interminably dinned into him that he could never possibly be quite careful enough, and for even closer protection he was put into a sanitarium where every bite he ate and breath he drew could be professionally policed. As a result he became virtually paralyzed by timidity; "I haven't the slightest doubt," he still says, "that if things had gone on like that I'd have died inside a few more months." His only weapon was a blind desperation of instinct, and by day not even that was any use. Nights, however, when everyone was asleep, he used to sneak out, strip, dive into a stream which sped across the grounds and ride it down quite a steep and stony waterfall, over and over and over. "The first few times," he recalls, "it scared the living hell out of me, but I realized—instinctively anyhow—it was exactly fear I had to get over." He kept at it until it was the one joy in his life. When they first caught him at this primordial autotherapy the goons were of course aghast; but on maturer thought they decided he might live after all.

The traits revealed in this incident are central and permanent in Huston's character. Risk, not to say recklessness, are virtual reflexes in him. Action, and the most vivid possible use of the immediate present, were his personal salvation; they have remained lifelong habits. Because action also is the natural language of the screen and the instant present is its tense,

Huston is a born popular artist. In his life, his dealings and his work as an artist he operates largely by instinct, unencumbered by much reflectiveness or abstract thinking, or any serious self-doubt. Incapable of yesing, apple-polishing or boot-licking, he instantly catches fire in resistance to authority.

Nobody in movies can beat Huston's record for trying to get away with more than the traffic will bear. *San Pietro* was regarded with horror by some gentlemen of the upper brass as "an antiwar picture" and was cut from five reels to three. *Treasure*, which broke practically every box-office law in the game and won three Oscars, was made over the virtually dead bodies of the top men at Warners' and was advertised as a Western. *The Asphalt Jungle* suggests that in some respects big-town crime operates remarkably like free enterprise. Huston seldom tries to "lick" the problem imposed by censorship, commercial queasiness or tradition; he has learned that nothing is so likely to settle an argument as to turn up with the accomplished fact, accomplished well, plus a bland lack of alternative film shots. And yet after innumerable large and small fights and a fair share of defeats he can still say of his movie career, "I've never had any trouble." Probably the whitest magic that protects him is that he really means it.

Nonetheless his life began with trouble—decorated with the best that his Irish imagination, and his father's, could add to it. He was born John Marcellus Huston on August 5, 1906, in Nevada, Missouri, a hamlet which his grandfather, a professional gambler, had by the most ambitious version of the family legend acquired in a poker game. John's father, a retired actor, was in charge of power and light and was learning his job, while he earned, via a correspondence course. Before the postman had taught him how to handle such a delicate situation, a fire broke out in town, Walter overstrained the valves in his effort to satisfy the fire department, and the Hustons decided it would be prudent to leave what was left of Nevada before morning. They did not let their shirttails touch their rumps until they hit Weatherford, Texas, another of Grandfather's jackpots. After a breather they moved on to St. Louis (without, however, repeating the scorched-earth policy), and Walter settled down to engineering in dead earnest until a solid man clapped him on the shoulder and told him that with enough stick-to-itiveness he might well become a top-notch engineer, a regular crackerjack. Horrified, Walter instantly returned to the stage. A few years later he and his wife were divorced. From there on out the child's life lacked the stability of those early years.

John divided his time between his father and mother. With his father, who was still some years short of eminence or even solvency, he shared that bleakly glamorous continuum of three-a-days, scabrous fleabags and the cindery, ambling day coaches between, which used to be so much of the essence of the American theater. John's mother was a newspaperwoman with a mania for travel and horses (she was later to marry a vice-president of the Northern Pacific), and she and her son once pooled their last ten dollars on a 100-to-1 shot—which came in. Now and then she stuck the boy in one school or another, but mostly they traveled—well off the beaten paths.

After his defeat of death by sliding down the waterfall, there was no holding John. In his teens he became amateur lightweight boxing champion of California. A high-school marriage lasted only briefly. He won twenty-three out of twenty-five fights, many in the professional ring, but he abandoned this promise of a career to join another of his mother's eccentric grand tours. He spent two years in the Mexican cavalry, emerging at twenty-one as a lieutenant. In Mexico he wrote a book, a puppet play about Frankie and Johnny. Receiving, to his astonishment, a $500 advance from a publisher, he promptly entrained for the crap tables of Saratoga where, in one evening, he ran it up to $11,000, which he soon spent or gambled away.

After that Huston took quite a friendly interest in writing. He wrote a short story which his father showed to his friend Ring Lardner, who showed it to his friend H. L. Mencken, who ran it in the *Mercury*. He wrote several other stories about horses and boxers before the vein ran out. It was through these stories, with his father's help that he got his first job as a movie writer. He scripted *A House Divided*, starring his father, for William Wyler. But movies, at this extravagant stage of Huston's career, were just an incident. At other stages he worked for the New York *Graphic* ("I was the world's lousiest reporter"), broke ribs riding steeplechase, studied painting in

Paris, knocked around with international Bohemians in London and went on the bum in that city when his money ran out and he was too proud to wire his father. At length he beat his way back to New York where, for a time, he tried editing the *Midweek Pictorial.* He was playing Abraham Lincoln in a Chicago WPA production when he met an Irish girl named Leslie Black and within fifteen minutes after their meeting asked her to marry him. When she hesitated he hotfooted it to Hollywood and settled down to earn a solid living as fast as possible. Marrying Leslie was probably the best thing that ever happened to him, in the opinion of Huston's wise friend and studio protector during the years at Warner Brothers, the producer Henry Blanke. Blanke remembers him vividly during the bachelor interlude: "Just a drunken boy; hopelessly immature. You'd see him at every party, wearing bangs, with a monkey on his shoulder. Charming. Very talented but without an ounce of discipline in his make-up." Leslie Huston, Blanke is convinced, set her husband the standards and incentives which brought his abilities into focus. They were divorced in 1945, but in relation to his work he has never lost the stability she helped him gain.

At forty-four Huston still has a monkey and a chimpanzee as well, but he doesn't escort them to parties. His gray-sleeted hair still treats his scalp like Liberty Hall and occasionally slithers into bangs, but they can no longer be mistaken for a Bohemian compensation. He roughly suggests a jerked-venison version of his father, or a highly intelligent cowboy. A little over six feet tall, quite lean, he carries himself in a perpetual gangling-graceful slouch. The forehead is monkeyishly puckered, the ears look as clipped as a show dog's; the eyes, too, are curiously animal, an opaque red-brown. The nose was broken in the prize ring. The mouth is large, mobile and gap-toothed. The voice which comes out of this leatheriness is surprisingly rich, gentle and cultivated. The vocabulary ranges with the careless ease of a mountain goat between words of eight syllables and of four letters.

Some friends believe he is essentially a deep introvert using every outside means available as a form of flight from self-recognition—in other words, he is forever sliding down the waterfall and instinctively fears to stop. The same friends suspect his work is all that keeps him from flying apart. He is wonderful company, almost anytime, for those who can stand the pace. Loving completely unrestrained and fantastic play, he is particularly happy with animals, roughhousers and children; a friend who owns three of the latter describes him as "a blend of Santa Claus and the Pied Piper." His friendships range from high in the Social Register to low in the animal kingdom, but pretty certainly the friend he liked best in the world was his father, and that was thoroughly reciprocated. It was a rare and heart-warming thing, in this Freud-ridden era, to see a father and son so irrepressibly pleased with each other's company and skill.

He has an indestructible kind of youthfulness, enjoys his enthusiasms with all his might and has the prompt appetite for new knowledge of a man whose intelligence has not been cloyed by much formal education. He regrets that nowadays he can read only two or three books a week. His favorite writers are Joyce, his friend Hemingway (perhaps his closest literary equivalent) and, above all, O'Neill; it was one of the deepest disappointments of his career when movie commitments prevented his staging the new O'Neill's *The Iceman Cometh.* His other enjoyments take many forms. He still paints occasionally. He is a very good shot and a superlative horseman; he has some very promising runners of his own. He likes money for the fun it can bring him, is extremely generous with it and particularly loves to gamble. He generally does well at the races and siphons it off at the crap tables. He is a hard drinker (Scotch) but no lush, and a heavy smoker. Often as not he forgets to eat. He has a reputation for being attractive to women, and rough on them. His fourth wife is the dancer, Ricky Soma; their son Walter was born last spring. He makes most of his important decisions on impulse; it was thus he adopted his son Pablo in Mexico. The way he and his third wife, Evelyn Keyes, got married is a good example of Huston in action. He suggested they marry one evening in Romanoff's a week after they met, borrowed a pocketful of money from the prince, tore out to his house to pick up a wedding ring a guest had mislaid in the swimming pool and chartered Paul Mantz to fly them to Las Vegas where they were married that night.

Huston's courage verges on the absolute, or on simple obliviousness to danger. In Italy during the shooting of *San Pietro*, his simian curiosity about literally everything made him the beau ideal of the contrivers of booby traps; time and again he was spared an arm, leg or skull only by the grace of God and the horrified vigilance of his friend Lieutenant Jules Buck. He sauntered through mine fields where plain man feared to tread. He is quick to get mad and as quick to get over it. Once in Italy he sprinted up five flights of headquarters stairs in order to sock a frustrating superior officer; arriving at the top he was so winded he could hardly stand. Time enough to catch his breath was time enough to cool off; he just wobbled downstairs again.

Huston is swiftly stirred by anything which appeals to his sense of justice, magnanimity or courage: he was among the first men to stand up for Lew Ayres as a conscientious objector, he flew to the Washington hearings on Hollywood (which he refers to as "an obscenity") and sponsored Henry Wallace (though he voted for Truman) in the 1948 campaign. Some people think of him, accordingly, as a fellow traveler. Actually he is a political man chiefly in an emotional sense: "I'm against *anybody*," he says, "who tries to tell anybody else what to do." The mere sight or thought of a cop can get him sore. He is in short rather less of a Communist than the most ultramontane Republican, for like perhaps five out of seven good artists who ever lived he is—to lapse into technical jargon—a natural-born antiauthoritarian individualistic libertarian anarchist, without portfolio.

A very good screen writer, Huston is an even better director. He has a feeling about telling a story on a screen which sets him apart from most other movie artists and from all non-movie writers and artists. "On paper," he says, "all you can do is say something happened, and if you say it well enough the reader believes you. In pictures, if you do it right, *the thing happens, right there on the screen.*"

This means more than it may seem to. Most movies are like predigested food because they are mere reenactments of something that happened (if ever) back in the scripting stage. At the time of shooting the sense of the present is not strong, and such creative energy as may be on hand is used to give the event finish, in every sense of the word, rather than beginning and life. Huston's work has a unique tension and vitality because the maximum of all contributing creative energies converge at the one moment that counts most in a movie—the continuing moment of committing the story to film. At his best he makes the story tell itself, makes it seem to happen for the first and last time at the moment of recording. It is almost magically hard to get this to happen. In the *Treasure* scene in which the bandits kill Bogart, Huston wanted it to be quiet and mock-casual up to its final burst of violence. He told two of his three killers—one a professional actor, the other two professional criminals—only to stay quiet and close to the ground, and always to move when Bogart moved, to keep him surrounded. Then he had everyone play it through, over and over, until they should get the feel of it. At length one of them did a quick scuttling slide down a bank, on his bottom and his busy little hands and feet. A motion as innocent as a child's and as frightening as a centipede's, it makes clear for the first time in the scene that death is absolutely inescapable, and very near. "When he did that slide," Huston says, "I knew they had the feel of it." He shot it accordingly.

Paradoxically in this hyperactive artist of action, the living, breathing texture of his best work is the result of a working method which relies on the utmost possible passiveness. Most serious-minded directors direct too much: "Now on this word," Huston has heard one tell an actor, "I want your voice to break." Actors accustomed to that kind of "help" are often uneasy when they start work with Huston. "Shall I sit down here?" one asked, interrupting a rehearsal. "*I* dunno," Huston replied. "You tired?" When Claire Trevor, starting work in *Key Largo*, asked for a few pointers, he told her, "You're the kind of drunken dame whose elbows are always a little too big, your voice is a little too loud, you're a little too polite. You're very sad, very resigned. Like this," he said, for short, and leaned against the bar with a peculiarly heavy, gentle disconsolateness. It was the leaning she caught onto (though she also used everything he said); without further instruction of any kind, she took an Oscar for her performance. His only advice to his father was a whispered, "Dad, that was a little too much like Walter Huston." Often he works with actors as if he were gentling animals; and although Bogart says without total in-justice that "as an actor he stinks," he has more than enough mimetic ability to get his ideas across. Sometimes he discards instruction altogether: to get a desired expression from Lauren Bacall, he simply twisted her arm.

Even on disastrously thin ice Huston has the peculiar kind of well-earned luck which Heaven reserves exclusively for the intuitive and the intrepid. One of the most important roles in *Treasure* is that of the bandit leader, a primordial criminal psy-chopath about whom the most fascinating and terrifying thing is his unpredictability. It is impossible to know what he will do next because it is impossible to be sure what strange piece of glare-ice in his nature will cause a sudden skid. Too late for a change, it turned out that the man who played this role, though visually ideal for it, couldn't act for shucks. Worried as he was, Huston had a hunch it would turn out all right. It worked because this inadequate actor was trying so hard, was so unsure of what he was doing and was so painfully confused and angered by Huston's cryptic passivity. These several kinds of strain and uncertainty, sprung against the context of the story, made a living image of the almost unactable, real thing; and that had been Huston's hunch.

In placing and moving his characters within a shot Huston is nearly always concerned above all else to be simple and spon-taneous rather than merely "dramatic" or visually effective. Just as he feels that the story belongs to the characters, he feels that the actors should as fully as possible belong to themselves. It is only because the actors are so free that their several indi-vidualities, converging in a scene, can so often knock the kinds of sparks off each other which cannot be asked for or invented or foreseen. All that can be foreseen is that this can happen only under favorable circumstances; Huston is a master at cre-ating such circumstances.

Each of Huston's pictures has a visual tone and style of its own, dictated to his camera by the story's essential content and spirit. In *Treasure* the camera is generally static and at a middle distance from the action (as Huston says, "It's imper-sonal, it just looks on and lets them stew in their own juice"); the composition is—superficially—informal, the light cruel and clean, like noon sun on quartz and bone. Most of the action in

Key Largo takes place inside a small Florida hotel. The problems are to convey heat, suspense, enclosedness, the illusion of some eighteen hours of continuous action in two hours' playing time, with only one time lapse. The lighting is stickily fungoid. The camera is sneakily "personal"; working close and in almost continuous motion, it enlarges the ambiguous suspensefulness of almost every human move. In *Strangers* the main pressures are inside a home and beneath it, where conspirators dig a tunnel. Here Huston's chief keys are lighting contrasts. Underground the players move in and out of shadow like trout; upstairs the light is mainly the luminous pallor of marble without sunlight: a cemetery, a bank interior, a great outdoor staircase.

John Huston discusses a scene in "Key Largo" with Humphrey Bogart and Lauren Bacall.

Much that is best in Huston's work comes of his sense of what is natural to the eye and his delicate, simple feeling for space relationships: his camera huddles close to those who huddle to talk, leans back a proportionate distance, relaxing, if they talk casually. He loathes camera rhetoric and the shot-for-shot's-sake; but because he takes each moment catch-as-catch-can and is so deeply absorbed in doing the best possible thing with it he has made any number of unforgettable shots. He can make an unexpected close-up reverberate like a gong. The first shot of Edward G. Robinson in *Key Largo*, mouthing a cigar and sweltering naked in a tub of cold water ("I wanted to get a look at the animal with its shell off") is one of the most powerful and efficient "first entrances" of a character on record. Other great shots come through the kind of candor which causes some people to stare when others look away: the stripped, raw-sound scenes of psychiatric interviews in *Let There Be Light*. Others come through simple discretion in relating word and image. In *San Pietro*, as the camera starts moving along a line of children and babies, the commentator (Huston) remarks that in a few years they'll have forgotten there ever was a war; then he shuts up. As the camera continues in silence along the terrible frieze of shock and starvation, one realizes the remark was not the inane optimism it seemed: they, forgetting, are fodder for the next war.

Sometimes the shot is just a spark—a brief glint of extra imagination and perception. During the robbery sequence in *Asphalt Jungle* there is a quick glimpse of the downtown midnight street at the moment when people have just begun to hear the burglar alarms. Unsure, still, where the trouble is, the people merely hesitate a trifle in their ways of walking, and it is like the first stirrings of metal filings before the magnet beneath the paper pulls them into pattern. Very often the fine shot comes because Huston, working to please himself without fear of his audience, sharply condenses his storytelling. Early in *Strangers* a student is machine-gunned on the steps of Havana's university. A scene follows which is breath-taking in its surprise and beauty, but storytelling, not beauty, brings it: what seems to be hundreds of young men and women, all in summery whites, throw themselves flat on the marble stairs in a wavelike motion as graceful as the sudden close swooping of so many doves. The shot is already off the screen before one can realize its full meaning. By their trained, quiet unison in falling, these students are used to this. They expect it any average morning. And that suffices, with great efficiency, to suggest the Cuban tyranny.

Within the prevailing style of a picture, Huston works many and extreme changes and conflicts between the "active" camera, which takes its moment of the story by the scruff of the neck and "tells" it, and the "passive" camera, whose business is transparency, to receive a moment of action purely and record it. But whether active or passive, each shot contains no more than is absolutely necessary to make its point and is cut off sharp at that instant. The shots are cantilevered, sprung together in electric arcs, rather than buttered together. A given scene is apt to be composed of highly unconventional alternations of rhythm and patterns of exchange between long and medium and close shots and the standing, swinging and dollying camera. The rhythm and contour are very powerful but very irregular, like the rhythm of good prose rather than of good verse; and it is this rangy, leaping, thrusting kind of nervous vitality which binds the whole picture together. Within this vitality he can bring about moments as thoroughly revealing as those in great writing. As an average sample of that, *Treasure*'s intruder is killed by bandits; the three prospectors come to identify the man they themselves were on the verge of shooting. Bogart, the would-be tough guy, cocks one foot up on a rock and tries to look at the corpse as casually as if it were fresh-killed game. Tim Holt, the essentially decent young man, comes past behind him and, innocent and unaware of it, clasps his hands as he looks down, in the respectful manner of a boy who used to go to church. Walter Huston, the experienced old man, steps quietly behind both, leans to the dead man as professionally as a doctor to a patient and gently rifles him for papers. By such simplicity Huston can draw the eye so deep into the screen that time and again he can make important points in medium shots, by motions as small as the twitching of an eyelid, for which most directors would require a close-up or even a line of dialogue.

Most movies are made in the evident assumption that the audience is passive and wants to remain passive; every effort is made to do all the work—the seeing, the explaining, the understanding, even the feeling. Huston is one of the few movie artists who, without thinking twice about it, honors his audience. His pictures are not acts of seduction or of benign enslavement but of liberation, and they require, of anyone who enjoys them, the responsibilities of liberty. They continually open the eye and require it to work vigorously; and through the eye they awaken curiosity and intelligence. That, by any virile standard, is essential to good entertainment. It is unquestionably essential to good art.

The most inventive director of his generation, Huston has done more to extend, invigorate and purify the essential idiom of American movies, the truly visual telling of stories, than anyone since the prime of D. W. Griffith. To date, however, his work as a whole is not on the level with the finest and most deeply imaginative work that has been done in movies—the work of Chaplin, Dovzhenko, Eisenstein, Griffith, the late Jean Vigo. For an artist of such conscience and caliber, his range is surprisingly narrow, both in subject matter and technique. In general he is leery of emotion—of the "feminine" aspects of art—and if he explored it with more assurance, with his taste and equipment, he might show himself to be a much more sensitive artist. With only one early exception, his movies have centered on men under pressure, have usually involved violence and have occasionally verged on a kind of romanticism about danger. Though he uses sound and dialogue more intelligently than most directors, he has not shown much interest in exploring the tremendous possibilities of the former or in solving the crippling problems of the latter. While his cutting is astute, terse, thoroughly appropriate to his kind of work, yet compared with that of Eisenstein, who regarded cutting as the essence of the art of movies, it seems distinctly unadventurous. In his studio pictures, Huston is apt to be tired and bored by the time the stages of ultrarefinement in cutting are reached, so that some of his scenes have been given perfection, others somewhat impaired, by film editors other than Huston. This is consistent with much that is free and improvisatory in his work and in his nature, but it is a startling irresponsibility in so good an artist.

During his past few pictures Huston does appear to have become more of a "camera" man, and not all of this has been to the good. The camera sometimes imposes on the story; the lighting sometimes becomes elaborately studioish or even verges on the arty; the screen at times becomes rigid, overstylized. This has been happening, moreover, at a time when another of Huston's liabilities has been growing: thanks to what Henry Blanke calls his "amazing capacity for belief," he can fall for, and lose himself in, relatively mediocre material. Sometimes—as in *Asphalt Jungle*—he makes a silk purse out of sow's ear, but sometimes—as in parts of *Strangers* and *Key Largo*—the result is neither silk nor sow.

Conceivably Huston lacks that deepest kind of creative impulse and that intense self-critical skepticism without which the stature of a great artist is rarely achieved. A brilliant adapter, he has yet to do a Huston "original," barring the war documentaries. He is probably too much at the mercy of his immediate surroundings. When the surroundings are right for him there is no need to talk about mercy: during the war and just after he was as hard as a rock and made his three finest pictures in a row. Since then the pictures, for all their excellence, are, like the surroundings, relatively softened and blurred. Unfortunately no man in Hollywood can be sufficiently his own master or move in a direct line to personally selected goals. After *Treasure*, Huston was unable to proceed to *Moby Dick* as he wanted to; he still is awaiting the opportunity to make Dreiser's *Jennie Gerhardt* and Dostoevski's *The Idiot* although he is at last shooting Stephen Crane's *The Red Badge of Courage*, which he has wanted to make for years. "This has got to be a masterpiece," he recently told friends, "or it's nothing."

There is no reason to expect less of it than his finest picture yet, for the better his starting material, the better he functions as an artist: he is one of the very few men in the world of movies who has shown himself to be worthy of the best. He has, in abundance, many of the human qualities which most men of talent lack. He is magnanimous, disinterested and fearless. Whatever his job, he always makes a noble and rewarding fight of it. If it should occur to him to fight for his life—his life as the consistently great artist he evidently might become—he would stand a much better chance of winning than most people. For besides having talent and fighting ability, he has nothing to lose but his hide, and he has never set a very high value on that.

Time
1941-1948

For almost seven years Agee was the movie reviewer for Time. *Out of this massive amount of material it was necessary to select. The selection could not be based on any systematic, critical criteria. On rereading, two main characteristics emerged. One, his ability to find something admirable or amusing in even the worst kind of movies, and second, the ability to say what he wanted to say within a fairly tight given form. Of course, another was his gift to have fun with it all.*

November 24, 1941

*N*ever Give a Sucker an Even Break (Universal) is not a movie; it is 70 minutes of photographed vaudeville by polypnosed W. C. Fields, assisted by Gloria Jean, Franklin Pangborn and other stage properties. As such, it is strong drink for cinemaddicts who believe that the Great Man can do no wrong, small beer for those who think that even a Fields picture should have a modicum of direction.

Sucker has no plot and needs none. It is just Fields trying to peddle a scenario to Esoteric Studios. He reads a scene, then plays it. Upshot: a maelstrom of slapstick, song, blackout episodes, old gags, new gags, confusion. That much of it is truly comic is testimony to the fact that Comedian Fields is one of the funniest men on earth. Whether he is offering a cure for insomnia ("Get plenty of sleep"), refusing a bromo ("couldn't stand the noise"), nasally vocalizing ("chickens have pretty legs in Kansas"), meticulously blowing the head off an ice cream soda, Fields is a beautifully timed exhibit of mock pomposity, puzzled ineffectualness, subtle understatement and true-blue nonchalance.

Now 62, Fields has spent most of his adult life battling babies, dogs, censors, producers, directors, the world in general. From the shape of his latest picture, it is apparent that he has Universal licked. The only round Fields is known to have lost was the production's title: he wanted it called *The Great*

Man: After the present title was selected, the comedian snarled: "What does it matter; they can't get that on a marquee. It will probably boil down to *Fields—Sucker*."

Recently Fields drew blood. Universal sent him a legal document threatening court action if he didn't mend his studio manners (*i.e.*, references to company executives, language in front of cinemoppets, general demeanor). Back came a reply: "Dear Sir, Mr. Fields and I read your letter and did we laugh." It was signed "Adele" (Fields's Negro housemaid).

Largely as a result of such bickering, *Sucker* is far from being the kind of picture that only W. C. Fields could turn out. His unique talent needs intelligent direction. It does not need all the props that its owner thinks are a necessity for his performance. The great comedian can play straight better and more firmly than anyone in the business.

February 2, 1942

Hellzapoppin (Mayfair Productions; Universal). The firm of John Sigvard Olsen and Harold Ogden Johnson has been manufacturing calculated lunacy for 27 years. In all that time their product has changed no more than a hooked rug.

Three years and four months ago this pair of astute businessmen of vaudeville assembled their lifetime's wares in a single prize package called *Hellzapoppin*. It ran 1,404 performances (an all-time Broadway musical-show record), grossed over $4,000,000, sent nearly 5,000,000 customers temporarily insane.

On celluloid, *Hellzapoppin* loses the frenetic quality it achieved on the stage. Lena still wanders through the set calling for Oscar; the little flowerpot whose owner won't claim it still grows by stages into a gigantic tree; homicide and suicide are amiably rampant; gags rise and fall by the bushel; some skits succeed, more fail.

But Olsen and Johnson's ability to exude a kind of ectoplasm which engulfs a theater audience and makes it participate in the show is necessarily cut off when the show is confined to the screen. The stage show, a cross between a fire in a lunatic asylum and the third day at Gettysburg, becomes only a small Balkan war in the movies. Stripped of its unsurpassable insanity, the name for it is ham vaudeville. Olsen and Johnson do not deny it. They call it "gonk."

Sample gonk: Olsen, in a grotesque mask, takes a seat among the audience and tries to scare some crusty, upperclass dames. They fail to frighten. He removes the mask, turns his face to the lady next to him. She takes one look and shrieks.

February 23, 1942

Roxie Hart (20th Century–Fox) is dedicated "to all the beautiful women in the world who have shot their men full of holes out of pique." A rewrite by Producer Nunnally Johnson of Maurine Watkins' 1926 Broadway hit *Chicago*, it is a bawdy farce of the bad old '20s when a pretty murderess was as likely to get ten weeks in vaudeville as the electric chair.

"This county wouldn't hang Lucrezia Borgia," a reporter (Lynne Overman) informs Roxie Hart (Ginger Rogers), redheaded, gum-chewing, wisecracking dancer, whose husband has just shot her lover and pinned the murder on her. Convinced that she can't have a career and be innocent, too, Roxie agrees to stand trial and let the newspapers "put her right up there" with Peaches Browning, Queen Marie, Ruth Snyder and Red Grange.

She hires the town's best criminal lawyer (Adolph Menjou), a "simple, barefoot mouthpiece" who knows no law but does know juries, enjoys the run of her jailhouse, overcomes the headline competition of Two-Gun Gertie (Iris Adrian) by professing to be with child, stampedes the jury into freeing her. A telling point: Menjou, bearing the swooned Roxie in his arms, stands before the judge and elocutes: "The defense rests."

Although *Roxie Hart* makes a hilarious burlesque of Chicago's Keep-Cool-With-Coolidge, Keep-Cockeyed-With-Capone era, it is often too overdone for superior farce. Mouthpiece Menjou and Newsman Overman make mincemeat of their fat roles; America's own Ginger Rogers is attractive but unbelievable in hers. The star plays second fiddle to the era.

Classic sequence: Roxie's farmer father, informed by long distance that his daughter may lose her life, returns unruffled to his rocker, meditates awhile before observing to his wife: "They're going to hang Roxie." Replies the mother with equal equanimity: "What did I tell you?"

The Gold Rush (Chaplin; United Artists) is a revival of Charlie Chaplin's most successful comedy (gross: $7,112,000). Printed from the original 1925 negative, it has been modernized by its producer-director-author-star only to the extent of substituting his own narration for the old subtitles, editing out 1,000 feet of film and adding a musical background score. The result is a sight for sore eyes, for old-style Chaplin fans and novitiates alike.

Although it was another generation's children who promised to be good all week if they could see a Chaplin comedy, the bantam tramp with his flapping shoes, battered derby hat, jaunty bamboo cane, absurd black mustache, shabby, defiant clothes, is not dated. The craftsmanship of his effortless performance—the innocent waddle, the peculiar childlike kick, the desperate elegance, the poignant gallantry—is still high comedy.

The hero of *The Gold Rush* is billed as The Lone Prospector, a tenderfoot out for Alaskan gold. In his running narrative, Chaplin calls him "the Little Fellow." With eloquent timing he jaunts along the rim of a ledge high in Chilkoot Pass, unknowingly trailed by a black bear, and the picture is away.

That the Little Fellow eventually becomes a multimillionaire wearing two fur coats, one over the other, is unimportant. What matters are the delicious beads of humor strung on the thread of his unique personality. Chaplin cinemaddicts will recognize with tears of joy two famed scenes: trapped by a blizzard in a lonely mountain cabin with a friendly prospector named Big Jim (Mack Swain), Charlie hopefully removes a shoe and places it in the stewpot. Tenderly basting the foul boot with its own juices, he nurses it along to Big Jim's bursting point. "Not quite done yet," soothes the Little Fellow. "Give it two more minutes." He serves it up with a shoestring for potatoes, munches it contentedly.

Other great scene: the dance of the rolls. Unable to speak his happiness at having Georgia (Georgia Hale), the dance hall girl he hopelessly adores, take dinner with him, the Little Fellow impales two rolls on forks and transforms them into the lyric legs of a ballet dancer, footing it with furious featness.

The dubbed-in narrative is as simple as its author's pantomime (*e.g.*, "With cheerful optimism our little Columbus descended into the vast uncharted waste—then stopped, stepped, slipped and slid"). It kids the stylized exaggerations of Big Jim, a notable heavy, by referring to him as "the noble type . . . Oh, how he loved to suffer"; it anticipates Georgia's atrocious, kittenish, dated antics by introducing her to the audience with the single expletive: "Georgia!"

Chaplin spent $125,000 refurbishing *The Gold Rush*, which had cost $2,000,000 to make. While editing out whole sequences and shortening others, he added film which had been cut from the original version, lengthening, in particular, the shoe-stewing sequence and another in which Big Jim, dizzy with hunger, sees the Little Fellow as an enormous chicken.

Despite the fact that silent films of *The Gold Rush* era were photographed for projection at 60 feet a minute, the picture unrolls with hardly a jerk at today's 90-feet-a-minute speed. The photography is remarkably good for its age, and the stronger light of modern projection machines considerably improves it.

For the last ten years movie distributors have begged Chaplin to reissue some of his great comedies. Chaplin now 52, and as fiscally astute as ever, is ready to pretty-up *The Circus* for reissue if *The Gold Rush* box office warrants it.

September 7, 1942

The Big Street (RKO-Radio) is a pleasant bit of paranoia that cannot possibly displease anyone, but may baffle some cinemaddicts for a while. It is also the first of Damon Runyon's homely tales about Times Square to be produced by him.

When Her Highness (Lucille Ball), an imperious nightclub queen, gets publicly slapped downstairs and fetches up at the bottom hopelessly crippled, it looks as if she or

Author-Producer Damon Runyon were crazy. It turns out that she is. A doctor explains that Her Highness is a paranoiac, which means, he says, that she wants to be what she can't be, and if she can't be, she will die. So Pinks (Henry Fonda), a lovelogged busboy, takes care of her.

Pinks feeds her on leftover champagne and caviar from the nightclub where he works. He plays butler for her, trundles her all the way from Manhattan to Miami in her wheel chair, plants her in the path of the playboy she is trailing. Risking a 20-year jail turn, Pinks blackmails the crook who slapped her (Barton MacLane) into a one-night loan of a nightclub (complete with Ozzie Nelson), stages a blowout to bolster Her Highness' fading delusions of grandeur. To cap the climax, Pinks appears in full dress, and Her Highness sees him for the first time as he really is. Galvanized by his love (and hers), she dances a few miraculous steps with him only to die, happy, in his arms.

This harmless charade has a certain honky-tonk charm for which those who liked Damon Runyon's *Butch Minds the Baby* will be warmly prepared. The talk is the patented Runyon brand of Times Square Swahili, in which a worn-out race horse is "practically mucilage," and marriage is described as "one room, two chins, three kids." There is the usual Runyon *corps de ballet* of ham-hearted grifters, heisters and passers, played by a friendly crowd of veterans from Hollywood (Eugene Pallette, Louise Beavers) and Broadway (Sam Levene, Millard Mitchell). Carefully solemn Henry Fonda has the dignity of a wax grape of wrath among satiated little foxes. Pretty Lucille Ball, who was born for the parts Ginger Rogers sweats over, tackles her "emotional" role as if it were sirloin and she didn't care who was looking. There is also a headwaiter played by sinister, saturnine Hans Conried. He packs so much cold, superb style into his half minute that he makes everybody else's fun look forced.

Good shot: Miss Ball, crippled and propped up in bed, trying to do a conga from the hips up. She does it very nicely.

Hollywood's best bet on why Damon Runyon became a producer is that he glumly watched Mark Hellinger move up from script writing to producing, swore that he could do anything Hellinger could do and do it better. At first he so loathed California that his wife bet him a dozen of his famed cacophonous Charvet ties that he wouldn't last four weeks. He stuck it out five months at RKO, signed a contract with 20th Century–Fox, and has since become, in most respects, an acclimated if eccentric Hollywoodsman.

Runyon is the community champ at gin rummy. He never drinks, loves to eat, spends every available hour holding levees at Mike Lyman's restaurant on Vine Street. He is inordinately proud 1) of the fact that nobody has ever paid a check while he was at the table, 2) of his ties (people on the lot swear he wore a new one, each louder than the last, every day for five months), 3) of a wire from his good friend Lord Beaverbrook: "Thanks for the ties. They ought to get me more attention in my present work. Max."

Runyon's prime beefs about living in Hollywood are that he has to pay his own telegraph tolls on his syndicated column, and that he has to get up early. He has a mole's dislike of daylight and fresh air. His office windows and shades are in perpetual blackout, and on the set this summer he wore, even on the hottest days, an ankle-length suede overcoat, griped mildly but continuously at every intrusive breeze.

Unlike many producers, Runyon leaves the technical jobs to those who understand them. He develops no stomach ulcers by throwing around his employers' money. He keeps well within his budget. He does most of his real work—endless attention to details of wardrobe, characterization, dialogue—alone, at night. He is calm. He stays out of Director Irving Reis's hair. When Runyon kidnapped smart young Director Reis from RKO's low-budget *Falcon* series, he took Reis to Manhattan, walked him through four solid hours of old friends (Mike Jacobs, bookies, shirtmakers, etc.), then said: "Good night. I think you can direct the picture now."

Reis attributes Runyon's success as a producer to the fact that he is an incurable, archetypical film addict: "He sees every scene through the lay eyes of the average audience, unburdened by any technical knowledge."

If Reis is right, *The Big Street* should be a howling success. Runyon has seen it at least 100 times. No matter how familiar he is with the tear-jerker scenes, he can still be relied on to cough loudly into his handkerchief or to grope on the floor for an imaginary object, in order to be alone with thoughts too deep for public tears. One day he saw it with the "Deathwatch," a group of sound, camera and musical technicians who are so-called because they have no interest in, or comment to make on, any film as entertainment. "Gee, Irving," he said to Reis, "It didn't play so good today, did it?"

June 28, 1943

The Russian Story (Artkino) gives such U.S. audiences as can get to it* a chance to see several great episodes from the ill-distributed Soviet film masterpieces of the past two decades. They are, however, grossly mulled and mauled into an attempted movie history of Russia. The history is propagandistic and sketchy (one notable omission is Napoleon) and the end result is a considerable cinematic crime.

The picture was flung together in the U.S. with the blessing of the National Council for American Soviet Friendship. A flatulent commentary with lines like "Fly, you banners—there is no wind strong enough to blow you down" is ping-ponged between Blues-Singer Libby Holman and mopey Actor Morris Carnovsky. The famous suspense with which Director Sergei Eisenstein prefaced the battle in *Alexander Nevsky* has been unmercifully hacked when half a minute of editorial discretion would have kept it whole, and the excellent battle music which Prokofieff contrived for that sequence becomes an aural trunk murder. Eisenstein's appalling scene in which soldiers drive civilians down a great flight of steps in Odessa (*Potemkin*) has also been tampered with—it is now a shambles instead of a few minutes of cinema as brilliantly organized as a movement in a Beethoven symphony.

Yet the picture is worth seeing—its great excerpts from the past are tributes to directors of genius and to a nation which, for a while, gave them a chance to work as cinema talents have

---

*Soviet films used to reach only a few big U.S. cities; now the chances are better. *Moscow Strikes Back* has played some 3,500 U.S. theaters. The average U.S. film plays around 12,000.

seldom been permitted to work. Even in mangled form, such scenes as the silver blaze of ripe wheat and sunflowers full of struggling men, crazed horses and black explosions (in Director Alexander Dovzhenko's *Shors*) are still able to make any perceptive U.S. filmgoer who has seen only the best advertised native films wonder, seriously, whether he has ever seen a real moving picture before. These Russian classics shine against the cheap, easy sheen of most films (and much of this film) as nobly as a battle flag against the patriotism worn by a chorus girl for a breechclout.

January 31, 1944

The Song of Bernadette (20th Century–Fox) will doubtless be one of the box-office bingos of the new year. It may not be, as its producers gasp, "a motion picture so powerful . . . so majestic . , . so deep in its understanding . . . that for one immortal moment you touch the eternal truth . . . the final fulfillment . . . of everything you are . . . or ever hope to be." Nevertheless, it is a remarkably good moving picture—an improvement on Franz Werfel's reverent novel about the French peasant girl who saw the Blessed Virgin and, with her help, discovered a miraculously healing spring at Lourdes.

When Bernadette Soubirous first saw, or believed she saw, her shining Lady (1858), the local rationalists hauled her before the police, hired a psychiatrist for her, boarded up her healing spring, did everything possible to discredit her. At first only the primitive, the wretched, the poor, believed in her with the intensity of their massive, sorrowful faith. Bernadette's priest (Charles Bickford) found it painfully hard to believe her. The Roman Catholic Church was cautious, but at last was convinced, and Bernadette spent her last years in a convent.

The Song of Bernadette lacks the razor-edged realism, the urgent poetry, the freshet-like creative vitality of great cinema or great religious vision. Sometimes its too high cinematic and religious gentility betrays itself awkwardly, as in the efforts of the cast to say *maman* (French for "mamma"), which is pronounced practically every way except mammy. But within its limits, most of *The Song of Bernadette* is reverent, spiritually forthright, dignified. The photography is continuously elegant. Most of the cast (especially Gladys Cooper as a Mistress of Novices) plays with unusual soberness and intensity.

As Bernadette, Newcomer Jennifer Jones (real name: Phylis Isley) makes one of the most impressive screen debuts in many years. It remains to be seen whether or not Cinemactress Jones can do in other roles the delicately dynamitic things she achieves as this little peasant saint. If she can, Hollywood should watch and guard Miss Jones as sedulously as the Church watched over Bernadette.

February 14, 1944

The Miracle of Morgan's Creek (Paramount) is a little like taking a nun on a roller coaster. Its ordinary enough subject —the difficulties of a small-town girl, pregnant, without a husband—is treated with the catnip giddiness to be expected from Writer-Director Preston Sturges (*The Great McGinty, The Lady Eve*). The overall result is one of the most violently funny comedies, one of the most original, vigorous and cheerfully outrageous moving pictures that ever came out of Hollywood. The picture also has its faults—both as fun and as cinema.

Morgan's Creek is the home town of Trudy Kockenlocker (Betty Hutton), a daftly endearing innocent who gradually remembers one morning that she married a transient soldier the night before—his name was something, she recalls, like Private Ratzkywatzsky. Presently she also realizes that she is pregnant. Fond as she is of her widower Poppa (William Demarest), she knows better than to confide in him; he has the worst film temper since the twilight of the Keystone Cops. But her young sister Emily (Diana Lynn) knows precisely what Trudy must do. She must marry Norval before he knows what he is in for.

Norval (Eddie Bracken) is Trudy's unwanted steady, a poor stammering loon of a 4-F whose stupidity is excelled only by his utterly selfless devotion. As Trudy watches him gratefully writhing in her clutches, she begins for the first time to love him. His efforts to save her good name, fantastically inept and deeply touching, would melt much colder hearts than hers. At the picture's end Norval, through no doing of his own, is at once ridiculous, pitiful and a national hero. As he shows up in his splendid new uniform, flash-bulbed, bewildered, happy, homely, still unaware of what is in store for him, he receives the brass-band salute aptly paraphrased as "AND the MONkey wrapped his TAIL a-round the FLAG POLE. . . ."

That salute is characteristic of Preston Sturges' treatment of a theme which might more normally interest Theodore Dreiser or some true-confessions Dumas. Sturges, like René Clair, has always understood the liberating power of blending comedy and realism, wild farce and cool intellect. But the best of the domestic and anarchic satire cannot be suggested on paper; it is too thoroughly cinematic. It reaches its perfection in William Demarest, whose performance is one of the few solidgold pieces of screen acting in recent years. But chief credit for *The Miracle* must go to Sturges, who has given the slick, growing genteelism of U.S. cinema the roughest and healthiest shaking up it has had since the disease became serious.

The chief failures are his, too. Some of the fun is painfully unfunny, because it is like a joker who outroars his audience's reaction. Some of the pity is not pitiful because it is smashed before it has a chance to crystallize. Most of the finest human and comic potentialities of the story are lost because Sturges is so much less interested in his characters than in using them as hobbyhorses for his own wit. His good friend and master, René Clair, is near the heart of it when he says, "Preston is like a man from the Italian Renaissance: he wants to do everything at once. If he could slow down, he would be great; he has an enormous gift and he should be one of our leading creators. I wish he would be a little more selfish and worry about his reputation."

The life of Preston Sturges might read as dizzily as one of his own comedies if it were not, in essence, so intensely bitter. On his first day at school in Chicago, Preston rode a bicycle and wore a Greek chiton. The bicycle was his stepfather's influence—Solomon Sturges, stockbroker and socialite, was a champion cyclist and a good amateur baseball player. The Attic haberdashery was his mother's idea. Mary Dempsey, who changed her name to Beatricci D'Este and finally settled for Mary Desti, was the bosom friend of Isadora Duncan.

Preston's mother was determined that he should be a genius.

"I was never allowed," Sturges says, "to play with other kids. They wedged art into me from every side. I was dragged into every goddamn museum in the world." There were gay moments, but they usually stank of culture.

The effect of such training was predictable. "They did everything they could," he says, "to make me an artist, but I didn't want to be an artist. I wanted to be a good businessman like my father." He was accordingly delighted when, at 16, he became manager of the Deauville branch of Mary's Paris cosmetics firm. When the U.S. entered World War I he joined the Air Corps, served in Tennessee and Florida till the Armistice.

After the war, Sturges returned to the Maison Desti. He knew a good deal about cosmetics, invented a kissproof lipstick. His mother, in England with a fourth husband, was on the rocks again. She claimed the business; he handed it over and went to work as a free-lance inventor. By the time he was 30 he was about as flat a failure as a man of his age and background could be. Then his appendix ruptured, and saved his life.

For six weeks, in a Chicago hospital, Sturges lay flat on his back. He emerged with an absolute determination to become a playwright, a no less absolute confidence in his ability. Sturges' second play, *Strictly Dishonorable*, which he wrote in six days, was a great Broadway comedy hit, running 69 weeks.

After three flops, Sturges went to Hollywood. For eight years he pestered producers to let him direct his own pictures; finally, after he had written 13 screen plays, Paramount's William Le Baron gave him his chance with *The Great McGinty*. This was the surprise hit of 1940. Some Hollywoodians even accepted Sturges' startling theory—that one man with a good head is better than any hundred men bumping heads.

Sturges' brilliant, successful yet always deeply self-sabotaging films suggest a warring blend of the things he picked up through respect for his solid stepfather, contact with his strange mother, and the intense need to enjoy himself and to succeed which came from 30 years of misery and failure. From his life with his mother he would seem to have gotten not only an abiding detestation for the beautiful *per se*, the noble emotion nobly expressed, but also his almost corybantic intelligence. From Solomon Sturges, on the other hand, Preston may have derived his exaggerated respect for plain success, which leaves him no patience towards artists of integrity who fail at the box office. The combination might explain his match-less skill in producing some of the most intoxicating bits of nihilism the screen has known, but always at the expense of a larger excellence.

Meanwhile Sturges has two pictures waiting in the can. One is called *Hail the Conquering Hero*. The other, *Great Without Glory*, is an adaptation of René Fülöp-Miller's *Triumph Over Pain*, which was the story of anesthesia. It is still the story of anesthesia—but it is also a Sturges farce. It remains to be seen what Sturges might do with really major material, such as *Seven Against Thebes*, or the Oberammergau Players.

April 24, 1944

Follow the Boys (Universal) is a glorification of the service which cinemice and men are rendering the Armed Forces. It is well described by an old subtitle from a comedy of the silent movies. The subtitle introduced the heavy as "muscle-bound from patting himself on the back."

Once in a great while a biceps unflexes, and the result is a good act. W. C. Fields, looking worn-and-torn but as noble as Stone Mountain, macerates a boozy song around his cigar butt and puts on his achingly funny pool exhibition with warped cues. Donald O'Connor continues to prove himself a Mickey Rooney with some unspoiled, big-Adam's-apple charm to boot. Orson Welles, as a nice parody of a magician, saws Marlene Dietrich in two and watches her better half walk off with the act. Sophie Tucker, the Manassa Mauler of her field, shouts a 1½-entendre salute to the boys through a meat-grinder larynx. Dinah Shore, singing *I'll Get By* over the short waves, soothes the entire planet in generously buttered mush. Ted Lewis talks through his top hat, and everybody who has ever liked Lewis—or John Barrymore—is happy. There are at least a dozen other acts, some of them all right. But they seem like three dozen, and the air gets so thick with self-congratulation that it is hard to see the patriotism.

Wriggling through all this dense tedium-laudamus, like a

Pekingese lost in a shopping rush, is a story. George Raft, a hoofer, marries Vera Zorina, a dancer. But George can think of nothing but camp shows and Vera can think of nothing except their impending baby (about which she is too miffed to tell him), so they part. Before they can make it up Raft dies, a hero, in the Pacific. His widow becomes the pride of the USO.

It Happened Tomorrow (United Artists). The idea which Dudley Nichols and René Clair picked up from an obscure one-acter by Lord Dunsany—what happens to a man who beats the world to the next day's news—sounds more comically appetizing than it is. Dick Powell, cub reporter for a Manhattan newspaper of the '90s, is the man who thinks it would be fun to know the future. An old city-desk pensioner (72-year-old Newcomer John Philliber), on the point of death, decides the boy needs a lesson, hands it out to him in easy doses in the form of three issues of the paper, neatly printed, a day ahead of time. Thanks to this ectoplasmic tip-sheet, Reporter Powell scores a beat on a box-office holdup, runs foul of irate Police Inspector Edgar Kennedy as a suspected accomplice, saves pretty Linda Darnell from pseudo suicide, sees a chance to stack up a quick fortune at the races—and comes smack against the third day's headlines, which announce his own violent death. The picture's funniest moments show him trying to worm his way out of that one.

Students of cinematic style will find many shrewdly polished bits in *It Happened Tomorrow* to admire and enjoy; and Dick Powell's graceful sportiness and Linda Darnell's new-minted loveliness are two arresting samples of what wise directing can do. But by and large the simple comic pleasures of the picture lose themselves in intricate artifice, until the last half-hour. Then, with the crowded, horse-playful race-track scenes and with the long, romping cops-and-robbers chase which ends the picture, cinemaddicts will know for sure that this film is the work of René Clair, the French cinemagician whose *Le Million, Sous les Toits de Paris* and *À Nous la Liberté* are among the most inspired screen comedies ever made.

May 1, 1944

G*oing My Way* (Paramount) goes the way of tons of Hollywood flesh this season: it is a religious picture. It is also one of
the year's top surprises. It presents Bing Crosby as a Catholic
priest, and gets away with it so gracefully that Crosby, the
priesthood and the audience are equal gainers. It offers, in the
performance of nutcracker-faced, 56-year-old Barry Fitzgerald,
the finest, funniest and most touching portrayal of old age that
has yet reached the screen. In so doing, it points the way to the
great films which will be possible when Hollywood becomes
aware of the richness and delight of human character observed
for its own sake.

The story, without rich characterization, would be nothing
much. A young priest (Bing Crosby) is sent by his bishop
to help out an old one (Barry Fitzgerald) in Manhattan's
mortgage-ridden St. Dominic's. For a while, they do not get
along; but young Father O'Malley fixes up everything else almost too easily. He deals with a delinquent girl (Jean Heather)
so silkily that before long she is married. He handles the jail-
fodder kids of the street so astutely that before long they are
singing Mozart's *Ave Verum* and liking it. He even teaches old
Father Fitzgibbon how to play golf. He also writes songs
which, with the help of an old friend who sings in opera (Metropolitan Diva Risé Stevens), he sells so effectively that the
parish, despite a disastrous fire, rises clear of all financial problems. And just before he leaves St. Dominic's to trouble-shoot
for another decrepit priest, he brings Father Fitzgibbon's
mother across on a surprise trip from Ireland, for the picture's
unusually valid and powerful tear-jerking climax.

Strictly speaking, this hardly has a right to pose as a religious
film. There is no real contest with evil or with suffering, and the
good itself loses half its force, because even the worst people in
Going My Way are as sugar-coated as *Mrs. Wiggs of the Cabbage
Patch*. Yet it has, inadvertently, a good deal of genuine religious quality, and is often a beautiful piece of entertainment in
spite of its Sunny-Jim story. Leo McCarey's leisured, limpid
direction and Steven Seymour's splendid sets are partly responsible for this—the coarse lace half-curtains, waxed floors
and seldom-used ashtrays of the rectory are evocative just short

of genius. But the best reasons are the loving attention to character, and some magnificent acting. Father Fitzgibbon might have been any brogue-rippling old male biddy. But as Fitzgerald portrays him—senile, vain, childish, stubborn, good, bewildered, stupid—he is the quintessence of the pathos, dignity and ludicrousness which old age can display. Father O'Malley, still more dangerously, might have been one of those brisk, bland up-and-comers who have made an impure science of "not acting like a priest at all." Instead he is subtle, gay, debonair —a wise young priest whose arresting resemblance to Bing Crosby never obscures his essential power.

Going My Way is a sort of friendly contest between two diametrically different kinds of acting: Fitzgerald's, the immensely experienced, stagewise sort which leaves mere virtuosity miles behind, and Crosby's, which is hardly acting at all, but merely the unaffected exploitation of an amiable personality. The picture shows that neither kind, at its best, can possibly be beat, and that together, they bring just about the last word in teamwork. It will surprise nobody who sees Crosby's performance, and the breadth of his control over the film as a whole, that he has just signed a ten-year contract with Paramount and is preparing—on the side—to make his debut as a producer (first picture: *The Great John L.*). Even so the picture is not his; it is Fitzgerald's.

Back in 1914 a tiny (5 ft. 3 in.), easygoing Irish civil servant named William Joseph Shields stood on the stage of Dublin's great Abbey Theatre, quakingly ready to deliver himself of his first speaking role. It was brief. The play was Sheridan's *The Critic* and his entire role, as "2nd Sentry," was to meet the cue "All this shall to Lord Burley's ear" with a yes-man's "'Tis meet it should." Just before the cue, the malicious actor next him whispered, and the terrified Mr. Shields repeated, loud and clear, "'Tis sheet it mould." He has been a comedian ever since.

Before long Shields was known to Dublin theatergoers as Barry Fitzgerald; he picked up the name, he remembers, from "the man in charge of programs."

For 15 years Fitzgerald acted only part-time, working part-time, too, as a "nominal" student at the Abbey. Gradually he got more important roles and a deeper interest in them; at last he quit his civil service desk for good. His first full-time professional appearance was in *The Silver Tassie*, in 1929. His friend Sean O'Casey wrote it especially for him.

The Abbey Theatre has never stultified itself with a starring system; if it had, Fitzgerald and Sara Allgood would undoubtedly have been headliners. When the Players toured the U.S. in 1934, a passel of critics and actors gave Fitzgerald a scroll calling him "the most versatile character comedian in the world today." A lot of reputable people still refer to him, automatically, as the finest living actor.

In spite of such abilities and encomiums, Fitzgerald had a run of negligible roles in Hollywood from the time he and three other Players put *The Plough and the Stars* on film (under John Ford's direction, 1937) to *Going My Way*. Said he, on a return trip to the Manhattan stage: "I didn't have the energy to come away. I made a little money and I thought I'd take a holiday. Weeks stretched into months and months into years. . . . I didn't like Hollywood. It is a dull and enervating place. And the girls are not half so lovely as they are cracked up to be. They have a hard and anxious look about them." What he did like was the mountaineers of West Virginia, whose reticence and modesty remind him of people in remote parts of Ireland. Even better, Fitzgerald likes to stroll around Harlem. "The Negroes there seem to live so casual a life. And there is much in a casual life."

Fitzgerald is a slow "study," not because of dull memory but because he learns the character instead of the lines. The role of Father Fitzgibbon was built up bit by bit from Fitzgerald's remembrance of a priest in Ireland; he and McCarey did a good deal of restyling on the set; and a lot of the character emerged for the first time in the shooting, as fresh as nascent oxygen.

July 3, 1944

Bathing Beauty (MGM) plunges streamlined swimming Champion Esther ("Prettiest Girl in Hollywood") Williams into her first starring role. The splash is celebrated in Technicolor, to the music of Harry James and Xavier Cugat. Red

Skelton lends the show comedic water wings. A song writer preparing a score for a water pageant, he falls in love with Miss Williams, crashes a girls' college where she teaches. There, with the help of numerous undergraduate cuties (notably pert, pint-sized Jean Porter), he revolutionizes the music department and, in wrinkled pink tights and a *tutu* as graceless as the hind elevation of an under-privileged hen, turns a class in eurythmics into the picture's funniest scene.

Miss Williams, a pretty young woman in the pink of condition, should have a pleasant and pleasing career on the screen. Dry and dressed, she suggests Ginger Rogers. Wet and peeled, as she slithers her subaqueous charms before underwater cameras, she suggests a porpoise amused by its own sex appeal.

July 17, 1944

Since You Went Away (Selznick–United Artists). The duck that hatched a swan was lucky compared to David Oliver Selznick. He hatched *Gone With the Wind* and has been trying to hatch another ever since. Last week he punctuated four pictureless years* with *Since You Went Away*, a marathon of home-front genre-filming. Sure enough, it was no *Gone With the Wind*. *The Wind* blew for four solid hours; *Went* goes on for ten minutes short of three. *The Wind* cost $4,000,000 to make; *Went*, a mere $2,400,000. *The Wind* was photographed in some of the most florid Technicolor ever seen; *Went* is in Quaker black and white and Hollywood's pearliest mezzotones. *The Wind* was perhaps the greatest entertainment natural in screen history; *Went*, though its appeal is likely to be broad, is essentially a "woman's picture." But it is obviously, in every foot, the work of one of Hollywood's smartest producers.

Since You Went Away is simply the story of a year (1943) and the things it does to the inmates of "that fortress, the American Home." If The Home is not an average U.S. reality, it is an average U.S. dream.

Head of this Home is Mr. Hilton who is a captain away at

* *Rebecca*, released after GWTW, was finished by the time GWTW was premièred.

war. Only his photograph ever appears in the film. Mrs. Hilton the U.S. dream housewife, is Claudette Colbert, acting her age. She is graciously patronizing to tradesmen, affectionate toward her servant (Hattie McDaniel) patient even with her bitchy cocktail-acquaintance (Agnes Moorehead) and a good mother to her two daughters.

Daughter Jane (Jennifer Jones) is dewily luminous. Daughter Brig is Shirley Temple. Chief reason U.S. cinemaddicts have breathlessly awaited *Since You Went Away* was to see Miss Temple in her first grown-up part. She is charming.

When Mrs. Hilton, to make ends meet, takes in a roomer, he is Monty Woolley, a retired colonel almost as crustily beaverish as "The Man Who Came to Dinner," but a lot nicer to have around. His G.I. grandson is Robert Walker, all feet, thumbs and fumbling charm. Miss Jones (in real life the former Mrs. Walker) falls in love with him and gives him self-confidence. Another visitor is the Hilton's dearest friend, Naval Lieutenant Joseph Cotten. Rejected by Miss Colbert, he has become a perennial bachelor.

As the year 1943 unwinds, these characters change and grow as they seldom get time to do in films. Miss Colbert greys preceptibly and learns to be a welder. An immigrant welder (Alla Nazimova) tells her that she embodies her own dearest dreams of America. Startling cinemaudacity: months after her husband is reported missing, Welder Colbert toys with the idea of accepting Mr. Cotten at last. Earlier Cotten seriously considers trying to seduce her.

Miss Jones begins the film with a nubile crush on her gallant "Uncle" Cotten. Before it is over, she is a full-fledged nurse's aide, whom war has robbed of Fiancé Walker. Miss Temple, too young for boys, misses her father intensely and has an innocent crush on Monty Woolley. Mr. Woolley becomes so thoroughly domesticated in the U.S. Home that he even calls a truce with Soda, a huge, wallowing, old, white bulldog who is perhaps the surest-fire character in this sure-fire picture.

What makes *Since You Went Away* sure-fire is in part its homely subject matter, which has never before been so earnestly tackled in a film, in part its all-star acting (everybody registers with all his might, down to Lionel Barrymore's few seconds as a preacher and Newcomer Guy Madison's brief, effective appearance as a sailor), most of all David Selznick's extremely astute screen play and production.

Selznick has given Claudette Colbert the richest, biggest role of her career. She rewards him consistently with smooth Hollywood formula acting, and sometimes—especially in collaboration with Mr. Cotten—with flashes of acting that are warmer and more mature. He has brought his newest find, Jennifer (*The Song of Bernadette*) Jones out of the cloister and made her an All-American girl. She rewards him with a nervous, carefully studied, somewhat overintense performance. Selznick placed a big bet on Shirley Temple's comeback and she pays off enchantingly as a dogged, sensitive, practical little girl with a talent for bargaining.

Though idealized, the Selznick characterizations are authentic to a degree seldom achieved in Hollywood. When a high-school graduating class sings *America the Beautiful*, the voices are touchingly inchoate, the singers' faces as stolidly reverent, and the shot of the Lincoln statue which begins the song and the meowing cat which ends it, are a deft, valid blend of showmanship, humor and yard-wide Americanism. The wounded men in *Since You Went Away* really look wounded, for almost the first time in a U.S. fiction war film. There are scores of such evidences of a smart showman's eye, mind and heart. Added up, they give the picture taste, shrewdness, superiority, life. Now and then the idealization runs too far ahead of the normal reality. But by and large the blend of flesh and fantasy is pretty close to Hiltonesque life in the U.S. Home.

August 21, 1944

*H*ail the *Conquering Hero* (Paramount), the newest cinematic caprice from Preston Sturges (*The Great McGinty*, *The Miracle of Morgan's Creek*), beats a satirical tattoo on the American small town. But it tells a story so touching, so chock-full of human frailties and so rich in homely detail that it achieves a reality transcending the limitations of its familiar slapstick.

Expertly sandwiched between the pratfalls and the broad pie-throwing burlesque of suburban manners lies a richer comedy idea—the alchemy by which a phoney hero is trans-

muted from the base metal of conventional heroics to the pure
gold of true heroism.

Woodrow Lafayette Pershing Truesmith (Eddie Bracken), an
awkward, befuddled but eager son of suburbia, is the "hero."
Given a rousing-send-off by fellow citizens of Oakridge, California, he marches confidently off to war, only to be ignomini-
ously bounced out of Marine boot camp because of his chronic
hay fever. Burning with shame, he thinks of his father, Hinky
Dink Truesmith, a hero who died gloriously at Belleau Wood
on the day his son was born; of his mother, so proud and radiant, weeping on the station platform; of the brass bands
tootling and banners proudly declaiming: "Like father, like
son."

So mortified is Hinky Dink's boy that he heroically hood-
winks his mother into thinking he really is leathernecking it on
Guadalcanal, writes his girl (Ella Raines) that he has fallen in
love with someone else and goes miserably off to work in a
shipyard.

What happens when six real Marines take Woodrow in hand
and forcibly escort him home, his ill-fitting uniform bristling
with extemporaneous decorations, is the stuff which makes
Hail the Conquering Hero one of the year's most ingratiating
pictures. When grateful townspeople solemnly burn the mortgage on the old Truesmith homestead and make plans to erect
a suitable monument in the town square, Woodrow's misery
seems to have reached its bearable limit. But it touches new
depths when, in one of the most uproarious political cam-
paigns in cinema history, the desperately reluctant Woodrow is
nominated for Mayor.

In vain he explains that it's all a mistake, he did it for his
mother's sake, and what is more he loves his mother very
much. One city father simply turns to another and whispers
gleefully: "See, he has a natural flair for politics." The sight of
so much suffering inevitably makes Woodrow's ultimate ascent
from his excruciating little comic hell an uncommonly heart-
warming experience.

Take It Or Leave It (20th Century–Fox) is easy to take as
light summer's entertainment. Seaman Eddie Collins (Edward

Ryan) returns to Brooklyn and his lovely and expectant wife Kate (Marjorie Massow). For her confinement she wants the services of eminent Dr. Preston, whose fee is $1,000 and who has no time for the case anyway. Determined to bypass these difficulties, the expectant couple go to a broadcast of Phil Baker's *Take It Or Leave It* program. Eddie succeeds in answering not one but six $64 questions in the breathless interval before Kate leaves the radio audience for the delivery room, while Phil Baker (himself) halts the program to page Dr. Preston over the air.

The six questions and one extra try answered by Eddie deal exclusively with the movies, giving 20th Century–Fox a thrifty opportunity to trot out Betty Grable, Alice Faye, Shirley Temple, Jack Oakie, Sonja Henie, George Montgomery and other high spots clipped from 20th Century–Fox films. Like the picture's obstetrical exigencies, the pace is brisk. Benjamin Stoloff's direction is gingersnappy.

October 23, 1944

To *Have and Have Not* (Warner), having jettisoned a solid 90% of the Ernest Hemingway novel, for which Warner Bros. paid plenty, may make devotees of Hemingway the sourest boycotters since Carrie Nation.* But the sea change which Producer-Director Howard Hawks supervised—for the benefit of Humphrey Bogart, Hoagy (*Star Dust*) Carmichael, and a sensational newcomer named Lauren Bacall (rhymes with McCall)—results in the kind of tinny romantic melodrama which millions of cinemaddicts have been waiting for ever since *Casablanca*.

The screen story of *To Have and Have Not* is still about a couple of low characters named Harry Morgan and Marie, and Harry is still a rugged individualist who takes rich men out fishing and earns side money in whatever nefarious ways turn up. But Harry's beat is no longer the axis between bourgeois Key West and revolutionary Havana; he now works out of

---

*The jettisoning was largely due to censor trouble, caused by the Hays office and by Government worries over Latin American relations.

wartime Martinique, and the villains are Vichyites. Marie is no longer an idealized image of happy marriage; she is a tall, hoarse, egregious, 22-year-old tramp, so worldly-wise that when a policeman all but slaps her jaw out of joint she hardly bats an eye.

Harry Morgan's adventures are also considerably altered. He smuggles Gaulists, slams pistols against Vichyites. Harry Morgan becomes, in fact, one of Humphrey Bogart's most edged portrayals of Nietzsche in dungarees, without whose hard resourcefulness one is forced to infer that the rest of the effete world would quickly fall apart.

But *To Have and Have Not* is neither an action picture nor a Bogart picture. Its story is, in fact, just a loosely painted background for a kind of romance which the movies have all but forgotten about—the kind in which the derelict sweethearts are superficially aloof but essentially hot as blazes, and seem to do even their kissing out of the corners of their mouths. This particular romance is decorated by some sinister yet friendly bits of low-life café atmosphere. Hoagy Carmichael's performance as a cokey-looking ivory-prowler is especially useful for some spidery Caribbean jazz, and for two wryly elegant Carmichael songs. But the most valuable fixture in the show is 20-year-old Lauren Bacall.

Lauren Bacall has cinema personality to burn, and she burns both ends against an unusually little middle. Her personality is compounded partly of percolated Davis, Garbo, West, Dietrich, Harlow and Glenda Farrell, but more than enough of it is completely new to the screen. She has a javelinlike vitality, a born dancer's eloquence in movement, a fierce female shrewdness and a special sweet-sourness. With these faculties, plus a stone-crushing self-confidence and a trombone voice, she manages to get across the toughest girl a piously regenerate Hollywood has dreamed of in a long, long while.

Her lines have been neatly tailored to her talents. They include such easy lines of cryptic folk poetry as "Was ya ever bit by a dead bee?" An even easier line, sure to bring down any decently vulgar house, is her comment on Bogart's second, emboldened kiss: "It's even better when you help." Besides good lines, there are good situations and songs for Newcomer Bacall. She does a wickedly good job of sizing up male prospects in a low bar, growls a *louche* song more suggestively than any-one in cinema has dared since Mae West in *She Done Him Wrong* (1933).

Lauren (real name, Betty) Bacall was born on 103rd Street in New York City in September 1924. According to her employ-ers, "she is the daughter of parents who trace their American ancestry back several generations." According to herself, she is part Rumanian, part French, part Russian (she thinks). Her father sold medical instruments. She is an only child. By the time she got out of Julia Richman High, Bette Davis was her idol, and she had seen enough Davis pictures to realize that it takes training to be an actress.

She got a certain amount of training at the American Acad-emy of Dramatic Arts, more as a walk-on, more as an ingénue (directed by George Kaufman). She also worked as an ush-erette, and got a job modeling for *Harper's Bazaar*.

In April 1943 Mrs. Howard Hawks, leafing through the *Bazaar*, caught on her face the way a skirt catches on barbed wire. She showed it to her husband; Producer Howard Hawks was caught too. He wired the magazine, asking whether she was available. The answer came fast, on the Hawks's doorstep, in person. In May 1943 Miss Bacall signed a contract with Hawks; this was shared by Jack Warner as soon as he saw her screen test, a bit of *Claudia*. The test alone is proof of her abilities; for Lauren Bacall (as seen in *To Have and Have Not*) to make even a mediocre stab at such a role is like Tom Dewey's successfully impersonating Lincoln.

For the better part of a year Hawks worked her out mainly in a vacant lot, bellowing anything from Shakespeare to odd copies of shopping news. In the fullness of time Hawks had achieved his purpose: he had developed her voice from "a high nasal pipe to a low guttural wheeze." He instructed her now to speak softly and naturally, paying no attention to the tradi-tional voice-culture style which he surrealistically compares with "digging post-holes."

Hawks carried his shrewdly contrived campaign of artificial-ized naturalness still further. Time and again he left it up to Lauren to decide for herself about how to play a scene, basing her decision on how she would handle the situation in real life. One of the most successful scenes in the picture is her own invention. After a highly charged few minutes with Bogart, late at night in a cheap hotel room, Marie reluctantly retires to her own quarters. At this point in the shooting, Miss Bacall complained: "God, I'm dumb." "Why?" asked Hawks. "Well, if I had any sense, I'd go back in after that guy." She did.

Lauren Bacall may or may not become a star. Yet only last fortnight, Hawks turned down a rival producer's $75,000 bid for her services. He understands her pretty well, and he has plans.

November 27, 1944

Meet Me in St. Louis (MGM) is a musical that even the deaf should enjoy. They will miss some attractive tunes like the sure-fire "Trolley Song," the graceful "Have Yourself a Merry Little Christmas," the sentimental "You and I" and the naively gay title waltz. But they can watch one of the year's prettiest pictures.

Based on Sally Benson's *New Yorker* stories, *Meet Me in St. Louis* has a good deal more substance and character than most musicals. It is the story of the well-heeled Smith family during the summer and fall and winter of 1903 and, more particularly, of the four Smith Sisters. Rose (Lucille Bremer), the eldest, is merely waiting for a proposal, which at length she gets. Esther (Judy Garland) is tremulously interested in the shy basketball player (Tom Drake) next door. Agnes (Joan Carroll) is still chiefly interested in things like swimming and hunting knives. Tootie (Margaret O'Brien) has a passion for letting her dolls die off so that she can bury them in the backyard.

Tragedy, of a gentle sort, threatens the Smiths when their father (Leon Ames) accepts a business promotion which means their permanent removal to New York. During the later reels of the picture they realize with considerable poignancy just how cherishable the spacious and innocent securities of early 20th-Century life in a good provincial city could be. Director Vincente Minelli and his colleagues are so profitably absorbed in such everyday matters that they make only a curtain-bow to the St. Louis Fair.

The solidest single achievement of the movie, in fact, is to give the Smiths something to be sorry about: the real love story is between a happy family and a way of living. Technicolor has seldom been more affectionately used than in its registrations of the sober mahoganies and tender muslins and benign gaslights of the period. Now and then, too, the film gets well beyond the charm of mere tableau for short flights in the empyrean of genuine domestic poetry. These triumphs are creditable mainly to the intensity and grace of Margaret O'Brien and to the ability of Director Minelli and Co. to get the best out of her. Her song ("Drunk Last Night") and her cakewalk, done in a nightgown at a grown-up party, are entrancing little acts. Her self-terrified Halloween adventures, richly set against firelight, dark streets and the rusty confabulations of fallen leaves, bring this section of the film very near the first-rate. To the degree that this exciting little episode fails, it is because the Halloween setup, like the film as a whole, is too sumptuously, calculatedly handsome to be quite mistakable for the truth.

May 14, 1945

The Clock (MGM), at its best, is so good that it inspires ingratitude for not being great. Its basic story is about as simple and moving as they come. A country-bred corporal (Robert Walker) arrives in New York to spend his last two days' leave before going overseas. After one brief look at the overwhelming city he ducks back into Penn Station. There he stumbles across a girl (Judy Garland), a little Manhattan office worker as lonely as he is.

Together they spend the afternoon sightseeing, the evening strolling in a tamed glade overlooking the Hudson River. A milkman (James Gleason) gives them a lift that turns into a night-long ride through the city; his wife (Lucile Gleason) gives them breakfast and some easygoing advice about marrying in a hurry. Almost against their will, they come to suspect that they are in love. The suspicion becomes a desperate certainty when, still without knowing each other's last names, they get separated in a subway crush.

When they finally find each other again, there is no question about it: they are going to get married. All afternoon, working against the city's implacably ticking clocks, they fight their way through the cruel bureaucratic mazes of getting a blood test, a license, a waiver of the 72 hours' invalidity. They tear in just under the wire for a grimy little civil ceremony that is shattered to bits by the passage of elevated trains. There follows a beautiful, bleak scene in an off-hours lunchroom where a munching stranger at the next table looks on and listens in as they droop over their inedible food, trying to fight off their bewilderment, their disappointment, their misery, their freezing shyness.

There are quite a few things wrong with this picture—some of them basic. The average lonely soldier in New York doesn't have the good luck to pick up Judy Garland, or true love, or anything remotely resembling either. But it could be justly argued that such things do occasionally happen—and ought to happen more often. Once you accept the basic premise, however, there are still drawbacks. The young lovers wouldn't be likely to spend the night so whimsically, to lose each other so casually in the subway, to find each other if they did, or to run into quite so picturesque a combination of gruffly kind metropolitan types. The trouble is more detailed than that. The pretty-enough "background music" (one of Hollywood's worst habits) reduces some of the story-telling from the sadly tender grandeur which the players and the monumental close-ups earn to a sort of oversweetened, high-grade M. G. Mush.

But Director Vincente Minelli's talents are so many-sided and generous that he turns even the most over-contrived romanticism into something memorable. He has brought the budding dramatic talents of his betrothed, Judy Garland, into unmistakable bloom. He has helped give Robert Walker an honest, touching dignity in place of the shucks-fellers cuteness he has sometimes seemed doomed to. It is Director Minelli who gives a passage like the silent breakfast scene its radiance. He has used most of his bit players and extras and crowds and streets so well that time and again you wonder whether some swarming, multitudinously human scenes were made in the actual city, with only a few of the actors aware of concealed cameras.

The Clock is a pleasant, well-told romance rather than the

great, true picture it might have been; but few films in recent
years have managed so movingly to combine first-grade truth
with second-grade fiction.

Vincente Minelli has a number of predilections which normally don't go down too well in Hollywood. Boom shots,
for instance, are generally under suspicion, both esthetically
and economically. A boom shot must either be perfect or be
scrapped. Constant use of a finder, too, is regarded as an affectation. Further, Minelli often reports at the end of a day's
work with only one shot perfected, and he is likely to make
such remarks as: "The accidental juxtaposition of people and
things makes for surrealism. The surrealists are the court
painters of the period. They sum up an age which is at best
utter confusion."

All such arty goings-on would ordinarily mean the kiss of
death to a Hollywood career; but not in Minelli's case. His
semi-surrealist juxtapositions, accidental or no, help turn *The
Clock* into a rich image of a great city. His love of mobility, of
snooping and sailing and drifting and drooping his camera
booms and dollies, makes *The Clock*, largely boom-shot, one
of the most satisfactorily flexible movies since Friedrich Murnau's epoch-making *The Last Laugh*.

Before ordering a shot, he peers forever through his finder,
working to make each shot the most abundant and expressive
possible (he was once a photographer). Besides being "boom-
happy" Minelli is "extra-crazy," taking infinite pains to invent
minor bits of business with anonymous individuals and groups.
No man in the business gets more satisfactory results.

Much of the time, in his slow, expensive efforts at perfection, Minelli drives writers, producers, actors and technicians
quietly out of their habit-hardened professional minds. But he
does it so gently, and always for such excellent reasons, that
they end up, as his producer Arthur Freed says, by "loving
him." Says his cutter, George White, "He may drive you crazy
but he gets what he's after. For a guy who has that much on
the ball, I'll string along."

Chicago-born 38 years ago, of theatrical stock (his mother
was a French actress), fraily handsome Vincente Minelli got
into New York theaters via musical comedy, as a designer of costumes, sets and ballets. Once dropped from Paramount (where

he was paid $2,000 a week), he returned to Hollywood in 1940. Up to now, he has made musicals exclusively (*Cabin in the Sky, I Dood It*, the luscious *Meet Me in St. Louis*). He was frightened at first by the straight-dramatic *Clock*. But he turned it into a directorial tour de force. Studiously as he researches and plans his films, Minelli is no theorist: "The exciting thing about pictures," he says, "is not to have a future plan. I like to work in a new quality every time." At the moment, his only future plan is to marry Judy Garland this June, if studio schedules permit.

June 11, 1945

Pillow to Post (Warner) puts several normally serious-minded Warner properties—notably Ida Lupino, Sydney Greenstreet and Director Vincent Sherman—over the hurdles and through the hoops of a fast, old-fashioned farce. The confusions develop when a young lady (Miss Lupino), in order to make sure of a night's rest in a tourist camp, persuades an Army lieutenant (William Prince) to pose as her husband. The picture plants every grain of corn—from a Negro manservant named Lucille to a small boy who puts a bullfrog in the heroine's valise —which might serve to make it indistinguishable from the old Samuel French masterpieces so dear to pre-Coolidge provincial dramatic societies.

Fortunately, however, corn is edible, and the serious thinkers (Miss Lupino, for that matter, started in comedy) turn out to have a nice knack for foolishness. Typical dialogue: Lieut. Prince (lugubriously eyeing Miss Lupino's knee-length nightgown): "I suppose it gives you freedom." Miss Lupino: "Well, that's what we're fighting for isn't it?"

January 7, 1946

Leave Her to Heaven (20th Century–Fox) is an obviously costly production of the best-selling (more than a million copies) novel by Ben Ames Williams. The story's central idea might be plausible enough in a dramatically lighted black-and-white picture or in a radio show with plenty of organ background. But in the rich glare of Technicolor, all its rental-library characteristics are doubly glaring.

Leave Her's heroine is jealous Ellen (Gene Tierney), whose somewhat too-intense love for her husband (Cornel Wilde) leads her to drown his brother, throw herself downstairs, and eventually poison her own coffee. The unhappy story moves through breath-takingly stylish country interiors which make no particular point except to show that the characters have plenty of chintz-upholstered leisure for getting into mischief.

It is a story of in-law trouble carried to awful extremes. But it is hard to work up any sustained sympathy for the upright characters. Audiences will probably side with the murderess, who spends all of the early reels trying to manage five minutes alone with her husband. Just as it looks possible, she picks up a pair of binoculars and sees his brother, her mother, her adopted cousin and the caretaker approaching by motorboat.

No amount of strenuous plot trouble—or even a long fall down a flight of steps—seems to jar Gene Tierney's smooth deadpan. Waking or sleeping, in ecstasy or anger, joy or sorrow, her pretty, composed features seem to be asking the single, gamin-and-spinach question: "Huh?"

April 8, 1946

MASTERPIECE

THE movies have produced one of their rare great works of art.

When Laurence Olivier's magnificent screen production of Shakespeare's *Henry V* was first disclosed to a group of Oxford's impassive Shakespeare pundits, there was only one murmur of dissent. A woman specialist insisted that all the war horses which take part in the Battle of Agincourt should have been stallions.

The film was given its U.S. premiére* this week (in Boston's

*Producer Filippo Del Giudice says the film will pay for itself in Great Britain (cost: almost $2,000,000). Paralleling Hollywood's bookkeeping on exports, he looks to the U.S. and elsewhere for profits. But United Artists, uneasy about the mass audience, is handling the film timidly. The plan: after

Esquire Theater). This time, the horses engendered no complaint. At last there had been brought to the screen, with such sweetness, vigor, insight and beauty that it seemed to have been written yesterday, a play by the greatest dramatic poet who ever lived. It had never been done before.* For Laurence Olivier, 38 (who plays Henry and directed and produced the picture), the event meant new stature. For Shakespeare, it meant a new splendor in a new, vital medium. Exciting as was the artistic development of Laurence Olivier, last seen by U.S. cinemaddicts in films like *Rebecca* and *Wuthering Heights,* for his production of *Henry V* was even more exciting.

As Shakespeare wrote it, *The Chronicle History of Henry the Fifth* is an intensely masculine, simple, sanguine drama of kinghood and war. Its more eloquent theme is a young king's coming of age. Once an endearingly wild Prince of Wales, Henry V (at 28) had to prove his worthiness for the scepter by leading his army in war. He invaded France, England's longtime enemy. He captured Harfleur, then tried to withdraw his exhausted and vastly outnumbered army to Calais. The French confronted him at Agincourt. In one of Shakespeare's most stirring verbal sennets, Henry urged his soldiers on to incredible victory. English mobility (unarmored archers) and English firepower (the quick-shooting longbow) proved too much for the heavily armored French. Casualties (killed): English, 29; French, 10,000.† With victory came the courtly peacemaking at Rouen, and Henry's triumphant courtship of the French Princess Katherine.

There were important minor touches. In one of the most moving scenes in Shakespeare, Falstaff was killed off. To replace him, his pal, Pistol, the quintessential burlesque of the

---

opening in the most English and academic of U.S. cities, *Henry V* will play twice-a-day in all major cities at legit prices. Heavy play will be made for Mr. Gallup's estimated 15,000,000 who thinks most movies worthless. There will be special rates for colleges, etc. No date has been set for general release.

A Midsummer Night's Dream and *Romeo and Juliet*, the two bravest attempts, were neither good cinema nor good Shakespeare.

†According to Shakespeare and medieval chroniclers, the English lost just 29. (Says Shakespeare's Duke of Exeter in magnificent understatement: " 'Tis wonderful!") English historical estimates: English losses 500. French losses 7,000. French estimates: French losses 10,000. English 1,600.

Elizabethan soul, was played far down to the groundlings. Because in writing *Henry V* Shakespeare was much hampered by the limitations of his stage, there was heavy work for the one-man Chorus, who, in persuasive and beautiful verbal movies, stirred his audience to imagine scenes and movement which the bare and static Elizabethan stage could not provide.

Olivier's *Henry V* frees Shakespeare from such Elizabethan limitations. The film runs two hours and 14 minutes. Seldom during that time does it fudge or fall short of the best that its author gave it. Almost continually, it invests the art of Shakespeare—and the art of cinema as well—with a new spaciousness, a new mobility, a new radiance. Sometimes, by courageous (but never revolutionary) cuts, rearrangements and interpolations, it improves on the original. Yet its brilliance is graceful, never self-assertive. It simply subserves, extends, illuminates and liberates Shakespeare's poem.

It begins with shots of 17th-Century London and Shakespeare's Globe Theater, where *Henry V* is being played. The florid acting of Olivier and his prelates and the Elizabethan audience's vociferous reactions are worth volumes of Shakespearean footnotes. For the invasion, the camera, beautifully assisted by the Chorus (Leslie Banks), dissolves in space through a marine backdrop to discover a massive set such as Shakespeare never dreamed of—and dissolves backward in time to the year 1415. Delicately as a photographic print in a chemical bath, there emerges the basic style of Shakespearean cinema.

Voice and gesture exchange Shakespeare's munificence for subtlety, but remain subtly stylized. Faces, by casting, by close-up and reaction, give Shakespeare's lines a limpid, intimate richness of interpretation which has never been available to the stage. One of the prime joys of the picture is the springwater freshness and immediacy of the lines, the lack of antiquarian culture-clogging. Especially as spoken by Olivier, the lines constantly combine the power of prose and the glory of poetry. Photographic perspectives are shallow, as in medieval painting. Most depths end in two-dimensional backdrops. Often as not, the brilliant Technicolor is deliberately anti-naturalistic. Voice, word, gesture, human beings, their bearing and costumes retain their dramatic salience and sovereignty. The result is a new cinema style.

Falstaff's death scene, for which the speeches were lifted bodily from *Henry IV*, Part 2, is boldly invented. The shrunken, heartbroken old companion of Henry's escapades (George Robey, famed British low comedian) hears again, obsessively, the terrible speech ("A man . . . so old and so profane. . . .") in which the King casts him off. In this new context, for the first time perhaps, the piercing line, "The king has kill'd his heart," is given its full power. In the transition scene which takes the audience from Falstaff's death to the invasion of France, the Chorus makes a final appearance alone against the night sky, then recedes and fades as the movie takes over from him. In a flash of imagination, Britain's armada is disclosed through mist as the Chorus, already invisible, says: *Follow, follow. . . .*

The French court, in fragility, elegance, spaciousness and color, is probably the most enchanting single set ever to appear on the screen. Almost every shot of the French court is like a pre-Renaissance painting. The French King (Harcourt Williams), is weak-minded and piteous as he was in history, if not in Shakespeare. There is one beautiful emblematic shot of his balding, pinkish pate, circled with the ironic gold of royalty.

The French Princess (Renee Asherson) has the backward-bending grace of a medieval statuette of the Virgin. Her reedy, birdlike exchange of French-English with her equally delightful duenna, Alice (Ivy St. Helier), is a vaudeville act exquisitely paced and played beyond anything that Shakespeare can have imagined. Her closing scene with Henry—balanced about equally between Olivier's extraordinarily deft delivery of his lines and her extraordinary deft pantomimic pointing of them —is a charming love scene.

The Battle of Agincourt is not realistic. Olivier took great care not to make it so. To find the "kind of poetic country" he wanted, and to avoid such chance anachronisms as air raids (the picture was made in Britain during the war), Olivier shot the battle sequence in Ireland.*

---

*On the estate of land-poor gentry who, perhaps in gratitude for the sudden prosperity the film brought them, named one of their donkeys for Olivier's wife, Cinemactress Vivien Leigh.

Making no attempt to over-research the actual fight, he re-duced it to its salients—the proud cumbrousness of the ar-mored French chevaliers, and Henry's outnumbered archers, cloth-clad in the humble colors of rural England. A wonderful epitomizing shot—three French noblemen drinking a battle-health in their saddles—is like the crest of the medieval wave. The mastering action of the battle, however, begins with a prodigious truckshot of the bannered, advancing French cav-alry shifting from a walk to a full gallop, intercut with King Henry's sword, poised for signal, and his archers, bows drawn, waiting for it. The release—an arc of hundreds of arrows speeding with the twang of a gigantic guitar on their victorious way—is one of the most gratifying payoffs of suspense yet contrived.

But the most inspired part of Shakespeare's play deals with the night before the Battle of Agincourt. It is also the most in-spired sequence in the film. Olivier opens it with a crepuscular shot of the doomed and exhausted English as they withdraw along a sunset stream to encamp for the night. This shot was made at dawn, at Denham (a miniature British Hollywood) against the shuddering objection of the Technicolor expert. It is one of many things that Olivier and Cameraman Robert Krasker did with color which Technicolor tradition says must not or cannot be done.

The invisible Chorus begins the grandly evocative descrip-tion of the night camps:

> *Now entertain conjecture of a time*
> *When creeping murmur and the poring dark*
> *Fills the wide vessel of the universe.*

The screen sustains this mood with a generalized shot of the opposed camps, their fires like humiliated starlight. There are no creeping murmurs, neighing steeds, crowing cocks, clanking armorers. Instead, William Walton's score, one of the few outstanding scores in movie history, furnishes sub-dued, musical metaphors. Midway through the Chorus, the film boldly breaks off to interpolate, to better effect, a scene in the French camp which in Shakespeare's version precedes it.

This scene itself also improves on Shakespeare. His French-men, the night before their expected triumph, were shallow,

frivolous and arrogant. By editing out a good deal of their foolishness, by flawless casting, directing and playing, and by a wonderfully paced appreciation of the dead hours of rural night,
Olivier transforms the French into sleepy, over-confident,
highly intelligent, highly sophisticated noblemen, subtly disunified, casually contemptuous of their Dauphin—an all but
definitive embodiment of a civilization a little too ripe to
survive.

The hypnotic Chorus resumes; the camera pans to the English camp and strolls, as if it were the wandering King himself,
among the firelit tents.

And here poem and film link the great past to the great
present. It is unlikely that anything on the subject has been
written to excel Shakespeare's short study, in *Henry V*, of men
stranded on the verge of death and disaster. The man who
made this movie made it midway in England's most terrible
war, within the shadows of Dunkirk. In appearance and in
most of what they say, the three soldiers with whom Henry
talks on the eve of Agincourt might just as well be soldiers of
World War II. No film of that war has yet said what they say so
honestly or so well.

Here again Olivier helped out Shakespeare. Shakespeare gave
to a cynical soldier the great speech: *But if the cause be not
good*, etc. Olivier puts it in the mouth of a slow-minded country boy (Brian Nissen). The boy's complete lack of cynicism,
his youth, his eyes bright with sleepless danger, the peasant patience of his delivery, and his Devon repetition of the tolled
word *die* as *doy*, lift this wonderful expression of common
humanity caught in human war level with the greatness of the
King.

Henry V is one of the great experiences in the history of motion pictures. It is not, to be sure, the greatest: the creation of
new dramatic poetry is more important than the recreation of
old. For such new poetry, movies offer the richest opportunity
since Shakespeare's time, and some of them have made inspired use of the chance. But *Henry V* is a major achievement
—this perfect marriage of great dramatic poetry with the
greatest contemporary medium for expressing it.

Producer-Director Olivier is very earnest in his desire to
share the honors of his production with those who helped him.

His friend Dallas Bower, a producer for BBC, was responsible for the idea of the production.

The Royal Navy had given Olivier leave to make *Demi-Paradise* (*Adventure for Two*) in the interest of Anglo-Russian relations, and extended it so that he could make *Henry V* "in the interests," says Olivier, "of Anglo-British relations."

Producer Filippo Del Giudice (who promoted Noel Coward's *In Which We Serve* on an original £15,000 shoestring) furnished some, and raised more, of the £465,000 (a little under $2,000,000) which *Henry V* cost.

Del Giudice did something more remarkable: he never interfered with Olivier's work; he never let him know that there were money difficulties. It was Del Giudice who suggested the excellent cameraman who had never worked in Technicolor before. He also suggested that Olivier should direct and produce the film as well as star in it. For those scenes in which Olivier played, his cutter, Reginald Beck, took over the direction. Their collaboration resulted in a mere twenty-five per cent throwaway of film, instead of the usual British fifty per cent and Hollywood ninety per cent. Olivier and Alan Dent (the London *News-Chronicle*'s ace theater critic whose long suit is Shakespeare) teamed inextricably on the superb editing of Shakespeare's play. The final preparation of the shooting script was a team effort by all hands. But it was Olivier who called in Costume Designers Roger and Margaret Furse and Roger Ramsdell (an old Yaleman). It was Olivier who sought out William Walton, whom he regards as "the most promising composer in England." It was he who recruited all-important Art Directors Paul Sheriff and Carmen Dillon. He made use, in fact, of a good deal of talent which most professional moviemakers overlook. And within the profession, he respected professionals more than they usually respect each other.

It was chiefly Olivier who did the brilliant casting; he who gave the French court its more-than-Shakespearean character. Many of the most poetic ideas in cutting and transition were also his. Above all, his was the whole anti-naturalistic conception of the film—a true Shakespearean's recognition that man is greater, and nature less, than life.

The career of Laurence Olivier (pronounced O'lívvy yay) was decided at fifteen, when he played Katherine in a boys-school production of *The Taming of the Shrew*. When he announced that he wanted to go on the stage, his father, a rural Anglo-Catholic clergyman, did not groan: "Better that I should see you dead." Instead, he gave his endorsement and financial support. At seventeen, young Olivier enrolled at the Central School of Dramatic Art, which is second only to London's Royal Academy of Dramatic Art. At eighteen, he was able to tell the Oliviers' old housekeeper, who asked what Laurence did in his first professional engagement: "When you're sitting having your tea during the interval [intermission], and you hear the bell summoning you back to your seat, you'll know that my finger is on the bell."

Later, more substantial parts in plays like *Journey's End*, *The Green Bay Tree*, *No Time for Comedy* proved Olivier to be one of the thoroughly good English actors. His performances as Hamlet, Sir Toby Belch, Macbeth, Henry V, Romeo, Iago, Coriolanus, Mercutio earned him a solid, if by no means pre-eminent, reputation as a Shakespearean actor—and gave him invaluable experience. He also picked up a good deal of experience, which he scarcely valued at all, acting intermittently in movies.

For years Olivier "just thought of movies as a quick way to earn money." In the '30s, his work with sincere, painstaking Director William Wyler made him realize that they can amount to a lot more. His fine performance as Heathcliff in *Wuthering Heights* first suggested that Olivier might be a great actor in the making. But Olivier was never really happy in Hollywood. He disliked the climate; he was homesick for the stage.

When England went to war, he planned, like his good friend Cinemactor David Niven, to join the air force. But he could not get out of his contract. While sweating it out, he took flying lessons and, in an unusually short time, piled up 200 hours.

In two years' service Olivier became a lieutenant in the Fleet Air Arm. He stepped unhurt out of a number of forced or crash landings, gave ground and gunnery instruction, never saw combat. But when he got back to work once more as an actor, theatrical London realized that a remarkable new artist had appeared. Olivier has no explanation for the change in himself except to say: "Maybe it's just that I've got older."

Now, as co-manager (with his friend, fellow flyer and fellow actor Ralph Richardson and with John Burrell) of London's Old Vic Theater, Olivier works at least ten hours a day. For recreation he spends quiet evenings after work at the home of friends, listening to phonograph music (Mozart is a favorite). When possible, he runs up to his country home, the 15th-Century Notley Abbey in Buckinghamshire, where his second wife Vivien Leigh is convalescing from tuberculosis.

Next month Olivier and Richardson will bring the Old Vic troupe to Manhattan for six weeks of Sophocles, Shakespeare, Sheridan and Chekhov. Later Olivier would like to film *Macbeth*, *Hamlet* and *Othello*. But he is in no hurry. He has not had enough plain rest to satisfy him since Britain went to war.

March 3, 1947

Odd Man Out (Two Cities; Universal-International), a rare attempt to use the screen for poetic tragedy, is the story of the last eight hours in the life of an Irish revolutionist named Johnny McQueen (James Mason). Robbing a Belfast factory for party funds, Johnny unwittingly kills a man and is himself gravely wounded. In confusion and terror, his comrades abandon him. By nightfall one of the most extensive man hunts in movie history is in full swing. So is an elaborate screen allegory.

The fatally wounded fugitive hero, at large in the gnashing city like a loose bolt in a machine, is Man in the extremity of anguish and dereliction. As such, he is a quick test of the presence or absence of true charity among those with whom he collides. And among all these people, who combine with the dark city into a moral image of the modern world, very little true charity is evident.

The constable (Dennis O'Dea), representing law and justice, is a humane and intelligent policeman, but his motives are as implacably businesslike as his search. Johnny's fellow revolutionists try to rescue him (and are killed or captured in the attempt), not for his own sake but as a point of honor, because he is their leader. The girl (Kathleen Ryan) tries to help Johnny because she would rather die—and if need be kill him—than endure a loveless life without him. An old priest (W. G. Fay) negotiates subtly for Johnny, because he feels that his business —a dying man's soul—is the really important issue. In his journey-toward-death, Johnny does encounter moments of compassion, but the charity is as shallow as the courage that goes with it: those who will not turn him over to the police will risk nothing for him, either.

At length Johnny falls into the hands of three shoddy, half-mad symbols of three strong human drives. An artist (Robert Newton), foaming with delusions of genius, tries to paint the death in his eyes; a doctor (Elwyn Brook-Jones) patches him up for the sake of his own lost pride; the third man (F. J. McCormick) schemes to sell him to the highest bidder. Under these frenzied circumstances, the delirious hero shouts his own conversion and the story's master theme: "Though I speak with the tongues of men and of angels and have not charity, I am become as sounding brass . . . and though I have all faith, so that I could remove mountains, and have not charity, I am nothing."

Odd Man Out is an extraordinarily ambitious movie. Director Carol (*The Stars Look Down*) Reed has a sensitive, often inspired eye for people and for cities, and Robert (*Henry V*) Krasker is one of the best cameramen alive. For perhaps its first hour, their film has excitement enough to oversupply any dozen merely "good" pictures. An outstanding achievement: the film paints a melancholy, multitudinous portrait of a night city. Yet its beauty is at times so profuse and lovingly planned that it weighs the film down much as over-descriptive prose harms a novel. And the story, after a stunning start, branches and over-extends itself and gradually loses contact with humanity. The hero is so near death that he hardly exists as either man or dramatic force; he becomes merely a passive symbol of doomed suffering. James Mason, though rich in glamor, rather embraces than combats the character's monotony. And some of the people he meets (vividly performed by Abbey Players) are even less human and more allegorical than he.

Dostoevskian in conception and design, the story progressively becomes more wildly adventurous, more mystical, more half-baked. But even in its failures, *Odd Man Out* is admirable. It is a reckless, head-on attempt at greatness, and the attempt frequently succeeds.

April 14, 1947

Ivan The Terrible (Artkino) is Part I of a three-part biography of Russia's first Czar (1530–84). It was written and directed by Sergei Eisenstein, one of the few men of genius who have made moving pictures. It is a great change and, many critics will feel, a great comedown from Eisenstein's early films, *Potemkin*, *Ten Days That Shook the World*, *Old and New*. Nonetheless it is obviously, and in every frame, the work of a great creative intelligence.

Ivan is the story of a ruler whose passion was to extend and unify a Russia dismembered among foreign enemies and predatory boyars; of the constant writhe of intrigue against him; of how he dealt with his enemies both foreign and domestic; and of how the man and his policies changed in the process. Major scenes are Ivan's coronation; his destruction of the Tartar city of Kazan; his rising from his supposed deathbed to abash those who are plotting against his son's succession. Half mad with grief and self-doubt after his wife's murder and his best friend's treachery, Ivan abdicates. At the end of the picture, by request of the common people, he returns to the throne, confident of "everlasting rule." As Eisenstein tells it, this vindication of Ivan becomes, by many parallels, a vindication of Stalin and his regime.

In part because it concentrates on making its political points this film is as little like an ordinary movie as could be imagined. But Eisenstein, the artist, never gives way wholly to Eisenstein, the protagonist. Every movement in it is exciting, but, springing as it does against the tensions of near-standstill, it is exciting as if a corpse moved. Besides restricting motion in his movie, Eisenstein has also fought shy of realism. All of his characters, their faces and their gestures are superhuman rather than human. Most of the action takes place as closely within palace walls as if the cameras had been confined to a theater stage. The lighting, too, is closer to florid Russian theater than to cinema.

Aside from powerful composition and exquisite cutting, the chief cinematic device is a prodigal use of close-ups—but these are also used to enhance the anti-naturalism.

Actually, the film is a visual opera, with all of opera's proper

Sergei Eisenstein, a unique blend of poetic, intellectual and purely animal energy.

disregard of prose-level reality. As such, it is an extraordinary bold experiment, fascinating and beautiful to look at. But Eisenstein has denied himself so much that is native to cinema and has concentrated so fiercely on political pedagogy that the film is also tiring and disappointing. It is saddening as well, when compared with his earlier films, which were not only more vigorous, free and poetic, but far more "revolutionary."

The finest moments in *Ivan* come when Eisenstein gets his head out of the ideological window for a breath of simple poetic excitement—with no ax-grinding to do. Ivan's deathbed scene has deep spear thrusts of grandeur, savagery and terror; and during the coronation scene there are wonderful surprises. Historians will find plenty of room for argument over whether Eisenstein's Ivan is 1) a whitewashing job—with a low bow to Stalin, 2) restitution towards a maligned monarch, or 3) a little of both. Under political attack, Eisenstein confessed that Ivan was even less terrible and more progressive than he shows him, and he is revising Part II accordingly.

May 5, 1947

Monsieur Verdoux (United Artists), Charles Spencer Chaplin's first film since *The Great Dictator* (1940), is the story of a middle-aged French bank clerk who loses his job during a depression. Tenderly devoted to his invalid wife, his little boy, and their security, and disastrously ill-equipped to fend for them in a prolapsed economy, he nevertheless manages to set up in business for himself. The business: murder.

His victims are stupid, wealthy women. His difficult task is to woo them, marry them, pry their money loose, murder them, dispose of the corpses, and invest his take. He is exceedingly hard-working, skillful and, in his way, ethical at his job; he takes the least possible emotional advantage of his victims, and he is careful to kill them painlessly.

He gets a certain esthetic pleasure out of his work, but on the whole it is distasteful and tiring; whenever he can, which is all too rarely, he escapes from the hurly-burly of breadwinning and relaxes at the lovely home his efforts secure.

Like many a man who drives a ruthless bargain, M. Verdoux has his good side. He exhibits an exquisite gentleness toward children, the sick and the maimed, and even the humblest animals. He spares one prospective victim (a new Chaplin protégé named Marilyn Nash), when he learns that she is the widow of a disabled war veteran and shares his burning pity for the helpless. He fails to close his deals with certain other clients too. He makes several brilliantly funny attempts on the life of rambunctious Martha Raye, but she was born lucky and is plainly indestructible. He nibbles interminably toward the heart and pocketbook of rich, socialite Widow Isobel Elsom—and is all but caught in his hazardous career as he is about to marry her.

Long after he has lost his family and, heartbroken, has retired from "business," he does get caught. By this time he is firmly convinced that good and evil are inextricably mingled— and has come to believe that he is not more essentially evil than good.

Chaplin has remarked that Verdoux paraphrases Clausewitz' idea that the logical extension of diplomacy is war. Verdoux's version: "The logical extension of business is murder." War, he tells the court which condemns him, is merely a grandiose multiplication of the crime he is dying for. But wholesale murder is condoned by the state. "Numbers . . . " (of killed men), he tells the fat-mouthed journalist who interviews him in his death cell, "numbers sanctify." An earnest priest, his last offices rejected, murmurs solemnly, "May God have mercy on your soul." "Why not?" replies M. Verdoux. "After all, it belongs to Him"—and walks out to be guillotined, away from the camera, down that straight road where most Chaplin movies end.

Monsieur Verdoux has serious shortcomings, both as popular entertainment and as a work of art. But whatever its shortcomings, it is one of the most notable films in years. It is not the finest picture Chaplin ever made, but it is certainly the most fascinating.

If it had no other virtues—and it has many—the film is a daring individual gesture, dared in an era when such acts are rare. One of the world's most inspired and most popular artists —a man who for decades has delighted people of all races, from children to highbrows—now deliberately releases a film which almost nobody can wholly like. Many will detest the product and despise Chaplin for producing it. He has replaced his beloved, sure-fire tramp with an equally original, but far less engaging character—a man whose grace and arrogance alone would render him suspect with the bulk of the non-Latin world. He has gone light on pure slapstick and warm laughter, and has borne down on moral complexity, terror and irony with an intensity never before attempted in films. At a time when many people have regained their faith in war under certain conditions and in free enterprise under any conditions whatever, he has ventured to insist, as bitterly as he knows how, that there are considerable elements of criminality implicit in both.

Unlike most of the few films which try with any honesty to say anything remotely worth saying, this one does not, in its last reel or so, duck out from under. In Chaplin's last minutes, instead, he opens up with his heaviest guns, and sticks by them to the bitter end. In the whole two hours of the film, there is not one instant of bidding in any shabby way for the audience's sympathy. Morally alone, this is a remarkable thing to have done.

Artistically, the film is no less extraordinary. It has its blurs and failures. Finely cut and paced as it is, the picture goes on so long, and under such darkness and chill, that the lazier-minded type of cinemagoers will probably get tired. Chaplin overexerts, and apparently overestimates, a writing talent which, though vigorous and unconventional, weighs light beside his acting gifts. As a result, a good deal of the verbal and philosophic straining seems inadequate, muddled and highly arguable—too highbrow for general audiences, and too naive for the highbrows.

A majority of Manhattan critics found the film baffling, disappointing, offensive, and, in stretches, plain boring. But a few enjoyed the subtle, tragicomic ironies germinated by Chaplin's powers of intuition, of pure feeling, and of observation. The set pieces of pure slapstick are as skilled and delightful, and as psychologically penetrating, as any Chaplin has ever contrived. The casting (including Victim Margaret Hoffman) is excellent and there are a couple of dozen fine pieces of characterization and acting, notably by Isobel Elsom and Martha Raye. Working with a new character, and adapting his old, mute artfulness to a medium new and basically hostile to him, Chaplin still has his sure virtuosity; his is one of the most beautiful single performances ever put on film.

June 16, 1947

Possessed (Warner) gets off to an exciting start with some suspenseful shots of a dazed derelict (Joan Crawford) wandering the streets of a great city at dawn, in search of a man named David. When she collapses, Miss Crawford is taken to a psychopathic ward. By the time the psychiatrist's drugs loosen her locked tongue enough to tell her story, Joan's desperate beauty and her fine, florid movie personality have aroused an intensity of interest which only a top grade picture could satisfy.

Possessed is not quite top grade, but most of it is filmed with unusual imaginativeness and force.

Joan's story, told in flashbacks, is cluttered with woman's magazine heartthrobs and too much elementary psychology. Her trouble really started when she fell possessively in love with David (Van Heflin), a cold-blooded man who can take his women or leave them. Joan got left. She had other troubles, too: Raymond Massey's mentally sick wife, whom she was nursing, was jealous of her without cause, and committed suicide. Since she was getting nowhere with Heflin, Joan married Massey. His daughter, Geraldine Brooks, believing her late mother's fantasies about the treacherous nurse, hated Joan. And every time Heflin turned up, Joan got wobbly in her loveless marriage. Worse still, she saw an affair ripening between Heflin and her stepdaughter.

It was no wonder that Joan's mind began to come apart. A prey to confused motives, she tried to "save" the girl from Heflin when she was really trying to save him for herself. She also gradually became convinced that she had murdered Massey's wife. Even more frightening hallucinations followed. After a fierce burst of melodrama, Joan winds up on the hospital cot. The cautious prognosis: she is a schizophrene, but conceivably curable.

Some of this story could better be embroidered on a housemaid's knee than on film. But the picture's writers, director and musicians have done some effective things with sound (heartbeats, exaggerated rain, distorted musical flashbacks, etc.) and with storytelling; they have even risked confusing the audience by taking it a little way inside Joan's split sense of reality. Other moviemakers ought to take more such risks: the results are much more exciting than confusing.

The film is also uncommonly well acted. Van Heflin puts a lot of bite into his work; Newcomer Geraldine Brooks has looks, talent and vitality. Miss Crawford, though she is not quite

up to her hardest scenes, is generally excellent, performing
with the passion and intelligence of an actress who is not content with just one Oscar. In fact, the weaknesses in this unusual
movie do not greatly matter beside the fact that a lot of people
who have a lot to give are giving it all they've got.

June 23, 1947

They Won't Believe Me (RKO-Radio) is a skillful telling of a
pretty nasty story about a man (Robert Young) who loves
money and women almost equally well, and finds that they get
in each other's way.

Mr. Young first falls for Jane Greer, but abjectly drops her
when his rich wife (Rita Johnson) yanks at the leash. She yanks
him from Manhattan to Los Angeles and he tries to play safe
in the new job she buys him. Unfortunately, Susan Hayward
glides out of a filing cabinet, and in no time at all he is a dishonest man again. Again his wife calls him to heel; this time
they move to a ranch. There isn't even a telephone and Mr.
Young can't stand it. Because of his complicated efforts to run
away but stay rich, both Miss Johnson and Miss Hayward die,
and he is suspected of murder. In a courtroom, he tells his
whole shameful story in flashbacks, understandably sure that
nobody will believe him.

Thanks to the fact that the ice was broken with the Wilder-
Sistrom movie of James M. Cain's *Double Indemnity*, Hollywood can now get by with filming this kind of shabby
"realism." The blessing is mixed. Apparently, U.S. moviegoers
have matured to the point where they will stand for reasonably
frank images of unhappy marriage, sour love affairs, and of a
disease so gravely epidemic as Mr. Young's obsessive desire to
stay in the money at all costs. But in this, as in most such
"adult" movies, the semi-maturity is well mixed with trashi-
ness.

Producer Joan Harrison and associates have brought the
story to the screen with considerable skill. Mr. Young and Miss
Johnson are excellent as the ill-mated man and wife; Susan
Hayward proficiently sells her special brand of sexiness; Miss
Greer is a comely beginner. And many of the minor roles are

more sharply drawn and cast than the leads. The jury, for instance, may be caricatured, but it is frightening to consider
that such a group holds in its hands a life even so patently
worthless as Mr. Young's.

September 1, 1947

*D*own to Earth (Columbia). In *Here Comes Mr. Jordan* (1941),
a suave master of celestial ceremonies helped the soul of a dead
prize fighter to inhabit the body of a surviving one, with happy
results in the ring and at the movie box office. This time
Mr. Jordan reaches higher for heavenly intervention, and escorts it a bit lower. The rosy shade of Terpsichore (Rita Hayworth), outraged by a Broadway work-in-progress called
Swinging the Muses, comes down to earth and gets into the act.
She immediately dances herself into the lead of the show, and
into a fine kettle of fish.

The show's producer (Larry Parks) has staked his life as collateral against a gangster's backing of the show. He plans to
put on one of the most sodden of those productions whose
success depends on a snarling contempt for any form of art
higher than a Rockette's hip joint. Terpsichore nags him into
trying the only thing worse: really bad "Art." Played her way,
the show flops in Philadelphia. Played his way, it is a smash
hit in New York. At this point Terpsichore is reluctant about
returning to heaven: she has, of course, fallen for the Duffy
Square Diaghilev.

The film may annoy those who do not thoroughly enjoy
"swinging" everything in sight. It is also mildly dismaying to
see that when the Muse of Dancing is really being herself, in
her own ballet sequence, she can't even get up on her points.
But after all, *Down to Earth* is a musical, and musicals are forgiven almost anything.

There are saving graces. Some of the side comedy, especially
as handled by James Gleason as a Broadway agent, is very
helpful. Miss Hayworth's first dance, in a vivid sea-green dress,
is a pleasure to watch. At moments it looks as if the ballet
number might amount to something; and the finale—a sort of
genteel *Walpurgisnacht* in an enormously enlarged Gramercy

Park—nearly picks the heavy show up and carries it places. The picture has really attractive songs by Allan Roberts and Doris Fisher (best: "Let's Stay Young Forever" and "People Have More Fun Than Anyone").

September 15, 1947

*K*iss *of Death* (20th Century–Fox) illustrates a new and vigorous trend in U.S. moviemaking. One of the best things that is happening in Hollywood is the tendency to move out of the place—to base fictional pictures on fact, and, more importantly, to shoot them not in painted studio sets but in actual places. In making this kind of realistic "locale" movie, 20th Century–Fox has been the leader—with *The House on 92nd St.*, *13 Rue Madeleine* and *Boomerang*.

Boomerang achieved a physical and moral portrait of an entire community. *Kiss of Death*, working in a darker, narrower field, among the criminals and policemen of a great city, lacks the older picture's richness of theme and its warmth, variety and brilliance. But in its own way it, too, is a clean knockout. It is also something new and welcome in U.S. crime movies. None of its criminals is glamorous, nor does anyone piously point out that crime does not pay. Nobody has to. The whole picture amply demonstrates the fact.

Kiss of Death is the story of a burglar named Nick Bianco (Victor Mature), and of the difficulties he encounters first as a criminal, then in trying to extricate himself from the underworld. Nick is paroled from Sing Sing when his wife's suicide, his love for his small daughters, and a partner's treachery cause him to turn state's evidence. Thereafter he belongs, body and soul, to Assistant District Attorney D'Angelo (Brian Donlevy). His liberty depends on his cooperativeness as a stool pigeon. His life, and the safety of his children and his second wife (attractively played by newcomer Coleen Gray) depend much too precariously on secrecy and on police protection. Tommy Udo (Richard Widmark), against whom Nick is forced to appear in court, is unexpectedly acquitted; and Udo is a sure killer. The rest of the picture shows how Nick, with the help—and hindrance—of the law, tries to win permanent safety for himself and his family.

The fright and suspense of the closing sequences depend largely on the conception of the pathological Udo and on Richard Widmark's remarkable performance of the role. He is a rather frail fellow with maniacal eyes, who uses a sinister kind of falsetto baby talk laced with tittering laughs. It is clear that murder is one of the kindest things he is capable of.

The earlier sequences of *Kiss of Death* are as hard, cold and clear as so many sheets of glass; but these relatively quiet scenes, too, are fascinating. They were well photographed (by Norbert Brodine) entirely in actual surroundings—Manhattan's Tombs, Sing Sing, an orphanage, Manhattan's streets and tenements and dives, even a Chrysler Building elevator—with none of the overhead lights which bathe all possible reality out of most Hollywood movies.

This bleakly beautiful actuality is so valuable to the movie that the writing (by Ben Hecht and Charles Lederer), the direction (by Henry Hathaway) and the playing all take their measure against it. With hardly a moment's exception, they measure up. Particularly good are the performances of Taylor Holmes as a crooked lawyer, and of Victor Mature, who apparently needed nothing all this time but the right kind of role. For once, he has it.

October 6, 1947

Wild Harvest (Paramount) revives the once profitable Quirt-Flagg* formula: two high-skilled bums carom around odd corners of the world, working at the same jobs, tomcatting after the same girls, fighting each other, and unable to do without each other. *Wild Harvest* adds something new to the formula: this time the heroes are migratory workers, involved in the robust job of wheat harvesting with combines. The harvesting job gives the audience something novel and vigorous

---

*Sergeant Quirt and Captain Flagg, head men in Laurence Stallings' and Maxwell Anderson's *What Price Glory?* (1926), launched a series of movies that continued through the '30s.

to look at, and it also gives the players something better to do than talk and make faces at each other. But there is still too much talking and face making.

Alan Ladd, boss of the gang, can take women or leave them alone, and believes in leaving them alone when there is work to do. Robert Preston, the gang's mechanic, can't leave them alone. He causes so much trouble chasing girls, and boot-legging wheat for chasing-funds, that he would be fired if he weren't indispensable to mechanized harvesting.

The worst of the trouble revolves around Dorothy Lamour, who is marooned on a farm but can think of only one good use for hay. She points this good use out to Ladd, who spurns her advances. So she marries Preston in order to keep in touch with her quarry. Finally Ladd and Preston slug it out in a bar and find that they mean much more to each other than the disconcerted Miss Lamour does.

Wild Harvest was directed by Tay Garnett, who has a flair for directing men and melodramas (*Bataan, Cross of Lorraine*) Whenever his men are hard at work or at their more believable kinds of play, Director Garnett shows what a good movie this might have been. His harvesters' dance is a fine, forlorn scene, and he stages quite a hair-raising wheat fire and a particularly violent chase. But he seems to have realized that nothing could be done with the tense Lamour-Ladd relationship except to treat it as slightly ridiculous.

October 27, 1947

The Unconquered (Paramount) is Cecil Blount DeMille's florid, $5,000,000, Technicolored celebration of Gary Cooper's virility, Paulette Goddard's femininity and the American Frontier Spirit. The movie is getting such stentorian ballyhoo that a lot of cinemagoers are likely to think less of it than it deserves. It is, to be sure, a huge, high-colored chunk of hokum; but the most old-fashioned thing about it is its exuberance, a quality which 66-year-old Director DeMille preserves almost single-handed from the old days when even the people who laughed at movies couldn't help liking them.

The story is set in the early 1760s. Miss Goddard, an English girl, is accused—unjustly, of course—of crime, and is sentenced to 14 years' slavery in North America. The highest bid comes from Captain Cooper of the Virginia militia. A scoundrel, Howard DaSilva, tricks Cooper out of his new property. The picture thereupon settles down in and near Fort Pitt, which every schoolboy will presumably recognize as early Pittsburgh.

Fort Pitt is a stockaded outpost, threatened by Indians. Scoundrel DaSilva wants war with the Indians and a weak frontier (he is a fur trader). Patriot Cooper wants peace and a strong frontier (he is the stuff that the unborn U.S. is to be made of). DaSilva gets his war and it remains for Cooper to rescue Miss Goddard from the aborigines (Boris Karloff and friends).

All this is made easier by Mr. DeMille's ability to make shot after shot bulge with energy. A suggestion about a white-skinned female slave—an angle that first inspired DeMille to make the picture—is played with vigorous naiveté for not-quite-censorable leers and laughs. Miss Goddard, stripped down within an inch of the Johnston Office, is tethered for torture by the Indians and writhes exquisitely. She also takes the bath which has for many years been virtually a DeMille signature. It cannot compare with Claudette Colbert's champion dip, as Poppaea (*The Sign of the Cross*, 1932) in what press-agents described as $10,000 worth of grade A asses' milk; but in its crude frontier way (a cramped wooden tub) the Goddard bath is effective.

Mixed with all the 19th Century theatricalism, the early 20th Century talent for making movies move, and the over-all impression of utter falsity, *The Unconquered* has some authentic flavor of the period.

When Cecil B. DeMille went to California in 1913 and rented half a barn in which to film *The Squaw Man*, there was a village there called Hollywood. But none of the innocents lived in the village dreamed, in their wildest nightmares, how radically Mr. DeMille and his followers would alter the community.

DeMille is a movie pioneer in various other respects, too. He did as much as any other man to develop "spectacle" movies. He doubtless did more than any other man, with his extravagant bathing scenes, to turn the U.S. bathroom into a national pride. He was the first Hollywoodian to risk a movie on an all-out religious theme (*The Ten Commandments*, 1923). He was among the first to use "effect lighting." He pioneered with the camera boom and the "blimp" (silencing insulation which permits the sound camera to move freely). He was among the first to use color in a feature (hand-tinting, in *Joan the Woman*, 1917).

His *Ten Commandments*, *King of Kings* and *Reap the Wild Wind* are among the biggest moneymakers in movie history; *King of Kings* is still going strong, on parish-house screens. For three decades DeMille's name has been loosely used as shorthand for fustian and splendiferous vulgarity. Because he is an artist in ham, his artistry has sometimes not been widely enough appreciated. Yet many a long-haired critic has recognized his cinematic talent.

DeMille still does his job, as he always has, in a royal style. Wherever he goes on the set, one man follows to whip a chair under him, another to shove a mike in front of him, while a secretary devotedly notes down every word he says. He has often been laughed at for his historical inaccuracies;* actually he has a great interest in research and knows how to use it.

"People may say I'm lavish," says DeMille, "but they can't say I'm wasteful." As a picturemaker, he is not wasteful. He allows very little film to die on the cutting-room floor. Moreover, he is efficient—and effective at the box office—in proportion to his lavishness. A nonlavish DeMille is not DeMille. A medium-budget picture (*Four Frightened People*) was one of his few flops.

Next spectacle: *Samson and Delilah*.

*One anonymous verse read:
    Cecil B. DeMille,
    Much against his will,
    Was persuaded to keep Moses
    Out of the Wars of the Roses.

November 3, 1947

Forever Amber (20th Century–Fox) is every bit as good a movie as it was a novel. But it may not be as sensationally popular as Kathleen Winsor's account of a Slut's Progress.

Many who admired the book may be disappointed to learn that in the picture Amber is allowed only four of her numerous lovers. What's more, she gets an even crueler comeuppance, without (as far as the camera can see) having much fun earning it. During the 140 minutes of the movie the famous hussy is never even kissed hard enough to jar an eyelash loose; and it comes as a mild shock when she suddenly announces her pregnancy.

But *Amber* enthusiasts may not realize that they are not getting what they paid for. By way of insuring a reputed $6 million investment in the picture, Darryl Zanuck and Company have performed near-miracles of cinematic legerdemain that distract attention from Amber's uninteresting innocence. Chief distractions:

The picture is mounted with a radiant opulence. Items: $250,000 to recreate and cremate 17th Century London; $100,000 to reconstruct a wing of Whitehall Palace; $90,000 for Amber's wardrobe; $100,000 to film one kiss (which was later cut).

Leon Shamroy's camera gives *Amber* a highly appetizing protective Technicoloration that dotes with equal affection on furniture and flesh, brazen sconce and brazen bust.

To keep *Amber* stepping, scene after scene had to be chopped out. These gaps have been plugged with some of the loudest cinemusic ever soundtracked—obviously in hope that audiences literally will not be able to hear themselves think. The scheme backfires in a curious way: with eyes drugged by the Technicolor and ears numbed by the weight of sound, cinemaddicts are in no shape to appreciate the movie's Big Attractions (The London Fire, The Green Plague, The Duel, Amber in Childbirth).

The first-magnitude cast is headed by a blonde Linda Darnell who makes a handsome but unexciting Amber. Cornel Wilde, as Amber's steady, Lord Bruce Carlton, uses both of his facial expressions frequently. George Sanders, as King Charles II, is at least a periwig above the other players and very nearly gives the show away when he says: "Madam, your mind is like your wardrobe—many changes but no surprises."

Nightmare Alley (20th Century–Fox) is a hair-raising carnival sideshow. At the dead end of the alley lives the Geek, an is-he-man-or-is-he-beast carnival exhibit that tears up and eats live chickens. He is able to stomach this job because he is in the last stages of dipsomania, and is paid a bottle a day and a place to sleep it off.

This ultimate pit of carnival-life degradation fascinates shrewd, up and coming young Stan Carlisle (Tyrone Power), but it takes Stan nearly two hours' playing time to learn that in spite of all his talents he was born to be a Geek. Stan is one of the most wholehearted and resourceful heels yet to leave a print on the U.S. screen. He climbs a ladder made of ladies. Rung Number 1 is Zeena (Joan Blondell), the midway's mentalist. He plays cozy with her just long enough to swipe a pseudo-telepathic formula through which he can graduate to the big time. Number 2 is a luscious, loyal dimwit named Molly (Coleen Gray), whom he marries. Number 3 is Lilith (Helen Walker), a pseudo-psychiatrist who outsmarts him at his own racket.

Nightmare Alley would be unbearably brutal for general audiences if it were played for all the humor, cynicism and malign social observation that are implicit in it. It would be unbearably mawkish if it were played too solemnly. Scripter Jules Furthman and Director Edmund Goulding have steered a middle course, now and then crudely but on the whole with tact, skill and power. They have seldom forgotten that the original novel they were adapting is essentially intelligent trash; and they have never forgotten that on the screen pretty exciting things can be made of trash. From top to bottom of the cast, the playing is good. Joan Blondell, as the fading carnival queen, is excellent and Tyrone Power—who asked to be cast in the picture—steps into a new class as an actor.

November 24, 1947

Mourning Becomes Electra (RKO Radio). The eye glides like a skiff across the black, lurching waters of a New England harbor. The sound track blares the black, lurching music of the chantey, *Shenandoah*. And on the screen the dreadful, faintly ludicrous enginery of Eugene O'Neill's tragedy of incest lurches, and begins.

The Mannons were the first family of a small New England seaport of 1865. Through the body of their Freudian existence, O'Neill has rammed the misfitting dramatic skeleton of the Greek trilogy, *Oresteia*.

An unfaithful wife murders her husband, just home from the war, whereupon her daughter, who has always loved father as immoderately as she has loathed mother, persuades brother to murder mother's lover. When mother hears of this event (from her son's cruel lips), she shoots herself. Her monstrously affectionate children then suffer a monstrous expiation. Demented by remorse and ingrown desire, the son shoots himself in order to join mother. Daughter determines to "live alone with the dead, and keep their secrets, and let them hound me, until the curse is paid out and the last Mannon is let die!"

Mourning Becomes Electra (produced on Broadway in 1931) was never a great play—let alone a great Greek play. But it is a play that hankers after greatness (and Greekness) like a schoolgirl with a crush on a bust of Aeschylus. By attempting to dramatize the Oedipus complex on a framework of Greek drama, O'Neill produced a travesty of Freudian thought and something like a parody of Greek tragedy.

Nonetheless, O'Neill is one of the finest theatrical craftsmen of his day, and *Electra* has a gnashing vitality. The cinemadaption is, as Playwright O'Neill himself concedes, "magnificent." The rough edges of the incestuous theme have been ground smooth in the dialogue without losing a jot of theatrical shock. The Grecian mood, though it echoes rather tinnily through the New England characters, reverberates grandly on the superloud sound track, in what O'Neill calls the "sumptuous simplicity" of the Mannon mansion, in the classic drape of the costumes, in the still, pure lighting of the picture.

The film also boasts some fine performances, notably

Rosalind Russell as the cold-blooded daughter and Katina Paxinou as the hot-blooded mother.* Michael Redgrave, as the unweaned son, illumines a tortuous, hazily written role with great imagination. Raymond Massey, as the statue-warm father, acts with variety and sensitivity. Leo Genn may not be the romantic Adam that O'Neill had in mind, but he is still entirely plausible. There are several minor quibbles but only one broad complaint to be lodged with the moviemakers. The film is far too long (2 hrs. 59 min.).

All praise and blame for a daring effort belong to Dudley Nichols. O'Neill, an old friend, would not permit the film to be made unless Nichols produced, directed and wrote the script. All credit for risking $2,250,000 in the venture belongs to RKO, which may have some trouble getting its money back. As one critic put it: "Average moviegoers are going to talk back to this picture."

Producer Nichols disagrees: "I think they'll accept it. It'll be a road show with Theatre Guild backing. It might even become a cultural 'must.' If not—well, sometimes our greatest [financial] failures give the films their greatest vitality."

December 8, 1947

*T*he Exile (Fairbanks; Universal) is one of those shy wildflowers which occasionally spring up almost unnoticed in the Hollywood hothouse. But because of its forced growth, half the freshness is off the bloom.

The story is a pleasant little fraud. A trumped-up anecdote of King Charles II's gay undernourishment in continental garrets, it is designed chiefly to purvey the Tarzantics of Actor Douglas Fairbanks Jr. But *The Exile* is also Young Doug's first fling as a producer, and he has concealed most of the fraud with both legitimate and handsome cinematic tricks.

The script (which he is said to have written) has a charming, blank-verse hauteur that just possibly may be a bit asinine— but the direction saves the day by insisting on a witty, natural

*Greta Garbo, 42, turned down the Paxinou role because she could not bring herself to play the mother of Rosalind Russell, 39.

reading. Fairbanks has also inflicted an extreme lilt on the rhythm of the film—a lilt that would be annoying if it were not necessary to keep the lame plot marching along.

The mock-ups of 17th Century garrets, inns and windmills are engagingly naive, and often drafty enough to send a chill through a steam-heated audience. The camera seems to eye everything with a cavalier detachment, and the sepia film gives the illusion that everything is seen through a blear of centuries.

Few cinemaddicts will stand up to cheer these tender graces, but fewer will want to miss those of a Fairbanks find: a 23-year-old, Tahiti-born "Tyrolean blonde" named Paule Croset. Her performance (as a Dutch farm girl) is as clear as a brook, and audiences may well object that the camera does not linger longer on her cool, inviting beauty.

December 15, 1947

O*ut of the Past* (RKO Radio) is a medium-grade thriller about a not-very-smart young man (Robert Mitchum) who is hired to hound down the runaway mistress (Jane Greer) of a hard guy (Kirk Douglas). Mitchum finds the girl, sets up housekeeping with her, and lets himself in for no end of melodramatic consequences. Fairly well played, and very well photographed (by Nicholas Musuraca), the action develops a routine kind of pseudo-tension.

When he performs with other men (most memorably in *The Story of G.I. Joe*), Robert Mitchum is a believable actor. But it seems to be a mistake to let him tangle—as a hero, anyhow—with the ladies. In love scenes his curious languor, which suggests Bing Crosby supersaturated with barbiturates, becomes a brand of sexual complacency that is not endearing. Jane Greer, on the other hand, can best be described, in an ancient idiom, as a hot number.

April 5, 1948

I *Remember Mama* (RKO Radio), an adaptation of John van Druten's stage hit, turns out much better than most such translations. A deeply domesticated "family" movie, *Mama* is a leisurely, kitchen-life chronicle of a tribe of Norse-American San Franciscans, in and around 1910. There is much less plot than incident, and the quality of the incidents increases in proportion to their deceptive simplicity.

Mama (Irene Dunne), who is very much the boss in her home, carefully allocates her husband's weekly pay. Katrin (Barbara Bel Geddes), who wants to grow up to be a writer, listens enraptured while the family's roomer, a worn-out old actor (Sir Cedric Hardwicke), reads aloud from Dickens and Shakespeare. Mama's painfully timid old-maid sister (Ellen Corby), who wants to marry an equally timid undertaker (Edgar Bergen), seeks Mama's moral support. Little Dagmar is operated on for mastoiditis (by Dr. Rudy Vallee, with a beard).

The bellowing Head of the Family, Uncle Chris (Oscar Homolka), who loves to scare and scandalize all the relatives

George Stevens, always one of Hollywood's better directors.

he dislikes, dies, with a drinker's gasp of satisfaction, after tossing off his last neat drink. Mama, by swapping recipes, wheedles a successful authoress (Florence Bates) into reading Katrin's stories and passing on the secret of literary success (write about what you know); Katrin grows up, to write the stories that tell the whole movie in flashbacks.

A great deal of the credit for *Mama* belongs to Producer-Director George Stevens. Always one of Hollywood's better directors (*Alice Adams,Woman of the Year*), he developed while he was away at war, like a few other talented picture-makers (notably William Wyler, John Huston, John Ford). In *Mama*, his first movie since his return, he felt no timidity about tackling a script that lacked action and a strong plot. He concentrated, with confidence and resourcefulness, on character, mood and abundant detail, and on the continuous invention of satisfying and expressive things to look at.

The picture is not without faults. Often some heavy trick of tearjerking or laugh-getting or some exaggeration in acting or in the story shatters the unusually rich and pleasant moods that Stevens develops. At such moments, the whole business becomes tinny or unbelievable. And although a leisurely pace is often as happily used as in *Going My Way*, and the picture has the easy, sweet-tempered continuity of a growing crop, there is too little reason why it shouldn't be an hour shorter than its two hours and 17 minutes.

Above everything else, the picture has obviously been made with the lively affection and pleasure which are the life blood of good popular art. The casting is wise and the acting is almost entirely satisfying. Miss Dunne, who has been prone to hurt her serious roles with snobbish or ironic undertones, takes her tongue out of her cheek and gives a performance that is warm, disciplined and unaffected. Homolka is a blend of good actor and bag-of-tricks; but most of the tricks are good, and seem appropriate to his florid role (one trick—a sudden shifting of his bulk on the deathbed—is almost magical). Barbara Bel Geddes has little to do except register gentle, clear emotions, but she does it exceedingly well and even manages not to make it monotonous. Rudy Vallee does nicely in his minor role and Edgar Bergen does some funny and touching things with his slightly larger one.

May 3, 1948

Anna Karenina (Korda; 20th Century–Fox) is the latest movie version (there have been four U.S. ones) of Tolstoy's lesser masterpiece. It is by far the costliest ($2,000,000) but far from the best.* Sir Alexander Korda and his British bankers provided the money; France's famed Director Julien Duvivier (*Pepe Le Moko, Panic*) contributed his talents.

With so much dough riding the throw, Duvivier carefully hedged his bet. His script tore down Tolstoy's complex scaffolding of historico-religious theory, eliminated the sub-plots, preserved only the central study of a falling woman, with a few glimpses of the high society she fell from. This might have been sufficient if the film had also saved a suggestion of the dreadful glacier-creep of Tolstoy's characterization. Instead, the camera work is uniformly uninspired, and the psychological glacier dissolves into teary slush.

Vivien Leigh is lashed about by the tremendous role of Anna like a pussy cat with a tigress by the tail. She is not assisted by a script which insists on sentimentally ennobling one of fiction's most vehemently average women. Irish-born Kieron Moore, Britain's newest cinematinee idol, is badly miscast as the debonair Vronsky; he appears to be an idol with feet of peat. The principals suffer further by comparison with Sir Ralph Richardson, whose Karenin fairly lumps out the screen with its three-dimensional reality.

June 14, 1948

The Time of Your Life (United Artists) is William Saroyan's rosy look-in on a San Francisco saloon and, in the late Charles Butterworth's enduring phrase, its habitués and sons-of-habitués.

Most of them are just on hand for the fun of it—a fine dancer (Paul Draper) who wants to be a comic; a lyric poet (Reginald Beane) of the hot piano; a cop (Broderick Crawford) so kind-hearted he wants to hand in his badge; an old

*Two better ones: *Love* (1927) and *Anna Karenina* (1935), both starring Greta Garbo.

Arab (Pedro de Cordoba) with exquisite hands and a diagnosis of the world's ills: "No foundation all down the line." The bartender is Bill Bendix at his gentlest.

The story, such as it is, evolves among five characters: a sort of bush-league saint (James Cagney) who tries to make people happy; a dim Man Friday (Wayne Morris); a B-girl* (Jeanne Cagney) who claims to have been prominent in burlesque; a fine old pathological liar (James Barton) in fringed buckskins; an itinerant sadist (Tom Powers) who has to supply, single-handed, Saroyan's conception of the power and proportion of evil in this world.

As a play, *The Time of Your Life* made its author a modest fortune. Whether it will do as much for the Cagney brothers, who turned it into a movie, remains to be seen. It is a skillfully calculated improvisation for live actors on a rigid stage, and has an almost cabaret dependence on flesh-and-blood intimacy with the audience. Wisely, in this case, the screen imitates the stage rather closely. The whole rhythm of entrance and exit, bit and buildup is strictly theatrical, and the camera scarcely ever leaves the redolent barroom set.

The performances—notably those of James Barton, Reginald Beane and James Cagney, are as deft a compromise between stage and screen as you are likely to see. Nevertheless, a good deal which would be as taut and resonant as a drumhead on the stage is relatively dull and slack on the screen. On the other hand, those who made the picture have given it something very rare. It's obvious that they love the play and their work in it, and their affection and enjoyment are highly contagious. They have done so handsomely by Saroyan that in the long run everything depends on how much of Saroyan you can take.

Saroyan is an entertainer of a kind overrated by some people and underrated by others—a very gifted schmalz-artist. In the schmalz-artist strength and weakness are inextricably combined—the deeply, primordially valid, and the falseness of the middle-aged little boy who dives back into the womb for pennies.

*A girl paid to talk (and listen) to lonely bar customers, keep them buying drinks.

The schmalz-artist requires more belief, more wishful thinking on the part of his audience, than better artists would dare require. Reality is as much his deadly enemy as it is the superior artist's most difficult love affair. At his best, Saroyan is a wonderfully sweet-natured, witty and beguiling kind of Christian anarchist, and so apt a lyrical magician that the magic designed for one medium still works in another. At his worst, he is one of the world's ranking contenders for brassy, self-pitying, arty mawkishness, for idealism with an eye to the main chance, for arrogant determination to tell damnably silly lies in the teeth of the truth.

Except in Saroyan's world, barroom philosophers who intrude on new customers with the words "What's the dream?" are seldom answered courteously; and when euphoria enchants any saloon for more than five consecutive minutes, you can expect a quick return of trouble, or boredom, or both. The face on Saroyan's barroom floor has something unassailably good about the eyes. But the smile is that of a swindling parson who is sure his own swindle is for the greater glory of God.

June 28, 1948

OLIVIER'S HAMLET

THE question used to be: Can Shakespeare's plays be made into successful movies? With his film production of *Henry V* Sir Laurence Olivier settled that question once and for all. But *Henry V* raised another question that it could not answer: Can the screen cope with Shakespeare at his best? Olivier undertook to answer that one, too. One evening next week, at simultaneous previews in Manhattan and Hollywood,* the first U.S. audiences will see the result.

The answer is yes. The screen is indeed adequate to Shakespeare at his greatest—and Director-Actor Olivier's *Hamlet* is the proof. With this admirable filming of one of the most difficult of plays, the whole of Shakespeare's dramatic poetry is thrown wide open to good moviemakers.

There is also a strong suggestion, in this film *Hamlet*, that

---

*General U.S. release will begin in Boston in August.

the movies have more than an enlarged medium to give to Shakespeare. A young (19) actress named Jean Simmons, who plays Ophelia, is a product of the movie studios exclusively. Yet she holds her own among some highly skilled Shakespeareans. More to the point, she gives the film a vernal freshness and a clear humanity which play like orchard breezes through all of Shakespeare's best writing, but which are rarely projected by veteran Shakespearean actors.

The man who dares to bring Hamlet, his friends and his antagonists to life has tackled one of the most fascinating and thankless tasks in show business. There can never be a definitive production of a play about which no two people in the world agree. There can never be a thoroughly satisfying production of a play about which so many people feel so personally and so passionately. Very likely there will never be a production good enough to provoke less argument than praise.

It can be said of Olivier's version—purely for the sake of argument—that it contains no single unquestionably great performance, but a complete roll call of fine ones; that it is worked out with intelligence, sensitivity, thoroughness and beauty; that it has everything which high ambition, deep sobriety and exquisite skill can give it.

Henry V was all simple, engaging action, and Olivier gave it a clarion confidence and sweetness. *Hamlet* is action in near-paralysis, a play of subtle and ambiguous thought and of even subtler emotions. Olivier's main concern has been to keep these subtleties in focus, to eliminate everything that might possibly distract from the power and meaning of the language. He has stripped the play and his production to the essentials. In the process, he has also stripped away a few of the essentials. But on the whole, this is a sternly beautiful job, densely and delicately worked.

The film is black and white, not Technicolor; color feeds the senses and cloys the mind, and this is not a poem of sensuousness, but of sensibility. There is something approaching, if not quite achieving, absolute depths of focus. There is no pageantry and no ornament; the great, lost creatures of the poem move within skull-stark Elsinore like thoughts and the treacherous shadows of thoughts. (Roger Furse's sets, as nobly severe and useful as the inside of a gigantic cello, are the steadiest beauty in the film. Next best: the finely calculated movement and disposal of the speakers, against his sounding boards.)

There is little novel interpretation of character: even that might distract from the great language, or distort it. There is no clear placement in time, no outside world except blind sky, faint landscapes, ruminant surf, a lyrical brook. The camera, prowling and peering about the cavernous castle, creates a kind of continuum of time and space. Such castles were almost as naked of furniture as the Elizabethan stage; Olivier uses both facts to the film's advantage. Not even the costumes are distracting; they are close to the simplest mind's-eye image: A King and Queen like playing cards; Hamlet in black and white, with a princely silver chain; Ophelia, a flowering draught of white. The production is as austere, and as grimly concentrated, as *Henry V* was profuse and ingratiating. Only the wild, heart-felt, munificent language is left at liberty.

Olivier was determined to make the play clear in every line and every word—even to those who know nothing of Shakespeare. For the most part, he manages to elucidate even the trickiest turns of idiom by pantomime or a pure gift for thought transference. But wherever it has seemed necessary, old words have been changed for new. "Recks not his own rede" becomes "Minds not his own creed." In all, there are 25 such changes. Some are debatable, but the principle is sound. It is equally sound, of course, to cut the text. There are purists who will yell bloody murder at the very idea that Shakespeare can possibly be "improved" on in any way at all. Nonetheless, Olivier has treated him to some shrewd editing.

In the process of cutting a 4½-hour play to 2½ hours' playing time, the editing has also been very drastic in places. The soliloquy "O what a rogue and peasant slave am I," which is cut in the film, is about as happily dispensed with as half the forebrain, for in it Hamlet tries more desperately than at any other time to come to terms with himself. "How all occasions do inform against me" is important self-revelation and great poetry as well; but that, too, had to go—along with Fortinbras. Sometimes Olivier and his co-editor, Alan Dent, have gone out of their way to save a small jewel ("The bird of dawning singeth all night long"). But now and then, apparently for the sake of pace, they needlessly throw something overboard.

Olivier and Dent are neither vandals, boobs nor megaloma-niacs. They knew what they were doing. They felt, mostly with very good reason, that they had to do it. Mostly as a result of cutting, their *Hamlet* loses much of the depth and complexity which it might have had. *Hamlet* is a sublime tragedy, but it is also the most delightful and dangerous of tragicomedies. Some of the tragicomedy remains and is the best thing in the film. But some of the best went out with Rosencrantz and Guildenstern.

Unluckiest of all, the audience is allowed to know less than it might about the Prince himself (nobody can ever know enough about him). It sees too little of his dreadful uncertainty, his numbed amazement over his own drifting, his agonized self-vilification. It understands too little of him as "passion's slave." Between the cutting and the conception of the role, it is small wonder that when, early in the play, Olivier comes to "The time is out of joint: O cursed spite, that ever I was born to set it right!" he all but throws the crucial couplet away.

But within his chosen limits, Olivier and his associates have done excellently—from grandiose poetic conceptions (e.g., the frightfully amplified heartbeats which introduce the Ghost) to clever little captures of mood (e.g., the cold, discreet clapping of gloved hands which applaud the half-drunken King). The film is built with a fine sense of form and line, and some of the editing worked out very well. Hamlet's big scene with Ophelia ("Get thee to a nunnery") comes immediately before, rather than after, his most famous soliloquy ("To be, or not to be"). Thanks to this transposition, and to the manner of playing, the possibility of Ophelia's madness is planted early, its causes are enriched, and Hamlet soars to his soliloquy with acute, imme-diate reasons for contemplating suicide.

The play-within-a-play is handled with high elegance and tension, in sinister dumb show, accompanied by the snarling archaic charm of the music William Walton composed for the occasion. The camera, always holding the mimes at distant center, steals in a lordly semicircle past the enormous heads of the guilty, the guileless, and the pitilessly watchful; and rising whispers, like leaves in a storm-foreboding wind, underline the shock and horror of this deadly piece of court satire. From there on, the film arches in unbroken grandeur and intensity.

The Graveyard Scene gets down to earth as it never can on the stage. The whole dueling sequence is splendidly shaped, dipping from the high quietness of Hamlet's great words with Horatio ("The readiness is all") into the steely clamor of as slashing a piece of swordplay as the movies have offered since the prime of the elder Fairbanks.

Ordinarily the stage, at the close of *Hamlet*, is so heavy with corpses that it looks like a hold full of haddock. But Olivier's camera threads among the dead and dying with special tact.

As for the asides and soliloquies, Olivier gives them on the sound track but plays them as mental monologue. His lips move with the words only when he would think aloud. This device is worked even more deftly in *Hamlet* than in *Henry V*, and has already become as standard in movies as the close-up. Shakespeare's descriptive and narrative speeches are pictured on the screen, and by the device, Olivier sometimes even manages to enhance the language. Ophelia's description of Hamlet's "madness" ("As I was sewing in my closet") gives the two of them a lovely passage of pantomime, never played before. Ophelia's drowning ("There is a willow grows aslant a brook") is derived from the Millais painting, and improves on it.

Any production of *Hamlet* stands or falls, in the long run, by the quality of its leading actor. Most productions have little to recommend them except a good Hamlet; few have that. This one, in every piece of casting, in every performance, is about as nearly solid as gold can be. It is hard to imagine better work, along traditional lines, than that of Felix Aylmer, snuffling and badgering about as Polonius; or of Basil Sydney (who once played a memorable Hamlet, in modern dress) as the corrupt, tormented usurper; or of Norman Wooland as a gentle, modest, steadfast and wise Horatio. Stanley Holloway, as the Gravedigger, is blessedly out-of-tradition;* he seemed to have learned his lines from the earth itself, not from "Shakespearean" pseudo-rustics. Terence Morgan, as Laertes, is the quintessence of an old aristocrat's fine, somewhat spoiled son. For once, Queen Gertrude is young enough, and beautiful enough, to explain all the excitement she generates in the Ghost, his murderer and her son. Indeed, Eileen Herlie, who

---

*The Second Gravedigger is blessedly out of the picture.

is only 27, has some trouble looking old enough to be the beauteous Majesty of Denmark. But her performance is a profoundly exciting job of tragedy in the grand manner.

Ophelia is not an easy role, nor is it any too clearly written. Most actresses who try it (besides being old enough to spank Polonius) are likely to play the sane scenes like mad scenes and the mad scenes like a little-theater production of Ring Lardner's *Clemo Uti, or the Water Lilies.*

Jean Simmons was only eighteen when she played Ophelia. She plays the sane scenes with a baffled docility, a faint aura of fey, and a tender suggestion of nascent maturity. All this may go a long way toward persuading 20th Century audiences that a young girl really could so sedulously obey a meddlesome old father, and really could lose her mind when her estranged lover killed him. She plays the mad scenes as if she had never heard that Ophelia is one of Shakespeare's most shameless tear-jerkers, and as if her lovely language and her cracked, ribald little songs were drifting out of a broken soul for the first time, rather than for the third century.

Young Miss Simmons has an unspoiled talent for speaking with an open voice or, in an old Shakespearean phrase of Robert Benchley's, from the heart rather than the roof of the mouth. She has an oblique, individual beauty and a trained dancer's continuous grace. As a result, she jerks genuine tears during scenes which ordinarily cause Shakespeare's greatest admirers to sneak out for a drink. Compared with most of the members of the cast, she is obviously just a talented beginner. But she is the only person in the picture who gives every one of her lines the bloom of poetry and the immediacy of ordinary life.

Was it an advantage to Miss Simmons to have nothing but movie training before this role? She would doubtless have the same freshness and the same talent for heartfelt speech (if not her useful knowledge of movie acting), if she had never heard of movies. But she has had as her constant mentors J. Arthur Rank's excellent dramatic coach, ex-actress Molly Terraine, and one of the best imaginable teachers, Laurence Olivier.

Jean Simmons has lived in Golders Green, a suburb of London, since she was a year old. Rank's publicists like to emphasize this honest supersuburbanity. Jean's grandfather was a music-hall artist who took great care that his children should stay off the stage. Her father won third prize (in Gymnastics) at the 1912 Olympics; the certificate still hangs proudly in the hall. When Jean was 14 her mother started her in a dancing school conducted by a Miss Aida Foster. Miss Foster took one look at the child, and had a little talk with her mother. Lying about her age, Jean promptly landed the first movie role she ever tried for, or dreamed of: as Margaret Lockwood's twelve-year-old sister in *Give Us the Moon*. (Miss Foster has been collecting an agent's percentage ever since.)

During the next couple of years Jean played small roles in such films as *Mr. Emmanuel* and *Caesar and Cleopatra*. Dancing, however, still looked like her real profession, and at 16 she earned her license as a teacher. But just then she got her first big chance, as the haughty young Estella in *Great Expectations*. Soon after, she appeared as a speechless but physically eloquent native girl in *Black Narcissus*.

Olivier and his friends began, still half-consciously, to think of her as Ophelia. David Lean, who directed *Great Expectations*, helped out by telling them how quickly she caught on to direction. But by then Jean was so heavily scheduled for minor movies that Olivier had to wheedle her away from Boss Rank by special dispensation.

Hamlet was the absolute news to Jean Simmons that it is to most people who "had to read it once in school." Olivier and Molly Terraine explained it to her line by line, in terms that she could understand. (When they came to Hamlet's "That's a fair thought to lie between maids' legs," and asked her if she knew what it meant, she replied, with embarrassment, that she supposed it was like when people are married.) Much of this touching sense of the newness, strangeness and beauty of the over-familiar lines helped Jean to make them sound new and living on the screen.

"We know what we are," the mad Ophelia says, in one of the most bemusing lines in the play; "but know not what we may be." It is clear to Olivier, as to many others, that Jean Simmons is "an exceptionally bright and promising actress." It is not so clear what she may become. Olivier offered her the chance of a lifetime: a modest and gradual seasoning, first in minor roles, then in larger ones, at the Old Vic in Bristol.

There is probably no more propitious training ground for legitimate acting in the English-speaking world. However, Jean has signed a five-year, million-dollar contract with J. Arthur Rank. She will next appear in *The Blue Lagoon*, in which she wears a sarong, and dies, after having an illegitimate baby in a rowboat, somewhere in the South Pacific.

She is a sweet-natured, spirited, unaffected girl, and unquestionably a talented one; she also has the makings of a big, popular movie star. She already gets 2,000 fan letters a week. Among them there have already been twelve proposals of marriage, and a proposition from an Indian chiropodist which is the ultimate sort of accolade a movie star must get used to. Would Miss Simmons be so kind, the Indian fan asked, as to send him a photograph of her feet, and a sliver of toenail?

If Miss Simmons had gone along quietly to Bristol, she could doubtless continue to call her soul—and even her toenails—her own. She might even, in time, become such an artist as Olivier is today. The most moving and gratifying thing in this film is to watch this talented artist, in the prime of his accomplishment, work at one of the most wonderful roles ever written.

In its subtlety, variety, vividness and control, Olivier's performance is one of the most beautiful ever put on film. Much of the time it seems a great one. But a few crucial passages will disappoint some people. There is hardly a line that he speaks, or a gesture he makes, which falls short of shining mastery, in the terms in which he conceives the role. But the conception is in some important ways limited. It is clear that Olivier has a laudable distaste for the pompous, the pansy and the pathological Princes who have so often dishonored the poem. He sees—and plays—Hamlet as a brave, resolute, delicate-souled man who was required, as Goethe said, to do the one thing on earth which happened to be impossible for that particular man to do. But Olivier hardly begins to suggest why (nobody has ever done more than suggest it), and he does not richly enough suggest the sidelights and terrifying silences within the greatest of the music Hamlet speaks.

Once or twice, as in the dance-like shouting of "The play's the thing," he verges on hollow flamboyance; and he may fall to the floor once too often. But such excesses are rare and disarming; mostly, insofar as he errs, he errs nobly on the side of restraint. He pours out the marvelous liquids of the first soliloquy ("O! that this too, too solid flesh would melt") very tenderly and melodiously, but with little of the anguish which lies half-awakened beneath the bitter mildness. "To be, or not to be" is spoken in a stoical quietude and levelness, but the subtler possibilities are not very clearly realized in those definitive, eroded lines; and with that insufficient realization their deepest humanity, along with their deepest art, slips away, much as the suicidal dagger slips from his hand and slants into the sea. In the terrific scene with the Queen, magnificent as he is, Olivier seems to stop at the brink of the cyclic, self-devouring, sadistic desperation which Shakespeare so clearly wrote into that page.

Short of such majestic challenges, Olivier is as sure in his work, and as sure a delight to watch, as any living artist. No other actor except Chaplin is as deft a master of everything which the entire body can contribute to a role; few actors can equal him in the whole middle register of acting. He takes such little words as "My father's spirit in arms!" and communicates and is worthy of their towering poetry. He can toss off lines like "For every man hath business and desire" in a way to make Shakespeare congratulate himself in his grave. His inflection of Hamlet's reply to Ophelia's "You are keen, my lord, you are keen (It would cost you a groaning, to take off my edge)" is enough to make the flesh crawl with its cruelty, the complexity which leaps into view behind the cruelty, and the brilliance of the actor who hides behind that.

That lightning rational sharpness which is among Olivier's surest assets may also account for a weakness. He freezes such a jet of enchantment as"Nymph, in thy prisons be all my sins remembered" with cold irony; but on the words, "Are you honest?" he is like a scalpel. He is a particular master of the sardonic, of complex reaction and low-keyed suffering, of princely sweetness and dangerousness of spirit, and of the mock-casual. On the invention of business, he is equally intelligent and imaginative. "I am glad to see thee well" is delivered with a pat on the head to a performing dog; Yorick's skull is poised with piercing ironic grace, cheek to cheek with his own living skull; the lost eyes stare into the audience as Hamlet says, very quietly, "Now get you to my lady's chamber, and tell her, let her paint an inch thick, to this favour she must come; make her laugh at that."

Broad as his range and virtuosity are, it seems possible that Olivier's greatest gifts are for comedy, especially for comedy which works close to the tragic. Like every first-rate comedian's, his sense of reality is strong and cool; his understanding of "the modesty of nature," and his regard for it, are exceptionally acute. Those who venerate the best in acting will easily forgive the rare excesses in this Hamlet, and will easily get over disappointments as beautiful as these; they will not soon forget the lively temperateness, the perfect commingling of blood and judgment, the high grace and spirit, which inform the performance as a whole.

It is not likely that Shakespeare will ever again reach the lusty, semi-literate mass audience for which he wrote; today's equivalent fills the neighborhood movie houses. *Henry V* was seen by an estimated five per cent of the people in each U.S. city where it was shown (as against a rough thirty-forty per cent who see the average Hollywood movie hit). Some who did see *Henry* must have gone to see it out of culture-snobbery, or because they were led by the ears. The heartening fact is that the picture better than paid for itself in cold cash, not to mention prestige, in its U.S. run. And for years to come *Henry V* and *Hamlet* will refresh and enchant every moviegoer who has it in him to love great dramatic poetry, beautifully spoken and acted.

A man who can do what Laurence Olivier is doing for Shakespeare—and for those who treasure or will yet learn to treasure Shakespeare—is certainly among the more valuable men of his time. In the strict sense, his films are not creative works of cinematic art: the essential art of moving pictures is as overwhelmingly visual as the essential art of his visually charming pictures is verbal. But Olivier's films set up an equilateral triangle between the screen, the stage and literature. And between the screen, the stage and literature they establish an interplay, a shimmering splendor, of the disciplined vitality which is art.

August 2, 1948

Hollywood was his invention. Charlie Chaplin said, "The whole industry owes its existence to him." Yet of late years he could not find a job in the town he had invented. He clung to the shadows, a bald, eagle-beaked man, sardonic and alone. At parties, he sat drinking quietly, his sharp eyes panning the room for a glimpse of familiar faces, most of them long gone. David Wark Griffith had been The Master, and there was nobody quite like him afterwards.

It was a long stretch from the genteel poverty of the Kentucky farm where D. W. Griffith was born in 1875 to the international renown he achieved. He had wanted to be a writer, but all that he wrote floundered and failed. In the beginning he was ashamed to be an entertainer: he toured with road shows as Lawrence Griffith. He was stranded in tank towns, fired, overworked and underfed. Between roles, he did slob labor.

Griffith tried writing for pictures, but the Edison Co. rejected his scenarios. When (in 1907) they hired him as an actor, to wrestle with a stuffed eagle in an old-fashioned cliffhanger, he attached himself to the movies and never, voluntarily, left them again. But until his third contract as a director with Biograph, his pride would not permit him to sign himself David Griffith.

As a director, Griffith hit the picture business like a tornado. Before he walked on the set, motion pictures had been, in actuality, static. At a respectful distance, the camera snapped a series of whole scenes clustered in the groupings of the stage play. Griffith broke up the pose. He rammed his camera into the middle of the action. He took closeups, crosscuts, angle shots and dissolves. His camera was alive, picking off shots; then he built the shots into sequences, the sequences into tense, swift narrative. For the first time the movies had a man who realized that while a theater audience listened a movie audience watched. "Above all . . . I am trying to make you see," Griffith said.

Griffith brought a strange, yet significant, heritage to his work. His father was Colonel Jacob Wark ("Roaring Jake") Griffith, a Confederate cavalry officer given to florid reading of

Shakespeare. Like him, young D. W. had a stentorian voice, a tough physical frame, and a character that mixed moral austerity with poetic sentiment. He absorbed the attitude of the post-bellum Southerner to the Northern carpetbagger and the problems of the new freed men. When his talents and his viewpoint merged in *The Birth of a Nation*, a story of the Civil War, the Reconstruction and the first Ku Klux Klan, the cinema had its first "colossal." But on the heels of the picture came race riots and cries of racial bigotry.

Griffith was hurt and astonished at the cries. By way of answer, he sank all the money he had in another super, *Intolerance*. The film ran 20 hours, before cutting, and undertook to prove, in four parallel stories from history, that intolerance and injustice never pay. *Intolerance* itself was a failure at the box office. Like his later successes (*Broken Blossoms, Orphans of the Storm* and *Way Down East*), it perhaps only proved that Griffith would never again match *The Birth of a Nation*.

Griffith tried the talkies twice. One had Walter Huston as Abraham Lincoln and was a box-office dud. The other, called *The Struggle*, was considered too faulty for general distribution. Yet in his lifetime, Griffith made 432 movies. They grossed about $60 million, some $25 million of it clear profit for Griffith and his associates.

When he died last week at 73 of a cerebral hemorrhage, in the Hollywood hotel where he lived alone, his lawyer said that the estate would not exceed $50,000. Of this, $20,000 had been found in a safe some years ago during the audit of an ancient hotel. It was wrapped in brown paper and marked "D. W. Griffith—Personal." D. W., his mind on the remote intangibles of a lifetime, had forgotten all about it.

In Hollywood last week, many people were offering epitaphs for Griffith. But perhaps the most succinct was the one presented years ago by another man who could claim to know about such things, the Frenchman René Clair. "Nothing essential," he said, "has been added to the art of the motion picture since Griffith."

February 2, 1948

Treasure of Sierra Madre (Warner) is one of the best things Hollywood has done since it learned to talk; and the movie can take a place, without blushing, among the best ever made. But unlike many films of high quality, it does not wear its art on its sleeve. This admirable reticence may earn *Treasure* some peculiar awards. Movie trade papers are treating it as a western; *Daily Variety* called it "action stuff with heavy masculine appeal." Reviewer Virginia Wright wrote in the Los Angeles *Daily News*: "[The] audience . . . seemed to find [*Treasure*] hilariously funny and, once having decided the spectacle was comic, they laughed indiscriminately at murder, fear and irony."

Treasure is not essentially either a western or a comedy. The squeamish and the lovelorn may be wise to stay away, for it has no heroine and a few scenes are shatteringly brutal. But it is a magnificent and unconventional piece of screen entertainment.

John Huston (*San Pietro*, *Let There Be Light*), who wrote the screen play and directed the film, adapted it from a novel by Mexico's Mysterious Stranger, B. Traven (*see below*). The story, ideal for movie purposes, is a sardonic, intensely realistic fable, masterfully disguised as an adventure story. It is a tale about three Americans of the mid-1920s, on the bum in Tampico. Running into modest luck in a lottery, they strike off into the depths of Mexico's mountains in search of gold.

Old Howard (Walter Huston, the director's father) has nosed around after gold a good deal of his life; he cheerfully warns the greenhorns of what gold can do to a man's character. They don't believe him, but they find out for themselves. Dobbs (Humphrey Bogart), a morally chaotic child of perhaps 40, starts coming apart early with bluster, fear and suspicion of his partners. Curtin (Tim Holt), a relatively stable youth, nearly cracks, too, under pressure, but gradually comes of age. The men run into jungle Indians, have to deal with a Texan (Bruce Bennett) who wants to muscle in on their little mine, and are hounded by bandits.

But the meat of the story is its simple revelation of three types of human character, altering in the presence of the sinister catalyst, gold. The story is told with intelligence, humor and suspense. It is by turns exceedingly funny and completely terrifying. It is as rich in symbolic overtones as it is in character and drama. For the treasure of the mountain is a fair image of most human goals; and the men who seek it are fair representatives of man.

Movies have always been expert at picturing cities, but *Treasure* excels most of them in the streets, park benches, eateries, bars and flophouses that are the backgrounds for its opening reels. The main characters make most so-called simple men in the movies look two-dimensional and sentimentalized. In the superb camera work (by Ted McCord), there is not one fancy or superfluous shot.

Walter Huston's performance is his best job in a lifetime of good acting. Humphrey Bogart cannot completely eliminate the existence of Humphrey Bogart—but he makes a noble effort to lose himself and does far and away the best work of his career. Tim Holt is less an actor than a presence, but it is a powerful and right presence. Bruce Bennett is a fine Texan. Alfonso Bedoya, as the bandit leader, gives the toothy smile a new lease on life as a sinister property (he is known in Mexico as "The Face That Kills").

It has never been easy, in Hollywood, to make a first rate, out-of-the-routine movie. *Treasure* would never have been made, or would have been hopelessly compromised and watered-down, but for several stalwart heroes. Director John Huston, the chief hero, sold the idea of doing the picture to Producer Henry Blanke. Blanke persuaded the leary moguls to buy the screen rights (Traven got a niggardly $5,000). At one point, Bogart saved the picture by refusing, against front-office pressure, to play his role except as Huston had written it.

With *Treasure*, John Huston, 41, establishes himself in the top rank of contemporary moviemakers. John is a leathery, ski-nosed man with hard, arresting eyes, who suggests a hammered-out version of his father, Walter. He is as tough in mind and performance as in looks.

John was born in 1906 in Nevada, Mo., a town which (he claims) his grandfather, a professional gambler, won in a poker game. When John was about seven, his parents were divorced. Living with his father, John picked up a profound knowledge of the theater. With his mother he traveled extensively ("Mother hated France, but she was nuts about Turkey"). At twelve he went to military school in California; as a boxer he became amateur lightweight champion of the state.

At 20 he joined the Mexican cavalry. He began to write stories. His father gave one to Ring Lardner, who gave it to H. L. Mencken, who printed it in the old *American Mercury*. John also wrote "a kind of a book" (it was a play) called *Frankie and Johnny*, illustrated by Covarrubias. To his surprise, Boni and Liveright gave him a $500 advance for it. John immediately entrained for Saratoga, where he picked up $11,000 in a dice game.

The "kind of a book" also got him a kind of a job in movies. He worked briefly for Sam Goldwyn and for Universal. He went on the bum for a while in London (he and Director William Wyler still ride the freights now and then). Later he wrote Hollywood scripts until he made a name for himself with his first job of directing (*The Maltese Falcon*, 1941). As an Army officer he made the sullenly beautiful documentary *Report from the Aleutians* and the magnificent *San Pietro*.

During the scripting of *Treasure*, Huston was in constant correspondence with its author, the mysterious B. Traven (*The Death Ship*, *The Bridge in the Jungle*). Novelist Traven has an enormous following in Europe, but nothing is known of him except that he has lived invisibly, somewhere in Mexico, for many years. Many of Traven's suggestions for movie treatment were so intelligent and knowledgeable that Huston was fascinated, and wanted to meet him.

In Mexico City's Reforma Hotel, one day, a frail little man in faded khaki, his shirt held together with a cheap gold pin, presented to Huston a card: Hal Croves, Translator. Traven, Croves explained, couldn't come; but as Traven's old friend and translator, he, Croves, knew the author and his work better even than Traven himself did. Huston hired Croves at $150 a week as technical adviser. By the time Croves had done his job and disappeared, Huston was pretty certain that uneasy little Mr. Croves was Traven himself.

Huston has no truck with theories of esthetics or questions of style; his sharp directing is intuitive. He has a coldly intelligent knowledge of how much to leave free within the frame, and the born artist's passion for the possibilities of his medium. "In a given scene," he says, "I have an idea what *should* happen, but I don't tell the actors. Instead I tell them to go ahead and do it. Sometimes they do it better. Sometimes they do something accidentally which is effective and true. I jump on the accident."

Does he think *Treasure* is his best work to date? The question is virtually meaningless to him. He says, drily and without self-consciousness: "It is as a picture-maker would have it."

Miscellaneous

"Pseudo-Folk" appeared in The Partisan Review *and pro-voked a good many bitter comments. It also provided a caustic item for the "Talk of the Town" in the* New Yorker. *"Sunset Boulevard" appeared in* Films in Review *and was reprinted in the British* Sight and Sound, *and is an illu-minating description of two basic types of directors.*

PSEUDO-FOLK

THE folk tradition, Louise Bogan writes in a recent issue of *Partisan Review*, "has become thoroughly bourgeoizified. At present there is no way for the artist to get at it, for it has been dragged into a region where nothing living or nutritious for his purposes exists." I want to extend this statement, or at least to specify it, in a few random notes.

Miss Bogan goes on to observe that in jazz, "American folk has never been more vigorous than at this moment." I entirely share her basic excitement over jazz and her basic hopes for it, but I think it is worth pointing out that roughly in ratio to the relative richness of its vigor, jazz has also suffered corruption. Even the best of it, I believe, has gone a long slope downward into an ever more unsophisticated sophistication, from the middle and late twenties to the present, and its progress and decay has the proliferant, geometrically increasing, frightening celerity of a galloping cancer. In twenty years, though formally it has never successfully transcended theme-and-variation, it has in some other respects covered roughly the ground which composed Western music took four hundred years to go over. There is hope, of course, in the fact that all of these stages of jazz are still operating. If you are lucky you can still hear the oldest and purest kind of boogywoogy (as against its Café Society softenings and elaborations). And you can still hear, in the back country South and on the best records by Mitchell's Christian Singers, the incunabular sort of music which holds, to jazz, roughly the relation which the first century of sung polyphony holds to later Western music, both religious and secular. In street bands and in dives, now and then, and now and then for a moment on the "race records" of little-known and unknown musicians, you can hear true lyric jazz at the point when the deep-country and the town have first fertilized each other, and before imitation, ambition and the possibility of earning much of anything have destroyed it. But at the same time you can hear Ellington and understand why he is compared to Delius, even if the comparison depresses rather than pleases you; and you can hear nasty, tricky little midgets like Raymond Scott, "sophisticating" this extremely sophisticated art out of all relation to its source and, in the same gestures, achieving a once-over-lightly loving-up betrayal of the unaroused body of all the rest of music. And you can see, if you can stand it, the sort of people who enjoy this sort of decay, beside which men like Sinatra and Crosby are very respectable folk-artists indeed, being strictly, genuinely, sincerely and skillfully of their special kind and class.

The quintessence of this special kind of vicious pseudo-folk, in my opinion, is Hazel Scott. She plays the sort of jazz one could probably pick up, by now, through a correspondence school. She plays her "classics" with a slobbering, anarchic, vindictive, rushing affectation which any mediocre elementary piano teacher would slap her silly for. Her "swinging" of these "classics" is beyond invective. So is her own manner towards herself, her work, her audience; it makes the reading-manner of Edna Millay seem as decent at least as that of Little Egypt. As for the manner of those who accept and applaud her, it is, if possible, even more noisome; and is precisely what you must expect of the sort of "democrat" who, if he happens to read these notes, will wish to call me an anti-Negro, an anti-Semite, a Nazi, and whatever other overdigested derogatives remain in his vocabulary.

The pity of it is that Negroes themselves seem to be as often fooled by this sort of decadence as whites are. Miss Scott is a concentrated symbol of corruptive self-deceit upon whom I can waste little personal regret; but there are others, well-known and unknown, about whom I feel very badly. Paul Robeson, I am sure, is essentially a good man, and he has sometimes used his fortuitous power bravely and well on behalf of his race. But what can one think of the judgment of a man who, over and over and over, to worse and worse and worse people, has sung the inconceivably snobbish, esthetically execrable

"Ballad for Americans"? And what has happened to our theater critics that not one has observed that the Robeson-Webster production of *Othello*, and its record-breaking success, are both painfully dubious phenomena? What is one to think of the all but unqualified praise for *Carmen Jones*; and what is sorrier than to think of Negroes in the audience, and in the cast, who obviously enjoy this traduction and zoo-exhibition of their race as intensely as the whites do?

Tolstoy's opinion that the one reliable judge of art was a clean old peasant has never convinced me, but it has strongly moved, interested and unsettled me. But thanks to our nominal democracy and to the machines for universal manure-spreading which have done so much towards making it what it is, the "peasants" themselves, the sources of folk art, are if possible even more dangerously corrupted than the middle-class audience. Advertising is a kind of bourgeois-folk art to which they are quite as vulnerable as the target audience; and we may have a jew's-harp President yet. I remember how shocking and convincing it was, a few years ago, to play a ten-years-old and a new version of "West End Blues," to some Negro high-school children. Both versions were by Louis Armstrong and both versions, in their very different ways, were good. But the older record was pure, sweet, unforcedly forceful, and great; and the new was adulterated, sugared-and-spiced, forcedly much less forceful, and sadly urbane, saved only by the musicians' essential innocence of their decline, and by their instinctive equilibrium and scarcely impaired skill, and by what remained of Armstrong's great warmth and talent. The children liked both records. But the one they played, over and over again, was the new one. It was in their idiom; and it was like the difference between Mozart and Wagner. They liked the elastic, leaping weave of the sumptuous saxophone choir which shrouded the whole performance in theatricality, false energy and stylish self-pity; and they loved Armstrong's last chorus, which no longer attempted the simple, squared, heart-felt declamation of the old one (though it was built in reference to it), but sloped and relaxed its dwindled passion along chromatics, elisions, incompletions—the popular-musical equivalent, in fact, to much of our poetry and prose, which is no longer capable of embodiment and of statement, but only of the evocation, the third-remove sensuous hint, the exquisite sub-detail, the romantic actor's catch-in-the-throat, the dying fall which the worst of such writers emphasize with dotdotdot.

I think this sort of deceit and decay is most disastrous and most conspicuous among Negroes, and I am interested again to observe that that is so in rough proportion as they are our richest contemporary source of folkart, and our best people en bloc. But it does not by any means stop with Negroes. The mock-primitive, demagogic style of the great bulk of WPA and leftist painting is a white disease, mainly, and seems to me almost entirely distinct in source and cause from the primitivism of Parisians or even the puniest of their imitators.

A white disease too is such a show as *Oklahoma*, the best of whose tunes have a certain pseudo-folksy charm, but whose accents, premises and success seem to me as questionable as those of Carl Sandburg, once he came to be "recognized," and in many respects before. Indeed we have a tradition for this sort of badness. The humor of men like Ward and Billings has always been spoiled for me not only by its low comic content but by its innocent-crafty, lucrative inverted snobbery; all but the best of Mark Twain is terribly tainted by his professional-Americanism; a man like Will Rogers is wholly explained by our national weakness for congratulating ourselves upon our special forms of disgracefulness; and there are not many of us who realize that Irving Cobb, C. B. Kelland, Edgar Guest and John Steinbeck have a great deal of shame in common; that the "talk-American" writer, the Common Man as normally represented in left-wing, liberal and tory fiction alike, and the pseudo-Biblical diction which chokes so much of our writing once we try to "dignify" the vernacular, are all at least as dangerously "literary," snobbish, affected and anti-human as the mock-Mandarin prose and the mock-Oxford speech of the self-caricatured Seaboard Anglophile.

On page 134 of *The Pocket Book of Quotations* you may read:

"I'm learnin' one thing, learnin' it all a time, ever' day. If you're in trouble, or hurt or need—go to the poor people. They're the only ones that'll help—the only ones."

On page 136:

> *"It takes a heap o' livin' in a house t'make it home*
> *A heap o' sun an' shadder, an' ye sometimes have t' roam*
> *Afore ye really 'preciate the things ye lef' behind,*
> *An' hunger fer'em somehow, with 'm allus on yer mind."*

The latter passage is by Edgar Guest and is quoted from his poem, "Home." The former is by John Steinbeck and is quoted from his novel, *The Grapes of Wrath*. The very small body of writing you might find which would not incriminate itself by comparison, which attempts to use the vernacular, and which at the same time shows good judgment both in using and in depriving itself of the Mandarin manner, is the prospect we have for the development of a popular literary art which I join Miss Bogan in looking towards.

(Postscript: I should explain that I have not seen *Othello, Carmen Jones* or *Oklahoma*, because I felt sure they would be bad. People who spoke well of the shows have reinforced me in this feeling and have helped give it detail. People who spoke ill of them, I regarded as even more trustworthy.)

With a sense of having very limited space I have made no attempt to analyze the pressures which seem to me to produce this pseudo-folk art and its audience and its character. I cannot hope to do so here, but do want to put down a few categories and suggestions.

1. The non-folk crosses to the folk or the pseudo-folk (Hazel Scott) or (again Miss Scott) presumes to "dignify" the folk by "classicizing" it, the "classical" by folksifying it. Here, in the artist and in the audience, there is an essential ignorance of, contempt for, or lack of confidence in, both ends or kinds of art; and there is, on both sides, through tacit semi-conscious mutual contempt, a lowering or full dismissal of ethical and moral standards.

2. The folk crosses to the non-folk: Paul Robeson; his pathetic vocal imitator at Café Society Uptown; Duke Ellington's more ambitious arrangements and compositions; the dreadful pseudo-savage, pseudo "cultured" dancing of Katherine Dunham and her troupe; Chaplin; Disney and Co.

3. The entertainer who relies chiefly on being "niggery": Miss Scott's grimaces of creative mock-orgasm and her exploitation of her bust and armpits; Cab Calloway; Cootie Williams' wahwahs and burrs; Armstrong's more frenzied skatting and his repeated high-notes, which used to run around 150 in a string. Both Negro and white audiences love this sort of thing, and pay for it. (White equivalents: the Professional American; Benton and Rockwell; the words of such Marc Blitzstein songs as "The Purest Kind of a Guy.")

4. A more refined, insidious version of the same thing, crossed with the idea that the folk are raised in dignity by becoming "classical": Robeson as Othello; the Negro men and white women of the audience who are excited by his scenes with Desdemona.

5. One aspect of the greater vulnerability of Negroes: their need, even more intense and more shut-in in its possible satisfactions than that of most "folk" whites, to rise both economically and in the world's love or, at least, adulation. Also the richness of their initial wares and the breadth of contrast for the audience-bourgeois, who feels a licensed loosening of his inhibitions—as he does also, say, in Latin countries—which he would never dare or live down among "his own kind."

6. One pseudo-saving grace of many pseudo-folk artists: contempt towards the audience which accepts and pays for their bad work. You will find this contempt in many Harlem entertainers and in many Hollywood writers—though I doubt that it explains the appalling camaraderies of the vernacular as employed in *Tunisian Victory* or in the most richly dreadful and fascinating of recent films, *Tender Comrade*. For that, you have to be hopelessly detached from, and benevolently interested in, and unconsciously patronizing towards "the folk," like Roosevelt.

7. One all but guaranteed effect, upon the folk-artist, of deliberately or through self-deceit corrupting his work: the ultimate destruction of his powers as an artist, instinctual, critical and merely shrewd.

8. One all but sure way towards this self-destruction: ever to work for a non-folk audience. It is perhaps particularly dangerous for a Negro artist to please moneyed whites. But in both

races such notable exceptions as Jimmy Savo and Pete Johnson remind us that the sufficiently subsumed and powerful individual, and he alone, is indestructible.

9. One all but sure way, still, for the non-folk artist to destroy himself: trying to work for a folk audience or, still worse, for the great middle audience which now includes not only the middle class but most of the working class.

10. The folk artist and the non-folk artist have this in common: that their living—if they try to get it from their work—all but entirely depends upon an audience which, if the artist succeeds with them, virtually assures the destruction of his art.

11. The three present conceivable but very dangerous exceptions and possibilities: work in jazz; work in moving pictures; work in nominally "light" poetry. Just possibly also work in soap-operas.

12. How much of the great corrupted audience, if it were presented with any proper sort of uncorrupted work, would prove to be so incurably corrupt as, by its current tastes, it suggests it must be? (I suspect that a very great part of this audience is diseased chiefly with passiveness, and might be teachable.)

13. Who, except the artist capable of it, may be qualified to distinguish between "the proper sort" of work and the merely compromised, not to mention the slavish? A few critics and amateurs, I should think, and some of the general audience; but is there any such work around? The last I can confidently distinguish is that of Armstrong in the late twenties and of Chaplin in *The Circus*. Clair's best films are a beautiful blend of folk and non-folk art, but I doubt that even in France they were designed for, or deeply satisfied, the full folk audience. Preston Sturges' latest film reaches the great audience if only through its vivacity, but it is hardly a work of art, popular or unpopular; it fails through snobbery, cynicism, cowardice and a radical lack of love.

Partisan Review, Spring 1944

SUNSET BOULEVARD

CHARLES BRACKETT and Billy Wilder have a long and honorable record in bucking tradition, breaking rules, and taking risks, according to their lights, and limits. Nobody thought they could get away with *Double Indemnity*, but they did; nobody thought they could get away with *The Lost Weekend*, but they did; apparently nobody thought they could get away with *Sunset Boulevard*, but they did; and now, one gathers, the industry is proud of them. There are plenty of good reasons why *Sunset Boulevard* (a beautiful title) is, I think, their best movie yet. It is Hollywood craftsmanship at its smartest and at just about its best, and it is hard to find better craftsmanship than that, at this time, in any art or country.

It is also, in terms of movie tradition, a very courageous picture. A sexual affair between a rich woman of fifty and a kept man half her age is not exactly a usual version of boy meets girl; nor is it customary for the hero and his best friend's fiancée to fall in love and like it; nor, as a rule, is a movie hero so weak and so morally imperfect that he can less properly be called a "Hero" than an authentic, unlucky and unadmirable human being. "Unhappy endings" are not so rare, by now, but it is rare to find one as skillful, spectacular and appropriate as this one. Besides all that, *Sunset Boulevard* is much the most ambitious movie about Hollywood ever done, and is the best of several good ones into the bargain.

It is unlikely that any living men know Hollywood better than Brackett and Wilder; most of their portrait is brilliantly witty and evocative, and much of it is also very sharp. It seems to me, however, that this is essentially a picture-maker's picture. I very much enjoy and respect it, but it seems significant to me that among other interested amateurs there is a wide difference of reaction, ranging from moderate liking or disappointment all the way to boredom, intense dislike, or even contempt. Judging by that it is hard to imagine that it will do very well before the general audience, interesting and exciting as it is, unless through some miracle of ballyhoo. I suspect that its main weakness as popular art lies not so much in unconventionalities of story or character, as in its coldness. And if it falls short of greatness—and in my opinion it does—I suspect that coldness, again, is mainly responsible. However that may be, I am willing to bet that it will be looked at and respected long after most of the movies too easily called great—not to mention the "heartwarmers"—have been sat through and forgotten. However that may be, it is certainly something for anyone interested in movies to see here and now. It may not be all it might have been, but it is completely faithful to its own set, intelligent terms and, within those terms, all but perfect.

A moderately corrupt script-writer (William Holden), down on his luck and in flight from trouble, dodges his car into a chance driveway and into a world as strange and obsolete as that of ancient Peru: a home and grounds which are Hollywood of the mid-twenties in extremis, now in irremediable decay. The chatelaine is a great ex-star (Gloria Swanson). Half mad, suicidal, with the obsessed narcissistic arrogance of the once adored and long forgotten, for years she has been working on the awful script in which she plans her return to glory. Her only companion, her servant (Erich von Stroheim), was once a director as brilliant in his way as she, and was her first husband; he devotes his wrecked life to mending the leaks in her delusions. In part because of his need for a hideout, but fully as much because he is bewitched by curiosity, incredulity and a gradual crystallization of awe and pity, the writer stays on in this hermetic world, as script-doctor, as half-imprisoned house-guest, ultimately as gigolo. He watches, while the woman is deluded into the belief that her return to the screen is only a matter of weeks; he watches while she uses every art and science available to Hollywood in her effort to turn fifty years into a camera-proof twenty-five; he watches while she sinks her talons and her desperate needs so deeply into him that escape, or the mere truth, without tragedy, becomes inconceivable. Meanwhile he carries on as best he may his effort to write a script of his own, with his best friend's girl (Nancy Olson); another love affair develops. The whole business culminates, inevitably, in a head-on collision between illusion and reality and between the old Hollywood and the new; and in staring madness, and violent death.

There is no use pretending to discuss all the virtues, or even all the limitations, of this picture: it is one of those rare movies which are so full of exactness, cleverness, mastery, pleasure, and arguable and unarguable choice and judgment, that they can be talked about, almost shot for shot and line for line for hours on end. The people of the present and their world are handled with a grimly controlled, mock-easy exactness which seems about as good as a certain kind of modified movie naturalism can get; this exactness is also imposed on the obsoletes and their world, but within that exactness they are treated always, with fine imaginativeness and eloquence, as heroic grotesques. Mr. Holden and his girl and their friend (Jack Webb), not to mention Fred Clark acting a producer, are microscopically right in casting, direction and performance. Miss Swanson, required to play a hundred per cent grotesque, plays it not just to the hilt but right up to the armpit, by which I mean magnificently. Mr. von Stroheim, with the one thoroughly sympathetic role, takes every advantage of that which is permissible to an artist's honor, and is probably the best single thing in the show. Miss Swanson's lonely New Year's Eve party, and the loud, happy little party to which Mr. Holden escapes, are two of dozens of smashing proofs of mastery in conveying, and evoking the living and the posthumous Hollywood.

Much of the detail is marvellously effective and clever; Miss Swanson watching her young face in an old movie and standing up into the murderous glare of the projector to cry: "They don't make faces like that any more!" (they certainly don't and it is our loss); or the lighted swimming pool, so nicely calculated for the ultimate catastrophe. Sometimes the picture is a shade too clever for its own good: von Stroheim playing Bach on the organ, with gloves on, is wonderful in a way but possibly too weird, even for the context; and now and then a camera set-up or a bit of business or a line is so overcalculated, so obviously cherished, that it goes a little sour, much as the same thing can happen in prose which has gone rigid with overtraining. Yet one of the oddest and most calculated moments in the picture is also one of the best: the lingering, silent, terribly close close-up in which a soft, sleek clerk whispers to the slightly nauseated kept man: "After all, if the lady is paying . . ." The intense physical and spiritual malaise of the young man's whole predicament is registered, through this brilliantly indirect shot, as it can never be, even in so bravely intransigent a movie, in a scene between him and Miss Swanson; and the clerk (and his casting) are as much to be thanked for that, as the man who conceived the shot.

Movies about Hollywood have always been better than novels about Hollywood (barring only Nathanael West's) because they are made by people who know the world and the medium they are talking about instead of by people who don't, and who have dropped in only to visit, hack or, in their opinion, slum. But almost inevitably, the view from inside is also limited. The manner of telling the story is apt to be gimmicky or too full of mere "effectiveness" because that is apt to become a habit with nearly anyone who works in movies for long. Superficially, the self-examination and self-criticism are often a lot of fun and sometimes amount to more than that, but essentially they are apt to be easygoing or even complacent, because that seems nearly always to happen to those who work in movies long enough to know their business really well. (Literary standards, to be sure, are as seldom higher; but literary men who write about Hollywood seldom know—or care—how little they know, and perhaps accordingly, feel all the better qualified as annihilative critics.) It seems to me that the makers of *Sunset Boulevard* are at times too gimmicky, contriving, and "effective"; on self criticism I am confused, as perhaps they are.

Largely through what is done with Miss Swanson, the silent era, and art, are granted a kind of barbarous grandeur and intensity, but the inference seems to be that they are also a good deal hammier than they actually were at their best. Further inference appears to be that the movies have come a long way since then. In many ways they have; in many other and important ways, this is open to argument and no such argument appears in this picture. On the other hand a great deal of truthfulness is achieved virtually without pointing or comment, by the people themselves. The lost people are given splendor, recklessness, an aura of awe; the contemporaries by comparison, are small, smart, safe-playing, incapable of any kind of grandeur, good or bad; and those who think they can improve or redeem the movies are largely just a bunch of what Producer Fred Clark aptly calls Message Kids, and compares with the New York critics. This is certainly a harsh picture of Hollywood; too harsh, considering some of the people who work there. By still quieter inference, of course, Hollywood is still essentially all right because it can produce such a picture as *Sunset Boulevard*; and with that, the considerable distance it goes, one is bound to agree.

Various observers have objected that the picture is "lifeless"; that the characters are unsympathetic; that neither tragedy implicit in the story—that of the obsolete artist, or that of the obsolete woman—is sufficiently developed, or explored, or is even risen to. Some of this seems to me true, some I disagree with; most of it, I think, comes from a temperamental unwillingness to accept Messrs. Brackett and Wilder as the kind of artists they happen to be. They are evidently much more concerned to make a character interesting, than sympathetic, and the interest itself is limited by the quality of their insight, which is intelligent and exceedingly clever, rather than profound. But the interest is real, and so far as I was concerned, sympathy developed accordingly; moreover, I am deeply grateful to artists who never try to cheat, coerce or seduce me into sympathy, and such artists are particularly rare in movies. On the charge of lifelessness I can only say that in my opinion there are two main kinds of life in art, not just one. The warmer, richer kind comes, invariably, from the kind of artist who works from far inside himself and his creatures. For the other kind, we can thank the good observer. Brackett and Wilder apparently have little if any gift for working from inside, but they are first rate observers, and their films are full of that kind of life. It is true, I think, that they fail to make much of the powerful tragic possibilities which are inherent in their story; they don't even explore much of the deep anguish and pathos which are still more richly inherent, though they often reveal it, quickly and brilliantly. But this does not seem to me a shameful kind of failure, if indeed it is proper to call it a failure at all: they are simply not the men for such a job, nor was this the kind of job they were trying to do. But they are beautifully equipped to do the cold, exact, adroit, sardonic job they have done; and artists who, consciously or unconsciously, learn to be true to their limitations as well as to their gifts, deserve a kind of gratitude and respect they much too seldom get.

Sight and Sound, November 1950

UNCOLLECTED FILM WRITING

Uncollected Film Writing

Wake Island (Paramount) is the first attempt to make a document of the U.S. troops in action in World War II. As a straight Hollywood show, the result is better-than-average. As an effort to fill civilians with the image and meaning of a terrible and magnificent human event, it is as good, and as far short of good enough, as can be expected of producers who underrate their subject, their audience, their moment in history and the tremendous powers of the medium they work with.

For the strictly military action, Scriptors W. R. Burnett and Frank Butler, and Director John Farrow stuck to the Wake Island log and made their record "as accurate and factual as possible." But the participants and their conduct at ease and in combat are fictional. The people who are supposed to give flesh & blood to *Wake Island*—a tough major (Brian Donlevy), a tough lieutenant (Macdonald Carey), a tough contractor (Albert Dekker), a tough team of comic privates (Robert Preston & William Bendix)—are sincerely invented and acted, but hopelessly unreal in so stern a context. Not even Brian Donlevy, who does his job as soberly as if it were a military assignment, can quite convince anyone that he is anything but the too-familiar, patriotic young actor, doing his best not to look like one.

The combat scenes are better, because battling machines and anonymous faces under stress carry an impact no self-conscious actor can give. When enemy planes swirl like gulls to machine-gun a helpless, bailed-out pilot, or when the screen is hammered full of recoiling guns, pressure dials, the disciplined metal of the air, and spasmodic twisted faces, *Wake Island* becomes a moving effort to record an action on a heroic scale.

But such moments are few, brief as flash bulbs, and continually let down by carelessness, conventionality, lack of imagination, lack of insight into faces, minds, motions. Some characteristic letdowns:

▶ Even the celluloid film is wrong. The silky panchromatic light which properly drenches a grade-A romance softens the strongest images of courage or death into a comfortable fiction.

▶ Men who are bombed or shot down in droves do not lie unanimously still. Some must show, by sound or motion, that to die or be wounded is not easy.

▶ After a fleet has made its impressively slow approach, models of it should not be knocked to pieces in an obvious tank of water.

The purpose of a film like *Wake Island* is to convince, startle, move and involve an audience to the highest possible degree. Toward that end, faces, bodies, machines, rhythms, darkness, light, silence & sound must build up a tension which is a plausible parallel to human fact. *Wake Island* is a cinematic defeat because it builds up this tension for brief moments, then relaxes.

Time, September 14, 1942

Exit Tony

A Los Angeles veterinarian and a taxidermist drove out one day last week to the San Fernando Valley ranch of the late Tom Mix, walked into a shed where the most famous horse since Pegasus stood in the mildness of his last few moments alive. The horse was Tony, who was a scrawny yearling following a vegetable wagon around a small town in Arizona when Tom Mix gave $12.50 for him. In the years that followed, Tony became the valiant central symbol of a cinematic age of innocence, the hero of millions of small boys and some of the best juveniles ever made.

Tony was in no sense a trick horse. But he was intelligent, utterly trusted Mix, and had what Tom called "a genius for acting." He leapt chasms, he dashed down precipices, he received Mix (an indifferent horseman) from a parachute. He carried Mix through a blast of dynamite which knocked a hole in Tony's side. He developed social graces. He managed to keep a straight face when he was honored in the dining rooms of the Savoy in London, the Crillon in Paris, the Astor in Manhattan, and when he was given quarters in the check room of Detroit's Book Cadillac. Tom Mix used to boast gratefully that Tony had earned him more than any race horse in history. (Earnings of Whirlaway: $511,406; of Tom & Tony: $4,000,000.)

All this had been in Tony's glamorous youth. Now Tony was very old (39). Most of his teeth were gone. It was no longer easy to get the molasses he needed for his diet. His front knees, broken in a film scene long ago, had grown so painfully stiff that someone had to be kept in his stall to help him to his feet. Since Tom Mix's death two years ago, there had been a vacant look in Tony's eye. He was scarcely aware of the veterinarian and taxidermist when they came in. A few seconds later he was no longer aware of anything. The veterinarian had injected five ounces of chloral hydrate into Tony's heart. At once the taxidermist set about flaying the cadaver so that Tony (stuffed) may tour the country for the benefit of Boy Scouts, other boys' organizations.

Time, October 19, 1942

For Whom?

In a human omelet which included Dorothy Lamour and Myrna Loy, an audience of 2,089 packed into Manhattan's Rivoli Theater to witness the most important screen première since *Gone With the Wind*—the first showing of *For Whom the Bell Tolls*.

For months, for years, the buildup had been developing; and not just the buildup but all the rest—the astronomically expanding budget, the ten thousand rumors and denials of political censorship, the interminable and ill-explained delays, like those whirs, buzzes and bangings which take place behind the curtain on the night Hamlet turns up drunk in a Hawaiian skirt. The audience was getting restless. But it was still eager. It knew Paramount had in Ernest Hemingway's novel the possibilities of one of the best pictures, greatest popular entertainments and most colossal money-makers ever produced. It wanted to see the new super-production, the *Gone With the Wind* with hair on its chest and ideology in its hair. It wanted to see precisely for whom, in Paramount's endlessly considered and fabulously invested opinion, *The Bell* did, or did not, toll.

As it turned out, the tremendous *Bell*, upon whose casting Paramount had spent three years and nearly three million dollars, tolled for nobody in particular, and tolled off key at that.

There was fine stuff in it, in great ill-digested, nervous chunks. But *For Whom the Bell Tolls* was not, by the kindest stretching of critical standards, a good picture. Nor was it reliable entertainment. Nor was the likelihood that it would pay its way more than a string of subjunctives.* It was, on a grand scale, a defeat of Hollywood by Hollywood. Censorship defeated it, and timidity; heavy investment defeated it, and pretentiousness; the very expectation of the public defeated it; and the desperate, driven, split, muddled desire to make a great picture and a great hit. It was a spectacular public demonstration of a fact often neglected in Hollywood—the fact that great entertainment depends upon some degree of good artistry, and that the effective functioning of artistry can be crippled by too anxious attention to entertainment.

For the person who was most likely to salvage the picture was also the best artist in the company, and the most simply attentive to an artist's job. Whoever else may have fumbled at the rope or muffled the clapper, the 27-year-old Swedish actress, Ingrid Bergman, hit the *Bell* such a valiant and far-sounding clang that there had been nothing like it since her great compatriot Greta Garbo enchanted half the world.

Whatever might be said for and against the production— and there was much to say—one fact was beyond argument: a great new star had been born; perhaps even, many felt, a great new actress.

Five years ago, when David Oliver Selznick, like a disguised Zeus, first started pawing up the turf and lowing in her vicinity, Ingrid Bergman was no easily-carried-away Europa. She was turning down offers, with the cool statement that she was doing very nicely as she was.

Nobody could argue the point. Her last three pictures had won her an international reputation. The Stockholm *Daily News* had named her as one of Sweden's ten outstanding women. It was only a year since she had led a fan-magazine poll as the most popular screen actress, any weight or country,

---

*Nevertheless, Paramount will road-show it, until 1945, at 75¢ and $1.10 minimum (matinee & evening), demanding 70% straight percentage and guaranteeing the exhibitor a 12½% profit. For GWTW, M.G.M. took 70%, guaranteed 10%.

in Sweden.* Although she was being sought by every major studio in Hollywood, it seemed to her a little worse than foolish to let anyone, at any price, try to improve on her life.

By that time, however, one of the cagiest men in one of the cooniest communities in the U.S. had seen Miss Bergman's *Intermezzo*. He usually got what he was after; and he was determined to get her. While calm Miss Bergman sat in Stockholm flicking off her wrist offers which nearly every actress in Europe would have rolled over and begged for, she reckoned without David O. Selznick. In that failure of reckoning began a sort of duel, and a sort of wooing, as rare in Hollywood as victorious talent.

It was simple enough, from Miss Bergman's point of view. Look at Charles Boyer since he went to the states, tiptoeing his great abilities across roles too thin to support a minimum human intelligence. Look at all the individual talents, as inimitable and irreplaceable as thumbprints, which had been turned into just so many highly decorative zombies. "Hollywood," she told the press, "has a queer way of taking an individual and fitting her into the American mold. I have worked hard to develop my style and I don't want anything to do with bathing suits and plucked eyebrows."

This was the sort of talk the Hollywood pashas had heard for years from fourth-raters and sour-grape sideliners. If a proved professional talked like that it was just a come-on. The proper reaction was either to snort your opinion and move off or to up your offer. They upped their offers—and clonked in mild faints again as Miss Bergman again said, no thank you. But this sort of talk suddenly dazzled David Selznick with a new, if incredible, idea. The idea was that Miss Bergman meant precisely what she said. She was genuinely less interested in becoming one of the apotheosized queen bees in the dream hive of millions, less interested even in great wealth, than she was in getting good parts and doing them as well as she knew how without interference. That, accordingly, was the only basis on which to approach her. And on that basis, for twelve months, David Selznick sedulously stalked his prey.

*No. 1 today, according to the Swedish Gallup Institute: Greer (*Mrs. Miniver*) Garson; No. 2, Miss Bergman.

This protracted wheedling of Beauty by what Beauty regarded as the Beast might have gone on until Miss Bergman
inherited the shawl of Ouspenskaya but for a second Selznick
brainstorm. Selznick decided that vociferous blandishments,
promises and temptations by cable were still a shade too Hollywood, and quit wearying the wires with them. This was a task,
he now realized, for flesh and blood. Considering Miss Bergman's mental picture of an American female executive, the
casting of the role was brilliantly lucky. He sent over a particularly tactful lady named Kay Brown. And that did it. Miss
Bergman was braced to resist something in unshaven tweeds
with a Cremo breath and a voice like a moose decoy. What she
met was "so sweet and human that I decided that anyone she
worked for" (Mr. Selznick walked up the walls in devilish glee)
"couldn't be nearly so crazy as I expected." When, in early
April 1939, the *Queen Mary* docked at Pier 90, the remarkable
Miss Brown had in tow the richest screen potentiality of a
decade.

"The Palmolive Garbo" was David Selznick's epithet for his
new property. The hard-veined, soft-souled gentlemen of the
press felt differently. There was something about Miss Bergman
—they clawed the air for adequate words—which made them
coo and baa like fatuous old uncles. "Lunching with her,"
sighed Thornton Delehanty, "is like sitting down to an hour
or so of conversation with a charming and highly intelligent
orchid." An A.P. feature writer uttered the glad cry, "As unspoiled as a fresh Swedish snowfall." Bosley Crowther in the
Times, after some startling lyricism involving a Viking's sweetheart, Ivory Soap, peaches, cream and Dresden china, concluded: "This reporter would like to go on record that he has
never met a star who compares . . ."

The ladies have been less abandoned in their eulogies, but
even among them Miss Bergman has managed very nicely. She
even got past the Scylla and Charybdis of the screen press
without shipping any water: Hedda Hopper has had nothing
but good to say of her, and Miss Bergman is probably the only
woman in Hollywood who can say of Lolly Parsons, with transparent sincerity, that she is "really sort of sweet."

Hollywood itself, normally a paradise of private snidery,
feels just as the press does. Not only is Ingrid Bergman with-

out an enemy in the whole community: people like the way she works, too. If she muffs a line, her apology is so obviously sincere that there is not a man or woman on the set who would not overwork to please her.

Victor Fleming, who directed her in *Dr. Jekyll & Mr. Hyde*, calls her Angel. Sam Wood calls her "a fine wholesome girl," and gratefully credits her and Cooper with the excellent morale of the whole outfit during difficulties on *The Bell*'s location. Deafening Gregory Ratoff shouts: "Haffing diracted Meese Boergmann in her foerst two Amerrican peetures, I vould say puzzitiffly I hope I do de same tvanty-two timeps more. She is sansahtional!"

As with the press and Hollywood, so also with the nation. But not even David Selznick's Palmolive epithet, though it is first-rate poetry, affords an analysis of Miss Bergman's peculiar assets. There has been no such analysis. Yet in some degree her assets could be listed:

▶ The abundance, in Hollywood, of women who are much more like each other than they are like Miss Bergman.

▶ Miss Bergman's particular kind of beauty. By external standards it is unremarkable. What makes it hard to compete with is that, coming from within, it is the beauty of an individual.

▶ The individual herself, who happens to be an uncommonly well-balanced and charming one.

Miss Bergman was an only child. Her mother died when she was three. Her father, a big, merry, popular photographer-artist, who liked to flex his basso in the bathtub, hoped his daughter would become an opera star, and early accustomed her to the enjoyment of routines before cameras. Ingrid was deeply attached to her father, but even before he died, when she was 13, she was much alone and without playmates. As soon as she learned to walk, and about as naturally, she learned her famous self-sufficiency and intactness. And she learned the thing that made it possible and preferable—her total absorption in acting. It began with rigging herself in her mother's old dresses. It went on with spouting poetry—and old poetry so long as it gave her histrionic impulses a canter. Later, at boarding school, though she was a prize winner at declamation, her tall, sensitive awkwardness increased her isolation.

Such solitude, which destroys some people, strengthens others. It seems to have strengthened her.

Born into a moderately well-to-do family of the upper middle class, Ingrid Bergman is, in addition, a European gentlewoman, who has lived less among the stultified members of her class than among the cultivated, the flexible, the gifted and the gay. As such, in Europe, she would be no more than an idealization of an attractive, not uncommon type. As such, in the U.S., she is as noticeable as a Negro President.

Even without talent, Miss Bergman would bring something rare to U.S. films. To cite one single asset which is hers almost exclusively, her photographed flesh looks neither like a Crane fixtures ad nor sponge rubber nor the combined efforts of a fashionable portraitist and a rural mortician; it looks like flesh. Many people, since life must go on, find this attractive, even when it surprises them to see it on the screen. The same thing goes for her poise, sincerity, reticence, sensitiveness and charm.

Also for talent, of which Miss Bergman has a lot. And she knows how to use it. Hollywood's talented people have developed marvelous skill in a tradition as rigid and elaborate as Javanese dancing, and almost as remote from life. Miss Bergman comes of a tradition in which an interest in realism, in the huge and various wealth of actual life, is as natural to a good actress as to a good novelist.

The U.S. will always like its great dancers and ritualists with good reason. But its fondness for Miss Bergman indicates, as well, an appetite for the sudden lights, edged shades and flexibilities of reality. As an actress, Miss Bergman has just one basic rule: "Never speak a line which does not make sense for the part." She is probably the best reader of lines in the business just now; and it appears to pay. Ingrid Bergman's first five U.S. pictures have brought her to an enviable position, which, for better or worse, her present role destroys for her forever. Hitherto people have liked her with the illusion of personal discovery: she has been the most widely recognized unrecognized player in the country. Everybody waited for her Maria with almost unhealthily sharpened interest.

The lovers and guerrillas and actions in Ernest Hemingway's novel were motivated and given their meaning by political intensities and by depths of human strength, weakness and need which Paramount has seen fit, or been forced, to remove. But the screen version of Ernest Hemingway's novel is still a story of love and violence in the Spanish Civil War. Gary Cooper is Robert Jordan, Hemingway's young Montana schoolteacher who has come to Spain to fight for democracy everywhere. Gary Cooper, over the years, has so cornered the beloved American romantic virtues of taciturnity, melancholy, tenderness, valor and masculine gauche grace that he has become, for millions, a sort of Abraham Lincoln of American sex. He plays modestly, sometimes beautifully.

As the guerrilla leader, Pablo, Hemingway's terrible symbol of a man devastated by the fear of death, Akim Tamiroff has some magnificent, all but tragic moments. As Pilar, Hemingway's salty symbol of Spain's people, Greek Actress Katina Paxinou would walk away with any less leaden show. Her hawk-fine face, wallowing walk, Goyaesque style and Noah Beery laugh assure her a rich future, if only she can find roles spacious enough. As the Soviet journalist, Karkov, Konstantin Shayne makes his characterization of a political commissar the most electrifying bit in years.

But those are the surprises. The rest of the time these actors go corky on their lines, overact operatically or sit and talk. Above all they talk. A tremendous effort has been made in this adaptation to keep Author Hemingway's characters intact. But the adaptation is too literary, too theatrical.

So is the cinema treatment of the central action of Hemingway's book. In Paramount's version Jordan's dynamiting of the strategic bridge is a genuinely exciting bit of suspense. But two dozen grade-B melodramas handle the same theme better every year.

And on the screen Hemingway's most delicate episodes, the nights that Jordan and Maria spend together in a sleeping robe, are expertly elusive. Paramount's answer to one wag's question, whether the Hays Office would let sleeping bags lie, is: Yes, but don't go near the water. The closest study cannot determine whether either or both the lovers are or are not in or out of the bag at any time.

Equally deft is Paramount's political touch & go. The rumors started as far back as the spring of 1941 that outside forces were tampering with the script and even with the production. Paramount's denials were prompt. So were everybody else's.

Paramount must be credited, to be sure, with letting Mr. Cooper murmur the no longer sensational news that Spain was a training ground for World War II. But that is about as impressive as the hindsight volubility of an upside-down parrot. Considering the particular hour and climate of world history which the *Bell* dramatizes, Paramount's executives have kept an almost divine political detachment. Says Chairman of the Board Adolph Zukor: "It is a great picture, without political significance. We are not for or against anybody." Says Director Sam Wood: "It is a love story against a brutal background. It would be the same love story if they were on the other side." Says Paramount President Barney Balaban: "We don't think it will make any trouble."

It won't. For when all the political whoopdedoodle about the film is over, there remains the only fact that, when all is said & done, anybody cares about—the fact that, whatever Hollywood's *Bell* tolled for, Ingrid Bergman rang it.

Time, August 2, 1943

The Battle of Russia (Special Services; Army Service Forces) is the most eloquent film yet made about Russia's part in this war. It was made for U.S. soldiers (it is the fifth of the Army orientation films*) but it has just as much to tell U.S. civilians.

Colonel Anatole Litvak, who made *The Battle of Russia*, is Russian-born, but his nostalgic love for Russia and its people is uncomplicated by political finepoint. As a director in France, Colonel Litvak made one of the best screen romances (*Mayerling*). As a director in Hollywood, he found out (*All This and Heaven Too, This Above All*) what U.S. filmgoers want to see. Colonel Litvak's special qualifications converge, in *Battle of Russia*, to create a superb and deeply moving film.

The Battle of Russia moves in three great waves of action: the first seven months of invasion; the siege of Leningrad; the

---

*Their purpose: to show U.S. troops, in international detail, what the war is about.

Stalingrad campaign. There are serious weaknesses: figure-skating around the Russian revolution and the German-Soviet Pact which Sonja Henie could envy; blurring into romancing (as in some specious shots of gibbeted civilians); surprising failures to make the most of great material (Leningrad's fortitude is reinforced by only a hint of Leningrad's semi-starvation). But overall and in most of its detail the film has remarkable power. Its power results from a simple fact: the greatest shots from Russia's great war records, out of which *The Battle of Russia* is made, are never used merely to tell a story, never for propaganda, always for the maximum of human and emotional force. Literal sound and suggestive music are used in the same way.

Samples:

▶ Russians, most of them elderly, their faces drawn, stiff, heart-broken, seek among frozen corpses for those who were dear to them. In an intensifying series, the shots show: a dead mother and baby, so frozen that the child's head stands rigid in the air above her bosom; an old woman, crying and stupefied, trying to limber the upthrust frozen arm of a dead man.

▶ Even music—which usually drowns moving pictures in sugar —adds greatly to this one. The sudden naïve, triumphal avalanche of scales which opens the finale of Tschaikovsky's Fourth Symphony—used here at the moment when the tide turns against the Germans at Stalingrad—is an astute and thrilling use of cinemusic.

I Dood It (M.G.M.) To spite a faithless fiancé, a dancing actress (Eleanor Powell) marries a man (Red Skelton) who, she believes, owns a gold mine. She kicks him out when she learns that he is really a pants-presser, grabs him back when he foils a saboteur's attempt to blow up a munitions warehouse.

While this musical-comedy plot thickens to the curdling point, a good many variously gifted people are kept busy making the show entertaining. Jimmy Dorsey's band establishes one hit (the smoothly meandering *Star Eyes*) and one bidder (the galumphing *So Long, Sarah Jane*). Hazel Scott blends swing and quasi-classical music to the disadvantage of both and the delight of millions. Comely Lena Horne proficiently marshals Count Basie's band and numerous choristers through a particularly unpleasant stretch of sub-operatic Afri-corn about the walls of Jericho. Eleanor Powell, who is the best female tap dancer on tap, proves it in a rope dance, a modified hula and a rampant straight number on a milk-white stage battleship. But Red Skelton is the best bet of all.

Most of Skelton's comedy is Bob Hope laid on with a ball bat. Red goofed up over a kiss, Red getting off lines like "I press men's pants but this is the slack season," appeals chiefly to the primordial. But now & then Skelton's broad and cheer-ful silliness—notably in one stretch of pantomime, uphol-stering himself in a false beard—comes so thick & fast that the effect is like being held down and tickled.

His Butler's Sister (Universal) first appears with her back to the camera, walking through a train. As she passes, the faces of male passengers light up as if she were at worst an improve-ment on Botticelli's Venus. Then she turns around. She is Deanna Durbin, ready to burst into song at the tap of a baton.

Miss Durbin portrays a young middle-western lady with an ambitious voice. She wants nothing so much as a chance to display it before Hit-Composer Franchot Tone. Her surprise and delight may be imagined when she discovers that her brother (Pat O'Brien) is the boozy butler of Composer Tone's Park Avenue penthouse. But it is Butler O'Brien's special busi-ness to keep thrushes out of this quiet nest, and for several reels Miss Durbin, though she crowbars her way into a maid's job there, has to content herself with charming some comic local lackeys and an eager Broadway producer (Walter Carlett). At last, at a Butlers' Ball, she utters some high notes which pierce the heart of her brother's boss. She also sings a slice of hickory-smoked Victor Herbert and an aria from Puccini's *Turandot* with her familiar verve. But as the verses go on, on, on and, by way of variation, on, some customers may feel that Art is the longest distance between two points.

Time, November 29, 1943

Lifeboat (20th Century–Fox) is one of the most ambitious films in years. It begins with a close-up of a foundering ship's funnel that might stand for the end of an era. Then the camera closely meditates a dissolving frieze of floating debris, and lifts its eye to frame, in the light of pre-dawn, its compact symbol of our time: a damaged boat, its compass smashed, its sole occupant a trullish photo-journalist who has lived through so much that she calls herself "practically immortal." Further survivors clamber aboard, masked and anonymous with floating oil. As the little boat gets moving, the film suggests Poet E. E. Cummings':

> *King Christ this world is all aleak;*
> *and life preservers there are none . . .*

The idea for *Lifeboat* first occurred to Director Alfred Hitchcock. John Steinbeck wrote the idea into a story (still unpublished). With Hitchcock's help, Scripter Jo Swerling wrote the story into a screen play. The cinematic problems involved in keeping nine characters and their story dancing for two hours upon the pin point of one lifeboat were staggering. Result: a remarkably intelligent picture, almost totally devoid of emotion. Its characters are not so much real people, derelict upon a real sea, as they are a set of propositions in a theorem. Their story is an adroit allegory of world shipwreck.

One survivor is a shipbuilder and owner named Rittenhouse (Henry Hull). He symbolizes the virtues and vices of capitalism. He assumes command as his natural right. "We're under way," he cries gaily, rubbing his hands as the sail bloats to the breeze. "Where to?" someone asks. "Uh?" he says, searching their faces; "Doesn't anyone *know*?" But there is no compass.

Another passenger is a German (Walter Slezak), captain of the destroyed U-boat which sank the lifeboat's ship. His life is saved when Shipbuilder Rittenhouse insists on democratic procedure and the observance of international law. When a dance-hall addict (William Bendix) develops gangrene, it is the German captain, an ex-surgeon, who amputates the gangrened leg. As the passengers grow weaker, the German takes charge and rows, hour after hour, comforting the derelicts by singing *Lieder.*

But he conceals his compass, steers not for Bermuda but for a German supply ship. And while everyone sleeps, he pushes overboard the man who catches him drinking from a concealed bottle of water. His apparently superhuman strength comes from this water and from energy tablets. In a burst of horror and rage his boatmates force him overboard, beat him under water. Rittenhouse delivers the *coup de grâce*—with the shoe from the amputated foot of the man the German saved.

The survivors have no water, no food, no energy, no destination, no prospect but death. "When we killed the German," they say, "we killed our motor." Says religious Negro Joe (Canada Lee): "We still got a motor." He means God.

Melodramatically salvation heaves in sight. A German supply ship and an Allied ship stage a shelling duel. The German ship is sunk.

A boy of 16, symbol of postwar Germany, clutches the lifeboat, is hauled aboard. Cinemactresses Mary Anderson and Tallulah Bankhead rush to help him. "Kill him!" cry the men —among whom only the gentle radio operator (Hume Cronyn) has any doubt. As the trembling boy holds them at bay with his water-soaked pistol, the Negro disarms him. They debate whether or not to kill him. Tallulah Bankhead recalls the man the German captain drowned and a young mother (Heather Angel) who was pulled aboard the lifeboat, later jumped overboard after her dead baby. When *Lifeboat* ends, they are still debating, like the world, what to do with the German.

Globular Alfred ("Hitch") Hitchcock has lately become an oblate spheroid by jettisoning some 90 lb. of flesh. (His starting weight was 295 lb., his favorite food, beefsteak.) But asceticism has not reduced Hitchcock's abilities as a humorist, raconteur, deadpan artist and the greatest director of cinema thrillers. At a large stag dinner party, when his turn came to enrich the traditional ambience of brandy & cigars with an off-color story, he murmured diffidently: "I have a story, but I'd best not tell it because it's rather long." The clamor for it was insistent. Then for three-quarters of an hour Hitch held a dozen grown men breathless, waiting for the *double-entendre*, while he told the story of Cinderella—straight.

This accomplished sadist was born of solid middle-class parents (his father was a poulterer) in London, 43 years ago. For a while he was a layout man for an advertising firm. In idle moments he jotted down elaborate titles for hypothetical films.

He took them to British International Pictures, was immediately hired as title artist. At 26, Hitch was a director.

In his younger days in London, Hitch was an insatiable first-nighter, a sort of rolling encyclopedia of stage lore. Another consuming interest was transportation. He could tell any Thamesside character who would listen the tonnage, type and country of every craft on the Thames. He loves to ride on trains, and two of his best pictures (*The 39 Steps, The Lady Vanishes*) have thrilling train sequences.

His memory for detail is photographic. After half an hour in one Swiss village, he reproduced it in a set down to the last lintel and *Lederhosen*. When he came to the U.S., he flabbergasted David O. Selznick's representatives by telling them precisely where everything in Manhattan was and how best to get there. And he could scarcely wait to see the police line-up, a treat to which he had been looking forward for years.

After he made *The 39 Steps* (1935), Hollywood had its eye on Hitchcock. He was not only England's leading director; he was, with René Clair, possibly the most brilliant of all directors of fiction films. In 1938 he signed with David O. Selznick, because he thought Selznick produced Hollywood's best pictures. But he takes no back talk from Selznick. As a result, he fares better than any other Selznick property. Selznick lend-leased Hitchcock to 20th Century–Fox to make *Lifeboat* for $200,000. Hitch pocketed $120,000 of it.

Hitchcock is no improviser. By the time shooting starts he knows the script by heart, knows to the last foot every effect he proposes to get out of the picture. He is a good actor, a superb teacher, a meticulous director. He will spend ten minutes not only demonstrating but explaining why a certain effect will be achieved if the actor gets less animation into his hands. Then he will do the scene himself. He never enacts a love scene; he will not risk a laugh.

Director Hitchcock always appears for a moment in each of his films. It is his way of "signing" his pictures. But there was no room or excuse for him in the lifeboat. So in the middle of a news page—which has precious little business in *Lifeboat* either—Hitchcock planted himself in bulbous profile, as the before-&-after model in a reducing ad.

Time, January 31, 1944

Phantom Lady (Universal) is the maiden production of Joan Harrison, who used to be Alfred Hitchcock's Girl Friday and who now becomes one of the few women producers in Hollywood's history.* *Phantom Lady* lags behind Hitchcock's best films, but it has picked up enough from them to sprint laps ahead of most thrillers.

The night when Architect Scott Henderson (Alan Curtis) meets her in a Manhattan bar and takes her to a show, the Lady (Fay Helm) is no phantom. Her handsome dolor is made the more memorable by a fiercely rhetorical hat. At the evening's end she drifts off without giving her name, and Architect Henderson drifts homeward to find detectives chewing cigars and chicle over his strangled wife. All efforts to find his alibi prove useless. The bartender (Andrew Tombes) has never seen her. Neither has the randy little drummer (Elisha Cook Jr.) who ogled her all evening. Neither has the Latin singer (Carmen Miranda's sister, Aurora), who threw a jealous tantrum because she and the Lady were wearing duplicate hats. Henderson is convicted of murder.

But his Secretary Carol (Ella Raines) realizes that somebody has stopped a lot of mouths with a lot of money. She hounds the nervous bartender. He is killed by a car. She starts pumping the drummer. He is strangled. Escorted by her boss's good friend, Jack Lombard (Franchot Tone), she even locates the maker of the special hat and its elusive wearer. But nothing really becomes clear to her until Good Friend Lombard tips his paranoiac hand.

Miss Harrison, with notable help from mood-wise Cameraman Elwood Bredell, invests this grade-B plot with a lot of style and scare. Some of the dialogue is ham, and toward the end the picture's edginess blunts noticeably. But the bar and bartender, the damp night streets, a late-night elevated platform, and a jam session that looks like an expressionistic death dance, have a good deal of Hitchcock's sinister melo-realistic melancholy.

Asked in what respect she differs from other Hollywood producers, Joan Harrison, 34, tilts one blonde eyebrow, grins,

*Some others, past & present: Mary Pickford, Fanchon Royer, Louella Parsons' daughter Harriet.

and replies, "I use my sex." When, against Universal's better judgment, she became a Universal producer, the studio sent around a photographer to immortalize the event. "Well," snapped Miss Harrison, "do you want some leg art?" Besides using a pair of ah-inspiring legs, she also uses a mind trained at the Sorbonne, at Oxford, and by England's shrewdest director.

Ten years ago, a friend roused her from a late morning hangover with the news that Alfred Hitchcock was advertising for a secretary. Hangover & all, Miss Harrison hurried 30 miles to London, bluffed her way past twelve applicants, and won out over 40 others whom Hitchcock had already interviewed.

As a secretary, Joan Harrison says she was terrible, but one important thing she did well. Hitchcock will never read a prospective script or even a synopsis for a script. It became Secretary Harrison's job to give him stories by word of mouth. Soon she began to improve on the originals as she went along. Miss Harrison became more & more useful to Hitchcock as an idea woman. With *The Girl Was Young* (1937) she did her first screen writing. With *Jamaica Inn* (1939) she did her first full script, got her first screen credit. By 1941 Secretary Harrison was 1) perhaps the most highly esteemed member of Hitchcock's permanent crew, 2) desperate. Her desperation was simple: she had ideas and an ego, and she was too close to a great man to do what she wanted with either. She left Hitchcock.

During the next two years several of Joan Harrison's scripts were ditched or manhandled by Paramount, Columbia, M.G.M., Warners. She was about ready to toss in the sponge when an agent turned up with a whodunit about a disappearing alibi in a conspicuous hat. Would she do a script? If so, Universal might be induced to produce it. Miss Harrison saw possibilities in the novel, but two years' freelancing had made her intensely leery of the handling it might receive. So she told the high muckymucks of Universal exactly how the picture was to be made. Few men, far less a woman, far less a woman so neatly made, had ever talked to them like that. But if they were startled they were also impressed. If the lady knew their business so much better than they knew it themselves, how would she like to produce the picture? Miss Harrison said that nothing would give her greater pleasure.

From the first Joan Harrison's working methods were rather unconventional: they showed foresight and sharp common sense. Miss Harrison lined up her art director (John Goodman) before she did anything else. Then she chose Scripter B. C. Schoenfeld, collaborated with him and, like Hitchcock, gave him full screen credit. She also teamed closely with Director Robert Siodmak. She did her own casting, down to the most insignificant bit. She sank $60,000 of her budget in Franchot Tone for the maniac, on the theory that "unusual casting brings a different flavor to your picture." She persuaded Alan Curtis to play without make-up, on the equally startling theory that a hero looks more heroic if he looks like a human being. She talked Ella Raines into wearing the simple dresses and coiffures a secretary might reasonably wear. She was better aware than most Hollywoodians of the value of silence—a good half of *Phantom Lady* is without the doubtful benefit of either talk or music. She was also cagey in her handling of the baser emotions: in *Phantom Lady* the jam session is quite an orgy, portrayed metaphorically, without a line of dialogue, suggestive or otherwise.

After she finished *Phantom Lady* three months ago, Producer Harrison was offered her choice of 1) a Western, 2) a stale-ale melodrama. She refused both: "I am a specialist. I am proud of being a specialist. I don't want to make pictures with the Andrews sisters." Her current ideas are 1) a film to be made entirely by women; 2) "a murder story involving only children."

Time, February 28, 1944

With the Marines at Tarawa (U.S.M.C.; edited by Warner Bros.; distributed by Universal) is war in the least expurgated form most U.S. cinemaddicts are likely to see. It has long been a question how much battle experience should be communicated to civilians. *With the Marines at Tarawa* should settle the question once for all. Some things have been left out (in battle the camera cannot be everywhere). And there is no shot of any American being wounded or killed. Nevertheless, the picture's 19 minutes of unflagging pity, terror and intense action make a film whose power no U.S. documentary has matched.

There is the endlessly cautious, catlike approach that a few marines make, across the open sand, to a blasted revetment which may still hold Japanese life, American death. There is the attempt on the part of a few others, as careful and painful as the probing of a complex wound, to climb a bunker and clean out its far side with rifles, flame-throwers, grenades. There is the weird, exquisite variety of individual expressions of skill and fear, which are the cross-texture of the violence of combat. Smoke, ruined palms, a boundless sense of death choke the screen. Men quickly fire into blindness, take quick cover, each moving jerkily with a quality of loneliness in the midst of action with which no loneliness of peace is comparable.

And there are touches, tender beyond the reach of invention. A boy who has withdrawn from the fight stands by a tree, exhausted, pinching the bridge of his nose. A young man holds gauze to his shot mouth and retires from the battle with precisely the hunched, half-stumbling gait of an athlete taken out of a game. There are two moments of greatness: the slow, tentative wading ashore of the relief troops on the fourth day (no camera recorded the slaughter of 300 to 400 on the second); the faces of the marines as they watch the flag rise to the peak of the pole they have won for it.

With the help of the Marine Corps, Warner Bros. has given this film fine reticence of sound effect and commentary. The very rawness of the color helps to give a rawer reality to some of the most real things ever fixed by a camera. But after all its fierceness *With the Marines at Tarawa* ends quietly, with one of the most powerful shots it records. The marines are trooping back from battle. They march toward the camera. One young fellow on the sidelines is smiling, almost with jubilation. There are no other smiles. One gaunt man, his face drawn with sleeplessness and a sense of death, glances up. His eyes reveal both his lack of essential hostility and his profound, decent resentment of the camera's intrusion. Just as he leaves the picture he makes a face, as a father might make a face at a child. In his eyes, in his grimace, he looks into the eyes of every civilian and whatever face that civilian is capable of wearing in reply. And in the eyes of the camera, with that salute, he meets the eyes of history.

—

See Here, Private Hargrove (M.G.M.) is war training expurgated by comedy. The picture dubs the title of 1942's best-selling, cubbish comedy of barracks life onto a swatch of slightly whimsical photographed cartoons. Typical cartoon: a soldier, agonizingly wriggling forward under barbed wire and live ammunition, exclaims: "My, this is exciting, isn't it?"

Private Marion Hargrove (Robert Walker) is typical of the half-grown, brash, good-natured boys whom the vast drafts of World War II have passed between the Army's shaping rollers. How to standardize such a kid into a soldier so disturbs Private Hargrove's captain that after one look at him the officer thinks of transferring to the Navy. In the long run Hargrove and his equally unmilitary comrades learn their trade. But the film devotes most of its time to the comic aspects of their training (mostly polishing garbage cans) and their vestigial private life.

Private Hargrove's particular pals are a slick con man, Private Mulvehill (Keenan Wynn), his buck-toothed, leering side-kick, Private Esty (George Offerman Jr.), and a solemn, proletarian, Private Burk (Bill Phillips). Private Burk tries to explain to Private Hargrove the puzzled sources of his patriotism, but Mulvehill and Esty simply gyp Hargrove right & left. As co-executives of a mythical Date Bureau, they sell him an evening with a girl (Donna Reed) who never heard of their scheme. They also form the Marion Hargrove Beneficial Association to raise funds for his New York furlough. The catch: he signs over to them the proceeds of his literary future. Later Mulvehill wangles good safe desk jobs for himself and Hargrove. But as their unit embarks for war, their sense of war's comradeship gets the better of them, and they plead their way back into the artillery.

Funniest shot: a monologue by Hargrove's girl's paunchy father (Robert Benchley), who buzzes away about his experiences in World War I while baffled Private Hargrove tries to get in a word.

Time, March 20, 1944

The Fighting Lady (U.S. Navy–20th Century–Fox) is the fiercely beautiful and thrilling color record of an aircraft carrier's career from her launching through her first half-dozen engagements.* It was shot during the past couple of years by a crew of six enlisted men, coached by famed photographer Captain Edward Steichen, and directed by Lieut. Commander Dwight Long. Their combined mileage was cut to its present 7,500 feet and 60 minutes by Fox's Louis de Rochemont, first producer of the MARCH OF TIME, whose first Hollywood film this is. John Stuart Martin, formerly of TIME, wrote the script; Lieut. (j.g.) Robert Taylor, formerly of M.G.M., narrated it. More responsible, in a sense, than any one of these men for the film's magnificence were the automatic cameras which peered down the barrels of the guns of fighters and bombers to record the picture's overwhelming shots of combat and flaming death.

The story of this flattop begins with green young men, many of them unbelievably boyish, endlessly rehearsing their deck and air routines, or loafing in the sunlight as their floating town lounges through the improbable colors of the Gulf Stream and edges her way through the Panama Canal. While they loaf, they wonder. Their destination is still as dead a blank to them as their experience of combat. Then, well out in the Pacific, in some rough, wonderful shots, they meet a tanker and refuel, and know at least that their job is to be long and businesslike.

In the course of their long voyage out, you get some sense of knowing the whole 3,000-odd personnel, from the cobbler and barber and tailor to the princely-looking royally treated pilots.

At length, some 7,000 miles out of Panama, they approach and learn their target—the small, elegant triangle of Marcus Island. The night before their first experience of combat—a night crowded with taciturn faces, with letters home, with prayers and last Communions, with the subdued, systematic turmoil of spotting the deck, with athletes' breakfasts served

*The carrier is no one actual ship; it is typical of carriers of the *Essex* class (27,000 tons). Much of the action was shot on one particular carrier, which the Navy does not wish to identify.

by artificial light, and finally with just waiting—is one of the most moving sequences in the film.

It is followed by something even more powerful—the take-off of the planes against an extravagant dawn which one might only smile at on a calendar. That in turn meets more than its match in the pictures which follow—the first of those many gun-barrel shots of combat in color which, in their effortless achievement at once of superhuman force and grandeur and of jewel-like delicacy, might well make this film the envy of good poets and painters for the rest of time. Later on, over Truk and Kwajalein and the Marianas, these shots—plus some hair-raising ones of crash-landings on the carrier deck—heap one astonishment so thickly upon another that the eye and mind can hardly keep pace. For violent air action and for pure visual magnificence, *The Fighting Lady* is not likely ever to be beaten.

I'll Be Seeing You (Selznick–United Artists) is Hollywood's first attempt to focus on the predicament of a shell-shocked soldier, trying to find his way back to normal life. Good and moving as it sometimes is, it leaves much to be said which, for the sake of the many neuro-psychiatric casualties who are already returning from the war, badly needs saying to American civilians. The picture's crucial weakness: it confronts its fumbling, humiliated, pitiful soldier Zack (Joseph Cotten) with a girl (Ginger Rogers) who, instead of being reasonably average, is also a decidedly special case. Zack is on Christmas furlough from an Army psychiatric hospital; Mary is on Christmas furlough from a penitentiary.

Such artificiality, falling far short of universal human interest, also leads to painfully irrelevant storytelling: the girl spends a large part of the picture deceiving Zack, first for her own good, later for his. And in the course of pampering this sort of overspecialized pathos, the far more pathetic and important story which the picture pretends to tell gets pretty thoroughly tear-dimmed.

Yet the picture is very far from being a total loss. Joseph Cotten's muted, excruciating performance is the best single guarantee of that; some moments of deep warmth and sympathy from Miss Rogers are also valuable. And the rest of the cast and David O. Selznick, Producer Dore Schary and Director

William Dieterle have done a good many unpretentiously remarkable things.

At the home of the girl's aunt (Spring Byington) there is
some touching domestic business (by Miss Byington, Shirley
Temple and the accomplished Tom Tully)—memorably a
Christmas supper at which everybody sings *O Come, All Ye
Faithful*. There are also moments of franker pain and shock
than most films dare to hand an audience without Boris
Karloff to reassure them it is all in fun—a scene with a screwily
bellicose veteran of World War I (Chill Wills), a horrible fracas
between Zack and a dog, a still grimmer scene in which Zack,
alone in his Y.M.C.A. room, all but drowns in a maelstrom of
the unforgettable noises of combat.

When Zack and his girl stroll through subdued, snowless
winter country, the landscape is photographed with an appreciation of the power and subtlety of weather that most U.S.
movie-makers seem to lack. When Zack invites his new friends
to a New Year's Eve party at the Y, the crowd there is precisely
as it should be. So are the decorations and so—a typical
Selznick touch—is the sailor, off at the side, solemnly working
himself into a lather on the parallel bars. (Other Selznick
touches: a stuffy senator asking Zack how the boys overseas
are thinking politically and getting a quite unpleasant answer;
a woman scolding her little boy—his name: Franklin.)

There are dozens of such indications that Selznick knows
and cares more about getting American life into good moving
pictures than any other man with his combined power and
talent.

Time, January 22, 1945

Salome, Where She Danced (Universal) has got practically
everything except the rise of Silas Lapham and the decline &
fall of the Roman Empire, and there seems to be no reason except pure niggardliness that they should not have been worked
in too. Items: defeated General Robert E. Lee telling a Confederate soldier (David Bruce) that "we must move with the ages";
a Berlin correspondent for *Leslie's Weekly* (Rod Cameron)
scooping the world on the opening of Bismarck's Austro-

Prussian War, with the help of a dancer named Anna Maria (Yvonne de Carlo); Anna Maria emerging from a shell to the strains of *The Blue Danube* to dance some elementary ballet; an energetic cavalry battle in which her lover, a Hapsburg Prince, loses the war and his life rather than cause her political embarrassment in Berlin; a scene in a raw Western U.S. town, in which Anna Maria calms the beavered natives by executing, as Salome, the hootchy-kootchy; a scene in which she reforms the quondam Confederate, turned local bandit, by her snarling contralto rendition of *Der Tannenbaum* (*Maryland! My Maryland!*); San Francisco in its heyday, which includes 1) an infatuated Russian multimillionaire (Walter Slezak), 2) the attempted pirating of a Chinese junk, 3) its sagacious proprietor, who speaks Oriental proverbs in Edinburr dialect, 4) a duel with rapiers on a blood-red floor, 5) a hair-raising stagecoach chase, 6) a happy ending. This does not, perhaps, give a very clear idea of the story, but that is no great loss.

One of the odd things about this odd picture is that there really is an Arizona town called Salome—Where She Danced. It was named, however, after a native, a Mrs. Grace Salome Pratt; and it is called, for short, Suhloam. The oddest thing of all, though, is that the show is quite a lot of fun. Most of the color and costuming is garishly pretty; the dialogue is richly flavored with such tongue-in-cheek lines as one man's description of the heroine: "She was always a great artist—but above all—a woman." Miss de Carlo, a newcomer to the screen, is not exactly persuasive as the great artist, but as a woman, especially in her Salome number, she brings the house down.

Dillinger (Monogram) is the story of a Public Enemy No. 1 whose misbehavior seems so innocuous, beside the work of later international candidates, that you can almost smell the sachet along with the tear gas and gunpowder. The picture recalls how this born delinquent knocked over a string of banks, a mail train, a harmless elderly couple and two of his associates; and how at last his girl betrayed him to G-men, who shot him down as he walked out of a nickelodeon. Fortunately, this old-fashioned story is told in an old-fashioned way. The result: a tough, tight, tense, tricky little melodrama.

This sort of storytelling, related to balladry but a lot less

long-winded, is not new to the screen. But it has been neglected so long that it is as good as new. Combined with evocative sets and appropriate performance (by Lawrence Tierney,
Edmund Lowe, Anne Jeffreys and others), and admirably
terse, it provides a tinnily entertaining, cinematically energetic
antidote to the two-hour doses of pure unflavored gelatin now
alarmingly on the increase. Significantly, it was made quickly
on very little money, as pictures go, and for a humble but reliable audience—the general equivalent of the audience which
reads pulp magazines. Its overall cost was $150,000. It was
shot in 21 days. The screen play was slapped together in a week.

Time, May 7, 1945

T*o the Shores of Iwo Jima* (Paramount), a nine-minute newsreel taken by Navy, Coast Guard and Marine Corps cameramen
of the fiercest fight in Marine Corps history, is worthy, or almost worthy, to rank with such great war records as *With the
Marines at Tarawa* (TIME, March 20, 1944). Shot chiefly on a
terrain as shapeless as an ash-heap, as mortally featureless and
cryptic as the flank of Captain Ahab's White Whale in their ultimate engagement, it lacks the relative coherence and clarity
of most of its predecessors. It demonstrates, in fact, more
clearly than any previous film, that war in its crucial essence is
neither dramatic nor even particularly human, but paroxysmic:
that it is simply hell on earth.

Even as you watch the immensities of a sea choked with
craft, and realize the incalculably great massing and bran-
dishing of skill and purpose assembled there, the whole motion
forward has the involuntariness of a convulsion. Even as you
look from a plane steep into the sea, and note the amazingly
regular patterns of the wakes, it is more as if a stone had been
gashed by the claws of a great beast. And along the ashen island, men and machines flounder and founder as desperately,
and with as little apparent clarity of intention, as if they themselves were phantasms of dust.

Yet all the chaos is flashed full of human light and meaning.
There is a row of mournfully dazed, wounded men in a boat,
their shoulders festooned by a long sheet-like strip of white

cloth. There are Japanese prisoners, by that fact presumably among the softest defenders of their island; and in their bleak, barrelbodied, flintlike power you will recognize if you never did before that the enemy is indeed tough. There is a closeup of a bullet-hole in flesh, at once as intimate and as impersonal as if it were your own wound, so new you cannot yet feel it. There is a shot made through the slot of a tank of a Japanese soldier trying to evade the machine-gun bullets which stitch the ashes all around him. Bemused, almost hypnotized in his dreadful slowness, fumbling in the footless dust with much the clumsiness of a terrified rat, he half falls, at last, behind a mound. For a moment, before you think, you may hope he has made it alive; but you will never know.

There is also a moment, inside the same tank, of intercom dialogue which was recorded on the spot. It is spoken, against insane din, in voices so local, so familiar, that your impulse is to look into the face of the last man who spoke and say something in reply. But the speaker's face does not appear; and if you are a civilian, it is unlikely that there are any words you could find to say.

Time, March 26, 1945

Uncle Harry (Universal) is a thriller, produced by Alfred Hitchcock's onetime secretary, Joan Harrison, whose murder thriller *Phantom Lady* (TIME, Feb. 24, 1944) established her as one of Hollywood's talented producers. Her second offering, a Broadway play adaptation, is again directed by able Robert Siodmak, and again features a vivid performance by Ella Raines. *Uncle Harry* is better done than its predecessor, more human, subtler, more exciting.

Harry (George Sanders) is the kind of man everybody likes and nobody quite respects—a man rendered permanently infantile by his own gentleness, by his family's standing in their small New England town, and above all by his bickering, manless sisters, the widow Hester (Moyna Macgill) and the semi-invalid Lettie (Geraldine Fitzgerald). Lettie in particular takes care that life shall never disturb him with a breath of fresh air.

When a strong cool blast of it (Ella Raines) wakes him up and threatens to make a man of him, everyone except Harry realizes that Sister Lettie's feelings about him exceed the sisterly. From there on the story is ever-crueler melodrama, culminating in a tacked-on ending which the audience is requested not to tell—presumably on the assumption that everybody has the right to feel sold out.

Despite its silly ending, *Uncle Harry* is worth seeing. Its hints of psychological incest, which are so arranged that you can take them or leave them, are even more interesting in their Hays Office aspects than as drama. The acutely recorded small-town characters and atmospheres, and the intense performances of all four principal players, are something more. Especially notable is Geraldine Fitzgerald's portrayal of the harboring sister —the first role in years which has given this actress opportunity to show more than a fraction of her worth.

Watching her play minor roles in major films like *Wilson*, major roles in minor films like *Shining Victory*, discerning cinemaddicts have long been puzzled by Geraldine Fitzgerald's fourth-magnitude stardom.

Because this particular victim of Hollywood's wonderful ways happens to be 1) intelligent, 2) candid, 3) now free to talk —her long-term contract with Warner has just expired ("thank God")—Miss Fitzgerald has finally explained all. Any Hollywoodenhead would insist that it was entirely her own fault, and, in a measure, she would cheerfully agree.

The trouble started in the rush of her first success when *Dark Victory* and *Wuthering Heights* made it clear that she would soon become a major star. David Selznick wanted her for the title role in Hitchcock's smash *Rebecca*, but she turned it down. She was under contract to Warner for half of each year; if she worked for Selznick, he would own the other half. She preferred to spend it with her husband, in Ireland. That sort of independence is neither admired nor understood in Hollywood. It didn't exactly enhance her stock, either, when she returned from Ireland pregnant.

She began getting second-grade, leftover and plain trash roles. She was done out of a long-promised chance to play Emily Brontë. She went to Broadway and enjoyed herself thoroughly in a play by Irwin Shaw (*Sons and Soldiers*). The fact that it flopped sent her Hollywood stock still lower.

Miss Fitzgerald was now well-foundered in that strange limbo where it is far worse to have started brilliantly and to have sloped off, than to be just starting; where everyone, forgetting what went wrong and why, assigns it simply to lack of ability; where it is silly to think of getting a release from a strangling contract; where boredom, frustration and hopelessness conspire against the will until, as she says, "all you can hope for is that sooner or later you will hit bottom. . . ." She hit bottom in the appalling *Ladies Courageous.*

When her friend Joan Harrison offered her the role of Lettie, Miss Fitzgerald wanted no part of it. ("You can see," she says, "I plan my career very carefully.") She knew it was a good role, but she thoroughly disliked it.

Robert Siodmak sold it to her—as an artist's duty toward a good piece of work, likable or not. When she finally got into the part she fell in love with it. She fell so hard that Director Siodmak, whose worries about Hays Office approval must have been a little like a man wondering how Queen Victoria would take to an off-color joke, had to tone down her performance. But despite all precautions, Miss Fitzgerald's salvation from limbo gleams handsomely through the Hays.

Time, August 27, 1945

The Big Sleep (Warner) is wakeful fare for folks who don't care what is going on, or why, so long as the talk is hard and the action harder. The message, if any, seems to be that the life of a private detective is ill-paid, full of social embarrassment, yet not without its compensations.

Author Raymond Chandler's hero Marlowe (Humphrey Bogart) hires on to help a tough old millionaire out of a bit of blackmail. Before he even knows her, one of the old man's daughters (Martha Vickers), a thumbsucking type with beautiful legs, indicates her depravity by trying, as the detective says, to sit on his lap while he is standing up. Her elder sister looks like, and is Lauren Bacall (Mrs. Humphrey Bogart); she seems to be interested in buying Marlowe out of the case, either by fiscal or physical currency. Still another compensation (Dorothy Malone), after only a few minutes' talk about rare editions, pulls off her glasses, shuts down her bookstore, and spends the balance of a rainy afternoon drinking rye with Sleuth Bogart.

But such pleasures, like the ring on the merry-go-round, cannot be enjoyed at leisure. Marlowe's more serious work takes him to a glass-eyed bookseller's orgy-nest just in time to find him dead, with Miss Vickers, squiffed in a Chinese gown, giggling over the remains. He takes the heiress home and hurries on to watch a painfully inept blackmailer (Louis Jean Heydt) catch a bellyful of lead; no time later, Marlowe is kicking the killer in the face.

He has no sooner wound up a mild flirtation with a lunch-room girl than two men chivvy him into an alley and work him back & forth like a rockinghorse, one hammering at his solar plexus, the other at his kidneys. And he has hardly got his breath back when he has to watch a huge criminal (Fred Steele) force a small damp grey one (Elisha Cook Jr.) to drink a glass of poison. After that it is only a question of time before the big man has laid out Marlowe with a fistful of small auto parts.

The picture itself may give a clearer idea than all this of why such things happen, but only under the most patient analysis. Actually, the plot's crazily mystifying, nightmare blur is an asset, and only one of many. By far the strongest is Bogart, who can get into a minor twitch of the mouth the force of a slug from an automatic. Another is Producer-Director Howard Hawks's fellow feeling for the Chandler world: even on the chaste screen Hawks manages to get down a good deal of the glamorous tawdriness of big-city low life, discreetly laced with hints of dope addiction, voyeurism and fornication. A round dozen minor players help him out with great efficiency—not to mention Miss Bacall, who is like an adolescent cougar.

Time, August 26, 1946

A STAR IS BORN

ONE fateful day in 1940, a would-be actress named Deborah Kerr (rhymes with star) was sitting in a London restaurant with an acquaintance of British Producer-Director Gabriel Pascal.

When Pascal himself was introduced, he promptly chanted in his richest Magyar overtones: "Sweet lady, you have a spiritual face."

That, as some Englishmen would say, tore it. For, as a result of that brief encounter, the bigwigs of Metro-Goldwyn-Mayer are now immodestly slapping their own backs with the fervor of flagellant monks. They have acquired little Miss Kerr, and they suspect that she might be the biggest thing that has happened to M-G-M since Greer Garson.

Somewhat more modestly, Miss Kerr will very soon be exposed to U.S. cinemaddicts. The exposure is a clever little British-made melodrama about Nazi spies in Ireland called *The Adventuress* (Eagle-Lion; English title: *I See a Dark Stranger*). Whatever the result of this more critical encounter, few who see her can miss the fact that Cinemactress Kerr carries *The Adventuress* as effortlessly as a hat box. Almost nobody at all will miss the fact that Cinemactress Kerr looks like everything Englishmen mean when they become lyrical about roses. Given this primary stuff that stars are made of, it is clear that Deborah is well on her way to becoming, as quickly as possible, the brightest and best movie star that the biggest and most proficient star factory in the world can make of her.

The origins of this dawning luminary lay in biographical penumbra beyond the visual range of Hollywood scouts. She was born in Helensburgh, Scotland, Sept. 30, 1921. Her family was neither down-&-out nor well-to-do. Her Scottish father's handsomeness was distilled, in her, to a gentle beauty. She still shows the benign effects of a limpid childhood and shines quietly with another unpurchasable endowment—an ineradicable gentility. Thanks to an ex-professional aunt in Bristol, Deborah, early in life, had several years' stiff training as an actress. Later she took a whirl at ballet. But her well-padded, 5 ft.-7 in. frame was a bit bulky for ballet, and realizing, as she now says, that "this [indicating her face] was the only thing I had to work with," she began hunting jobs on the stage.

She read children's stories over the BBC. She took part in open-air Shakespeare productions in Regent's Park, rising from walk-ons to lines like "Will you go hunt, milord?" There was one incandescent moment when Producer-Director Michael Powell noticed her in an agent's office (he remembers her as "a plump little dumpling who was obviously going places") and wrote a bit for her into *Contraband*. But the bit wound up on the cutting-room floor. So Deborah continued to live at a Y.W.C.A. on 35 shillings ($7) a week and spent most of her waking hours being turned out of producers' offices. By the time Gabriel Pascal saw her, plain living and plenty of walking had etherealized the dumpling to that lithe spirit which Pascal singled out.

And from the moment Pascal saw her, unknown Deborah Kerr was in. In a flash, he perceived that Miss Kerr was the ideal Salvation Army lass to be slapped around by Robert Newton in *Major Barbara*. It was not much of a part, but Deborah slapped so photogenically that within the next year she suffered modified mayhem in four more pictures, of which the most memorable was *Love on the Dole*. Then came Powell & Pressburger's *Colonel Blimp*, the best of her films to date, and one of the two most fate-fraught in shaping her career.

Blimp's big moments left Deborah emotionally starved, but in range of type it was a feast. She played three archetypes of English womanhood—a governess in Berlin circa 1900; a county-family debutante of the early 1920s; a merry Motor Corps girl of World War II. And she played them in color. Miss Kerr's natural coloring would have reduced Renoir to a quivering jelly. It is so vivid that she faced the Technicolor cameras with little more than simple street make-up. She was dissolvingly lovely to look at; and she acted her modest roles with a quiet finish, shrewdness and grace which were already (she was then 21) unqualifiedly her own style. Ben Goetz of Metro British, as soon as he saw *Blimp*, determined to snatch Miss Kerr away from Pascal at once.

Luckily, Pascal was short of funds (since *Major Barbara* he had merely farmed Deborah out to other studios, in Selznick fashion). Goetz bought half of Pascal's contract with Deborah and decided to use her opposite Robert Donat in Alexander Korda's war film, *Perfect Strangers* (U.S. translation: *Vacation from Marriage*). In the first part of *Vacation from Marriage* Deborah played mousiness right down to the bottom of the mousehole, then, transfigured by the experience of war, she devoted the closing reels to looking a little more beautiful and vibrant than unmartial mortals can ever hope to look.

It was quite a pleasant little picture and, in the U.S., quite a solid little flop. Nevertheless, it was *Vacation* which landed Cinemactress Kerr on that planet-girdling conveyor belt which ends, implacably, in Hollywood.

A Hollywood screening of *Blimp* did not provoke Cinemagnate Louis B. ("L.B.") Mayer and his paladins to a joyful dog-fight for a full Kerr contract. It served, rather, as a come-on, by planting Miss Kerr so fruitfully in the M-G-M unconscious that when these unimpulsive executives assembled, some time later, to see *Vacation from Marriage*, they were most pleasantly disposed to watch her work again. *Vacation from Marriage* bored them to tears. But Deborah Kerr did not bore them a bit. In fact, L.B., without a moment's hesitation, uttered the flat pronouncement: "That girl is a star."

But scarcely had Metro's massive procurement machinery begun to move than it stalled. L.B. was ready & willing; Miss Kerr was more than ready & willing. But Pascal had so thoroughly snarled up his half of the contract that it seemed impossible to untangle. The chief difficulty was that Pascal had guaranteed Deborah a certain sum after British taxes. To Hollywood the price seemed prohibitive. Poor Deborah languished as helplessly as the rich man with the needle's-eye view of heaven. Then, suddenly, she became more like a bone at the vortex of a dogfight. M-G-M, Sam Goldwyn, Loew-Lewin, Hal Wallis and J. Arthur Rank were all trying to get at her. It was M-G-M which finally bought out Pascal, and gave her a new contract. For an unknown it was fairly fabulous—a document to raise loud whistles in front offices and low moans in dressing rooms; seven years at $3,000 a week, 52 weeks a year, no options; Miss Kerr to be starred or co-starred in all films.

Miss Kerr was bought but she still had to be sold—to her employers. The obstetrics of star-bearing often seem to have as little apparent relation to the finished star as forceps have to a baby. How Miss Kerr came into her first Hollywood role is a fair sample.

M-G-M had paid $200,000 for the screen rights to Frederic Wakeman's cross, best-selling novel about radio, *The Hucksters*; Mayer had thought it would be good for Gable. Gable claimed shudderingly that the hero's flagrantly libertine outlook would ruin him forever as a great lover. The book's big

sales and a denatured script brought Gable around. Metro decided to create its own star (Metro can create a star overnight
as surely as Hormel creates Spam). Why not Deborah Kerr?
But the producer, Arthur Hornblow Jr., was still worried. *The
Hucksters*, he pointed out, is budgeted at $2,500,000 and
Gable is one of the most valuable properties in pictures; why
risk a new girl? The High Council compromised. It scheduled
Miss Kerr tentatively for the role, pending a screen test, and
cabled her marching orders.

From that moment, she entered a strange, new, hermetic
world, beguiling, hypnotic and gently self-destructive. Thence-
forth she would be bombarded by the ultraviolet and infrared
rays peculiar to Hollywood, and the anthropophagous at-
tentions most peculiar of all to M-G-M. She might imagine
M-G-M saying, like the doctor in James Thurber's cartoon:
You're not my patient, Miss Kerr, you're my meat.

Solicitude is nine-tenths of stellar possession, and M-G-M's
solicitude began with the choice of transatlantic passage. As an
R.A.F. pilot, Deborah's husband, Anthony C. Bartley, had shot
down 15 confirmed planes. But in her new studio's opinion, it
was inadvisable to risk flying flesh & blood that is worth many
times its weight in gold. So Deborah and Tony crossed on the
Queen Elizabeth.

The studio formalities were a human test before the screen
test. Deborah and Tony arrived shortly before noon. The first
order of business was meeting Benny Thau, padishah of new
talent and liaison officer between Mt. Olympus and sea level.
Benny was most cordial. Casually Gable strolled in. One by
one, Benny flicked the switch to all the members of the High
Council—Eddie Mannix, Sam Katz, Howard Strickling, Arthur
Hornblow. One by one they filed in to look over their corporate purchase. They were charmed by this lovely girl. They recognized her at once as a lady. They thought that she handled
herself well. In fact, they were more convinced than ever that
she was perfect for Kay, *The Hucksters'* heroine. Said Deborah
later: "It was like being anesthetized. I was cross-eyed looking
at everybody."

Then the big moment arrived. L.B. himself would give
them audience. In fact, he had arranged a little *intime* lun-
cheon in the fourth floor executive dining room, next to the

gymnasium and steam room. The hard, magnificent old man was graciously interested in Tony's war record. He was even more interested if less conversational about Miss Kerr. But the demitasses were hardly drained before things began to hum at the studio. Deborah knew that she had passed Test No. 1.

She was taken down to Publicity and introduced to Melvina Pumphrey (Mel is very good with new girls). It would be Mel's job to help Miss Kerr "adjust" to a new way of life. Mel would be her immediate contact with the public and press. She would instruct Deborah in what to say and what not to say. She would be present at every interview and would report to the studio on what had been said. Deborah and Tony were reminded, in velvet tones, that they were "on the team" now and were expected to "play ball."

Meanwhile, Producer Hornblow was furiously at work. He called in Irene (Irene is a superb couturière) and discussed Deborah's wardrobe. Within a week he wanted to shoot the scene in which *The Hucksters'* hero makes a pass at *The Hucksters'* heroine, and he wanted a dress for it right away. While Irene rushed to obey, Deborah was rushed to Make-up and Hairdressing. Make-up did everything to Deborah Kerr's face that the most ingenious cosmetic artists in the world can do. In the end, it decided that it was impossible to do anything for her that nature had not done already. Hornblow agreed (Jack Dawn really knows his stuff). Deborah's face photographs beautifully with nothing but a base, lipstick, eyebrow pencil and a minimum of highlighting. Then Hornblow and Director Jack Conway studied the hairdressing tests very carefully (L.B. believes in trying everything on film), expressing their feelings in low hieroglyphic grunts.

Somehow Deborah also had to squeeze in two sittings in the portrait gallery (the national magazines would be clamoring for pictures). Then there was the housing problem. The studio took care of that. By the greatest good fortune, Screenwriter Casey Robinson (*noblesse oblige*) had made his Pacific Palisades house available, a charming English-type cottage spang in the middle of an orange grove. This was a great load off Deborah's and Tony's mind (L.B. believes that a good star is a happy star).

A week after Deborah's arrival, Hornblow was ready to

shoot the crucial test. Gable, Deborah was told, had agreed to make it with her. An old set was found and redressed. Gable sent flowers. Hornblow sent flowers. The cameras rolled. Gable made his pass and his proposition. Kerr gently but firmly rebuffed him.

Hornblow was elated. That well-bred strain certainly came through. Gable was swept off his feet (Clark recognizes talent when he sees it). Next day Hornblow cut the test. It looked wonderful. The High Council declared it had never seen a better one. By orders from on high, the rest of the studio was allowed to see it, too. Louella Parsons noted in her column that they "all but cheered." Deborah was officially announced for the part.

Until then, Miss Kerr had been on trial. But at 2 o'clock one afternoon, she was called in unexpectedly, and by 3 she was in front of the cameras. This time it was no test; it was for keeps. Gable had managed to materialize six dozen red roses. He sent them to her dressing room with a note: "Good luck on your opening night from your leading man, Clark Gable."

The script called for Miss Kerr to make an exit from the elevator of a swank Manhattan apartment building on Gable's arm, and gracefully to sidestep a mild verbal pass. Gable's palms were sweating, as they always do before a scene. Deborah, a paragon of self-composure, sailed through without a slip. Cried Gable: "My leading lady, hell! I'm her co-star!" Said Deborah: "I always wondered what it would be like. You come 6,000 miles and then suddenly—bang! crash! wallop!—you've done it. It's like having a tooth out."

Hornblow was completely won over. Studio executives began shyly to confess that from the beginning they had suspected that Deborah had the makings of a great star. But the credit really belonged to L.B. The scuttlebutt in the fourth floor steam room was thicker than the steam: never had there been a girl better suited to the studio's peculiar requirements. That flowerlike beauty would thrive in a hothouse atmosphere. Between sessions on the massage table, it was noted that, while she could act like Ingrid Bergman, she was really a kind of converted Greer Garson, womanly enough to show up nicely in those womanly roles which have always proved so soothing to Metro audiences.

All that remained was for people to see *The Hucksters*, and Deborah would be a star, and quite possibly a major star overnight. L.B. had bet close to $3,000,000 on that, and L.B. would not have that kind of money to throw around if L.B. had been wrong very often. Down from Olympus rang the declaration; the day after the picture is released, Deborah Kerr will be a big star.

And how about Deborah? It is hard to tell about Deborah. During her first few days in the U.S., before the cosmic rays had peppered her very deeply or the great steel rollers had swept over her, she was an excited, self-confident, ambitious girl, not snobbish, or arty, very ready with humor and irony, keenly determined not to be standardized, or forced into dull or silly roles. But by now she has probably realized more clearly that very few things are really up to her. She can simply use her beauty and her talent as honestly as possible under the circumstances. But the circumstances are wholly in the keeping of other people. Metro is giving her her prodigious chance; Metro pays her salary; she is "on the team." "All I can do," she says, "is put my faith in my employers."

Whatever comes of it, she has managed to charm the town, and this includes her employers. Her warmth, her grace and her willingness to accept anyone and anything at face value fascinates Hollywood. So does her husband, who, as a war ace and a son of a knight,* is by no means dismissible as Mr. Deborah Kerr. And they in turn are fascinated. In England, they had been in a land of privation. In their small house in Pacific Palisades, there is a Bendix washing machine, a Westinghouse refrigerator and a gas pipe in the fireplace which makes kindling unnecessary. Says Deborah: "We lean out a window and squeeze a lemon in our drinks. If that isn't the height of debauchery, I don't know what is."

In time Miss Kerr may "adjust" even to Hollywood's spectacular social life. She and her husband had scarcely been in town a week when they were asked over to Nunnally Johnson's. Under the impression that this was to be an informal little cocktail spread, they innocently walked in on time (they

---

*His North-of-Ireland father, the barrister Sir Charles Bartley, was knighted (1942) after able service in India.

have not yet learned how to be late). The first bit of Hollywood home life to meet their eye was four men in white coats carrying, to her station behind the roast beef, a half-naked mermaid. Says Deborah: "We were terrified."

Time, February 10, 1947

The Macomber Affair (Bogeaus-Robinson; United Artists) is a screen version of Ernest Hemingway's excruciating study of the relationships between an ill-married American couple and their hired English hunter-guide, and of the relations of all three to what Hemingway once called "grace under pressure."

Since the three are hunting big game in Africa, the pressures are primitive, and considerable. Macomber (Robert Preston) is a good shot but he lacks courage in a crisis and the sportsman's sense of honor towards his quarry. Besides, he talks too much about himself. The hunter (Gregory Peck), on the other hand, is everything a Hemingway hero should be. Mrs. Macomber (Joan Bennett) is not slow to choose between them nor delicate in showing her preference—in several almost unbearably ugly scenes of cruelty and humiliation. Under the pressures, Macomber finds his courage for the first time in his life. Finding it, his life really begins and his abjectness towards his wife is at an end. Mrs. Macomber promptly shoots him through the head.

According to Hemingway, she shoots him deliberately. According to Mrs. Macomber, in the movie, it was just a tragic accident—and the audience is left to make up its own mind.

Up to this point, *Macomber* is a brilliantly good job—the best yet—of bringing Hemingway to the screen. None of the three principal players could possibly be improved on; the African landscapes and hunting scenes (which were made in Africa and Mexico) are as believable as a neighbor's backyard. Director Zoltan Korda (*Sahara*) has already made two films in Africa, which is a help in this particular picture; still more important, he knows people, and style, and atmosphere, and how to make them vivid on a screen. There is hardly a point that Hemingway made in this savage, complex communiqué about the war between the sexes that Korda and his actors fail to make in movie terms. In fact, a good 95% of *Macomber* is a remarkably exciting picture for mature audiences. The worst of Hollywood's "improvements" on the original story is the did-she-or-didn't-she ending, which pulls the fuse out of Hemingway's whole payoff.

It Happened in Brooklyn (M-G-M) features Frank Sinatra, Jimmy Durante and Kathryn Grayson at the tops of their respective voices. It needn't have bothered, so far as the box office is concerned, to do anything more. What little more it does is nearly all to the good. Aside from an overdose of jokes about Brooklyn, everything about the picture is not only unobjectionable but, in a modest way, definitely enjoyable.

Sinatra, as usual, is a shy type who fails to get the girl; he not only sings with great effectiveness (best new song: *Time After Time*), but performs naturally and unaffectedly. Durante, as a high-school janitor, hasn't much to do beyond proving, without any strain, that he is one of the most likable entertainers in the business. Miss Grayson, prettier and more animated than ever, warbles an aria from *Lakmé* like an eisteddfod of thrushes, and does even better by Mozart's *Là Ci Darem la Mano*, in which she is supported by Sinatra. For good measure young Billy Roy plays the piano impressively, and Peter Lawford hangs around amiably as the shy son of an English duke.

The story doesn't matter much, except that it gives these entertainers a chance to do their work in a relaxed manner and, no less important, to be very nice to each other. By no particularly strange coincidence, that makes an audience feel good too. Metro has a particular fondness for these experiments in *Gemütlichkeit*. When they go wrong, they go awfully wrong. But when they go right—and Scripter Isobel Lennart, who also wrote *Anchors Aweigh*, seems to have a hand for it— they are something for cinemagoers to be thankful for.

The Farmer's Daughter (RKO Radio) takes a story that is almost as moss-green as its title, and turns it into amusing, lifelike entertainment. The story is not The One About the Traveling Salesman; it is The Other One—about the country girl (Loretta Young) who comes to the big city, gets work as a maid in a mansion, softens up the crusty butler (Charles Bickford), wins over the lady of the house (Ethel Barrymore), takes part in the conversation as she passes the canapés, and eventually romps off with the son of the house (Joseph Cotten).

With minor variations, this story has been used by the movies since movies began. For a long time before that, it was used in paper-backed novels. The chief variations in this one: 1) the family is one of the great political families of its state, 2) the son is a Senator and the dowager is the Party Boss and 3) the country girl herself, no slouch at politics, runs for the Senate on a sort of Common-Woman ticket, against dirty opposition. Like some of Frank Capra's films, the picture teaches a few easy-to-take lessons about the good & bad that is possible in a democracy.

But *The Farmer's Daughter* turns out to be excellent entertainment because Producer Dore Schary and his associates evidently know a good deal about the special kinds of people they are telling about. Whenever the political and bluebook friends of the family gather for cocktails or a council of war, it is a notably convincing and specialized kind of party or council, with minor characters that are beautifully drawn. Miss Young, blonde for the occasion and sporting a Swedish accent,* acts rather like a nice girl playing a charade, yet she is very likable. Messrs. Cotten and Bickford are exceedingly competent. And Ethel Barrymore, besides being invincibly persuasive as a great lady, suggests, with a mere flick of her eyes, that she has enough political savvy to save the nation.

Time, April 7, 1947

This Happy Breed (Rank-Universal) is Noel Coward's proud and loving tribute to the unbreakable British backbone. It tells the story of the lower-middle-class Gibbons family between Wars I & II. The film opens and ends with a fine Technicolor shot of the roofs of London. In the closing shot the roofs lie defenseless to the hell that is soon to crack them open. But by then, Coward has made clear how ready the people under the

---

*Rumpled into her diction by Ruth Roberts, who irons it out of Ingrid Bergman's.

roofs are to endure the worst and to prevail against it. He shows this never through flat heroics, but through the quiet, immense courage, patience, kindliness and common sense which give structure, and a certain majesty, to 20 years of one family's life.

The plot is simple. It shows the family life of Frank Gibbons (Robert Newton), his wife Ethel (Celia Johnson) and their three children. Vi (Eileen Erskine), a docile creature, gives little trouble. She marries a young pinko, but quickly domesticates him. Reg (John Blythe), a charming, rather irresponsible boy, messes about on the left side of the general strike but marries and turns out well in the end. Then he is killed in an auto wreck. Queenie (Kay Walsh) is the real problem. A spirited, rebellious girl, with ideas above her class, she runs off with a married man and suffers the consequences. It is years before she is reunited with her gentle, sailor sweetheart (John Mills).

That is about all there is to the story. Comic relief and pathos are added by an addulous grandma, a neurasthenic maiden aunt and an old wartime friend of Frank's (Sterling Holloway). But the real meat of *This Happy Breed* is in the many plotless little human studies which Coward writes with such relish— Frank's advice to his bridegroom son, delivered in the privacy of the bathroom, just before the wedding; snappish, jagged family quarrels; a touching drunk scene between the two aging ex-soldiers; Ethel's silent, terrible way of absorbing bitter news. The real hero of the film is time, as designated on the face of every player, in the growth, bloom and final bleakness of a fruit tree in the backyard, and by the deathly resonance of the empty house as the family leaves it.

If the film has any serious fault (occasional jerkiness and slowness of episodes are minor ones), it lies close to the heart of Noel Coward's particular kind of talent. His deep affection and respect for his subject cannot be questioned, nor can his deep knowledge of it (he came from just such a background). But he is an extremely clever man, with a great flair and fondness for theatrical trick and design, which, at their worst, can use emotions as if they were stage properties. When clever men try to write with complete sincerity and, at the same time, to apply their sophistication to simple matters, the result is sometimes specious and sentimental. There are ways of insisting that a character is the salt of the earth which are essentially patronizing. For example, the noble character of Frank (extremely well played by Mr. Newton) is often hurt by this unconscious patronage.

But Coward nearly always writes with much purer feeling about unsophisticated women, and Celia Johnson and Kay Walsh make the most of some beautiful opportunities. Miss Johnson has a subtly balanced melancholic power, and an ability to convey complex emotions simply, which derive from the great days of the stage, and are almost never seen in a film. And the excellent director, David Lean (*In Which We Serve*, *Blithe Spirit, Brief Encounter*), has again rendered Mr. Coward as rich a service as Mr. Coward has rendered him.

Time, April 21, 1947

Shoeshine (Alfa; Lopert) may strengthen a suspicion that the best movies in the world are being made, just now, in Italy. U.S. audiences have seen only one other important Italian picture, *Open City. Shoeshine*, in some respects, is even better.

In subject and story, *Shoeshine* is deceptively modest. It traces the gradual destruction of two boys of the Roman streets, twelve-year-old Giuseppe (Rinaldo Smordoni) and his close friend, 14-year-old Pasquale (Franco Interlenghi). They are attractive and resourceful children, at first appearance, living the anarchic, hand-to-mouth life of most of Italy during the chaotic period between the Italian and German surrenders. Then they become front men for Giuseppe's older brother, in a small-time black market deal. They are caught and locked up for questioning. If they had informed on their elders promptly, they would probably have been released; but courage and their loyalty to Giuseppe's brother forbids informing. They are caught into the awful, rickety rollers of the State, and there they are ruined.

Some of the State's representatives are kind and well meaning, but they are hardly more helpful than the brutes, the prigs, the fools and the merely indifferent. The boys are locked in separate cells and come under new influences. Pasquale is tricked into informing; neither boy ever quite understands how they have been betrayed. The seraphically charming Pasquale dwindles into a corrupted, potential criminal. The stolid Giuseppe grows into a grave embodiment of vengeance. Deceit, bewilderment, loss of affection and of faith drive them to the edge of sanity. Finally Pasquale kills his friend. Over the dead body, he first begins to realize what he has done to his friend and to himself—and a little of what has been done to both of them.

Shoeshine was intended as a furious and moving indictment of a postwar society, and of a world, in which such things could happen. It is all of that, and more. It makes the oversimplified diagnosis and prescription of most social tracts look like so much complacent blueprint. It is filled, in every scene, with an awareness of the pitiful complexity of the causes of even simple evil. The jailers, bureaucrats, magistrates, lawyers and priests who are cogs in the machinery of destruction are savagely caricatured, but each one of them is presented with compassion and understanding, as well as rage. Institutions and individuals alike are shown to be staggering not only under their own intrinsic sins but also under the extra burdens which defeat, and war, and a generation of bullying and corruption, have bequeathed. And the crucial destruction takes place, as it must, in the heroes themselves.

Like all true tragic heroes, *Shoeshine*'s boys are destroyed less by outside circumstance than by their inability, under the worst of circumstances, to keep faith with themselves and with all that they have reason to trust. And like all true tragic heroes, they are destroyed by a combination of their noblest traits and their weakest ones.

Cinematically the picture is, without pretentiousness, a masterpiece: wonderfully rich and supple, bursting at the seams with humane sympathy, wisdom and creative energy. There is nothing visually fancy about it, and nothing notably original; its beauty rests on its simple and impassioned use of basic principles which most studios have abandoned or emasculated. It is devoted to that fundamental of movie reality: picturing the way that places and things and people really look and act and inter-act, and making the information eloquent to the eye.

By American standards, *Shoeshine* was made on a shoestring: 31 million lire ($138,000). (*Open City* cost only $100,000.) But it was a long, hard scrimmage in the making. Neither Producer Paolo W. Tamburella (who thought up the idea), nor Director Vittorio De Sica, nor Sergio Amidei (who wrote *Open City*) and his three fellow writers are exactly yes-men. Finding the right actors and getting fine performances out of young amateurs—they were all shoeshine boys—was no small job in itself. And there were plenty of subsidiary difficulties. (When Allied authorities forbade G.I.s to act in the film—and G.I.s were indispensable to the Roman scene of that period—the producers made-do with five Italian ex-P.W.s in U.S. uniforms.)

And once the picture was finished, Government authorities were horrified. They were still more horrified when Signor Tamburella warned them of the publicity stench he could raise out of their refusal to allow the film's release. The authorities gave in.

Time, September 8, 1947

*L*ured (Stromberg; United Artists), an agreeable, tongue-in-cheek murder mystery by Leo Rosten, enlists an American taxi-dancer (Lucille Ball) in the service of Scotland Yard (Charles Coburn). A maniacal killer of women, at large in London, lures his victims through want ads. It is Miss Ball's precarious business to follow up all ads that seem to promise danger. One of her narrow squeaks is Boris Karloff, a decaying impresario who turns out to be mad as a hatter. In the course of her researches she also tangles with some shady characters who ship girls to South America, with a highly suspect wolf (George Sanders) and with his mousy associate (Sir Cedric Hardwicke). The picture is too busy with laughs to worry much about chills, but no one ought to complain about that.

I Know Where I'm Going (Rank; Prestige) doesn't even try to be a great movie, but it is a very good one in its charming, unpretentious way. It was written, directed and produced by Michael Powell and Emeric Pressburger (out of J. Arthur

Rank's pocket, of course), who made *Colonel Blimp* and *Stairway to Heaven*.

The story: an imperious English girl (Wendy Hiller), very sure of what she wants out of life, is sure that she wants to marry one of England's richest men. The wedding day is set; they are to marry on an island he has leased—Kiloran, off the Scottish coast. She has only to get there; her itinerary, like everything else in her life, is planned to the minute. But neither Nature nor True Love sees it quite her way.

Nature sends a fog, and strands her on the nearby island of Mull. When she prays for a wind to lift the fog, she prays up a gale that frustrates her for several days more. True Love, meanwhile, takes every gentlemanly advantage. An impoverished laird (Roger Livesey), who owns Kiloran, squires her all over the beautiful island, and deep among the equally attractive natives. Their Scottish virtues, and his own, get implacably under her hide. Her struggle to keep her will and her pride on their course involve her and the laird in a thrilling piece of melodrama. She never does get to Kiloran. But she does find out where she is going.

The love story develops, deftly and gently, not between the customary movie paper dolls, but between two sympathetic, strongly individualized human beings, beautifully embodied by Miss Hiller and Mr. Livesey. It is no mere ripening towards a clinch. Before she is capable of love, the heroine has come of age by learning how much better a woman she is than she had ever realized. In the course of watching her grow up, Messrs. Powell & Pressburger achieve, unobtrusively, a remarkable study of a place and a people. This study is never quaint, traveloguish, educational or condescending.

The film is an achievement in civilized comedy; even in its grave and noble moments it preserves a graceful, tender gaiety.

Deep Valley (Warner) is a story about lonely people, and what the breakdown of their loneliness does for them—and to them. A remote California farm is abruptly opened to contact with the world when a convict road gang bulldozes its way into the neighborhood. The daughter (Ida Lupino), a loveless, stammering slavey, runs off and hides in the woods with a fugitive convict (Dane Clark). Her malingering mother (Fay Bain-

ter) and her embittered father (Henry Hull), forced to depend
on each other, strike off the shackles of their years of hatred.
The main story centers, of course, on the transfigured Miss
Lupino, her violent sweetheart and their hopeless romance.

It is a rather pathetic picture because everyone concerned
with it is obviously trying very hard to do something good,
powerful and out of the ordinary. Occasionally, this effort
brings the picture to life. There are also a few good flashes of
melodrama. But on the whole, *Deep Valley* is reminiscent of
many of the solemn little-theater plays of the early '20s: *i.e.*, it
is lost in mawkishness and pseudopoetic feeling masquerading
as art.

Time, September 15, 1947

LEADING MAN

THREE or four nights a week, he has an odd, recurring
dream. He is an athlete in a jampacked, outsized stadium. He
takes off for an efficient, unspectacular broad jump. But he
suddenly soars past the pit and over the heads of the officials,
zooms right on over the stadium wall in a long, majestic arc,
and wakes before he lands.

Except for his good looks, which are considerably above average, Gregory Peck is an average young man who has made a
fairly fast and dizzying jump to movie stardom. Since his arrival in Hollywood four years ago, he has carried a large part of
the burden of an aggregate Hollywood investment of some
$23 million, and has been instrumental in grossing a total of at
least $50 million. With his ninth—and newest—picture, *The
Paradine Case* (*see below*), he is in such demand that he has had
to turn down starring roles in some 30 other pictures, most of
them major productions.

During 1947, cinemaddicts watched him as a gentle back-
country father in *The Yearling*, as a lady-killing hunter in *The
Macomber Affair*, as Lascivious Lewt in *Duel in the Sun*, and as
the crusading journalist in *Gentleman's Agreement*—performances which established him as an actor of solidity and range.

Peck, at 31, has moved up into a secure place on the list of
the nation's top ten box-office draws. He can count on 5,000

fan letters a week. He has been respectfully mentioned four times as a candidate for the Academy Award; his performance in *Gentleman's Agreement* makes him a red-hot contender for the 1947 Oscar.

Like the average man that he is, Peck is nobody's fool. He knows that his talents, though real, are not extraordinary. He is acutely aware of the wide gap between his natural abilities and his smashing success. He knows pretty well how much of his spectacular rise he can credit to himself, how much to pure luck, how much to the peculiarities of the flying-trapeze world he works in. He fully expects to wake up one of these days and find himself in San Diego again, driving a truck.

Peck's boyhood, like his current dreams, was up in the air. His parents were divorced when he was a small child, and he was split up and parceled out among relatives, as he was later to be divided among the studios. He felt something like security only with his father, a charming, easygoing ex-basketball star who had failed in business as a druggist and hoped his son might become a doctor. Although Gregory was a handsome boy, he tended to stand back and watch while the cheerleaders and backfield men made off with the only girls who interested him. When at last he got a girl of his own, he fell as much in love with her secure family life as with her. Hoping to get married, he threw over medicine and took a job driving an oil truck. He lost direction again when he lost the girl; and, with nothing better to do, began putting himself through the University of California by waiting on table.

He pulled an A in Elizabethan literature, but he wasn't much of a student. One thing he did enjoy was rowing. His crew was good enough to row at Poughkeepsie; but his career as an oarsman ended abruptly when he hurt his spine.

The injury was the shrewdest twist Fortune has given Peck's career. Because of it he took up acting, which he had never before considered. Because of it, he was draftproof at a time when the war brought Hollywood disastrously close to total emasculation.

With sports out of the question, Gregory landed a part as Starbuck in a college production of *Moby Dick*. In this first try at acting he was so terrible that self-respect forced him to try again. In the next plays, he was better. By the time he played

Matt in the drama club's *Anna Christie*, he knew what he wanted. He could not even wait five days to pick up his diploma, he was in such a hurry to reach Broadway.

Broadway was less excited. He did get a job speaking lines, of a sort. They were spoken very sharply and very fast at a World's Fair ride called the Meteor Speedway. The lines began: "*A-thrill-a-second-a-mile-a-minute-around-the-walls-of-an-upright-BOWL!. . . Come on, brother . . . defy the laws of gravity! . . .*" Shortly before the venture folded, Peck took a job ushering tourists around Rockefeller Center, where his performances were no more outstanding. Until he learned better, he innocently assured other eager outlanders that Brooklyn was a part of New Jersey. He once fell asleep in a box while his charges outstayed (by an outrageous 20 minutes) their free glimpse of a Radio City show.

In 1939, he won a two-year scholarship at Manhattan's Neighborhood Playhouse. Broadway Producer Guthrie McClintic saw him and signed him for a last-act bit in the road tour of Katharine Cornell's *The Doctor's Dilemma*. On that tour, Peck met and later married Greta Konen, a tiny, bright-blonde Finnish girl who was Cornell's hairdresser.

After a dreary series of revivals, summer stock and out-of-town closings, McClintic gave him a role in a 1942 Broadway show, Emlyn Williams' *The Morning Star*. The show soon folded, but the critics had some nice things to say about a new juvenile named Gregory Peck.

The kind notices encouraged Peck and interested Hollywood enormously. The young actor earnestly wanted to become a good artist in a good Broadway play. But after three flops in a row, he began to feel that a little ready money, quickly made, would be very nice indeed—so long as it was clearly understood by everyone that after one picture he was going straight back to Broadway.

Hollywood, a hard place to get into, is even harder to leave, once you're in. Peck's "one" picture, *Days of Glory*, was a rather pathetic Hollywood attempt to make a Russian-style "art" movie. It was not a box-office success; but before it was released and before most of Hollywood had even seen it, Peck was one of the most sought-after properties in town.

Louis B. Mayer was anxious to sign him up for a seven-year contract. Darryl Zanuck was eager to trust him with the leading role in a $3,000,000 production (*Keys of the Kingdom*), regardless of the fact that Peck was unknown and unwilling even to make a screen test. David Selznick, who now claims to have recognized Peck's talent from the first, was also in there nibbling (characteristically, Selznick eventually walked away with the lion's share). There is a touch of more than Hollywood's habitual fantasy in these frantic negotiations for the services of a promising, impoverished, idealistic, unknown young stage actor.

Peck himself was both obliging and obstinate. He obstinately asked for clauses permitting him, for instance, half-time on Broadway (something unheard-of for a movie beginner)— and he obligingly, in the long run, let himself in for enough commitments to keep him hopelessly busy in the studios for a solid seven years. When the moguls were through shuffling around their pieces of Mr. Peck, he was the most owned and least available leading man in Hollywood, and one of the most valuable.

At present, he is partitioned as follows: to M-G-M for two more pictures; to 20th Century–Fox for two; to David Oliver Selznick for three.

In spite of Hollywood's bad reputation for misusing talent, studios normally try hard with anyone they regard as promising. With Peck, the moviemakers were inclined to outdo themselves. Each studio needed a major male star, and Peck looked like a good risk. Moreover, since no studio had been able to snare him outright, each was determined to sweat the best possible use out of him. Peck was inadvertently handed some bum pictures; but each one was a major production. And during his first years, he had the run of a virtually clear field. Since he ran it as seriously and efficiently as if the field were swarming with tacklers, he had established himself solidly by the time his competitors got back out of uniform.

Peck's fleeting resemblance to Gary Cooper was undoubtedly helpful, at the start. Neither moviemakers nor moviegoers take quickly, as a rule, to a wholly unprecedented face. But it was soon clear also that Peck was no carbon copy, but a distinct and engaging new personality. He has a face which Mary Morris of *PM* has aptly described as "early American." It can, of course, be dangerous to look enough like Abraham Lincoln to suffer by comparison or to seem to be plagiarizing. At certain unfortunate moments Peck looks merely like a pretty Lincoln; but he never looks like a silly one, a road-show impersonator, or a sandwich man for the Republican Party.

One of his gravest dangers as an actor may be his good looks, which invest any role he undertakes with a certain idealized, legendary quality. But his fine-featured face gives him enormous range as a movie hero: while remaining a virile 6 ft. 3 in., he can suggest, if the plot demands it, a man who is delicate, ill, or even morally weak. Peck appeals, as a very popular male star must, to both bobby-soxers and their mothers. He manages this feat without presenting himself as a big brother, as a cute, asexual nephew, or as a sophisticated porch climber. Men also immediately like him and wish him well; they feel that he is, in fact, an average human being—luckier, better looking and more gifted than they, but essentially one of themselves.

Caught neck-deep among Hollywood's peculiar blessings and obligations, Peck likes being regarded as a good actor. But he takes little pleasure in his fame, and none, apparently, in the standing, prestige or power he might have. He admits to some laziness, but adds, with proper self-respect: "I can be conscientious as hell under pressure."

His deepest interests are after-hours. They center in his home, his wife, and, above all, in his sons, 3½-year-old Jonathan and Stephan, 1½. The three-man romps, in which he hurls the youngsters against the softer pieces of furniture like a couple of shrieking medicine balls, give him the best moments of his day. Sociable, in a non-Hollywood way, he spends two or three evenings a week over a home dinner, whiskey, and talk with one or two of his handful of close friends (closest: Richard Conte). He actively dislikes nightclubs.

A friend has suggested that Peck virtually never goes out evenings because he is terrified at the possibility of running into some of the community's better-known Bright Boys. "I am short of the old I-am," he explains. "When I get mixed up with Nunnally Johnson or Herman Mankiewicz or Ben Hecht, I am struck dumb. I feel more comfortable in front of a camera." Actually, the very sound brain in his head doesn't run either to wit or to high-brow intellectual discussion. Alfred Hitchcock has said of him that he is probably the most anecdoteless man in Hollywood; it does not come natural to him either to tell anecdotes or to inspire them. David Selznick has called Peck the best-informed actor in Hollywood, which is probably an exaggeration. Selznick may have meant to say that Peck has one clear sign of a vigorous intelligence: an eagerness to keep on learning.

Like many actors, he is sanguine about a piece of work while he is at it, but he soon cools into a stern self-critic. During the filming of *Duel in the Sun*, he talked—jocosely, to be sure—about out-heeling Satan and out-Laurencing Olivier. Now he says of *Duel*: "I didn't do much acting. I rode horses, necked with Jennifer, and shot poor old Charley Bickford." Of *Valley of Decision*: "My agent wanted me to be seen with a big female star. Greer's audience, he said, will be a good thing for you. It was a very good maneuver. The movie? I didn't like it." Of *Spellbound*: "I was lousy." Of *The Yearling*: "I would have liked the picture better with its Walt Disney aspects pushed into the background. It was much too lushly done, and we have to take part of the rap."

By Hollywood standards, Peck is shamefully underpaid. Up to last year, he was still at the mercy of his own commitments and of the studios to which he was committed. He still suffers from being an obliging man more interested in acting than in money. In order to get the part of the millowner's son in *Valley of Decision*, he had to sign for three additional pictures at $45,000, $55,000 and $65,000 respectively. One of these, *The Yearling*, has been made. At the time Peck made it he was worth at least $150,000 a picture (standard fee for topflight stars). Today, if he chose to operate that way, he might command and get $200,000 or more. But he will make two more pictures for M-G-M—at $55,000 and $65,000. His sensible attitude: "Every good picture lengthens your screen life."

In his first really profitable year, 1946, his income was $220,000, of which he kept $46,000. He recently bought a $50,000 house in the Thomas Mann–Joseph Cotten neighborhood of Pacific Palisades, and is putting whatever money he can salvage into a heavy annuity program.

Peck still clings doggedly to the notion of being a stage actor. It is not that he considers himself too good for movies (he doesn't think he is good enough), nor even that he thinks plays are better than pictures. But he still believes that the theater is the best place to learn how to act. He has been instrumental in organizing a Selznick-financed group of movie people (Cotten, Jennifer Jones, Dorothy McGuire, *et al.*) who do stage-acting in their spare time. But it will be a long time—three years at least—before he can hope to work again on Broadway. "The stage, yes," he now says with a hounded look, "when I get through with these commitments."

In his new picture, Peck contends manfully with a role which only a virtuoso might have saved. But there is no good reason why either Peck or his admirers need worry about his future. For the camera's purposes, his lean, bony face is the sort that is practically indestructible. For the next 20 years, he is not likely to look enough older to damage him as a leading man. And his place in movies is already high, secure and respectably unique.

He is U.S. cinema's first male idol to resist typing: the first to devote himself successfully to the art of acting, rather than a stylized display of physique and personality. He has shown no signs of that depth of intuition which would suggest that he will ever become a great actor—as Olivier, for instance, may become. But he seldom fails to turn in a performance that is honorably beyond the line of movie duty. He is diligent, definitely if quietly talented, intelligent about his work; and he has an obvious capacity for study and for growth. Unless he succumbs to boredom, frustration, wealth, or the hideous difficulties of trying to be both a matinee idol and an honest artist, he is certain to become a thoroughly good actor.

The Paradine Case (Selznick) stars Gregory Peck as a gifted, happily married English lawyer who falls in love with the client he is defending. Mrs. Paradine (Valli) is accused of poisoning her blind husband, and Lawyer Peck recklessly sets out to pin the crime on the dead husband's valet (Louis Jourdan). In his infatuation for his client, he is incapable of imagining that she may be guilty. In his jealousy, he suspects an affair between the valet and the accused lady. Making a headlong effort to defend her, he brings on a suicide and his own virtual ruin.

This tale is put on film with the high polish, the intelligence, and the mastery of tension that are to be expected of Director Alfred Hitchcock. But Robert Hichens' basic story is so intricate in plot and pattern—there are four interlocking triangles, and hints of two more—that only an inspired talent for drama and for characterization could have saved it from obvious artificiality. No such talent is in evidence; nor has Producer David O. Selznick improved matters in his screen play. The only characters who come sharply to life are the barrister's wife (Ann Todd) and her confidante (Joan Tetzel); some of the others are acted with solid skill (by Charles Laughton, Charles Coburn, Ethel Barrymore), but they remain lay figures—interested but lifeless participants in a rigid, theatrical dance.

One expects, in a Hitchcock movie, a few moments as shockingly vivid as a fire alarm. There are no such moments here. There are many clever little shots-in-the-arm that are unrelated to the story. Innumerable tricks of lighting and mood are moderately effective but irrelevant.

It is hard to figure who is at fault, or why, in the case of the much heralded Italian newcomer, Valli. Her beauty, or better-than-beauty, has an almost reptilian fascination; she is, indeed, the most *fatale*-looking *femme* since Garbo. But it remains an open question whether she can act. Hitchcock, keeping her nearly motionless, plies her with one slow, cold, lambent close-up after another. Some of these close-ups function forcefully in the story-telling; but too many are as non-functional as her frequent changes of hairdo. It looks as if Hitchcock, one of the smartest directors of women in the business, had been required, in Valli's case, merely to glamorize a new Selznick star. Newcomer Jourdan does respectably by his limited chance—which is to look handsome and intense.

Gregory Peck turns in the first performance that may trouble his well-wishers. Although he has worked exceedingly hard to become an Englishman (he studied a recording of an Anthony Eden speech), he remains unmistakably American in appearance and bearing. A tremendously cagey and accomplished actor might conceivably have made a convincing character out of this attorney, in spite of the inadequacies of the script. Peck is not yet cagey or accomplished enough. He carries his trial scenes with considerable style; and he comes close to some first-rate acting in his difficult crack-up scene. But his lawyer is never one of the most brilliant in England, as the story claims; the role is not brilliantly conceived or written, and Peck, for all his virtues, is not a brilliant man.

Time, January 12, 1948

Red River (Howard Hawks–United Artists). When people discuss the real artists in picture-making, they seldom get around to mentioning Howard Hawks. Yet Hawks is one of the most individual and independent directors in the business. Even when he has a vapid chore to do, he gives it character; when a picture really interests him, he gives it enough character to blast you out of your seat. *Red River*, which Hawks produced and directed, clearly interested him a lot. It is a rattling good outdoor adventure movie.

Red River is a yarn about the first cattle drive over the Chisholm Trail, from deep Texas into Abilene, Kans., soon after the Civil War. It is also the story of the fierce character duel which develops, along the way, between the tyrannical boss cattleman (John Wayne) and his intrasigent foster son (Montgomery Clift). Mr. Clift takes time out for a little romance with a "dancing girl"* (Joanne Dru), but essentially this is a movie about men, and for men.

The story originally appeared in the *Satevepost* and, in many respects, is just an average piece of hack fiction. But it is worked out with sincerity and vigor, and is amenable to movie treatment. Director Hawks gives even the relatively silly episodes with the girl a kind of roughness and candor which make them believable and entertaining. And when Hawks concentrates on men working, or contesting leadership, or merely showing what they are made of, the picture practically blows up with vitality and conviction.

There is a constant illusion that you are watching an extraordinary effort to get cattle across a certain immense expanse of difficult and threatening country, that you are learning a lot about how such a job feels and gets done, and that the perpetually wrangling players are important not so much of

*Johnston Office euphemism for prostitute.

themselves, but because the whole success or failure of the attempt depends on these people. The attempt is really the story, and the "background" is really the hero of the piece, and its villain.

Hawks obviously likes and understands men, grand enterprise, hardship, courage and magnificent landscape. The greatest satisfaction of this picture is continuous and unobtrusive. It is the constancy with which all outdoors, and all human endurance of it and effort to conquer it, keeps bulging the screen full of honest and beautiful vitality, like a steady wind against a well-trimmed sail.

Time, October 11, 1948

THE MARX BROTHERS. By Kyle Crichton. New York; Doubleday & Co., *310 pp., 18 illus.,* 1950. $3.00.

LEONARD (Chico) and Adolph (Harpo) and Julius (Groucho) and Milton (Gummo) and Herbert (Zeppo) Marx were the sons, in that order, of an endearing and invincibly feckless father whom they called Frenchy, and of a fantastically sanguine and resourceful mother named Minnie. The Marxes' existence might fairly be described as bare, and as almost nightmarishly improvisatory, but never as melancholy and seldom even as anxious. The family's career during the nine or ten decades (or so it seems) before they hit the jackpot was rather like a slackwire act, blindfold, in Laocoonic tandem, without a net. The boys showed few special aptitudes and such as they were, they never got the debatable blessing of formal development.

Apparently Chico's one burning interest in life was chasing (and grounding) girls; moreover, he inherited his mother's vertiginous optimism; so he oscillated between business and show business without much caring which he was in or where he was headed. Harpo cared even less what he did; it is fairly clear that in his own way he was always as natural-born a natural as the comic character he sleep-walked into. Groucho, the brainiest, most sensitive and glummest of the brothers, always wanted to be a doctor and was constantly reading whatever he could lay hands on; but for the grace of Minnie and a lack of even minimal funds he might well have wound up wearing a frock-coat in earnest or, quite as possibly, as just a good run-of-the-mill intellectual. Gummo was always apparently the calmest and most conservative of the boys; after serving a long and faithful term in Minnie's Bohemia he escaped into commerce and lived happily ever after. Little Zeppo got a late start, but by the evidence he had the markings of a topnotch juvenile delinquent, and if only he had been permitted to follow his natural bent there is no telling where he might have gone, or for how long.

Essentially, Kyle Crichton's book is simply a straightforward account of how skeleton-stark necessity, and Minnie's implacable vitality, whipped this unpromising gaggle into what must have been one of the very worst acts in the history of vaudeville; and of how, painfully slowly, by accident and by instinct and nine-tenths blindly, they evolved into some of the most wonderful clowns (if a word so genteel can be used of them) of a century most happily distinguished in its inspired low-comedians. The word straightforward is used advisedly but it may be misleading. Since Mr. Crichton's straightforwardness is disciplined by a relaxed and pleasant narrative skill, and since his calm straight gaze mainly examines slaphappy hard luck on a heroic scale, the book is fine entertainment at its best and at its average is something almost better; a warmly unsentimental and unforced account of how one whacky, brave, loyal, indestructible family managed by hook or as often by crook to stay alive and intact. But by straightforward I also mean to suggest that Mr. Crichton is in some ways too simple and modest to do a complete, or even a completely satisfying, job on this subject.

The book is of course inevitable reading for anyone who has ever thanked God, or points South, for the Brothers. And as far as it goes, it is a happy and irreproachable piece of work. Whether it should have gone farther is arguable. Those top-heavy critics who like to require of a writer that he guess what they insist he ought to do, and take care to do it, will doubtless think and speak very ill of Mr. Crichton for choosing, instead, to do what *he* wants to. I feel no such wish—let alone any such right—to blame him for being himself; I do however feel certain regrets, and some of them are rather grave. I am deeply grateful to Mr. Crichton for not psychoanalyzing or class-angling his friends or their comedy, or in any other way adding to the monument of nonsense which has been raised in their name; Harpo in particular has been treated as if he were Pan on a unicycle, and certain French commentators (to mention only the most pretentious offenders) have parlayed the whole act into something between a Masque of Anarchy and the Id Kids on a busman's holiday.

I also realize that it is very hard, and risky at best, to write seriously about comedy, and that to do so would have altered the tone and structure of an unusually well-informed and harmonious book. But on the evidence of what he has done, both in this book and in his movie articles for *Colliers*, Mr. Crichton so obviously has the wits to do that, and so obviously lacks the intellectual pompousness which so often louses up the attempt, that I am grieved that he did not choose to take the risk. After all, the men he is writing about are comedians, and are about as skilful and as deeply satisfying as comedians could ever be, short of greatness. We are given beautifully clear and lively and sometimes very suggestive or touching images of them in private life, and behind-scenes in their professional life, and we get a glimmering idea of what they were like on-stage, before they were any good; but once they become a great act—for they were certainly that, whether any single one of them touched greatness—we scarcely see them *at work*, at all; and there is very little writing about the work, or comment upon it. We get virtually no idea of what makes Groucho (to me) so much the most deeply gifted and durable and funny of them, or of what, strangely enough, gives him a surprising nimbus of glamor (perhaps the tantalizing sense that something even more remarkable, but Lord knows quite what, is lost or strayed in him, then he has ever become).

There is no attention to the development of Harpo (a development, in my opinion, from a dazzling anomaly into a merely very likable clown and man inferred behind the clown, unhappily tinged with something like artiness). Even within my own not very wide or odd acquaintance, quite a few women of discerning and independent tastes have felt that Chico has enough humane warmth to supply a dozen tearjerkers, and enough sex-appeal to abash any twenty matinée idols; I thereby infer that that must be the opinion of quite a respectable minority and would think it worth mentioning, if a bit special. I have never yet seen anyone give Zeppo adequate appreciation in print, and had hoped to find that here, but no; except in the excellent illustrations his peerlessly cheesy improvement on the traditional straight-man is never recorded; I regret, too, the absence of a long quiet sigh over his replacement by Alan Jones and one hundred interminable songs. Alan Jones, who furnished another and funny but distinctly less rare kind of fatuousness, and a somewhat more cultivated singing voice, is not mentioned. Neither is S. J. Perelman, whose hand is clear in their most brilliant scripts. Neither is the Godsent stooge Margaret Dumont, the century's noblest matron, who was consistently as funny as the Brothers at their funniest; and that, I would suppose, must stand as the most disconcerting measure of the book's incompleteness, for most people who love the Marx Brothers.

I would give a lot to see some attempt at analyzing, and evaluating, and placing, and accounting for, the unprecedented kind of free-wheeling, deep-city humor that Marxes developed —the more so because it was not in every way unique but was also just the wildest and best of a kind, as deeply native to this country as, for instance, the "tall tales" of the frontiersmen or the professional-American gallus-twangings of the dialect humorists ever were, and any amount funnier. I wish too that Mr. Crichton might have pointed up more clearly how they fumbled their way through to it. By inference from the rich raw materials he supplies, it was about equal parts a use of professional experience grimly acquired, deep in the sticks, where savage roughness was still rather admired, and a gradual, all but subconscious emergence of the kind of weirdness this unconventional family was used to every day, around home or whatever circuit fleabag passed for home: in other words, like all good artists, they began really to know themselves and to learn how to make use of the knowledge. But how in God's name can one account for the fact that they had their first smash success, with this new kind of humor, in Philadelphia, of all cities! By my own meager but paralyzing impressions of Philadelphia, anthropologists (or, heaven prevent it, humorologists) might puzzle over that mystery for the balance of Western Civilization; Mr. Crichton doesn't even speak of it as odd.

It would also be worth mentioning that after the late Irving Thalberg told the Marxes what was wrong with the pictures they had made at Paramount, and they moved to Metro, they made better movies so far as the Art of the Cinema is concerned but—many people including myself think—incomparably less funny shows. If only, for that matter, the book contained more straight reminiscence about their shows. What little there is— notably a few passages from *Cocoanuts* and Groucho's blandly immortal adlib during a soporific harp solo, "I wonder what ever happened to Rhinelander?"—is a delight, and I'd suppose any follower of the Marxes could enjoy any amount more of it. For just one instance it certainly ought to warm anybody's remembrance I can care for, to read a rehash of, and salute to, the beautiful little act in *Duck Soup*, in which all the brothers, dressed as Groucho in nightshirt and tasseled cap and candle-stick, try to kid each other that they are mirror images. Not to mention that seems almost like writing a biography of Joyce without mentioning *Ulysses*. But as a matter of fact Mr. Crichton skimps gravely, even on straight story-telling, once his friends stop suffering hilariously and begin to enjoy life; they have their first great success at the Palace on pages 221–23 and the book ends, with a graceful cutback to Minnie's death, on page 310. That is appropriate to the form and theme he chose, but an awful lot has been sacrificed.

It begins to occur to me that I may be writing an unfair re-view. Certainly, anyhow, I have spent a lot more time regret-ting what isn't in the book, than commending what is; and more than once I have thrown in a personal opinion, or preju-dice, as if it were common knowledge, or even a biographer's obligation. Let me earnestly repeat, however, that I am not pretending to say that Mr. Crichton should have done what I wish he had done. I only wish that somebody would do it, and he seems finely qualified to. Also I assume that most readers of this magazine will read the book, or have already read it. So I will waste no time telling them what a pleasure it is; that is a foregone conclusion.

Films in Review, 1950

THE NIGHT OF THE HUNTER

The Night of the Hunter

FULL SHOT—THE STARLIT SKY

VOICE: *And He opened His mouth and taught them, saying. . . .*

FADE sky to day. LAP DISSOLVE TO

LONG SHOT—HELICOPTER—OHIO RIVER COUNTRY
High over the country, CENTERING the winding river.

VOICE: *Beware of false prophets. . . .*

LOWER LONG SHOT—HELICOPTER—RIVER COUNTRY
We approach a riverside village.

VOICE: *. . . which come to you in sheep's clothing . . .*

A CLOSER, LOWER HELICOPTER SHOT
We descend low over a deserted house; CHILDREN in yard run and hide; we hear "IT" counting "*five, ten, fifteen, twenty. . . .*"

VOICE: *. . . but inwardly they are ravening wolves.*

MEDIUM SHOT—"IT"
He finishes his count with a loud "*Hundred*" and turns, then:

"IT": what's wrong?

We PAN as he comes towards a little boy, beside an open cellar door, who gestures towards the open door. "IT" looks down.

"IT": (a low gasp) Heyy! (then he shouts to all and to us) Heyy!

We DOLLY IN fast to, and TILT DOWN into open cellar, into:

CLOSE SHOT—A LEG
A skeletal leg in a rotted fume of stocking and a high-heeled shoe. We HOLD a moment, then PULL UP and AWAY over the converging heads of several CHILDREN. A CHILD whimpers softly.

HELICOPTER SHOT
The yard and the CHILDREN, same angle and height as the last descending helicopter shot. We PULL BACK and AWAY.

VOICE: *Ye shall know them by their fruits.* DISSOLVE TO

HIGH LONG SHOT—HELICOPTER

CENTERING the river.

VOICE: *A good tree cannot bring forth evil fruit.* . . .

LOWER LONG SHOT (HELICOPTER)
CENTERING on open touring car, as it drives along a river road.

VOICE: *Neither can a corrupt tree bring forth good fruit.*

We STOOP LOW towards the car.

VOICE: *Wherefore by their fruits ye shall know them.*   CUT TO

CLOSE SHOT—PREACHER
He is the driver of the car. Pleasant river landscapes (PROCESS) flow behind him. He is dressed in dark clothes, a paper collar, a string tie. As he drives he talks to himself.

PREACHER: What's it to be, Lord, another widow? Has it been six? Twelve? . . . I disremember.

He nods, smiles, and touches his hat. We see a farm couple in a poor wagon.

PREACHER: You say the word, and I'm on my way.

LAP DISSOLVE TO

CLOSE SHOT—PREACHER DRIVING
He brakes his car in a small riverside town; then proceeds.

PREACHER: You always send me money to go forth and preach your *Word*. A widow with a little wad of bills hidden away in the sugar-bowl.

LAP DISSOLVE TO

CLOSE SHOT—PREACHER DRIVING
He shifts into second gear, climbing a steep little hill.

PREACHER: *I am tired*. Sometimes I wonder if you really understand. (pause) Not that you mind the killin's . . .

The stones of a country graveyard gleam in the last daylight.

PREACHER: Yore Book is *full* of killin's.

He starts fast and noisily down a steep hill.

PREACHER: But there *are* things you *do* hate, Lord: per-fume-smellin' things—lacy things—things with *curly hair*—

CUT TO

INT. A BURLESQUE HOUSE—MEDIUM CLOSE SHOT—A DANCER
She is hard at work, to music o.s.

FULL SHOT—AUDIENCE—CENTERING ON PREACHER, IN AISLE SEAT

Among the members of the sad burlesque audience, he is in strong contrast: a sour and aggressive expression. Music o.s. We MOVE IN fast to a

HEAD CLOSE-UP.

MEDIUM CLOSE SHOT—THE DANCER

INSERT—PREACHER'S LEFT HAND
Labeled H-A-T-E in tattoo across four knuckles, it grips and flexes.

INSERT—HIS RIGHT HAND
Before we see the lettering he slides it into his pocket.

EXTREME CLOSE SHOT—PREACHER
His head slants; a cold smile; one eyelid flutters.

INSERT—RIGHT HAND AND POCKET
We hear the snapping open of a switch-blade knife and the point of the knife cuts through his clothes.

LESS EXTREME CLOSE SHOT—PREACHER
He seems to "listen" for something.

PREACHER: No, there are too many of them; you can't kill a *world*.

A hand descends firmly onto his shoulder. He glances up behind him as we   TILT TO

CLOSE SHOT—A STATE TROOPER
He bends down and speaks quietly next PREACHER'S ear.

TROOPER: You driving an Essex tourin'-car with a Moundsville license?   LAP DISSOLVE TO

INT. COURTROOM—CLOSE THREE-SHOT—JUDGE AND CLERK, OVER PREACHER

JUDGE: Harry Powell, for the theft of that touring car you will spend thirty days in the Moundsville Penitentiary.

PREACHER: (correcting Clerk) *Preacher* Harry Powell.

JUDGE: A car thief! Picked up where *you* were! A man of God? (to Clerk) Harry Powell.   LAP DISSOLVE TO

FULL SHOT—MOUNDSVILLE PENITENTIARY—DAY (HELICOPTER)

A grim stone turretted façade; an American flag idles at top center.   LAP DISSOLVE TO

CLOSE DOWNWARD TWO-SHOT—JOHN AND PEARL HARPER

They sit in the grass, a sentimental picture. JOHN is nine; PEARL is five. They are working together on PEARL'S doll; PEARL is dressing her, while JOHN gets on a difficult shoe.

PEARL: Stand still, Miss Jenny!

JOHN: (across her) There! What's so hard about that!

He proudly exhibits the shod foot.

They hear the sound of an auto engine o.s. They look o.s. and get up, PEARL dangling the doll.

LONG SHOT—OVER THE CHILDREN—BEN HARPER'S FORD

A Model-T Ford approaches at maximal speed on uneven dirt road.

PEARL: (to John, happily) Daddy!

The car careens towards us; then swings into the sideyard as we PAN, and stops.

They run towards their father fast; then JOHN looks puzzled and they stop short.

BEN HARPER half-falls out of the far door, his shoulder blood-stained, his eyes wild. A hefty, simple man of thirty. He looks at them, dazed, across the car.

MEDIUM SHOT—BEN HARPER

BEN: Where's your Mom?

JOHN: Out shopping—you're bleeding, Dad—

BEN: Listen to me John.

On this he comes around clear of the car with a revolver in one hand and a bloody roll of banknotes in the other.

CLOSE SHOT—JOHN

He screams. BEN slaps him with the back of the money hand, leaving blood on JOHN'S cheek.

CLOSE GROUP SHOT—JOHN, BEN, PEARL

PEARL, and the house, are in BACKGROUND. PEARL just clutches her doll. During BEN'S next lines, JOHN touches his cheek and looks at the blood on his fingers and at the bloody money—of which we FLASH-CUT an INSERT.

BEN: (rushing) Listen! This money here! We got to hide it before they get me! There's close to ten thousand dollars. (his eyes dart wildly) Under a rock in the smokehouse? Ah no. Under the bricks in the grape arbor? No, they'd dig for it.

CLOSE SHOT—BEN

BEN: (sudden triumph) Why *sure*! *That's* the place!

He moves forward and OUT and in his place we see two police cars, small in distance, coming fast. We hear sirens.

INT. FRONT POLICE CAR—THROUGH WINDSHIELD
. . . and OVER two STATE TROOPERS. They move at high speed, with sirens.

BEN and his CHILDREN, tiny in the distance, dilate.

TROOPER: (driving) That's him.

2ND TROOPER: (over his shoulder, as if to us) He prob'ly still has that gun.

CLOSE GROUP SHOT—BEN AND CHILDREN
. . . police cars approaching in BACKGROUND. PEARL hugs her doll. JOHN is dazed. BEN stands, pistol in hand.

BEN: Here they come.

JOHN: Dad, you're bleeding. . . .

He grabs JOHN's shoulder and stoops as we TIGHTEN IN.

BEN: Listen to me son. You got to *swear. Swear* means promise. First swear you'll take care of little Pearl. Guard her with your life, boy. Then swear you won't never tell where that money's hid. Not even your Mom.

JOHN: Yes, Dad.

BEN: You understand?

JOHN: Not even her?

In b.g. the TROOPERS get out of their cars and fan out cautiously to surround BEN: guns in hand.

BEN: You got common sense. She ain't. When you grow up that money'll be yours. Now *swear.* "I will guard Pearl with my life . . ."

JOHN: (fumbling) I will guard Pearl with my life. . . .

BEN: . . . . "and I won't never tell about the money."

JOHN: And I won't never tell about the money.

PEARL: You, Pearl. You swear too.

CLOSE SHOT—PEARL

PEARL: (giggling) Who's them Blue Men yonder?

HEAD CLOSE-UP—JOHN

JOHN: (under breath) Blue men.

GROUP SHOT—TROOPERS IN BACKGROUND

A TROOPER: Ben Harper!

BEN: I'm goin' now children. Goodbye.

BEN backs away from his CHILDREN, raising his hands, gun in one hand. We PULL BACK a little, enlarging the GROUP SHOT and the role of the TROOPERS in it.

TROOPER: Drop that gun, Harper. We don't want them kids hurt.

TWO TROOPERS approach BEN from behind.

BEN: Just mind what you swore, son. *Mind*, boy!

GROUP SHOT—JOHN
He runs forward and clasps his stomach, with his mouth open.

MEDIUM SHOT—BEN AND TROOPERS—JOHN'S VIEWPOINT
One TROOPER smacks the back of BEN'S head with a pistol barrel.

CLOSE SHOT—JOHN

JOHN: (shouting; a sickly smile) Don't!

MEDIUM SHOT—BEN AND TROOPERS—AS BEFORE
Another TROOPER, with a pistol barrel, knocks the pistol from BEN'S lifted hand.

CLOSE SHOT—JOHN

JOHN: (shouting) Don't!

BEN sinks to his knees as both men, and two others from the front, close in on him.

HEAD CLOSE-UP—JOHN

JOHN: Dad!

He takes in the GROUP with his mouth open.
O.s. we hear the slamming of car doors, and car starting away.

FULL SHOT—JOHN'S VIEWPOINT—THE CARS
They drive away fast in road dust.

THREE-SHOT—THE CHILDREN AND WILLA HARPER
Carrying a shopping bag, their mother, WILLA, runs up from
BACKGROUND between the CHILDREN, looking always to cars
O.S.

CLOSE SHOT—WILLA
She has a rich body.

RESUME THREE-SHOT

PEARL comes to her and she picks up PEARL and the *doll*;
JOHN, laden with his oath, walks quickly into the house.
WILLA does a bewildered take, then looks again towards the
cars O.S.   LAP DISSOLVE TO

INT. COURTROOM—CLOSE THREE-SHOT—JUDGE AND CLERK,
OVER BEN

JUDGE: Ben Harper, it is the sentence of this Court that for
the murder of Ed Smiley and Corey South, you be hanged by
the neck until you are dead, and may God have mercy on your
soul.   LAP DISSOLVE TO

FULL SHOT—THE MOUNDSVILLE PENITENTIARY
SAME VIEW AS BEFORE; BUT NOW IT IS NIGHT.
                                              LAP DISSOLVE TO

INT. BEN'S CELL—NIGHT—CLOSE DOWN-SHOT—BEN
He lies on his back, chuckling and murmuring indistinctly in
his sleep.

BEN: I got you *all* buffaloed! You ain't never gonna git it
outen me; not none o' you!

PREACHER'S VOICE: (o.s., very low) Where, Ben? Where?
Where?

BEN: (distinctly) And a little child shall lead them.

CLOSE TWO-SHOT—NEW ANGLE—BEN, THEN PREACHER
BEN lies in profile. From the bunk above, the face of PREACHER
stretches down into the SHOT, upside down, snake-like.

PREACHER: (softly) Come on, boy: tell me.

BEN wakes, sees PREACHER, and hits him so hard in the face that he falls from bunk to floor. PREACHER collects himself into a squat, nursing his face. BEN sits up in bed.

PREACHER: (with wholesome dignity) Ben, I'm a Man of God.

BEN: Tryin' to make me talk about it in my sleep!

PREACHER: No, Ben.

BEN: What'd I say? (he grabs Preacher's throat and shakes him) What? What? What? What?

PREACHER: (choking) You was quotin' Scripture. You said—you said, "And a little child shall lead them."

BEN: Hm!

He lies back, amused. PREACHER sits on the bedside; manner of a parson visiting the sick.

PREACHER: (gravely) You killed two men, Ben Harper.

BEN: That's right, Preacher. I robbed that bank because I got tired of seein' children roamin' the woodlands without food, children roamin' the highways in this year of Depression; children sleepin' in old abandoned car bodies on junk-heaps; and I promised myself I'd never see the day when *my* youngins'd want.

PREACHER: With that ten thousand dollars I could build a Tabernacle that'd make the Wheeling Island Tabernacle look like a chicken-house!

BEN: Would you have free candy for the kids, Preacher?

He picks up and wads a sock.

PREACHER: Think of it, Ben! With that cursed, bloodied gold!

BEN: How come you got that stickknife hid in your bed-blankets, Preacher?

PREACHER: I come not with Peace but with a Sword.

BEN: *You*, Preacher?

PREACHER gets and pockets the knife.

PREACHER: That Sword has served me through many an evil time, Ben Harper.

BEN: What religion do you profess, Preacher?

PREACHER: The religion the Almighty and me worked out betwixt us.

BEN: (contemptuously) I'll bet.

PREACHER: Salvation is a last-minute business, boy.

BEN: (sock near mouth) Keep talkin', Preacher.

PREACHER: If you was to let that money serve the Lord's purposes, He might feel kindly turned towards you.

BEN: Keep talkin', Preacher.

He wads the sock into his mouth and lies back, sardonic.

PREACHER: (his voice fading into Dissolve) You reckon the Lord wouldn't change his mind about you if . . .

                                                    DISSOLVE TO

EXT. PENITENTIARY COURTYARD — NIGHT   DISSOLVE TO

INSERT — PREACHER'S HANDS
They rest on sill of cell window, the lettered fingers legible. The right hand is lettered L-O-V-E. The hands open, disclosing his open knife. They close over it.

CLOSE SHOT — PREACHER, AT CELL WINDOW
His eyes lift from his hands, heavenward. Moonlight on his face. He prays, quietly.

PREACHER: Lord You sure knowed what You was doin' when You brung me to this very cell at this very time. A man with ten thousand dollars hid somewhere, and a widder in the makin'.   DISSOLVE TO

EXT. PENITENTIARY COURTYARD — NIGHT
Same SHOT as before, but now, prison lights are on; and a man, a prison GUARD, waits close inside door. BART the HANG-MAN joins him with a silent salute. BART wears a hard derby.

EXT. PENITENTIARY — THE DOOR — (REVERSE)
They walk in silence into MEDIUM, MOVING SHOT, the GUARD talkative, BART reluctant to talk.

The Penitentiary recedes in b.g.

GUARD: Any trouble?

BART: No.

GUARD: He was a cool one, that Harper. Never broke.

BART: He carried on some; kicked.

EXT. BART'S HOUSE—MEDIUM SHOT—BART AND GUARD
On porch, by door, is a doll's perambulator. BART and GUARD walk into the SHOT.

GUARD stops, BART starts up his front steps.

GUARD: He never told about the money.

BART: (walking up steps) No.

GUARD: What do *you* figure he done with it?

BART: (turning, at door) He took the secret with him when I dropped him.

The GUARD leaves the SHOT; BART goes in.

INT. BART'S HALLWAY—CLOSE SHOT—BART
He hangs up his coat and hat. Across this his wife speaks o.s.; a lighted door is ajar at rear of hall. A clatter of dishes and pans o.s.

BART'S WIFE: (o.s.) That you, Bart? Supper's waitin'.

BART just nods, and, tiptoeing, walks into a door next the kitchen and snaps on a light and turns on water o.s. His wife comes out of the kitchen and goes in.

INT. BART'S BATHROOM—CLOSE TWO-SHOT—BART AND WIFE
He is washing his hands in thick lather. Passing, she pecks his cheek and, as we PAN, looks into the next room. He looks past her, and we see two small CHILDREN asleep in a big brass bed. BART registers, turns again to the basin, and we PAN them back into the original TWO-SHOT.

BART: (low) Mother: sometimes I think it might be better if I was to quit my job as guard.

His WIFE's eyes go sharp and quiet.

WIFE: (low) You're always this way when there's a hangin'. You never have to be there.

BART rinses his hands. A sigh; he takes up the towel.

BART: Sometimes I wish I was back at the mine.

WIFE: And leave me a widow after another blast like the one in '24? Not on your life, old mister!

He looks at her a moment. She goes out. He looks o.s. towards his CHILDREN. He goes into their room on tiptoe.

MEDIUM SHOT—BART
He approaches his children, across whose bed WE SHOOT without yet seeing them. He comes into MEDIUM CLOSE-UP. As he leans and we TILT DOWN, he extends his large hands.

CLOSE DOWNWARD TWO-SHOT—HIS CHILDREN
Two rose-and-gold little GIRLS lie in sleep; BART'S hands enter the SHOT and gently rearrange the covers so that their mouths and throats are free. We watch, for a moment more, the two sleeping faces.   LAP DISSOLVE TO

HEAD CLOSE-UP—BART, HOVERING HIS CHILDREN

CHILDREN'S VOICES: (o.s. chanting) Hing, hang, hung.
See what the Hangman done!   LAP DISSOLVE TO

EXT. CRESAP'S LANDING—DAY
We are in *Peacock Alley*. The tree-shaded dirt street of a small, one-street river town; a picturesque, mid-19th-century remnant of the old river civilization, which general Progress has left behind. Chiefly we see, in this order: A *schoolhouse* (on far side of street); *Miz Cunningham's second-hand shop*; a *Grange House* sporting a poster for a Western movie; *Spoon's Ice Cream Parlor*. At the end of this street, down the river-bank, is a brick wharf and UNCLE BIRDIE'S *wharf-boat*. In b.g. and in passing, suggestions of sleepy small-town life.

From the HEAD CLOSE-UP of BART the *Hangman* o.s. chanting, we   LAP DISSOLVE TO

HEAD CLOSE-UP—JOHN HARPER
Chanting VOICES o.s. complete *"see what the Hangman done!"*
                                                    PULL BACK TO

CLOSE PULLING TWO-SHOT—PEARL AND JOHN
They stroll barefoot down the empty dirt sidewalk. They look towards the voices, PEARL friendly, JOHN hostile.

MEDIUM SHOT—THE CHILDREN, OVER JOHN AND PEARL
Several, within the door of the *Schoolhouse*, stick their heads around the edge. They chant at the HARPER CHILDREN. Another, next the door, is drawing something on the wall.

CHILDREN: (chanting) Hung, hang, hing! See the Robber swing!

OVER these lines we CUT briefly to—

CLOSER SHOT—THE CHILDREN
. . . chanting, drawing. The ARTIST completes in chalk, a large simple sketch of a man hanging from gallows. As the verse ends we CUT TO:

MEDIUM SHOT—THE CHILDREN, OVER JOHN AND PEARL
They look towards OUR CHILDREN; JOHN pays them no attention. The drawing is revealed. JOHN takes PEARL'S hand. The other CHILDREN giggle.

CHILDREN: (chanting) Hing, hang, hung! Now my song is done!

Between lines one and two JOHN turns away from them into—

CLOSE TWO-SHOT—JOHN AND PEARL—THROUGH WINDOW
WE SHOOT them through the window of MIZ CUNNINGHAM'S second-hand store. The back of a watch is silhouetted large in FOREGROUND; JOHN'S eyes instantly fix on it; in b.g. the SCHOOL-CHILDREN finish their song and vanish, giggling, into the schoolhouse. We hear the ticking of the watch.

INSERT—THE WATCH
A watch with a moving sweep-hand, ticking.

CLOSE TWO-SHOT—JOHN AND PEARL

PEARL: Are you goin' to buy it, John?

No answer. JOHN'S eyes are fixed on the watch. OVER a shop-doorbell we hear:

MIZ CUNNINGHAM'S VOICE: (o.s.) Uh-Hawwww! (They glance toward her.)

MEDIUM SHOT—MIZ CUNNINGHAM
Fantastically dirty and fantastically dressed, she hustles to them and we PAN her into a THREE-SHOT. She talks like a Tidewater Cockatoo.

MIZ CUNNINGHAM: (continuing) So your Mommy's keepin' you out of school! Poor little lambs!

PEARL watches her; JOHN, the watch.

MIZ CUNNINGHAM: And how is your poor, poor mother?

JOHN: She's at Spoon's Ice Cream Parlor.

MIZ CUNNINGHAM: (she snuffles) The Lord tends you both these days!

JOHN doesn't take his eyes off the watch.

CLOSE SHOT—JOHN

His eyes are fixed on the watch o.s.

MIZ CUNNINGHAM'S VOICE: (o.s.) Didn't they never find out what your father done with all that money he stole?

Eyes as before till *"money,"* then he looks up towards her.

MEDIUM SHOT—MIZ CUNNINGHAM

MIZ CUNNINGHAM: When they caught him, there wasn't so much as a penny of it to be seen! Now what do you make of that! Eh, boy?

She grins horribly.

TWO-SHOT—OVER JOHN AND PEARL

JOHN: Pearl and me, we have to go.

He walks off fast as we DOLLY BEHIND THEM; he leads PEARL, who hugs her doll.

PEARL: (chanting) Hing, hang, hung.

JOHN: You better not sing that song.

PEARL: Why?

JOHN: 'Cause you're too little.

A few paces in silence; now they come to the big window of *Spoon's Ice Cream Parlor.*

PEARL: Can we get some candy?

WILLA'S face is seen within; serving a customer, she sees them and waves them away.

JOHN: No.

He keeps her strolling. WALT SPOON, comes out, proffering two lollypops.

WALT: Howdy, youngins.

PEARL drags at JOHN'S hand but JOHN, pretending not to see or hear, drags her out of the SHOT, shaking his head. We

DOLLY IN on WALT, who looks after them, surprised and touched, then goes inside.

INT. SPOON'S PARLOR—GROUP SHOT—WALT, WILLA, ICEY SPOON

We PAN WALT across a little of his Parlor; he plants the lolly-pops back in a jar on the counter and leaves the SHOT as we TIGHTEN IN on WILLA and ICEY. WILLA slides used dishes into wash-water; ICEY jaws down her back, from first moment of shot.

ICEY: Willa Harper there is certain plain facts of life that adds up just like two plus two makes four and one of them is this: No woman is good enough to raise growin' youngsters alone! The Lord meant that job for two!

WILLA: Icey, I don't want a husband.

CLOSE SHOT—ICEY

ICEY: (fiercely) *Fiddlesticks!*   LAP DISSOLVE TO

FULL SHOT—EXT. STREET—NIGHT

The weekly movie audience is letting out, next door to SPOON'S. Some start cars or wagons, others stroll to SPOON'S.
          LAP DISSOLVE TO

INT. SPOON'S PARLOR—EVENING—TWO-SHOT—ICEY AND WILLA

We start with a CLOSE SHOT as ICEY'S hands slap together a gooey banana split; TILT UP to TWO-SHOT, favoring ICEY; fin-ish on WILLA, on "it's a *man* you need," etc.

Murmur of CUSTOMERS o.s.

WALT'S VOICE: (calling o.s.) One solid brown sody, one Lovers' Delight.

ICEY: 'Tain't a matter of wantin' or *not* wantin'! You're no spring chicken, you're a grown woman with two little youn-gins; it's a *man* you need in the house, Willa Harper!
          LAP DISSOLVE TO

LONG SHOT—NIGHT—A TRAIN

A short, lighted, toy-like train departs the town along the river-bank, whistling. The whistle TIES OVER the previous DIS-SOLVE. STARLIT SKY.   LAP DISSOLVE TO

FRAMING SHOT—EXT. HARPER HOUSE—NIGHT
A square, HEAD-ON SHOT, river water below and vibrant starlight above; featuring a gas-lamp by the road; a tree; and pretty tree-shadows which work across a window.

INT. HARPER CHILDREN'S BEDROOM—NIGHT—TWO-SHOT—JOHN, PEARL, SHADOWS
PEARL lies in their bed, her doll snug on her shoulder. JOHN sits on the edge of the bed, in his underwear.

PEARL: Tell me a story, John.

JOHN: Once upon a time there was a rich king . . . (he sees the shadows on the wall and gets up and looks at them) . . . and he had him a son and a daughter and they all lived in a castle over in Africa. Well, one day this King got taken away by bad men and before he got took off he told his son to kill anyone that tried to steal their gold, and before long these bad men come back and—

PEARL: The Blue Men?

He moves, and as his shadow moves away we see the shadow of PREACHER, motionless. PEARL sits up and points at it. JOHN notices her and sees it. We PAN JOHN to the window. He looks out.

FULL SHOT—PREACHER—THROUGH WINDOW, JOHN'S VIEWPOINT.
He stands motionless.

RESUME PREVIOUS SHOT—JOHN AT WINDOW
He turns and we PAN him to bed.

JOHN: (casually) Just a man. (he climbs into bed and pulls up the covers) Goodnight Pearl, sleep tight; and don't let the bedbugs bite.

PEARL: (to doll) 'Night Miss Jenny; don't let the bedbugs bite.

As they settle down we hear PREACHER'S singing, sweet and quiet o.s.: *"Leaning on the Everlasting Arms."*   DISSOLVE TO

EXT. RIVER AND TOWN—MORNING—FULL SHOT—A GINGER-BREAD SIDE-WHEELER

She steams around a bend towards a toy-like small town. PREACHER'S song, o.s., ties over. People are waving from shore and boat.

FULL PANNING SHOT—THE BOAT, FROM SHORE
We PAN her into frame UNCLE BIRDIE STEPTOE'S toy-like little wharf-boat. As she passes broadside we CUT TO:

MEDIUM SHOT—BIRDIE, THEN JOHN
. . . as boat passes. BIRDIE'S head sticks through a porthole. He is a wiry old river character. The boat whistles. As BIRDIE speaks we PAN JOHN, and foundered skiff, into TWO-SHOT with BIRDIE.

BIRDIE: She don't put in at Cresap's Landing no more, but she still blows as she passes. Come on in and have a cup of coffee.

JOHN: (starting towards him) Ain't nobody stole Dad's skiff.

BIRDIE: Ain't nobody goin' to neither, long as Uncle Birdie's around.

He vanishes from the porthole. We PAN JOHN from skiff to wharf and Birdie's door.

BIRDIE'S VOICE: (calling o.s.) First day my jints is limber enough I'll haul her up and give her a good caulkin'.

INT. BIRDIE'S boat—TWO-SHOT—JOHN AND BIRDIE

JOHN enters and sits on a box. BIRDIE, in a ramshackle rocking chair, pours coffee. BESS'S photograph on chest near BIRDIE.

BIRDIE: Ain't seen you in a coon's age, Johnny.

JOHN: I been mindin' Pearl.

BIRDIE: Pshaw now! Ain't it a caution what women'll load onto a feller's back when he ain't lookin'?

He gives JOHN a cup of coffee.

BIRDIE: 'Scuse me, Cap, while I sweeten up my coffee.

He fetches a liquor bottle from beneath the rocking chair; about to pour he does a take at BESS'S PHOTOGRAPH.

INSERT—THE PHOTOGRAPH
It stands in a cabinet frame: A fine-looking young woman in archaic dress, with sharp, accusing black eyes.

BIRDIE'S VOICE: (o.s.) Dead and gone these twenty-five years and never takes her eyes off me.

CUT OVER his line to—

CLOSE TWO-SHOT—JOHN AND BIRDIE
He turns the picture away and splashes liquor into his coffee.

BIRDIE: (pouring) Man o' my years *needs* a little snort to get his boiler heated of a morning.

They drink. BIRDIE, satisfied, sighs and rocks.

BIRDIE: This mornin' I was talkin' to this stranger up at the boarding-house. He knowed your Dad!

CLOSE SHOT—JOHN
JOHN looks cautious.

JOHN: Where did he know Dad?

CLOSE SHOT—BIRDIE
BIRDIE'S face falls; he takes another drink.

BIRDIE: Well, boy, I'll not hide the truth; it was up at Moundsville Penitentiary.

CLOSE TWO-SHOT—NEW ANGLE
JOHN puts his cup down and gets up.

JOHN: I got to go now, Uncle Birdie.

He heads for the door.

BIRDIE: Why shucks boy, you just got here.

He follows JOHN to the door. JOHN runs up the bank, not looking back.

JOHN: (running) I told Mom I'd be back to Spoon's for Pearl.

EXT. STREET—MEDIUM SHOT—JOHN
He runs up the street close to Spoon's and stops dead.

CLOSE SHOT—JOHN
He is horrified by what he sees.

INT. SPOON'S ICE CREAM PARLOR

GROUP SHOT through door-glass, from JOHN'S VIEW POINT

PREACHER, WILLA and PEARL surround a little table. WALT stands by, puffing his pipe. ICEY in BACKGROUND, stirs fudge at a little soda-fountain stove. WILLA looks both moved and pleased. PEARL, shyly flirting with PREACHER, all but hides in WILLA'S skirts. PREACHER dandles PEARL'S doll on his knee as he talks. All the grownups are avid for his words, which we don't hear through the glass.

CLOSE SHOT—JOHN
We SHOOT THROUGH the DOOR; he quietly enters.

GROUP SHOT
They look casually to JOHN, and continue talking.

ICEY: (stirring; with a meaningful glance at Willa) God works in a mysterious way, His wonders to perform.

OVER this JOHN ENTERS the SHOT and stands at the fringe of the GROUP, staring at PREACHER'S hands and at the doll.

PREACHER: I was with Brother Harper almost to the end; . . .

GROUP SHOT—NEW ANGLE—FAVORING JOHN AND PREACHER

PREACHER: (continuing) . . . and now that I'm no longer employed by the Penitentiary it is my joy to bring this small comfort to his loved ones.

FLASH-CUT CLOSE-UP—JOHN
On "Penitentiary" he glances quickly at PREACHER'S face; then back to his hands.

GROUP SHOT—ICEY

ICEY: (sniffing) It's a mighty good man would come out of his way to bring a word of cheer to a grieving widow!

CLOSE SHOT—WALT

WALT: So you ain't with the State no more?

GROUP SHOT—FAVORING PREACHER AND JOHN

PREACHER: No, Brother; I resigned only yesterday. The heart-renderin' spectacle of them poor men was too much for me.

He becomes aware of JOHN'S staring.

PREACHER: Ah, little lad, you're staring at my fingers.

He hands the doll to PEARL. JOHN'S eyes follow the doll.

PREACHER holds up both hands to JOHN. JOHN looks back at his hands.

PREACHER: Shall I tell you the little story of Right-Hand-Left-Hand—the tale of Good and Evil?

JOHN stands still. PEARL, with her doll, crosses to PREACHER and twines about his knee.

CLOSE SHOT—JOHN
He looks on, in dumb alarm.

CLOSE SHOT—PREACHER

PREACHER: H-A-T-E! (he thrusts up his left hand) It was with this left hand that old brother Cain struck the blow that laid his brother low! L-O-V-E! (he thrusts up his right hand) See these here fingers, dear friends! These fingers has veins that lead straight to the soul of man! The right hand, friends! The hand of Love!

GROUP SHOT—ICEY, WALT, WILLA—OVER PREACHER'S HANDS
They are impressed in their different ways.

PREACHER: (o.s.) Now watch and I'll show you the Story of Life. The fingers of these hands, dear hearts!—They're always a-tuggin' and a-warrin' one hand agin' t'other. (he locks his fingers and writhes them, crackling the joints) Look at 'em, dear hearts!

MEDIUM SHOT—JOHN—OVER PREACHER'S HANDS
He looks on with unseeing eyes.

PREACHER: (o.s.) Old Left Hand Hate's a-fightin' and it looks like Old Right Hand Love's a goner!

GROUP SHOT—WALT, ICEY, WILLA, OVER HANDS

PREACHER: (o.s.) But wait now! Hot dog! Love's a-winnin! Yessirree!

CLOSE SHOT—PREACHER

PREACHER: It's Love that won! Old Left Hand *Hate's* gone down for the count! (he crashes both hands onto the table)

FULL SHOT—THE WHOLE GROUP
Slight applause from the ADULTS. PREACHER takes PEARL, with her doll, onto his lap.

ICEY: I never heard it better told. I wish every soul in this community could git the benefit. You jest *got* to stay for our church pick-nick Sunday!

PEARL offers PREACHER the DOLL to kiss. PREACHER complies.

CLOSE SHOT—JOHN'S REACTION

RESUME GROUP SHOT

PREACHER: (finessing it) I must wend my way down River on the Lord's work.

ICEY: You ain't leavin' in no hurry if *we* can help it!

WILLA: John: take that look offen your face and act nice.

PREACHER: He don't mean no impudence; do you, boy? (no answer) Do you, boy? Ah, many's the time poor Brother Ben told me about these youngins.

JOHN: What did he tell you?

CLOSE SHOT—PREACHER
He does a little take. His eyes twinkle palely.

PREACHER: Why, he told me what fine little lambs you and your sister both was.

GROUP SHOT

JOHN: Is that all?

CLOSE SHOT—PREACHER
Something new enters his eyes; a game has begun between them.

PREACHER: Why, no, boy; he told me lots and lots of things. Nice things, boy.

A tight silence. ICEY pours fudge into a buttered pan.

PREACHER: *My*, that fudge smells *yummy*!

CLOSE SHOT—ICEY

ICEY: (with horrid archness) It's for the pick-nick. And you won't get a *smidgen of my fudge* unless you stay for the pick-nick!

Over her line, o.s., hymn-singing begins and now, OVER her "the case rests" smile we bring up the singing and

LAP DISSOLVE TO

EXT. THE RIVER BANK—CHURCH IN BACKGROUND—FULL
SHOT—THE SINGING PICKNICKERS

A pleasant, grassy river-bank. Few men in proportion to
women and children. We CENTER PREACHER. They are
singing "*Brighten the Corner*;" PREACHER sings conspicuously
well. The women watch him and admire him. He gives WILLA
the eye as we PAN to CENTER WILLA, who looks wooed and
self-conscious. ICEY enters the SHOT and whispers and beckons
WILLA and, as the singing continues, they leave the group and
start towards a shade tree in MEDIUM GROUND, which we PAN
TO CENTER.

FULL SHOT—WILLA AND ICEY
They walk; singers in BACKGROUND.

ICEY: Don't he have the grandest singin' voice?

WILLA nods. ICEY, looking ahead, is displeased.

MEDIUM SHOT—THE TREE, JOHN AND PEARL
They sit on the bench, their backs to us, partly concealed by
the tree trunk.

ICEY'S VOICE: (sharp) John! Pearl!

They look around. ICEY and WILLA enter the SHOT, their backs
to us.

ICEY: Run along and play, you two.

JOHN: Where?

ICEY: Down by the river. My goodness!

Docile, they leave the shot as WILLA and ICEY approach the
bench.

CLOSE TWO-SHOT—WILLA AND ICEY
They sit on the bench, their backs to us. The CHILDREN recede
towards the river in BACKGROUND. WILLA meekly keeps her
head down. Singing continues o.s.

ICEY: That feller's just achin' to settle down with some nice
woman and make a home for himself.

WILLA: It's awful soon after Ben's passing.

ICEY: If ever I saw a Sign from Heaven!

WILLA: John don't like him much.

ICEY: Pearl *dotes* on him.

WILLA: The boy worries me. It's silly, but it's like there was something still between him and his Dad.

ICEY: What *he* needs is a dose o' salts!

WILLA: There's something else.

ICEY: What?

WILLA: The money, Icey.

ICEY: I declare, you'll let that money haunt you to your grave, Willa Harper!

WILLA: I *would* love to be satisfied Harry Powell don't think I've got that money somewhere.

ICEY: You'll come right out and *ask* that Man of God! (turning and yelling) Mr. Paow-well! (to Willa) Clear that *evil mud* out of your soul!

PREACHER starts towards her. ICEY pivots and we PAN OVER her to CHILDREN by river.

ICEY: (yelling) John! Pearl!

CLOSE SHOT—PEARL AND JOHN

JOHN looks up from pebble-skimming and loosens his tie.

ICEY: (yelling o.s.) Come along *hee-ere* and get some *fuu-udge*!

JOHN: (calling) I don't want no fudge.

His brow is furrowed. He skims another pebble.

ICEY: (shouting o.s.) *You'll do what you're told!*

They unwillingly get moving.

RESUME TWO-SHOT—ICEY AND WILLA

ICEY: You go set down by the River.

WILLA: (getting up) Oh, Icey, I'm a sight!

ICEY: Get along with you.

Both women set off, WILLA to River, ICEY towards GROUP. We TRACK after ICEY. PREACHER approaches. ICEY, crossing him, gives him a little shove towards WILLA and a coy—

ICEY: *You ! ! !*

We FOLLOW her to the women who are busying themselves with the fudge.

CLOSE GROUP SHOT—ICEY AND WOMEN, FAVORING ICEY
. . . a few men in BACKGROUND, and, beyond them, PREACHER sits down by WILLA at water's edge. JOHN and PEARL approach. As ICEY starts yammering the men, WALT among them, shyly withdraw.

ICEY: That young lady'd better look sharp or some smart sister between here and Captina's a-gonna snap him up right from under her nose! (they nod and agree, ad lib) She's not the *only* fish in the river! (more agreement. John and Pearl join Icey. Icey speaks to John) Now you two *stay put*!

CLOSE SHOT—JOHN
He looks hard towards WILLA and PREACHER o.s.

ICEY: (o.s., to women) Shilly-shallying around . . .

LONG SHOT—WILLA AND PREACHER
. . . from JOHN'S VIEWPOINT in tableau of decorous courtship, framed by heavy domestic bodies.

ICEY: (o.s.) A husband's one piece of store goods ye never know till you get it home and take the paper off.

CLOSE TWO-SHOT—WILLA AND PREACHER
They sit by the water; drooling willows; almost in travesty of a romantic scene. WILLA dabbles one hand in the water.

WILLA: (very shy) Did Ben Harper ever tell you what he done with that money he stole?

HEAD CLOSE-UP—PREACHER
His head goes slantwise and he smiles oddly.

PREACHER: My dear child, don't *you* know?

CLOSE SHOT—JOHN
He watches intently towards his mother; PEARL holds his hand. ICEY'S voice o.s.

GROUP SHOT—WOMEN, JOHN AND PEARL

ICEY: She's moonin' about Ben Harper. That wasn't love, it was just flap-doodle. (agreeing nods and murmurs) Have some fudge, lambs. (she hands some down to John and Pearl. Pearl smears her mouth with it; John, watching always towards his mother, takes one nibble and throws the rest away). When you're married forty years, you know all that don't amount to a hill o'beans! I been married to my Walt that long, and I'll swear in all that time I'd just lie there thinking about my canning.

In BACKGROUND WALT looks sheepish.

WILIA'S VOICE: (calling o.s.) John! John?

All look towards her.

LONG SHOT—OVER GROUP
WILLA is standing, beckoning JOHN

MEDIUM TWO-SHOT—JOHN AND PEARL
They start towards their mother.

GROUP SHOT—ICEY AND WOMEN—NEW ANGLE

ICEY: A woman's a *fool* to marry for that. It's something for a *man*. The good Lord never meant for a decent woman to want *that*—not *really* want it! It's all just a fake and a pipe-dream.

The others agree with her. She puts a piece of fudge in her mouth.

CLOSE GROUP SHOT—PREACHER, WILLA, CHILDREN
. . . as JOHN and PEARL (with DOLL) come shyly up. WILLA is seated again. She is radiant.

WILLA: John, Mr. Powell has got something to tell you.

PREACHER: Well, John, the night before your father died, he told me what he did with that money.

CLOSE SHOT—JOHN
He desperately conceals his reaction; he thinks BEN has betrayed him.

RESUME GROUP SHOT

PREACHER: That money's at the bottom of the river wrapped around a 12-pound cobblestone.

CLOSE SHOT—JOHN AND PEARL
He now conceals his *new* reaction.

RESUME GROUP SHOT

WILLA touches PREACHER's hand, warmly.

WILLA: Thank you, Harry.

She looks all around her, glowing, and stands up, hands to hair.

PEARL: John . . .

JOHN: Sshhh . . .

WILLA: I feel clean now! My whole body's just a quiverin' with cleanness!

She walks away towards ICEY and the WOMEN.

CLOSE SHOT—PREACHER

PREACHER: John: here.

CLOSE SHOT—JOHN AND PEARL

JOHN moves to stand in front of him; PEARL, to stand beside PREACHER, with the DOLL.

CLOSE SHOT—PREACHER AND CHILDREN

From JOHN'S eye-level; as JOHN steps in front of him and PEARL beside him.

PREACHER: Your tie's crooked.

HEAD CLOSE-UP—JOHN

The hand named LOVE and the hand named HATE come in to straighten the necktie. JOHN looks down. He looks up and sees:

GROUP SHOT—JOHN'S viewpoint

PREACHER, in close up, hands busy o.s.; PEARL, with doll; and between them, in BACKGROUND, WILLA. She is now running fast towards ICEY, who walks towards her with arms outstretched. Behind them, the group of women. BIRDIE'S guitar music begins o.s.   DISSOLVE TO

EXT. BIRDIE'S BOAT—EVENING—MEDIUM SHOT—BIRDIE, JOHN AND SKIFF

Birdie sits beside his open door, strumming a guitar and singing. The scene is lamplighted from within. Ben's skiff is inverted on trestles in FOREGROUND. At start of scene we see only JOHN'S feet; he's under the skiff, examining it. After three lines of song he comes out from under, and lounges against the skiff, tracing a tarry seam with his forefinger.

BIRDIE: (singing) 'Twas down at Cresap's Landing, Along the River Shore, Birdie Steptoe was a Pilot in the good old days of yore. Now he sets in his old wharf-boat . . .

JOHN: (across him) When'll Dad's skiff be ready?

BIRDIE: Can't hear ye, boy. (singing) . . . So the big boats heave a sigh, They blow for Uncle Birdie . . .

JOHN: (across him) When'll the skiff be ready?

BIRDIE: (singing) And the times that are gone by. I'll have her ready inside of a week; and then we'll go fishin'. How's your Maw?

Through rest of scene, Birdie picks lazily at his guitar.

JOHN: O, she's all right.

BIRDIE: How's your sister Pearl?

JOHN: Just fine.

He gets up.

BIRDIE: Leavin', boy?

JOHN: Yep; gotta watch out for Pearl, Uncle Birdie.

BIRDIE: Well goodnight, boy. Come again—any time.

JOHN leaves the SHOT.

BIRDIE: And mind now—I'll have your Paw's skiff in ship-shape, 'side of a week.

MOVING SHOT—JOHN
As he runs past SPOON's, looking in, he is curious.

MOVING SHOT—SPOON'S, HIS VIEWPOINT
ICEY embraces WILLA or waltzes her around; WALT looks on, pleased.

FULL SHOT—JOHN
He hurries away from us towards home.

FRAMING SHOT—THE HARPER HOUSE
In the otherwise dark house, one window is lighted. JOHN enters the shot, his back to us. Seeing the lighted window, he hesitates.

JOHN: (softly) Is somebody there?

Silent pause, listening; then he walks cautiously towards us.

FULL SHOT—JOHN
A tall, narrow shooting-frame; right and left thirds of screen are black.

We SHOOT from inside the screen door. JOHN crosses the porch and softly opens the door and enters on tiptoe and pauses, close to us, in the dark hallway, listening sharp.

JOHN: (softly) Is anybody here?

Silence. Relieved, but puzzled, he tiptoes along towards the rear of the hallway in CLOSE-UP as we PULL AWAY. We bring in the bottom of the stairs.

PREACHER'S VOICE: (o.s.) Good evening, John.

JOHN gasps, peering, and looks up.

TWO SHOT—JOHN AND PREACHER—NARROW SCREEN

PREACHER looks at JOHN; JOHN sinks onto the edge of a chair. PREACHER sits opposite. A bar of light from door falls across PREACHER'S face.

PREACHER: I had a little talk with your mother tonight, John; and your mother decided it might be best for *me* to—let you know the news.

From JOHN, just a questioning helpless reaction.

PREACHER: Your mother told me tonight she wanted me to be a daddy to you and your sister. We're going to get married, son.

JOHN is still.

PREACHER: Did you hear what I said, son?

JOHN: Huh?

PREACHER: Married! We have decided to go to Sistersville tomorrow, and when we come back—

JOHN: (just breathing it) You ain't my Dad! You won't never be my Dad!

PREACHER: (obsessed, disregarding him)—and when we come back, we'll all be friends—and *share our fortunes together, John!*

JOHN: (screaming) You think you can make me tell! But I won't! I won't! I won't!

He gawks at his own folly, covers his mouth with his hand and looks up at PREACHER.

PREACHER: (softly) Tell me *what*, boy?

JOHN: Nothin'!

PREACHER: Are we keeping secrets from each other, little lad?

JOHN: No. No.

PREACHER stiffens, relaxes, and chuckles softly.

PREACHER: No matter, boy, we've got a long time together.

CLOSE TWO-SHOT—JOHN AND PREACHER

JOHN starts for the stairs.   DISSOLVE TO

EXT. HARPER YARD—MORNING—CLOSE SHOT—BEN'S FORD
It stands vibrating, then moves out of shot with receding engine sound o.s., disclosing:

TWO-SHOT—JOHN AND PEARL

ICEY'S skirts in BACKGROUND. They are awfully spic-and-span; they even wear shoes.

ICEY: (o.s.) *Wave yer hands! Great sakes!*

They wave after the car, bewilderedly.

ICEY: (o.s.) You wait here while I get your night-things.

She hustles out of shot.

PEARL: *Now* can I tell?

JOHN: Hm?

PEARL: When Mr. Powell's our Daddy then I can tell him about—

His hand clamps over her mouth. She struggles and whimpers.

JOHN: You *swore*, Pearl!

PEARL: (across him) John! Don't!

JOHN: You promised Dad you wouldn't *never* tell!

He takes his hand away but holds it ready.

PEARL: I *love* Mr. Powell *lots* and *lots*, John.

JOHN grabs her by the shoulders and glares.

JOHN: *Don't you tell! Don't you* NEVER DARE *tell!*

Over them we   LAP DISSOLVE TO

SHOULDER CLOSE-UP—WILLA

She is caressing her shoulders.

FULL SHOT—WILLA
Her back is to us. She is in a pathetic night dress; she stands before a mirror in a hotel bedroom in Sistersville. She walks to the door.

INSERT WILLA'S HAND
It hesitates on the doorknob.

CLOSE SHOT—WILLA
Shooting OVER her as she opens the door, we see PREACHER in bed, his back to us. Beyond him, a window. The drawn shade rustles quietly.

CLOSE SHOT—THE DOOR
. . . from within the room. WILLA closes the door, on which PREACHER'S coat hangs. The closing brings a knocking sound. WILLA feels the outside of the coat; feels something hard; takes out the knife and looks at it.

INSERT—THE KNIFE IN HER HAND—CLOSE SHOT—WILLA
A moment of perplexity; then a little smile.

WILLA: (whispering) Oh! It's . . . uh . . .

She puts it back in the pocket and gives the pocket a pat. She starts towards the bed.

TWO-SHOT—WILLA AND PREACHER
We SHOOT OVER PREACHER as she approaches modestly and stands by the bed.

WILLA: (softly) Harry . . .

His hand comes up; she puts out her own, expecting a loving hand-clasp; but PREACHER points to the window.

PREACHER: Fix that window shade.

Startled, then again tender, she moves to:

CLOSE SHOT—WILLA AT WINDOW
She adjusts the shade, looking always towards the bed. She smiles maternally. As we PULL BACK and PAN into FULL SHOT OF BED she comes to the bed and sits on the edge and slips off her mules. PREACHER'S back is to her.

WILLA: (softly) Harry!

PREACHER: (cool and clear) I was praying.

WILLA: Oh, I'm sorry, Harry! I didn't know! I thought maybe—

With a sounding of bedsprings PREACHER turns. His voice is quiet and cold.

PREACHER: You thought, Willa, that the moment you walked in that door I'd start in to pawing you in the abominable way men are supposed to do on their wedding night. Ain't that right, now?

WILLA: No, Harry! I thought—

PREACHER: I think it's time we got one thing perfectly clear, Willa. Marriage to me represents a blending of two spirits in the sight of Heaven.

He gets out of bed. WILLA puts her face down to the pillow and moans.

PREACHER snaps on a harsh bare bulb at center of room.

PREACHER: (quietly) Get up, Willa.

WILLA: Harry, what—

PREACHER: Get up.

She obeys.

PREACHER: Now go and look at yourself yonder in that mirror.

WILLA hesitates.

FULL SHOT—OVER PREACHER—CENTERING A STAINED BU-REAU MIRROR

PREACHER: Do as I say.

WILLA walks to meet her image in the mirror; her eyes on PREACHER.

PREACHER: LOOK at yourself.

Her head drops, facing the mirror.

CLOSE SHOT—WILLA, PREACHER, BULB
WILLA is in HEAD CLOSE-UP; bulb hangs at center; PREACHER, in his nightshirt, is beyond it.

PREACHER: What do you see, girl?

Her mouth trembles; she can't talk.

PREACHER: You see the body of a woman! The temple of creation and motherhood. You see the flesh of Eve that Man since Adam has profaned. That body was meant for begetting children. It was not meant for the lust of men.

WILLA just opens her mouth.

PREACHER: Do you want more children, Willa?

WILLA: I—no, I—

PREACHER: It's the business of our marriage to mind those two you have now—not to beget more.

WILLA: Yes.

He stands watching her for a moment; then he snaps off the light and gets into bed.

PREACHER: You can get back into bed now and stop shivering.

WILLA, in the darkness, does not move. She folds her hands in prayer and lifts her eyes.

WILLA: (whispering) Help me to get clean so I can be what Harry wants me to be.   LAP DISSOLVE TO

INSERT—A TORCH OR RAILROAD FLARE

VOICES: (o.s.) AAA-MEN!

GROUP SHOT—CONGREGATION
A dozen country men and women in religious ecstasy.
(NOTE: No set necessary for this scene. Flare, or flares, in every SHOT. Faces lighted by flares.)

CONGREGATION: AAA-MENN!

WILLA: (o.s., very loud) You have all sinned!

CONGREGATION: Yes! Yes!

HEAD CLOSE-UP—WILLA

WILLA: But which one of you can say as I can say: I drove a good man to *murder* because I kept a-houndin' him for clothes and per-fumes and face paint!

GROUP SHOT—CONGREGATION

WILLA: (o.s.) And he slew two human beings and he come to me and he said: *Take* this money and *buy* your per-fumes and paint!

FULL FIGURE SHOT—WILLA, STANDING; PREACHER STAND-
ING IN B.G.

WILLA: But Brethren, that's where the *Lord* stepped in!
That's where the LORD *stepped in!*

PREACHER: Yes!

CONGREGATION: (o.s.) Yes! Yes!

GROUP SHOT—CONGREGATION

WILLA: (o.s. screaming) And the Lord told that man—

CONGREGATION: Yes! Yes!

CLOSE SHOT—WILLA

WILLA: The Lord said, Take that money and throw it in the
River!

CONGREGATION: (o.s.) Yes! Yes! Hallelujah!

WILLA: Throw that money in the River! In THE RIVER!

CONGREGATION: (o.s.) IN THE RIIV-ER!   CUT TO

EXTREME CLOSE DOWN-SHOT—PEARL'S DOLL
It lies face down on arbor bricks, its back wide open; money
spilling out. A little breeze toys with the money. HOLD, a moment, in silence. Then we hear a snipping sound o.s. TILT UP-
WARD into—

CLOSE SHOT—PEARL
She sits at the end of the grape-arbor. She finishes cutting a
skirted paper-doll out of a hundred dollar bill and lays it down
beside a male hundred-dollar paper-doll. She pats the dolls.

PEARL: Now! You're John—and you're Pearl.

JOHN'S VOICE: (o.s. calling) Pearl? . . . Pearl?

PEARL starts guiltily and looks towards him, scrambling money
together. JOHN's footsteps o.s.

PEARL: You'll get awful mad, John. I done a Sin!

CLOSE SHOT—JOHN—PEARL'S ANGLE

JOHN: You what?

He hears the frantic rustling of paper—

JOHN: (aghast) Pearl! You ain't—

CLOSE SHOT—PEARL, OVER JOHN

PEARL: John, don't be mad! Don't be mad! I was just playing with it! I didn't *tell* no one!

FLASH CUT CLOSE-UP—JOHN
. . . as he stoops toward her, dumb with horror.

CLOSE SHOT—PEARL
She continues to gather the money together.

PEARL: (pleading) It's all here.

CLOSE TWO-SHOT—JOHN AND PEARL

JOHN: Pearl! Oh, Pearl!

She's stuffing bills back into the torn doll. They slide through her fingers. He helps.

FLASH INSERT—PREACHER'S FOOT
. . . as he plants it, with sound, in damp grass.

CLOSE SHOT—THE CHILDREN
JOHN freezes.

PREACHER'S VOICE: (o.s.) John?

JOHN: Oh—yes?

LONG SHOT—PREACHER—CHILDREN'S VIEWPOINT
He stands at far end of arbor.

PREACHER: What are you doing, boy?

LONG SHOT—CHILDREN—PREACHER'S VIEWPOINT

JOHN: Getting Pearl to bed. I—

PREACHER: What's taking you so long about it?

FLASH INSERT—THEIR FRANTIC HANDS, MONEY, THE DOLL

JOHN: (o.s.) It—she—

CLOSE SHOT—PREACHER—PEERING TOWARDS THEM

PREACHER: What's that you're playing with, boy?

LONG SHOT—CHILDREN—PREACHER'S VIEWPOINT

JOHN: Pearl's junk. Mom gets mad when she plays out here and don't clean up afterward.

PREACHER: *Come on*, children!

INSERT—JOHN'S HANDS PIN THE DOLL TOGETHER

FULL   SHOT—CHILDREN   STAND   UP,   LOOK   TOWARDS
PREACHER, AND SLOWLY START TOWARDS HIM. THE TWO FOR-
GOTTEN PAPER-DOLLS ARE BLOWN TOWARDS HIM TOO.

MOVING SHOT—PREACHER—JOHN'S VIEWPOINT

PREACHER'S watch-chain gleams. The shot SLOWLY CLOSES
DOWN on it and becomes still. We see the paper-dolls blow
past him.

PREACHER'S VOICE: Now, up to bed with the both of
you.

CLOSE SHOT—JOHN AND PEARL

JOHN starts to laugh uncontrollably. We PAN them past
PREACHER'S stomach into FULL SHOT.

PREACHER'S VOICE: Come here, John.

PREACHER'S VOICE: Run along, Pearl.

PEARL goes, JOHN comes towards PREACHER.

PREACHER—JOHN'S VIEWPOINT

PREACHER: Your mother says you tattled on me, boy. She
says you told her that I asked you where that money was hid.

JOHN: (o.s.) Yes. Yes.

PREACHER: That wasn't very nice of you, John. Have a
heart, boy.

CLOSE SHOT—JOHN
His helpless reaction. Pause.

PREACHER'S VOICE: Run along to bed.

As JOHN turns away we   LAP DISSOLVE TO

CLOSE SHOT—WILLA IN PROFILE
. . . and PULL AWAY showing JOHN as he turns to her. (PEARL'S
head is turned away; she's asleep.)

WILLA: Were you impudent to Mr. Powell, John?

JOHN: Mom, I didn't mean—

WILLA: What were you impudent about?

JOHN: He asked me about the money again, Mom.

WILLA: You always make up that lie, John! There *is* no
money, John. Can't you get that through your head?

                                          LAP DISSOLVE TO

CLOSE SHOT—A GAR, UNDERWATER

CLOSE UPWARD TWO-SHOT—JOHN AND BIRDIE
They look down into the water.

BIRDIE: Meanest, orneriest, sneakinest critter in the whole river, boy! A gar!

CLOSE TWO-SHOT—JOHN AND BIRDIE

They sit up into it.

JOHN: Here's your can o' hooks, Uncle Birdie.

BIRDIE: There hain't nary hook in the land smart enough to hook Mister Gar. What a feller needs is mother-wit—and a horse-hair.

Over this, he pulls horse-hair out of his hatband. He sets to work rigging his noose.

JOHN: Won't he bust it, Uncle Birdie?

BIRDIE: Shoot, a horse-hair'll hold a lumpin' whale.

He puts over his line. Pause.

BIRDIE: Do you mind me cussin', boy?

JOHN: No.

BIRDIE: Tell you why I ask—your step-pa being' a Preacher an' all . . .

JOHN's lips go like string. BIRDIE sees it.

BIRDIE: Never was much of a one for preachers myself. I dunno what's wrong up at your place, but just remember one thing, Cap—if ever you need help you just holler out and come a-runnin'. Old Uncle Birdie's your friend.

A powerful strike. BIRDIE lands the gar. The air is full of sparkling water.

BIRDIE: There! You slimy, snag-toothed, egg-suckin', bait-stealin' so-and-so!

QUICK INSERT—THE THUMPING FISH IN BOTTOM OF BOAT

FULL SHOT
He beats the fish with the heel of an old shoe.

BIRDIE: (beating) Mind what I told you. If ever you get in a crack, I just come a-runnin'.

Now there is no sound of thumping or beating.

CLOSE SHOT—JOHN
Admiring BIRDIE, he squares his shoulders, full of confidence.

JOHN: Can we eat him, Uncle Birdie?

BIRDIE: If you got an appetite for bones and bitterness.

On this, he flings the dead gar in a wide arc out into the river.

LAP DISSOLVE TO

INT. CHILDREN'S BEDROOM—NIGHT
The children are ready for bed.

CLOSE SHOT—PREACHER
Smiling, quiet, awaiting an answer.

CLOSE SHOT—JOHN

JOHN: I don't know.

TWO-SHOT—JOHN AND PREACHER

PEARL plays unconcernedly in background.

PREACHER: (intimately) She thinks that money's in the river, but you and me, we know better, don't we, boy?

JOHN: I don't know nothin'!

PREACHER: The summer is young yet, little lad. (he turns away from John) Pearl?

He holds out his hands to her; she comes to his lap, dropping her doll at his feet. JOHN turns his back and looks out the window beside bureau.

PREACHER: John's a feller who likes to keep *secrets*.

PEARL: Mm-hm.

PREACHER: I'll tell *you* a secret.

PEARL: Yes?

PREACHER: I knowed your Daddy. (PEARL frowns) And do you know what your Daddy said to me? He said, "Tell my little girl Pearl there's to be no secrets between her and you."

INSERT—JOHN'S HAND COMES TO REST BESIDE A HAIRBRUSH

RESUME TWO-SHOT—PREACHER AND PEARL, JOHN IN B.G.

PEARL: Yes?

PREACHER: Now it's *your* turn.

PEARL: What secret shall I tell?

PREACHER: How old are you?

PEARL: That's no secret. I'm five.

CLOSE SHOT—JOHN—PREACHER AND PEARL IN B.G.
A look of impotent hatred.

PREACHER: Sure, that's no secret.

RESUME TWO-SHOT

PREACHER: (continuing) What's your name?

PEARL: (giggling) You're just foolin'! My name's Pearl.

PREACHER: Tst-tst! Then I reckon I'll have to try again! Where's the money hid?

JOHN throws the hairbrush, striking PREACHER'S head.

JOHN: (screaming as he throws) You swore you wouldn't tell! (he beats the air with his fists) You swore! You swore! You swore!

CLOSE SHOT—PREACHER
He is sure now PEARL knows.

THREE-SHOT—PEARL, PREACHER, JOHN

PEARL: (awed) You hit Daddy with the hairbrush!

Another silence.

PREACHER: (cheerfully) You see? We can't have anything to do with John. (light off) You and me will go down to the parlor.

PEARL: Miz Jenny! Miz Jenny!

She gets the doll. We PAN them through the door.

TWO-SHOT—PREACHER AND PEARL
Outside door as he closes it.

PREACHER: John's just plumb bad through and through—

CLOSE SHOT—PEARL
As PREACHER'S hand locks the door.

PEARL: (at door) Yes, John's just plumb bad.   CUT TO

INT. SPOON'S ICE CREAM PARLOR—THREE-SHOT—WILLA, ICEY, WALT

We shoot over ICEY as WILLA opens the door to leave. WILLA is in outdoor clothes and is not dressed for work in the parlor.

WILLA: That boy's as stubborn and mulish as a sheep!

ICEY: It's a *shame*!

WILLA'S face shines like one possessed.

WILLA: Goodnight.

WALT enters shot, his back to us.

ICEY: Goodnight, honey.

As WILLA starts away we DOLLY THROUGH DOOR and PAN her to deserted street. There is a river mist.

TWO-SHOT—WALT AND ICEY
WALT is ill at ease.

RESUME SHOT ON WILLA

ICEY: (o.s. calling) Plan on a longer visit next time.

WALT: (o.s.) You don't hardly get settled till you're frettin' to git home again.

Again WILLA pauses and turns.

WILLA: (with sweet radiance. To Walt) I'm needed to keep peace and harmony between them. (to Icey) It's my burden and I'm proud of it, Icey!

She walks off into the mist.   LAP DISSOLVE TO

EXT. HARPER HOME—NIGHT—MEDIUM SHOT—LIGHTED PAR-
LOR WINDOW; REST OF HOUSE DARK
Distant muffled sound of river-boat whistle.

PEARL: (o.s.) John's bad.

WILLA enters, her back to us; she stops.

PREACHER: (o.s.) Yes; John's bad.

PEARL: Tell me another secret about my Dad.

CLOSE SHOT—WILLA
She smiles benignly.

PREACHER: (o.s.) *O* no! *Your* turn!

PEARL: All right.

PREACHER: Where's the money hid.

WILLA keeps smiling.

PEARL: John's bad.

PREACHER: Where's the money hid? Tell me, you little wretch, or I'll tear your arm off!

Still smiling, shaking her head as in disbelief, WILLA makes for house as PEARL screams.

INT. HARPER HALLWAY—TWO-SHOT—WILLA AND PREACHER
Narrow screen, same set-up as in earlier corridor scene, PREACHER and WILLA. Their eyes meet. Pause.

PREACHER: (stunned) I didn't expect you home so soon.

CLOSE SHOT—WILLA
She still smiles; her eyes turn to sound of PEARL'S sobbing.

TWO SHOT—AS BEFORE

PREACHER stands still; WILLA in BACKGROUND opens closet door where PEARL sobs.   CUT TO

TWO-SHOT—WALT AND ICEY
. . . washing and drying glasses. ICEY is washing briskly, WALT is drying slowly.

WALT: Icey, I'm worried about Willa.

ICEY: How do you mean?

WALT: I'm figurin' how I can say it so's you won't get mad.

ICEY: Say *what*, Walt Spoon!

WALT: There's somethin' wrong about it, Mother.

ICEY: About *what*!

WALT: About Mr. Powell. All of it!

ICEY: Walt!

WALT: Now, Mother, a body can't help their feelin's.

ICEY: May the Lord have mercy on you, Walt Spoon!

WALT: Mother, I only—   CUT TO

INT. WILLA'S AND PREACHER'S BEDROOM—FULL SHOT—WILLA ON BED—PREACHER IN BACKGROUND

WILLA lies in profile on the bed along the bottom of the frame. A prim, old woman's nightdress makes her look like a child. Her hands are clasped. PREACHER, fully dressed, stands at the window, which is in BACKGROUND towards foot of bed. His coat, hung over a chair, is in silhouette. River mist outside window halated by exterior gas-lamp. The window shade is up. She is mumbling in prayer. She stops.

PREACHER: (his back still turned) Are you through praying?

WILLA: I'm through, Harry.

He turns. WILLA is calm and immobile with the ecstasy of a martyr.

PREACHER: You were listening outside the parlor window.

WILLA: It's not in the river, is it Harry?

PREACHER: *Answer me!*

WILLA: Ben never told you he throwed it in the river? Did he?

PREACHER hits her across the mouth. A pause.

WILLA: (continues, unruffled) Then the children know where it is hid? John knows? Is that it? (a pause) Then it's still here, somewhere amongst us, tainting us?

CLOSE SHOT—PREACHER, LISTENING FOR A VOICE

RESUME TWO-SHOT

WILLA: So you must have known it all along, Harry.

CLOSE SHOT—PREACHER, LISTENING

After a moment, the river boat whistle blows, nearer. HOLD CLOSE-UP a moment after whistle.

CLOSE DOWN-SHOT—WILLA, SAINT-LIKE

WILLA: But that ain't why you married me, Harry. I know that much. It couldn't be that because the Lord just wouldn't let it.

RESUME TWO-SHOT—WILLA

WILLA: He made you marry me so's you could show me the Way and the Life and the Salvation of my soul! Ain't that so, Harry?

CLOSE SHOT—PREACHER

He has heard the VOICE and starts to move out of CLOSE SHOT.

RESUME TWO-SHOT

He has moved over to the coat on back of chair.

CLOSE SHOT—COAT

His hand goes into the pocket and brings the knife out. (It is the same coat, and pocket, as in the wedding-night scene.)

RESUME TWO-SHOT

WILLA: So you might say it was the money that brung us together.

He pulls down the blind. He moves toward the bed.

WILLA: The rest of it don't matter, Harry.

INSERT—PREACHER'S HAND AND KNIFE

It clicks open.

RESUME TWO-SHOT

As he raises his arm to strike:

HEAD CLOSE-UP—WILLA

. . . with foolish, ecstatic eyes.

WILLA: Bless us all!   DISSOLVE TO

INT. CHILDREN'S BEDROOM—FULL SHOT—THE SHADOWS ON THE WALL

They are shaped as in earlier scene, but altered by mist. Set-up as in earlier scene. Over them we hear the whinny-and-catch and the failure of the Ford being cranked; once; then again: then JOHN's shadow moves on the wall and on a third cranking which engages the engine, we PAN TO WINDOW, shooting over JOHN, who peers out, into blind mist. The gears of the car shift; the car moves away, unseen; its sounds diminish slowly, and die. A moment of silence; then JOHN turns and we PAN him to the bed. He gets in beside PEARL, who is asleep, and, as we TIGHTEN IN CLOSE, puts his hand across the face of the doll.   DISSOLVE TO

HEAD CLOSE-UP—ICEY

An ominous expression. She looks sharp to WALT, beckoning secretly; through rear screen door of kitchen, onto porch.

ICEY: (loud whisper) Walt! Come quick!

FULL FIGURE SHOT—WALT

He is scrubbing out an ice cream container on the back porch. He looks up and moves towards her.

WALT: (natural voice) What's wrong, Mother?

MEDIUM CLOSE—ICEY, THEN WALT

ICEY: (whisper) *Sshhh!* He's in there.

WALT ENTERS SHOT with pipe.

WALT: Who?

ICEY: (whisper) Mr. Powell! (Walt looks enquiry) Willa has run away!

WALT: I'll be switched! . . .

They enter the kitchen. We hear muffled sounds of sobbing o.s.

MEDIUM CLOSE TWO-SHOT

WALT: Just *went?*

ICEY: She took out some time durin' the night,—in that old Model-T—

WALT clucks his tongue.

WALT: Is he hit pretty bad?

ICEY: All to pieces!

WALT moves towards kitchen cabinet.

WALT: There's a little peach brandy—maybe a sip?

ICEY: A man of the Cloth?

MEDIUM CLOSE SHOT—WALT

He pours, snaps it down; weak-defiance.

MEDIUM CLOSE SHOT—ICEY

ICEY: Walt Spoon, that's for sickness in the house!

MEDIUM CLOSE SHOT—WALT

He looks towards o.s. sobbing.

WALT: What can we do, Mother?

TWO-SHOT

ICEY: I thought if you went and talked to him—another man—

MEDIUM SHOT—PREACHER

He sits at a table, his back towards us, mumbling over his Bible.

TWO-SHOT—WALT, ICEY BEHIND HIM, ENTERING THROUGH DOOR

WALT: Mister Powell?

PREACHER: (suddenly loud) A strange woman is a narrow pit!

ICEY: (a reverent whisper) Amen! Amen!

PREACHER: She lieth in wait as for a prey. And increaseth the transgressors among men.

He closes his Bible and turns to them with weepy eyes and a brave little smile.

PREACHER: My dear, dear friends! Whatever would I do without you!

CLOSE SHOT—ICEY

ICEY: (wailing) Mister Powell!

THREE-SHOT—NEW ANGLE

WALT: Is there anythin'—*any*thin' . . . ?

PREACHER: It is my shame—my crown of thorns. And I must wear it bravely.

ICEY: What could have *possessed* that girl!

PREACHER: (simply) Satan.

ICEY: Ah.

WALT sits across from PREACHER. ICEY is at PREACHER's elbow.

WALT: Didn't you have no inkling?

PREACHER: Yes; from the first night.

WALT: The first night?

PREACHER: Our honeymoon.

CLOSE SHOT—WALT

WALT: How's that?

TWO-SHOT—PREACHER AND ICEY

PREACHER: She turned me out of the bed.

ICEY: (with pleasure) *Nnnoooo!!*

CLOSE SHOT—WALT
Filling his pipe.

WALT: *What* do you figure to do?

TWO-SHOT—PREACHER AND ICEY

PREACHER: Do? Why stay and take care of them little kids. Maybe it was never *meant* for a woman like Willa to taint their young lives.

ICEY: (hands clasped; with approval) *Mmmmm!*

CLOSE SHOT—WALT

Dabbing at moisture in the corner of his eye.

WALT: That's mighty brave of you, Reverend.

TWO-SHOT—PREACHER AND ICEY

PREACHER: I reckon it's been ordained this way, Brother Spoon.

CLOSE SHOT—WALT

WALT: Didn't—didn't she leave no word?

TWO-SHOT—PREACHER AND ICEY

PREACHER: A scrawl. On a piece of notepaper on the bureau.

ICEY smiles sideways.

PREACHER: I burned it. (Preacher holds out his hand, stares in disgust, and wipes his palm dramatically on his coat-sleeve) I tore it up and burned it—it stank so strong of hellfire.

ICEY: *Amen.*

PREACHER: The pitcher has went to the well once too often, my friends.

CLOSE SHOT—WALT

WALT: She'll come draggin' her tail back home.

CLOSE SHOT—PREACHER

PREACHER: She'll not be back. I reckon I'd be safe in promisin' you that.

CLOSE SHOT—WALT

WALT: Maybe she's just run off on a spree.

PREACHER'S VOICE: (o.s.) No!

WALT: Well, there's no harm in hopin'.

TWO-SHOT—PREACHER AND ICEY

PREACHER: Ain't no sense in it, neither. I figured somethin' like this was brewin' when she went to bed last night.

ICEY: (all woman) How?

PREACHER: She tarried around the kitchen after I'd gone up, and when I went downstairs to see what was wrong . . .

ICEY: (eagerly) What!

PREACHER: She'd found this fruit jar of dandelion wine (Icey touches him) that the husband—Harper—had hid somewheres in the cellar. (playing his ace) She was drinking.

CLOSE SHOT—ICEY
ICEY is happy to let her mouth fall open and let out a gasp.

CLOSE SHOT—WALT
Sniffling.

THREE-SHOT—PREACHER, ICEY, WALT

PREACHER: I tried to save her.

ICEY: I know you did, Reverend. Oh, I know how you tried!

PREACHER: The devil wins sometimes!

CLOSE SHOT—PREACHER

PREACHER: (eyes upturned) Can't nobody say I didn't do *my* best to save her! DISSOLVE TO

CLOSE UNDERWATER SHOT (Tank)

We PAN, with slowly streaming weeds, and bring in WILLA in close profile; the current, coming from behind her, drifts her long hair across her throat.

MEDIUM SHOT—WILLA AND CAR
She is in profile as before—

CLOSE SHOT—A BAITED HOOK
It descends, and catches on the windshield, and the line tautens; then tugs. We start to follow the line up.

CLOSE SHOT—ABOVE WATER—THE LINE
We continue to follow the line up, and bring in, close, the stern of BEN HARPER'S skiff.

MEDIUM SHOT—UNCLE BIRDIE
He sits back, tugging unconcernedly at the line. Then he leans over to see what's wrong.

CLOSE SHOT—BIRDIE
. . . as he peers over side.

DOWNSHOT—FULL SHOT OF CAR AND WILLA; BIRDIE'S VIEW-POINT

CLOSE SHOT—BIRDIE, HORROR-STRICKEN

MOVING UNDERWATER SHOT—WILLA
We hear PREACHER'S voice o.s., singing:

PREACHER: (o.s.) *Leaning! Leaning! Safe and secure from all alarms!*
Meanwhile we move vertically DOWNWARD TOWARDS HER FACE, serene in death. We may or may not glimpse the gashed throat, through drifting hair.   LAP DISSOLVE TO

EXT. HARPER HOME—FULL SHOT—THE HOUSE AND TREE

PREACHER leans against the tree; he continues singing:

PREACHER: *Leaning! Leaning! Leaning on the Everlasting Arms!* (seductively) Children!

CLOSE MOVING SHOT—PREACHER
We start moving before he does. LOW CAMERA; full figure. We TILT to frame him from the waist downward and follow close behind him. As he leaves the tree and walks along the side of the house; we TILT DOWNWARD and CLOSE IN, to follow only his feet; he steps past a tiny cellar window and we PAN and TIGHTEN IN CLOSE ON IT, into—

CLOSE TWO-SHOT—JOHN AND PEARL
Their noses are flat against the glass; their cheeks touch; their window isn't quite big enough to hold both their heads. It is on the ground; we don't see their chins. They look towards the departed PREACHER.

PREACHER'S VOICE: (o.s.) *Chill-dren?*

PEARL, who is on the side PREACHER has left by, turns her head towards JOHN.

INT. CELLAR—MEDIUM CLOSE TWO-SHOT—JOHN AND PEARL
They are standing on a coal heap, faces at window.

PEARL: John, why do we have to hide?

JOHN has taken charge. He speaks very quietly, but calmly and cheerfully, as to an invalid. He starts down the rustling coal-heap, helping PEARL down.

JOHN: Careful . . .

The following dialogue as they climb down, making as little noise as possible.

We PULL slowly away.

PEARL: Where's Mom?

JOHN: She's gone to Moundsville.

PEARL: To see Dad?

JOHN: Yes, I reckon that's it.

They have achieved the cellar floor.

PREACHER'S VOICE: (more peremptorily outside) Children!

During the following dialogue we hear, o.s., the opening of a door, and PREACHER's footsteps indoors as he crosses floor, climbs stairs, and opens another door.

JOHN: Someone is after us, Pearl.

PEARL: I want to go upstairs. It's cold and spidery down here. I'm hungry.

JOHN: Now listen to me, Pearl. You and me is runnin' off tonight.

PEARL: Why?

JOHN: If we stay here somethin' awful will happen to us.

PEARL: Won't Daddy Powell take care of us?

JOHN: No, that's just it. No.

FULL SHOT—A ROOM UPSTAIRS
PREACHER looks under the bed.

RESUME CELLAR TWO-SHOT—THE CHILDREN

PEARL: Where are we goin', John?

JOHN: Somewheres. I don't know yet.

o.s., PREACHER's footsteps come down stairs; JOHN leads PEARL carefully past a rake, a hoe, and a shelf-prop and they crouch down into—

CLOSE TWO-SHOT—JOHN AND PEARL

. . . beside an apple barrel. PREACHER's footsteps cross kitchen o.s.

PEARL: I'm hungry, John.

JOHN: We'll steal somethin' to eat.

PEARL: It'll spoil our supper.

PREACHER'S VOICE: (o.s.) Pearl?

Both look sharp towards cellar door o.s.

THE CELLAR DOOR—CHILDREN'S VIEWPOINT

The door opens; PREACHER'S head, carrying a candle in holder; a whitewashed wall and stairs are lighted.

PREACHER'S VOICE: I hear you whisperin', children, so I know you're down there. I can feel myself gettin' awful mad, children.

CLOSE TWO-SHOT—THE CHILDREN

PEARL: (whispering) John . . .

JOHN claps his hand over her mouth.

CELLAR DOOR

PREACHER'S VOICE: My patience has run out, children. I'm comin' to find you now.

He clop-clops nearly to the bottom of the stairs. ICEY'S voice cuts cheerfully across his descent.

ICEY: (calling o.s.) Yoo-Hooooo! Mis-ter Paow-welll!

He goes up the stairs and vanishes. Light on wall through open door to kitchen.

ICEY'S VOICE: Just a little hot supper I fixed for you and the children.

PREACHER'S VOICE: Bless you, bless you!

ICEY'S VOICE: And how are the children?

PREACHER'S VOICE: They're down there playin' games in the cellar and they won't mind me when I call 'em. I'm at my wit's end, Miz Spoon.

ICEY clucks her tongue o.s.

ICEY'S VOICE: (yelling) John: Pearl:

She appears at head of stairs. Her voice crackles with authority.

ICEY: John! Pearl! Shake a leg! (she claps her hands sharply)

FULL SHOT—THE KITCHEN—OVER ICEY

ICEY: (continuing) I won't have you worryin' poor Mister Powell another minute!

A short pause; then the children, covered with coal-dust, emerge into the light and climb the stairs. JOHN's head is hung in defeat. As they enter the kitchen we PULL BACK.

ICEY: Just *look* at you! Dust and filth from top to toe!

GROUP SHOT—THE CHILDREN, OVER PREACHER AND ICEY

ICEY: Want me to take 'em up and wash 'em good?

PREACHER: Thank you, no. Thank you, dear Icey. I'll tend to them. Thank you.

ICEY pats JOHN's head.

CLOSE SHOT—JOHN

ICEY'S VOICE: Don't be too hard on 'em, Reverend. Poor motherless children.

JOHN looks to PEARL and we PAN HER IN as PREACHER's hand named LOVE moves through her locks. We PAN with PREACHER and ICEY as they move towards the door.

ICEY: Remember now Mister Powell, don't be afraid to call on us. Good night.

CLOSE SHOT—JOHN
He watches ICEY leave, o.s.

PREACHER: (o.s.) Good night Miz Spoon, and thank you again.

FULL SHOT—PREACHER AND ICEY
ICEY goes away along path outside. PREACHER, his back to us, watches her a moment, then turns.

PREACHER: Weren't you afraid, my little lambs, down there in all that dark?

HEAD CLOSE-UP—JOHN
Wondering what to do next.   LAP DISSOLVE TO

CLOSE SHOT—BIRDIE, OVER BESS'S PICTURE
We begin with HEAD CLOSE-UP of BIRDIE as he rocks, and PULL BACK
He is rocking; and drunk. A bottle stands beside the picture. He turns and speaks to the picture.

BIRDIE: They'll think it was me! They'll think it was old Uncle Birdie!

CLOSE SHOT—BIRDIE—NEW ANGLE

His hands grip the edge of the chest on either side of the picture, which we now see.

BIRDIE: If you'd o' seen it, Bess! I'm drunk as a lord and I know it, but . . .

INSERT—BESS'S PICTURE

BIRDIE'S VOICE: (o.s. continuing) Sweet Heaven, if you'd o' seen it!

RESUME PREVIOUS SHOT

BIRDIE picks up the bottle. His hand and the liquor tremble.

BIRDIE: (continuing) Down there in the deep place . . . her hair wavin' lazy and soft like meadow grass under flood waters and that slit in her throat just like she had an extry mouth.

INSERT BESS'S PICTURE

BIRDIE'S VOICE: (o.s.) And there ain't a mortal human I can tell but you . . .

RESUME PREVIOUS SHOT

BIRDIE: (continuing) . . . Bess, for if I go to the Law they'll hang it on to me.

The bottle falls from his hand onto its side on the edge of the chest.

CLOSE SHOT—BIRDIE—NEW ANGLE

The reverse angle of the opening shot. BIRDIE rocks heavily; liquor gurgles from bottle to floor.

BIRDIE: Sweet Heaven save poor old Uncle Birdie!

LAP DISSOLVE TO

MEDIUM THREE-SHOT—PREACHER, JOHN, PEARL

PREACHER sits at head of table. JOHN stands to PREACHER'S right, around corner of table; he remains expressionless and immobile, until he speaks. PEARL stands to JOHN'S right, hugging the DOLL. The table is loaded with good food.

PREACHER, well-fed and at leisure, dabs his mouth delicately with his napkin, folds it, puts it in a ring, and folds his hands. He waits.

PEARL: (at last) I'm hungry.

PREACHER: Why, sure. And there's fried chicken and candied sweets and cornsticks and apple cobbler!

PEARL: Can I have my supper please?

PREACHER: Naturally.

PEARL: Can I have milk too?

PREACHER: Yes. But first of all we'll have a little talk.

PEARL frowns and puts her finger in her mouth; she remembers he twisted her arm.

PREACHER: (softly) About our secrets.

PEARL: No.

PREACHER: Why, pray tell?

PEARL: Because John said I mustn't.

THREE-SHOT REVERSE—PREACHER, OVER NECKS OF CHILDREN
He slaps the table; his eyes crackle.

PREACHER: NEVER—MIND—WHAT—JOHN—SAID!

PEARL starts to snivel.

PREACHER: John is a meddler. Stop sniveling. Looky here a minute!

He brings out the knife.

PREACHER: Know what this is?

PEARL shakes her head for *no*.

PREACHER: Want to see something cute? Looky now!

He touches the spring; the blade flicks open.

PREACHER: How *about* that! This is what I use on meddlers.

He lays the open knife on the table.

PREACHER: John might be a meddler.

THREE-SHOT—THE CHILDREN, OVER PREACHER
PEARL thinks the knife is a toy and crosses behind JOHN to pick it up.

PREACHER: NO—*no*, my lamb. Don't touch it! Now don't touch my knife! That makes me mad. Very, very mad.

She hugs the DOLL and he puts the hand named LOVE on her curls.

PREACHER: Just tell me now; where's the money hid?

PEARL: (affectionately) But I swore. I promised John I wouldn't tell.

CLOSE SHOT—PREACHER

PREACHER: JOHN—DOESN'T—MATTER! Can't I get that through your head, you poor, silly, disgusting little wretch!

HEAD CLOSE-UP—PEARL

Her mouth quivers; a large tear brims in her eyes.

CLOSE SHOT—PREACHER

PREACHER: There now! You made me lose my temper!

THREE-SHOT—CHILDREN, OVER PREACHER

PREACHER: I'm sorry! I'm real sorry!

PEARL sniffles and wipes her eyes with her free fist.

PREACHER: (in a caressing tone) Now! Where's it hid, honey?

JOHN: (suddenly and lightly) I'll tell.

THREE-SHOT—PREACHER, OVER NAPES OF CHILDREN

PREACHER: (lightly) I thought I told you to keep your mouth shut—

JOHN: (light and quick) NO,—it ain't fair to make Pearl tell when she swore she wouldn't. I'll tell.

PREACHER'S EYES CRINKLE and he turns to PEARL, smiling brightly.

PREACHER: (chuckling) Well I declare! Sometimes I think poor John will make it to heaven yet!

His eyes snap back to JOHN and his voice is like a whip.

PREACHER: All right boy: where's the money?

HEAD CLOSE-UP—JOHN

JOHN: In the cellar. Buried under a stone in the floor.

THREE-SHOT—PREACHER OVER CHILDREN

He closes and pockets the knife. His eyes never leave JOHN'S.

PREACHER: It'll go hard, boy, if I find you're lyin'.

THREE-SHOT—PREACHER OVER CHILDREN
PEARL gapes up at JOHN as he speaks.

JOHN: I ain't lyin'. Go look for yourself.

CLOSE SHOT—PREACHER
. . . as he gets up, cellar door in BACKGROUND.

PREACHER: All right . . . (he turns towards the door; then glances around) Come along.

HEAD CLOSE-UP—JOHN

JOHN: What?

THREE-SHOT—PREACHER, OVER CHILDREN

PREACHER: Go ahead of me—the both of you.

They cross him, towards the door.

FULL SHOT—THE CELLAR STEPS—FROM THE BOTTOM
The CHILDREN precede PREACHER, who carries a candle in holder. PEARL is gaping at JOHN'S lie. JOHN is looking left and right, casing the joint.

PREACHER: (continuing) You don't reckon I'd leave you.

JOHN: (with forced lightness) Don't you believe me?

PREACHER: (sardonically) Why sure, boy, sure.

Now they are at bottom of stairs. JOHN sees PEARL'S expression and takes her hand.

PREACHER: Now where, boy? Mind; no tricks. I can't abide liars.

JOHN: Yonder.

He squeezes PEARL'S hand harder, and points.

FULL SHOT—NEW ANGLE-OVER THE THREE
JOHN points out a place beneath a shelf laden with Mason jars; it is at the most distant part of the cellar from the stairs.

PREACHER starts toward it, leaving them at foot of stairs, then turns, catching JOHN'S ruse.

PREACHER: (sardonic) O no you don't!

He shepherds them ahead of him.

THREE-SHOT—NEW ANGLE
They arrive beneath the shelf.

PREACHER: Now: Where?

JOHN: (lying magnificently, meeting Preacher's eyes) Under the stone in the floor.

PREACHER sets the candle on a barrel near the shelf-prop and sinks to his knees below shot as PEARL gapes at JOHN and JOHN looks stony. She seems about to speak.

FLASH INSERT—JOHN SQUEEZES PEARL'S HAND HARD

CLOSE SHOT—PREACHER, FEATURING FLOOR
His hands sweep dust and expose concrete. He straightens on his knees and turns to the children in close BACKGROUND.

HEAD CLOSE-UP—PREACHER
. . . as he turns.

PREACHER: This is concrete.

CLOSE TWO-SHOT—THE CHILDREN
A moment's silence.

PEARL: John made a Sin. John told a lie.

THREE-SHOT—FAVORING PREACHER
PREACHER gets slowly to his feet and puts on his "listening" look. His sincerity is beyond doubt.

PREACHER: The Lord's a-talkin' to me now. He's a-sayin', "a liar is an abomination before mine eyes."

He takes his knife out, and springs it open.

CLOSE TWO-SHOT—FAVORING JOHN

PREACHER: Speak, boy: Where's it hid? (the knife pricks the flesh under John's ear) Speak, before I cut your throat and leave you to drip like a hog hung up in butcherin' time!

CLOSE SHOT—PEARL
She starts to sob.

CLOSE TWO-SHOT—JOHN AND PREACHER

JOHN: Pearl, shut up! Pearl, you swore!

PREACHER: You could save him, little bird.

HEAD CLOSE-UP—PEARL

PEARL: (crying) *Inside my doll! Inside my doll!*

TWO-SHOT—JOHN AND PREACHER, FAVORING PREACHER

PREACHER is astounded. His hands fall away from JOHN. He leans back against the wall and talks through laughter.

PREACHER: In the doll! Why sure! Sure!

HEAD CLOSE-UP—JOHN
His eyes are all over the place.

PREACHER'S VOICE: (o.s.) The last place anyone would look!

THREE-SHOT—PREACHER, JOHN, PEARL

PREACHER makes a lunge across JOHN for the doll; JOHN ducking under his arm, pulls PEARL forward with his left hand; he turns backwards and with his free hand, in one movement, knocks over the candle and pulls out the support on the shelf.

CLOSE SHOT—PREACHER
Jars shower over him; one crowns him and breaks, shedding guck, which he wipes from his eyes.

TWO-SHOT—THE CHILDREN
They start up the stairs.

FULL SHOT—PREACHER
He makes one step forward, steps on a rolling jar, and falls.

TWO-SHOT—THE CHILDREN
They are near the top of the stairs. We hear PREACHER below them. JOHN slips and they nearly fall backward. As JOHN recovers, PREACHER enters the shot, his back to us. The children get through the open door as PREACHER reaches top. JOHN slams the door, catching PREACHER's hand. PREACHER screams. JOHN's astonished eyes peer through the crack in the door; the door loosens; PREACHER yanks his hand loose and sucks it, groaning; the door slams to; the bolt is shot home.

HEAD CLOSE-UP—PREACHER
. . . over sound of slamming bolt. He snarls like the Big Bad Wolf.
All the above happens at once.

INT. KITCHEN—CLOSE TWO-SHOT—JOHN AND PEARL, BY DOOR
PEARL, dangling her doll, cries. JOHN panting, leans against wall by door. JOHN is wondering what to do now. Pause.

PREACHER'S VOICE: (o.s., sweetly) Chilll-dren?

PREACHER'S VOICE: (continuing) The only reason I wanted that money is so's you could have it.

JOHN: (to himself; panting) The river. That's the only where! Uncle Birdie Steptoe!

PREACHER'S VOICE: (cooing) Puhr-urrl? Want your Mommy back? (Pearl hugs her doll) Want me to get her right now?

PEARL: (sharply) John?

JOHN: Hush, Pearl. Come on.
They fly out of the house.

PREACHER'S VOICE: (bellowing, as they go) OPEN THAT DOOR, YOU SPAWN OF THE DEVIL'S OWN STRUMPET!

FRAMING SHOT—EXT. THE HARPER HOUSE
A pretty, pastoral shot of the house in light mist, as they run across and leave the shot. Before they disappear, we hear PREACHER'S fists hammering against the door. We stay on the house at leisure; we hear him lunging, shoulder to door; we begin to hear squeaking of hinges and splintering of wood.

FULL CIRCLE SHOT—FRAMING BIRDIE'S WHARF-BOAT
An ultra romantic image of shelter and peace. Frogs or river noises o.s., then the rattle of running footsteps. The children center, their backs to us, sprinting towards the boat. Light mist as in previous shot.

JOHN: (calling) Uncle Birdie! Uncle Birdie!

INT. BIRDIE'S BOAT—GROUP SHOT—BIRDIE AND CHILDREN
We shoot over BESS'S turned photograph and over BIRDIE, close, passed out in his rocker. The children run through open door in BACKGROUND and JOHN runs up to BIRDIE.

JOHN: Uncle Birdie!

CLOSE SHOT—BIRDIE

BIRDIE: (gesturing feebly) Don't!

CLOSE TWO-SHOT—NEW ANGLE—BIRDIE, OVER JOHN

JOHN: Hide us Uncle Birdie! He's a-comin' with his knife!

He grabs BIRDIE'S shoulder; BIRDIE half-rises, and falls face down on floor.

CLOSE TWO-SHOT—BIRDIE ON FLOOR, OVER JOHN

JOHN: It's me! John Harper and Pearl! You said to come a-runnin' if we needed you!

BIRDIE rears on one elbow and looks up at him.

BIRDIE: (in friendly recognition) Johnny!

He falls face down again.

CLOSE TWO-SHOT—NEW ANGLE—FAVORING JOHN

JOHN grabs BIRDIE by one ear, turning his face up.

JOHN: Uncle—Birdie! Oh—please! *Please wake up!*

CLOSE TWO-SHOT—FAVORING BIRDIE
He looks up earnestly at JOHN.

BIRDIE: I never done it, boy. Sweet Heaven I never done such a terrible thing! I'll swear on the Book to it, boy! I never done it! I never!

CLOSE SHOT—JOHN
He is lost; and he becomes a man.

BIRDIE'S VOICE: (o.s.) Lord save poor old Uncle Birdie Steptoe that never hurt a fly! (he snores, softly)

JOHN: (quiet) There's still the river.—The skiff is down by the willows.

He masterfully takes PEARL by the hand and leads her into the night.

LONG SHOT—THE CHILDREN
We shoot from the river. They struggle through the sumac and pokeberry weeds at edge of river, towards skiff, whose prow, tethered to willow, we see throughout this un-moving shot, at our extreme right. When they come opposite skiff—which is a few yards out from shore—   WE CUT TO

TWO-SHOT—THE CHILDREN
PEARL, frankly bored, dangling her doll, is yawning. JOHN, as he finishes undoing rope from a willow root, looks up and around, checking on pursuit. His eyes fix.

FULL SHOT—PREACHER'S SHADOW

On the bank above, it is huge in the mist. Same camera position as foregoing; new angle.

TWO-SHOT—THE CHILDREN
BACK view: skiff in BACKGROUND. Same camera position; new angle.

JOHN: (whispering) Please be quiet—Oh *please*, Pearl!

PEARL: (natural voice) John, where are we g—

JOHN: Hush.

FULL SHOT—SHADOW, THEN PREACHER
Same position and angle as before.

PREACHER'S own figure advances to supplant his shadow. He peers downward, his open knife catching the light.

PREACHER: (businesslike) Children?

He starts slashing his way down through the brush-filth.

FULL SHOT—THE CHILDREN
Same camera position as before. They are floundering through mud, half-way to the skiff.

FULL SHOT—PREACHER
Same position and angle as in previous shot of him. He is half-way down the bank. With his knife, he hacks at an entangling vine.

FULL SHOT—THE CHILDREN
Position and angle as before. They reach the skiff. Hacking sounds o.s.

JOHN: Get in the skiff, Pearl, goodness, goodness, *hurry!*

PEARL: (hesitant) That's *Daddy!*

He picks her up and throws her into the skiff.

CLOSE SHOT—PEARL AND DOLL
. . . as they land, sprawling, in bottom of skiff among fish-heads and bait cans. JOHN gets in after them.

FULL SHOT—PREACHER—CHILDREN'S VIEWPOINT
He tears free of brush to edge of river, knife glittering.

CLOSE SHOT—JOHN
With his oar, he tries to push the boat free of mud.

FULL SHOT—PREACHER—CHILDREN'S VIEWPOINT

He wades towards them, knee-deep in mud.

CLOSE SHOT—JOHN
He is shoving at the oar even more desperately.

INSERT—JOHN'S HANDS
Straining.

FULL SHOT—PREACHER—CHILDREN'S VIEWPOINT
He flounders deeper and more heavily through the mud; much closer.

CLOSE SHOT—JOHN
He pushes the boat free of mud.

CLOSE SHOT—PREACHER—CHILDREN'S VIEWPOINT
He hurries much closer through shallow water. Prow of boat in FOREGROUND.

PREACHER: *Wait*, you little whelps! *Wait!*

Another step forward and he does a pratt-fall and makes a splash.

CLOSE SHOT—JOHN—PEARL IN BACKGROUND
He is trying to feather the boat out to where the current will catch it. In panic and haste he is clumsy.

JOHN: Why can't I do it when I know *how* to do it!

FULL SHOT—PREACHER
. . . as he gets up, at edge of mud.

PREACHER: *Wait! Wait! I'll slit your guts!*

FULL DOWN-SHOT—THE SKIFF, THEN PREACHER
The current catches it and spins it round like a leaf. JOHN'S efforts with the oars are useless. PREACHER enters, wading fast. His hands are within an inch of reaching the helpless skiff; capriciously the current takes it downstream.

TWO-SHOT—JOHN AND PEARL
The skiff is taken steadily by the current. PEARL sits up, doll in arms. JOHN is almost asleep with exhaustion.

FULL SHOT—THE SKIFF, OVER PREACHER
It is well away from him and getting smaller. Waist-deep, he wades a couple of steps after it, then just looks.

HEAD CLOSE-UP—PREACHER

He begins a steady, rhythmical, animal scream of outrage and loss.

LONG SHOT—THE RIVER AND LANDSCAPE, FEATURING STAR-LIGHT; AND THE DRIFTING BOAT—PEARL IN STERN

TWO-SHOT—THE CHILDREN—FRONT ON
JOHN is asleep. PEARL sits sleepily whispering to her doll.

PEARL: Once upon a time there was a pretty fly, and he had a wife, this pretty fly. . . .

MEDIUM LONG SHOT—THE DRIFTING BOAT THROUGH FIRE-FLIES

PEARL'S VOICE: (o.s.) . . . and one day she flew away, and then one night his two pretty fly children . . .

SPECIAL SHOT—THE MOVING SKIFF, THROUGH DEW-JEWELED SPIDER-WEB

PEARL'S VOICE: (o.s., continuing) . . . flew away too, into the sky, into the moon . . .

SPECIAL SHOT—A FROG, AND SKIFF
A big frog is profiled; the skiff drifts by in distance; the frog twangs out a bass-note.   DISSOLVE TO

INSERT—A PICTURE POSTCARD— A COUNTY COURTHOUSE
As the card is turned to the handwritten side we   CUT TO

CLOSE TWO-SHOT—WALT AND ICEY

WALT: (reading aloud) Dear Walt and Icey: I bet you been worried and gave us up for lost. Took the kids down here with me for a visit to my sister Elsie's farm. Thot a little change of scenery would do us all a world of good after so much trubble and heartache. At least the kids will git a plenty of good home cooking. Your devoted Harry Powell

ICEY: Now ain't you relieved, Walt?

WALT: Sure, but you was worried too, Mother; takin' off with never a word of goodbye. I even got to figurin' them gypsies busted in and done off with all three of 'em.

ICEY: You and your gypsies! They been gone a week!

WALT: Not before one of 'em knifed a farmer and stole his horse. Never caught the gypsies nor the horse.

                              LAP DISSOLVE TO

DESCENDING HELICOPTER SHOT—THE RIVER—DAY
A man is going along a river lane on horseback.
It is PREACHER; he walks the horse away from us.

DISSOLVE TO

DESCENDING HELICOPTER SHOT—ANOTHER BEND OF THE RIVER
We descend to a poor riverside farmhouse; JOHN and PEARL tether a boat in front of it.

GROUP SHOT (FROM GROUND) THREE HOMELESS CHILDREN, OVER JOHN AND PEARL
They are eating hot boiled potatoes. A glance at JOHN and PEARL, and they turn away towards lane in BACKGROUND. JOHN and PEARL proceed towards the house.

MEDIUM SHOT—JOHN, PEARL, WOMAN, THROUGH DOOR
We shoot from within open door of kitchen. JOHN and PEARL advance to edge of porch. A TIRED FARM WOMAN stands by door, within. We shoot over her.

TIRED FARM WOMAN: Hungry, I s'pose. Well, I'll see if there's any *more* potatoes to spare. Where's *your* folks?

JOHN: Ain't got none.

Woman leaves shot briefly. (we HOLD ON CHILDREN) She re-enters and goes to them with a bowl of steaming potatoes. They take hands-ful, and make to eat.

TIRED FARM WOMAN: Go 'way; go 'way.

They turn away and walk towards boat. She looks after them.

TIRED FARM WOMAN: Such times, when youngins run the roads!

She leaves the SHOT. We frame them briefly, walking away, then;

DISSOLVE TO

CLOSE SHOT—A PLACARD—NIGHT
It is lit by firelight. It reads:

PEACH-PICKERS WANTED
WEEKLY HIRE

PREACHER'S VOICE: (o.s.) An ungrateful child is an abomination . . .

LAP DISSOLVE TO

GROUP SHOT—PREACHER AND MEN

PREACHER stands behind the flames; in FOREGROUND an OLD MAN sits profiled on a box. Other workers, all men, sit around fire.

PREACHER: (continuing) . . . before the eyes of God. The world is fast going to damnation because of impudent young-ins a-flyin' in the face of Age.

Short silence, as the other men look at PREACHER without liking. Then the old man spits into the fire.

CLOSE SHOT—THE FLAMES
A spurt of steam as spit strikes.

CLOSE SHOT—A HOOT OWL
. . . hooting. LAP DISSOLVE TO

CLOSE SHOT—A TURTLE—NOONDAY
He comes down to water.

JOHN'S VOICE: (o.s.) They make *soup* out of them . . .

LONG SHOT—THE CHILDREN IN PASSING SKIFF
Full landscape in BACKGROUND.

JOHN: (continuing) . . . but I wouldn't know how to go about gettin' him open. LAP DISSOLVE TO

LONG SHOT—CHILDREN AND SKIFF, OVER RABBITS IN GRASS
We shoot over two sitting rabbits as they watch, their ears up. The skiff passes. PEARL plays with doll. JOHN unsnarls line.
LAP DISSOLVE TO

FULL SHOT—THE CHILDREN AND SKIFF, FRAMED BY WILLOWS —TWILIGHT
The skiff passes. Baa-ing of sheep o.s.

MOVING SHOT—FROM RIVER—A SHEEP
The sheep bleats. We PAN in a big barn near the river, then a lighted house; willows along shore.

FULL SHOT—THE SKIFF—FROM THE BANK

JOHN re-sets his oar. They angle towards us for the shore.

JOHN: We're gonna spend a night on land.

UP-SHOT—THE CHILDREN, OVER THE MOORED SKIFF
. . . they reach top of the bank. Corner of barn and lighted window in BACKGROUND. Sounds of mouth-organ and girl singing o.s.

FULL SHOT—A LIGHTED WINDOW, THE SHADE DRAWN
A wire bird-cage hangs close to the shade, silhouetted. On the perch, a canary. Lullaby and mouth-organ continue o.s. After a moment the CHILDREN enter, backs to us, and stop, looking.

CLOSE TWO-SHOT—THE CHILDREN
Window-light on faces, song over. A moment.

PEARL: Are *we* goin' home, John?

JOHN: *Ssh . . .*

He turns, her hand in his. We PAN as they tiptoe towards the big, open door of barn; big open hayloft window above.

INT. ROOM—LOW TRACKING SHOT—THE CHILDREN
As they walk down aisle of barn we shoot them past bellies and legs of row of cows. Sounds of munching and soft lowing o.s. JOHN helps PEARL up a little ladder to the hayloft.

MEDIUM SHOT—THE CHILDREN, WINDOW—TWILIGHT
. . . as the CHILDREN bed down in hay, only legs visible, protruding into frame of window, which frames a middle-distant white lane beyond house, and a landscape. Whippoorwill o.s. A DARKENING OF LIGHT.   LAP DISSOLVE TO

SAME SET-UP
The full moon is half-risen. Whippoorwill o.s.
                                          LAP DISSOLVE TO

SAME SET-UP
The moon is well above the horizon. Whippoorwill o.s.
                                          LAP DISSOLVE TO

SAME SET-UP
The moon is still higher. A pause; the whippoorwill stops in mid-phrase. Brief pause; then John sits up into silhouette.

CLOSE SHOT—JOHN
He listens intently. We hear nothing. His eyes alter. We hear, distantly

PREACHER'S VOICE: (o.s., singing) *Leaning, Leaning . . .*
At various distances o.s., we hear dogs barking at the sound of the singing.

PREACHER'S VOICE: (continuing; louder) . . . *safe and secure from all alarms;*

The dog from the farm rushes braying to his gate. Other dogs continue o.s. PREACHER appears, astride his walking horse, singing.

PREACHER: *Leaning . . .*

CLOSE SHOT—JOHN
Watching; dread and despair. Sounds go.

PREACHER: (o.s.) *Leaning; Leaning on the Everlasting Arms.*

FULL SHOT—PREACHER
He approaches and crosses center screen, continuing the hymn. (We do not PAN with him; he crosses the frame of the great window.)

CLOSE SHOT—JOHN
Eyes following PREACHER. PREACHER and dogs continue o.s.

JOHN: (to himself) Don't you *never* sleep?

FULL SHOT—PREACHER
He vanishes beyond trees, his singing more distant. Dogs continue.

CLOSE SHOT—JOHN AND PEARL—NEW ANGLE
He wakes her. PREACHER's singing o.s.

JOHN: (scared whisper) Pearl, wake up! Come on, Pearl!

FULL SHOT—PREACHER
He vanishes; scuttling of children in hay, o.s.; dogs quiet; his song dies. Brief silence. The whippoorwill resumes.

MEDIUM LONG SHOT—THE CHILDREN, NEAR BARN
Hand in hand, they hurry out of barn and, as we PAN, along its side, towards River, o.s. Whippoorwill o.s.

FULL SHOT—A BRIGHT FULL MOON
The whippoorwill's singing continues o.s.

FULL SHOT—CHILDREN AND SKIFF

JOHN steers through turbulent, moonlit water. Whippoorwill continues. Low moon.

CLOSE SHOT—A FOX, BARKING

CLOSE DOWN-SHOT—CHILDREN ASLEEP IN SKIFF (TANK)

Blank, calm water; the skiff enters and passes full length below us, the CHILDREN asleep in it; blank water again; again the fox barks.

MEDIUM SHOT—THE SKIFF, DRIFTING SHOT THROUGH RIVER-SIDE GRASS
Crickets o.s. The skiff nears a sand-bar.

INSERT—THE PROW, GROUNDING
The prow softly grates against sand.

MEDIUM SHOT—THE GROUNDED SKIFF, AGAIN THROUGH GRASS
Crickets fainter. TILTING UPWARD.   LAP DISSOLVE TO

FULL SHOT—THE STARLIT SKY   LAP DISSOLVE TO

FULL SHOT—RIVER LANDSCAPE—SUNRISE
Distant; medium; the near; roosters crow o.s.

CLOSE SHOT—JOHN WAKING
He looks to PEARL o.s.

FULL SHOT—PEARL, THEN RACHEL, OVER JOHN
PEARL is picking daisies. A fence up beyond her. Beyond the fence, a woman, RACHEL COOPER, appears. She carries a berry-basket on her arm. JOHN scrambles up, grabs an oar, and holds it defensively. PEARL freezes.

RACHEL: (loud) You two youngsters get up here to me this instant!

TWO-SHOT—JOHN AND PEARL—RACHEL'S ANGLE

RACHEL: (o.s.) Mind me now!

JOHN lowers the oar at the female authority in her voice.

RACHEL: (o.s.) Now git on up to my house.

They hesitate.

THREE-SHOT—OVER JOHN

RACHEL: I'll git me a willow switch.

They still hesitate. She breaks off a switch and comes for them, squishing through the mud. She surrounds them and drives them like geese up the bank.

LOW FULL SHOT—THE THREE, FROM SIDE

They move across the meadow like a nursery frieze. She tweaks with her switch. As she goes near PEARL'S calves, JOHN turns.

JOHN: Don't you hurt *her*!

RACHEL: Hurt her *nothin'*! *Wash* her's more like it! (hand to mouth, yelling) Ruby!

FULL SHOT—A TOMATO PATCH

Three crouching figures pick tomatoes beyond a low white fence; Rachel's house in background. RUBY, thirteen, pops her head up like a rifle-target.

RACHEL: (o.s.) Clary!

Clary, eleven, pops up.

RACHEL: (o.s.) Mary!

Mary, four, pops up.

THE GIRLS: (in chorus) Yes Miz Cooper!

GROUP SHOT—RACHEL AND HARPERS, MOVING TOWARDS FENCE

She has JOHN and PEARL by their napes.

RACHEL: Bring yer baskets.

The three girls enter, their backs to us, carrying baskets of tomatoes.

GROUP SHOT—THE GIRLS, OVER RACHEL AND HARPER CHILDREN

She holds JOHN and PEARL very firmly, inspecting baskets, across gate of fence.

RACHEL: Nicely picked, Clary. Mary; put the big ones on top. Ruby, most o' them ain't fit to go to market. Put them baskets down. Ruby, fetch the washtub and put it by the pump. Mary, Clary, fetch me a bar o' laundry soap and the scrub brush.

GIRLS: (in chorus) Yes Miz Cooper!

They hurry off.

RACHEL: Come on, now; up to the house.

She opens the gate, pushes the Harper children through, shuts the gate, and walks between them, her back to us. The children hesitate. She turns to them and stops.

THREE-SHOT—THE CHILDREN, OVER RACHEL
She looks them up and down. If we saw her face, her lips would be pursed and working with anger.

RACHEL: Gracious! If you hain't a sight to beat all! Where you from?

No answer; their eyes are wide with curiosity.

RACHEL: Where's your folks?

CLOSE SHOT—JOHN

RACHEL: (o.s.) Speak up now!

His eyes go down to her feet. He, and we, start to examine her from foot to head; for this is our heroine at last.

CLOSE TILTING SHOT—RACHEL
. . . from JOHN's eye-level. We TILT SLOWLY UP her height. She wears man's shoes, heavy with mud; a rough skirt; a shapeless sweater hangs over her shoulders; she is in her middle sixties and wears a man's old hat. Her face says:

RACHEL: (sort of roughly) Gracious! So I've got two more mouths to feed!

CLOSE SHOT—JOHN
For no reason at all he feels he has come home.

LAP DISSOLVE TO

GROUP SHOT—JOHN, PEARL, RACHEL, RUBY, DURING WASHING

RACHEL mercilessly scrubs JOHN; JOHN doesn't like it; RUBY washes PEARL with a cloth.

CLOSE SHOT—JOHN
Hating the scrubbing. He breaks away.

FULL SHOT—JOHN AND RACHEL
JOHN dodges behind a bush, RACHEL in hot pursuit.

CLOSE SHOT—THE BUSH; RACHEL
RACHEL's head bobs up and down above the bush; we hear the unmistakable sound of a female hand on a child's bottom.

LAP DISSOLVE TO

FULL SHOT—A SHELF, FULL OF MARKET BASKETS, NEATLY COVERED WITH DAMP MUSLIN   LAP DISSOLVE TO

FULL SHOT—THE CARRIED BASKETS, IN MOTION

EXT. MOUNDSVILLE STREET—TRACKING SHOT—RACHEL AND HER BROOD

All carry baskets. RACHEL charges along at the head of the procession. A CATTLE DEALER strolls the other way.

CATTLE DEALER: Howdy Miz Cooper—you goin' to sell me yer hog this year?

RACHEL doesn't stop walking.

RACHEL: With the price o' pork what it is?

CLOSE TRACKING SHOT—RACHEL
She keeps walking.

RACHEL: (talking to herself) I'm butcherin' my hog myself, smokin' the hams, and cannin' the sausage. (she calls to children over her shoulder) *You*-all have your work cut out!

CLOSE TRACKING TWO-SHOT—JOHN AND CLARY IN MID-PROCESSION

JOHN: She talks to herself.

CLARY: All the time.

JOHN: Your Maw's funny.

CLARY: She ain't our Maw. We just live at her house.

They walk in silence.

JOHN: Where's your folks?

CLARY: Some place.

MARY: My Daddy's in *Dee*-troit.

JOHN: (to Ruby) Who's *your* folks?

RUBY: I dunno.

FULL SHOT—THE STREET

A WAITRESS, wearing an apron labeled EMPIRE EATS, hurries across the street towards the GROUP. We PAN her in to MARY. The procession halts briefly. She embraces MARY.

WAITRESS: Mary! Honey! Mornin' Miz Cooper. (to Mary) Guess what! I'm savin' up to buy ye a charm bracelet!

CLOSE SHOT—RACHEL

RACHEL: Never mind the gewgaws; don't you miss your visit this Sunday; and come to Church with us.

FULL STREET SHOT

The WAITRESS hurries away. She dodges past a car.

WAITRESS: See ye Sunday, love!

CLOSE SHOT—RACHEL

She follows WAITRESS, then LOVERS in car, with her eyes.

FULL STREET SHOT

The car CENTERS, held up in traffic; two lovers in it, sitting close.

CLOSE SHOT—RACHEL

She takes in the LOVERS.

RACHEL: Women is durn fools! *All* of 'em!

She sighs, angry at all women, herself included, and turns away. We are at the door of a GROCERY STORE. The GROCER is on his doorstep.

FULL SHOT—GROUP AND GROCERY

RACHEL: (to children) Take yer baskets in.

The CHILDREN file in past her and GROCER.

RACHEL: (to Grocer) Looky there. (she indicates the lovers) *She*'ll be losin' her mind to a tricky mouth and a full moon, and like as not I'll be saddled with the *consequences.*

She starts into store with the GROCER.

INT. STORE—GROUP SHOT—RACHEL, GROCER, CHILDREN

RACHEL and GROCER come up to counter.

RACHEL: (continuing; she takes a list from her bosom and gives it to Grocer) Here's what you owe me. (she counts baskets) One, two, three, four, five . . . where's the other basket? Where's Ruby?

CLARY: She went.

RACHEL: John: *you* go fetch Ruby. (John goes. As Grocer empties baskets and tots up, Rachel continues:) Big Ruby's my problem girl. She can't gather eggs without bustin' 'em; but Ruby's got mother hands with a youngin, so what're you to say?

EXT. DRUG STORE—FULL SHOT—RUBY

She stands with her market-basket, reacting to wolf whistles o.s.; she is seeking the world.

THREE-SHOT—RUBY, OVER TWO YOUNG LOAFERS

1ST LOAFER: How 'bout tonight, Ruby?

RUBY gestures RACHEL'S nearness.

2ND LOAFER: (to 1st) What gives?

1ST LOAFER: The Old Lady's around. (to Ruby) How 'bout Thursday?

RUBY nods.

1ST LOAFER: (to 2nd) The old gal thinks she comes in fer sewin' lessons o'-Thursday.

FULL SHOT—RUBY; JOHN IN BACKGROUND

JOHN: (calling) Miz Cooper wants you.

He turns and goes; RUBY, with an eye to 1ST LOAFER, turns and follows.

INT. GROCERY STORE—GROUP SHOT—CENTERING RACHEL

GROCER: (to Pearl) And will you show me your dolly, little lady?

JOHN has entered in BACKGROUND. PEARL holds the doll to her, and JOHN moves in quietly to her side. They stand together, as so often before.

GROCER: See ye got *two* more peeps to your brood.

RACHEL: Yeah, and ornerier than the rest.

GROCER: How's your *own* boy, Miz Cooper?

RACHEL: Ain't heard from Ralph since last Christmas. Don't matter—I've got a new crop. (she laughs. Loudly) I'm a strong tree with branches for many birds. I'm good for something in this old world and I know it, too! We know that she will rout the Devil.

GROCER: (a good tradesman) Got a good buy in soap, Miz Cooper.

RACHEL: (triumphant) Don't need no soap. I'm boilin' down the fat from my hog.   DISSOLVE TO

INT. RACHEL'S SCREENED PORCH—EVENING—GROUP SHOT
—RACHEL, GIRLS, JOHN ASIDE

CENTERING RACHEL as she takes a book from table, and the
GIRLS MOVE to sit at her seat, and JOHN stands to one side.
RACHEL glances at him.

CLOSE SHOT—JOHN
He looks suspiciously to the Book in her hands, for to him it
has come to mean only Preacher.

INSERT—THE BIBLE
. . . as she opens it on her lap o.s. we hear a screen door open.

GROUP SHOT—RACHEL, CHILDREN, JOHN IN BACKGROUND
We see the door closing as JOHN goes out. The girls sit on low
stools in semi-circle at RACHEL'S feet. We CENTER RACHEL.
RACHEL, keenly aware of JOHN, pretends to ignore him. JOHN
crosses behind her and stands with his back to us. We see the
back of his head through the screen. RACHEL, changing her
mind about what story to tell, finds the new page she's after,
and spreads her hands flat on the pages. She never glances at
the text. She is fishing for JOHN.

RACHEL: Now old Pharaoh, he was the King of Egyptland!
And he had a daughter, and once upon a time (louder) she was
walkin' along the river bank and she seen somethin' bumpin'
and scrapin' along down on a sandbar under the willows.

CLOSE SHOT—THE BACK OF JOHN'S HEAD, IMMOBILE

RACHEL: (o.s.) And do you know what it was, children?

RESUME GROUP SHOT

RUBY, CLARY, MARY: (excited) No!

PEARL: No!

RACHEL: (still loud) Well, now, it was a skiff, washed up on
the bar. And who do you reckon was in it?

RUBY: (confidently) Pearl and John!

RACHEL: (still loud) Not this time! It was just one youngin
—a little boy babe. And do you know who he *was*, children?

CLOSE SHOT—JOHN'S HEAD
. . . as he turns around.

RUBY, MARY, CLARY, PEARL: (o.s. in unison) No!

RESUME GROUP SHOT

RACHEL closes the Bible; she knows the Lord's battle is won. As she continues, she puts aside the book and takes up her mending.

RACHEL: (very quietly) It was Moses!—A King of men, Moses, children. Now. Off to bed. Hurry.

On "off to bed," JOHN turns his back again.

CLOSE SHOT—RACHEL; JOHN IN BACKGROUND
She mends for a few moments.

RACHEL: (commandingly) John, git me an apple.

JOHN crosses behind her and off, towards door. We hear it open and close.

RACHEL: Git one for yourself, too.

MEDIUM SHOT—JOHN
He approaches with two apples. We PAN him into a:

TWO-SHOT—JOHN AND RACHEL
He gives her an apple. She immediately takes a bite. He doesn't bite his. She looks up at him from her apple.

RACHEL: (suddenly) John, where's your folks?

JOHN: (plainly) Dead.

RACHEL: Dead. (she nods with finality)

JOHN starts to eat his apple.

RACHEL: Where ye from?

JOHN: Up river.

RACHEL: I didn't figger ye rowed that skiff from Parkersburg!

JOHN makes a move; he slowly and tenderly reaches out his hand and lays his fingers on her knuckles.

JOHN: Tell me that story again.

Our heroine would like to thank the Lord openly, but she knows she must not show her feelings; she speaks gruffly—

RACHEL: Story, honey? Why, what story?

JOHN: About them Kings. That the Queen found down on the sandbar in the skiff that time.

RACHEL: Kings! Why, honey, there was only one.

JOHN: I mind you said there was two.

RACHEL: Well, shoot! Maybe there was!

CLOSE SHOT—RACHEL
Maybe we see—though JOHN does not—the thanksgiving in her eyes.

RACHEL: Yes, come to think of it, there *was* two, John.

O.s., in distance, we hear the whistle of a river boat.

DISSOLVE TO

EXT. MOUNDSVILLE STREET—EVENING—MOVING SHOT—RUBY
Her head and shoulders from behind as she walks down the neon-lighted street; drugstore and loafers in b.g.; jazz music o.s.

FULL SHOT—RUBY, OVER DRUGSTORE LOAFERS
Our two loafers lounge on a bench. RUBY approaches.

2ND LOAFER: (to 1st) Hey. Must be Thursday.

1ST LOAFER: Here we go.

He gets up and starts towards RUBY, who catches his eye.

RUBY, FROM BEHIND
She turns to a magazine stand and fingers a magazine, awaiting LOAFER, who approaches in BACKGROUND.

INSERT—RUBY'S HAND; MAGAZINES
They are lurid, tawdry fan and pin-up magazines.

PREACHER enters, between RUBY and LOAFER, and turns to RUBY into CLOSE TWO-SHOT. LOAFER pauses in BACKGROUND.

PREACHER: You're Ruby, ain't you, my child?

RUBY: Can I have this?

PREACHER: Surely. I'd like to talk to you, my dear.

RUBY: Will you buy me a choclit sody?

PREACHER: O' course.

LOAFERS: Watch out Preacher! Why, *Preacher!*

PREACHER: (sternly) Shet yer dirty mouths!

CLOSE SHOT—RUBY

She looks up at him admiringly; then to LOAFERS; back to PREACHER.

LAP DISSOLVE TO

INT. DRUGSTORE — CLOSE TWO-SHOT — PREACHER AND RUBY
RUBY is finishing her soda.

RUBY: Ain't I purty?

This is a familiar clue to PREACHER.

PREACHER: Why, you're the purtiest girl I've seen in all my wandering. Didn't nobody never tell you that, Ruby?

RUBY: (hoarsely) No. No one never did.

PREACHER: (moving in) There's two new ones over at your place, ain't there Ruby?

She nods.

PREACHER: What's their names?

RUBY: Pearl and John.

PREACHER: Ahhh. (whispering) And is there—a doll?

RUBY: (nods) Only she won't never let me play with it.

PREACHER: Ahh!

He gets up and heads for door. RUBY, dismayed, hurries after him.

PREACHER: (firmly) Yes!

He strides through door, RUBY following.

THREE-SHOT — PREACHER AND RUBY ON SIDEWALK, 2ND LOAFER IN B.G. 1ST LOAFER HAS GONE.

PREACHER comes out fast, RUBY touches his arm, he turns on her. They are in close TWO-SHOT. RUBY goes on tiptoe. PREACHER inclines his ear.

CLOSE SHOT — RUBY

RUBY: Did you ever see such purty eyes in all your born days?

CLOSE SHOT — PREACHER

INSERT — PREACHER'S HAND
It slides into his knife pocket. We hear a click.

2ND LOAFER: (o.s.) Don't let him git away, Sugar!

THREE-SHOT—PREACHER AND RUBY, LOAFER IN B.G.

RUBY: He ain't like you-all! Next time I won't even ask him to buy me a sody!

She turns to PREACHER, but PREACHER, on "next time," has left the SHOT.

CLOSE SHOT—RUBY
She looks after him, clasping the magazine under her chin.

FULL SHOT—PREACHER
Her hero strides away into darkness.

CLOSE SHOT—RUBY
Gazing after him.

RUBY: I been bad!   DISSOLVE TO

CLOSE DOWN-SHOT—THE MAGAZINE, OPEN, IN RACHEL'S LAP

We PULL UP and AWAY into:

TWO-SHOT—RACHEL, SEATED; RUBY STANDING BESIDE HER

RACHEL: Ruby, you didn't have no money to buy this.

RUBY: You'll whip me!

RACHEL: When did I ever?

RUBY: This man down at the Drugstore . . .

RACHEL: The *Drugstore?*

RUBY: Miz Cooper. I never went to sewin' lessons all them times.

RACHEL: What you been up to?

RUBY: I been out with men.

RUBY collapses face down over RACHEL'S lap and sobs, as we TRACK IN CLOSE.

RACHEL: Dear God, child!

Now RACHEL also weeps. She bends low over RUBY, stroking her hair.

RACHEL: You was lookin' for *love*, Ruby, the only foolish way you knowed how. (she lifts Ruby's face cheek to cheek beside her own) We all need love. Ruby, I lost the love of my son—I've found it with you-all.

They weep together.

RACHEL: You must grow up to be a fine, full woman; and I'm goin' to see to it you do.

She starts making up RUBY's hair like that of a young woman.

RUBY: This gentleman warn't like *them*! He just give me a sody and the book.

RACHEL: Now who was this?

RUBY: He never asked me for nothin'.

RACHEL: He must have wanted *somethin'*, Ruby. A man don't waste time on a girl unless he gets *something*.

RUBY shakes her head.

RACHEL: What'd you all talk about?

RUBY: Pearl and John.

RACHEL: John and Pearl!

RUBY nods.

RACHEL: Is he their Pap?

RUDY shrugs.

RACHEL: Why hasn't he been to the house?

DISSOLVE TO

FULL SHOT—PREACHER ON HORSE ON ROAD

FULL FIGURE SHOT—RUBY

Seeing PREACHER, she drops two eggs.

RUBY: (shouting) Miz Cooper!

RACHEL: (o.s. from within house) What?

RUBY: The man! The man!

TRACKING SHOT—PREACHER
He tethers his horse and, as we PAN and TRACK on behind him, walks to the bottom of the steps; RUBY moves into side of SHOT: beyond PREACHER, RACHEL stands behind her screen door, hands folded under apron.

PREACHER: Mornin', ladies.

FULL FIGURE SHOT—RACHEL, BEHIND SCREEN

RACHEL: How'do.

FULL FIGURE SHOT—PREACHER

RACHEL'S VIEWPOINT, through screen.

FULL FIGURE SHOT—RACHEL, BEHIND SCREEN

PREACHER: You're Miz Cooper, I take it.

RACHEL: (coming through door) It's about that John and that Pearl?

THREE-SHOT—PREACHER, RACHEL, RUBY IN BACKGROUND

PREACHER'S face twitches with emotion. He breaks out into great thankful sobs. He falls to his knees.

PREACHER: My little lambs! To think I never hoped to see them again in this world! Oh, dear Madam, if you was to know what a thorny crown I have borne in my search for these strayed chicks!

CLOSE SHOT—RACHEL
She takes him in. He doesn't take *her* in.

THREE-SHOT—AS BEFORE

RACHEL: Ruby, go fetch them kids.

RUBY minces off around the side of the house.

CLOSE SHOT—PREACHER—RACHEL'S ANGLE
He wipes off tears with the heel of his left hand, watching her.

PREACHER: Ah, dear Madam, I see you're looking at my hands!

CLOSE SHOT—RACHEL
She is.

CLOSE SHOT—PREACHER—AS BEFORE
He holds up the right hand.

PREACHER: Shall I tell ye the little story of Right-Hand-Left-Hand—the tale of Good and Evil?

CLOSE SHOT—RACHEL

PREACHER: (o.s.) It was with this left hand that old brother Cain struck the blow that laid his brother low—

RACHEL: (wanting to know) Them kids is yours?

CLOSE SHOT—PREACHER

PREACHER: (recovering from the interruption) My flesh and blood!

CLOSE SHOT—RACHEL

RACHEL: Where's your Missus?

TWO-SHOT—PROFILING RACHEL AND PREACHER
PREACHER gets to his feet.

PREACHER: She run off with a drummer one night. Durin' prayer-meetin'.

RACHEL: Where's she at?

PREACHER: Somewheres down river! Parkersburg, mebbe! —Cincinnati!—One of them Sodoms on the Ohio River.

RACHEL: She took them kids with her?

PREACHER: Heaven only knows what unholy sights and sounds those innocent little babes has heard in the dens of perdition where she dragged them!

CLOSE SHOT—RACHEL

RACHEL: Right funny, hain't it, how they rowed all the way up river in a ten-foot john-boat!

CLOSE SHOT—PREACHER
. . . recovering, and by-passing it.

PREACHER: Are they well?
He turns his head.

FULL SHOT—RACHEL AND PREACHER, FROM SIDE
All the CHILDREN enter, around corner of house. As they move in, RACHEL replies:

RACHEL: A sight better than they was.

By now JOHN is on the top step beside RACHEL. One of his hands holds on to her skirt, as if he were pulling her towards him. His eyes never leave hers. All the CHILDREN freeze, PEARL is on ground, just beyond JOHN. Others in BACK-GROUND; RUBY as near PREACHER as she can get.

PREACHER: Gracious, gracious! You are a good woman, Miz Cooper!

RACHEL: How you figgerin' to raise them two without a woman?

PREACHER: The Lord will provide.

PEARL, with a wail of happiness, drops the DOLL on the step and runs to PREACHER, who picks her up. JOHN instantly picks up the DOLL and holds it to him. He looks up at RACHEL.

CLOSE TWO-SHOT—JOHN AND RACHEL
JOHN looks deep into RACHEL'S eyes.

PREACHER: (o.s.) The Lord is merciful! What a day is this!—And there's little John!

RACHEL: What's wrong, John?

JOHN: Nothin'. (he smiles)

PREACHER: (o.s.) Come to me, boy!

RACHEL: What's wrong, John?

TWO-SHOT—PREACHER AND PEARL

PREACHER: Didn't you hear me, boy?

TWO-SHOT—JOHN AND RACHEL

RACHEL bends a little over him. She wants the situation clarified.

RACHEL: John, when your Dad says 'come', you should mind him.

JOHN: He ain't my Dad.

HEAD CLOSE-UP—RACHEL
She takes this in; JOHN has sold her. She looks to PREACHER o.s.

RACHEL: He ain't no Preacher neither. I've seen Preachers in my time, an' some of 'em was saints on earth. A few was crookeder'n a dog's hind leg, but this 'un's got 'em all beat for badness.

She starts to turn.

GROUP SHOT
She walks purposefully into the house. PREACHER lunges for JOHN and the DOLL.

CLOSE TWO-SHOT—PREACHER AND JOHN

JOHN ducks under the porch and PREACHER tries to follow him. He can't get under. O.s. we hear the slam of the screen door. PREACHER'S head comes up to see and we TILT UP, shooting over the back of his head. RACHEL stands there, full figure, with a pump-gun.

RACHEL: Just march yourself yonder to your horse, Mister.

Back of PREACHER's head is still immobile.

RACHEL: March, Mister! I'm not foolin'.

CLOSE SHOT—PREACHER, OVER GUN-BARREL

PREACHER gets to his feet. The open knife is in his hand. As we see it, the gun-barrel twitches. PREACHER backs away towards his horse, bouncing the knife lightly in his hand.

PREACHER: (screaming) You ain't done with Harry Powell yet! The Lord God Jehovah will guide my hand in vengeance! You devils! You Whores of Babylon! I'll come back when it's dark!

As he mounts his horse we   DISSOLVE TO

FULL SHOT—RACHEL'S HOUSE—NIGHT
It is dark. O.s. we hear PREACHER singing *Leaning*.

FULL FIGURE SHOT—RACHEL
She sits in profile, her gun across her knees. Song continues o.s.

FULL SHOT—THE CHILDREN, ASLEEP
. . . in a big bed. RUBY sits up, listening to song o.s.

FULL FIGURE SHOT—RACHEL, AS BEFORE
Song continues o.s. We PAN to PREACHER outside. We see him through window. He sits hunched on a stump.

FULL SHOT—THE HOUSE, OVER PREACHER
He continues singing.

HEAD PROFILE—RACHEL
After a moment we see her mouth open; and either to comfort herself or to drown out PREACHER's voice, she joins in the hymn.

FULL SHOT—THE HOUSE—AS IN OPENING SHOT
A descending candle moves past a window; RACHEL and PREACHER sing o.s.

FULL SHOT—PREACHER ON STUMP
. . . over back of RACHEL's head. The song ends. RUBY enters SHOT carrying a candle. Its light blacks out the window-glass. RACHEL looks up.

RACHEL: Moonin' around the house over that mad dog of a Preacher! *Shame*, Ruby!

She blows out the candle. We see through the window. PREACHER has gone.

CLOSE SHOT—RACHEL

RACHEL: Merciful Heaven!

She stands up.

CLOSE TWO-SHOT—RACHEL AND RUBY

RACHEL: Ruby, get the children out of bed. Bring them all down here to the kitchen.

RUBY leaves the SHOT. RACHEL moves towards window. She puts her hand over her eyes.

RACHEL: Women is such fools!

The soft hoot of an owl o.s. RACHEL looks up.

CLOSE SHOT—AN OWL ON A BRANCH, LOOKING DOWN

CLOSE SHOT—A BABY RABBIT

CLOSE SHOT—THE OWL SPREADS HIS WINGS AND SWOOPS

CLOSE SHOT—RACHEL
Still for a second; then o.s., the scream of a rabbit.

RACHEL: It's a hard world for little things.

OVER this line we have heard the patter of feet down staircase. She turns.

GROUP SHOT—THE CHILDREN
They look at her with complete trust.

GROUP SHOT—RACHEL, OVER CHILDREN

RACHEL: (snapping) Children, I got lonesome. I figgered we might play games.

PEARL and MARY jump up and down, patting their palms. RACHEL extends her hands and they gather close to her.

PEARL: Won't you tell us a story?

CLOSE SHOT—RACHEL

RACHEL: I might (a swift furious glance into the moonlight) I might tell A Story.

She sits down, the gun across her knees.

GROUP SHOT—RACHEL AND CHILDREN
. . . as MARY and PEARL sit at her feet. RUBY stands beside
RACHEL. JOHN stands near RACHEL.

CLARY: I'll light the lamp.

RACHEL: It's more fun hearin' stories in the dark.

CLARY sits at RACHEL'S feet.

CLOSE PANNING SHOT—JOHN
He is alert now. He moves in close beside RACHEL, whom we
PAN into

CLOSE TWO-SHOT with him, and presses the whole of his right
arm against her arm. RACHEL registers quietly.

CLOSE GROUP SHOT—RACHEL AND CHILDREN

RACHEL: Well . . . mind what I told you about little Jesus
and his Ma and Pa and how there was No Room at the Inn?

HEAD CLOSE-UP—RACHEL
Her eyes, sharp and glittering, look outside.

FULL SHOT—THE OUTSIDE, FEATURING EMPTY STUMP,
RACHEL'S VIEWPOINT

GROUP SHOT—RACHEL AND CHILDREN
She gets up with gun; we PULL AWAY; in BACKGROUND, CHIL-
DREN turn faces to keep watching her. She comes close to win-
dow, gun ready, CHILDREN in BACKGROUND

RACHEL: Well now, there was this sneakin', no-'count,
ornery King Herod! She turns round and walks back to her
chair; CHILDREN'S eyes always on her.

RACHEL: And he heard tell of this little King Jesus growin'
up and old Herod figgered: Well, shoot! There sure won't be
no room for the both of us! (she sits down) I'll just nip this in
the bud.

GROUP SHOT—RACHEL AND CHILDREN, FROM SIDE

RACHEL: (continuing) Well, he never knowed for sure
which one of all them babies of the land was King Jesus.

HEAD CLOSE-UP—RACHEL
Her eyes glittering as she turns to look towards us.
RESUME SIDE GROUP SHOT

RACHEL gets up, with gun. Again we PULL AWAY, as faces of all CHILDREN in b.g. turn to watch her.

RACHEL: And so that cursed old King Herod figgered if he was to kill all the babies in the land, he'd be sure to get little Jesus.

Without speaking, she goes back to her chair.

FRONT GROUP SHOT

RACHEL: (more relaxed) And when little King Jesus' Ma and Pa heard about that plan, what do you reckon they went and done?

CLARY: They hid in a broom closet!

MARY: They hid under the porch!

HEAD CLOSE-UP—JOHN

JOHN: No; they went a-runnin'.

TWO-SHOT—RACHEL AND JOHN

RACHEL: Well now, John, that's just what they done! *They* went a-runnin!

The clock starts striking three. RACHEL looks to sound o.s.

FULL SHOT—CLOCK AND HALL MIRROR, BEYOND DARK KITCHEN
In the mirror, a shadow ducks.

FULL GROUP SHOT—RACHEL AND CHILDREN

RACHEL gets up, gun at port, and faces into the darkness.

PREACHER: (o.s.) Figured I was gone, eh?

Eyes on the darkness, she bends low to the CHILDREN.

RACHEL: (whispering) Run hide in the staircase! Run quick!

They scatter out of shot; RUBY lingers.

RACHEL: (without turning to her) Ruby, git.

RUBY obeys in a trance. RACHEL, gun at ready, looks into the darkness.
FULL SCREEN—DARKNESS
Pause.

RACHEL: (o.s.; in a high, steady voice) What do you want?
PREACHER: (o.s.) Them kids!

RACHEL: (o.s.) What are you after them *for*?

PREACHER: (o.s.) None of your business, Madam.

RACHEL: I'm givin' *you* to the count of three to get out that screen door; then I'm a-comin' across this kitchen *shootin*'!

A stepped-on cat screams o.s. and PREACHER'S satanic face, and his hand lifting the open knife, rise swiftly from floor.

FULL FIGURE SHOT—RACHEL—SAME SHOT AS BEFORE
She fires off her gun.

FULL SHOT—SCREEN DOOR

PREACHER staggers out and runs yelping with pain into the barn. O.s. we hear the zing-zing of a country phone being cranked.

GROUP SHOT—RACHEL, OVER BACKS OF CHILDREN'S HEADS
They huddle on the stairs in reverent silence. RACHEL, her gun slung sportily under one arm, talks into wall phone which hangs just within the box stairway.

RACHEL: Miz Booher? Rachel Cooper. Git them State Troopers out to my place. I done treed somep'n up in my barn.   DISSOLVE TO

FULL SHOT—RACHEL AND JOHN
RACHEL sits on the screened porch, awake, gun on knees. JOHN sits on floor, asleep, his head leaning against her. Barn in BACKGROUND. Sunrise.

CLOSE SHOT—RACHEL AND JOHN
Same position. JOHN awakes.

JOHN: I'll see to Pearl.

RACHEL: I'll make coffee.

They get up and start into kitchen.

GROUP SHOT—THE CHILDREN, OVER RACHEL AND JOHN
They lie huddled in calm sleep. JOHN and RACHEL watch a moment.

JOHN: She's all right.

They start for the stove.

TWO-SHOT—RACHEL AND JOHN, AROUND STOVE

RACHEL puts her gun beside the stove, ready to hand, and picks up a coffeepot; JOHN puts kindling in stove.

RACHEL: John, you know? When you're little you have more endurance than God is ever to grant you again? Children are Man at his strongest. They abide.

JOHN looks at her a moment. O.s. we hear police car sirens. They look towards the sound.

FULL SHOT—THROUGH POLICE CAR WINDSHIELD
We SHOOT OVER two TROOPERS. Sirens loud, they rapidly approach RACHEL'S house as RACHEL, without gun, holding JOHN'S hand, comes down to fence. Presently, the other CHILDREN hurry out of house behind. The car brakes.

FULL SHOT—RACHEL AND CHILDREN OVER TWO POLICE CARS—BARN IN BACKGROUND
The TROOPERS, fanning wide, advance towards barn. RACHEL and the CHILDREN are grouped a short distance behind them. The barn door gapes black. Short pause; then PREACHER appears.

A TROOPER: (shouting) Is that him, Ma'am?

RACHEL: (shouting) Yes! Mind where you shoot, boys! There's children here!

TROOPER: Whyn't you call us up before?

RACHEL: Didn't want yer big feet trackin' up my clean floors.

CLOSE SHOT—PREACHER
He stands, swaying; his left arm is bloody and helpless. In his right hand the open knife hangs apathetic. His eyes are glazed. He does not seem to care whether they come or not.

TROOPER'S VOICE: (o.s.) Harry Powell, you're under arrest for the murder of Willa Harper!

MEDIUM SHOT—PREACHER AND TROOPERS—JOHN'S VIEWPOINT
TROOPERS close in on PREACHER, from before and behind, exactly as for BEN'S arrest.

CLOSE SHOT—JOHN
The same sickly look, as at BEN'S arrest.

MEDIUM SHOT—PREACHER AND TROOPERS—JOHN'S VIEW-POINT

One TROOPER smacks the back of PREACHER'S head with a pistol-barrel.

CLOSE SHOT—JOHN

JOHN: (shouting) Don't!

RESUME VIEWPOINT SHOT

Another TROOPER, with a pistol barrel, knocks the knife from PREACHER'S lifted hand.

CLOSE SHOT—JOHN

JOHN: (shouting) Don't!

RESUME VIEWPOINT SHOT

PREACHER sinks to his knees as both men, and two others from the front, close in on him. The tableau is the same as in BEN'S arrest.

CLOSE SHOT—JOHN

JOHN: (shouting) Dad!

FRONT GROUP SHOT—RACHEL AND CHILDREN

JOHN grabs the DOLL from PEARL and starts to run.

RACHEL: John! John!

She starts after him.

FULL SHOT—TROOPERS, JOHN, RACHEL, OVER PREACHER

PREACHER prostrate along bottom of screen. TROOPERS are beating him. JOHN runs up from background followed by RACHEL. JOHN rushes among the TROOPERS, flogging PREACHER over the head with the DOLL. The TROOPERS, astounded, lay off. RACHEL is stopped in her tracks.

JOHN: Here! Here! Take it back! I can't stand it, Dad! It's too much, Dad! I don't want it! I can't do it! Here! Here!

The DOLL has burst open and the money has spilled over PREACHER. Now two TROOPERS gently lift JOHN away. RACHEL lifts him in her arms; she turns towards house.

FULL FIGURE PULL SHOT—RACHEL AND JOHN—GROUP IN BACKGROUND

She carries JOHN towards the house. His head hangs back over her arm. We hear his dry, exhausted sobs.

INT. COURTROOM—DAY—CLOSE SHOT—ICEY

ICEY: (yelling) Lynch him! Lynch him!

TWO-SHOT—WALT AND ICEY

ICEY: (yelling) Bluebeard!

WALT: (yelling at all the men around him) Twenty-five wives!

ICEY: And he killed every last one of 'em!

GROUP SHOT—WALT, ICEY, MEMBERS OF COURTROOM AUDIENCE

Perhaps ten faces. Most are frenetic. Our two LOAFERS are having fun. General hubbub o.s. A gavel o.s.

ICEY: (yelling) If the People of Marshall County . . .

LOAFERS: (cynically, across her) Bluebeard! Bluebeard!

CLOSE SHOT—JOHN

He looks to sound of gavel. The hubbub and the gaveling stop.

LAWYER: (o.s.) Will you identify the prisoner?

JOHN looks over his shoulder in same direction as the gavel.

LAWYER: (o.s.) Please, little lad. Won't you look yonder . . . (his pointing finger enters the shot. John shakes as if he had a cold) . . . and tell the Court if that is the man who killed your mother?

JOHN looks at the finger. Short pause.

LAWYER: (o.s.) It's all right, Mrs. Cooper. You can take the little fellow away.

The LAWYER's hands gently help him from chair.

GROUP SHOT—RACHEL AND CHILDREN

. . . as LAWYER's hands consign JOHN to RACHEL.

LAWYER: Merry Christmas to you and yours, Mrs. Cooper.

The CHILDREN bob and reply, ad lib, "Merry Christmas to *you*." RACHEL sniffs.

LAWYER: (o.s.) And what's Santy Claus going to bring *you*, little man? Above JOHN's head, by winding and holding to ear, RACHEL pantomimes a watch.

LAWYER: (o.s.) *O-ho-oo-o!*

ICEY: (o.s.) Them is the ones he sinned against, my friends!

Gaveling starts.

LOAFER: (o.s.) Bluebeard! Bluebeard!

CROWD: (o.s.) Bluebeard! Bluebeard!

As RACHEL and CHILDREN turn to go, gaveling and hubbub
fade and we   LAP DISSOLVE TO

INT. A CAFE—NIGHT

RACHEL and her CHILDREN sit in two booths, in a corner, next
to a big front window. Christmas parcels on bench at RACHEL'S
right.

FULL SHOT—RACHEL AND HER GROUP, THEN CAFE AND
WINDOW

Sound o.s. of approaching crowd. As we PULL BACK we bring
in a few other customers and the big window. There are
Christmas decorations in the cafe and the street outside is
hung with them. Thirty feverish people, some of whom carry
torches, enter the scene; ICEY stares in the window and screams.

ICEY: (high-pitched) Them's hers!

Everyone in the cafe stands up. RACHEL gathers her parcels.
ICEY rushes to door and opens it.

ICEY: Them's her orphans!

She turns to crowd.

RACHEL: Where's Ruby?

CLARY: She went.

ICEY shouts into the cafe.

ICEY: Them poor little lambs!

ICEY turns to the street mob. RACHEL hurries her CHILDREN
to door.

ICEY leaves door to yell at mob.

ICEY: Them's the ones he sinned against, my friends!

CASHIER: (across Icey) Go out the back way, Miz Cooper.

As RACHEL leaves SHOT, the CASHIER shuts and locks the door.

EXT. BACK ALLEY—NIGHT—PANNING SHOT—RACHEL AND
COMPANY EMERGING FROM DOOR

MARY and CLARY come out first and start walking to our left.
RACHEL comes out and hurries off to our right, followed by
JOHN, holding PEARL'S hand.

We PAN to MARY and CLARY.

CLARY: Ain't we goin' to the Bus Depot?

No answer. They turn and we PAN with them as they hurry
after RACHEL, and we bring in RACHEL, charging away from us
with her brood hustling to keep up.

GROUP SHOT—FEATURING WALT AND ICEY

ICEY carries torch. She is flanked by rabid faces and by smiling
LOAFERS, one of whom carries an axe. As she speaks, a MAN
rushes up to WALT and gives him a rope.

ICEY: (shouting; high-pitched) Draggin' the name of the
Lord through the evil mud of his soul!

WALT: (bellowing) Come on!

They all start marching, in step.

PANNING SHOT—RACHEL AND CHILDREN
Marching and voices o.s. and in BACKGROUND.

Carrying Christmas parcels, they hurry alongside a building
and, at CENTER of PAN, cross the end of a street.

The MOB marches down the street TOWARDS CAMERA; MEN
run to join it.

ICEY: (high-pitched) He lied!

WALT: Tricked us!

ICEY: He taken the Lord's name in vain and he trampled on
His Holy Book!

WALT: String that Bluebeard up to a pole!

ICEY: He's Satan hiding behind the Cross!

OTHERS: (ad lib) Lynch him! String him up!

We PAN RACHEL and CHILDREN past this street and they hurry
towards RUBY, who stands alone in BACKGROUND, facing the
jail.

HEAD CLOSE-UP — RUBY'S ECSTATIC FACE

In BACKGROUND, RACHEL and CHILDREN hurry towards her. MOB noise o.s. Hearing the approach of RACHEL'S GROUP, RUBY turns the back of her head towards us. Now there are no mob voices; only the ominous sound of fifty-odd people marching in step.

RUBY: I love him!

TRACKING SHOT — RUBY
Ominous silence.

RUBY: He loves me because I'm so purty! You think he's like them others!

SIDE TRACKING SHOT — RUBY, RACHEL AND GROUP
Marching sound o.s.

RACHEL firmly takes RUBY'S arm and drags her off in our direction. RACHEL shoos MARY and CLARY ahead of her. JOHN and PEARL flank RACHEL, clinging to her wide skirts. RUBY, nearest us, keeps looking back over her shoulder. We TRACK them along side of JAIL to rear of JAIL.

RUBY: (continuing) You took on something awful about him buying me that there movie book. You was so mad you shot him and the blue men took him.

On "blue men," we stop TRACKING and, as GROUP leaves SHOT, CENTER a POLICE CAR, waiting at rear door of JAIL. PO-LICEMEN start out of door.

MEDIUM GROUP SHOT — POLICEMEN AND PREACHER
They roughly hustle PREACHER into the car. Marching sound o.s.

SHOT — FROM WITHIN CAR — BART
PREACHER and POLICE are in b.g. Through car window we see BART the HANGMAN come out of his door. He wears his derby. A POLICEMAN puts head out of window. Marching sound o.s.

MEDIUM SHOT — BART THE HANGMAN
On porch, by door, is a doll's perambulator, but this time there is a Christmas wreath on the door. Marching o.s.

POLICEMAN: (o.s.) Hey *Bart*!

Auto engine starts up o.s.

HEAD CLOSE-UP—BART

BART: Yeah?

MEDIUM SHOT—BART
Marching o.s.

POLICEMAN: (o.s.) We're savin' this bird up fer *you*!

HEAD CLOSE-UP—BART
Marching o.s.

BART: This time it'll be a privilege.

FULL PANNING SHOT—POLICE CAR, THEN RACHEL AND GROUP
The car jumps fast out of SHOT and we PAN PAST BART and CENTER RACHEL and GROUP, walking fast away from us. Mob voices o.s.

A VOICE: (o.s., over departing car) Bust the door down!

CLOSE GROUP SHOT—RACHEL AND CHILDREN
Clutching Christmas parcels they hurry away from us into darkness. RUBY, hanging back, dragged by RACHEL, babbles over her shoulder.

RUBY: (happily) They'll git him out. I'll git my things ready—my shawl and my Mickey Mouse wristwatch that don't run and the straw hat with the flower, and we'll be married and live happily ever after!

VOICES: (o.s. ad lib, cutting across Ruby) Bust the door down! Set *fahr* to it! Where's that axe! Climb up on the balcony! You six git 'round to the *back*!

ICEY: (o.s., screaming) *People of Marshall County*!

DISSOLVE TO

FULL SHOT—NIGHT LANDSCAPE—PINE TREES, AND SOFTLY FALLING SNOW   DISSOLVE TO

EXT. RACHEL'S HOUSE—EVENING; SNOWING—CLOSE SHOT— RACHEL AT MAILBOX
She peers into empty mailbox.

RACHEL: Nothing!

She slams the box shut and, as we TILT and PAN, walks away from us through snow towards her lighted house.

RACHEL: I'm glad they didn't send me nothing! Whenever they do it's never nothing I want but something to show me how fancy and smart they've come up in the world.

She goes into the house.

INT. RACHEL'S KITCHEN
It is decorated for Christmas.

GROUP SHOT—RACHEL AND CHILDREN

Rachel enters; the four girls stand in line, packages ready; JOHN stands in b.g., in doorway to next room.

MARY: Can we give you your presents now?

CLOSE SHOT—RACHEL

RACHEL: Shoot! You don't mean to say you got me a present!

Their hands hold packages up to her.

RACHEL: Shoot now!

She takes a package.

CLOSE SHOT—JOHN

RACHEL: (o.s.) Why, Ruby!

Embarrassed, JOHN leaves the shot.

RACHEL: (o.s.) A POT-HOLDER!

CLOSE SHOT—JOHN—NEW ANGLE
From a fruit bowl, he selects the biggest apple, shines it on his shirt, wraps it in the doily under his bowl, opens a drawer and gets out a clip clothespin, clips his package, and leaves shot.

RACHEL: (o.s., continuing) And much neater than last year's, Ruby!

(Sound of tearing gift-paper o.s.)

RACHEL: (o.s.) And Clary! *ANOTHER POT-HOLDER!* Ain't that thoughtful. I'm always burnin' my hands.

FULL SHOT—RACHEL, AND CHILDREN, OVER JOHN
. . . as he enters with present. RUBY and CLARY are standing aside; MARY and PEARL hold up a third pot-holder.

RACHEL: And did you two make this *together*?

Both nod.

MARY: You hop us, *some.*

CLOSE SHOT—RACHEL, ACCEPTING JOHN'S GIFT
She opens it.

RACHEL: (quietly) John, that's the richest gift a body could have. (continued, briskly) You'll find *your* presents in the cupboard under the china-closet.

GROUP SHOT—RACHEL AND CHILDREN

RACHEL: You know where, Ruby.

All turn and run through door except Ruby, whom RACHEL detains.

RACHEL: Ruby: (she takes a box from her apron pocket) This is yours.

RUBY opens it quickly; it is a cheap costume-jewelry flower-spray. RUBY and RACHEL kiss like grown women and RUBY goes to join the others.

FULL SHOT—RACHEL
She turns to her stove and is framed by Christmas garland in b.g.; banging pots about and stirring; praying as she works, which is the best way to pray.

Appropriate noise, o.s., of opening presents.

RACHEL: Lord save little children! (bang) You'd think the world would be ashamed to name such a day as Christmas for one of them . . . (bang) . . . and go on the same old way. (she starts stirring) My soul is humble when I see the way little ones accept their lot. (she pauses in stirring) Lord save little children! The wind blows and the rain is cold. Yet, *they abide.*

In BACKGROUND, the girls run upstairs, their new dresses over their arms. RACHEL glances over her shoulder.

MEDIUM SHOT—JOHN—RACHEL'S VIEWPOINT
JOHN stands in next room, looking at something in his hand.

CLOSE SHOT—JOHN—IN OTHER ROOM
We see he holds a watch. He looks like any boy, rich or poor, with his first watch.

HEAD CLOSE-UP—RACHEL

RACHEL: (whispering, so that he does not hear) For every child, rich or poor there's a time of running through a dark place; and there's no word for a child's fear. A child sees a shadow on the wall, and sees a Tiger. And the old ones say, "There's no tiger; go to sleep." And when that child sleeps, it's a Tiger's sleep, and a Tiger's night, and a Tiger's breathing on the windowpane. Lord save little children!

JOHN enters boldly behind her and, with a scrape, masterfully swings a chair around close to her and straddles it. RACHEL turns her back to us. She expects him to speak, he doesn't, so she fills in:

RACHEL: That watch sure is a fine, loud ticker!

JOHN gives her a burning, proud smile.

RACHEL: It'll be nice to have someone around the house who can give me the right time of day.

JOHN finds his tongue.

JOHN: This watch is the nicest watch I ever had.

RACHEL: A feller can't just go around with run-down, busted watches.

She turns back, face to us, and goes on with her stirring. JOHN goes off towards the staircase to join the girls; then turns back.

CLOSE SHOT—JOHN

JOHN: I ain't afraid no more! I got a watch that ticks! I got a watch that shines in the dark!

He turns and hurries to the stairs.

HEAD CLOSE-UP—RACHEL

Over the sound of his running upstairs:

RACHEL: (telling us) They abide and they endure.

LAP DISSOLVE TO

FULL SHOT—STARRY SKY

FADE IN TITLE:

THE END

SELECTED JOURNALISM
AND BOOK REVIEWS

Tennessee Valley Authority

THE Tennessee River system begins on the worn magnificent crests of the southern Appalachians, among the earth's oldest mountains, and the Tennessee River shapes its valley into the form of a boomerang, bowing it to its sweep through seven states. Near Knoxville the streams still fresh from the mountains are linked and thence the master stream spreads the valley most richly southward, swims past Chattanooga and bends down into Alabama to roar like blown smoke through the floodgates of Wilson Dam, to slide becalmed along the crop-cleansed fields of Shiloh, to march due north across the high diminished plains of Tennessee and through Kentucky spreading marshes toward the valley's end where finally, at the toes of Paducah, in one wide glass golden swarm the water stoops forward and continuously dies into the Ohio. The watershed encompasses some 44,000 square miles, a valley about the size of England and within a day's journey of all between Boston, Duluth, Key West, a valley whose climate is excellently mild (the mean annual temperature is 60 degrees), a valley which is the heart of the Southeast. Within that valley are—a number of things. Four cities: *Asheville*—in the eastern mountainous land of summer resorts, a city which has never quite got over the shock of Mr. Thomas Wolfe's novel *Look Homeward Angel* (he was a local boy and should have done more kindly by them). *Knoxville*—at the head of the Tennessee, girdled with mines and quarries and timber, the first capital of the state of Tennessee, the seat of the University of Tennessee, the erstwhile (1931) twenty-eighth most murderous city, big or little, in the U.S. *Chattanooga*—self-styled Dynamo of Dixie and great center for religious publications, whose 400 factories more or less and hospitable attitude toward Yankee industrialists and whose strategic location as a distributor do much to give point to the Dynamic epithet but hardly explain the more typically native boast of more churches per capita than any other city in the U.S. *Paducah*—set among the western lands of Kentucky tobacco and among the great tobacco buyers (American Tobacco and Axton-Fisher have "interests" there).

There are also the towns up-and-coming like Bristol and Kingsport and Johnson City and the villages down-at-heel like Dayton of blessed memory and Jacksboro and Tracy City. And but for the fine soft slur of speech in the streets and the still goodly number of Model T Fords and the few deciduous southern mansions with their hitching posts and the "nigger-towns" with their clay beaten down by bare heels and the whitewashed clapboard shacks and the odd predilection of the valleyite for "lawing,"* these towns might as easily be in Massachusetts or Minnesota with Main Street much the same the country over. And there's the Negro, too, who might be better off in Charleston or in Harlem. And here and there a Southern Gentleman of the old school, who still nuzzles "burbon" juleps and quotes Horace and talks "hosses" and loves his country as the greatest battleground of all the war, next to Virginia. And here and there a farmer prosperous enough to spend five to ten thousand a year on fertilizer alone. And the mountaineer, of whom more later. And the crops, which are varied and which are often as not poor in the bargain. And many a mine and knitting mill and lumber camp in the valley and a smattering of the outposts of big companies like International Harvester at Chattanooga and Aluminum Co. of America near Knoxville—all to remind you that in the past two generations men came in from the North and men came to in the South and a New South grew up and twisted its roots through the Old. These industries and these companies are of less significance to TVA by title and size and balance sheet than for what they have done for the valley. There are these things among many others and there is the open country itself by the millions of acres—some of the loveliest and most somber and some of the cruelest and most haggard you will find in all America. There are also, all told, some 2,000,000 people.

This is the Tennessee Valley you might see as a visitor. It is more or less the valley you'd know if you lived there. It is the valley that is newly TVA's to have and to hold for better, for worse. To TVA there are things about the valley still more important and not so easily seen. The mountains are profoundly

---

*Valley vernacular for hanging about the courthouse on one's own—or others'—legal business. No dispute is too small to "go to law over." Of the valleyman's indoor sports, "lawing" is among the most popular.

muscled with some forty of the minerals most useful to man. Coal and iron ore and limestone (which, properly handled, add up to spell "Ruhr") are there in huge quantities and are convenient to the river; there is much copper and zinc and marble and bauxite (the ore of aluminum) and lead; immense deposits of manganese scarcely touched (the natives condition their rutty roads with it) and phosphate rock in huge abundance and asphalt rock; even traces of silver and gold. Of chestnut oak and oak pine there are excellent stands, billions of board feet, and there are dense forests of the temperate trees. The soil is as varied as the stones under it. The river is a powerful and far-falling river constant in its course, and its bed of limestone and tough clay is in general a good bed for big dams. Indeed, nature set the stage for something of a Utopia. And if you believed only the Chambers of Commerce and the first signs you saw on every road you might believe that 2,000,000 people haven't done so badly. From the forests of the seven states which the valley involves, 7,000,000,000 board feet are cut each year. In sixty years Tennessee has produced nearly a quarter of a billion tons of coal. The yearly value of natural resources (exclusive of timber) in Tennessee alone is $38,500,000. Fine figures, these. You could paint the whole valley with such figures. You might find business pretty bad but they'd be nice figures just the same, and the picture a good clear-cut picture of the sort it is nice to look at.

But here is the other side of the picture: careless fires and unregulated cutting have ruined and are ruining great stands of timber on watersheds where trees should have stood forever. Because natural resources which should have sustained local industries indefinitely have been shipped away in crude form and exhausted, whole communities have been and are being pauperized, abandoned. Where the forests are no more, where the farms are steep, where the land is light, where copper fumes wander, vast acreages of farmland are rapidly being totally laid waste by erosion. The waste land descends unimpeded into the river slowly but surely to choke the channels and to fill in great natural reservoirs that cannot be replaced. Scarcely under control and highly capricious in its flow, the Tennessee River floods the bottom lands and does an estimated $1,780,000 damage every year and adds its more than mite to the springtime disorders of the Mississippi. The river is poorly developed for navigation. Its power possibilities have scarcely been touched. Muscle Shoals was a try; it cost the government some $150,000,000 and, as everyone knows, is now a muscle-bound white elephant.

Of the 2,000,000 inhabitants perhaps one in six lives in a large city. But more important to TVA are the small-towners, still more important are the farmers. Over half the people live on farms. Some of the soil is good. Some of the best is in danger of flood. Much more, thanks to erosion, is being slaked of its life. Still more is light and sandy and inherently unfit for cultivation. The farmer in the mountains who takes apart the long sick land between the tilted racks of stone calls eight bushels of wheat and ten of corn to the acre a right good crop.* The farmers are backward in their methods; machinery in these times even less used than ever; fertilizer is expensive; power is unavailable to the poorer people at reasonable prices, virtually unheard of on many farms and for that matter in many communities; families are large; food is poor; pellagra and hookworm and dysentery are general among the mountain people. To these farms, from the factories of stricken midland cities, jobless prodigals have returned by the tens and scores of thousands in no hope of work but with some hope for mere existence.

There are, to be sure, prosperous men who till good lands but where TVA has looked it has found the typical valley farmer and his family getting along on $100 cash a year.

When the farmer lives up the shadowy coves and deep among the mountains on farms so steep that, in native parlance, a man "falls outen his own garden" and "swings in his back door on a grapevine," in a country so wild that he "keeps possums for house cats," he is more and less than a farmer: he is a mountaineer. He is the strong backbone of the Tennessee Valley. His forefathers settled this country in the 1700's when the effete civilization east of the Alleghenies stuck in their craws. They whipped the Britishers and Loyalists at King's

---

*Between 1918 and 1927 Iowa farmers averaged a yield of 39.8 bushels of corn to the acre; the average yield of Kansas wheat was thirteen bushels. Averages for Tennessee for the same period were: for corn, twenty-four bushels; for wheat, 10.6 bushels.

Mountain. They kept much to themselves and their great-grandsons do likewise and live in much the same way, while slowly the sawmills and the mines and the railways and the highways and now TVA burn seclusion from about them. Many of them are illiterate; many are lawless in the bad sense and the good of that word. They never heard of Margaret Sanger and they have little interest in Mazda bulbs and little respect for this century of progress. Homespun and feuds and "mountain dew" are not so rife among them as some dreamy souls would have you believe, but you would find them all if you looked around a bit. Their language is pidgin-Elizabethan and some of their songs are still of the sea and of England and strong in their blood is a species of rugged individualism which makes the Gary brand look more pallid than usual. In short, for all the cheap romancing the fact has had, they are of that incomparably pure American stock which produced such men as Lincoln and Chief Justice Marshall and, for that matter, Cordell Hull. TVA has a deep but realistic respect for what it calls the native culture of the valley and, far more directly than the citizen of Knoxville, the mountaineer is a part of TVA's plans.

Such is the laboratory for a great experiment. Such are the raw materials good and ill from which TVA prepares to fashion a civilization which, in a certain important way, is new and is significant to all the U.S. That important way is well enough known: the past four years have filled the air with it in various forms. Most simply, it is this: the Tennessee Valley and the continent as a whole had many riches in common when, in 1492, those riches began to be suspected. And the development of the valley up to the present has had much in common with the development of the U.S., the opening up of any rich, new land in the westward course of empire. It has been praised as a pioneer development. Other salient characteristics are these: it has been consistently shortsighted, wasteful, uncoordinated. Far and wide the opinion—sound, bad, and indifferent—grows that we are approaching a turning point in civilization, that among other things an ancient human habit must be corrected. Man must learn to cooperate with his surroundings instead of disemboweling and trampling and hoping to discard them. On the crest of this wave of talk and overrapid action

TVA is the first American attempt to tackle the problem specifically and bit by bit to build at the pace which scientific advancement requires. If TVA succeeds in its valley, it will be of significance not merely to the whole Southeast and not merely as a classic model for similar work in other valleys* but ultimately of importance to all the U.S. At least that is the way the Authority looks at it.

Of TVA's experiment these, briefly stated, are the prime ultimate objectives:

To regulate river flow. To develop navigation to a maximum. To eliminate flood. To develop and use electric power as a yardstick to gauge the practices of private power companies. To distribute as much power as possible as cheaply as possible to as many people as possible. To try to develop cheap fertilizers. To control soil erosion. To classify and improve the soil and put it to its best uses. To promote better farming methods. To conserve the forests. To develop all resources in the valley in good relation to one another.

These are the outward and visible signs of something else again. Apparently it isn't quite possible to undertake such comprehensive responsibilities without a somewhat Utopian gleam in the eye: at any rate TVA has it. The coordination TVA seeks is social as well as industrial. In other words, it involves human beings. The TVA vision runs something like this: the natural forces and resources in the valley will be developed with one eye on the long future and the other on the immediate welfare of the people. Farmers will till only the good and tillable soil. The rich resources of the valley will be developed by relatively small industrial groups; production will be governed more by local than by outside demand.

The factories will be not in the cities but in the open valley. The leaders, by preference, will be valley men—the workers

---

*The valleys of the great Columbia and Missouri rivers have been mentioned as eligible for similar treatment. And last August California's Governor Rolph signed legislation establishing a state water project Authority which will have charge of a $170,000,000 development to which, it is expected, the federal government will contribute $48,000,000. Chief objectives: to build Kennett Dam (as great in bulk as Boulder Dam); to impound the flood waters of the Sacramento; to pump excess water into dryish San Joaquin Valley; to develop and sell electric power.

must be—until unemployment is no more in the valley. Not only will farmers and villagers earn a prospering penny; people will move out from the cities and work the land and the machine as well. In short, a number of familiar phrases flow readily to mind: what TVA is after is a decentralization of industry, regional planning on a large scale, a well-wrought and well-controlled balance between the Jeffersonian dream of an agrarian democracy and the best characteristics of what so many people like to call the Power Age.

In this enormous machine the balance wheel is human. And here TVA becomes almost mystical in its earnestness and speaks of preserving and developing the native culture. For what that means, you must look again at the man and woman who sit on their front porch. These mountaineers must be raised and reconciled to such higher standards of living as obtain in more prosperous parts of the valley. They must also be taught responsibility to society. On the other hand the more prosperous valleyites must be raised to that high standard of Americanism which is peculiarly the mountaineer's.

It is no easy task and it is not easily definable, but it is important to TVA and it is therefore to be considered. How seriously, if not indeed fanatically, TVA is taking these social issues its employment policies will serve to show. From the very first the stand has been notably firm against political appointments, to the slight irritation of Postmaster General Jim Farley, and just as firm, though more kindly, against unemployed "outsiders." TVA's work is indeed to be of, by, for the valley people. As for the valleyite who applies for work, he is faced with a peculiarly searching questionnaire, is asked much in detail about his schooling and his relationship with spirituous liquors during the past outlawed decade. To gather such strange if valuable data requires, to say the least, tact—if you wish an independent countryman to take your job rather than starve in protest. Evidently TVA has tact, too, for men are taking jobs. The men who build Norris Dam will live in the carefully pioneer-style model town which will rise at Cove Creek. They will work only three days a week. (Three days' wages will go far in mountain families used to getting along on $100 and less a year—and will go to twice as many families.) On the free days these workmen may, if they like, attend vocational school and learn plumbing and masonry and carpentry and other crafts. Not, as TVA points out, for the purpose of annoying the trade unions, but primarily to supply good handymen to remote neighborhoods which have had none before.

All of which is very fine. It has an epic quality—and a quality more easily put in words than in deeds. Who are the men who are to translate it? They are more important to the plan than their titles suggest, for like many another Rooseveltian conception, the Tennessee Valley Authority can be visualized only in terms of the men he chose to administer it.

The TVA is a corporation created by the Tennessee Valley Authority Act, which in turn was created by warlike little Senator Norris of Nebraska and by a President who saw more in it than "putting the Government into the power business" (which had brought two prompt Republican vetoes) and by careful study of the legal set up of Port of New York Authority and—like any great and farsighted idea—by a number of men who also ran. To the extent of having a corporate name and seal, the right to sue and be sued, to make contracts, to adopt by-laws, to purchase or lease property, it is an independent corporation. It is under no government department but it is entitled to the help and advice of any federal office, including the Patent Office. It is armed with the right of eminent domain. Fifty million dollars of the President's $3,300,000,000 recovery program is at its disposal to begin with, and there are possibilities of additional income from the sale of power and fertilizer. For future work the Board is authorized to issue, on the credit of the U.S., $50,000,000 in 3½ per cent bonds having a fifty-year maturity. (So far as power is concerned, there will be no subsidy. TVA must sell its power at a rate which will not only return all operating costs but will also, over a term of years, retire the capital invested.) The task has no deadline. TVA has only to submit an annual report to the President and to Congress. From time to time the President may recommend additional legislation. He it is who appoints and may at any time remove the Directors.

The Directors are three: two elderly college presidents named Morgan and a very lively young lawyer named Lilienthal.

As Chairman of the Board, Roosevelt promptly appointed Dr. Arthur Ernest Morgan, self-taught President of Antioch

(Work-and-Study) College, which in ten years he has built up from an obscure experiment. His first official act was to submit a careful inventory of his personal properties, a thing no U.S. public officer had ever thought of doing before. Dr. Morgan is as well known among hydraulic engineers as among educators. It was he who put the wild Miami River in its place after the Dayton (Ohio) flood in 1913; it was he who lent an authoritative hand to the drafting of the drainage codes of half a dozen states. President Roosevelt was impressed by something more when he first read Dr. Morgan's *Antioch Notes.* Dr. Morgan's friends know him as a man of considerable human wisdom, of breadth and integrity and originality of mind.

The other Morgan is a college president too. He is Dr. Harcourt Alexander (no kin to Dr. A. E.) Morgan, who leaves behind fourteen years' service as President of the University of Tennessee. He is an authority on artichokes, bugs, cats, dogs, eggs, fish, geraniums, hay, iguanas, jam, and so down the alphabet. He is also, by dint of years of study, an authority on agriculture and industry in his valley. To balance industry and agriculture is his assigned task.

David E. Lilienthal, Director and General Counsel, is more the "wonder boy" type. He has a brilliant past at thirty-four, especially as a legal authority on public utilities. At Harvard Law he was (like a few other headliners today) one of Felix Frankfurter's star pupils. Later he became the friend and associate of Donald Richberg, was Special Counsel for the city of Chicago in the telephone-rate controversy which Chicagoans will well remember. At thirty-two he left Chicago to help Wisconsin's Governor Philip La Follette reorganize the State Railroad Commission. His revision of the public-utility statutes of Wisconsin has already served as a model for several other states.

The Directors serve nine-year terms (staggered to begin with at nine, six, and three at a $10,000-a-year salary—less, for the time being, the government's 15 per cent cut in basic salaries. Each is entitled to one of the numerous empty government houses on the Muscle Shoals reservation where by requirement of the creative act, official TVA headquarters must be. They also get traveling expenses.

Preliminaries are if anything harder than the job itself. It takes time to learn just where such a corporation stands in relation to the statutory framework of seven states and many municipalities.* It takes time to make your own definitive studies geological, social, and industrial; time to know all there is to know about every square mile of a great valley.

Granting all these points, eyebrows have yet been raised at the record of the Authority's first months in its valley. TVA's reluctance to issue detailed statements, its practice of giving such items as employment figures in round and sometimes conflicting numbers (even when asked to specify), the fact that not until August 10 did TVA allocate specific duties to its three Directors to execute preliminary projects "with the least possible delay"—at such small straws in a large wind, no few people have looked askance, have suggested that two elderly academicians, however at home with round phrase and round idea, have limitations when confronted with a mass of cold hard detail demanding stern organization. They have at any rate been less specific than gentlemen handling the public's money usually are. By the end of the summer, TVA had begun to assert itself as we shall presently see. But with much theory still to be translated into practice, it is perhaps as well to bear these criticisms in mind.

The critics, however, mislead if they imply that valley workers are idle, have no immediate plans. Many a valley venture hums. On September 1, after 200 men had spent the summer taking inventory, TVA inherited Muscle Shoals and sixty (sometimes called eighty) Shoals men from the War Department (and in all is absorbing between 400 and 600 men from the War and other departments). The Authority will arrive at its own valuation of this property through "an appraisal by disinterested engineers." What will be done with the Shoals nitrate plants is yet to be decided. As they stand, they're pretty

---

*Late in August a situation arose which will force a definition of TVA's position and powers. Southern Industries & Utilities, Inc. applied to the Federal Power Commission for a fifty-year permit, against the issue of which Counsel Lilienthal, in the name of TVA, made formal protest. S.I.& U.'s proposed development: a dam and powerhouse at Aurora (near Paducah), an immense valley-gulfing reservoir 167 miles long. Grounds for protest: Congress granted TVA exclusive jurisdiction in all developments on the Tennessee. The matter is to be settled at a public hearing.

useless and outdated. But TVA, experimenting in cooperation with agricultural colleges and farmers' organizations, hopes in time to learn how to make fertilizers which will sell at about a third their present cost. Perhaps on the "four-county" plan—a central plant to each four counties, each to serve the needs of its limited territory. TVA doesn't know yet. In the mountains northwest and southeast of Knoxville, two CCC camps and 400 men are beginning the great task of reforestation and erosion control which in time, Dr. Morgan estimates, will absorb 5,000 workers at the very least. In a secluded laboratory a one-time Alabama Rhodes Scholar is developing a new method of transmitting power over long distances—a method which may make today's transmission as obsolete as a wooden plow. What the method and who the man are TVA's secrets. In Knoxville's Sprankle Building, in 106 offices, TVA draftsmen are busied over plans; in the wild country twenty miles above Knoxville, where Cove Creek steps into the Clinch River, more men on the TVA payroll explore the countryside. In these last two activities center TVA's most immediate, most important present undertaking: the Norris Dam.

The wild honeycomb of caves upstream has been found safe against reservoir leakage, and now TVA's men are laying out highway and railway connections, clearing the three miles of land where a model and permanent town will rise to house the workers. An able body of able-minded men is going over the plans for Norris Dam, among them Colonel George R. Spalding (St. Louis office of the War Department), Mr. S. M. Woodward of the University of Iowa (whom Chairman Morgan describes as "one of the ablest men the United States ever produced in hydraulics"), Mr. J. L. Savage (designer of the Boulder and Madden dams), and Mr. Savage's colleagues in the Denver office of the Reclamation Bureau. Who will boss the job of building, TVA can't tell. Some other government agency snitched from under the TVA nose the able gentleman chosen (his name is withheld), and all the Authority can say is that Norris Dam will *not* be built by public contract.

However that may be, construction will start early in 1934. The 250-foot Norris Dam and the powerhouse will take four years to build and, together with the transmission line that will link the development with Muscle Shoals, will cost nearly

$45,000,000. The deep tangle of valleys above the dam will brim with a ragged lake of some eighty-three square miles, impounding 140,000,000,000 cubic feet of water.*

The average March–October flowage ratio of the Tennessee River at Muscle Shoals has been estimated at ten to one (peak divergence was fifty-three to one). The Norris Dam, with its immense storage, will go far toward bringing this flow into balance. Which will mean:

For navigation:

At present, navigation is governed by the seasons, and the channels are poor. Every year 2,000,000 tons of cargo ply the river below and the river above Muscle Shoals, but only 12,000 tons use its locks. Water storage and the clearing of a nine-foot, 650-mile channel will give this tonnage free passage from Knoxville to Paducah. In time to come the valley's raw materials will have cheap passage by water, and cheaply by water valley products may reach any port on earth.

Flood:

Norris Dam will greatly reduce; subsequent dams will eliminate.

Power:

At present Muscle Shoals can count on only about 120,000 horsepower of "firm" (constant, year-round) waterpower—and only firm power is worth talking about. The powerhouse at Norris Dam will generate 220,000; by balancing the flow of the Tennessee is sure to raise Muscle Shoals well toward its ultimate capacity of 610,000 horsepower. Subsequent dams not yet scheduled will do still more. The ultimate horsepower possible to wrench out of the river is estimated at 3,000,000.

What TVA could do with this power is what scared Presidents Coolidge and Hoover into vetitive spasms. Nine power companies under two great holding corporations, Commonwealth & Southern and Electric Bond & Share, now serve 550,000-odd valley customers with power at an average production and transmission cost estimated at nine mills per

---

*From ninety-two cemeteries to drier territory, tactful TVA will transfer the occupants of 4260 graves, "with signal honor to the dead and with due deference to the living."

kilowatt hour.* Wholesale power to other utilities and to manufacturers is generally cheap, but it is alleged that domestic
users and small municipalities have been known to pay six to
eighteen times the average production cost.

These private companies, combined, are equipped to supply
33 per cent more power than the valley is using.

Within a very few years, thanks to TVA, excess production
will jump to 66 per cent. And TVA hopes to sell its power at a
uniform switchboard rate considerably lower (how much, nobody can be sure) than rates have a habit of being. How on
earth the valley is to absorb all this excess power and what on
earth it will mean to the power companies and a $400,000,000
investment in private power (the figure is Wendell L. Willkie's,
President of Commonwealth & Southern), powermen would
like very much to know.

Many an interested party was trying to find out during the
summer months—while TVA issued broad missionary statements and while TVA's Directors kept dumb and looked wise.
Not even yet, not for years to come, may powermen or TVA or
any human agency know all it wants to know about TVA's
power problems, yet when, on August 25, the Authority put its
cards on the table, powermen recognized a New Deal and a
strong hand indeed.

Lawyer David Lilienthal, in charge of TVA's electric power,
will act on these basic policies: "Private and public interests in
the business of power are of a different kind and quality and
should not be confused. The right of a community to own and
operate its own electric plant is undeniable . . . one of the
measures which the people may properly take to protect themselves against unreasonable rates. Such a course of action may
take the form of acquiring the existing plant, or setting up a
competing plant, as circumstances may dictate. The fact that
(TVA) action . . . may have an adverse economic effect upon

*This, as applied to all nine companies, is the merest estimate-derived-from-
an-estimate. Carl D. Thompson's "Confessions of the Power Trust" contains,
among much else, a study of Alabama Power Co. (subsidiary of Commonwealth & Southern) as a representative company, and Alabama Power's average production cost is therein estimated at .882 cents a kilowatt hour.

a privately owned utility . . . a matter for the serious consideration of the Board in framing and executing its power program . . . is not the determining factor. The most important considerations are the furthering of the public interest in making power available at the lowest rate consistent with sound financial policy, and the accomplishment of the social objectives which low cost power makes possible." (Power is indeed the lifeblood of TVA's social-industrial-agrarian scheme; of the local industries and of the well-run farms TVA hopes to foster. And already more than fifty towns have applied for power service.)

"To provide a workable and economic basis for operations," TVA plans first "to serve certain definite regions" (those in the vicinity of Muscle Shoals and Norris Dam, and the belt of land that will lie near the transmission line connecting these dams) "and to develop its program in those areas before going outside." Later, the development will include the whole Tennessee Valley and "to make the area a workable one and a fair measure of public ownership . . . several cities of substantial size (such as Chattanooga and Knoxville) and ultimately, at least one city of more than a quarter million . . . such as Birmingham, Memphis, Atlanta, or Louisville."

Although TVA's present intention is to develop its power program in the valley before thinking of going outside, it may go outside "if there are substantial changes in general conditions . . . government policy" . . . or if the private companies "do not cooperate in the working out of the program."

And, possibly more sinister still to powermen, since conceivably it foreshadows a great buying-over campaign: "Every effort will be made . . . to avoid the construction of duplicate physical facilities, or wasteful competitive practices. Accordingly, where existing (transmission) lines of privately owned utilities are required to accomplish the Authority's objectives . . . a genuine effort will be made to purchase such facilities . . . on an equitable basis."

Accounting will show "details of costs, and will permit of comparison of operations with privately owned plants, to supply a 'yardstick' and an incentive to both private and public managers." TVA's power accounts and power records "will always be open to inspection by the public."

Powermen bitterly recall that day in War-time when Alabama Power forked over the site of Muscle Shoals—on which it had already spent some $5,000,000—to the government. All that for $1. They remember, too, what happened later when for publicity purposes Alabama Power reproduced that $1 check: Alabama Power was fined $500 for reproducing a government document. Nowadays even louder and funnier things are afoot. Tossing reminiscences aside, the same gentlemen as bitterly observe that (through a 3 per cent tax on the gross revenues from sales of energy both commercial and domestic, through the $1 tax on every $1,000 worth of capital stock which, as NRA boys, they must hand over) they along with thousands of investors in private power and along with U.S. citizens by the millions the country over, are forced to pay for TVA's program. Bitterly they agree with Professor Richard J. Smith, legal authority on utilities (who, in the *Yale Law Journal*, June 1933, points out that municipal control and state regulation of private power have often as not been merely negative in properly directing the expansion of the industry), and again bitterly they expand upon his observations, cry that if the government *must* take the utilities in hand there's a sounder, wiser way of doing it than by TVA's proposed policy of serving isolated municipalities, or breaking down the great transmission systems whereby the load may be balanced and the rates may be kept down. That wiser way, say the powermen, is by out-and-out, comprehensive acquisition of such systems. And as for that, Wendell L. Willkie recalls the offer he made before a House Committee last April when TVA was imminent: to absorb all power TVA might generate and to sell it over his own lines at rates congruent with such savings as TVA might effect. Not a move was made about that but Mr. Willkie's offer still stands.

As for what can be done about it, powermen will remind you of certain rights which are theirs according to the Fourteenth Amendment. And will observe that TVA cannot enter into direct competition without nullifying the franchise which grants a utility exclusive right to operate within its given territory. And will remark that even in these dizzy times there are courts where, perhaps, such matters will be granted a fair hearing.

In fact, TVA has swung a bold foot through a beehive of problems both practical and ethical, of significance not merely in themselves but as they apply to the whole theory of relationships between private and public interests. These are problems and this is a theory which have yet to be solved and defined. Meanwhile, one corner is quite clear of doubt: in very truth, the U.S. government is "in the power business."

Such is the program of the Tennessee Valley Authority. (And be it observed that power, important though it is, is to be the mere spine of the whole living animal.) Such are the mere first inklings of the action which must, through years to come, carry it out. And such are a few of the problems yet to be solved by the men who have committed themselves by oath to a belief in "the feasibility and wisdom" of TVA's program. Meanwhile, nothing is built and all is planning and a ruffling of blueprints. Not until 1938, when Norris Dam stands tall and solid to the memory of the men who fought for it, when the great hive-shaped dynamos down the river begin to whine their hearts out, will TVA begin to realize returns. Not until then will the world be qualified to begin to judge the men now busy with beginnings.

Fortune, October 1933

Cockfighting

You are a gentleman. You have a taste for sport (most likely horses), leisure to indulge it, and an estate. One quiet morning you walk down to your stables. As you come around the side of the barn, you hear a soft but violent fluttering of wings, an agitated hissing, a passionate exclaiming of low voices. You look down, and there are your Negroes (if you happen to be a southern gentlemen) crouched in a wide circle on the ground, leaning on bent knuckles, peering into the center of the ring. They are watching two birds, large and brightly colored, that cling together beak to beak with arched necks, dancing up and down, while their wings whir and they slash at each other viciously, rapidly, with their spurs. The birds are gamecocks, most ferocious of all domestic creatures, and their dance is fatal—it can end only in death. And you are present at one of the many new births of man's most ancient sport, legally extinct in at least forty of the United States, frowned on in all, minor and surreptitious pleasure of the rich, secret passion of the poor, purpose of the Heel Tap Club, most exclusive in the world: cockfighting.

Since 1879* there has been next to no open pitting of game-cocks in the U.S. Breeders who engage in it, hangers-on who watch it, may be subject to fines or imprisonment, their accessories seized; the birds themselves may be "arrested" and destroyed. Rarely, an obscure paragraph or two may appear in your newspaper: a cockfight has been raided, a few anonymous gentlemen fined. But for all the public knows, this sport, which kings and presidents have favored, might be as obsolete as dueling. Only its few devout followers can hint at the number of matches fought yearly in the U.S. (perhaps a few hundred, perhaps a few thousand) or the amount of money which changes hands in fees and purses (from $5,000,000 up); and neither gentleman nor gangster, whose codes after all have much in common, will reveal where these mains are fought

*When the last public main (between Georgia and Kentucky) was held at the old Spanish cockpit in New Orleans, scene of America's most famous cockfights.

or who fights them. But cockers will tell you this: that the American Society for the Prevention of Cruelty to Animals (which gets a slice of all fines imposed by its initiative in most states) collects thousands of dollars every year. And slaughters hundreds of thoroughbred cocks.

Around cockfighting, centuries older than most other sports, has grown a host of rules, customs, and traditions, but in essence it is the simplest of combats. Two breeders or their handlers, cocks under their arms, step into the pit (a twenty-foot circle inclosed within a low wall), set the birds down face to face on the ground, and stand back, attentive. The cocks do the rest—fly at each other and fight until one is dead or unconscious. For weapons they use gaffs, slender, curving needles of murderous steel fitted to their legs over the filed stumps of their natural spurs. The gaffs may be long or short (one and one-quarter to two and one-half inches); with them the cock slashes forward and upward, turning his leg as a boxer turns his arm in an uppercut, using his beak to bite and hold and balance. The longest gaffs give the shortest, bloodiest fights. They are used chiefly in the South, where heat, sloth, and sudden temper discourage lengthy argument among cocks as among men. Little can be done to aid the fighters. If a blood clot forms in a cock's throat, his handler may (when the referee calls time out on some technicality) suck at the cock's beak to remove it; if he is wounded (blind or paralyzed) so that he cannot fight, he may rest while his opponent's handler scoops up his own cock and runs through a complicated count; then, if he is still helpless, he forfeits the match.

There are three ways of pitting cocks. Most frequently, on impulse or to settle a discussion of their birds' merits, two breeders may set their favorite cocks against each other informally and bet on the result: such a fight is a "hack." Formal cockfights require weeks of training and preparation. Two promoters may collect teams of cocks, their own and/or their friends', match them by weight in an odd number of fights, and so make a "main" to which come spectators from miles around. Besides the betting on individual performances, there is usually a big wager on the outcome of the main. Greatest events of the cocking world are tournaments held annually where enthusiasts are thickest. To these travel breeders who come hundreds of miles for the chance to win a purse and a championship, perhaps to make their strains famous, and so valuable commercially. An entry fee is charged each contestant, the sum divided into purses for the winners. Such tournaments may last for several days, and the winning cocks meet in elimination matches from which emerge the champions. To U.S. Breeders, the Orlando (Florida) and Jersey Breeders' tournaments are the Kentucky Derby and Preakness of cockfighting.

If you doubt the color and gravity of these spectacles, read one of the four national magazines devoted exclusively to fighting cocks. *Grit and Steel, Feathered Warrior, Knights of the Pit*, and *Game Fowl News* are the four, with a combined circulation of some 25,000 copies a month. Correspondents in all parts of the country report the outcome of important mains and tournaments; exciting matches, valorous birds are described; breeders advertise the courage and cunning of their fowl. For (obscure and furtive as it is) cockfighting is a sport and a business, with thousands of followers who give their lives and fortunes to it. Absent though it may be from the sports columns of the New York *Times* or the Chicago *Tribune*, it has its definite place in the sporting life of the nation. The tout who haunts the race tracks, the gangster who feeds on boxing and wrestling matches, the gentleman who hunts with thoroughbreds at Warrenton or Radnor—all these are likely to be found around the pit when two fine cocks are matched.

Those who love the sport are not discouraged by its clandestine nature. With the fanatic fervor of all enthusiasts, they gather covertly in dark, deserted places, from Christmas until Independence Day, to see their birds win a main or two, then die. The pit may be erected in a neighbor's barn, in an abandoned shed, a basement, or a gymnasium—sometimes even in gloomy, unrented lofts of Manhattan office buildings. In all parts of the country (but chiefly in rural districts) news of a coming main passes among the devotees discreetly, by word of mouth. Like members of some sinister secret order, they meet silently on the appointed day; gentlemen, breeders, yokels, gangsters—society's highest and its lowest, seldom those in between who comprise the Public. A file of cars follows its leader down a road, turns off, halts in a field beside some ominous black building yawning against the night sky. The headlights vanish; the obscure company melts through a doorway. Then, within, the cautious mumbling of their voices may be heard, and the sport begins.

Like members of a secret order, too, these sportsmen have their unwritten code of honor. Nothing unites them but their common passion and the peril of the Law. They sign no legal contracts, give no tokens of good faith; none are needed. Their bets are made verbally and paid without question. They expect no trickery in the pit, for a gamecock fights eagerly to the finish, without aid or urging, and such prearranged decisions as grace the prize ring and the track are next to impossible. The cocking clan has also its High Moral Purpose: its value of the gamecock as an example of ideal courage. They love to quote the speech Themistocles made to his Athenian army in 480 B.C., on the way to Salamis: "These animals fight not for the gods of their country, nor for the monuments of their ancestors, nor for glory, nor for freedom, nor for their progeny, but for the sake of victory, and that one may not yield to the other." Rugged individualists are these rooster worshipers, and they will remind you that the eagle was chosen to symbolize the U.S. by only two votes over the cock.

What makes a *game* cock is courage. It is a superlative kind of courage, blind, stubborn, and uncompromising, which has only two ends: victory or death. And therein lies the fascination of this spectacle—it is the most primitive combat a man may be privileged to see in these times. The birds are bred for gameness alone; they are delicately cared for, fed, and conditioned, with no purpose except to die in battle. Other cocks, bred for poultry or for exhibition, may be as pure in blood, but to a cocker they are only "dunghills." A dunghill cock will fight for supremacy in the poultry yard, sometimes to the death; but in the cocking pit, armed with gaffs, he will turn and run. His business is to eat and to reproduce his kind. A gamecock, confronted by any rival rooster, will ignore the most alluring hens, the most delicious food, while he glares with beady hatred at his instinctive enemy for days on end; restrained from fighting, he will fall dead of hunger and exhaustion.

There is an axiom among breeders: "A cock is as good as he proves himself in the pit." The purest ancestry, the best training and handling are no guaranty that a cock will be truly game. For gameness, in this sport, is an absolute quality, not a comparative one; and there is no certain proof of gameness except death. That they may judge as best they can the quality of a bird for the pit, breeders have only one test. They take two stags (to a cock what pups are to a dog—after their first molting, when they are about a year old, they become cocks) and let them spar with muffs fitted over their spurs.* But such a trial is little more than a test of form and tactics.

And there's another axiom of the pit, following logically from the first: "You can't *buy* a gamecock. You can borrow or steal it, or it may be given to you." For the cost of fine cock-flesh is an indeterminate matter. Fresh from a victory in the pit, after winning a $5,000 stake, a bird may be worth $5,000. A few weeks later, after losing his next fight, he may be worth nothing. The breeder who owns a fine cock values him beyond any cash reckoning. Those cocks which *are* sold may sell for as little as twenty-five dollars. They are the birds you see advertised in the cocking journals or changing hands among the grooms in your stable. What their genealogy is, nobody can say, but they are likely to be sufficiently pure in blood, sufficiently game. Other cocks, or notable strains which have produced good fighters for four or five generations, may now and then be had privately from friendly breeders for a few hundred dollars.

The cost of raising a cock is almost negligible. You can breed two hundred for little more than the cost of breeding two. To compete in an ordinary main you may hatch as many as a hundred eggs and select from them as many as twenty-one promising cocks. That will take you about a year and a half, at an average expense of $5 a week—in all, $350. If you hire a man to train and diet them for the pit, you will pay $75 for his work. All your equipment, including gaffs, can be bought for another $25 or less. That brings your total expenses to less than $500. Each of your twenty-one cocks has cost you about $20 —to breed a thoroughbred yearling for the Futurity would take $5,000—and a winner may bring you anywhere from $50 to $5,000, or more: whatever stake has been agreed upon. Or

---

*From this practice, in 1725, Jack Broughton got the idea of boxing gloves for prizefighters.

you can compete in the tournament at Orlando, which costs $1,000 to enter, and win from $1,500 to $8,000 in prizes. Its rich patrons put big money into cockfighting. But it's a game a poor man can afford to play.

If this were the normal margin of profit in cockfighting it would be easy money indeed. There is this catch, however: unlike human fighters, cocks rarely lack courage, never lay down. Their gameness is absolute. And so, if his birds are properly trained, a breeder can count himself normally lucky to win his 50 per cent of the fights he enters. To win six times out of ten is an astonishing average, and few exceed it. There is the case of the prosperous plumber. He bred some gamecocks for his own amusement and found that he had a genius for handling them, as some men have for handling bees. So he gave up plumbing and went in for cockfighting in earnest. His string of victories was considered extraordinary, but in 1930 he made only $8,500. And 1930 was his banner year. To a plumber that may be a mighty good income; to a boxing promoter it would look trifling. Obviously a man doesn't take up cocking for the money in it. Illegal or not, it couldn't be called a racket.

Actually the only real money to be gained from the pit is in bets. And that may be as much or as little as the better's purse allows. There is no sport more purely dependent on chance than cockfighting. To the rich (who are careless of money) it is a game above suspicion; to the poor (who have none) it is a game they can afford. Racing or boxing or baseball may be the national pastimes of the masses in all great U.S. cities. But in the little towns and the lonely rural stretches which are still America, cockfighting is the people's sport. Especially in the South; no spectacle excites a Negro like a cockfight. That's why, until some remote time when the nation turns wholly urban, in countless barnyards the gamecock will remain a telltale evidence of lawbreaking, as (until lately) was the whiskey bottle. You cannot have fine poultry without a cock or two. And where there are cocks you will surely come upon your servants some fine morning, gathered in a ring to watch them fight. Being a gentleman, you will as surely pause to watch yourself.

The genealogy of the gamecock is as vague and anonymous as the genealogy of the masses who have bred him. Where he first came from is a fruitless inquiry: farmers, slaves, and soldiers have had their fighting birds for as long as man remembers. In Persia cockfighting was ancient when Alexander the Great made his conquest; Japanese game fowls are as old as the Japanese imperial family (First Family of the World); and the Spaniards, most passionate of all cockfighters,* found cocks before them in Mexico and Peru. Because in early times voyages were long and fresh stores necessary to efficient soldiers, where armies went the hen (and therefore the cock) was likely to go also. Is that how roosters came into Britain, with Caesar's legionaries? Or were they there already? There, at any rate, they were; and the British watched them assassinate each other in 55 B.C., were still watching them in 1655 A.D. when already they were drifting into the American colonies. First sport of the New World (after boxing, for which a man required no accessories) was cockfighting.

U.S. gamecocks have an honorable but confused ancestry. Until the Revolution most were of pure English blood. Such were the birds General Washington imported from New Orleans and asked Thomas Jefferson over to Mount Vernon to see. Such also were the valiant cocks Andrew Jackson bred even after he got to the White House. But after the Revolution American seamen began to bring back outlandish fowls from the Orient and turn them loose in native barnyards. There were some odd results. From a red Malay cock (now stuffed in the Peabody Academy of Science), brought home to Salem in 1846 by Captain Richard Wheatley, and a hen of English blood sprang the first Rhode Island reds. Other miscegenetic unions produced breeds with exotic names known only in the cockpit: Crazy Snakes, Kansas Sluggers, Roughhouse Blues, Strychnine Greys, Stone Fences, White Mules, many another as threatening. Some 250 native strains have been distinguished, but interbreeding has so mingled them that few are pure. Intermixture makes them no less aristocratic. Game fowl crossed with dunghill blood soon disappear from the pit, and so rarely corrupt the noble strains. Famous U.S. names (which mean little): Warhorses, Whitehackles, Shufflers, Roundheads.

---

*In all Spanish-speaking countries cocks share with bulls the honor of dying most often to amuse the people.

How to breed gamecocks is a question steeped in controversy and superstition. But from the lore of all breeders, whether intuitive or scientific, three simple and universal rules emerge. They are these:

The blood must be kept fresh. Almost all American cockers agree that inbreeding has brought ruin upon English, Scotch, and Irish fowl. A certain amount of inbreeding is practiced, to fix new strains, to keep famous strains pure, especially to reproduce in their children the qualities of great and valorous sires. Some line breeding (matings between nephews and aunts, which to a cocker are not incest) is necessary—how much depends upon the breeder's own discretion, perhaps more upon the purity of the strain itself. Some cockers claim to have produced fine birds after forty years of strict inbreeding. But the majority seek fresh blood after four incestuous generations at most.

The blood must be kept game. The fierce valor of fighting cocks hangs upon a delicate thread of training and selection. A single drop of dunghill blood, as all breeders agree, will destroy it for all time, produce birds fit only to strut about the barnyard.

The hen must be as game as the cock. Oldtime breeders used to say that "one good hen is worth a dozen cocks." Few modern breeders, though they grow lyrical over the strength and spirit of a fine hen, go quite so far. They do grant that sire and dam may have equal influence on the heredity of their young; the sisters of great fighters are prized, and mated with fine cocks.

Cocks differ in the pit as boxers differ in the ring. Each has his own personality, readily felt by a true devotee of the sport, and the methods of no two are quite alike. But, like boxers too, they may be divided by temperament into two rough classes: shufflers and single strokers. A shuffler is a swift, aggressive fighter; he strikes as fast and as often as he can move his legs; he gives his enemy no rest. Single-strokers are powerful, slower and more cunning; they wait for an opening, then thrust accurately and deep, conserving their strength. In the long northern matches these cocks are deadly: they are the Gene Tunneys of the pit. Shufflers do better in the short, violent matches of the South: like Jack Dempsey, they are killers.

But the greatest cocks are those which know both methods. To live long, a cock should crowd his opponent when he can, trying for a quick death, but dawdle when he must and wait for a chance to strike.

Because among most game birds there is little to choose in courage, and because victory depends as much on chance as on skill, physical condition is of first importance in the pit. They are matched by weight, usually within a limit of two ounces; so that any needless fat is a big handicap. And either too much weight or too little is likely to hurt the cock's wind, his greatest asset, whether in a short, violent fight or in a long, exhausting one. Once it took six weeks to feed and train a cock for the pit; now ten or twelve days is considered enough. He is kept alone in a small coop, his weight and vitality closely watched. Daily his feeder puts him on a cushioned table for exercise, tosses him up, lets him fall with flapping wings. The cock finds it very pleasant.

Talented feeders and handlers command great respect among their own kind, high and low. Usually they work under the patronage of wealthy sportsmen; sometimes their reputation grows until they can afford to work for whom they please. Greatest figure in U.S. cocking, now grown almost legendary, was Michael Kearney, who came over from Ireland in 1875 with his birds under his arm. Strains which he developed first for August Belmont and other sportsmen, later for Herman Duryea, biggest gentleman breeder of his time, still dominate American pits. Duryea and Kearney fought their cocks in England and France, won some twenty mains, lost none. In thirty years of breeding they lost only one main, to John Hoy. Today Harry Kearney, Michael's son, is considered a fine handler.

Andrew P. O'Conor, born in America of Irish parents, is a famous handler who has fought cocks for more than forty years. O'Conor's banner years were 1905–06, when he made a triumphal tour abroad, handling for the Earl of Clonmell, who became his friend and patron. Out of three mains, he won two, the third was a draw; a quarter of million dollars changed hands in purses and bets. When O'Conor was in his prime, Dr. H. B. Clarke of Indianapolis was also a notable figure, fighting his own cocks abroad. Dr. Clarke still makes an occasional match. Because so many strains have lost their identity few breeders today achieve the fame of Kearney, O'Conor, and many others thirty years ago. Currently most successful are Peter Horrocks of Cleveland, Col. John H. Madigin of Buffalo, and Thomas W. Murphy of Poughkeepsie. Col. Madigin has won four purses (two of them firsts) in the Orlando tournament, where meet the finest cocks in the South.

Nobody will tell you who are the eight top breeders (socially) of gamecocks in the U.S. And for a very good reason: all but one are rich, all are prominent socially and members of that small, secretive society of cockers: The Heel Tap Club. Founded in 1922, the club centers its roving headquarters about Boston and New York. To its tournaments each season came the eight members with their friends and retainers and their retainers' friends, bringing their own birds which they handle themselves. Once a year it meets as a club, at a dinner given by one member for the other seven.

The names of these reticent enthusiasts, like the name of Yahweh, may not be spoken; nor are their names, for all this silence, high in the councils of government or business. Five are Bostonians, Mr. A and Mr. B are relatives by marriage, both hunting enthusiasts; Mr. A sells insurance, Mr. B is a dog fancier. Mr. C is a partner in a prominent brokerage firm. Mr. D has a woolen textile business. Two others do nothing but manage their estates. Mr. E was a pioneer breeder of polo ponies, Mr. F races horses, is a famous shot. Mr. G is one of the oldest members of the New York Stock Exchange, but none too active on it. His only sporting interest is cockfighting. Only Southerner in the club is Mr. H, a Virginian of the old planter tradition, without money, but a lover of cocks and horses: a typical southern sportsman.

Mysterious this roster may be; but mystery has become a necessity (at least in the North) among cock lovers whose social prominence would otherwise bring them under the spotlight of the Law. Only in the rural South has the Law remained so feudal that it knows better than to molest gentlemen. And even there, publicity outside of their own circle is avoided by these sportsmen. But they protest. Many a Courtesy Colonel grows apoplectic over his julep, reflecting on the indignity offered by animal cruelty laws to an old, honorable, and patrician pastime. It is the timid, weakspirited bourgeoisie, they say, who take away cockfighting from both their inferiors and their betters.

"What happens to the dunghill chicken?" a cocker will exclaim. "At best, his neck is wrung to fit him for the family dinner. At the worst, he is mutilated and fattened, then sent off to a poultry house where pickers with sharp knives slash the roof of his mouth, so that he may bleed to death slowly while he is stripped of his feathers."

To the sportsman a gamecock's death is triumphant and exalted. Even cockers grant that the bird is stupid. Probably he feels no pain—only an irresistible urge to annihilate the enemy who stands for an abstract challenge to his supremacy. Out of the pit, he is well fed and housed, parades at his ease in a small universe of his own. Perhaps three times in a season he fights, and if he is powerful enough to survive, his taste for battle is only whetted. He may live four years (some cocks have lived and fought to be eight) before age and boredom make a victim of him. Then he dies, still in such fury of hatred that no spectator can pity him. And a score or so of gamblers and poor farmers, a sprinkling of fine gentlemen, are happy. To all this the A.S.P.C.A. makes no answer. But faithfully, each year, it gathers up its unrepentant horde of blue-blooded birds. Sometimes (in the great cities) it puts them to die in lethal chambers. More often it turns them over to the police, who wring their necks to feed prisoners or the poor. Many a sergeant who knew no better has locked his sullen flock of criminals in a cell overnight, returned in the morning to find them dead. For gamecocks love nothing better than to fight: like sailors ashore, they can imagine no happier paradise than one in which rages an endless free-for-all, ending constantly in death.

Fortune, March 1934

The U.S. Commercial Orchid

You should know right at the start that there are no less than 15,000 species of orchid, of which a good many of the more restrained types, such as the moccasin flower, and the lady's-slipper, thrive familiarly in our own temperate woodlands. From now on when we say orchid we mean orchid as you understand it: the big, flagrant, tropical job whose normal career runs from hothouse to Milady's collar bone to the garbage can, rustling up, in transit, considerable satisfaction to Milady, considerable expense to her decorator, and considerable profit to the fellow who raised the orchid.

Today, in the U.S., 800,000 to 1,000,000 of these commercial orchids are sold in a year at retail prices ranging from seventy-five cents (off season, for cheap skates) to $8 and $10 and even $12 (in season, for non-pareils) per single blossom and in quantities varying from a very few hundred per midsummer day to a great many daily thousands around Christmas and Easter. The florist who retails the orchid, in spite of the fancy price he puts on it, doesn't stand to make much off it; the man who grows and wholesales it, in spite of the fancy costs he poured into it and in spite of the strong irregularities of the season, does. There are about forty such growers in the U.S., and most of them don't amount to much. A scattering of them have the Pacific Coast trade more or less to themselves; a half dozen or so more, located in Westchester and New Jersey, ship flowers into Greater New York. Of these eastern orchidists the most notable are shrewd Mr. Sam Gilbert, who represents the Richmond Floral Co. of Staten Island, and Lager & Hurrell of Summit, New Jersey. But by and large these growers concentrate on developing and selling individual plants, and ship on the cut flowers as a sideline. There is just one company that really counts in a large way in the commercial-orchid field, and that is Thomas Young Nurseries, Inc., of Wall Street and also Twenty-eighth Street in New York, of Bound Brook in New Jersey, of Cleveland, and of Chicago. Thomas Young Nurseries: whose 160,000 mature plants in two flocks of hothouses produce no less than 70 and as high as 80 per cent of the U.S. orchids sold in season—and a strong 50 to 60 per cent of all U.S. commercial orchids; whose monopoly is nicely protected on the one hand by the high price of good orchid plants, on another by seedling problems, and on still another by a strict government quarantine* against imported orchids as bearers of insect pests. So you can see that all in all, in any story of the U.S. commercial orchid, this one company is pretty much the whole show.

The story in brief is simple. In 1929 big business got hold of a good commodity, which was nevertheless untouched by any save the most tentative and erratic business methods, and took just those large if obvious advantages of it that any gentleman who knew his business would be bound to take. For one thing, the orchid had known only localized distribution; big business gave it national distribution. For another, the orchid had never known promotion; big business promoted merry hell out of it. For the rest, this success story can thank a combination of competent management with those talents peculiarly native to the orchid itself. If, to begin with, you want some picture of the orchid "business" prior to 1929, old Thomas Young himself will furnish a fair one.

In 1922 the Cornell plant physiologist Lewis Knudson discovered that orchid seed will germinate much more dependably in solutions of agar-agar than in anything else; and thus solved the toughest single problem of the orchid hybridist. One of these, the Bound Brook, New Jersey, fancier Thomas Young, took such proliferous advantage of the find that by 1927 he was orchid poor. Thousands upon thousands of unexpected new plants forced him to a choice. Either he must enormously expand his greenhousing facilities, and go into business in a large way if only to defray that expense, or he must sell out. Now for a long time Young had done some business in gardenias and had carried on a sporadic and fortuitous trade in cut orchids, but he was no sort of businessman at all—never even kept any books, and had always raised the orchid pretty much

*Framed in 1919, the quarantine forbids any grower to import more than 400 plants in a year; the orchids face government fumigation; most of them die along with their pests in the process. This quarantine appears to discourage growers: of 14,000 plants authorized for import in 1934, only 9,000 were actually brought in.

for the orchid's sake. Also, he was now sixty-five years old, and tired. He chose to sell out, named the naively low price of $800,000, and sat down and waited.

People came, florists and wholesalers, and yearned around, and went away: big money wasn't highly concentrated in the florist trade. Two of the nibblers are worthy of mention, one because of an act of mercy, and the other because, if he had taken hold, this might be quite a different story. The shrewd and ritzy Manhattan florist Max Schling, good friend to Young, wanted to buy and couldn't, and told Thomas Young his $800,000 price was loony low. The spectacular Morton Goldfarb (M. Goldfarb—My Florist, Inc., the Philadelphia Gimbel's, Macy's, Bamberger's, Abraham & Straus), who is reputed to have grossed $2,000,000 in flowers in 1934, wanted to buy, too, and also couldn't, and is still sore he didn't have the money. My God, if he'd had that outfit by now he'd have flower shops on the corners of every major city in the country, like United Cigar; and he'd sell nothing but orchids, gardenias, and roses, at set prices; he'd mass produce; and he'd be cleaning up.

But time went on, and there were no takers. In the next couple of years Young had to double his hothouse space, rent his own wholesale store (first of its kind in the orchid trade) in New York, and in fact was on the verge of being forced into big business if only by default. He felt awful.

And then with opening of the febrile and outlandish year 1929, a very different kind of fish swam past, struck, and swallowed Young's bait right to the armpit. And Young drops out of our story, free of his burden. Free of most that had comprised his life, for that matter.

Wall Street's Charles D. Barney & Co., through its new "new business" man, Carl Beckert, and through the promoter Arthur Bunker, got wind of Thomas Young's plight and investigated: and before long it was a deal. Barney's Reybarn Investments, through Barney's Selected Industries, Inc., bought out Young for $2,750,000 cash, rewarded idea-man Bunker with 25,000 of its 150,000 common shares and the temporary presidency of the new company, shook out the rest of the stock in the laps of Barney partners, named its officers, filed away newborn Thomas Young Nurseries, Inc., in its fat portfolio, and sat down to await statements on something novel in history: the handling of orchids as a big business.

The results at the end of 1929, which were reported in the first issue of *Fortune*, were pretty indeed: net earnings of $800,000 on a $2,750,000 investment. Earnings in the years since have of course diminished considerably—have even, two years, blushed red. But they have diminished by no means so much as you'd have every reason to expect of earnings on one of the most eminently useless commodities in existence during six of the most eminently lean years of an era. Gardenias have, to be sure, done their part—10 per cent gross and doubtless a lot less net; but the gardenia market has been stuffed so full it has busted. (Few years ago the flower wholesaled at $14 to $18 a dozen; now the best are $1.50 to $6.) Scarcely assisted the orchid has, in fact, done very well indeed by its impresarios: so well that today, though all the Young properties, green goods included, are assessed at only $2,800,000 you couldn't buy Thomas Young Nurseries, Inc., for $30,000,000. Here, for the past six years (each ending May 31), are gross sales and net profits or losses as listed:

	Gross Sales	Profit
1930	$ 718,630	$333,890
1931	593,040	105,850
1932	348,650	(80,010) loss
1933	266,490	(56,070) loss
1934	384,290	32,240
1935	387,540	24,790
	$2,698,640	$360,690

Indeed, thanks to the breadth of Young's depreciation policy, the story is really happier than that. On an average, during each of the past six years, $67,500 has been written off to equipment depreciation, a total so far of $405,000 or 49 per cent amortization of Young's $903,000 plant. Seven or eight years at that average, which Young's intends to continue, will reduce the book value of the plant to $1 and returns from then on will be almost pure gravy.

Thomas Young Nurseries, Inc., breaks down into three corporations: the New York, the New Jersey, the Cleveland. The New York company, the small and rather dingy wholesale store on Twenty-eighth Street, is operated by Vice President H. E. Kenyon (under Beckert's surveillance) and is owned 100 per cent by the Jersey company (thirty greenhouses, 300,000 square feet of glass, 25,000 gardenia plants, 130,000 mature orchid plants, 175,000 orchid seedlings). The Jersey company also owns 76 per cent of the Cleveland company (ten green-houses, 40,000 square feet of glass, 30,000 mature plants, no seedlings), which still again in turn rents and runs another wholesale store, likewise small and dingy, in behind the world's biggest hotel, the Stevens, in Chicago. And of course all these companies are owned by Reybarn Investments, which again is owned by Barney & Co. Twenty-four per cent of the Cleve-land company is owned by its President, Parmely Webb (son of Myron T.) Herrick, who made news in Paris eight years ago when he lent a suit to a weekend guest of his father's, Charles A. Lindbergh.

As a heavy Cleveland socialite, Herrick was a particularly fortunate appointment for that branch of the business. But then too, setting up a plant in Cleveland and opening a store in Chicago were both thoroughly smart moves in the first place. Subtle but definite climatic differences between Ohio and Jersey are such that one plant can often ably complement the other by season as well as geography. It's mostly a geo-graphical advantage, though. Bound Brook serves the thick, surrounding herd of seaboard cities; Cleveland is generally free to serve Chicago and the great breadth of hinterland. When Barney's went into the business, remember, the orchid was al-most purely a short-haul, indeed a metropolitan, commodity. Within a year Barney's had extended the shipping radius to 1,000 miles and now, thanks no less to distributive machinery than to heavy promotion, Young's gets orders steadily from small cities and small towns which never entered the conjec-ture of the old-time orchidists. A fourth of Young's orchids to-day fill provincial orders. Within the first year after it opened, the Chicago store was doing almost as well as the one in New York; of late it has done rather better.

Boss of the whole outfit since 1932 is Carl Beckert, President and Treasurer of the New York company, President at Bound Brook, Vice President at Cleveland, and a pleasant and intelli-gent commercial type who quite precisely looks his part: an olympiad at Yale and a couple of decades of upper-middle-class business activity. None of the Barney partners meddle in much, being chiefly interested in Beckert's annual statements. Beckert himself has no need to overstrain: Cleveland and Chicago, which are carbon copies of the eastern outfit, are in capable hands, and so, for that matter, are Bound Brook and the New York store, and so is the important job of promotion.

Be well advised, before we proceed along the Thomas Young assembly line at Bound Brook, that you are seeing the merest sketch of what is there for the trained horticulturist to see. For the orchid has unbearably complicated reproductive habits and through all the stages of its life must be watched over with a carefulness whose specific lore would fill volumes and which in the long run thaws off the deep end into pure intuition.

A modest one-story affair with beaverboard walls and linoleum floors serves to house the brunt of the purely business end of the whole company: the rest is a shining, hypnotic realm of glass by the acre and of coal and water and moss and moist cinders and quietude and tender care. Beckert's office allows itself a few touches of executive dignity—a gleaming desk, a bookcase full of treatises on financial management, advertising, orchid culture. For a layman, Beckert has learned quite a bit about orchids, but he puts on no authoritative facade. He comes out from New York, not perfectly regularly, early of a morning, runs through things with Mr. Babey (pronounced Bobby), and often as not leaves for town by noon, for an engagement. Mr. Babey, who looks scarcely thirty, is in actual charge not only of the office force and of the packers and shippers, but of the hothouse staff (most of which worked under Young) and even of Godfrey Erickson. Erickson, however, is given plenty of latitude, and that is well: for this silent, curiously gentle, all but mystical Swedish ex-sailor, who has no interest in Young's beyond the flowers as flowers, is possibly the most valuable man in the whole outfit. He has spent twenty of his forty-five years in these greenhouses and he knows, as none of the management makes any claim to, just about all any one man can know about raising orchids.

The two biggest greenhouses (65 by 200 feet) and six of the standard size (35 by 250 feet) are devoted to 25,000 gardenia plants; the rest of the thirty to orchids. The orchid houses may strike you as surprisingly cool for tropical plants; the average temperature is 62 degrees to 66 degrees Fahrenheit. When a crop needs forcing the temperature may be raised as high as 90 degrees. The houses are steam-heated. Air conditioning was once considered, but it was discovered it would cost $27,000 to condition one twenty-five-by-forty-foot greenhouse, and the idea was dropped like a hot potato. Young's uses aluminum paint in its greenhouses for cleanliness as well as erosion resistance, and repaints every year. Cleanliness is of immense importance, and every square foot of earthen floor is turned and freshly cindered once a year to keep down weeds and fungi. Orchid plants used to hang in baskets, but the roots dried out too quickly, and now ordinary pots do the job. There is no standard way of benching the pots; the matter rests with the individual grower. Erickson is for stadium-wise tiers rather than level benches, arranges his plants in one vast geometric alignment, and centers immense importance on such abstruse minutiae as the distance a given plant should occupy, at a certain age, between the roof and the floor; a matter of mere inches. A strange man, Erickson, and an able one. Able to say that his orchids "tell" him "what they need" and to make that, somehow, not fatuous but almost credible.

All of the Young orchids, except for a few thousand lady's-slippers, are of the great division of epiphytes (devourers of air) and average two flowers per plant per year and are generally productive for around twenty years. The nurseries are specially distinguished as having the world's largest and best collection of whites. No orchid is pure white, but the whiter the better: they're particularly popular for weddings, and bleaching is a common practice among some growers. Keeping, of course, only the commercially useful plants, Young's has also more varieties of orchid than any other grower, and is the largest if not indeed the only grower interested in crops rather than in the development of individual plants. Most popular orchids are members of a showy family called *Cattleya*: each hybrid differs, and blooms at a different time of year so that—if you want it—a continuous supply is obtainable. In 1935, 318,000 of the flowers Young's sold were cattleyas. For its crop in general, the company must depend on two sources, the mature plant itself, and the one to three bulbs into which it subdivides each year—bulbs which themselves are blowing off flowers a year later. Raising from the plant and bulb is, as orchids go, fairly simple; merely a matter of taking all sorts of care. Here, very briefly sketched, is the extremely important job of hybridizing, of raising seedlings—a job which at Bound Brook is handled by three men.

The raw materials are simple enough: coal, pots, water, osmundi for orchid plants to grow in, agar-agar to nourish the orchid seeds themselves. Coal, pots, and a lot of water are necessary to any greenhouse. Osmundi, the stuff any orchid plant, seedling or not, grows in, is a springy, nitrogenous sort of moss which looks like matted horsehair, smells a little like a zoo house, grows like a lot of footstools in Florida bogs. Young's buys about 7,000 sacks of it (2,000 for Cleveland) a year at about $1 a sack.

Even less expensive is the agar-agar. Bound Brook uses only about five pounds of it a year, at $3 a pound, in its 1,600 test tubes. Agar is a tawny, powdery derivative (translucent gray in solution) of Oriental seaweeds which has long been important as a culture medium in bacteriology. Since 1922 it has been a godsend to orchid hybridizers. For the orchid seed, unlike that of any other plant, does not wear enough food to nurse life into it, and orchid men in the past had fed it peat moss, fungi, pure manure, burlap, turkish toweling, and virtually everything else short of a bit of old lace, without any predictable success.

The new generation begins with the flower; and with the genital subtleties of the orchid Charles Darwin managed to fill a thick book. Discretion is the better part of valor and we had best say little more here than this: nature contrived every flower, as you must know, as nothing more nor less than an invitation to the rape; and the orchid takes advantages of that privilege spectacular and complex far beyond the point of mere abuse. A bee, lured among those lordly floral leaves, hikes his thighs around many unusual corners, departs woolly with pollen, and, falling for another labyrinthine love trap, leaves that yellow dust against the sexual organs of another orchid. Shortly the flower droops shut against any later invasion; down the stem a plant womb swells in the course of nine to fourteen months to the size of a child's fist and, gently exploding, delivers posterity upon the mercy of the air and of nature. In the nursery, of course, the plants are fertilized not by random bees but by careful, selective hand and, long before ripeness, the womb is sealed in a waxen sack. And the seed, five hundred thousand to a million of them, looking like fine wheat flour, are taken to the laboratory, which looks hardly more elaborate than the kitchen of a modern farmhouse. And there begins a job years long.

With platinum-pointed, flame-sterilized needles the seeds are sown, 200 to a test tube, in a solution of agar which hardens and shrinks, holding the roots of the seedlings firmly in place. Plugged with cotton, and entered in the studbook, the tubes go to a small hothouse where they are kept under high temperatures for a year or more. If fungus gets in (and nobody knows how it does or whence it comes) it will kill practically the whole batch; otherwise, the losses in this most critical stage seldom run above 2 or 3 per cent. Out of each unharmed tube, however, only the fifty or so hardiest are selected. At this stage the seedlings, infinitesimally exploded into three or four leaves, are only about a quarter of an inch high. At the ends of long steel needles they are lifted from their stiff jelly bed and put, fifty together, into community pots packed tight with fine-chopped osmundi. At the end of a year of hogging nitrogen, the thirty hardiest are taken out and planted five to a pot. The weaklings are thrown away. At the end of another year each plant gets its own pot: and again only the sturdiest are kept. By this time the original 200 seeds have produced possibly twenty-five or thirty plants, of which fungus has killed far fewer than Young's rigid selection.

Once the plants assume individual status, it takes them another four years to flower, six to put out a full crop. And trouble doesn't end there. For orchids are hybrids from wayback; and they are as subject to Mendelian law as any fruitfly or human being. In short, for all the care you've put into the matchmaking, you can never be perfectly sure what will come of it. Some otherwise healthy plants refuse to bloom at all. Others flower minus the baroque lip which is the esthetic point and purpose of the orchid. Others run all to lip. Others are hideously miscolored. Moreover they're as likely to bloom in summer as in winter, and the attempt to force or curb the plants into step with the season accounts for a 5 to 6 per cent crop loss and is seldom, as yet, a howling success at best. The sexless, the deformed, and the bruise-colored, then, reward the grower's years of care with total loss, and the same is pretty much the story when the good ones flower off season. However, once the plant has put forth its flower, all chance ends: it will dependably duplicate that flower for the rest of its natural life. And in the long run this work with seedlings, which is virtually the whole fascination to the fancier and which for the commercial orchidist corresponds to lab work in any industry, is eminently worth the candle for the sake of the occasional windfalls which could occur along no other channel. Such a windfall is the bestselling *Cattleya*, Athena, a cross made by Young himself and so named by Beckert because he hoped the word would be easily pronounced by Greek florists, of whom there are many. Last year was the tenth birthday of the Athena seedlings, the first Athena crop; and Young's now has 2,400 Athena plants, a big productive regiment. The special goal now is a dark purple cattleya which will bloom in season. They've got a good cross already between a couple named Fabia and Brilliant but it blooms in August at the season's very nadir. About 20 per cent of Young's orchids sold today come from seedling-born plants; the rest from plants bred out of bulbs.

After such a trip you may begin to gather something of the why of the ultimate high retail cost of the orchid. The Young nurseries bring to flower 450,000 orchids, more or less, a year. Three-fourths of the mature plants are at Bound Brook. Bound Brook costs run over $300,000 a year. Counting off a probably generous 10 per cent of that to gardenia culture, the cost of raising the average single cut orchid can therefore be figured, if quite roughly, at around eighty cents.

For a number of good reasons, moreover, you'd probably best stay out of the business. To say nothing further of the quarantine, the plants cost money. Finest hybrids that bloom in wearing season can't be had for less than $200 each; some have been sold for as much as $5,000; and a few years ago Lager & Hurrell reported getting upward of $10,000 for a plant bearing a pure white flower. So, you can see, it would cost quite a handsome penny indeed to buy, say, just 20,000 mature plants. It may occur to you then to build yourself a crop out of seeds. It has already occurred to a number of small growers, and they are having a tough time of it indeed. Not merely is seedling culture a hard, delicate job; you have to increase your equipment like a snowball as time goes on (a handful of seed can populate 7,500 pots) and your overhead snowballs for years before you've flowers for sale. Young's, with many plants both mature and young, and plenty of capital, can afford to discard the expensively curable sick and the exhausted (has done away with 45,000 mature plants since mid-'32) and to take supremely good care of its stock. Less well equipped firms take a beating. They can't expand in step with the expansion of their seedling army and, reducing care costs such as re-potting to a minimum, they get a low yield of orchids that are inferior at that.

A lot of care is taken in cutting and packing orchids. They are never plucked till they're in full bloom for unlike other flowers they fail to develop further if taken from the plant in bud. Once cut they are quickly popped into individual, water-filled tubes, racked in trays, taken to the sorting room, sorted by kind, size, and color, and placed in a refrigerator for the several hours of "hardening" thanks to which an orchid, given a reasonable amount of care from then on, will last a week to a fortnight without wilting and can be transported anywhere in the country. Carefully arranged in boxes braced against crushing, the floral leaves closely watched against folding under, which cracks and blackens, the orchids are sewed into place with cloth tape. The boxes are filled with macerated waxed paper which absorbes no moisture, and tightly sealed. In warm weather the case is closed in another, much heavier: in cold, within two, swathed in many layers of paper. For long journeys each flower takes along its own tight-stoppered flask and the boxes are labeled Handle With Care in flashy red italics. On any long haul they are shipped by express; last Christmas the Twentieth Century tacked on a special car for the sole benefit of Young orchids. Back in 1929–1930 there was even some smart talk about airplane shipment. It hasn't come to much for two good reasons: packaged orchids are bulky, and such rapid transit is uncalled for. The orchid at this stage, in spite of general impressions to the contrary, is a hardy flower.

Young's packs its orchids in the evening. At four in the morning a truckman comes around. He has a key to the shipping room and another to the New York store, and he generally reaches the store about seven. If a special call comes during the morning another lot is rushed off by train, reaches the store about eleven. In town, Vice President H. E. Kenyon and his three assistants never know how many they'll get that day.

Young's New York wholesale store is a good plain job, three steps down from West Twenty-eighth Street's sidewalk near Sixth Avenue, in the heart of the wholesale florist district. Only note of swank about this little box which orchidizes the whole eastern seaboard are a few handsome color plates on the walls. Four smooth-topped benches run the length of the main room; a room behind is occupied by a big refrigerator similar to those used in meat stores; downstairs is a hide-out for flowers kept for favored customers. Young's ships in 300 to 500 orchids a day during the slack season, 3,000 to 5,000 during the rush. The season follows precisely the contours of the in-town social season, thickening all through the fall and rotting away from the bosoms of June brides, with a peak at Christmas time, smaller peaks (which Young's is working hard to develop) for Valentine's and Mother's days, and Mount Everest at Eastertide: within Holy Week U.S. orchidists get rid of 30,000 to 50,000 of the flowers.

By a little after seven of a morning, business begins to thicken up all along the street; Young's orchids are laid out the length of the benches and blue-faced quick little men are sidling and soon crowding alongside. Kenyon quotes a price to the first men who come into the store; they slope out down the street; he waits to see if they come back right away. If they do, he's all set; if they don't, he comes down on his price. The grapevine is in full swing: and prices may vary a lot from one hour to the next. The florists call *Cypripedia* Cyps ("sips" in New York, "sipes" in Chicago), *Cattleya* Catts, but generally don't bother with the technical names, just so the orchid looks salable, i.e., showy. If they want a special type they ask for it by description, Brasso with purple lip and such. Most of them buy only three to five flowers but some, like Schling or Morton Goldfarb, may buy hundreds and, in a big rush, thousands at a shot; and shippers usually buy a lot. Sometimes the haggling gets violent; Goldfarb is at times a star showman, throwing his hat around, breaking pencils, cuffing blossoms behind their ears, and shouting "Christ what lousy orchids!" The trading is as subtle and as merciless as any you'll locate in any market west of Bagdad, but it shakes down plain enough averages. To give you the summertime spirit of the thing, we quote the weekly *Florists Exchange and Horticultural Trade World*: "Orchids continue to drag; no one receives any great quantity but in spite of it, not a few have gone to waste. Good, clean, fresh blooms are commonly offered at fifty cents and seventy-five cents and small or stale samples, quite presentable, as low as twenty-five cents; no one even mentioned a dollar this morning." (A lot of "small or stale samples" are picked up by pushcart men, sold in Harlem.) As a rule, even in summer, Young's refuses any offer lower than seventy-five cents for fine hybrids, and rarer types run high as $1 and even $1.50. In season the low rises to $1 or $1.50, the general high from $4 to $6, and the extra-specials have rated as high as $10. Prices now are up from what they were in 1932 and 1933 but retailers still remember the Easter of 1930 when three orchids sewed together brought $45 and $50.

By ten any average morning, winter or summer, the day's business is virtually completed: from eleven or so on, the store is quiet as an attic, and smells like a recently used mortician's chapel.

By price, demeanor, and reputation the orchid is obviously tops in its field in what is politely describable as aristocrat appeal. Yet the most that the old-style orchidists had ever done about promoting it was to list off names and prices in the florists' trade sheets.

It wouldn't have been like the Young management to let such an opportunity slip by. The Young management didn't and doesn't: today Young's spends about $40,000 a year on promotion. Of that about 60 per cent goes for trade advertising, about 30 per cent for retail advertising. Since 1933 the latter job has been capably handled by a publicity organization known as June Hamilton Rhodes, Inc.

Rhodes, Inc., isn't at all the sort of organization that likes to call itself an "agent"; it is an "assistant." It has quiet tie-ups with producers of lace, velvet, jewelry, orchids, and such luxury commodities, and the service is of two sorts, both free of charge: furnishing raw materials for pictures or the pictures themselves to newspapers and style magazines; and writing, for these same organs, news releases. Rhodes has a round thousand outlets, of which the most important are those magazines whose livelihood is derived from amusing, flattering, and frightening the literate females of the land and giving them advisory service on what to buy. Rhodes is a particular master of indirect advertising: nothing so vulgar as brands, prices, company names, ever roughs up the tranquility of its copy; nor does copy ever accompany a picture. The picture alone the prose alone, is held to be quite, quite enough. So whenever you see in the fashion magazines appealing photographs of sweet young things from a hall bedroom who have about them that inescapable aura of refinement which undernourishment can lend the most ill-born demeanor, and who are molded slick as damp sea cows in velvets and chastely strung with costly jewelry, you will usually observe that they are garnished off to boot with a corsage of orchids, you will know who is responsible, and you may or may not be persuaded that it is after all rather a bloody shame that any woman must ever be deprived of copious supplies of any one of the triumvirate. The literature, which is of the same cut as the art, is perhaps best comparable to the voice of a female radio announcer: chilly contralto didacticism. Besides which, stylish, energetic Mrs. Rhodes herself, or more often her personable assistant Miss Fox, who handles the Young account, turns up in the flesh at fashion shows, wearing orchids and giving chats about them designed to overcome those scraps of prejudice against the flower which still, here and there, linger on. Of late, too, there have been tie-ups between orchids and other class commodities such as Fisher Bodies, Lux Soap, Pepperell Sheets, and Packard Motors. Even the trade ads have the Rhodes touch though they're written not by Rhodes but by the Franklin

Press in Philadelphia, which gets out the exceedingly handsome color plates—first ever used in orchid advertising—on whose hind side the copy is printed. Ordinarily the advertising, in the *Florists Exchange and Horticultural Trade World* for instance, is pretty forthright and plain-jane. Young's, in its trade copy, does stoop so low as to mention itself, but the general sentiments expressed are still and definitely on the flowery side, considering the surroundings. The slogan, "Never be without an orchid," has been found specially effective.

No man even half awake to the social, economic, and political realities of our time could for an instant doubt, after a glance at such methods, that Young's promotive expenditures are worth their salt and to spare. Young's does, to be sure, pay a price for the elegant reticence of its promotion: every other orchid grower in the country has steadily neglected to spend a red cent on advertising. Young's, by keeping its own name off the Rhodes copy, takes the whole trade for a free buggy ride. But Young's can afford it. The whole business has its effect, and not merely on the public but on the florists, who have no soft ideas about orchids; in Young's wholesale store they've even been known to sit on them.

It's a funny thing about the florists. They make money off orchids, to be sure, but that is by no means the only reason why they carry them. Confessed one, in a recent survey: "Any florist in the fashionable districts must carry orchids or have people conclude he is not a first-class florist." Which is one of the lines Young's plugs hardest in its trade advertising.

Carrying the orchid no more for profit than for prestige, the florist does his own valuable bits of promotion. A fat lot is added to the purchase price by the fact that satin-covered boxes, many of them in bizarre shapes, and ribbons of velvet and silk and incidental backgrounds of other flowers are used to exaggerate the sacred stature of the orchid as a gift. You can get it in heart-shaped boxes for Valentine's Day, for instance; and if you care enough about your dear deceased to want to express your grief in expenditure, you can buy a coffin cover woven of orchids.

Even so, retail prices aren't what they used to be, even with the smartest of the florists. They used to run high as $15 and more per single bloom. Today, this is the story of Max Schling, one of the smartest: of any thousand orchids in season, seven may bring $10 to $12; twelve as high as $8; twenty-five will go for $5 and $6; the rest at around $3.50. And in summer you can buy an orchid for seventy-five cents and can't pay more than $4 without insisting. But again even so, the principle remains strongly as you'd expect it to be. To quote another florist: "Society people want orchids because not everyone can have them due to their price. In this shop men won't buy the $6 and $7 orchids but choose the $10 and $12 blooms instead. In other words, it is necessary to keep the price of orchids up in the luxury range to continue their popularity with these people."

When Barney & Co. took over the Young Nurseries, Young had 129,000 mature and 25,000 immature plants and it had for years been possible, thanks chiefly to the agar discovery, to mass produce orchids. It still is. And instead of mass producing, re-member, Young's has thrown away 45,000 mature plants in three and a half years. You can credit depression, and good care, for this only in part. Orchid production has been ironed out to its present delicate balance by one chief and obvious consideration: for the people the orchid appeals to. What we have quoted one florist as saying, plenty of others will admit, and the admission tallies with a conclusion arrived at early in Barney's orchid career in a J. Walter Thompson survey of the New York market: that people like orchids because of their high price. And, though one glance at an orchid, another at any dozen orchid wearers, and a third at orchid promotion, will convince you that there's more to it than that, neverthe-less high price is inevitably and indispensably involved in the orchid. Manufactured at a rough cost of eight cents per blos-som and produced in great masses, it could profitably sell for a lot less than it does: and who would be the buyers? Morton Goldfarb would tell you, plenty and plenty of people who can't touch it now. But how can anyone be sure? No one can. The one reasonably predictable fact is that if the orchid be-came anywhere near as cheap and abundant as the rose, few of its purchasers would be those several sorts and degrees of ladies and gentlemen who at present so satisfactorily enjoy the privilege of supporting it.

Which of itself explains why Young's reduced its orchid

stock and why production and demand are so neatly geared to the present near-million a year. And why also none of the forty U.S. orchidists ever make any really vicious gestures toward underselling each other.

Fortune, December 1935

Book Reviews

"TIME AND CRAVING"
After Many a Summer Dies the Swan
—Aldous Huxley—Harper ($2.50).

THE Aldous Huxley whose early books so skillfully anatomized human viciousness and human hopelessness is no more. With *Eyeless in Gaza* he turned to painful self-searchings. With *Ends and Means* he grew stonily didactic. One of the gifted moral satirists of modern times, he had become, by logical development, a definitely religious man. He still is, but in his new book he turns to his earlier technique: uses once more the light realistic fantasy and the sharp surgical analysis which first made him famous, but uses them to say the most serious things he has ever had to say.

The "Swan" of Huxley's sour fable is Jo Stoyte: old, half-mad with wealth and power ("they are the same"), desperately hanging on to his sexual potency, desperately afraid of its loss, of age, of death. In his gigantic ferroconcrete chateau in Southern California he lives with his young mistress, Virginia Maunciple, a born courtesan with a short upper lip who frequently repairs, for penitence, to the "Lourdes Grotto," which "Uncle Jo" has built for her. Jo's other mainstay is sleek, Levantine Dr. Sigmund Obispo who keeps the old man hopped up with hormone injections, and searches, meanwhile, for the substance by which, in Marxist John Strachey's optimistic phrase, "death might be indefinitely postponed." The doctor enjoys Jo Stoyte's mistress, old Jo himself does a bit of murder, and finally they all go to England, where Obispo uncovers the Fifth Earl of Gonister, who nominally died a century ago. The secret of living indefinitely has already been solved: the Earl, at 201, has matured into a raging fetal ape.

In the proper hands, it could be pulp fiction. In Aldous Huxley's it is quite as plausible as highly intelligent satire need be. In his hands, too, it is the excuse and occasion for the things he particularly wants to talk about. Scattered in short (but stiff) doses throughout the narrative, they are spoken by a Mr. Propter, the straightest and maturest straight man Mr. Huxley has ever permitted himself. As he speaks them, they are some of the firmest, most beautifully articulate essays Huxley has ever written.

Simple in essence, but by no means so simple as they sound, Mr. Propter's ideas boil down to this: "Time and craving, craving and time—two aspects of the same thing; and that thing is the raw material evil." Good, impossible within time, exists only on the animal level and on the level of eternity, of "pure, disinterested consciousness." That level is attained in the loss of wilfulness, of desire, of personality.

With that leverage on good and evil, talking with a rational clarity most mystics have lacked, Mr. Propter makes moral mincemeat of everything in sight, "good" or "bad," within the purely human sphere of endeavor. Some of his enemies—war and fascism—are popular pushovers. Others will leave Propter few takers. A partial list of targets for his dialectic: politics, capitalistic society, organized religion, romantic love, science, socialism, humanitarianism, language, virtue, selfless devotion, sex, art—in brief, all activities on the purely human plane, however disinterested, are productive only of evil.

"I believe," remarks Propter, "that, if you want the golden fleece, it's more sensible to go to the place where it exists than to rush round performing prodigies of valour in a country where all the fleeces happen to be coal-black."

Aldous Huxley went to Southern California about 18 months ago, not to write film plays but because of his eyes. In 1911 he contracted keratitis, which he says "left one eye slightly, and the other almost completely covered with scar tissue, besides inducing large errors of refraction." He went to Los Angeles for instruction in the Bates method of training his eyes to "relax." Although he moves about like a partially blind man, and his right eye looks blind (a blue film), he now reads without out glasses, can do things "I couldn't have any more done than a fly a year ago."

In 1938 he wrote a film version of Eve Curie's life story of her mother. Garbo was to have played it, but the story was shelved. Just completed, in collaboration with Jane Murfin, is an adaptation of *Pride and Prejudice*, for Metro-Goldwyn-Mayer.

For the past six months his home has been a secluded wooden cottage in Pacific Palisades, overlooking Santa Monica. With his wife and niece he lives very quietly, takes long walks—sometimes 20 miles—in the Santa Monica hills. The only movie people he sees much of are Ronald Colman, Anita Loos, Directors Cukor and Mamoulian, and Charlie Chaplin, "an old and good friend." Another friend he sees fairly often is Bertrand Russell, now a professor at U.C.L.A. Recently he gave a picnic; the guests were Russell and Garbo.

As for rumors that he is developing a "new religion" he says: "There is no question of concocting a new religion. Certain people have been preoccupied with similar psychological experiments and with speculations concerning them for the past three thousand years. . . ."

Time, January 29, 1940

GENIUS-À-LA-KING
The Hamlet—William Faulkner—
Random House ($2.50).

THE locale of *The Hamlet* is Frenchman's Bend, a little clump of houses sunk 20 miles deep in the country from Jefferson (presumably Oxford), Miss. The time is the late 19th Century. What the story's essential subject is, God—and just possibly William Faulkner—knows. Apparently it is a study of the village itself, chiefly in terms of an evil clan of intruders named Snopes. The volume is built in four books, like the four movements of a symphony.

Book One is a sort of muted epic on those tricks of sharp rural trading which become the legendary material of country store gossips. It tells how cold Flem Snopes, a tenant farmer's son, gains complete power over Will Varner, who virtually owns the town. Other Snopeses turn up on the horizon.

Book Two is a piece of natural history in human terms; the story of a queen bee. Eula Varner is a semi-superhuman embodiment of unmitigated sex, already embarrassingly female at the age of eight. As she ripens, the male community establishes itself in quavering, fighting concentrics of courtship: first raw boys, the slick sports in shiny buggies. But it is Flem who finally gets her. He takes her to Texas.

In Book Three the idiot Ike Snopes falls in love with a cow. Mink Snopes murders a widower named Houston. The villagers, to cure the idiot of "stock-diddling," slaughter the cow and require him to eat of her. In a gruesome scene Houston's hound attacks Mink. Mink is caught and jailed.

In Book Four Flem returns from Texas with a string of insanely wild piebald ponies and sells them to his neighbors. They break loose in horrendous slapstick and pervade the countryside. Mink gets a life sentence; Cousin Flem doesn't lift a finger to help him. Two bourgeois and a desperate peasant invest all they have in a plot of land where Civil War treasure is known to be buried. They find Flem has hoodwinked them as he has everyone else. When last seen, Flem is on his way to larger operations in Jefferson.

If that were all there was to the book it would be plenty, though no man could quite judge of what. But for Dionysian William Faulkner the story is, as usual, a mere set of springboards and parallel bars for the display of one of the most dazzling and inchoate talents in contemporary letters. The reader who takes in the show exposes himself to so furious a narcotic cyclone of Poe, Melville, Mark Twain and original Faulkner that the best he can do is to hang on to his hat and wits. As the storm screams past he may discern a number of things, mainly favorable to the author and to his own pleasure:

Through his people, both normal and daemonic, through his animals, through his fascination in the mysteries of gesture, tones of speech, stature of objects, phases of weather, and through his magical ability to isolate them in words, William Faulkner records the much-investigated South more subtly and truly than any dozen more simple reporters on it.

If an anthology were made of it, this novel would contain perhaps 100 each of almost incredibly beautiful poems, lyric paintings, scenes from motion pictures. Faulkner has learned more from films, and could give them more, than any other writer.

Whatever their disparities, William Faulkner and William Shakespeare share these characteristics: 1) Their abundance of invention and their courage for rhetoric are bottomless. 2) Enough goes on in their heads to furnish a whole shoal of more temperate writers. 3) By fair means or foul, both manage to play not for a specialized but for a broad audience.

In passages incandescent with undeniable genius, there is nevertheless not one sentence without its share of amateurishness, its stain of inexcusable cheapness.

Time, April 1, 1940

EDIBLE SLICE-OF-LIFE
In the Money
—William Carlos Williams—New Directions ($2.50).

Ever since Zola, writers have tried to commit to paper the daily living of average families. "Naturalism" had a notion that an account of how such a family struggles through its oatmeal, breeds another generation to do likewise, could present all human life fearlessly and whole. The result of this literary theory has been some good amateur anthropology, a titanic amount of dullness, little art.

Part of that little is the work of William Carlos Williams. A Rutherford, N.J., baby specialist and poet, Williams in his best verse gives the simple objects of existence the glistening integrity of pebbles in a quick stream. In *White Mule*, three years ago, he trained his poet-doctor's eye on the ordinary living of a U.S. middle-class family, set down their record in noiseless, antiseptic prose. *In the Money* is a continuation of *White Mule*. It is also a broad advance on the naturalist front.

The materials of *In the Money* are so simple that, judged even by the flattest traditions of Naturalism, they scarcely exist. Joe Stecher is a German-American, his wife Gurlie is Norwegian, his daughters are Lottie, 5, and Flossie, 2. They live in Manhattan, on 104th Street, and the year is 1901. Joe has quit his job (he is a printer) and is trying against stiff, not to say dirty, opposition to set up in business for himself. He lacks the proper piratical zest; Gurlie is hell-bent to get him—and herself—In the Money. In the long run he succeeds, they get a house in the suburbs. Meanwhile Gurlie has snubbed her neighbors and fought bitterly with her mother; Joe has had a personal interview with President Theodore Roosevelt and has not been impressed; Flossie, her parents blandly unaware of it, has acquired the neurosis which will give her whole life shape; the children have been vaccinated and have visited aunts in Vermont; and Gurlie, at the end, is beginning to show a sourness toward Joe which suggests unhappy events for a few volumes to come.

It could be, as such things always have been, as dull as dipsomania. But *In the Money* is as fully fleshed, as complex, and as curiously beautiful as daily life. So Williams lifts his material clear of the stodgy fog banks of Naturalism. To this central ability he brings an impressive set of spare tools. Joyce himself has scarcely greater precision with dialogue, and only Richard Hughes has written so well of the behavior of children. Without one line of comment, Williams makes clear "social significances" which the authors of *Middle-town* can only bumble over. With scarcely a skid into deliberate lyricism, whole chapters become lyric. Dickens without gush, Dreiser without fat, Lardner without cynicism, might combine to approximate it. On his subtle, flexible, non-literary monotone, Dr. Williams seems to carry, without gasp or gesture, the whole load of daily living in the U.S.

Time, December 2, 1940

ABSTRACT PROSE
Ida
—Gertrude Stein—Random House ($2).

Most readers require of prose that it make concrete sense as they think sense should be made. So Gertrude Stein, who uses prose to build a series of abstractions, either infuriates most readers or elicits defensive jeers. But readers who are willing to read words as they are willing to listen to notes in music—as things without an explicit message—can get from her work a rare pleasure. The three stories in her earliest (1909) book, *Three Lives*, being anchored to sense, are good ones to start on. Her latest book, *Ida*, much more abstract, is a good one to go on with.

The heroine of *Ida* is purportedly modeled on the Duchess

of Windsor. That fact need trouble no one, short of a tenth reading or so. Ida is a woman who likes to rest, to talk to herself, to move around. In the course of her lifetime she has several dogs, marries several men (mostly Army Officers), lives in several of the 48 States. She seems at times to be some sort of dim, potent symbol or half-goddess, sometimes a plain case of schizophrenia, sometimes a stooge for Miss Stein. In the long run, after several icily beautiful pages of suspense, she appears to settle down with a man named Andrew.

How much or how little sense *Ida* makes as a story is not important. The words in which it is told are stripped of normal logic, and totally cleansed of emotion. The result is something as intricately clean as a fugue or a quadratic equation.

For those who wish to make the effort, the following suggestions:

> Read it with care, but require no sense of it that it does not yield.
>
> Read it aloud.
>
> Read it as poetry must be read or music listened to: several times.
>
> Read it for pleasure only. If it displeases you, quit.

Gertrude Stein says of Ida: "Ida decided that she was just going to talk to herself. Anybody could stand around and listen but as for her she was just going to talk to herself."

Time, February 17, 1941

A MIRROR FOR ENGLAND
Between the Acts
—Virginia Woolf—Harcourt, Brace ($2.50).

THE late great Virginia Woolf's last book is not one of her major works; it is almost a "light" novel. But it compares with the run of light novels as a Mozart opera compares with one by Sig Romberg. It is also the most nearly public of her exquisitely private books. Its subject is no individual, but the whole of England.

On the lawn of a country house, on a summer afternoon in 1939, a group of upper-class English people watch a village pageant and retire with its ambiguous messages fading on "the sky of the mind." By this time the afternoon is over. Mrs. Woolf has conjured up a heroic image of the whole splendor of English literature and history, from the age when rhododendrons crowded Piccadilly to the moment when, puzzled, uneasy, a little offended, the audience beholds itself torn to pieces among the flashing mirrors of the village players in their finale, called *England: Ourselves.*

These spectators are a sultry, mercifully drawn set: a restive wife, her sullen husband; his aged, beak-nosed, naive father, dreaming of youth in India; his delicate old Aunt, cherishing a crucifix between her bony hands; an assortment of eligible neighbors. The pageant they have come to see is a half-talented, half-parodied hodge-podge which in actual performance would have been sad, silly, and typically British, but which, in Mrs. Woolf's hair-line contexts, is moving too.

While Queen Bess and other principals hold the forestage, for instance, village supers clad in sackcloth creep among the trees, unable to make themselves heard through the wind as they chant: *"Digging and delving, hedging and ditching, we pass . . . Summer and winter, autumn and spring return . . . All passes but we, all changes . . . but we remain forever the same. . . ."* They remind you of Evelyn Waugh; yet in Mrs. Woolf's many-planned perspective they are also in truth the nameless human swarm.

Nature and machines are other characters in the larger drama. A wedge of planes blasts to bits the Rector's fuddling interpretation of the show; and butterflies are deluded by bright costumes on the grass: "Red Admirals gluttonously absorbed richness from dish cloths, cabbage whites drank icy coolness from silver paper."

After the show, the two elders of the household, dreaming of the glories of a vanished England move up to bed, to death. The younger couple, a sorrowful, sadly mismated Adam and Eve, are left alone to their marriage and to silence, sailing like disconsolate swans on the exhausted calm of a summer evening, and on the edge of one of the steepest chasms in history.

"Alone enmity was bared; also love. Before they slept, they must fight; after they had fought, they would embrace. From that embrace another life might be born. But first they must

fight, as the dog fox fights with the vixen, in the heart of darkness in the fields of night."

Virginia Woolf was the unlikeliest artist on earth to stoop to
propaganda, or to any form of public ingratiation. She did not
do so here. Yet England and its people, its present, past, innocence and disease, are here summarized in much the way a
night wind can summarize a continent.

Time, October 13, 1941

GUIDEBOOK FOR A LABYRINTH

James Joyce—Harry Levin—New Directions ($1.50).

THE review of *Finnegans Wake* by Harvard's Harry Levin was
one of the few that gave James Joyce the sense that his book had
a reader. Mr. Levin's volume on Joyce is designed to be read
along with Joyce's works. On Joyce's powers of characterization, on his Swiftian moral grandeur, and on that almost
Shakespearean humaneness which alone could delight the
plainest of readers, he is obtuse as only a hyper-intellectual can
be. But on those intricate obscurities which put off most plain
readers, and on Joyce as a technician and theorist, he has written the best guidebook and the most brilliant criticism to date.

Of all modern artists, Joyce was the most bitterly uncompromising, the most tortuously responsible to his vocation; as
a result, he was "the most self-centered of universal minds."
His obsessive subjects, the city and the artist, bracketed the
whole conflicted matter and spirit of modern civilization. *A
Portrait of the Artist* is self-centered, naturalistic; and Levin
tells a tantalizing little of its earlier 1,000-page version, which
was far more so. The multitudinous date of *Ulysses* vibrated
like cold made-lightning between the cathodes of the most
fluoroscopic symbolism and the most granitic naturalism. In
Finnegans Wake naturalism and the artist himself all but disappear; the book is a shimmering death-dance of chameleon-like
symbols; an attempt at nothing less than a complete serio-
comic history of human consciousness—in Levin's neat phrase,
a "doomsday book," culminating in a Phoenician paradox of
dissolution and resurrection.

Though history was, to Joyce, "a nightmare from which I

am trying to awake," he made some frightening images of the history of his time. *Finnegans Wake* derives much from the philosopher Giambattista Vico's cyclic theory of history, which is highly apposite to the present. According to Vico, and Joyce, the first of a civilization's four phases begins, and the last collapses, in fear of thunder, and a rush for underground shelter; and in that sheltering cave, religion and family life begin again. Today the ambiguous thunder talks above every great city of the earth and the shelters are crowded, and a civilization, if it is ending, is no less surely germinal. In one great warning work of literature after another, meanwhile, a similar mental cavern is retreated to and explored (Joyce's was a Dedalean Labyrinth). Levin quotes St. John's "Except a grain of wheat fall into the earth and die, it abideth by itself alone, but if it die, it beareth much fruit." That, says he, is "the burden of the manifold texts of *Finnegans Wake*," and of Dostoevski, Tolstoy, Ibsen, Zola, Gide, Eliot, Mann.

Time, January 19, 1942

INQUEST ON DEMOCRACY
Walt Whitman. Poet of Democracy
—Hugh l'Anson Fausset—Yale ($3).

THIS compact, brilliant critical biography is 1) an excellent life of Walt Whitman, 2) a just, if merciless, evaluation of him as poet, mystic and prophet of democracy, 3) an arduous, provocative sermon on the nature and responsibility of democracy and of art. Unlike most Whitman critics, Author Fausset avoids the extremes of most books about Whitman. He neither damns nor admires Whitman for being a homosexual. He does not claim that Whitman's poetry is as great as Homer's or merely a free verse Sears, Roebuck catalogue. He simply tries to explain what Whitman achieved in poetry and mysticism, what he failed to achieve—and why.

Critic Fausset's thesis is simple: if Whitman was a great poet, it was his business to fulfill the responsibilities of one. If he was the evangelist of democracy, it was his business to write a true, not a heretical, gospel. In Fausset's opinion, Whitman never quite succeeded in being either poet or evangelist. He wrote some great poetry and some amazingly energetic verse. But on the whole, he shrank even from such responsibilities as he was equipped to recognize. He perceived a great number of democratic half-truths. He lacked the intellectual equipment or spiritual stamina to make the half-truth whole. Reason: Whitman, the man, was never really whole.

Bisexual. All human beings, Critic Fausset observes, are to some extent bisexual. But Whitman had a great deal more of the woman in him than men normally have. This schism in his nature, Fausset believes, was in part the source of such greatness as he had. It was also the chief source of his failures. Whitman's femininity gave him his tremendous powers for the passive absorption of experience, for sympathy, for the almost bottomless endurance (as in the Civil War hospitals) of massive suffering. But it also accounts for the sentimentality, effusiveness, extreme over-assertiveness, pseudo-masculinity and egoism of many of his poems.

Because he feared and never quite understood himself, because, in all probability, he never felt normal sexual desire in his life, his hunger for the easy comradeship of simple men developed. "More intent on excluding none than on wholly finding one," it was inevitable that he should remain innocent to the end of his days of psychology, character, the true nature of individualism, personality, tragedy, evil—all of which considerably complicate the problems of the poet and of the democratic theorist.

Womblike. Due to the same schism, Whitman never really understood the essential duties of an artist. Real harmony of form is "created from within." It demands "an act of unified being in the artist himself"; the more he enters "into the depths of his own soul, the deeper he [enters] into the meaning of things." And "there [is] no other way of achieving creative insight in place of an external and generalized view." Whitman achieved such insight and such harmony only rarely; notably, Fausset points out, in a sense of death as womblike as his frame of mysticism or the childlike attachment to his mother, which he never broke. Much of the time he substituted, for truly distilled perception, declamations, loud affirmations, a catalogue of beloved objects, and worked in a vocabulary too superficial and meager, and in a formal pattern too loose, to produce anything that can be called true poetry.

His bisexualism also involved Whitman in other difficulties. One can be as hopelessly tethered to flesh by Whitman's sort of "false relish," Fausset observes, as by the Puritanism which he was over-reacting against. The errors and half-truths of Whitman's gospel in general are brought out most clearly, Fausset believes, in the celebration of sex, *Children of Adam* and *Calamus*. Whitman "affirmed far too easily the identity of body and spirit . . . and this evasion resulted in an almost complete sacrifice of the distinctively human values to biological forces."

In these poems, Fausset shrewdly remarks, "the faces of men and women in love, the eyes of their intelligence, hardly ever meet." He also finds symptoms of frustrated sexual impulse in Whitman's spurious "primitiveness": "A primitive man may think *in* his bodily organs. But he would be the last to think *about* them or to display or exploit them consciously." In short, "to attempt [as Whitman did] to resolve the conflict of self-consciousness and sex by merely sinking to the biological level . . . was to abandon the hope of human integrity without recovering an animal innocence."

War. By 1860 Whitman's work as the poet-propagandist of democracy (*Song of Myself, Song of the Open Road, Children of Adam*) was almost finished. Democracy's crisis, the Civil War, was to provide him with the source of his greatest poetry and the great central act of his life. Being a simple man, he liked the glamor of war, liked still more its courage and comradeship. He wrote half-Hitlerish lines on the glories of immolation en masse. He also wrote the maturest poems of his life, possibly the finest that have ever been written about war. And in the hospitals of Washington he lived his gospel of brotherhood more eloquently, truly and bravely than he had ever managed to write about it.

The rest of his life was decline. Like any old soldier, Whitman faced, and faced nobly, a different gambit of heroism: the slow endurance of anti-climax—failing poetic powers, the wrenching death of his mother (for which, at 54, he was as emotionally unprepared as a child), the paralysis which he endured for 20 years of his remaining 27.

Those years were not uniformly dreary. They were warmed by the half-filial, half-erotic friendship of many young men, notably the young Irish streetcar conductor, Peter Doyle. They were cheered by the startling letters of Mrs. Anne Gilchrist. She had read the *Leaves* and wrote their author: "Nothing in life or death can tear out of my heart the passionate belief that one day I shall hear that voice say to me, 'My mate. The one I so much want. Bride, wife, indissoluble, eternal' . . . O come, come, my darling, look into these eyes and see the long ardent aspiring soul in them."

Orbic. Whitman was still active. He went West, like the nation, and saw the Rockies. Their grandeur reminded him of his own poetry. But he was aging. He began to say he had never read Emerson before he wrote *Leaves of Grass* (he had), to be a little cagey about money, to blossom a little senilely at his few remaining birthday parties to welcome the less fantastic of his admirers. They were not the common workmen he had written for, but those poets and cultivated hangers-on who are the fate of poets in general. He kept adding to *Leaves of Grass*. It had become "a habit." He wrote *Democratic Vistas*, a book of prose more perceptive of the weak spots in U.S. democracy than anything Whitman had written before. He had outlived his pre-Civil War hopefulness, but he was still capable only of vague "orbic" statements about the leadership of "the divine literatus," and preached once again "his old back-to-nature illusion." He still professed his uncritical confidence in the deep instinctive virtues of "the People." Author Fausset believes that this confidence is part of Whitman's pathetic fallacy.

Like his masses, Whitman lacked the self-mastery, the intelligence and the creative idea whereby true democracy becomes possible. He glimpsed "the necessity of bringing the moral sense into a new relation with intelligence," but he could "only link them loosely and hopefully together." He vaguely foresaw "the basic problem of democracy, that of reintegrating the individual in a social whole and converting a semi-conscious mass into a community of responsible persons," but "he overlooked the cost of integration, as he had overlooked it in himself."

And "his lack of insight into the nature of imagination and the spiritual cost of creating great literature was paralleled by his ignorance of the nature and cost of the 'soul-consciousness,' whose development he insisted, rightly enough, it should be the one purpose of all government in a democracy to encourage."

Time, June 15, 1942

"It Is Written"
The Dream Department
—S. J. Perelman—Random House ($2).

S. J. PERELMAN picks up business where he left off with *Look Who's Talking* (*Time*, Aug. 12, 1940). One passage should suffice to give traffic signals to such readers as remain unfamiliar with Perelman's work. The passage was inspired by a notice to the effect that moving pictures would be used for department-store advertising. The title is *Kitchenware, Notions, Lights, Action, Camera!*

Scene: *The music room in the palatial villa of Mrs. Lafcadio Mifflin at Newport. Mrs. Mifflin, a majestic woman in a slim-pin Bemberg corselet well boned over the diaphram (Stern Brothers, fourth floor), is seated at the console of her Wurlitzer, softly wurlitzing to herself. Mr. Mifflin, in a porous-knit union suit from Franklin Simon's street floor, is stretched out by the fire like a great, tawny cat. Inasmuch as there is a great, tawny cat stretched out alongside him, also wearing a porous-knit union suit, it is not immediately apparent which is Mifflin.*

There are many other pieces under such titles as *Beat Me, Post-Impressionist Daddy, Caution—Soft Prose Ahead, P-s-s-t Partner, Your Peristalsis is Showing*. They handle, with the expertness required for delivering a two-headed baby, the aching half-lunacies which turn up as a normal part of U.S. life. They use one of the rangiest and most microscopically exact vocabularies in modern letters—a vocabulary drawn entirely from those ancient current and emergent clichés of which Flaubert and Joyce were both collectors and which are as diagnostic of a civilization as any ten themes on the *Zeitgeist*, and a thousand times as entertaining.

They are, as Perelman's pieces have been for some years, overformularized: yet even at their most manufactured they have a surface and a perfection of rhythm which little contemporary prose can touch. At their best, they stand with the best of Ludwig Bemelmans and of James Thurber as a shocking commentary on most of the nominally more solid and earnest books being written in English.

The Author is less well known than his work. Said he last week:

"Button-cute, rapier-keen, wafer-thin, and pauper-poor is S. J. Perelman, whose tall, stooping figure is better known to the twilit half-world of five continents than to Publisher's Row. That he possess the power to become invisible to finance companies; that his laboratory is tooled up to manufacture Frankenstein-type monsters on an incredible scale; and that he owns one of the rare mouths in which butter has never melted are legends treasured by every schoolboy.

"Perelman's life reads like a picaresque novel. It began on a bleak shelf of rock in mid-Atlantic near Tristan da Cunha. Transplanted to Rhode Island by a passing Portuguese, he became a man of proverbial strength around the Providence wharves; he could drive a spike through an oak plank with his fist. As there was constant need for this type of skilled labor, he soon acquired enough tuition to enter Brown University. He is chiefly remembered there for translating the epigrams of Martial into colloquial Ambaric and designing Brooks Bros.' present trademark, a sheep suspended in a diaper.

"Perelman like many another fledgling writer headed posthaste for Montparnasse. A redoubtable tosspot and coxcomb, he was celebrated throughout the Quarter for drinking Modigliani under the table; his fondness for this potent Italian aperitif still remains unabated. In 1925, disguised as Ashton-Wolfe of the Surete, he took to frequenting the *milieu*, the sinister district centering about the rue de Lappe. As 'Papa' Thernardier, he organized the gang that stole a towel from the Hotel Claridge and defaced the blotters at the American Express Co. A *demarche* from the Quai d'Orsay shortly forced him to flee Paris.

"When, in 1928, the meteoric career of Joe Strong, the Boy Plunger, ended abruptly with the latter's disappearance from

Wall Street, few knew that Perelman had ended another chapter. In bloody Cicero, Illinois, swart Sicilian mobsters fingered their roscoes uneasily, dismayed at lightning forays by a new rival. In a scant eight months, no shell of needled beer touched lip in Chicago County without previous tribute to 'Nails' Perelman. Implacable, deadly as a puff adder, the hand that triggered a steely automatic could caress a first Folio with equal relish. Able to snatch in fifteen minutes the rest most men required a night for, Perelman spent the balance dictating novels (*Jo Bracegirdle's Ordeal*, *The Splendid Sinners*), essays (*Winnowings*, *The Anatomy of Gluttony*, *Turns with a Stomach*), plays (*Are You There, Wimperis?*, *Musclebound*, *Philippa Steps Out*), and scenarios (*She Married Her Double, He Married Himself*).

"Retired today to peaceful Erwinna, Pa., Perelman raises turkeys which he occasionally displays on Broadway, stirs little from his alembics and retorts. Those who know hint that the light burning late in his laboratory may result in a breathtaking electric bill. Queried, he shrugs with the fatalism of your true Oriental. '*Mektoub*,' he observes curtly, 'It is written.'"

Time, February 1, 1943

U.S. at War:
"A Soldier Died Today"

IN Chungking the spring dawn was milky when an MP on the graveyard shift picked up the ringing phone in U.S. Army Headquarters. At first he heard no voice on the other end; then a San Francisco broadcast coming over the phone line made clear to him why his informant could find no words. A colonel came in. The MP just stared at him. The colonel stared back. After a moment the MP blurted two words. The colonel's jaw dropped; he hesitated; then without a word he walked away.

It was fresh daylight on Okinawa. Officers and men of the amphibious fleet were at breakfast when the broadcast told them. By noon the news was known to the men at the front, at the far sharp edges of the world's struggle. With no time for grief, they went on with their work; but there, while they worked, many a soldier wept.

At home, the news came to people in the hot soft light of the afternoon, in taxicabs, along the streets, in offices and bars and factories. In a Cleveland barbershop, 60-year-old Sam Katz was giving a customer a shave when the radio stabbed out the news. Sam Katz walked over to the water cooler, took a long, slow drink, sat down and stared into space for nearly ten minutes. Finally he got up and painted a sign on his window: "Roosevelt Is Dead." Then he finished the shave. In an Omaha poolhall, men racked up their cues without finishing their games, walked out. In a Manhattan taxicab, a fare told the driver, who pulled over to the curb, sat with his head bowed, and after two minutes resumed his driving.

Everywhere, to almost everyone, the news came with the force of a personal shock. The realization was expressed in the messages of the eminent; it was expressed in the stammering and wordlessness of the humble. A woman in Detroit said: "It doesn't seem possible. It seems to me that he will be back on the radio tomorrow, reassuring us all that it was just a mistake."

It was the same through that evening, and the next day, and the next; the darkened restaurants, the shuttered nightclubs, the hand-lettered signs in the windows of stores: "Closed out of Reverence for F.D.R."; the unbroken, 85-hour dirge of the nation's radio; the typical tributes of typical Americans in the death-notice columns of their newspapers (said one signed by Samuel and Al Gordon: "A Soldier Died Today").

It was the same on the cotton fields and in the stunned cities between Warm Springs and Washington, while the train, at funeral pace, bore the coffin up April's glowing South in re-enactment of Whitman's great threnody.

It was the same in Washington, in the thousands on thousands of grief-wrung faces which walled the caisson's grim progression with prayers and with tears. It was the same on Sunday morning in the gentle landscape at Hyde Park, when the burial service of the Episcopal Church spoke its old, strong, quiet words of farewell; and it was the same at that later moment when all save the gravemen were withdrawn and reporters, in awe-felt hiding, saw how a brave woman, a widow, returned, and watched over the grave alone, until the grave was filled.

Time, April 23, 1945

Victory: The Peace

T HE greatest and most terrible of wars was ending, this week, in the echoes of an enormous event—an event so much more enormous that, relative to it, the war itself shrank to minor significance. The knowledge of victory was as charged with sorrow and doubt as with joy and gratitude. More fearful responsibilities, more crucial liabilities rested on the victors even than on the vanquished.

In what they said and did, men were still, as in the aftershock of a great wound, bemused and only semi-articulate, whether they were soldiers or scientists, or great statesmen, or the simplest of men. But in the dark depths of their minds and hearts, huge forms moved and silently arrayed themselves: Titans, arranging out of the chaos an age in which victory was already only the shout of a child in the street.

With the controlled splitting of the atom, humanity, already profoundly perplexed and disunified, was brought inescapably into a new age in which all thoughts and things were split— and far from controlled. As most men realized, the first atomic bomb was a merely pregnant threat, a merely infinitesimal promise.

All thoughts and things were split. The sudden achievement of victory was a mercy, to the Japanese no less than to the United Nations; but mercy born of a ruthless force beyond anything in human chronicle. The race had been won, the weapon had been used by those on whom civilization could best hope to depend; but the demonstration of power against living creatures instead of dead matter created a bottomless wound in the living conscience of the race. The rational mind had won the most Promethean of its conquests over nature, and had put into the hands of common man the fire and force of the sun itself.

Was man equal to the challenge? In an instant, without warning, the present had become the unthinkable future. Was there hope in that future, and if so, where did hope lie?

Even as men saluted the greatest and most grimly Pyrrhic of victories in all the gratitude and good spirit they could muster, they recognized that the discovery which had done most to end the worst of wars might also, quite conceivably, end all wars—if only man could learn its control and use.

The promise of good and of evil bordered alike on the infinite—with this further, terrible split in the fact: that upon a people already so nearly drowned in materialism even in peace-time, the good uses of this power might easily bring disaster as prodigious as the evil. The bomb rendered all decisions made so far, at Yalta and at Potsdam, mere trivial dams across tributary rivulets. When the bomb split open the universe and revealed the prospect of the infinitely extraordinary, it also re-vealed the oldest, simplest, commonest, most neglected and most important of facts: that each man is eternally and above all else responsible for his own soul, and, in the terrible words of the Psalmist, that no man may deliver his brother, nor make agreement unto God for him.

Man's fate has forever been shaped between the hands of reason and spirit, now in collaboration, again in conflict. Now reason and spirit meet on final ground. If either or anything is to survive, they must find a way to create an indissoluble partnership.

Time, August 20, 1945

Europe: Autumn Story

THE fall of the year shone gently upon the broken cities and the exhausted fields of Europe. On Berlin's Kreuzberg, frost stiffened upon the worm-wrought, illegible features of an exhumed, Gestapo-killed cadaver to which someone had attached a tag reading, *Homo sapiens.*

Of the unrecounted millions of Europeans who survived him, few could greet the season with anything of its own tenderness. It was the first autumn of liberation, the first since the end of the war. It was the first autumn of the atomic age.

In the steep forests of Norway, German guerrillas still skulked and fought. In Denmark, for want of transportation, practically the only food surpluses in Europe were near standstill. Only butter, eggs, meat moved, thinly, to England, Norway, the U.S. Army.

By millions, in transverse migrations, Germans struggled westward out of New Poland, northward out of the Sudetenland and Austria, to swell a nation already overpopulated and reduced in size; while Russians struggled eastward, some out of slavery and some out of voluntary servitude, towards home and an uncertain welcome.

In Hamburg, hundreds of looted bells awaited restoration to the belfries of nations with bell-like names. Poland, The Netherlands, Belgium; provided, of course, that those belfries, and their churches, still existed.

In the Sudeten, those Germans who remained wore identifying armbands. In Berlin, Jews were entitled to extra rations. In the British zone, on behalf of Jews, the British commandeered clothes from Germans. Thanks to presidential demand, the first of many Jews in the American zone were removed from behind barbed wire and were installed in houses requisitioned from Germans. Into Germany, fleeing a new paroxysm of pogroms in New Poland, wandered still more Jews.

Mysteriously planted placards warned fraternizing Bavarian girls: "O God, if it depends on us, you will pay for it!" Daily, the snowline crept a little farther down the mountains of

Bavaria, hideout of SS men. A Sudeten German asked whether it was true that Americans were now fighting the Russians.

In Switzerland, Belgium's Leopold bowed to temporary exile, but by no means to permanent renunciation of his throne.

In The Netherlands, underfueled pumps sucked at flooded farmlands which for years to come would be sterile as salt.

The scraped Danubian plain blazed like brass: Hungary, one of the bounteous nations of Europe, would this year require six million quintals of wheat. Allied authorities started a vast woodcutting campaign in the Vienna woods, to supplement the capital's inadequate coal stocks.

In all the nations of eastern Europe, free and secret elections were still promised. Angered and fearful, a group of Bulgarian peasants told an American correspondent how an armed 23-year-old Communist mayor had lumped their long-held acreages and plowed the boundaries under.

National Actionists in Greece went armed and carried British Army passes certifying their "confidential work." The enemies, the hunted men of EAM, live in peril of arrest and beatings. In Rome, the first Italian democrats to meet in parliamentary Assembly since the murder of Matteotti set themselves to restore integrity and hope to a broken nation. The withdrawal of A.M.G. from Italy was indefinitely postponed; in liberal opinion, to protect Rightists and Monarchists.

In Paris a man's suit cost $500. A correspondent stopped to get his jeep repaired in Neufchâteau. The garage operator, a brawny Frenchwoman, immediately questioned him about American soldiers sleeping with German girls. "*C'est incroyable*," she mourned. "Yes, some French girls slept with Germans when they were here. But only bad girls. We do not understand why you Americans do it. You are not bad but you still sleep with Germans." An American sergeant lounged at a nearby corner watching the thin traffic in Neufchâteau's one big street; he turned loose barbaric French at passing girls; they giggled, and swept on. Wearily he jerked his thumb towards the hilltop graveyard on the edge of town. He said: "My division liberated this joint. A lot of the boys from the 79th are lying up there. And for what? To have these people spit on us now?"

French nuns and children sifted garbage against the lean chance of bits of food fit for children or nuns or pigs to eat.

Even in Marseilles, the sky muted its Mediterranean blare. Along the wide streets the plane trees turned pale yellow. In the still unmended tenements of Madrid, before long now, a people whom victory had passed by would be shuddering.

Man's hope, man's fate contested in the subtle autumn light. Winter stood just at the shoulder of the gentlest of seasons.

Europe had emerged from history's most terrible war, into history's most terrifying peace. Europeans said, again & again, that their aspirations were for liberty. They showed, again & again, their desperately seasoned respect for security. Now the struggle between liberty and security was engaged.

In London the Council of Foreign Ministers achieved only the disconsolation of all in the world who desired peace, not power. Eastern Europe was a Russian bastion; western Europe coalesced towards a "family" which, to the Russians, would be a bastion against the Soviet Union. Within nations, as among them, political forces jockeyed for power.

The totalitarian socialists, by far the most astute professionals in the field, moved toward their goals by methods which equally disturbed scoundrels and honorable men. The democratic socialists, maintaining that full liberty and full security can be combined and made enduring, were embarrassed by their new responsibilities in Britain, and by those problems of relative inefficiency which confront all democrats. Only in Czechoslovakia, one of the less unhappy nations in Europe, were socialist prospects very promising. But that country's fortunes depended chiefly on friendly relations with the Soviet Union; and democratic and totalitarian socialists are not notable for lifelong friendships.

Europe's peasants continued to be peasants. Materialists in a sense more primal than that of Adam Smith or Marx, politically inert and purchasable, they served less as anchorage than as ballast. As for Europe's conservatives, it seemed unlikely at the moment that ordinary people would ever trust them again.

In whom was man to put his hope? In himself? A Frenchwoman, remembering the magnificent selflessness of war and the millennial hours of the liberation of Paris, sorrowfully said: "We have returned to our own egos."

As winter moved down through Norway and, along the Gulf of Finland, rusted the dark green, springlike grass which heavy summer had never touched, many Europeans were pre-occupied with matters even more primitive than the ego. When winter came, they knew, it would trap a hundred million of them with less food for each, or little more, than American soldiers got last year in Japanese prison camps. They would be severely short of fuel, of shelter, of clothing. Millions of homes —and, in Berlin, hospitals—were without windowglass. Tuberculosis was rampant among adolescents and common among small children. Bubonic plague nuzzled at the ports of the Mediterranean.

Many would die. Many more would survive. They were no braver than other men; they could be expected, in sufficient anguish and embitterment and desolation, to turn to those stronger than themselves who offered both a will and a way.

They could also be expected, as winter tightened its vise, to confirm an enduring opinion of that nation which, in the unalterable conviction of Europeans, might have prevented much of the anguish and so might have prevented political dereliction. That nation was the U.S.

Countless millions of Europeans had all their lives seen in the U.S. a dream of liberty and security, of democratic generosity and efficiency. With the American armies had come the American reality, and it was not—it could not have been—the stuff of the dream.

The people of Europe had seen, and had not failed to value, the vigor and promise and individual generosity of the American soldier. They had also seen, with the deadly discernment of peoples experienced in disaster and disillusion, how ill-raised to understand this most sophisticated of wars, and how timidly briefed in its meanings, were these same Americans. Now, in France and the Lowlands, in Germany and Austria and Italy, the people saw Americans, homesick and purposeless and often misbehaved, affronting all around them and under them with their abundance amid want, their altogether human and altogether brutal longing to get the hell out of those ruined lands, and to go home.

The offenses were not universal, nor were they solely American. By a Dutch roadside stood a sign embossed with the Maple Leaf of the Canadian Army: REMEMBER! THE DUTCH ARE OUR ALLIES! But the Americans, in their overwhelming number and voice and strength, had made Europe supremely conscious of them, and of the country from which they came. In the end, and in this autumn of unfilled need, it was not the Americans, but America, that Europe judged.

Time, October 15, 1945

The Nation:
Democratic Vistas

O<small>UT</small> on the Montana range, rattlesnakes were unusually plentiful, and the old men predicted a long warm fall and a short easy winter.

In Chatsworth, Ill. First Lieut. Billie Wittler, an Army nurse, made Page One of the weekly *Plaindealer* when she got back home: "She has seen much front-line active duty in the European sector, including Italy and Germany. She was able to see the Alps in all their beauty and says Switzerland, especially, is beautiful."

In Manhattan, a nobly decorated veteran of the Pacific was passed along by a junior executive, who was unfavorably impressed by his willingness to take "anything," to a junior executive who told him, kindly, "You know, I don't think this is exactly the job for you." Upon hearing this, the young hero burst into tears.

Happy days, more or less, were here again. Despite prodigious achievements at home & abroad, the nation had not been essentially changed by war. Now, returning to peace rather than struggling through to it nine-tenths dead, the U.S. was more like itself than ever—in a world which would never again be remotely the same.

Butter pats were served again at Schrafft's and Henrici's; cases against cigaret blackmarketers were dropped. Along the highways, in whatever cars they had, people were blowing out tires and bumping into each other again; the city traffic tie-ups were something awful. Other moral equivalents to war were the fall's football games—which drew record crowds—and a shooting season so trigger-happy that Colorado's game department recommended manslaughter laws for hunters.

Army deaths were totaled 216,966, the Navy's 55,896; the National Safety Council announced that on the home front, since Pearl Harbor, 355,000 had been killed through accident, and 36,000,000 injured.

The great hit songs of the season were *Till the End of Time*,

I'll Buy That Dream, On the Atchison, Topeka & the Santa Fe. Best-selling novels were *The Black Rose* and *Forever Amber.* A big movie hit was *Love Letters,* a romance about amnesia. A psychologist claimed that *Superman* provided a beneficent Aristotelian catharsis; a Jesuit saw in him a fascist archetype. Young girls tried to look like Bacall with a dash of Hepburn. Their elders went in for cosmetics with manic names like Fatal Apple and Havoc. They also favored detachable daintiness features and phantom crotches. In ads as expressive as dreams, fathers forfeited their children's love because of denture breath, and women exclaimed: "Don't expect *me* to marry *you* with a mouthful of cavities!"

A Navy doctor, soon to come home, wrote warning his wife rather sadly that he had gotten bald and heavy. She wrote back gently: "You will find that three years has done quite a bit to me, too."

A partially paralyzed ex-defense worker gave his six-year-old daughter a doll, his nine-year-old son a pack of cards, told them to shut their eyes because more was coming, and shot them through their heads.

The war was over. The postwar world was born. Everywhere the returning traveler saw signs of change, signs of no change at all, signs of change but too fast, signs of change but not fast enough: signs by the millions.

In Seattle a 25-year-old veteran was sore about the skimpiness of his civilian shirttails. All over the U.S., businessmen read a brochure: *Among Convention Leaders Who Know—It's Chicago 81 to 65.* In New Haven a CIOrganizer told ralliers: "We want full employment and if free enterprise must go, let it go. The manufacturers want to return to normalcy—the normalcy of no labor movement."

In the window of a gas station–soda fountain in McFarland, Calif. (pop. 605), appeared a wobbly handmade sign: "Colored Trade Not Solisited at Fountain."

In New Orleans white housewives, proud for the first time in their lives of doing their own housework, said "those niggers all want $12 or $15 a week and they're no good at that." The editor of the Laurel, Miss. *Leader-Call* listened to servicemen on a train en route to mustering-out camp, talking of sports, and home, and their tremendous desire to get back to the joys of civilian life. He wrote: "I wonder if they aren't going to get a great jolt."

In Kansas City, which calls itself the heart of America, a veteran of the Pacific observed: "Over there in the line we talked about life and death, and who was going to get it next. So what happens when I get home? I no more get into the house the old man begins to tell me about his God-damned lawn mower."

A twelve-year-old delinquent phoned home at 3 a.m.: "Mom! Guess where I am? In jail again."

At the height of a historic, nationwide housing shortage, such classified ads as this were common in the *Star*: "Desperate. No place to go. Veteran, wife and two children need home immediately."

In Davey Markowitz' place two veterans, former friends and schoolmates, met for the first time in four years. The ex-sergeant gave his boyhood friend, an ex-lieutenant, only a perfunctory greeting: "I hate lieutenants," he snarled.

Over in Byers, Kans., Wayne Fisk came back from the Navy and said that a long rest would sure look good to him. But a day of loafing was enough. So while he was resting he painted his father's house.

In its own quiet way, it was a period as madly chaotic in the relatively unscathed U.S. as in the shattered rest of the world. Nobody seemed able to see much beyond the end of his nose. Business tossed on the greatest wave of labor unrest since the middle '30s. In vast numbers ex-war workers, some unwilling and some unable to live on reduced postwar wages, floated along on war savings or on unemployment compensation while, in vast numbers, jobs went begging. Veterans too wanted time to rest up and to enjoy themselves and to get readjusted, and they didn't want to be hurried about it either. Many were jealous of the high wages paid in wartime and paid no longer; many others, who took back their old jobs, left them within a few weeks.

Everywhere, people had expected an immediate, dreamlike postwar flow of the autos and refrigerators and radios and washing machines and farm machines and nylons and plumbing and good clothes which had been promised all through the war to the most machine-dependent and comfort-loving of nations. Everywhere, such hopes were sorely disappointed.

Underneath all the pleasure-bending, elbow-bending and tongue-bending (reflected perhaps—and perhaps not—in increased church attendance) lay a more mature awareness, a profound, bewildered foreboding, a tragic and justified uneasiness, a still more disturbing fatalism. Many Americans assumed that the nation's interracial troubles were barely beginning; that another great depression and another great war were dead certainties; that the next opponent was Russia; that nothing whatever could be done about such matters.

Almost without exception Americans realized that they might not like the neighbors but they had to live with them. Almost without exception they talked a good deal about the atomic bomb; many had it on their minds even more than they talked about it. But almost without exception they were so thoroughly absorbed in immediate troubles, pleasures, hopes, angers and disappointments—and perhaps so essentially far-gone in the basic kind of hope which holds human beings upright—that they were virtually incapable of even trying to take fate into their own hands.

The general attitude about atomic control got no farther than the first primitive reflex of greed and terror; the unkeepable secret must be kept. The general attitude toward racial problems was most sadly expressed by the more thoughtful Southerners, who said they only wished they could spend the next few years where there weren't any Negroes. The general attitude toward Europe was in the first place insufficiently informed, in the second place wearily or even scornfully indifferent.

Isolationism, in its old, simple, scarehead sense, was somewhere near being a thing of the past. But unconscious isolationism, far more insidious, was an all-powerful and increasing phenomenon of the present and future. If civilization, or time itself in the provincial, planetary sense, was to last more than another few decades, the responsibility rested chiefly on the American people. But for wholly understandable, nonetheless tragic reasons, the American people were not very responsible toward any major responsibility. If this troubled season was any indication, they would be too busy trying to buy that wholly unpurchasable dream.

Time, November 5, 1945

Chronology

1909   Born James Rufus Agee (known to his family as "Rufus")
        to Laura Tyler Agee and Hugh James Agee (known as
        "Jay") on November 27, in Knoxville, Tennessee. (Laura,
        devoutly Anglo-Catholic, comes from a prosperous, culti-
        vated Knoxville home; Jay's roots lie in the mountains
        north of town. At the time of his son's birth, Jay is work-
        ing for the Tyler family's construction business, after
        previous jobs with the U.S. Post Office Department, in-
        cluding an assignment in Panama, and the Louisville and
        Nashville Railroad.)

1912   Sister Emma born June 22.

1916   On May 16, as Jay Agee is returning to Knoxville after vis-
        iting his own ailing father in the hills, his car hits an em-
        bankment and flips over; he dies instantly. James, his
        mother, and his younger sister move out of the family
        house, but continue to live in Knoxville, near mother's
        family.

1918–22 Mother spends the summer of 1918 with the children in a
        cottage near the grounds of the St. Andrew's School, es-
        tablished by Episcopal monks of the Order of the Holy
        Cross on the Cumberland Plateau near Sewanee, Ten-
        nessee. Family moves in 1919 from Knoxville to St. An-
        drew's. Agee forms close, lifelong relationship with a St.
        Andrew's teacher, Father James Harold Flye, who serves
        as his mentor and as a kind of surrogate father. At his
        mother's direction, Agee lives in the dormitory; unable to
        visit her freely for the next half decade, he grows closer to
        Father Flye and his wife, Grace, and becomes deeply in-
        volved in the religious rituals of the school. Mother, who
        serves as a deaconess of the institution, becomes involved
        with a St. Andrew's staff member, Father Erskine Wright.

1923–24 To be near her sick father, mother takes the family back
        to Knoxville. Agee enters Knoxville High School mid-
        term freshman year. Mother marries Father Wright in the
        spring of 1924. Under medical advice to find a damp yet

temperate locale to suit Father Wright's constitution, the newlywed couple explore several southern towns, but eventually settle in Rockland, Maine. Disliking the household's atmosphere of pious gentility, Agee spends little time there.

1925–28   Following a bicycle tour of France and England with Father Flye, Agee enrolls at Phillips Exeter Academy in Exeter, New Hampshire. Writes for *The Phillips Exeter Monthly* and joins the literary society, the Lantern Club (eventually is elected editor of the former and president of the latter). The Lantern Club "is one of the big things to be in here," he writes to Father Flye. "It runs the *Monthly*, and is a literary club. It gets several authors up here each term who give very informal talks in the club room. Booth Tarkington, who graduated here, came several times, and Sinclair Lewis may come this winter. It's a swell idea to have such a thing in a school, don't you think?" Composes stories, criticism, and poetry, including verse narrative "Ann Garner." Develops a crush on a younger male student; begins an affair with a woman several years older than he, Dorothy Carr, an employee of the Exeter Public Library. Begins corresponding with Exeter alumnus and Yale undergraduate Dwight Macdonald. Macdonald and Agee share a love of movies. "To me, the great thing about movies," Agee writes to Macdonald in the summer of 1927, "is that it's a brand new field. I don't see how much more can be done with writing or the stage. In fact, every kind of recognized 'art' has been worked pretty nearly to the limit. Of course great things will undoubtedly be done in all of them, but, possibly excepting music, I don't see how they can avoid being at least in part imitations. As for the movies, however, their possibilities are infinite." Agee barely passes many of his courses, but his teachers, impressed by his literary gifts, provide him with strong recommendations to Harvard, where he is accepted.

1928–29   At Harvard, rooms with future television producer Robert Saudek. Before the end of his first year, contributes a revised version of "Ann Garner" to Lincoln Kirstein's magazine *Hound and Horn*, as well as poetry to *The Harvard Advocate*. Spends a great deal of time at concerts, plays, and movies, and is placed on academic probation. Spends summer as a migrant worker, hiking from one wheatfield to the next in Kansas and Nebraska, then hitchhikes to Tijuana and back to the Northeast; visits Saudek and his family in Pittsburgh. "I had a good summer," he writes Father Flye. "Hard work and little time or provocation to be unhappy." In the same letter he writes, "On the whole, an occasional alcoholic bender satisfies me fairly well. Don't, please, get the idea that this invariably ends in drunkenness. That seldom happens unless I'm down in the dumps at the time."

1930–31   Professor Theodore Spencer, Agee's Harvard tutor (a faculty counselor), takes him on a visit to the Clinton, New York, home of Dr. Arthur Percy Saunders, a chemistry professor at Hamilton College, and his wife, Louisa, a former lecturer in English literature at Cornell. The Saunders, who have social ties to such figures as Robert Frost and Alexander Woollcott, welcome Agee into their circle. Back at Harvard, Agee and poet Robert Fitzgerald take two courses given by the Saunders' friend, the literary critic I. A. Richards. Over Christmas, Agee breaks up with Dorothy Carr. Declares, in a letter to Father Flye, his ambition "to combine what Chekhov did with what Shakespeare did—that is, to move from the dim, rather eventless beauty of C. to huge geometric plots such as Lear." To do so, he says, "I've thought of inventing a sort of amphibious style—prose that would run into poetry when the occasion demanded poetic expression." The Saunders' daughter, Olivia, or "Via," six years older than Agee, moves to Cambridge; Agee begins courting her. Does well enough academically to regain full standing in his class.

1932   As president of *The Harvard Advocate*, Agee scores a popular success and publicity coup with a parody of *Time* that imagines how the news magazine would have covered the world of antiquity. With the help of Macdonald, secures a job at the business magazine *Fortune*, recently founded by Henry Luce. Writes and delivers the class ode at Harvard's commencement exercises. Hitchhikes to New York, where he begins working at Luce's headquarters on floors 50–52 of the Chrysler Building. Takes on various anonymous assignments as part of a staff that includes Macdonald, Archibald MacLeish, and Wilder Hobson (Macdonald's Yale roommate and Thornton Wilder's nephew). Often works alone in the middle of the night, blasting Beethoven on a phonograph. Resides in Brooklyn, first in a barely furnished apartment, then in larger rooms complete with telephone. Via Saunders moves to New York in October, and she and Agee make wedding plans for the new year.

1933   Via and Agee marry at an Episcopal church in Utica, New York, on January 28, and move into a basement apartment in Greenwich Village. Agee continues to write poetry, including "John Carter," a long narrative poem in ottava rima started at Harvard and never completed. At Archibald MacLeish's request, collects his other poems for consideration by the Yale Younger Poets series. Writes first substantial piece for *Fortune*, an evaluation of the Tennessee Valley Authority which attracts considerable attention. Declines offer by Henry Luce to enroll him in Harvard Business School.

1934   Is enthralled by James Joyce's *Ulysses*, which has just been published in America. The Yale Younger Poets series publishes Agee's collection as *Permit Me Voyage*. Contributes articles to *Fortune* including "Cockfighting," "The American Roadside," and "Roman Society." Is impressed by the work of photographer Walker Evans, one of whose pictures illustrated Agee's "American Roadside" article; for Agee, Evans' work "has a kind of Joycean denseness, insight and complexity resolved in its bitter purity."

1935   Agee writes 10,000 words of autobiographical material for a novel. Works hard on a major piece about the Tennessee Valley Authority for *Fortune*, but is frustrated by the magazine's editing of his piece on the orchid industry. In November, struggling to recharge his art and his marriage, travels with Via to Anna Maria, a small coastal town in western Florida. During the first months of an unpaid half-year leave of absence, reads Freud's *The Interpretation of Dreams* and *The Inner World of Childhood* by Francis Wickes, a follower of Jung; records and analyzes his own dreams.

1936   Louis Untermeyer includes four new poems by Agee in his anthology *Modern American Poetry*. Writes "Knoxville: Summer 1915," a lyrical prose recollection of his childhood. On the way back from Florida in April, Agee and Via stop in New Orleans and take in the jazz scene, then

observe Easter at St. Andrew's School with Father Flye
and Grace. Staying at the Flyes' for most of the month,
Agee befriends St. Andrew's student David McDowell
(who will be his future publisher). When Agee returns to
New York, *Fortune* assigns him a story about the struggle
of sharecroppers to survive in the Depression, and teams
him with Walker Evans, who has become a close friend.
The two travel to Alabama in July to make contact with
tenant farmers. Evans makes a first connection with a
sharecropping family, but will later credit Agee's seductive
"diffidence" for the pair's ability to win the trust of the
Tingles and two related families, the Burroughs and the
Fields. After three weeks of chronicling the families' lives
in intimate detail, Agee and Evans return to New York.
Fortune editors reject Agee's piece. He hopes to turn the
aborted feature into a book, but must persuade *Fortune*
to cede ownership of the research and writing on tenant
farmers that Agee has done for them while on staff.
Writes experimental movie treatment, "Notes for a Motion Picture: The House."

1937   Agee's marriage to Via continues to decline. Begins liaison with Alma Mailman, a young violinist and former
protégée of the Saunders. Grows more restless at *Fortune*—
his friends Macdonald, Hobson, and MacLeish have already left—and enters into a freelance, rather than staff,
arrangement with the magazine. Submits an application
for a Guggenheim fellowship listing 47 projects, from "an
anti-Communist Manifesto" to "reanalyses of the nature
and meaning of love"; the foundation turns him down.
Fortune permits Agee to use his Alabama work in a book.
He accepts a $500 advance from Harper & Brothers,
where he will work with editor Edward Aswell, who has
recently signed Thomas Wolfe. Agee's last published
piece for *Fortune* is a scathing account of a New York to
Havana vacation cruise. He visits Wilder and Peggy
Hobson on Long Island's North Shore, and the New Jersey retreat of ACLU director Roger Baldwin, Dellbrook
Farm. "Notes for a Motion Picture: The House" appears
in anthology *New Letters in America*, edited by Horace
Gregory.

1938   Via and Agee separate; their divorce becomes final at
year's end. Agee goes to live with Alma in a house in the

small town of Freetown, New Jersey. Hopes to finish
"Three Tenant Families," which he envisions as a short
book of "about 200 pages," but is unable to meet an August 1 deadline. "Knoxville: Summer 1915" appears in *Partisan Review*. Samuel Barber composes a musical setting
for a poem from *Permit Me Voyage*, "Sure on this Shining
Night." Agee and Alma marry in a brief civil ceremony in
December.

1939   Agee and Alma move into a Brooklyn home on St. James
Place owned by Wilder Hobson's in-laws. Agee accepts a
Fortune assignment to write about Brooklyn. After *Fortune* rejects the piece, Agee severs his connection with the
magazine. Leaves Brooklyn with Alma, who is pregnant,
for Monk's Farm in Stockton, New Jersey. Photographer
Helen Levitt, a volunteer darkroom assistant to her friend
Walker Evans, visits Agee and photographs him and an-
other visitor, Delmore Schwartz. Throughout the sum-
mer, Agee reads sections of his still-incomplete book to a
succession of guests. Submits an excerpt to the magazine
Common Sense (edited by Selden Rodman, Macdonald's
brother-in-law). Delivers the manuscript to Harper &
Brothers before Labor Day; Aswell dislikes the book's
profanity and eccentricity, and the publisher rejects it.
James and Alma move to 322 West 15th St. in Manhattan.
Robert Fitzgerald, now editing the "Books" section at
Time, gives him a place on his reviewing staff; Agee shares
an office with Whittaker Chambers at the new Time-Life
Building in Rockefeller Center, and contributes a handful
of unsigned reviews each week, starting with the January 1,
1940, issue. Houghton Mifflin accepts "Three Tenant
Families," now called *Let Us Now Praise Famous Men*,
and schedules it for publication in 1941. For his friend Jay
Leyda's journal *Films*, Agee contributes a screen treatment of a section from André Malraux's *Man's Fate* de-
picting the execution of Chinese Communists in 1927.
Becomes romantically involved with Austrian Catholic
émigré and *Fortune* researcher Mia Fritsch.

1940   Alma gives birth on March 20 to a son, named Joel for
Agee's maternal grandfather.

1941   Alma leaves Agee and takes one-year-old Joel with her to
Mexico, where she lives through most of the war years
with German Communist writer Bodo Uhse. Agee and

Mia Fritsch live together in a fifth-floor Greenwich Village apartment. Houghton Mifflin publishes *Let Us Now Praise Famous Men*, with Walker Evans' photographs, in August; the book sells only 600 copies before it is remaindered by the publisher. Critical response is marked by hostility or bewilderment; in an essay in *The Kenyon Review*, however, Lionel Trilling, while expressing some reservations, calls it "a great book" and "the most realistic and important moral effort of our generation."

1942   At Time-Life, Agee moves from book to movie reviewing, becoming the regular *Time* film critic in September. Continues to review books for *Time* on special occasions and for isolated two- or three-month periods. The cultural editor of *The Nation*, Margaret Marshall, invites him to become the journal's movie critic while he continues to hold down his position at *Time*. Inaugurates his *Nation* column in December.

1943   Originally classified 3-A, Agee is warned by his draft board of possible reclassification; however, the board passes him over. He and Mia agree to try to have a child.

1944   In the summer, Mia gives birth prematurely to a boy, who dies shortly after birth; soon after, she and Agee marry. For Archibald MacLeish, now Librarian of Congress, Agee compiles an annotated list of films most worthy of preservation. *Time* sends him to Hollywood, where he meets industry figures such as 20th Century–Fox executive Darryl F. Zanuck. His film-related features for the magazine encompass not merely new stars such as Ingrid Bergman and Gregory Peck, but behind-the-scenes forces such as producer Joan Harrison.

1945   Alma returns to New York from Mexico briefly with Joel, now five years old. She lives in Agee's writing studio before getting an apartment of her own. Her New York stay allows Agee to establish a relationship with the son he's barely known. Praises John Huston's battlefield documentary *The Battle of San Pietro* in a review for *The Nation*. Writes unsigned pieces for *Time* about the death of Roosevelt, the atomic bomb, and the American occupation of Europe.

1946   Mia gives birth to Agee's first daughter, Julia Theresa. He contributes the introduction to a collection of photographs by Helen Levitt (the book is not published until 1965).

1947   Begins novel *The Morning Watch*, based on Holy Week observances at St. Andrew's; continues to work on autobiographical novel that will be published as *A Death in the Family*. Samuel Barber sets "Knoxville: Summer 1915" to music for soprano and orchestra. At a New York press conference for Charlie Chaplin's *Monsieur Verdoux*, Agee rises to Chaplin's defense against reporters who charge him with being a fellow traveler and tax evader, asking what "people who care a damn about freedom—who really care for it" can think "when so many of the people of this country pry into what a man's citizenship is, try to tell him his business from hour to hour and from day to day and exert a public moral blackmail against him for not becoming an American citizen . . . in the way that they think he should?" With Chaplin in mind, writes a long film treatment called "Scientists and Tramps," which plunges the comedian's Little Tramp persona into the aftermath of a nuclear holocaust.

1948   Leaves *Time* and *The Nation* and gives up regular movie reviewing. Plans a series of longer pieces for *Life*. Writes his first dramatic screenplay, an adaptation of Stephen Crane's "The Blue Hotel," and continues collaboration with Helen Levitt. After doing some camerawork for her documentary "In the Street," contributes commentary and dialogue for a semi-documentary feature about a young boy in Harlem, *The Quiet One*, which Levitt photographs under the direction of Sidney Meyers. Agee and Mia, who is still on salary at *Fortune*, buy a country retreat in Hillsdale, New York, in the Berkshires. Son Joel is taken to live in East Germany with Alma and Bodo Uhse.

1949   Agee publishes nostalgic essay "Comedy's Greatest Era" in *Life*; the article generates enormous reader response and a revival of interest in comedians of the silent era.

1950   Mia gives birth to their second daughter, Andrea Maria. In a *Life*-sponsored symposium called "What's With the Movies?" Agee says, "Movies are made for respectable people now; were better when made for lowbrows and made with instinct and delight." John Huston agrees to be the subject of an Agee profile, which appears in *Life* as

"Undirectable Director," then hires Agee to help him adapt C. S. Forester's novel *The African Queen*. Before beginning work on the script, Agee spends time with Huston, Chaplin, and producer Frank Taylor and his wife, Nan, as well as her sister, Patricia Scallon, with whom he has an affair.

1951   Houghton Mifflin publishes *The Morning Watch* to respectful reviews. In Santa Barbara, California, Agee drives himself to keep up with Huston both on the tennis court and in their story conferences, while holding to his own insomniac schedule; suffers a heart attack. Peter Viertel, uncredited, helps Huston finish the script. A writer friend from Harvard, Bernard Schoenfeld, finds Agee a house in Malibu. Agee adapts Stephen Crane's story "The Bride Comes to Yellow Sky" and plays a small part in the movie, which is released along with an adaptation of Joseph Conrad's "The Secret Sharer" as a two-part film, *Face to Face*. Has second major heart attack in October; Mia and their children come to the West Coast and remain with him thereafter. Socializes with Bertolt Brecht, Charles Laughton, and Aldous Huxley at the salon of screenwriter Salka Viertel, mother of Peter Viertel.

1952   Agee and family spend the first half of the year in California, the second in New York. For French filmmaker Albert Lamorisse, writes English narration for *White Mane*, a 47-minute film about a wild horse, filmed in the Camargue region. Is commissioned by former Harvard roommate Robert Saudek to write a five-episode, two-and-a-half-hour dramatization of Lincoln's early life for television program *Omnibus*, in which Agee also acts as poet Jack Kelso. The series is a critical success, but historian Allan Nevins charges Agee with historical distortion in a televised discussion of the show. Agee's short story "A Mother's Tale" appears in *Harper's Bazaar*.

1953   Huston offers Agee the chance to adapt *Moby-Dick*, but he turns it down. Writes an original screenplay, "Noa Noa," about the life of Paul Gauguin.

1954   Mia gives birth to John Alexander Agee, the writer's second son. Agee writes screen adaptation of Davis Grubb's novel *The Night of the Hunter* and retains sole credit, although the director, Charles Laughton, drastically prunes his script. Continues to suffer from heart trouble. Contributes ideas and verses, which go unused, for the Lillian Hellman–Leonard Bernstein musical *Candide.* Writes script about young musicians at the Tanglewood Music Festival for director Fred Zinnemann and *New York Times* music critic Howard Taubman.

1955   Agee pushes *A Death in the Family* closer to completion. On May 16, while riding in a New York City taxicab, suffers massive heart attack and dies. Father Flye officiates at the funeral service at St. Luke's Chapel in New York. Is buried in Hillsdale, New York. (*A Death in the Family* is published in 1957 and wins the Pulitzer Prize the following year.)

Note on the Texts

This volume contains the reviews and essays by James Agee collected in the posthumous edition *Agee on Film: Reviews and Comments* (1958), along with 21 film reviews and profile pieces not included in that edition; the screenplay for the 1955 film *The Night of the Hunter*; and 15 pieces Agee published in magazines between 1933 and 1950.

Agee began reviewing movies for *Time* in September 1942 and for *The Nation* three months later. He served as the film critic for both magazines simultaneously until 1948, when he stopped regularly reviewing movies. His film writing for magazines was collected after his death in *Agee on Film: Reviews and Comments*, published in 1958 by McDowell, Obolensky. This collection is a historically significant edition, brought out as Agee's posthumous reputation was on the rise—his autobiographical novel *A Death in the Family* had just been awarded the Pulitzer Prize—and film reviewing in general was beginning to be regarded as serious writing, at least as practiced by gifted critics such as Agee. The present volume prints the complete text of the 1958 McDowell, Obolensky edition of *Agee on Film: Reviews and Comments*. Except for Agee's review of Kyle Crichton's *The Marx Brothers*, which is taken from *Films in Review* (1950), the reviews and profile pieces in this volume's "Uncollected Film Writing" section are taken from the following issues of *Time*:

Wake Island: September 14, 1942.

"Exit Tony": October 19, 1942.

"For Whom?": August 2, 1943.

The Battle of Russia; *I Dood It*; *His Butler's Sister*: November 29, 1943.

Lifeboat: January 31, 1944.

Phantom Lady: February 28, 1944.

With the Marines at Tarawa; *See Here, Private Hargrove*: March 20, 1944.

Going My Way: May 1, 1944.

The Fighting Lady; *I'll Be Seeing You*: January 22, 1945.

Salome, Where She Danced; *Dillinger*: May 7, 1945.

To the Shores of Iwo Jima: March 26, 1945.

Uncle Harry: August 27, 1945.

The Big Sleep: August 26, 1946.

"A Star Is Born": February 10, 1947.

The Macomber Affair; *It Happened in Brooklyn*; *The Farmer's Daughter*: April 7, 1947.

This Happy Breed: April 21, 1947.

Shoeshine: September 8, 1947.

Kiss of Death; *Lured, I Know Where I'm Going*; *Deep Valley*: September 15, 1947.

"Leading Man"; *The Paradine Case*: January 19, 1948.

Red River: October 11, 1948.

In 1954, Agee wrote the first draft of a screenplay adapting Davis Grubb's 1953 novel *The Night of the Hunter*. After reading the draft, the film's director, Charles Laughton, cut and substantially rewrote Agee's original version. Although Agee retained sole writing credit, the screenplay was the product of this collaboration; as Agee wrote in January 1955: "My feeling was, and is, that Charles had such an immense amount to do with the script, that it seems to me absurd to take credit, much as I'd like it. . . . I'm sure you know as well as I do or better, how embarrassed a writer should rightly feel in being given full credit, who has done a piece of work for and with Charles. It's on this basis that I feel very strongly that credit on the script should be double. At times, I've even felt that it should be given to him entirely: I can withdraw from that position only in realizing that I was useful, as a sort of combination sounding-board and counter-irritant." The film was released in September 1955, a few months after Agee's death. *The Night of the Hunter* screenplay printed here is taken from *Agee on Film: Five Film Scripts* (New York: McDowell, Obolensky, 1960).

This volume's "Selected Journalism" section consists of articles by Agee originally published in *Fortune* and *Time* that treat subjects other than film. The texts of "Tennessee Valley Authority," "Cock-fighting," "The U.S. Commercial Orchid," "U.S. at War: 'A Soldier Died Today,'" "Victory: The Peace," "Europe: Autumn Story," and "The Nation: Democratic Vistas" are taken from Paul Ashdown, ed., *James Agee: Selected Journalism* (Knoxville: University of Tennessee Press, 1985). The texts printed here of "'Time and Craving,'" "Genius-à-la-King," "Edible Slice of Life," "Abstract Prose," "A Mirror for England," "Guidebook for a Labyrinth," "Inquest on Democracy," and "It Is Written" are taken from Victor A. Kramer, ed., *Agee: Selected Literary Documents* (Troy, NY: The Whitson Publishing Company, 1996). The following list gives the original periodical sources for these articles:

Tennessee Valley Authority: *Fortune*, October 1933.

Cockfighting: *Fortune*, March 1934.

The U.S. Commercial Orchid: *Fortune*, December 1935.

"Time and Craving": *Time*, January 29, 1940.

Genius-à-la-King: *Time*, June 10, 1940.
Edible Slice of Life: *Time*, December 2, 1940.
Abstract Prose: *Time*, February 17, 1941.
A Mirror for England: *Time*, October 13, 1941.
Guidebook for a Labyrinth: *Time*, January 19, 1942.
Inquest on Democracy: *Time*, June 15, 1942.
It Is Written: *Time*, February 1, 1943.
U.S. at War: 'A Soldier Died Today': *Time*, April 23, 1945.
Victory: The Peace: *Time*, August 20, 1945.
Europe: Autumn Story: *Time*, October 15, 1945.
The Nation: Democratic Vistas: *Time*, November 5, 1945.

This volume presents the texts of the original printings chosen for inclusion here, but it does not attempt to reproduce nontextual features of their typographic design. The texts are presented without change, except for the correction of typographical errors. Spelling, punctuation, and capitalization are often expressive features and are not altered, even when inconsistent or irregular. The following is a list of typographical errors corrected in this volume, cited by page and line number: 15.9, Connecticut; 40.28, know; 62.39–40, sweeness; 78.13, Honorable Moon; 88.26, then; 85.32, Destiny,; 88.26, then; 88.30, cockatil; 102.38, possible; 119.8, vivacious; 121.7, telescopic; 123.3, Bryon; 139.19, think getting; 147.38, seen!; 158.14, only only; 169.3, *The*; 198.8, Esther; 208.28, Othewise; 209.22, brilliance; 215.9, *Marys*; 215.33, nabod; 225.30, plently; 229.6, title; 230.34, "wonderful; 235.10, wierdest; 237.17, housemaid.; 240.31, *Siam*,; 240.36, pratfall; 241.30, greately; 250.23, that it is; 253.16, 253.16, inconspicious; 253.26, Chandeler; 253.33, surrepitious; 266.11, title seems; 284.6, *Boomerang!*; 298.10, that it,; 309.25, of he; 309.26, Favisham; 311.17, relationship; 356.8, two often; 370.25, 1906; 408.34, certainly; 413.14, It's; 416.13, payoffs; 427.26, Massey'e; 439.33, RKO) Radio,; 442.14, Insead; 445.19, ones:; 447.32, a play; 457.22, have never; 458.2, champon; 460.2, *"Folk Art"*; 466.5, himself; 491.33, leary; 531.6, songs one hundred; 555.28, back; 595.21, briefly; 596.22, doll; 602.9, is is?; 603.7, she; 605.4, set; 605.20, Pharoah; 627.32, live; 633.6, scarely; 638.2, trades; 638.30, be so; 643.12, Wilkie's; 655.16, exercies; 662.37, hole; 671.22, cow; 675.19, Virgina; 675.22-23, Lavantine; 681.35, afternoon; 682.5, Piccadily; 683.29, lightening; 684.5, phrases; 684.6, last,; 686.10, *and*; 688.29, *Perstalsis*; 701.39, on train.

Notes

In the notes below, the reference numbers denote page and line of this volume (the line count includes headings). No note is made for material included in standard desk-reference books. Biblical quotations are keyed to the King James Version. Quotations from Shakespeare are keyed to *The Riverside Shakespeare*, ed. G. Blakemore Evans (Boston: Houghton Mifflin, 1974). For further biographical background than is contained in the Chronology, see Alfred T. Barson, *A Way of Seeing: A Critical Study of James Agee* (Amherst: University of Massachusetts Press, 1972); Lawrence Bergreen, *James Agee: A Life* (New York: E.P. Dutton, 1984); Victor A. Kramer, *James Agee* (Boston: Twayne, 1975); Erling Larsen, *James Agee* (Minneapolis: University of Minnesota Press, 1971); *Letters of James Agee to Father Flye* (New York: George Braziller, 1962); Michael A. Lofaro, ed., *James Agee: Reconsiderations* (Knoxville: University of Tennessee Press, 1992); James Lowe, *The Creative Process of James Agee* (Baton Rouge: Louisiana State University Press, 1994); David Madden, ed., *Remembering James Agee* (Baton Rouge: Louisiana State University Press, 1974); Genevieve Moreau, *The Restless Journey of James Agee* (New York: Morrow, 1977); Peter H. Ohlin, *Agee* (New York: Obolensky, 1966); Kenneth Seib, *James Agee: Promise and Fulfillment* (Pittsburgh: University of Pittsburgh Press, 1968); Ross Spears and Jude Cassidy, eds., *Agee: His Life Remembered* (New York: Holt, Rinehart and Winston, 1985).

AGEE ON FILM: REVIEWS AND COMMENTS

30.2   straw hats] The summer stock circuit.

30.2   *Three Men on a Horse*] Comedy (1935) by John Cecil Holm and George Abbott.

37.7   *Jalna*] Best-selling novel (1927) by Canadian author Mazo de la Roche.

40.4   Slavko Vorkapitch] Filmmaker and theorist (1892–1976) known for his work on montage and special effects in Hollywood features.

40.23   *Homage to Blenholt*] Novel (1936) by Daniel Fuchs.

42.12–11   a colored pianist . . . forget] Dooley Wilson (1894–1953).

43.6–7   Rupert Hughes's *The Old Nest*] A film of Hughes's 1912 novel was released in 1921.

45.23   Moody-and-Sankey-style hymn]   The evangelist Dwight Moody (1837–99) was associated with the hymn writer Ira D. Sankey (1840–1908), who compiled collections such as *Sacred Songs and Solos* (1873) and *Gospel Hymns* (1875–91).

49.14   *Querschnitt*]   An avant-garde cultural journal published in Berlin, 1921–33.

51.23   Manny Farber]   Writer and painter (b. 1917) who in the 1940s was film critic for *The New Republic.*

52.3   Basic English]   Simplified version of English with a vocabulary of 850 words, developed by I. A. Richards and Charles King Ogden, and described in Richards' *Basic English and Its Uses* (1943).

52.4   Madame Litvinov]   Ivy Litvinov (1889–1977), the English wife of Maxim Litvinov, who served as Soviet foreign minister, 1930–39, and as ambassador to the U.S., 1941–43.

52.24   Mr. Davies]   Joseph Davies (1876–1958), the U.S. ambassador to the Soviet Union, 1936–38.

53.8   Weber and Fields]   Comedy team of Joseph Weber (1867–1942) and Lew Fields (1867–1941); their shows included *Fiddle-dee-dee* (1900), *Hoity Toity* (1901), and *Twirly Whirly* (1902).

53.10   GPU]   Gosudarstvennoye Politicheskoye Upravlenie (State Political Directorate), the Soviet security police, 1922–34.

53.18   Daisy Ashfordism]   Daisy Ashford (1881–1972) was the author of *The Young Visiters*, published in 1919 but written when she was nine.

53.32   Professor Dewey]   John Dewey had headed a commission of inquiry into the treason charges made against Trotsky during the Moscow trials; its report, *Not Guilty*, was published in 1938.

54.12   the Mukden incident]   On September 18, 1931, a group of Japanese army officers provoked a clash between Japanese and Chinese troops at Mukden that led to the Japanese occupation of Manchuria.

55.32   Virginia Dare wine]   Popular brand of wine from scuppernong grapes, manufactured beginning in 1835 and sold with reduced alcohol content during the Prohibition era.

56.5   Stainer]   Sir John Stainer (1840–1901), English composer of religious music and organist at St. Paul's Cathedral.

56.38   OWI]   Office of War Information.

57.2–3   Hans Richter]   Painter and experimental filmmaker (1888–1976) associated with the Dada movement; his feature *Dreams That Money Can Buy* (1946) was based on scenarios by the artists Calder, Duchamp, Ernst, Léger, and Man Ray.

57.14   Major de Seversky]   Alexander Procofieff de Seversky (1894–1974), Russian pilot and aircraft designer; his 1943 book *Victory Through Air Power* was a best-seller.

60.37   Lidice]   German troops destroyed the Czech village of Lidice on June 10, 1942, in reprisal for the recent assassination of the senior SS leader Reinhard Heydrich by members of the Czech resistance. Before razing the village the Germans shot 192 men and seven women and deported 205 women and 96 children to concentration camps; of the deportees, 145 women and 15 children survived the war.

61.29   Earl Browder]   Secretary-general of the American Communist Party, 1930–45.

65.3–4   *Forbidden . . . Women*]   Feature films by Ernst Lubitsch, both released in 1924.

74.23   *ABCA*]   A film about the Army Bureau of Current Affairs.

75.36   raid on Kiska]   U.S. and Canadian troops landed on Kiska in the Aleutian Islands on August 15, 1943, expecting to encounter determined resistance, but then discovered that the Japanese had evacuated the island without being detected.

82.24   Dziga-Vertov]   Soviet filmmaker (1896–1954) whose films include *The Man with the Movie Camera* (1929) and *Three Songs of Lenin* (1934).

84.37   Captain Billy's *Whiz-Bang*]   Popular humor magazine, associated with occasionally off-color jokes, published by Captain Wilford H. Fawcett from 1919 to the late 1930s.

88.24–25   Mann's *Early Sorrow*]   "Unordnung und frühes Leid" (1926), story by Thomas Mann translated as "Disorder and Early Sorrow."

92.1   Florence Atwater]   A precocious teenage character in Booth Tarkington's novel *Gentle Julia* (1922).

99.17–18   Nordhoff and Hall]   Charles Nordhoff (1887–1947) and James Norman Hall (1887–1951), co-authors of novels including *Mutiny on the Bounty* (1932) and *Men Against the Sea* (1934).

101.1   Hardie Albright]   Movie actor (1903–75) whose films included *Cabin in the Cotton* (1932) and *Red Salute* (1935).

109.28   one of Joyce's finest stories]   "The Dead" in *Dubliners* (1914).

114.5   Alice Duer Miller]   Fiction writer (1874–1942) and campaigner for women's rights; her books include *Are Women People?* (1915) and *The White Cliffs* (1940).

118.2   Roger Touhy]   Touhy led a major bootlegging and gambling organization in northwest Cook County, Illinois, from the 1920s until his arrest on kidnapping charges in 1933.

119.20   fall of Cassino]   The town, and the monastery on nearby Monte Cassino, were captured by Allied troops on May 18, 1944, ending a four-month battle.

123.6–7   Norman Corwin]   Writer (b. 1910) best known for his plays and poems written for radio.

127.22   Oley Speaks and S. Parkes Cadman]   Speaks (1874–1948), American composer; Cadman (1864–1936), Protestant clergyman and author of inspirational books including *The Parables of Jesus* and *Ambassadors of God*.

129.32   *Sentimental Education*]   Novel (1869) by Gustave Flaubert.

131.7   Butcher-Leaf-Lang-and-Myers]   Samuel Henry Butcher (1850–1910) and Walter Leaf (1852–1927), British classicists who collaborated with Andrew Lang (1844–1912) on prose translations of *The Odyssey* and *The Iliad*, respectively; Ernest Myers also worked on the *Iliad* translation.

132.12   Dr. Gillespie]   Character portrayed by Lionel Barrymore in the film *Young Dr. Kildare* (1938) and its 14 sequels.

144.30   Kid Ory]   Edward "Kid" Ory (1886–1973), trombonist and jazz composer; he led an important New Orleans band (1910–19) whose personnel at various times included King Oliver, Sidney Bechet, and Louis Armstrong.

145.30–31   *esprit d'escalier*]   Literally "staircase wit"; an afterthought of what one ought to have said on an earlier occasion.

151.16–17   Hedwig's . . . *Duck*]   In Ibsen's 1885 drama, Hedvig, the presumed daughter of Hjalmar Ekdal, commits suicide after an emotional scene in which he rejects her after learning she is really another man's daughter.

157.28   Studs Lonigan]   Protagonist of a trilogy of novels (1932–35) by James T. Farrell.

162.15   Donald Culross Peattie]   Botanist (1898–1964) and author of books including *An Almanac for Moderns* (1935) and *The Road of a Naturalist* (1941).

166.6   Black Dragon agents]   Members of the Kokuryukai (Black Dragon Society), an ultranationalist Japanese secret society named after the Black Dragon (Amur) River on the Russian-Manchurian border.

166.25   Lonsdale]   Frederick Lonsdale (1881–1954), playwright whose successes included *Aren't We All?* (1923) and *The Last of Mrs. Cheney* (1925).

171.40–172.1   the mobbing . . . Caruso]   Donato Caretta, the former warden of Regina Coeli prison, was dragged from the Palace of Justice in Rome by a mob on September 18, 1944, beaten, and then drowned in the Tiber. Pietro Caruso, the former fascist police chief of Rome, was convicted by an Italian court and shot on September 22, 1944.

175.4 Ivan Albright] Painter (1897–1983) known for his painstakingly detailed, magical realist works.

176.18 Pegasus or the Houyhnhnms] Pegasus, immortal winged horse sprung from the blood of Medusa, and tamed by Bellerophon; Houyhnhnms, race of horses of superior intelligence, in the fourth book of Jonathan Swift's *Gulliver's Travels.*

178.17 William Bitzer] Billy Bitzer (1872–1944), principal cameraman for the Biograph Company, who worked with D. W. Griffith on all of his major films.

179.27 David Low] British political cartoonist (1891–1963) best known for his creation Colonel Blimp.

181.4 *Trio*] Controversial novel (1943) by Dorothy Baker about a lesbian teacher.

196.33 Jeeter Lester] Protagonist of the novel *Tobacco Road* (1932) by Erskine Caldwell.

197.35–36 Texas Guinan] Nightclub owner (1884–1933) who flourished in New York in the Prohibition era, known for her catchphrase "Hello, sucker!"

203.40 Mauldin] Bill Mauldin (1921–2003), cartoonist for *Stars and Stripes* during World War II. His cartoons were collected in *Star Spangled Banter* (1941), *Sicily Sketch Book* (1943), *Up Front* (1945), and other volumes; he won the Pulitzer Prize in 1945.

208.19–20 Y. Frank Freeman] Executive at Paramount Studios (1915–62).

219.5 Merton Gills] In *Merton of the Movies* (1922), a play by George S. Kaufman and Marc Connelly, based on a novel by Harry Leon Wilson, Merton Gill is a young Midwesterner who aspires to become a serious film actor. Film versions were produced in 1924, 1932, and 1947.

233.37 Landru] Henri-Désiré Landru (1869–1922), French serial murderer.

245.8 *PM . . .* the Lerner editorial] Max Lerner (1902–92) was the chief editorial writer for the left-wing New York tabloid *PM.*

254.4–5 Spike Jones] Musician (1911–65) known for the comic and musically adventurous recordings he made with his group The City Slickers.

255.1 a new girl whose name I missed] Lilli Palmer.

255.10 *The Scoundrel*] Film (1935) written and directed by Ben Hecht and Charles MacArthur and starring Noel Coward.

264.29 Little Eyolf] Title character in a play (1894) by Henrik Ibsen.

273.7 a colored singer] Caleb Peterson.

277.6 Dr. Siegfried Kracauer or Barbara Deming] Kracauer (1889–1966), German philosopher and critic resident in the U.S. from 1941, best known for his study *From Caligari to Hitler* (1947); Deming (1917–84), proponent of pacifism and nonviolence who was a film critic in the 1940s.

292.20 Lecuona] Ernesto Lecuona (1896–1963), Cuban composer and pianist who wrote music for Hollywood films in the 1930s and 40s.

314.24 Varga] Alberto Vargas (1896–1982), Peruvian artist who created the "Varga girl" pin-ups for *Esquire* in the 1940s.

320.5–6 *The Old Homestead*] Long-running play by Denman Thompson, first performed in 1887.

326.39–40 Milton Caniff] Cartoonist (1907–88) best known for the comic strip *Terry and the Pirates*, which began newspaper publication in 1934.

344.2 *Pervigilium Veneris*] Latin poem (c. 3rd century A.D.) of unknown authorship, celebrating the eve of the spring festival of Venus.

353.12 *Pépé le Moko* and *Algiers*] *Pépé le Moko* (1936), French film starring Jean Gabin and directed by Julien Duvivier; remade in Hollywood as *Algiers* (1938), starring Charles Boyer and directed by John Cromwell.

357.8 Julien Sorel] Protagonist of Stendhal's novel *The Red and the Black* (1830).

360.31 Joseph Shearing] Pseudonym of Gabrielle Margaret Long (1886–1952); her novels as Shearing include *Moss Rose* (1935) and *The Golden Violet* (1941).

385.21–22 Peaches . . . Grange] Newspaper headlines in the late 1920s were dominated by "Peaches" Browning's 1926 divorce suit against her much older husband, "Daddy" Browning; Queen Marie of Romania's 1926 visit to the United States; Ruth Snyder's 1927 trial for the murder of her husband (she and her lover Judd Gray were electrocuted at Sing Sing, January 22, 1928); and Red Grange's successes as All-American halfback (1923–24) and quarterback (1925) at the University of Illinois, which earned him the nickname "The Galloping Ghost."

395.28 Manassa Mauler] Heavyweight champion Jack Dempsey.

460.32–33 Mitchell's Christian Singers] North Carolina gospel quartet which began recording in 1934; John Hammond presented them in his "From Spirituals to Swing" concerts at Carnegie Hall in 1938 and 1939.

461.8 Raymond Scott] Composer and inventor (1908–94) whose compositions include "Powerhouse" and "The Toy Trumpet."

462.1   "Ballad for Americans"] Cantata with music by Earl Robinson and words by John Latouche, popularized in a 1939 radio broadcast by Paul Robeson.

462.2–3   Robeson-Webster production of *Othello*] Margaret Webster's successful 1943 production featured Paul Robeson as Othello, Uta Hagen as Desdemona, and Jose Ferrer as Iago.

462.5   *Carmen Jones*] Musical (1943) by Oscar Hammerstein II, based on Bizet's *Carmen* and using its music; the action is transposed to the American South and features a largely African-American cast.

463.27   Irving . . . Guest] Irvin Cobb (1876–1944), humorist and journalist, author of *Old Judge Priest* (1916); Clarence Budington Kelland (1881–1964), author of stories including "Top Hat," filmed as *Mr. Deeds Goes to Town*; Guest (1881–1959), popular poet whose books include *Just Folks* (1917).

465.3–4   Cootie Williams] Jazz trumpeter (1910–85) long associated with the Duke Ellington orchestra.

466.1   Jimmy Savo and Pete Johnson] Savo, vaudeville comedian (1892–1960); Johnson (1904–67), boogie woogie pianist.

UNCOLLECTED FILM WRITING

497.31   the rise of Silas Lapham] *The Rise of Silas Lapham* (1885), novel by William Dean Howells.

512.20   Mozart's *La Ci Darem la Mano*] Duet from act one of *Don Giovanni*.

THE NIGHT OF THE HUNTER

"In 1954 James Agee wrote the film script of *The Night of the Hunter*, based on the Davis Grubb novel. The motion picture, directed by Charles Laughton, and with Paul Gregory as producer, was released, in 1955, through United Artists. Agee, who died in May, 1955, never saw this picture in which leading roles were played by Robert Mitchum, Lillian Gish and Shelley Winters." [Note in the 1960 McDowell, Obolensky edition of *Agee on Film: Five Film Scripts*, the source of the text in the present volume.]

SELECTED ESSAYS AND JOURNALISM

665.29–30   Charles Darwin . . . a thick book] *On the Various Contrivances by which British and Foreign Orchids Are Fertilized by Insects, and on the Good Effects of Intercrossing* (1862).

681.32   Sig Romberg] Sigmund Romberg (1887–1951), composer of operettas including *Maytime* (1917) and *The Student Prince* (1924).

696.17   National Actionists] The National Action movement had collaborated with the German occupation.

696.19   EAM]   Ethnikon Apeleutherotikon Metopon (National Liberation Front), resistance movement founded by the Greek Communist Party in
September 1941.

696.21   murder of Matteotti]   Giacomo Matteotti, the anti-fascist leader
of the Italian Socialist Party, was murdered in 1924.

696.23   A.M.G.]   Allied Military Government.

Index

Library of Congress Cataloging-in-Publication Data

Agee, James, 1909–1955
    Film writing and selected journalism / James Agee.
        p. cm.—(The Library of America ; 160)
    Includes bibliographical references and index.
    Contents: Agee on film : reviews and comments—
Uncollected film writing—The night of the hunter—
Journalism and book reviews.
    ISBN 1–931082–82–0 (alk. paper)
        I. Books—Reviews. 2. Motion pictures—History. I. Title.
II. Series.

PS3501.G35A6   2005b
791.43'75—dc22   2005045095

THE LIBRARY OF AMERICA SERIES

The Library of America fosters appreciation and pride in America's literary heritage by publishing, and keeping permanently in print, authoritative editions of America's best and most significant writing. An independent nonprofit organization, it was founded in 1979 with seed money from the National Endowment for the Humanities and the Ford Foundation.

This book is set in 10 point Linotron Galliard,
a face designed for photocomposition by Matthew Carter
and based on the sixteenth-century face Granjon. The paper
is acid-free Domtar Literary Opaque and meets the requirements
for permanence of the American National Standards Institute. The
binding material is Brillianta, a woven rayon cloth made by
Van Heek-Scholco Textielfabrieken, Holland. Composition
by Dedicated Business Services. Printing and
binding by Courier Companies, Inc.
Designed by Bruce Campbell.